Reflective Teaching

Also available in the series:

Other books by Andrew Pollard published by Continuum

Reflective Teaching

Effective and Evidence-informed Professional Practice

Andrew Pollard

with contributions by

Janet Collins, Neil Simco, Sue Swaffield,
Jo Warin and Paul Warwick

continuum
LONDON • NEW YORK

CONTINUUM

The Tower Building, 11 York Road, London SE1 7NX

370 Lexington Avenue, New York, NY 10017-6503

www.continuumbooks.com

© Andrew Pollard 2002

First published 2002

British Library Cataloguing-in-Publication Data

A catalogue record for this book is available from the British Library.

ISBN 0-8264-5116-0 (hardback)
ISBN 0-8264-5117-9 (paperback)

Typeset by CentraServe Ltd, Saffron Walden, Essex
Printed and bound in Great Britain by
Bookcraft (Bath) Ltd, Midsomer Norton

CONTENTS

http://www.rtweb.info

PREFACE

Reflective Teaching has been produced following an extensive round of consultation among the profession (please see the acknowledgements), and with the assistance of an Editorial Team – Janet Collins (Open University), Neil Simco (St Martin's College, Ambleside), Sue Swaffield (University of Cambridge), Jo Warin (Lancaster University) and Paul Warwick (University of Cambridge). This has made it possible to develop the handbook and its associate resources in a number of ways.

In particular, we now offer three fully integrated and complementary resources:

- *Reflective Teaching* (the core handbook for school-based professional development)
- *Readings for Reflective Teaching* (for over 120 associated and fully integrated readings)
- *RTweb* (website for supplementary, updatable Notes for Further Reading, Reflective Activities, links, downloads, etc.)

Regarding the present text, there has been a complete update in relation to curriculum, pedagogy, assessment, social inclusion, inspection and many other topics, in response to changes of the past six years. Following devolution, we have tried to address the rather different UK contexts of England, Northern Ireland, Scotland and Wales. New chapters are included on mentoring, language and the role of newly qualified teachers, and imaginative design features make the book even easier to use. In particular, we have introduced signposts, where specific links or routes through the book are suggested. The underlying rationale for the structure of the book is to be found in Figure 4.1 and, of course, it is possible to travel around this territory in many different ways. It's your choice! The main contents page, content pages for each chapter and the overall index will help if you ever feel lost, or really want to 'start again'.

Selective *Key Readings* are provided at the end of each chapter. It is possible to sample some of these suggestions, and many others, by consulting *Readings for Reflective Teaching* (2nd edition). To assist in this, extensive cross-referencing is provided throughout the text, as indicated by the **Reading** icon.

Previous versions of the book were popular for the extensive guidance on reading after each chapter and we intend that these comprehensive *Notes for Further Reading* should remain available through the internet on *RTweb*. Their location there will enable us to provide regular updates of their content.

Also expected to be available on **RTweb** (in downloadable form) are additional *Reflective Activities* and many of the diagrams and figures contained in the book. We hope that these will prove useful and welcome ideas for the further development of the site. Please check it out!

As a whole, these resources are intended to provide flexible and comprehensive support for school-based teacher education and training, in a form that is suitable for a wide range of circumstances. In particular, whilst trainees and teachers early in their careers remain a prime audience, we believe that the materials offer strong support to mentors and to more experienced teachers in self-motivated continuing professional development activities. Whilst all chapters provide up-to-date overviews of key issues, they are also expected to be used selectively, depending on judgements of what is needed to meet specific learning objectives. As indicated above, there are many routes through these materials.

The book remains focused on primary education, though we are aware that it is also extensively used in relation to training at the Foundation Stage and early parts of Key Stage 3. Whilst we welcome this, we do not claim to have fully met these particular needs. A more focused secondary version was published in 1997 (Pollard and Triggs) and an early years version is under discussion.

My thanks again to those who have offered comments, criticisms and suggestions regarding previous editions. These are extremely helpful and users of these new resources are invited to continue to maintain the feedback loop so that they can be effectively developed in the future.

Andrew Pollard
University of Cambridge
January 2002

ACKNOWLEDGEMENTS

A very large number of people have contributed to this new *Reflective Teaching*, its associate *Readings* and *RTweb*. However, we continue to appreciate and build on the legacy of one of the original textbook authors, Sarah Tann. Pat Triggs' work on the secondary edition has also contributed to this text.

The publishing team at Continuum has been extremely supportive of our work and we would particularly like to thank Anthony Haynes for his imaginative support. More substantively, Emma Cook has provided extremely helpful and efficient assistance on a wide range of issues. Mark Bolland and Ben Pitcher have managed the production process very smoothly. Lesley Atkin did an excellent job as copy-editor and Hilary Cooper provided the index. Thanks too to Alexandra Webster for her innovative ideas on marketing which, we hope, will enable these *Reflective Teaching* materials to reach more people.

The secretarial work that supports a project of this sort is considerable, and we are particularly grateful for the contributions of Suzanne Fletcher and her colleagues at the Faculty of Education, University of Cambridge. Thanks too to Sarah Butler in Bristol and Susan Cockburn in Ambleside.

The photographs in this book were taken by Fiona Berry and we are grateful to her for her care and imagination. We are particularly grateful to the headteachers, staff, pupils and parents of the two schools in which photographs were taken. They are Kettlefields County Primary in Cambridgeshire, where Sarah Humphreys is Headteacher, and Rowland Hill Nursery in Haringey, which is led by Julie Vaggers.

 A major development in support of this new edition is the website, **RTweb**. For their ideas and support of this development we would like to thank Phil Hill, Ken Bingham and Sparrowhawk and Heald at Cambridge, and Henry Liebling at the University College of St Mark and St John, Plymouth. Mark Thomas, our webmaster, has been wonderful.

The new resources have been designed to support initial teacher education and the early stages of professional development throughout the UK. We would like to acknowledge the helpful advice from Jill Staley and Keith Brumfitt of the Teacher Training Agency; Joyce Hughes from the Northern Ireland Council for the Curriculum, Examinations and Assessment and Mary Mallon of the Northern Ireland Network for Education; Kath Cannon and Lisa Jenkins of the National Assembly for Wales Training and Education Department; Robin McKendrick of the Teachers and Schools Division of the Scottish Executive.

Eight stalwart colleagues from across the UK were kind enough to review the final draft of this Handbook, and comment on it from particular perspectives. We are very grateful to Anne Campbell, Manchester Metropolitan University; Ken Jones, Swansea Institute of Higher Education; Stuart Marriott, University of Ulster; Rod Parker Rees, University of Plymouth; John Robertson and Douglas Gullands, University of Paisley; Philippa Cordingly, Consultant to the TTA on Teacher Research, and her colleague, Don Evans, at the Centre for the Use of Research and Evidence in Education.

We gratefully acknowledge the work of professional organisations such as the *National Primary Teacher Education Conference*, the *National Primary Trust*, the *Association for the Study of Primary Education* and journals such as

Education 3–13 in supporting reflective practice and in influencing the development of these materials.

Particular thanks to the many teachers, headteachers and LEA advisers who have discussed with Andrew Pollard ideas that are contained in these books. This process has continued since initial publication of the first edition of *Reflective Teaching* in 1987. It often occurs informally during visits to school or LEA conferences, but it is always valuable and appreciated.

We would also like to record our appreciation of the work of the educational research community. In a sense, we see *Reflective Teaching*, **Readings** and **RTweb** as forms of dissemination of the excellent research that continues to be achieved in the UK and elsewhere.

We would like to thank the National Primary Teacher Education Conference (NaPTEC) for facilitating a wide-ranging consultation on how this new edition should be developed. This involved an initial survey followed by discussions with staff and students in over a dozen institutions. We are very grateful for all the support and advice that was offered. Other colleagues have provided advice as new drafts of the text have been developed. Those helping in such ways have included the following: *Birmingham LEA*: Francis Mallon. *Bishop Grosseteste College*: Marion Mence. *University of Bristol*: Patricia Broadfoot, Guy Claxton, Martin Hughes, Peter John, Malcolm Lewis, Marilyn Osborn and Susan Robertson. *University of Cambridge*: Holly Anderson, Grant Bage, Colin Conner, Eve Bearne, Mary Jane Drummond, David Frost, Peter Huckstep, Mark Lofthouse, John MacBeath, Jean Rudduck, John Siraj-Blatchford, Anne Thwaites, Jane Webster and David Whitebread. *Cheltenham and Gloucester College of Higher Education*: Alison Scott-Bowman and Sally Palmer. *Cardiff LEA*: Ros Pollard. *University of Cardiff*: John Furlong. *University College Chichester*: Gianna Knowles. *De Montfort University*: Paul Gardner. *DFID*: Terry Allsop. *University of Derby*: John Dolan, Viv Taylor-Basil, Jenny Ambrose, Claire Archer, Claire Bridges, Karen Cholerton, Mark Dobson, Louise Edwards, Melanie Fisher, Amy Frost, Sophie Gauntley, Patricia Grace, Ranjit Johal, Carl Jones, Pamela Kitching, Rubi Mahmood, Laura Mann, Kay McGinness, Ellen Roberts, Shelly Rogers, Caroline Rumbolt, Emily Shoolbred, Eva Simmons, Margaret Ward, Katherine Wheatley, Paula Whysall and Maggie Zarattinie. *University of Greenwich*: Laura Anthony, Joanna Atkinson, Claire Blake, Helen Brook, Julie Edwards, Rosemary Morgan, Sharon O'Callahan, Zoe Thomas and Robert Young. *City University of Hong Kong*: Kai Hung Wong. *Leeds Metropolitan University*: Kathy Hall. *University of Leeds*: Angela Anning, Roger Beard, Peter Tomlinson. *University of London, Institute of Education*: Sally Power and Iram Siraj-Blatchford. *University of Malta*: Anton Cardona and Joe Mifsud. *Manchester Metropolitan University*: Lesley Abbott, Mike Archer, Anne Campbell, Karen Carter, Dave Hustler, Olwyn McNamara, Carol Mindham, Helen Moglett, John Robinson, Bridget Somekh and Ian Sugarman. *National Leadership College*: Karen Carter. *University of North London*: Elizabeth Burn and Merryn Hutchins. *Open University*: Deidre Cook, Roger Handcock and Bridget Hoad. *Oxford Brookes University*: Simon Catling and Alison Price. *University of Plymouth*: Jennifer Nias and Rod Parker-Rees. *University of Queensland, Australia*: Tony Kruger. *University of Sheffield*: John Quicke. *Rebridge LEA*: Pete Dudley. *St John's College School, Cambridge*: Rachel Sparks-Lingfield. *St Martin's College*: Marion Dadds, Owain Evans, Tony Ewens, Karen Mills, Colin

Richards, Phil Sandell, Ian Simpson and Chris Sixsmith. *St Mary's University College*: Carolyn Olton. *Stoke Bishop Primary School, Bristol*: Pearl Wilson. *University College of Ripon and York*: Sue Tite. *University of Victoria, New Zealand*: Keith Sullivan. *University of Wales, Swansea*: Gill Harper-Jones, Janet John, Roy Lowe, Trisha Maynard and Sue Saunders. *University of the West of England*: Richard Eke, Liz Newman, Lynn Raphael-Reed, Ron Ritchie. *University of Wolverhampton*: Mike Lambert.

We gratefully acknowledge the following and thank them for giving permission to reproduce the materials cited below.

Hay McBer for Figure 1.3 from *Research into Teacher Effectiveness* (2000), a report for DfEE.

John Furlong and his colleagues Margaret Wilkin, Trisha Maynard and Sheila Miles for Figure 2.2 adapted from *The Active Mentoring Programme* (1994), Cambridge: Pearson.

Croom Helm Ltd and Patrick Easen for Figure 5.1 and other material from his *Making School-centred INSET Work* (1985), London: Croom Helm.

Inner London Education Authority, for the 'Me at School' form (Reflective Activity 5.6) designed by members of the Junior School Project team based at the Research and Statistics Branch.

Barry Fraser and Darrell Fisher for the short form of 'My Class Inventory', from their *Assessment of Classroom Psychosocial Environment: Workshop Manual* (1983), Bentley: Western Australian Institute of Technology.

Jenny Mosley Consultancies for Figure 6.2 from *Quality Circle Time: The Heart of the Curriculum* (1998).

Network Educational Press for Figure 7.6 adapted from Alistair Smith's *Accelerated Learning in Practice* (1998).

US National Research Council and David A. Goslin for the foundation of Figure 7.8. See NRC (1999) *Improving Student Learning*, Washington DC: National Academy Press.

Robin J. Alexander for Table 8.1 from *Primary Teaching* (1984), London: Holt, Rinehart and Winston.

Boynton/Cook Heinemann and Douglas Barnes for Figure 12.1 from *From Communication to Curriculum* (1975), London: Penguin.

Longman Group UK Ltd for Figure 12.2 from S. Alladina and V. Edwards (eds) *Multilingualism in the British Isles* (1991).

Routledge and Alec Webster, Mike Beveridge and Malcolm Reed for Figure 12.3 from *Managing the Literacy Curriculum* (1996).

Routledge for Figure 13.1 from G. A. Brown and R. Edmundson, 'Asking questions' in E. C. Wragg, (ed.) *Classroom Teaching Skills* (1984).

Neville Bennett and Elizabeth Dunne for Figure 13.2 from *Managing Classroom Groups* (1992), London: Simon and Schuster.

Department for Education and Employment for Figure 14.5 from DfEE, *From Targets to Action: Guidance to Support Effective Target Setting in Schools* (1997).

Chris Sixsmith and Neil Simco for Figure 16.1 from 'The role of formal and informal theory in the training of student teachers', *Mentoring and Tutoring*, Vol. 5, No. 1 (1997), pp. 5–13.

John MacBeath and Peter Mortimore for ideas which led to Figure 17.1. See MacBeath and Mortimore *Improving School Effectiveness* (2001), Buckingham: Open University Press.

Stephen Ball and Routledge for Figure 17.3 from *Micro-Politics of the School* (1987).

Finally, Andrew Pollard would like to offer particular thanks to the Editorial Team, Janet Collins, Neil Simco, Sue Swaffield, Jo Warin and Paul Warwick, whose generosity and expertise have contributed so much to the development of these materials.

INTRODUCTION

The main aim of this book is to support trainee teachers, school mentors, university tutors and all teachers, however experienced, who wish to reflect upon teaching in a systematic fashion. Together with its supplementary materials, *Readings for Reflective Teaching* and *RTweb*, we have tried to provide comprehensive support for the development of effective classroom practice. However, these resources are intended to be more than just a practical guide to the development of classroom expertise. The analysis and activities have been set within a framework that attempts to link classroom practice and research with current educational, political and social debates. This book thus offers a broad context – the context of the 'extended professional' – within which to reflect upon teaching.

Teacher education and training has been in a state of flux for many years. Undergraduate degree and post-graduate training routes, run by higher education institutions, remain the bedrock of our provision. This book, *Readings* and *RTweb*, should make a direct contribution to such courses and their associated mentoring activities in schools. However, there is also considerable momentum towards the development of alternative routes into teaching. In part, this is a response to problems of recruitment, but it also reflects belief in the practical effectiveness of employment-based routes. This is a very important development, and we have developed *Reflective Teaching* resources to support these distance-learning circumstances with the 'handbook', pocket library of readings and website.

This book and its associated resources thus have extremely serious intentions and contemporary relevance. We wish to support the continuing development of high-quality professionals who can enhance pupil attainment, and we also want to support new teachers in understanding the contexts in which they work and the significance of what they do. Because teachers are concerned with citizens of the future, with life-chances, social inclusion and with the quality of children's experiences in the present, they can never avoid value questions. Because they deal, from moment to moment, with a constant flow of dilemmas, they can never avoid the need to exercise professional judgement. Professionals for the rapidly developing new century thus need flexible and resilient approaches to continuing development, and it is important that the significance of reflective teaching has been explicitly recognised (DfEE, 2001a).

Indeed, for many years, 'reflective teaching' has been an extremely popular concept among professional educators in the UK and internationally. However, it has also been the focus of some criticism. In particular, some feel that it has sometimes been used rhetorically and with too little rigour. Others point to the importance of intuition for very experienced professionals. There have also been suggestions that reflection is only appropriate once initial skills have been established. On the other hand, it is important to maintain the very highest expectations for all teachers, at whatever stage of professional development.

In England, the Teacher Training Agency (TTA) endorses the need for high expectations and the core processes of reflective teaching, albeit somewhat obliquely in the case of the latter. For example, it requires those awarded Qualified Teacher Status to demonstrate that they 'are able to improve their own teaching, by evaluating it, learning from the effective practice of others, and from evidence' (standard 1.7). As we shall see, similar commitments to self-evaluative, reflective processes are sustained in Scotland, Northern Ireland and Wales.

When Sarah Tann and Andrew Pollard began writing the first edition of this book in the mid-1980s, they fully recognized that all forms of action inevitably involve people in making judgements based on values and commitments – and this is certainly true for teachers. They therefore tried to offer a framework that recognized the necessity of professional judgements by individual teachers and yet was also informed by a set of value-commitments that would command widespread support in moral and ethical terms.

At a fundamental level, they tried to emphasize the links between education, human rights and democracy. In this respect one can learn a great deal from looking at the Universal Declaration on Human Rights and the European Convention on Human Rights, which were both developed in the post-war years. Britain passed its Human Rights Act in 1998, which gave full effect to the Convention. The UK is also a signatory of the Council of Europe's special educational Recommendation (1985) and it is worth citing some parts of this document here. For example, it states:

> The understanding and experience of human rights is an important element of the preparation of all young people for life in a democratic and pluralistic society. It is a part of social and political education, and it involves intercultural and international understanding.
>
> (1.1)

> The study of human rights in schools should lead to an understanding of, and sympathy for, the concepts of justice, equality, freedom, peace, dignity, rights and democracy. Such understanding should be both cognitive and based on experience and feelings.
>
> (3.3)

> During teacher education, trainees should be: 'encouraged to take an interest in national and world affairs' and 'be taught to identify and combat all forms of discrimination in schools and society and be encouraged to confront and overcome their own prejudices'.
>
> (5.1)

The United Nations Convention on the Rights of the Child passed into international law in 1989. This provides children and young people with many fundamental protections, integrating economic and social rights indivisibly with civil and political entitlements. Article 12 is particularly interesting for teachers, since it recognizes each child's right to express views and feelings on all matters affecting the child, and to have those opinions taken into consideration (see Osler and Starkey, 1996, **Reading 13.9**, for more complete discussion of these issues). Is Article 12 fulfilled in your classroom?

These are challenging ideas, but ones which have to be faced if we are to provide the best possible quality of education for all the children in our societies. The work of a professional educator thus involves a heavy degree of social responsibility. We hope that this book and supplementary resources will help its readers to both improve their classroom effectiveness and reflect on such concerns.

This book has three parts, Part 1 is entitled 'Becoming a Reflective Teacher'.

It offers a theoretical rationale for the approach (Chapter 1) and an account of key issues for trainees and mentors (Chapter 2). It concludes with a review and examination of ways of investigating classrooms (Chapter 3).

Part 2, 'Being a Reflective Teacher', represents the classroom-focused, practical core of the book. Each chapter is devoted to a particular aspect of the teaching–learning process. Each has the same structure: a significant issue is discussed, reflective activities for classroom investigation are presented, follow-up points are suggested and selective guidance for further reading is given. Supplementary resources in **Readings** and **RTweb** are indicated.

The issues selected in Part 2 are ones which are basic to classroom life: the context and the circumstances of teachers and pupils (Chapter 4); values and the identity of teachers and pupils (Chapter 5); classroom relationships (Chapter 6); considering how children learn (Chapter 7); reviewing curriculum and subject knowledge (Chapter 8): specific planning of what to teach (Chapter 9); organizing a classroom (Chapter 10); behaviour management (Chapter 11); the characteristics of classroom communication (Chapter 12); classroom teaching strategies (Chapter 13); assessment issues (Chapter 14); social inclusion and the consequences of classroom practice (Chapter 15).

Part 3 looks 'Beyond Classroom Reflection' to consider reflective teaching and innovation in schools as a whole. We begin with guidance on learning as a newly qualified teacher (Chapter 16), before moving to consider the context of schools more generally and, in particular, continuing professional development (Chapter 17). The book concludes with consideration of the role and responsibilities of reflective primary-school teachers in society (Chapter 18).

ACRONYMS USED IN THIS BOOK

AAIA	Association of Assessment Inspectors and Advisors
ACCAC	Curriculum and Assessment Authority for Wales
APU	Assessment for Performance Unit
ASE	Association for Science Education
ASPE	Association for the Study of Primary Education
ATL	Association of Teachers and Lecturers
ATM	Association of Teachers of Mathematics
BECTA	British Educational Communications and Technology Agency
BERA	British Educational Research Association
CASE	Campaign for the Advancement of State Education
CASE	Cognitive Acceleration through Science Education
CCEA	Council for the Curriculum, Examinations and Assessment
CCW	Curriculum Council for Wales
CEP	Career Entry Profile
CERUK	Current Educational Research in the United Kingdom
CPD	Continuing Professional Development
DENI	Department of Education Northern Ireland
DES	Department of Education and Science
DfEE	Department for Education and Employment
DfES	Department for Education and Skills
EAL	English as an Additional Language
EEL	Effective Early Learning
GA	Geographical Association
GTC	General Teaching Council
GTCS	General Teaching Council Scotland
GTCW	General Teaching Council Wales
HMCI	Her Majesty's Chief Inspector
HMI	Her Majesty's Inspectorate
ICT	Information and Communications Technology
IEP	Individual Education Plans
INSET	In-Service Training
ITT	Initial Teacher Training
LDA	Learning Development Association
LEA	Local Education Authority
LINC	Language in the National Curriculum
LTS	Learning and Teaching Scotland
MA	Mathematical Association
MAPE	Micros and Primary Education
NAAIDT	National Association of Advisers and Inspectors of Design and Technology
NAHT	Natiional Association of Head Teachers
NAME	National Anti-racist Movement in Education
NAPE	National Association for Primary Education
NAPTEC	National Primary Teacher Education Conference
NAS/UWT	National Association of Schoolmasters/Union of Women Teachers
NATE	National Association for the Teaching of English
NCA	National Curriculum Assessments

NFER	National Foundation for Educational Research
NLS	National Literacy Strategy
NNS	National Numeracy Strategy
NPC	National Primary Centre
NPT	National Primary Trust
NQT	New Qualified Teacher
NUT	National Union of Teachers
OFSTED	Office for Standards in Education
PACE	Primary Assessment Curriculum and Experience
PGCE	Postgraduate Certificate of Education
PICSI	Pre-Inspection Context and School Indicator
PSHE	Personal, Social and Health Education
QCA	Qualifications and Curriculum Authority
QTS	Qualified Teacher Status
SCAA	School Curriculum and Assessment Authority
SCITT	School-Centred Initial Teacher Training
SED	Scottish Education Department
SEED	Scottish Executive Education Department
SEN	Special Educational Needs
SHA	Secondary Heads Association
STA	Specialist Teacher Assistant
TA	Teacher Assessment
TGAT	Task Group on Assessment and Testing
TTA	Teacher Training Agency
ZPD	Zone of Proximal Development

PART 1

BECOMING A REFLECTIVE TEACHER

CHAPTER 1

Reflective teaching

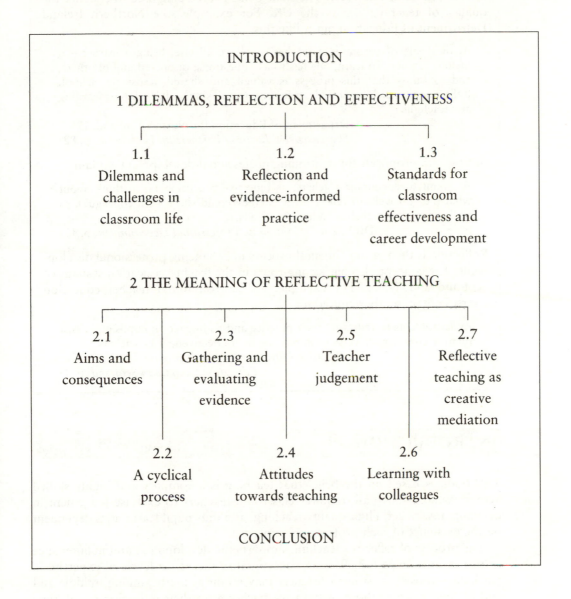

INTRODUCTION

1 DILEMMAS, REFLECTION AND EFFECTIVENESS

1.1
Dilemmas and challenges in classroom life

1.2
Reflection and evidence-informed practice

1.3
Standards for classroom effectiveness and career development

2 THE MEANING OF REFLECTIVE TEACHING

2.1
Aims and consequences

2.3
Gathering and evaluating evidence

2.5
Teacher judgement

2.7
Reflective teaching as creative mediation

2.2
A cyclical process

2.4
Attitudes towards teaching

2.6
Learning with colleagues

CONCLUSION

Enhancing professional standards and competences

Reflective activity makes a powerful contribution to the learning of many professionals – engineers, doctors and nurses, police officers, architects and lawyers, to name but a few. The same benefits are being used to enhance the quality of teaching across the UK. For example, the Northern Ireland Department of Education put it like this:

> At the heart of becoming a teacher is, above all else, being a learner – a lifelong learner. To learn, one has to ask questions, of oneself and of others, and to know that this process is valued and shared across the school. Reflecting on teaching provides a focus for analysing and developing learning and teaching.
>
> (Department of Education for Northern Ireland, 1999, *The Teacher Education Partnership Handbook*, p. 82)

In England, proposals for continuing professional development explain:

> We want to encourage teachers, as reflective practitioners, to think about what they do well, to reflect on what they could share with colleagues, as well as identifying their own learning needs.
>
> (DfEE, 2001, *Continuing Professional Development*, p. 12)

Reflection is then, a fundamental process in enhancing professional development. The concept also has strong roots in the teacher education systems of Scotland and Wales. For example, all Scottish initial teacher education courses are presently required to:

> Assist students to reflect on their practice and its impact on pupils and assist them to consider the ways of improving their effectiveness as teachers.
>
> (Scottish Office, 1998, *Guidelines for Initial Teacher Education Courses in Scotland*, p. 1)

INTRODUCTION

This book is based on the belief that teaching is a complex and highly skilled activity which, above all, requires classroom teachers to exercise judgement in deciding how to act. High-quality teaching, and thus pupil learning, is dependent on the existence of such professional expertise.

The process of reflective teaching supports the development and maintenance of professional expertise. We can conceptualize successive levels of expertise in teaching – those that student-teachers may attain at the beginning, middle and end of their courses; those of the new teacher after their induction to full-time school life; and those of the experienced, expert teacher. Given the nature of teaching, professional development and learning should never stop.

The process of reflection thus feeds a constructive spiral of professional development and capability (see Figure 1.1).

Reflective teaching should be personally fulfilling for teachers, but also lead to a steady increase in the quality of the education provided for children. Indeed,

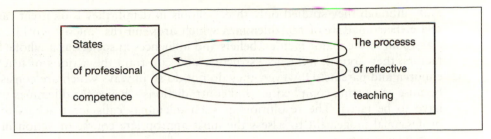

Figure 1.1 *The spiral of professional development*

because it is evidence based, reflective practice supports initial training students, newly qualified teachers and experienced professionals in satisfying performance standards and competences. Additionally, as we shall see, the concept of reflective teaching draws particular attention to the aims, values and social consequences of education (see also **Reading 1.5**).

This chapter has two main parts. The first introduces some of the dilemmas which teachers face and key issues surrounding evidence-based practice, professional standards and competences. In the second part, seven major characteristics of reflective teaching are identified and discussed.

RTweb also provides resources which supplement this chapter, such as a *compendium* of terms, issues, organizations and legislation.

1   DILEMMAS, REFLECTION AND EFFECTIVENESS

1.1   Dilemmas and challenges in classroom life

The complicated nature of educational issues and the practical demands of classroom teaching ensure that a teacher's work is never finished. When practicalities, performance standards, personal ideals and wider educational concerns are considered together, the job of reconciling the numerous requirements and possible conflicts may seem to be overwhelming. As a Key Stage 1 teacher explained to us:

> I love my work but it's a constant struggle to keep it all going. If I focus on one thing I have to neglect another. For instance, if I talk to a group or to a particular child then I have to keep an eye on what the others are doing; if I hear someone read then I can't be in position to extend other children's language when opportunities arise; if I put out clay then I haven't got room for painting; if I go to evening courses then I can't prepare as well for the next day; if I spend time with my family then I worry about my class but if I rush around collecting materials or something then I feel guilty for neglecting the family. It's not easy . . . but I wouldn't do any thing else.

Such dilemmas are frequently expressed – not only by experienced teachers, but even more by student-teachers.

One excellent analysis of the difficult dilemmas which teachers face has been provided by Berlak and Berlak (1981, **Reading 1.3**). The framework that they developed is a simple but very powerful one. Its strength derives from the fact that, although they studied only three schools in detail, they took great care to relate their analysis of the dilemmas which arose in the 'micro' world of the classroom to the major factors, beliefs and influences in society as a whole. Such factors, they argued, influence, structure and constrain the actions of teachers, children and parents. However, they do not do so in ways which are consistent, because of existing complexities and contradictions – hence the dilemmas which have to be faced. The resolution of such dilemmas calls for teachers to use professional judgement to assess the most appropriate course of action in any particular situation.

But what are the major dilemmas that have to be faced? Figure 1.2 presents a version of many of them and merits some study.

This book is intended to provide a practical guide to ways of reflecting on such issues and it offers strategies and advice for developing the necessary classroom expertise to resolve them.

1.2 Reflection and evidence-informed practice

There has been considerable discussion in recent years about the use of 'evidence' to inform educational practices (**Readings 3.3, 3.2**). Could this help to resolve endemic classroom dilemmas? Are we suffering, as Dadds (2001, **Reading 9.4**) suggested from a sort of 'hurry-along' survival instinct in which taking account of the next requirement is replacing principled, informed and considered judgement? Some policy-makers argue that large-scale scientific studies should be combined with systematic reviews of research to determine 'what works', with conclusions being passed down to teachers. Others point to the value of performance or benchmark evidence, such as assessment, inspection, or intake data, to challenge existing thinking. Many others however, advocate direct professional involvement in classroom enquiry, so that teachers take control of their own research and development. The latter, as we will see in Chapter 3, builds on the long tradition of action research which was established by Lawrence Stenhouse (**Reading 3.1**).

In England, the Department for Education and Skills and the Teacher Training Agency promote each of these approaches. For example, a research centre for Evidence-Informed Policy and Practice in Education (www.eppi.ioe.ac.uk) systematically searches and reviews available evidence; a database of Current Educational Research in the United Kingdom has been established (CERUK) (www.nfer.ac.uk/ceruk); 'Research Summaaries' are available from the DfES Standards website; and a National Education Research Forum has been established to advise on new issues for study (www.nerf-uk.org). In England, a national scheme of 'Best Practice Research Scholarships' is available to support classroom teachers and reflective classroom enquiry is encouraged in the DfES's policy for continuing professional development (DfEE, 2001a). There is regular publication of performance and inspection evidence across the system from the government departments of Wales, Scotland, Northern Ireland and England. More significantly however, there is considerable support from universities, local education authorities and government agencies for teachers who choose to reflect on school and classroom practices by conducting their own classroom research. Another increasingly significant set of institutions is the General Teaching Councils. Although the Northern Ireland GTC is not yet established, the new

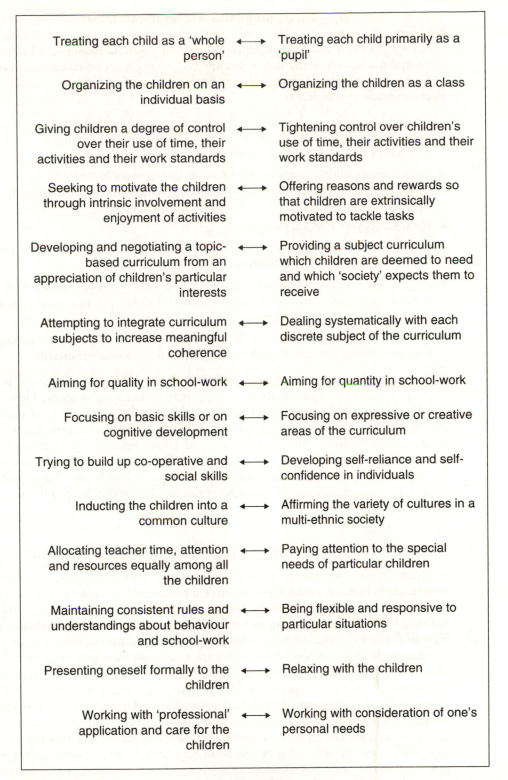

Treating each child as a 'whole person' ←→ Treating each child primarily as a 'pupil'

Organizing the children on an individual basis ←→ Organizing the children as a class

Giving children a degree of control over their use of time, their activities and their work standards ←→ Tightening control over children's use of time, their activities and their work standards

Seeking to motivate the children through intrinsic involvement and enjoyment of activities ←→ Offering reasons and rewards so that children are extrinsically motivated to tackle tasks

Developing and negotiating a topic-based curriculum from an appreciation of children's particular interests ←→ Providing a subject curriculum which children are deemed to need and which 'society' expects them to receive

Attempting to integrate curriculum subjects to increase meaningful coherence ←→ Dealing systematically with each discrete subject of the curriculum

Aiming for quality in school-work ←→ Aiming for quantity in school-work

Focusing on basic skills or on cognitive development ←→ Focusing on expressive or creative areas of the curriculum

Trying to build up co-operative and social skills ←→ Developing self-reliance and self-confidence in individuals

Inducting the children into a common culture ←→ Affirming the variety of cultures in a multi-ethnic society

Allocating teacher time, attention and resources equally among all the children ←→ Paying attention to the special needs of particular children

Maintaining consistent rules and understandings about behaviour and school-work ←→ Being flexible and responsive to particular situations

Presenting oneself formally to the children ←→ Relaxing with the children

Working with 'professional' application and care for the children ←→ Working with consideration of one's personal needs

Figure 1.2 *Common dilemmas faced by teachers*

English institution is actively promoting teacher research, and the Scottish GTC has been supporting professional development since 1966. In Wales, the GTC(W) has been awarded significant funds to promote professional development and teacher research, and is emerging as a significant voice for teachers.

In reviewing overall provision in England, the TTA (2000) advises that effective teachers should:

- know how to find and interpret existing, high quality evidence from a range of sources, such as research reports, other schools' experience, OFSTED inspection and performance data as a tool for raising standards;

- see professional development, which includes elements of research, as a means of improving classroom practice and raising standards, rather than as an end in itself;

- see pedagogy as integral to learning;

- interpret external evidence confidently, in relation to pupil or subject needs, rather than viewing it as a threat;

- accept that systematic enquiry into specific elements of teaching is a hard but crucial component of continuing professional development – and a key to raising the esteem in which the profession is held;

- be seen as equal partners with academic researchers in the process of producing evidence about teaching and in using it to raise standards.

Reflective professionals will thus be able to draw on, or contribute to, many sources of evidence, and use them to *inform* their teaching practice. However, we should note and *emphasize*, that a simple or direct translation of findings into action is not wise. This is because there are so many variables involved in teaching and learning, and direct 'cause and effect' findings rarely stand up to scrutiny. Simplistic answers to the question 'What works?' are thus unlikely to be secure, and professional judgement will remain a highly significant filter in interpreting the significance of research evidence for particular pupils or classroom contexts.

1.3   Standards for classroom effectiveness and career development

In recent years, competency criteria and latterly 'standards' have been set by governments in many countries to provide a framework for teacher training and further professional development. For instance, those for Scotland, Northern Ireland, Wales and England are set out on their respective agency websites (see **RTweb** for links) – and we have drawn on this to headline the relevance of each chapter of the book. Although such requirements may have great significance in their day, they seem to be altered quite frequently in the face of what often appear to be political imperatives. At the time of writing this text the DENI Inspectorate in Northern Ireland had just produced new set of competences focused on literacy, numeracy, classroom management and Information and Communications Technology (ICT), and a new 'Benchmark Statement for Initial Teacher Education' was being produced in Scotland. A new set of Standards had just been announced in England and a review for Wales was 'under consideration'. It would thus be prudent for students, mentors, teachers and teacher educators to get used to change though, of course, any requirements will still revolve around the enduring, fundamental concerns of teaching and learning.

For example, in England and, with minor adjustments, Wales, approximately 800 standards for initial teacher training were set by DfEE Circular 4/98 and Welsh Office Circular 13/98. They were presented within four major headings:

A. Knowledge and understanding

B. Planning, teaching and class management

C. Monitoring, assessment, recording, reporting and accountability

D. Other professional requirements.

In addition to these generic requirements, there were also subject-specific requirements. All primary trainees were required to have closely specified subject knowledge in both 'pure' and 'applied' ways, and to understand key teaching approaches within the core subjects of English, mathematics and science.

The criteria created a very heavily structured and regulated set of requirements which all trainees had to achieve prior to the award of Qualified Teacher Status (QTS). There was an inherent danger of atomization, with trainees focusing closely on the achievement of individual skills and standards rather than on a more integrated form of reflective capability (Calderhead, 1994, **Reading 2.4**). The requirements were challenged, notably by the National Primary Teacher Education Conference (NaPTEC) in terms of their implied model of teaching, learning and professionalism, and in terms of their manageability. Further, when policed through high-stakes inspection, they were also seen by some as part of an initiative to curtail the influence of higher education institutions (Furlong *et al.*, 2000).

In 2000, offering more benign support, the DfEE consulted on a new national framework for professional development through all career stages. As they put it:

> We believe that it would be helpful for teachers if we set out the standards of practice most teachers already aspire to in a national framework which all new and existing professionals could use to monitor progress and aid the planning of their professional development. The framework would map out the progression possible in a teacher's career, such as induction, passing the performance threshold and Advanced Skills Teacher, in terms of the skills and characteristics that they should expect to demonstrate at each point. The framework would also include the qualities needed for middle management roles such as subject leadership and the way these would develop for school leadership and headship.
>
> (DfEE, 2000:7)

Such a comprehensive framework already exists in Northern Ireland (DENI, 1999, see Chapter 16, Section 1.1). However, the new TTA circular of 2002 remains focused on initial teacher training alone. Structurally, it is possible to identify a framework of three levels:

Level 1 is the 2002 statutory framework for initial teacher training. Whilst still containing standards and course requirements, this is very much slimmed down from Circular 4/98. It covers much the same areas as its predecessor, but 'professional values' are now included as a discrete section and are seen as permeating sections on 'knowledge and understanding' and on 'teaching'.

Level 2 can be seen as the TTA Handbook, offering non-statutory guidance on areas such as assessment of the standards and partnership between higher education institutions and schools.

Level 3 consists of exemplars of good practice produced by providers and training schools. Such resources include this book, its accompanying **Readings** and internet site, **RTweb**, with their supplementary resources and ideas providing support on a chapter-by-chapter, topic-by-topic basis.

The new framework in England thus takes the form of a pyramid, with a small section of statutory requirement at the top, followed by non-statutory guidance on certain areas and then a large base of resources and examples of good practice. There is considerable scope here for high-quality reflective practice.

This new English framework for national standards is part of the 'New Labour' agenda for reform in education, a major part of which relates to restructuring the teaching profession. This was envisaged in two green papers, *Excellence in Schools* (DfEE, 1997) and *Teachers Meeting the Challenge of Change* (DfEE, 1998a). It was also influenced by a model of 'teacher effectiveness', as constructed by the Hay McBer Consultancy (2000). This envisaged three complementary factors contributing to pupil progress – teaching skills, professional characteristics and classroom climate (see Figure 1.3). For each of these factors, many subsidiary skills and elements of knowledge were identified, together with various 'levels' of capability for each.

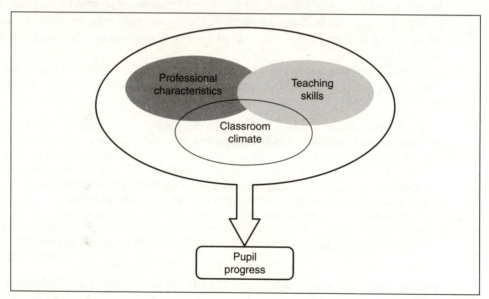

Figure 1.3 *The Hay McBer model of teacher effectiveness*

Broad standards and competences are helpful in defining goals for students, mentors, headteachers, tutors and others who are engaged in initial teacher education. As the TTA (2000) put it, they can:

- set out clear expectations for teachers at key points in the profession
- help teachers at different points in the profession to plan and monitor their

development, training and performance effectively, and to set clear, relevant objectives for improving their effectiveness

- ensure that the focus at every point is on improving the achievement of pupils and the quality of their education
- provide a basis for the professional recognition of teachers' expertise.

However, we need to be clear about the status of such models and criteria (BERA, 2001). The requirements described above (and, in more detail, at the start of each chapter in this book) set out the skills, knowledge and understanding which have been deemed to be appropriate for teachers in the particular context of England in the year 2002. However, those required where a centralized national curriculum and legally defined assessment procedure exist may well differ from those which are called for where teachers and schools are more engaged with a greater degree of partnership (as, for instance, in Northern Ireland and Scotland). Those called for where class sizes are high and resources scarce (as in many parts of the world) may vary from those needed when much smaller classes or groups are taught with good access to equipment. In particular, the standards required in 2002 are unlikely to remain constant. To illustrate this point, it is interesting to consider the requirements made of apprenticed 'pupil teachers' in England almost 160 years ago.

Regulations respecting the education of pupil teachers.

Minutes of the Committee of Council on Education, 1846.

Qualifications of candidates:

To be at least 13 years of age.

To not be subject to any bodily infirmity likely to impair their usefulness.

To have a certificate of moral character.

To read with fluency, ease and expression.

To write in a neat hand with correct spelling and punctuation, a simple prose narrative read to them.

To write from dictation sums in the first four rules of arithmetic, simple and compound: to work them correctly, and to know the table of weights and measures.

To point out the parts of speech in a simple sentence.

To have an elementary knowledge of geography.

To repeat the Catechism and to show that they understand its meaning and are acquainted with the outline of Scripture history. (Where working in schools connected with the Church of England only.)

To teach a junior class to the satisfaction of the Inspector.

Girls should also be able to sew neatly and to knit.

Figure 1.4 *Regulations respecting the education of pupil teachers, 1846*

We have to remember then, that officially endorsed standards are historically and contextually specific. Despite the moderating influence of available research, they are likely to be strongly influenced by the cultures, values and the priorities of decision-makers who happen to be in power at the time of their construction. In the case of teacher development in England, the framework for 'professional standards' describes the particular formulation of skills, knowledge and understanding which has been deemed appropriate for the particular time and circumstances. During a forty-year career, a teacher is likely to experience many such systems, and historical or comparative reflection will help keep them in perspective. Indeed, Hay McBer themselves caution against over-conformity when they emphasize that 'teachers are not clones' and assert that professionals always have to use their judgement about circumstances, pupils, contexts and teaching approaches (2000: para 1.1.4). This, of course, is an important element of reflective and evidence-informed teaching.

In summary, our view is that the notion of reflection applies throughout professional life but in different ways. Novice teachers, such as those in initial teacher training, may use reflection to improve on specific and immediate practical teaching skills. Competent teachers, such as Newly Qualified Teachers, may use reflection as a means of self-consciously increasing understanding and capability, thus moving towards a more complete level of professionalism (Calderhead, 1994, **Reading 2.4**. Expert teachers, such as those who have passed competency standards thresholds, will work at a higher level, understanding the various issues concerning children, curriculum, classroom and school so well that many decisions become almost intuitive. In these kinds of ways reflective teaching has a place throughout the profession from trainees and Newly Qualified Teachers (NQTs) to advanced skills teachers, teacher advocates, team leaders in performance management and subject leaders.

2 THE MEANING OF REFLECTIVE TEACHING

The notion of reflective teaching, around which this book is based, stems from Dewey (1933, **Reading 1.1**) who contrasted 'routine action' with 'reflective action'. According to Dewey routine action is guided by factors such as tradition, habit and authority and by institutional definitions and expectations. By implication it is relatively static and is thus unresponsive to changing priorities and circumstances. Reflective action, on the other hand, involves a willingness to engage in constant self-appraisal and development. Among other things, it implies flexibility, rigorous analysis and social awareness.

Dewey's notion of reflective action, when developed and applied to teaching, is both challenging and exciting. In this section, we review its implications by identifying and discussing what we have identified as seven key characteristics of reflective practice. These are:

1. Reflective teaching implies an active concern with aims and consequences, as well as means and technical efficiency.

2. Reflective teaching is applied in a cyclical or spiralling process, in which teachers monitor, evaluate and revise their own practice continuously.

http://www.rtweb.info

3. Reflective teaching requires competence in methods of evidence-based classroom enquiry, to support the progressive development of higher standards of teaching.

4. Reflective teaching requires attitudes of open-mindedness, responsibility and wholeheartedness.

5. Reflective teaching is based on teacher judgement, informed by evidence-based enquiry and insights from other research.

6. Reflective teaching, professional learning and personal fulfilment are enhanced through collaboration and dialogue with colleagues.

7. Reflective teaching enables teachers to creatively mediate externally developed frameworks for teaching and learning.

Each of these characteristics will now be considered more fully.

2.1 Aims and consequences

Reflective teaching implies an active concern with aims and consequences as well as means and technical competence

This issue relates first to the immediate aims and consequences of classroom practice for these are any teacher's prime responsibility. However, classroom work cannot be isolated from the influence of the wider society and a reflective teacher must therefore consider both spheres.

An example from the history of educational policy-making in England will illustrate the way in which changes outside schools influence actions within them. Following the initiation of a 'Great Debate' by Prime Minister Callaghan (1976) many of the 'taken-for-granteds' in education were progressively challenged during the 1980s and 1990s. Successive Conservative governments introduced far-reaching and cumulative changes in all spheres of education. Many of these reforms were opposed by professional organizations (see for example, Haviland (1988) and Arnot and Barton (1992)) but with no noticeable effect on political decision-making (see also **Reading 18.4**). Indeed, the allegation was made that educational policy was being influenced by a closed system of beliefs – an 'ideology' deriving from a small number of right-wing politicians and pressure groups. Meanwhile, teachers and pupils worked to implement the new forms of curriculum, assessment, accountability, management and control which had been introduced, despite the fact that the profession at the time was largely opposed to the principles on which the reforms were based (see Osborn *et al.*, 2000; Pollard *et al.*, 1994, **Reading 18.5**).

Such a stark example of the contestation of aims and values in education raises questions concerning the relationship between professionals, parents and policy-makers. It is possible to start from the seemingly uncontroversial argument that, in a democratic society, decisions about the aims of education should be 'democratically' determined. However, it has also been suggested (White, 1978) that teachers should adopt a role as active 'interpreters' of political policy. Indeed, that most teachers accept this argument is shown by the way in which they have implemented legislation even when they did not support it – though in the 1990s an unusual number of teachers in England did leave the profession. More recently, Bramall and White (2000) analysed the National Curriculum 2000 and suggested that, whilst there are explicit aims and a rationale, these may not be 'owned by' teachers and may not relate to the operationalization of these in the actual curriculum. Indeed, there may be a gap between the 'official' rationale of the National Curriculum and the day-to-day experience of many classroom teachers – a problem that reflective teachers may wish to address.

These kinds of stance are very different from the idea of the autonomous professional with which many teachers once identified. Yet it can be argued that the existence of unconstrained autonomy is only reasonable and practical if ends, aims and values are completely uncontroversial. However, as soon as questions about educational aims and social values are seriously raised then the position changes. In a democratic society, the debate appropriately extends to the political domain and this, of course, is what has happened in recent years.

This does not mean though, that teachers, even as interpreters of policy, should simply 'stand by' in the procedure. Indeed, there are two important roles that they can play. In the case of the first, an appropriate metaphor for the teacher's role is, as White suggested, that of 'activist'. This recognizes that primary school teachers are individual members of society who, within normal political processes, have rights to pursue their values and beliefs as guided by their own individual moral and ethical concerns. They should thus be as active as they wish to be in contributing to the formation of public policy. Second, whilst accepting a responsibility for translating politically determined aims into practice, teachers should speak out, as they have done in the past, if they view particular aims and policies as being professionally impracticable, educationally unsound or morally questionable. In such circumstances the professional experience, knowledge and judgements of teachers should be brought to bear on policy-makers directly – whether or not the policy-makers wish for or act on the advice which is offered (for interesting developments of this argument, see Thompson, 1997). Indeed, it is important that, within a modern democratic society, teachers should be entitled to not only a hearing, but also some influence, on educational policy. Professional and subject associations, such as the Association for the Study of Primary Education (ASPE) and the Geographical Association (GA) together with the General Teaching Council of each part of the UK, provide collective forms of organization for such voices. However, in recent years, teacher unions such as the NUT, ATL and NAHT have undoubtedly been the most effective in making their voices heard.

The reflective teacher should thus be aware of the political process and of its legitimate oversight of public educational services. However, they should also be willing to contribute to it both as a citizen and as a professional (see also Section 2.7 of this chapter and **Reading 1.4** on 'creative mediation', and Chapter 18 for activity beyond the school).

2.2 A cyclical process

Reflective teaching is applied in a cyclical or spiralling process, in which teachers monitor, evaluate and revise their own practice continuously

This characteristic refers to the process of reflective teaching and provides the dynamic basis for teacher action. The conception of a classroom-based, reflexive process stems from the teacher-based, action–research movement of which Lawrence Stenhouse was a key figure. He argued (1975, **Reading 3.1**) that teachers should act as 'researchers' of their own practice and should develop the curriculum through practical enquiry. Various alternative models have since become available (Carr and Kemmis, 1986; Elliott, 1991; McNiff, 1988) and, although there are some significant differences in these models, they all preserve a central concern with self-monitoring and reflection (see also Pring, 2000, **Reading 3.2**).

Teachers are principally expected to plan, make provision and act. Reflective teachers also need to monitor, observe and collect data on their own and the children's intentions, actions and feelings. This evidence then needs to be critically analysed and evaluated so that it can be shared, judgements made and decisions taken. Finally, this may lead the teacher to revise his or her classroom policies, plans and provision before beginning the process again. It is a dynamic process which is intended to lead through successive cycles, or through a spiralling process, towards higher-quality standards of teaching. This model is simple, comprehensive and certainly could be an extremely powerful influence on practice. It is consistent with the notion of reflective teaching, as described by Dewey, and, provides an essential clarification of the procedures for reflective teaching.

Figure 1.5 represents the key stages of the reflective process.

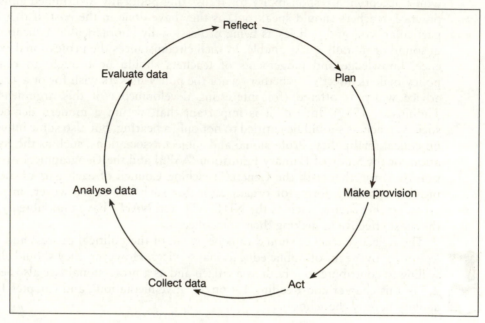

Figure 1.5 *The process of reflective teaching*

2.3 Gathering and evaluating evidence

> *Reflective teaching requires competence in methods of evidence-based classroom enquiry, to support the progressive development of higher standards of teaching*

We can identify four key skills here, reviewing relevant, existing research, gathering new evidence, analysis and evaluation, each of which contributes to the cyclical process of reflection (see Section 2.2). Drawing on the experience of colleagues receives particular attention in Section 2.6.

Reviewing relevant, existing research. The issue here is to learn as much as possible from others. Published research on the issue of concern, from teachers or from professional researchers, may be reviewed. Internet-based search techniques make this an increasingly straightforward task as do other resources – such as the *Key Readings* which conclude each chapter of this book, and the *Notes for Further Reading* which, chapter-by-chapter, are available on **RTweb**. Additionally, many web-sites are provided by summarizing agencies such as the *Times Educational Supplement*, National Foundation for Educational Research, education-online, DfES, TTA, QCA, Welsh Assembly, Scottish Parliament, Scottish Executive Education Department and the Northern Ireland Department of Education. For research project information, see the Current Educational Research Database in the United Kingdom (CERUK) at www.nfer.ac.uk/ceruk. More conventionally, higher education providers usually have excellent libraries which they will make available to partnership schools.

Gathering new evidence. This relates to the essential issue of knowing what is going on in a classroom or school as a means of forming one's own opinion. It is concerned with collecting data, describing situations, processes, causes and effects with care and accuracy. Two sorts of data are particularly relevant. Objective data are important, such as descriptions of what people actually do, but so too are subjective data which describe how people feel and think – their perceptions. The collection of both types of data calls for considerable skill on the part of any classroom investigator, particularly when they may be enquiring into their own practice.

Analytical skills. These skills are needed to address the issue of how to interpret descriptive data. Such 'facts' are not meaningful until they are placed in a framework that enables a reflective teacher to relate them one with the other and to begin to theorize about them.

Evaluative skills. Evaluative skills are involved in making judgements about the educational consequences of the results of the practical enquiry. Evaluation, in the light of aims, values and the experience of others enables the results of an enquiry to be applied to future policy and practice.

Further practical discussion on competence in classroom enquiry is offered in Chapter 3 of this book, in **Readings** and on **RTweb**. However, such competence is not sufficient in itself for a teacher who wishes to engage in reflective teaching. Certain attitudes are also necessary and need to be integrated and applied with enquiry skills.

2.4 Attitudes towards teaching

Reflective teaching requires attitudes of open-mindedness, responsibility and wholeheartedness

Open-mindedness. As Dewey put it, open-mindedness is:

> An active desire to listen to more sides than one, to give heed to facts from whatever source they come, to give full attention to alternative possibilities, to recognise the possibility of error even in the beliefs which are dearest to us.
>
> (Dewey, 1933, p. 29)

Open-mindedness is an essential attribute for rigorous reflection because any sort of enquiry that is consciously based on partial evidence, only weakens itself. We thus use the concept in the sense of being willing to reflect upon ourselves and to challenge our own assumptions, prejudices and ideologies, as well as those of others. However, to be open-minded regarding evidence and its interpretation is not the same thing as declining to take up a value-position on important social and educational issues. This point brings us to the second attribute which Dewey saw as a prerequisite to reflective action – 'responsibility'.

Responsibility. Intellectual responsibility, according to Dewey, means:

To consider the consequences of a projected step; it means to be willing to adopt these consequences when they follow reasonably ... Intellectual responsibility secures integrity.

(Dewey, 1933, p. 30)

The position implied here is clearly related to the question of aims that we discussed above. However, in Dewey's writing the issue is relatively clearly bounded and he seems to be referring to classroom teaching and to school practices only. Zeichner (1981–2) takes this considerably further. Moral, ethical and political issues will be raised and must, he argues, be considered so that professional and personal judgements can be made about what is worthwhile. It clearly follows that a simple instrumental approach to teaching is not consistent with a reflective social awareness (see also **Reading 1.5**).

Wholeheartedness. 'Wholeheartedness', the third of Dewey's necessary attitudes, refers essentially to the way in which such consideration takes place. Dewey's suggestion was that reflective teachers should be dedicated, single-minded, energetic and enthusiastic. As he put it:

There is no greater enemy of effective thinking than divided interest ... A genuine enthusiasm is an attitude that operates as an intellectual force. When a person is absorbed, the subject carries him on.

(Dewey, 1933, p. 30)

Together, these three attitudes are vital ingredients of the professional commitment that needs to be demonstrated by all those who aim to be reflective teachers.

In modern circumstances, these attitudes of open-mindedness, wholeheartedness and responsibility are often challenged, and the morale of many teachers has been low in recent years. Halpin (2001) argues that maintaining 'intelligent hope' and imagining future possibilities are essential for committed educationalists. Beyond simple optimism, this requires 'a way of thinking about the present and the future that is permeated by critique, particularly of the kind that holds up to external scrutiny taken-for-granted current circumstances' (p. 117). Maintaining a constructive engagement, a willingness to imagine new futures, and a self-critical spirit are thus all connected to reflective practice.

2.5 Teacher judgement

Reflective teaching is based on teacher judgement, informed by evidence-based enquiry and insights from other research

Teachers' knowledge has often been criticized. For instance, Bolster (1983) carried out an analysis of teachers as classroom decision-makers and suggested that, since teacher knowledge is specific and pragmatic, it is resistant to development. Bolster argued that teacher knowledge is based on individual experiences and is simply believed to be of value if it 'works' in practical situations. However, this gives little incentive to change, even in the light of evidence supporting alternative ideas or practices. On this analysis there is little need for teacher judgement, since teachers will stick to routinized practices.

For an alternative view we can draw on Donald Schon's work (Schon, 1983, **Reading 1.2**) on the characteristics of 'reflective practitioners'. Schon contrasted 'scientific' professional work such as laboratory research, with 'caring' professional work such as education. He called the former 'high hard ground' and saw it as supported by quantitative and 'objective' evidence. On the other hand, the 'swampy lowlands' of the caring professions involve more interpersonal areas and qualitative issues. These complex 'lowlands', according to Schon, tend to become 'confusing messes' of intuitive action. He thus suggested that, although such 'messes' tend to be highly relevant in practical terms, they are not easily amenable to rigorous analysis because they draw on a type of knowledge-in-action – knowledge that is inherent in professional action. It is spontaneous, intuitive, tacit and intangible but, it 'works' in practice.

Schon also argued that it is possible to recognize 'reflection-in-action', in which adjustments to action are made through direct experience. As he put it:

> When someone reflects-in-action, he [sic] becomes a researcher in the practice context. He is not dependent on the categories of established theory and technique, but constructs a new theory of the unique case. He does not keep means and ends separate, but defines them interactively as he frames a problematic situation. He does not separate thinking from action . . . His experimenting is a kind of action, implementation is built into his enquiry.
>
> (Schon, 1983, p. 68)

Such ideas have received powerful empirical support in recent years, with the sophistication of teachers' classroom thinking and 'craft knowledge' being increasingly recognized and understood by both researchers (Elbaz, 1983; Calderhead, 1987; 1988; Olson, 1991; Cortazzi, 1990, **Reading 5.2**; Brown, 1992 and policy-makers (TTA, 1998, 2000). It is clear that effective teachers make use of judgements all the time, as they adapt their teaching to the ever-changing learning challenges which their circumstances and pupils present to them. In recent years, there has also been much greater recognition of the role of intuition in the work of experienced teachers (Atkinson and Claxton, 2000; Tomlinson, 1999a, b) and decision-making. Nevertheless, one of the most exciting policy developments of recent years is the way in which forms of evidence-informed practice are being encouraged to support continuing professional improvement (DfEE, 2001a).

Educational researchers' knowledge has also often been criticized. Most of this derives from work undertaken by former teachers who have moved into academia. It may be based on comparative, historical or philosophical research, on empirical study with large samples of classrooms, teachers, pupils or schools, on innovative methodologies, or on developing theoretical analyses (see Chapter 3, Section 3). Additionally, many researchers regard it as their duty to probe, analyse and evaluate – particularly with regard to the impact of policy – even though this is not always popular with governments! Whatever its character, such educational research has the potential to complement, contextualize and enhance the detailed and practical understandings of practising teachers.

In recent years, considerable effort has been made to improve the relevance, significance and impact of educational research, and to engage with practitioners and policy-makers. Indeed, the best work is of very high quality and is an important source of ideas and evidence on teaching, learning, policy and practice. Over 130 selections of such work are provided in **Readings** and further advice on relevant publications (with regular updates) is offered through **RTweb's**

Notes for Further Reading. For ease of use, this material is organized using the chapter headings of the text of this book.

Politicians' knowledge of education has also often been criticized – and some will feel that this is an understatement! However, governments have a democratic mandate and are appropriately concerned to ensure that educational services meet national needs. Teachers would thus be unjustified if they ignored the views of politicians, though independence, experience, judgement and expertise remain the defining characteristics of professionalism. Indeed, where politicians' views appear to be influenced by fashionable whims, media panics or party considerations rather than established educational needs, then a certain amount of 'professional mediation' may be entirely justified (see Section 2.7).

Taken as a whole, we strongly advocate attempts to maximize the potential for collaboration between teachers, researchers and politicians. For such collaboration to be successful it must be based on a frank appreciation of each other's strengths and weaknesses. While recognizing the danger of unjustified generalization, we therefore identify these strengths and weaknesses (see Figure 1.6).

We arrive then, at a position that calls for attempts to draw on the strengths of the knowledge of teachers, researchers and politicians or policy-makers. By doing this, we may overcome the weaknesses which exist in each position. This is what we mean by the statement that reflective teaching should be based on 'informed teacher judgement'. The implied collaborative endeavour underpins this whole book.

2.6 Learning with colleagues

Reflective teaching, professional learning and personal fulfilment are enhanced through collaboration and dialogue with colleagues

The value of engaging in reflective activity is almost always enhanced if it can be carried out in association with other colleagues, be they trainees, teachers or tutors. The circumstances in primary schools, with very high proportions of contact-time with children, have constrained a great deal of such educational discussion in the past – though this is gradually changing as whole-school professional development assumes a greater priority. On teacher-education courses, despite the pressure of curricular requirements, reflection together in seminars, tutor groups and workshops, at college or in school, should bring valuable opportunities to share and compare, support and advise in reciprocal ways.

Wherever and whenever it occurs, collaborative, reflective discussion capitalizes on the social nature of learning (Vygotsky, 1978, **Reading 7.3**). This is as significant for adults as it is for children (see Chapter 7) and it works through many of the same basic processes. Aims are thus clarified, experiences are shared, language and concepts for analysing practice are refined, the personal insecurities of innovation are reduced, evaluation becomes reciprocal and commitments are affirmed. Moreover, openness, activity and discussion gradually weave the values and self of individuals into the culture and mission of the school or course. This can be both personally fulfilling and educationally effective (Kohl, 1986; Nias, 1989, **Reading 5.1**).

Recently, when the development of coherence and progression in school

	Strengths	Weaknesses
Teachers' knowledge	Often practically relevant and directly useful Often communicated effectively to practitioners Often concerned with the wholeness of classroom processes and experiences	May be impressionistic and can lack rigour Usually based in particular situations which limits generalization Analysis is sometimes over-influenced by existing assumptions
Researchers' knowledge	May be based on careful research with large samples and reliable methods Often provides a clear and incisive analysis when studied Often offers novel ways of looking at situations and issues	Often uses jargon unnecessarily and communicates poorly Often seems obscure and difficult to relate to practical issues Often fragments educational processes and experiences
Politicians' knowledge	Often responsive to issues of public concern May have a democratic mandate May be backed by institutional, financial and legal resources	Often over-influenced by short-term political considerations Often reflects party-political positions rather than educational needs Is often imposed and may thus lack legitimacy

Figure 1.6 *A comparison of teachers', researchers' and politicians' knowledge*

policies and practice have become of enormous importance, collaborative work is also a necessity. At one level, it is officially endorsed by the requirement to produce 'school development plans', a process which has been seen as 'empowering' (Hargreaves and Hopkins, 1991; see Chapter 17). More detailed work on the nature of primary-school cultures and the development of the 'intelligent school', whilst affirming the enormous value of whole-school staff teams working and learning together, has also shown the complexity and fragility of the process (MacGilchrist *et al.*, 1997; Southworth *et al.*, **Reading 17.2**).

Whatever their circumstances though, reflective teachers are likely to benefit from working, experimenting, talking, and reflecting with others. Apart from the benefits for learning and professional development, it is usually both more interesting and more fun!

2.7   Reflective teaching as creative mediation

Reflective teaching enables teachers to creatively mediate externally developed frameworks for teaching and learning

The 1990s in England were characterized perhaps more than any other decade of the twentieth century by increasingly centralized control of education. Following the Education Reform Act, 1988, this first impacted on the curriculum and was quickly followed by national assessment and inspection. There was steady critique of pedagogy (e.g. Alexander *et al.*, 1992) and at the end of the decade there was a massive change in the scope of teachers' pedagogic judgement through the introduction of the National Literacy Strategy (DfEE, 1998b) and National Numeracy Strategy (DfEE, 1999). Such detailed prescription had never previously occurred in England. Regarding literacy, 15 minutes of text-level work at whole-class level was to be followed by 15 minutes of word/sentence-level work, then 20 minutes of group work, including independent group activities and guided reading or writing, and finally a 10-minute plenary to consolidate learning. Echoes of such policies had considerable effect in Wales, but Scotland and Northern Ireland managed to retain a larger measure of partnership between teachers and policy-makers. Nevertheless, educational provision is being thought of in systemic terms all over the world, and there is no doubt that teachers must get used to coming to terms with the external requirements which are bound to ebb and flow over the period of a career.

Such developments place a premium on a particular form of reflective activity which we call 'creative mediation'. This involves the interpretation of external requirements in the light of a teacher's understanding of a particular context and bearing in mind his or her values and educational principles. For example, some teachers may share Frater's (1999) argument that the National Literacy Strategy in England neglects the needs of a substantial population of poor readers. They might therefore wish, through reflective practice, to imaginatively adapt and enhance the framework so that it fits more comfortably within their practice. The example of the National Literacy Strategy is a good one because it encompasses the essence of creative mediation, by showing how external developments and requirements are aligned with deeply held professional values.

In a study of change in primary education through the 1990s, Osborn *et al.* (2000) identified four different kinds of 'creative mediation' (see **Reading 1.4**).

- *Protective mediation* calls for strategies to defend existing practices which are greatly valued (such as the desire to maintain an element of spontaneity in teaching in the face of assessment pressure).

- *Innovative mediation* is concerned with teachers finding strategies to work *within* the spaces and boundaries provided by new requirements – finding opportunities to be creative.

- *Collaborative mediation* refers to teachers working closely together to provide mutual support in satisfying and adapting new requirements. As Osborn *et al.* (2000, p. 78) state: 'One of the unintended consequences of National Curriculum implementation was the unprecedented level of collaboration which emerged amongst primary teachers.'

- *Conspirational mediation* involves schools adopting more subversive strategies where teachers resist implementing those aspects of external requirements that they believe to be particularly inappropriate.

Such forms of mediation exemplify major strategies in the exercise of professional judgement. Clearly they need to be carefully justified.

See **RTweb** for links to supportive professional associations, and also the future discussion in Chapter 8, Section 3.4 and Chapter 18, Section 3.

CONCLUSION

In this chapter we have considered the spiral of professional development and the particular role of reflective teaching in raising standards of teaching. We have outlined the seven key characteristics of reflective teaching.

Some readers may well be wondering if this isn't all just a bit much to ask. How is the time to be found? Isn't it all 'common sense' anyway? Two responses may be made. First, it is certainly the case that constantly engaging in reflective activities of the sort described in this book would be impossible. The point, however, is to use them as *learning experiences*. Such experiences should lead to conclusions which can be applied in new and more routine circumstances. This is how professional expertise is actively developed. Second, there is certainly a good deal of 'common sense' in the process of reflective teaching. However, when reflective teaching is used as a means of professional development it is extended far beyond this underpinning. The whole activity is much more rigorous – carefully gathered evidence replaces subjective impressions, open-mindedness replaces prior expectations, insights from reading or constructive and structured critique from colleagues challenge what might previously have been taken for granted. 'Common sense' may well endorse the value of the basic, reflective idea but, ironically, one outcome of reflection is often to produce critique and movement beyond the limitations of common-sense thinking. That, in a sense, is the whole point, the reason why reflection is a necessary part of professional activity. The aim of reflective practice is thus to support a shift from routine actions rooted in common-sense thinking to reflective action stemming from professional thinking.

Teachers can confidently expect to raise their standards of professional competence through adopting processes of reflective teaching – and the remainder of this book is designed to provide support in that process.

Key readings

The dilemmas in educational decision-making, which suggest that reflection is a continually necessary element of teaching are analysed in:

Berlak, A. and Berlak, H. (1981)
Dilemmas of Schooling.
London: Methuen.   Reading 1.3

Two works by Dewey which have influenced our thinking are:

Dewey, J. (1916)
Democracy and Education.
New York: Free Press.   📖 **Reading 1.1**

Dewey, J. (1933)
How We Think: A Restatement of the Relation of Reflective Thinking to the Educative Process.
Chicago: Henry Regnery.

The work of Zeichner on reflective teaching is also very stimulating. See, in particular:

Tabachnick, R. and Zeichner, K. (eds) (1991)
Issues and Practices in Inquiry-Oriented Teacher Education.
London: Falmer.   📖 **Reading 1.5**

On the potential gains, embracing both practical competence and social emancipation, which are claimed to derive from self-evaluation and classroom enquiry, see:

Stenhouse, L. (1983)
Authority, Education and Emancipation.
London: Heinemann.   📖 **Reading 3.1**

Carr, W. and Kemmis, S. (1986)
Becoming Critical: Knowing through Action Research.
London: Falmer Press.

Elliott, J. (1991)
Action Research for Educational Change.
Buckingham: Open University Press.

Smyth, J. (1991)
Teachers as Collaborative Learners.
Buckingham: Open University Press.

For a range of views on the nature of professional knowledge and its relationship to more theoretical analyses, see:

Schon, D. A. (1983)
The Reflective Practitioner: How Professionals Think in Action.
London: Temple Smith.   📖 **Reading 1.2**

Calderhead, J. (1988)
Teachers' Professional Learning.
London: Falmer.

Brown, S. and McIntyre, D. (1992)
Making Sense of Teaching.
Buckingham: Open University Press.

For case studies of teacher's practical reasoning, see:

Elbaz, F.(1983)
Teacher Thinking: a Study of Practical Knowledge.
London: Croom Helm.

Clandinin, D. J. (1986)
Classroom Practice: Teacher Images in Action.
London: Falmer Press.

Cortazzi, M. (1990)
Primary Teaching How it is: A Narrative Account.
London: David Fulton.   📖 **Reading 5.2**

For an influential perspective on the 'art' of teaching, including the concept of 'connoisseurship', see:

Eisner, E. W. (1979)
The Educational Imagination.
New York: Macmillan.

For a sustained attempt to identify competences of reflective teaching, see:

Hextall, I., Lawn, M., Menter, I., Sidgwick, S. and Walker, S. (1991)
'Imaginative projects: arguments for a new teacher education',
Evaluation and Research in Education, 5 (1 and 2), 79–95.

For international comparisons of changes in teacher education which track a tightening of state control in many countries, see:

Popkewitz, T. (ed.) (1993)
Changing Patterns of Power: Social Regulation and Teacher Education Reform in Eight Countries.
New York: State University of New York Press.

Given the influence of Dewey on reflection in professional life, and the intellectual openness advocated by him, we should be prepared to engage with those who espouse very different views. For a direct attack on Dewey and on educationalists, see:

O'Hear, A. (1991)
Education and Democracy: Against the Educational Establishment.
London: Claridge.

 Readings for Reflective Teaching (the companion volume) offers other closely associated work on the issues raised in this chapter. This includes work by authors such as:

John Dewey, Donald Schon, Ann and Harold Berlak, Marilyn Osborn, Elizabeth McNess, Patricia Broadfoot, Robert Tabachnick and Ken Zeichner.

 RTweb offers additional professional resources for this chapter. These may include *Notes for Further Reading*, supplementary *Reflective Activities*, useful *Web Links*, *Extension Texts* and *Download Facilities* for diagrams, figures, checklists, activities.

CHAPTER 2

Learning through mentoring in initial training

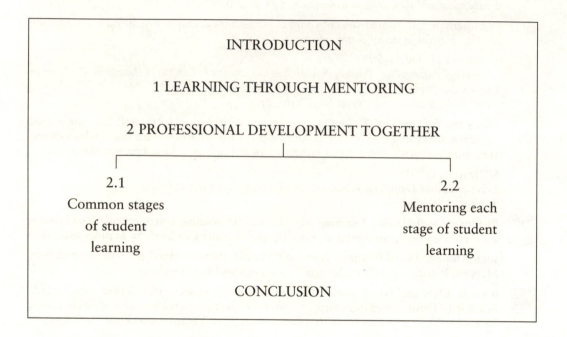

INTRODUCTION

1 LEARNING THROUGH MENTORING

2 PROFESSIONAL DEVELOPMENT TOGETHER

2.1
Common stages
of student
learning

2.2
Mentoring each
stage of student
learning

CONCLUSION

Enhancing professional standards and competences

The role of school-based practice in learning how to teach has a very long history, and is likely to remain saliant in teacher education. However, the way this is prioritized and organized changes over the years. Currently, the English TTA specifies that all providers of initial training must:

> Work in partnership with schools and actively involve them in planning and delivering ITT, selecting and assessing trainee teachers for Qualified Teacher Status.
>
> Set up partnership agreements which make clear to everyone involved each partner's roles and responsibilities.
>
> Make sure the partnership works effectively and that the training is co-ordinated and consistent, with continuity across the various contexts in which it takes place.
>
> (TTA, 2002, *Requirements for ITT*, R3)

Similar commitments and requirements exist in Northern Ireland, Wales and Scotland. For instance, the latter's guidelines for the approval of initial teacher education courses properly insists that:

> Schools are essential partners in the preparation of the next generation of teachers.
>
> (Scottish Office, 1998, *Guidelines for Initial Teacher Education Courses in Scotland*, p. 2)

INTRODUCTION

Mentoring is a means of providing support, challenge and extension of the learning of one person through the guidance of another who is more skilled, knowledgeable and experienced, particularly in relation to the context in which the learning is taking place. This chapter addresses mentoring in initial training and is written partly for mentors and partly for trainee teachers. Chapter 17 supports mentoring for newly qualified teachers and during the early years of professional development.

The importance of mentoring in modern initial teacher education reflects three trends. First, there is the growing professional recognition and understanding of the complexity of teachers' capabilities and of the need to study, practise and develop these within real school contexts. Second, the high proportion of time on initial training courses now spent in school-based training makes mentoring an absolutely key process in the development of high professional standards and the transfer of knowledge from one generation of teachers to the next. Third, there is a significant development, particularly in England, in the form of more flexible and employment-based routes into teaching. School-based mentoring will be a very important feature of such provision.

Mentoring, and being guided by a mentor, provides excellent opportunities for the development of teaching skills and reflective understanding, both within subjects and more generically. After all, that is the essential rationale for establishing a relationship between a trainee and an experienced teacher. This stands whether or not it is underpinned by a conventional 'partnership' arrangement between a school and a higher education institution, or is associated with a Training School's provision, School-Centred Initial Teacher Training or any other employment-based route into teaching. It stands whether access to training is full-time or part-time, BEd or PGCE, fast-track, established or 'flexible'. Whatever the route or form of training, there is a clear pattern in which increasing responsibility for mentoring students is being taken on a whole-school basis, with subject specialists and senior management supplementing the more continuous support of a class-based mentor.

In a sense then, as Edwards and Collison (1996, **Reading 2.2**) argued, trainee teachers join a community of existing practices, and mentoring activity can also be seen as contributing to the dynamics of a developing school. The learning of trainees is not just personal therefore, though this aspect is clearly vital, but it also refects and contributes to the culture of the school itself. As they put it:

> We recognise a constant and creative interaction between learners and contexts. The meanings of teaching and learning are constantly created, negotiated and tested by those who are acting and learning in those contexts.
>
> (Edwards and Collison, 1996, p. 7)

Agreement about roles and relationships within such arrangements is obviously crucial if their benefits are to be maximized, and this is true for teacher mentors, trainee teachers and, where appropriate, higher education tutors. If the roles are clear, then the learning potential of such situations is very considerable.

The role of the student is certainly the most important – and we will direct this text to you, the trainee-teacher reader, at this point. Your approach to the new challenges you will meet is crucial. We might identify three dimensions of the role as you begin to enter the school community and develop as a professional. First, you need to present and organize yourself so that you become accepted within the school. This means being sensitive to customs and practices. Second, you need to be receptive to the efforts which your mentor(s) and tutor make and be willing to develop a constructive relationship with them. Remember that being challenged by a mentor is an opportunity to learn – rather than an attack – though you should certainly feel able to enter into dialogue with them. Third, it is vital that you adopt an active, professional approach to the development of skills and understanding, and that that advice is received openly. You can also contribute a great deal to any necessary assessment phase, through the quality of your self-evaluation activities.

The role of the mentor has been usefully analysed by Sampson and Yeomans (1994, **Reading 2.1**). They suggest that it has three dimensions. These are *structural* – working across the school as planner, organizer, negotiator, inductor for the student placement; *supportive* – working with the student as host, friend and counsellor; *professional* – working with the student as trainer, educator and assessor. Recent developments in mentoring put further emphasis on providing analysis of performance, both generically and in relation to particular subjects, and in offering both advice and challenge.

The role of a tutor from a higher education institution, if the training route provides for this support, can also be seen in terms of these three dimensions.

Structurally, he or she would often have established relationships with 'link' or 'partnership' schools, so that the placement could be negotiated smoothly. The tutor would then facilitate and support the relationship between the student and mentor as it develops, so that the potential benefits of that learning relationship are forthcoming. Professionally, the tutor would expect to contribute to the educational process by offering comparative experience and knowledge from reading and research. In the assessment phase he or she must draw on their comparative judgement and may be able to enhance consistency of judgement across schools. There are interesting differences across the UK regarding the role of higher education tutors in school-based elements of teacher education. Broadly, this is stronger at present in Wales, Scotland and Northern Ireland than it is in England.

See RTweb for links to governmental organizations in each part of the UK.

1   LEARNING THROUGH MENTORING

If roles, relationships and channels for communication are established and open, then the potential for constructive professional learning is considerable. Focusing specifically on this, Peter Tomlinson (1995) has provided a very useful summary of four major forms of student learning activity and mentoring assistance, and these are set out in Figure 2.1.

---

1. Assisting students to learn from other people teaching by:
   explaining the planning
   guiding observation of the action
   modelling and prompting monitoring
   modelling and prompting reflection.

2. Assisting students to learn through their own teaching activities by:
   assisting their planning
   supporting their teaching activity
   assisting monitoring and feedback
   assisting analysis and reflection.

3. Progressively collaborative teaching involving:
   progressive joint planning
   teaching as a learning team
   mutual monitoring
   joint analysis and reflection.

4. Exploring central ideas and broader issues through:
   direct research on pupil, colleague, school and system contexts
   reading and other inputs on teaching and background issues
   organized discussion on these topics.

Figure 2.1 *Major forms of student learning activity and mentoring assistance (Tomlinson, 1995)*

This is an exciting agenda in which the mentor provides support at each stage of the teaching cycle (see Figure 1.5). Indeed, in many ways the mentor–student relationship is very close to that which is discussed in relation to social constructivist models of learning (see Chapter 7, Section 1.3). Thus the mentor 'assists the performance' and 'scaffolds the understanding' of the student learner, as he or she constructs his or her own skills and understanding in the classroom context. Initially then, as a trainee, you may need direct support by explanation, modelling and guidance with the analysis of issues and with evaluation. Gradually however, you will become sufficiently confident to teach more independently. Greater challenges will be faced (larger groups, longer teaching sessions, more complex teaching aims) and you will begin to monitor your performance more independently. Collaborative teaching will reinforce these emergent skills and understandings as you get more experience.

The mentor is thus uniquely placed to offer support and challenge in Tomlinson's first three ways (learning from others, learning from their own teaching, collaborating with others). Where available, tutors from higher education institutions are likely to be able to make a particular contribution to the fourth element of exploring key concepts, broader issues and recent research.

2 PROFESSIONAL DEVELOPMENT TOGETHER

2.1 Common stages of student learning

Effective mentoring involves the use of professional skills, such as those reviewed above, in appropriate responses to the changing learning needs of students. But what do we know about the way in which trainee teachers may develop?

An examination of research literature on the process of learning to teach confirms the common-sense observation that trainees typically go through a number of distinct stages of development, each with its own focal concerns. Maynard and Furlong (1993) argued that these concerns can be grouped under the following headings: early idealism; survival; recognizing difficulties; hitting the plateau; and moving on. Of course, things may turn out differently, but this is a useful progression to reflect upon!

Early idealism

Before training begins, new student teachers are often highly idealistic about teaching. For many, this involves wanting to identify closely with the pupils and their needs and interests. This identification with the pupils is hardly surprising, since, for the vast majority of students in training, their only experience of the teaching process has been as pupils themselves. Such commitments are highly commendable, and may continue to underpin professional values for many years. However, once trainee teachers enter the classroom, such idealism can fade very quickly.

Survival

The first days and weeks in the classroom are often extremely challenging for students both professionally and personally. A common complaint is that it is difficult to 'see' what is *really* going on. Indeed, it is often hard to disentangle

the complexities of teaching and to understand the processes involved. Either things appear to be straightforward – something that anyone can do – or they seem overwhelming in their complexity. In the early stages of school experience, time is often given for trainees to observe classroom practice. However, as Calderhead (1988) and (Doyle, 1977, **Reading 11.1**) confirm, this contact is often undervalued because interpretation of classroom noise and movement is difficult, and the significance of teacher actions may not be clear. In a nutshell, it is simply hard to know what it is one is supposed to be looking at and why! It is no wonder that at this stage students often go in search of 'quick fixes' and 'hints and tips' (Eisenhart, Behm and Riomagnano, 1991). Learning how to observe an experienced teacher and how to understand the different skills that he or she is using is thus an achievement in itself. It is something that students need to be supported in doing. In particular, one must allow time and avoid panic of any sort – things will eventually fall into place.

Another important feature of early classroom experiences is that trainees frequently become obsessed with their own survival; 'fitting in' and establishing themselves as a 'teacher' often become major issues for them. Rather than wanting to identify closely with the pupils, they become dominated by their concern to 'manage' them. However, if achieving classroom management and control becomes the overriding concern, then teaching and learning activities begin to be judged almost entirely in terms of whether they contribute to achieving that end. Maynard and Furlong suggest that trainees are often person-ally very stressed by this early period of learning to teach. In particular, many find it hard to come to terms with themselves as authority figures. They have to get used to a new persona, 'me-as-teacher' (see Chapter 5, Section 1) and for some, it is not a character they particularly like. As a consequence it is not uncommon for students to go through a period of resenting the pupils for forcing them to be more authoritarian than they really want to be.

Recognizing difficulties

Fortunately the confusion and challenges brought about by the first taste of teaching do not, in most cases, last more than a week or so. Slowly, the 'survival' stage gives way to a period where trainees can at least start to disentangle some of the complexities involved in teaching. They begin to identify some of the difficulties they face in learning to teach. However, this recognition brings its own pressures and they can be overwhelmed by the complexity of it all. As a result, despite assurances from teachers and tutors and attempts to help them view this is as a 'learning experience', the dominant concern for most students at this early stage is, 'Will I pass?', 'Will I satisfy the standards?' In this circumstance, a common reaction is for trainees to try to replicate or mimic other teachers' behaviour. They develop an apparent competence by focusing on teaching strategies and classroom organization, 'acting' like a teacher without necessarily understanding the underlying purpose or implications of those actions.

Hitting the plateau

Eventually, most trainees do manage to at least 'act' like a teacher; they learn how to control the class and engage the pupils in some purposive activity. However, Maynard and Furlong suggest that once students have achieved this level of competence, they may stop developing – they can 'hit a plateau'. After all, if we find a way of teaching that 'works' and offers security, there is certainly an incentive to stick to it! The challenge is then for school mentors to move the trainee on from 'acting like a teacher' towards 'thinking like a teacher'. We would suggest that the difference between these two states is that experienced teachers devote most of their attention to thinking about their pupils' learning rather than focusing on their own 'performance'. In other words, they are competent and confident enough to be able to 'de-centre' from themselves to the pupils. Evidence suggests that, in developing in this way, students benefit greatly from external support and some progressive development of practical teaching skills.

Moving on

There is one further stage of learning to teach and that involves the development of the trainee as a 'reflective practitioner' – a concept which was explored in Chapter 1 and to which this book contributes. To teach in this way is an appropriate ambition at any stage of a professional career, and a programme of initial teacher training can lay foundations. Nevertheless it is clear that, as we gain in confidence, we are capable of taking more responsibility for our own professional development, for broadening our repertoire of teaching strategies, deepening our understanding of the complexities of teaching and learning, and for considering the social, moral and political dimensions of educational practice. We are also in a better frame of mind to think seriously about subject knowledge. Mentors and higher education tutors, working collaboratively, are well placed to help students analyse and reflect on their own teaching.

2.2   Mentoring each stage of student learning

Mentoring should be developmental so that trainees are supported through the different stages of learning to teach. However, it is important to emphasize that, in arguing for a developmental approach, we are not suggesting that mentors should simply provide whatever support they are asked for. Indeed, there will be times when mentors will need to be more assertive in their interventions, providing students with what it is judged that they 'need', even when this may not be what they immediately 'want'. However, in essence, mentoring is no different from any other form of teaching and it is necessary to start from where the learners are and take typical patterns of development into account.

Following Furlong *et al.* (1994), we outline a number of different stages of mentoring (see also Maynard, 2001, **Reading 2.3**). In each stage we can identify different learning priorities for the trainee and a different 'role' for the mentor in supporting those learning needs. We also suggest a number of key mentoring strategies. The development of any one student will be much more complex than a simple stage model implies; they will develop at their own rate and will need to revisit issues because they have forgotten them or wish to relearn them in a different context or at a deeper level. We therefore intend these stages of mentoring to be considered flexibly and with sensitivity. In fact it is probably more appropriate to think of each stage as cumulative rather than discrete. As students develop, mentors will need to employ more and more strategies from the repertoire that we set out.

A summary of a developmental model of mentoring adapted from Furlong *et al.* (1994) is set out in Figure 2.2.

Beginning teaching

As we indicated earlier, when trainees first begin the process of learning to teach, they often have two particular learning needs. They need to learn how to 'see' – to disentangle and identify some of the complexities of the teaching process. In particular, they are most concerned to discover how teachers achieve effective control within the classroom.

In developing an understanding of how to achieve classroom control, trainees face two particular difficulties. The first is that teachers often find it extremely difficult to explain how it is they achieve discipline and order. To an experienced teacher, classroom management is such a 'natural' process that it is difficult to discuss it in isolation from other aspects of teaching. The second difficulty is that by the time that the student arrives in school, usually part way through the year, teachers have already established relationships with their pupils. Much of the 'work' that goes into achieving order takes place at the beginning of the school

	Beginning teaching	Supervized teaching	From teaching to learning	Reflective teaching
Stage of trainee development	Survival	Recognizing difficulties	Hitting the plateau	Moving on
Focus of student learning	Rules, rituals, routines and establishing authority	Teaching competences	Understanding pupil learning and developing effective teaching	Taking control and developing professionalism
Role of mentor and tutor	Providing models of effective practice	As trainers, providing focused advice and instruction	As critical friends, providing constructive critique for development	As co-enquirers, joining together in aspects of professional development
Key mentoring strategies	Student observation focused on class routines and teacher techniques	Focused observation by trainee, combined with structured observation of the trainee and feedback	Focused observation by, and structured observation of, the trainee Re-examination of lesson planning	Partnership in teaching and supervision

Figure 2.2 *A developmental model of mentoring*

 year and thereafter is simply understood by teacher and pupils alike (see Chapter 6 on establishing relationships). By the time trainees arrive, many of the teacher's management strategies may be almost 'invisible'.

Because much of what the student most wants to learn may be tacit, and invisible to the untutored eye, we would suggest the focus for students in the earliest stages of learning to teach must necessarily be on the rules, routines and rituals of the classroom. By observing and copying these 'ready-made' strategies, trainees can more quickly come to participate in the classroom and begin to 'act' like a teacher.

At this stage, students can best be helped to make sense of the classroom and understand its rules, rituals and routines by observing and teaching collaboratively alongside their mentor. By setting up focused observations and collaborative teaching, the mentor acts as a model for the trainees; interpreting events, guiding their observation, drawing their attention to what they are doing and why, and to the significance of what is happening in the classroom. Collaborative teaching also allows the trainee to begin to engage in substantive 'teaching', while the teacher, rather than the student, remains responsible for classroom management and control.

Supervised teaching

Once trainee teachers have gained some insight into the rules, routines and rituals of the classroom and, through carefully supported collaborative work, have themselves had some experience of teaching, then they will be ready for a more systematic and structured approach to training. As we indicated above, during this second phase of their teaching experience, trainees are likely to be mostly concerned with developing their own 'performance' as teachers. Their aim will be to achieve greater and greater control over the teaching and learning process. An important element of this will be developing more confidence with subject knowledge – and in particular the ways in which knowledge can be taught effectively. We suggest that this development can be supported best if the class mentor (and subject mentor(s), if appropriate) explicitly develop a formal 'training' role, focusing directly on the standards or competences of teaching.

In reality of course, teaching cannot be fully characterized as a series of discrete competences or standards because the whole is always more than the sum of the parts. Thus, to extract one particular element from a complex process like teaching is necessarily artificial. Nevertheless, to simplify the complexity for training purposes, there are benefits in mentors focusing on specific teaching competences in a structured way.

As part of their systematic training, students will continue to need to observe and investigate classroom practices, though now their focus might benefit by being even more tightly geared to issues which have been identified for further development. The Reflective Activities in this book should provide many ideas for worthwhile activities. In addition, we would suggest that mentors and tutors provide similarly focused observation and feedback on specific teaching competences.

In terms of the *content* of training, the broad focus is provided by 'official' standards and competences which may be set by a government or national agency. In this book, we have highlighted these at the front of each chapter, and also drawn attention to differences in emphasis in different parts of the United Kingdom. The degree of specificity of guidance the mentor and tutor need to give the trainee will vary depending on the stage of the student's development and their success in managing the particular competence successfully. The more difficulty a trainee has, the more helpful it is for the mentor and tutor to give specific guidance.

From teaching to learning

Once trainees have gained sufficient confidence in classroom management and control in order to 'act' like a teacher, then they are able to turn their attention away from their own performance, and look more deeply at the content of their lessons in terms of what their pupils are actually learning. As we saw earlier, Furlong *et al.* (1994) called this process 'de-centring'.

Developing the ability to de-centre, to reassess one's teaching in terms of pupils' learning rather than one's own performance, is a vitally important part of becoming an effective teacher. However, experience shows that trainees often fail to move on in this way unless they are given some direct help. They may be satisfied with having established a particular formula for teaching which keeps the children quiet and occupied, but then fail to look critically at what learning is taking place. This is understandable, but it is not good enough.

Students who find difficulty in moving on to consider pupils' learning often embody two basic misconceptions. First, they may hold views that are not supportive of the need for further development to focus on pupil learning itself. For example, they may believe that teaching is simply about the transmission of knowledge and the accumulation of factual information; that school learning is 'discrete' and separate from learning going on elsewhere in pupils' lives; that giving correct answers denotes understanding. Until these sorts of beliefs have been challenged and trainee teachers have begun to recognize the complexities involved in teaching and learning (see Chapters 4 to 15), they will not be open to developing a more appropriate approach to planning for pupils' learning over time.

A second difficulty may be that the student actually has insufficient confidence in classroom management and control (see Chapter 11). An appreciation of how pupils learn also demands a willingness to experiment with different strategies of classroom organization (see Chapter 10). In particular, it demands that pupils take an active role in their learning and, when appropriate, to participate in investigation and enquiry. For some trainee teachers, especially those who have only a tentative hold on classroom control, this may appear very threatening. How much easier to keep pupils sitting in their places and have their attention focused on you!

Trainees have to come to realise that effective classroom control is attained primarily through working *with* young pupils through *well-matched* activities that:

- address pupils' needs and interests
- take account of how pupils learn
- are supportive of pupils' developing understanding of the subject area.

The development of a fuller understanding of effective teaching is often a slow and difficult process for students. In particular, understanding of how pupils learn, and the appropriate role of a teacher in supporting them, takes years to develop.

If trainees are to move on to develop a more realistic understanding of the processes involved in effective teaching, they need to be encouraged to look critically at the teaching procedures they have established and to evaluate their effectiveness. The Reflective Activities in this book will help in this, but students will certainly need the consistent support and advice of their mentor. Careful collaboration between the two is essential at this point and the task for the mentor and the tutor is particularly challenging at this stage of the student's development. Furlong *et al.* (1994) characterize the role as providing 'critical friendship' through which the trainee is challenged to re-examine their teaching, while at the same time is offered practical support, encouragement and personal affirmation.

Reflective teaching

As we indicated above, there is one further stage of trainee development that needs to be considered and that is their development as reflective practitioners. We would suggest that the focus for student learning in this final stage of development should include:

- broadening the trainee's repertoire of teaching strategies
- encouraging the trainee to take more responsibility for their own professional development
- deepening their understanding of the complexities involved in teaching and learning, including its social, moral and political dimensions.

As the student begins to acquire greater skill and knowledge and develop a more appropriate and realistic understanding of the nature of teaching, so the mentor and the tutor should begin to modify their role yet again. While there will still be times when they need to act as 'model', 'trainer' or 'critical friend', they should also develop the role of 'co-enquirer'. As co-enquirers, mentors and trainees will develop a more open and equal relationship, spending more time working as equal professionals. Such a relationship has the advantage of encouraging students to take greater responsibility for their own learning and allows trainee, mentor and tutor to address some of the complexities of teaching in a spirit of more open enquiry.

However, its most valuable role is in providing a framework for mentor and trainee to discuss planning and teaching at a more fundamental level than before. No longer should mentors present themselves as an authority, knowing the 'right' answers. Rather, through discussion of their planning and teaching, mentors should attempt to 'open up' their work and invite questioning. This can be achieved by, for example:

- focusing on the *complexity* of thinking underlying professional decisions
- exposing the moral, practical and other *dilemmas* underlying professional decisions
- evaluating the social and educational *consequences* of particular professional decisions
- discussing the social, institutional and political *contexts* in which professional decisions have to be made.

It is by participating in such open, professional discussions in relation to their own practice that students can be encouraged to confront the complexities of teaching more deeply. From their initial beginning on the periphery of school life, the trainee should feel drawn into the culture of the school and should feel able to make a worthwhile contribution to its development.

3 | CONCLUSION

In this chapter we have reviewed the key role of mentoring in modern teacher education and drawn attention to important mentoring skills. Additionally, we have reviewed characteristic ways in which the competence and self-confidence of trainee teachers often develops, and considered the ways in which mentors might offer, challenge and support progress made. For further discussion of these issues, see Maynard, 2001, **Reading 2.3**; and Moyles, Suschitzky and Chapman, 1998, **Reading 16.4**).

As the chapter makes clear, becoming a 'reflective teacher' is almost bound to be challenging, but it is made considerably easier with appropriate support from mentors and tutors working together in a learning-oriented school. Chapter 16 continues discussion of such issues in respect of the induction of newly qualified teachers.

Key readings

Recent approaches to teacher education and training are premised on large proportions of school-based initial teacher education. Whilst many courses remain founded on close partnerships between higher education institutions and schools, mentoring on employment-based routes is likely to be even more significant.

An important influence on this approach to teacher education came from a project co-ordinated from the University of Oxford, centred on the development of school-based partnerships. An excellent overview of this work is provided by:

McIntyre, D. and Hagger, H. (eds) (1996)
Mentors in Schools: Developing the Profession of Teaching.
London: David Fulton.

Of course, the actual learning and development of trainees is at the heart of the mentoring process – hence the emphasis in this chapter. The best study of this remains:

Furlong, J. and Maynard, T. (1995)
Mentoring Student Teachers: The Growth of Professional Knowledge.
London: Routledge.   see also **Reading 2.3**

An excellent analysis of effective mentoring in primary schools comes from Edwards and Collison. Their book locates mentoring within a clear understanding of primary school cultures and the communities of professional practice within them. This is combined with practical advice.

Edwards, A. and Collison, J. (1996)
Mentoring and Developing Practice in Primary Schools: Supporting Student Teacher Learning in Schools.
Buckingham: Open University Press.   **Reading 2.2**

An explicit analysis of mentoring in the context of the development of reflection comes from:

Tomlinson, P. (1995)
Understanding Mentoring: Reflective Strategies for School-based Teacher Preparation.
Buckingham: Open University Press.

For a light-hearted fictional account of the trials and tribulations of mentors and mentees in school-based teacher education, see:

Campbell, A. and Kane, I. (1998)
School-based Teacher Education: Tales from a Fictional Primary School.
London: David Fulton.

Good books on mentoring skills are:

Caroll, C. and Simco. N. (2001)
Succeeding as an Induction Tutor.
Exeter: Learning Matters.

Moyles, J., Suschitzky, W. and Chapman, L. (1998)
Teaching Fledglings to Fly? Mentoring and Support Systems in Primary Schools.
London: Association of Teachers and Lecturers.

Stephens, P. (1996)
Essential Mentoring Skills: A Practical Handbook for School-based Educators.
Cheltenham: Stanley Thomas.

 Part 2 of this book provides an enormous bank of resources to support mentoring. There are comprehensive reviews of important issues, *Reflective Activities* to try, and notes on Key Readings, all of which can be selectively used to meet particular needs and support professional development. Additionally, the complementary book *Readings for Reflective Teaching* offers further resources.

 Readings for Reflective Teaching (the companion volume) also offers other closely associated work on the issues raised in this chapter. This includes work by authors such as:

John Sampson, Robin Yeomans, Anne Edwards, Jill Collison and Trisha Maynard.

 RTweb offers additional professional resources for this chapter. These may include *Notes for Further Reading, Reflective Activities*, useful *Web Links, Extension Texts* and *Download Facilities* for diagrams, figures, checklists, activities.

CHAPTER 3

Developing an evidence-informed classroom

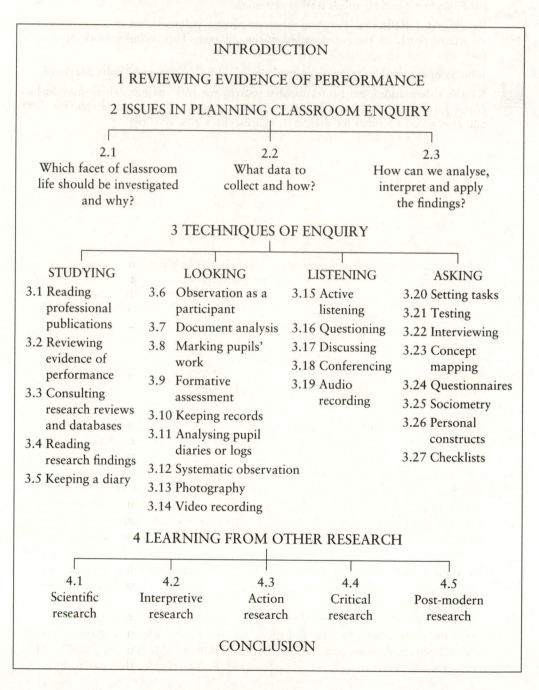

INTRODUCTION

1 REVIEWING EVIDENCE OF PERFORMANCE

2 ISSUES IN PLANNING CLASSROOM ENQUIRY

| 2.1 Which facet of classroom life should be investigated and why? | 2.2 What data to collect and how? | 2.3 How can we analyse, interpret and apply the findings? |

3 TECHNIQUES OF ENQUIRY

STUDYING
3.1 Reading professional publications
3.2 Reviewing evidence of performance
3.3 Consulting research reviews and databases
3.4 Reading research findings
3.5 Keeping a diary

LOOKING
3.6 Observation as a participant
3.7 Document analysis
3.8 Marking pupils' work
3.9 Formative assessment
3.10 Keeping records
3.11 Analysing pupil diaries or logs
3.12 Systematic observation
3.13 Photography
3.14 Video recording

LISTENING
3.15 Active listening
3.16 Questioning
3.17 Discussing
3.18 Conferencing
3.19 Audio recording

ASKING
3.20 Setting tasks
3.21 Testing
3.22 Interviewing
3.23 Concept mapping
3.24 Questionnaires
3.25 Sociometry
3.26 Personal constructs
3.27 Checklists

4 LEARNING FROM OTHER RESEARCH

| 4.1 Scientific research | 4.2 Interpretive research | 4.3 Action research | 4.4 Critical research | 4.5 Post-modern research |

CONCLUSION

Enhancing professional standards and competences

Developing an enquiring mind, research awareness and evidence-informed classroom practices can significantly enhance professionalism and the quality of provision at every stage of a teacher's career. This is recognized in national requirements. For example, at the time of writing, in Wales the standards for QTS state that trainees must:

> Understand the need to take responsibility for their own professional development and to keep up to date with research and developments in pedagogy and in the subjects they teach.
> (Welsh Office, *Standards for the Award of QTS*, standard D: e)

In England, new teachers are required to uphold the professional code of the General Teaching Council by demonstrating that they:

> are able to improve their own teaching, by evaluating it, learning from the effective practice of others and from evidence.
> (TTA, 2002, *Standards for the Award of QTS*, standard 1.7)

It is thus important to be able to conduct small-scale enquiries, and to understand and evaluate other evidence and research which might support improvement. In Northern Ireland and Scotland, similar capabilities are required. For example, in the latter students must:

> Demonstrate the abilities associated with analysing situations and problems, seeking solutions and exercising sound judgement in making decisions.
> (Scottish Office, 1998, *Guidelines for Initial Teacher Education in Scotland*, competence 4.5)

INTRODUCTION

The model of a reflective teacher, as outlined in Chapter 1, suggests that critical reflection and systematic investigation of our own practice should become an integral part of our daily classroom lives. This was the central idea of the great educationalist, Lawrence Stenhouse (1975, **Reading 3.1**; see also Pring, 2000, **Reading 3.2**). In some countries, such ideas have been developed in new directions, and now receive explicit, national endorsement. For example, in England the government has placed considerable emphasis on evidence-informed reflection as contributing to continuing professional development and the improvement of standards of teaching and learning (DfEE, 2001a; TTA, 1999, **Reading 3.3**). Further, the collection of classroom evidence has become a crucial element in the measurement of teaching performance for qualification, threshold and salary purposes.

With this increasing attention on the improvement and measurement of teaching performance, more and more teachers have begun to gather evidence about both classroom practices and pupil learning (McNamara, 2002). However, if such evidence is to be objective, valid and reliable, then an appreciation of the major issues involved in research and some knowledge of the main forms of enquiry and techniques available are essential. This chapter has been written as a simple introduction to such matters, and it does not aim to provide full guidance on technical aspects of research methods. Readers are strongly advised to follow up issues and techniques in which they may be particularly interested via *Key Readings* at the end of the chapter or *Notes for Further Reading* on **RTweb.** Links to various research organizations can also be found there.

Turning to the work of professional researchers, the chapter offers an introduction to five distinct approaches – each of which illuminates the world in powerful and interesting ways. When consulting such work, it is helpful to have a basic understanding of the theoretical perspectives from which they derive, and Section 4 of the chapter will help in this.

1   REVIEWING EVIDENCE OF PERFORMANCE

In many countries, there has been a massive increase in the quality and quantity of statistical and other information gathered by government agencies. Where this is significant, as in the English education system, many professional enquiries are likely to be stimulated by such data. However, all data must be careful interpreted, and those from official sources are no exception.

In England, a great deal of information is produced by the Office for Standards in Education (OFSTED). This derives from three main sources. The first is concerned with inspection evidence that is generated from an OFSTED inspection of a particular school. All inspection reports contain quantitative and qualitative data concerning the performance of particular schools and these reports are available to the public and can be found on the internet. The second concerns the annual Performance and Assessment (PANDA) reports which are published for each individual school and contain comparative information about the performance of that school in relation to national statistics concerning performance of pupils on national curriculum tests, attendance data and the annual schools' census data. Thirdly, and of more general application, OFSTED publish a range of national performance indicators, particularly concerning performance on National Curriculum Tests. In evaluating the impact of this kind of information, it is perhaps significant that in recent years primary education has been moving into a league table culture, where tables of schools' perform-ance, particularly in relation to tests and examinations, are published in local newspapers. It is also significant that, in the standards for the award of QTS identified in the TTA Standards, there is a clear requirement for this kind of data to be used in the development of pupil performance. For instance, it is suggested that all to be awarded QTS must 'understand how national, local, comparative and school data including national curriculum test data, where applicable, can be used to set clear targets for pupils' achievements' (DfEE, 1998).

Such information, offering performance measures, value-added analyses, benchmarking and local, national and international comparisons, is a very powerful factor in improving the measured educational performance of pupils, teachers, schools and LEAs. It should be used as such and acknowledged for its strength in posing challenging questions.

However, reflective teachers will also want to consider if such measurements offer valid representations of everything that is worthwhile and valuable in education. Do they, for instance, satisfactorily embrace all aspects of children's development, or of creativity and the arts? Are there measures of significant motivational issues such as learning disposition, or attitudes to lifelong learning? How do they account for innovation, or processes of transition over time? Additionally, it is important to note that the way in which information is represented can impact on priorities. In fact, neither information itself, nor the way it is presented, can be regarded as being neutral. It does affect our perception of 'reality'. Thus, whilst using information on pupil, class or school performance as important sources of evidence, it is vital to remain aware of its strengths and weaknesses.

Other, more collegial, forms of performance evidence are also available within schools, particularly in those with a strong learning culture (see Chapter 17, Section 1.1) or where staff support and mentor each other effectively (see Chapters 2 and 16). Insights into one's practice are particularly powerful when they come from those whom one respects, so that critical friendships, mentoring processes, performance reviews or even the outcome of school-based self-evaluation can each be an effective stimulus for further classroom enquiry.

2   ISSUES IN PLANNING CLASSROOM ENQUIRY

Before any research can begin there are general decisions to be taken concerning the overall design of the study. The most significant of these design issues will be discussed below.

2.1   Which facet of classroom life should be investigated and why?

Whilst pupil-performance evidence may suggest particular strengths and weaknesses, identifying the key issues for investigation is sometimes a problem in itself. Dillon (1983) offered a threefold categorization of the kinds of problems that might be explored: existing problems which we can already recognize; emergent problems which we discover in our initial investigations; and potential problems which we anticipate might develop if we took a particular course of action. The issue chosen for investigation may emerge from any of these three types of problem.

2.2   What data to collect and how?

These decisions are extremely important, for getting them wrong can easily lead to unintended distortion of findings. First, there is the question of what data to collect. The *sample* should be appropriate in focus and quantity to represent the range of events, pupils or phenomena that are to be studied. Additionally, data should be selected which are as *valid* as possible as indicators of what it is we really want to study. Judgements about which data to collect are thus crucial, but there is then a further challenge to collect data in a consistent and *reliable* way.

These three issues – sampling, validity and reliability – keep professional researchers worrying away throughout any programme of research, and reflective teachers should be just as aware. The harsh reality however is that what we choose to collect and the way we chose to collect it will directly affect what we find. It will therefore influence our understanding of the situation. One way of limiting this problem is to use several methods so that data on a single issue can be collected in several ways. This is known as 'methodological triangulation'. However, our choice must, to a certain extent, be determined by what is feasible, given the time we can set aside to collect data and the time we can spend analysing it.

2.3 How can we analyse, interpret and apply the findings?

The basic strategy is to look for patterns, for places where regularities and irregularities occur. In order to do this, the data have to be sorted using various sets of criteria. All patterns of frequencies, sequences and distributions of activity are likely to be of interest. In addition, it is also important to look for spaces and omissions – where something does not occur which might have been expected. Where examples of co-occurrence exist, they can be misinterpreted as implying a cause–effect relationship. Such judgements should be viewed with caution until further data reinforce the pattern.

The important question of interpreting findings leads us into the issue of the relationships between research and the theoretical explanations to which it can lead. Such theorizing is an integral part of reflective teaching because it represents an attempt to make sense of data and experience. It is an opportunity to develop creative insights and an occasion to consider any discrepancies between 'what is' and 'what ought to be'. In a sense, we are all theorists in our everyday lives in the ways in which we develop hunches and use our intuition. This might be a starting-point, but as reflective teachers we would need to go further. In particular, we would want to generate theory relatively systematically and consciously. One way of doing this is to engage in a continuous process of data collection, classification and analysis of our own practice. This could be extended by making the process more public, through the involvement of colleagues as 'critical friends' at interim points. The 'theory' which emerges is likely to be professionally relevant and may also offer insights with regard to other cases. This kind of theory resembles what Glaser and Strauss (1967) refer to as 'grounded' in that it is developed from and grounded in our own experiences.

Such theorizing is particularly important for conceptualizing teaching and learning processes and for developing a language with which they can be discussed and refined. Indeed it has been argued that the lack of such an appropriate conceptual vocabulary has been a serious constraint on professional development (Hargreaves, 1978b). However, it is to be hoped that discussion and critique of models, such as the Hay McBer (see Chapter 1), will gradually lead to the development of a robust professional language for teaching and learning. Perhaps such language will be echoed in national frameworks for curriculum, pedagogy, assessment and accountability.

For the most part then, teachers are likely to be concerned directly with improving specific aspects of their practice. This calls for the use of a range of techniques for gathering data, which we will now review.

3   TECHNIQUES OF ENQUIRY

For many teachers, it is difficult to collect the information we need to make necessary day-to-day decisions and judgements, much less the information needed for anything more systematic. Our usual impressionistic data are collected sporadically and are often incomplete. They are selective and are probably based on what we have found in the past to be useful (one of the reasons it is so difficult to break out of old habits). They also tend to be subjective, because we have so few chances of discussion to help us to see things from any other viewpoints. However, if we could manage it, the most helpful information would be:

- descriptive (so that they are evidence-based)
- dispassionate (so that they are free from supposition or prejudice)
- discerning (so that they are valid and insightful)
- diagnostic (so that they lead us towards improvements).

That data should be as valid and reliable as possible must be accepted, but technicalities should not blind us to some relatively simple underlying processes in research. Essentially, these boil down to *studying*, *looking*, *listening* and *asking*.

In Figure 3.1 this simple classification is used to produce an overview of data-gathering techniques. These are introduced in this chapter and then illustrated in use at various places in the book. Throughout such discussions, a distinction is drawn between those enquiry methods that occur routinely in professional and classroom life and those which must be undertaken specially. Whilst, for the most part, the former are more convenient to use, the latter often produce more structured data which may be easier to analyse. Readers should note that these are introductory descriptions only. For further guidance on research techniques many books such as Denscombe (1998), Bell (1987) and Hitchcock and Hughes (1989) are available. Please see **RTweb** for a comprehensive and updated list of suggestions.

3.1   Reading professional publications

Many teachers regularly read articles from the education press, whether it is an item in the local paper, a staff-room copy of the *Times Educational Supplement*, a magazine such as *Child Education*, or material from their professional association. We also receive a great deal of educational information and are exposed to educational debate through radio and television.

But what use do we make of all this information? It tends, of course, to come in thick and fast. On appropriately chosen topics, a reflective teacher may well want to organize this flow, so that rather than being overwhelming, it is put to work. For instance, if the issue of home–school liaison was a school priority

	STUDYING	LOOKING	LISTENING	ASKING
ROUTINELY OCCURING	Reading professional publications (3.1) Reviewing evidence of performance (3.2)	Observation as a participant (3.6) Document analysis (3.7) Marking pupils' work (3.8) Formative assessment (3.9) Keeping records (3.10)	Active listening (3.15) Questioning (3.16) Discussing (3.17) Conferencing (3.18)	Setting tasks (3.20) Testing (3.21)
SPECIALLY UNDERTAKEN	Consulting research reviews and databases (3.3) Reading research findings (3.4) Keeping a diary (3.5)	Analysing pupil diaries or logs (3.11) Systematic observation (3.12) Photography (3.13) Video recording (3.14)	Audio recording (3.19)	Interviewing (3.22) Concept mapping (3.23) Questionnaires (3.24) Sociometry (3.25) Personal constructs (3.26) Checklists (3.27)

Figure 3.1 *A typology of enquiry methods*

reflected in the school improvement plan, staff meeting time would be given to this issue. A focused discussion could be stimulated by relevant articles being collected, and notes made about items on other media. This could be shared among colleagues, and would provide a rich resource for collaborative discussion.

3.2   Reviewing evidence of performance

Agencies such as OFSTED and QCA now analyse large amounts of data on pupil and school performance. Baseline and value-added comparisons are possible so that pupil gains can be considered in relation to school characteristics. See Section 1 of this chapter for discussion of the use, strengths and weaknesses of such data.

3.3   Consulting research reviews and databases

With the increased emphasis on evidence-informed practice, new databases and reviewing resources are becoming available. Sources include the web-sites of the DfES, Welsh Assembly, Scottish Parliament and Northern Ireland's Network for Education (see below). The General Teaching Councils in each country may also offer information. These are complemented by facilities such as the National Foundation for Education Research's project database (CERUK) and the Centre for Evidence-Informed Policy and Practice in Education. Sometimes, there is publicity in the media for important reviews such as those concerning the National Literacy and Numeracy strategies. There are also specialist review journals. One of the best is the *Review of Educational Research*, published by the American Educational Research Association.

Databases, abstracts, journals and research indices are thus available. They may often be found on CD-ROM in specialist libraries, or through the internet. This range is developing and changing rapidly. For some examples, see:

Indexing and database services
British Education Index (BEI): www.leeds.ac.uk/bei
Current Educational Research in the UK (CERUK): www.nfer.ac.uk/ceruk
Educational Resources Information Centre (ERIC): www.ericir.syr.edu/eric
Social Science Information Gateway: www.sosig.ac.uk
Education On-line: www.leeds.ac.uk/educol
Regard (ESRC database of projects): www.regard.ac.uk/regard/home
BUBL Information Service: www.link.bubl.ac.uk/education

The UK centre for conducting systematic research reviews is:
Centre for Evidence-Informed Policy and Practice in Education:
www.eppi.ioe.ac.uk/education.htm

Research associations, institutions, funding bodies and charities:
British Educational Research Association (BERA): www.bera.ac.uk
European Educational Research Association (EERA): www.eera.ac.uk
Scottish Educational Research Association: www.sera.ac.uk
Collaborative Action Research Network (CARN): www.uea.ac.uk.care.carn
National Foundation for Educational Research (NFER): www.nfer.ac.uk
The Economic and Social Research Council (ESRC): www.esrc.ac.uk

The Nuffield Foundation: www.nuffield.org.uk
Scottish Council for Research in Education: www.scre.ac.uk
Association for the Study of Primary Education: www.aspe.org.uk

Government departments or agencies:
Department for Education and Skills: www.dfes.gov.uk
Teacher Training Agency: www.canteach.gov.uk
British Education and Communications Technology Association:
   www.becta.org.uk
National Grid for Learning: www.ngl.org.uk
Department of Education for Northern Ireland: www.deni.gov.uk
Northern Ireland Network for Education: www.nine.org.uk
The Northern Ireland Council for the Curriculum, Examinations and
   Assessment: www.ccea.org.uk
Learning and Teaching Scotland: www.LTScotland.org.uk
The Scottish Parliament and Scottish Executive: www.scotland.gov.uk
The National Assembly for Wales: www.wales.gov.uk
The Curriculum and Assessment Authority for Wales: www.accac.org.uk

Journals are increasingly online and offering supplementary services, but charge a subscription. For instance, the *Times Educational Supplement* has TES Book-find, offering English-language access to over a million titles, with powerful search facilities. See also:

Times Educational Supplement: www.tes.co.uk

A massive abstracting database is provided by Taylor and Francis, drawing on over 700 education journals. See:

Educational Research Abstracts: www.tandf.co.uk/era

Many university education departments also use the World Wide Web to provide excellent introductions to what they have to offer. You can find the web addresses of UK university sites at:

www.birmingham.ac.uk/webmaster/ukuwww.html
www.niss.ac.uk/sites/he_cis.html

Please see a specialist librarian or **RTweb** for further advice and links.

3.4   Reading research findings

Academic books, journals and other output provide a rich source of description, analysis, critique and innovation about education. Indeed, many excellent examples have been drawn together in **Readings**, the volume that complements this handbook. Having said that, it is true that academics often write for each other and may use specialist conceptual vocabulary. This is their 'tool-kit', enabling them to talk and work more effectively together. Such use of language occurs in many walks of life, for instance in the in-house jargon of journalists, politicians, and Chief Inspectors. Increasingly however, educational researchers are also working to develop more accessible texts for professional and public audiences.

Readers of academic work should, above all, read actively and must not be over-awed by the text. Key questions must be posed. What is the core argument? What is the evidence base? How convincing is this? What is its relevance for practice? Readers must, in other words, interrogate the material and put it to work for them. Searching for introductions, summaries and conclusions is a good strategy too. If this is done, then studying academic texts becomes a really fascinating way of enhancing the quality of professional knowledge and understanding.

In Section 4 of this chapter we offer a brief introduction to the major paradigms in social scientific research, within which most educational research can be located. It is worth considering this as it will enable research studies to be 'placed' and understood more effectively.

3.5 Keeping a diary

Keeping a written diary remains an excellent way of recording classroom or school experiences and one's feelings and perspectives on them. On the one hand, some would argue that the whole point of keeping a diary is that it should be personal and private. On the other hand, 'reflective diaries' are sometimes suggested as part of coursework, and might therefore be accessed by mentors or tutors and treated as documentary indications of a trainee's thinking. In any event, it is worth remembering that any document produced in relation to professional work should reflect ethical concerns and the rights of others.

A very personal diary can provide vivid and flexible accounts of ideas and feelings. It can offer a safe space to express the emotional side of teaching, as well as more systematic attempts to analyse and reflect. When a diary is 'unofficial' it may be a place to speculate, propose, theorize and generally enter into a conversation with oneself. This is extremely valuable, for the act of writing serves to 'scaffold' understanding (Tharp and Gallimore, 1988). A diary is also a record, and can be re-visited in later days, weeks or years to consider both specific issues or the process of continuing professional development.

Technical decisions are few, but will relate to your aims. Perhaps you may wish to record your experiences in a particular period of school experience, in which case, a regular daily record would be wise. This will record the days when not much happened of note, as well as those which seemed to 'explode' with activity. On the other hand, you may want to focus your diary on a particular topic – class management, a group of children, a subject. Further into a career, you may want to keep a diary note each half term – it would certainly be of great interest in years to come.

Whilst a diary can simply be a cathartic record, it has the potential to be more than this. Once you have it, then you do have a document which can be analysed. Some really excellent studies of primary-school classrooms have been made in this way (Armstrong, 1980; Dadds, 1995).

3.6 Observation as a participant

Of course, observation is an entirely natural, continuous process. However, as a method for gathering classroom evidence, it refers to the process of actively, carefully and self-consciously describing and recording what people do whilst one may be, oneself, part of the action (Wragg, 1999). Personal involvement is not necessarily seen as a weakness if the benefits of direct experience are complemented by care in avoiding judgements. The emphasis, in the first place, should be on rich description. Recording is usually done in the form of careful notes containing detailed descriptions of people, events, incidents or issues. Such notes may record individual or group activity. They may record conversations together with features of the situations in which conversations or events took place. It is often helpful to discuss the situation observed to elicit the participants' interpretations of events. Thus the observer's, teacher's and the children's views may be sought.

Child observation is a particularly important skill for early-years' educators, for the behaviour of young children often reveals more than they may be able to express easily at any particular stage of development. A notebook is particularly helpful for this (see 3.10 on keeping records).

Such records can contain a wealth of information and can be applied very flexibly. Over a period of recording, it is normally possible to discern recurring themes that may lead to a greater understanding of the complex whole of a classroom environment. This technique, because it is relatively open-ended, can be particularly comprehensive and responsive to the unique features of the situation.

3.7   Document analysis

It can be revealing to examine official documents. For instance, this is a very important aspect of policy analysis and of historical and comparative work. In such approaches, official documents will be 'interrogated' to generate an analysis. Do there appear to be any hidden aims, as well as those which are explicit? What are the underlying assumptions embedded in the document? Which groups are likely to gain from the document? Which groups are likely to lose? Does the document reflect the influence of any particular interest group, or a combination of concerns? How has it been created? Who was consulted? Who was not? How is this reflected in its final form?

Recent governments of the United Kingdom continue to helpfully provide a steady flow of education documents on which this form of analysis can be used, and those associated with other political parties may be just as interesting. At a school level, examination of documents such as the brochure for parents might reveal underlying assumptions about how children learn, what they should learn and how they should be taught, or maybe reveal tacit, taken-for-granted thinking about social diversity and inclusion issues. Similarly, school policy documents are likely to provide insights into collective staff thinking – their aims, values and commitments. Similarly useful and indicative documents are annual school-development plans, and minutes of governors' and parents' meetings. However, it is worth remembering that even school documents tend to be relatively 'official' products and may thus gloss over internal debates that took place in the process of their creation. It is important, therefore, to read 'between the lines' and to be aware of what is not recorded as well as the issues that are brought to our attention.

3.8 Marking pupils' work

Pupils' work is, of course, a really important source of evidence of their learning, and marking that work is a crucial form of teacher enquiry into the progress, or otherwise, of each child. This can be anything from a verbal comment (e.g. What an exciting story!), to setting spelling corrections at the end of an exercise, or a grade or mark. In Foundation and early Key Stage 1 classes, children's output is particularly interesting as an indicator of their thinking. For all children, their capability in the actual process of writing or recording must be considered in analysing the materials.

Marking can also be extended to offer more wide-ranging analyses. For instance, to study a pupil's development over time one can consider each piece of work as part of a sequence. It is only by comparing each example with previous work that it is possible to assess whether any learning has taken place and what significance to attach to any mistakes. If such mistakes, or 'miscues', are analysed carefully they can provide valuable clues to possible learning difficulties. It is revealing to note whether errors are consistent or one-offs. If a pattern emerges then a future teaching–learning point has been identified. Such diagnostic marking can provide useful information upon which to base subsequent discussion, or be used when making judgements about matching future tasks.

3.9   Formative assessment

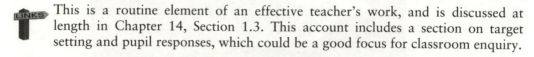 This is a routine element of an effective teacher's work, and is discussed at length in Chapter 14, Section 1.3. This account includes a section on target setting and pupil responses, which could be a good focus for classroom enquiry.

3.10   Keeping records

Keeping records is the subject of Section 4.1 in Chapter 14. This section describes twelve ways of collecting and organizing information about children's work and learning. There is a very strong tendency for such information to be collected, but not fully analysed. What sorts of enquiry could you develop from the records that you keep, or could keep?

3.11   Analysing pupil diaries or logs

Obviously, this is only possible when diaries or logs are kept. Children of appropriate writing capability write down their reflections of their learning experiences. This is particularly useful, for example, when children are doing self-directed work. They can use their diary or log book to comment on their ongoing progress, to keep the teacher 'in touch' without posing undue management problems.

A diary or log can take many forms. It might include the child's original plan of intended work, and the reason for doing it. It might also include a description of what was done, whether any changes were made and why. It could include an analysis of what knowledge or skills had been employed, which were reinforced, which were acquired and which extended. The child could then go on to comment on what had been enjoyed – or not enjoyed, and what had been worthwhile – or not. Finally, a log could include the children's view of what they would like to move on to next. Such self-analysis requires considerable sophisticated self-reflection from a child – the meta-cognitive skills discussed in Chapter 7. A useful extension of the use of pupil diaries or logs is the opportunity they also provide for parents and teachers to add comments and respond to issues which are raised.

3.12   Systematic observation

This is a way of observing behaviour in classrooms by using a schedule, or list of categories, of probable behaviour (see Croll, 1986). Categories are chosen by the observer, who therefore has to decide in advance what is important. Each category is then 'checked off' as the behaviour is observed. The technique assumes that the teacher has already carried out sufficient preliminary, exploratory investigations to be able to decide which behaviours are relevant. However, having devised the schedule, systematic observation can be a very quick and easy-to-administer technique for collecting information. It is used in two main ways. There is a 'sign system' procedure in which a record is made each time there is any sign of the listed behaviours, whereas in a 'timed system' behaviour is recorded only at predetermined time intervals.

Systematic observation might be useful, for example, in finding out how much use is made of the book corner and who seems to use it most. It could be used to produce a measure of how long individual children concentrate on particular set tasks. It could be used to note how teachers distribute their time among different children; which children seek attention; which ones avoid it; or which ones 'get forgotten'. Another common use is to measure the possible differences in the ways teachers interact with boys and with girls. Information collected in this way can easily be quantified, and the frequencies and distribution patterns of the listed behaviours can be calculated. However, such information cannot provide an explanation. The technique is also heavily reliant on the appropriateness of the predetermined categories on the schedule.

3.13 Photography

Recording what happens inside a classroom, by any of the next three techniques, provides a very valuable source of information, for they 'fix' events that are so fleeting. This is particularly valuable because no one can have ears and eyes everywhere and even the most alert of teachers misses a great deal of what goes on. The ethical principle of 'informed consent' applies here though, and the use of a camera should be discussed with children and others in the classroom beforehand.

Photography is a relatively unobtrusive form of visual recording, especially if fast film (with a high ASA/ISO rating) is used so that flash is not needed. Digital technologies are also opening up many new possibilities for using photography for rapid recording of classroom events. Photography, of course, only captures frames of action rather than the sequence of action itself, though multiple snapping can overcome this to some extent. A particular advantage is the ease of use of photographs once they are developed or downloaded into a computer. They can thus provide an excellent basis for reflective discussion with others – including the children who have been photographed.

3.14 Video recording

Video recording is particularly helpful in providing contextual information in classrooms and in capturing non-verbal behaviour as well as some speech. Although a video camera may seem to be capable of capturing a lot of classroom action, sampling selections must be made – as any film-maker would confirm. Before filming, even if a formal 'screenplay' is inappropriate, it is important to think through exactly what is required. What is the primary purpose of making the recording? This is likely to have implications for camera positioning and there may also be power source, sound, lighting, safety and other operational considerations. However, modern video cameras, with automatic focusing and low-light adjustment facilities, make the use of video a relatively easy task. The quality of the soundtrack is usually the weakest point and this should not be relied upon without testing or special provision.

This is a convenient and very powerful form of data, and the television broadcasting of 'video diaries' now offers a well-understood model on which work with children could be based. Whilst the presence of cameras is likely to affect some children and may distort the normality of the classroom, if done periodically the novelty usually soon wears off.

3.15 Active listening

Really attentive listening is particularly hard for busy people, such as teachers, who have to think about so many things at once. However, it is an excellent source of classroom evidence to stimulate ideas and enquiry. It is addressed in Chapter 13, Section 1.4.

3.16 Questioning

Questioning is, again, a very basic and highly valuable method of enquiry, as well as being key to teaching itself. It is discussed extensively in Chapter 13, Section 1.2.

3.17 Discussing

Discussion has innumerable roles in classrooms, both for teaching and learning and as a source of evidence for classroom enquiry. It is considered at length in Chapter 13, Section 1.3.

3.18 Conferencing

This is a term used to describe a particularly focused and extended discussion between teacher and child. Conferencing is similar to conducting an informal interview. Such a session offers an opportunity for a teacher and child to come to a mutual understanding of the nature of work in progress and to discuss what has been found to be enjoyable/not enjoyable or easy/challenging/hard. It also provides a chance to discuss any difficulties being experienced and to plan future activities. The length of the discussions will, of course, vary with the needs of the child. However, the teacher will need to plan to set aside a certain amount of time, perhaps at a set period each day, when the class know that the teacher must not be disturbed, if at all possible. In many situations discussions with a group or pair would be appropriate, though it is important that the group context does not inhibit some individuals within the group. It is often an advantage if there are some activities in which the whole class is taking part, as then some issues can be discussed collectively.

3.19 Audio recording

Audio recording of a class discussion is a common and simple procedure. However, tape recorders often only pick up a few of the children, or perhaps only the teacher's voice. Nevertheless, the procedure can provide excellent information about the amount, type and distribution of teacher talk – a very worthwhile, though often salutary experience.

Recording small groups or pairs of children can similarly provide valuable insights into the language strategies used and into social dynamics, and it is technically easier if background noise can be controlled. Children usually forget about the recorder, though its presence may affect some – either to put on a performance or to clam up. Time could be allowed for familiarization. A radio microphone or portable recorder could also be worn by an individual child for a period of time. The main advantage of this is that the quality of the recording is likely to be much improved. It must be remembered that it takes a significant amount of time to play back and study. Still more time will be needed for transcription.

3.20 Setting tasks

Perhaps the most routinely available source of evidence of pupil learning is that which arises, lesson by lesson, as children engage in the activities and tasks which the teacher has prepared for them. Something will inevitably happen. The important questions are 'what happens?' and 'is anyone paying attention?'

Teachers who are aware of the need for formative assessment and of the potential for gathering evidence from routine classroom activities should be able to focus tasks so that the pupil actions and performance reveal what they know, can do and understand. The skill, then, lies in providing tasks that are appropriate and accessible for all the children but which also enable you to discriminate constructively in terms of what particular children know and learn. This is a form of 'differentiation by outcome' – the development of understanding about the needs and capacities of the child by evaluating 'how they got on'. The strengths of using tasks for enquiry purposes derive both from the frequency and routine nature of the opportunities which are available and from the high validity which this form of assessment is likely to have. After all, it is embedded in everyday classroom processes. It should provide a rich source of insights about pupil learning strategies and attainments.

3.21 Testing

Tests take many forms and are used for a wide range of different purposes.

Teacher tests/published tests/national tests
Those which teachers devise themselves and are directly related to what has been taught. Compare these with published tests which are intended to be generally applicable to a wide range of situations. National tests, such as end of key stage and optional tests, are designed very specifically to test the objectives of the National Curriculum.

Criterion-referenced/norm-referenced tests
Those tests which use specific items to identify aspects of individual children's work; compare with tests which are used to compare individuals in terms of 'normal' expectations of achievement.

Diagnostic/prognostic

Those which aim to identify what the child can/can't do now; compare with tests designed to highlight future potential (e.g. IQ/eleven-plus tests).

Open/closed

Those which have questions to which there is room for imagination and creativity; compare these with tests to which there is one right answer.

Teachers often devise their own tests for particular diagnostic purposes in order to help them achieve the best possible cognitive match. Such tests could be used to discriminate between children's achievements, or used to assess a teacher's effectiveness in implementing specified learning objectives. Criterion-referenced, mastery tests, in carefully graded series, are popular in many sports award schemes, such as those for swimming, athletics and gymnastics. They also, of course, underpin the National Curriculum structure of levels, attainment targets and statements of attainment.

There is no doubt that appropriate comparative scores for children can be helpful in any review of the attainments of children, teachers or schools. Test scores are thus an important form of evidence of learning. However, whatever type of test is used, it is most important for a reflective teacher to try to identify its strengths, weaknesses and its underlying assumptions. For example, what does a reading test actually take to indicate 'reading', upon which theory of learning to read is it based, and, is it successful in what it aims to do? Is the test based on valid data so that it really measures what it is supposed to? Can the test be reliably used so that data collected are consistent?

3.22 Interviewing

Interviews are structured or semi-structured discussions which can be used to find out what people think or do, and why. The interviewer can explore and negotiate understandings because of the possibility of immediate feedback and follow-up. However, because of the person-to-person situation, some people may feel threatened – by the interviewer or, if it is a group interview, by other participants. The success of this technique of data collection rests heavily on the relationship established and on the way in which the event is conducted. Interviews can be used with varying degrees of formality and structure. The term 'interview' is usually reserved for the more formal, more structured one-to-one situations. As the event becomes more informal and less structured, it may be more appropriately seen in terms of a 'conference' or discussion.

3.23 Concept mapping

This term denotes a procedure which requires children to 'map' out what they have learned and how, to them, it appears to 'fit' together. Children might be helped to draw a web or flow chart to show what they have been learning about. Such a chart would, eventually, represent the ideas, concepts and knowledge that the children have been working with during a particular unit of work, as perceived by the child. The procedure might begin by listing aspects of the subject or topic that was covered. The children can then map the relationships between the different items – explaining how they see any links. This provides a way of seeing what they have understood. It can then provide a basis for teacher and child to talk over understandings and misunderstandings.

There are lots of ways of doing this. Each child can be asked to review things they have learned in a teaching session, and to write each item on small pieces of paper. These can be arranged on a larger sheet and moved around experimentally to eventually reflect, by their proximity to each other, the relationships between the various aspects of the topic as seen by the child. The small pieces of paper can then be glued on and lines drawn between them to represent the relationships. Finally, a few words expressing these relationships are written on each line. It should be possible to relate such concept maps both to teaching plans and relevant attainment targets. It is likely to underline the fact that, whatever we teach, children make sense of it in their own ways.

3.24 Questionnaires

This form of data collection uses questions and statements to stimulate responses to set items. Questionnaires are usually given to the respondents to fill in, which therefore demands a certain level of writing skill. The technique can be used for collecting factual information as well as opinions. Hence, it may provide data both about what people do or think, and why.

The format of a questionnaire may be closed (asking for specific data or yes/no responses) or open (asking for general and discursive responses). Open forms of response encourage relatively free answers, which has the advantage of enabling the respondent to express their thoughts and priorities in their own way. However, it also makes greater demands on the respondents' writing abilities and poses the problem of how to categorize the wide range of replies which such an item may well evoke.

Questionnaires can be useful in a variety of ways, such as providing information to include on school records; to discover how children feel about aspects of classroom life; or for evaluative purposes at the end of a unit of work. The answers may be required as written sentences, by ticking boxes, or by ringing a word/number on a rating scale (e.g. hard – quite hard – just right – easy, or 'exciting' 5–4–3–2–1 'boring'). For younger children, scales have been devised which require the child to colour the face which shows how they feel – in response to a statement which is read out by the teacher: the faces range from happy to neutral, bored, worried or angry.

3.25 Sociometry

Sociometric techniques have been developed to help children and teachers gain insights into friendship patterns. The basic procedure is to ask children, in confidence, to name a small number of children (normally three) from their class with whom they would like to work or play. This can also, with care, be extended to ask children to identify anyone with whom they would not like to work or play. The friendship groupings which emerge from an analysis of these choices as a whole can then be represented in diagrammatic form, known as a sociogram. Such representations provide a visual display of social relationships: mutual pairs and groups (where choices are reciprocated), clusters of friends (though not all with reciprocated choices), isolates and even rejectees.

We should note, however, that this technique does not tell the whole story. In particular, it provides a static picture of friendships and, given the dynamic nature of the social relationships of some children, this needs to be borne in mind. Nevertheless, the data are structured and descriptive and can provide a good starting-point for analysing further aspects of relationships between children.

3.26 Personal constructs

This is a structured method of indirectly finding out about the way people think and feel about each other. Personal constructs are evident in our thinking when, for example, we appraise or comment on children. A procedure for this situation might be to produce a small name card for each child, to successively draw three names and to identify which two are most alike, and then to explain why. In this way it is possible to elicit relatively instinctive reactions and the actual 'constructs', or criteria, which are used. Such a procedure is usually more effective than asking, in the abstract, what constructs are used to distinguish between children. Having obtained such a list, it is then possible to classify the constructs – for example, those that are academic, physical or social. The patterns that emerge could indicate underlying assumptions about perceptions of children. However, whilst construct elicitation helps respondents to 'surface' intuitive concepts, in itself it is unlikely to indicate why they feel it or to describe what they actually do.

3.27 Checklists

Checklists provide a simple and practical form of record that has been tried and tested by generations of teachers. Targets, levels, key skills or other competencies can be clearly listed and ticks, crosses or other symbol systems can be used to record children's achievements against these criteria. However, judgements should be checked with evidence before a checklist is completed. Sometimes checklists are completed relatively impressionistically, which is unlikely to be accurate.

4 | LEARNING FROM OTHER RESEARCH

Educational researchers have, over many years, produced a wonderful array of studies of classrooms, schools and educational issues. These offer excellent starting points for new school-based enquiries. It is helpful, however, to understand the background thinking behind different approaches to research. This section provides such guidance.

We will identify five major social scientific research approaches to educational research – the scientific, interpretive, action, critical and post-modern. This is a considerable simplification of a complex theoretical area (for instance, see Delanty, 1997), but will suffice for our purposes (for further simplification see Bassey, 1995, **Reading 3.4**). Enduring questions about the fundamental assumptions that underlie each of the research approaches nevertheless remain. For instance, which is more significant, measuring behaviours or understanding meanings? Is it better to do careful research before drawing conclusions for action, or should we try to improve practice by investigating it as we try things out? Do individuals act voluntarily to change their world, or do the circumstances into which we are born determine the people we become? Can society be improved though the application of reason, or does the post-modern world make this enlightenment ambition impossible? Indeed, in studying patterns of social practice, should we be trying to describe, understand, improve, transform or deconstruct?

	Major practical purposes	Characteristic research methods	Forms of research knowledge
Scientific research	To provide an empirically 'proven' basis for improvement	Systematic designs, involving large, structured samples and gathering of quantitative data	Objectivist, seeking generalizations and explanations
Interpretive research	To inform judgement as a basis for improvement	Flexible designs, involving detailed, holistic case-studies and empathic gathering of qualitative data	Subjectivist, describing cases and developing understanding
Action research	To directly improve practice through self-development	Cyclical designs, based on self-monitoring using a range of data in a practitioner's workplace	Evaluative, describing and analysing personal practice
Critical research	To illuminate inequalities and support emancipatory practice	Relational designs, using data eclectically to illuminate a dialectic between individual agency and social structure	Transformative, aspiring to reveal structural circumstances and support 'praxis'
Post-modern research	To deconstruct hidden power relations and affirm diversity	Reflexive, flexible and participatory designs, often interrogating cases from a particular stand-point	Perspectival, emphasizing complexity, uncertainty and difference

Figure 3.2 *Five major approaches to educational research*

As we will see, most teacher-initiated, classroom-based research is likely to be influenced by action research, but there are also rich resources from other research traditions to be drawn on. These will contextualize classroom studies and illuminate issues of practice and policy in novel ways.

Figure 3.2 provides a concise summary of the five research approaches that we have identified. In particular, we pick out their major practical purposes, characteristic research methods and forms of research knowledge. The following text explores such issues further.

4.1 Scientific research

The classical 'scientific' model is based on the research style that has served the physical sciences for many years. Its characteristic stages are to:

- recognize and define a problem
- develop an hypothesis
- design a controlled research procedure to test the hypothesis
- accumulate observations
- analyse the data
- interpret the data and form generalizable explanations.

The hallmarks of the scientific model are, therefore, that the investigation has an hypothesis, which is testable and replicable, which provides an explanation and is generalizable. When such research is referred to as scientific, it is usually to highlight two features that are believed by some to be crucial. These are, first, that the way the research is carried out is 'systematic' and, second, that the interpretation of the data collected is 'objective'.

When this model is transferred to the social sciences, certain inadequacies are evident. For instance, it is very much more difficult to test an hypothesis in a classroom situation with the same rigour as one might expect in a laboratory experiment. It is more difficult because we cannot isolate the variables being examined and we cannot control all the myriad factors that might influence the test. In addition, we are dealing with human beings for whom we must have proper ethical concern. Further, because of the complexity of the classroom and because of the ethics of any such research, any 'experiment' can never be exactly replicated. Researchers have had to rely on sophisticated statistical methods to try to measure the impact of variables.

Nevertheless, there has been a long tradition in education research of following the scientific model as far as possible. For example, much of the laboratory-based psychological testing and measurement research was of this nature (for example, Cattell and Kline, 1977). Similarly, the extensive work on teacher effectiveness in classrooms in the USA during the 1960s and 1970s used systematic observation techniques (for example, Flanders, 1970), and these are still positively regarded for some purposes (for example, Galton *et al.*, 1999; Pollard *et al.*, 2000).

In recent years there has been considerable pressure on educational researchers to demonstrate 'what works' to enhance the quality of policy-makers' judgements. The classical scientific paradigm is therefore enjoying something of a revival, for instance, through the use of school- and pupil-performance data, randomly controlled trials, naturally occurring experiments and longitudinal studies of large cohorts of pupils. Scientific reviews of previous studies are also accumulating.

One major criticism that has often been made of scientific research is that it fails to adequately address the subjective perceptions of the people who are the focus of the study. This concern led to the development of interpretive forms of research.

4.2　Interpretive research

Interpretive approaches to educational research have been strongly influenced by anthropology and the aspiration to understand, describe and analyse the cultures of particular societies and groups. Among the ethnographic methods that have been developed are participant observation and interviewing. These techniques are explicitly qualitative and are concerned with opinions and perspectives as well as observable facts or behaviour.

In the first place, interpretive researchers aim simply to describe the perspectives, actions and relationships of the people whom they are studying. Typically, they study a limited number of cases in depth and try to achieve a view of the whole situation in a way that is seen to be valid by the participants. This process often requires the personal involvement of the researcher and is rarely a neat, linear progression of research stages. The approach is pragmatic and flexible, as the researcher seeks data and understanding (Burgess, 1984; Hammersley and Atkinson, 1983; Woods, 1986). The outcome of such research is usually a detailed case-study within which concepts, relationships and issues are identified and analysed. Glaser and Strauss (1967) provided the classic statement of the challenge of such work when they argued that interpretive sociologists should start from the grounded base of people's perspectives. Then, through the simultaneous collection, classification and analysis of data, they should develop systematic and theoretically refined perspectives of the social institutions and relationships that they study. Some examples of such work are available concerning primary education (King, 1978; Pollard, 1985, **Reading 6.4**; Hartley, 1985, 1992; Grugeon and Woods, 1990; Troyna and Hatcher, 1992, **Reading 15.8**; Nias, 1989, **Reading 5.1**; Pollard, 1996, 1999, **Reading 5.5**).

Interpretive research has strengths and weaknesses, as does the scientific model. Indeed, in many respects, they can be seen as complementary. For instance, an interpretive researcher's 'generation' of theory may be balanced by a scientific researcher's 'testing'; qualitative data on perspectives may be balanced by quantitative data on behaviour; and a focus on detailed whole cases may be balanced by generalization from sampling across cases.

Whatever their differences, both the scientific and interpretive approaches to social science share an assumption that the prime responsibility of researchers is to describe and analyse social processes. Involvement in change is seen as a distinct, and secondary, consideration. For action researchers, this priority is reversed.

4.3   Action research

The term 'action research' originates from Lewin (1946). His model for change was based on action *and* research. It involved researchers, with teachers or other practitioners, in a cyclical process of planning, action, observation and reflection before beginning the whole process all over again.

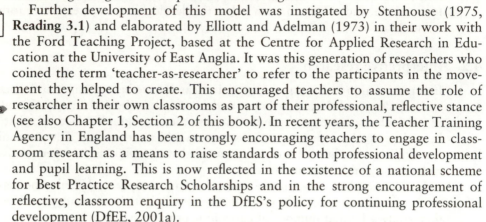

Further development of this model was instigated by Stenhouse (1975, **Reading 3.1**) and elaborated by Elliott and Adelman (1973) in their work with the Ford Teaching Project, based at the Centre for Applied Research in Education at the University of East Anglia. It was this generation of researchers who coined the term 'teacher-as-researcher' to refer to the participants in the movement they helped to create. This encouraged teachers to assume the role of researcher in their own classrooms as part of their professional, reflective stance (see also Chapter 1, Section 2 of this book). In recent years, the Teacher Training Agency in England has been strongly encouraging teachers to engage in classroom research as a means to raise standards of both professional development and pupil learning. This is now reflected in the existence of a national scheme for Best Practice Research Scholarships and in the strong encouragement of reflective, classroom enquiry in the DfES's policy for continuing professional development (DfEE, 2001a).

Action research has also been developed extensively by curriculum specialists working alongside teachers as can often be seen from the publications of subject associations. There are now many excellent published examples of teachers' action research (e.g. Hustler *et al.*, 1986; Nixon, 1981; Webb, 1991). For an excellent, up-to-date summary of the strengths of action research, see Pring (2000, **Reading 3.2**).

Despite the professional support for this approach, we should note that it has been criticized for encouraging a classroom focus while wider, structural factors are accepted as unproblematic (e.g. Barton and Lawn, 1980, 1981; Whitty, 1985). On the other hand, (Carr and Kemmis, 1986) argue that such work provides a means of 'becoming critical'. They suggest that action research involves the improvement of practice; improvement of the understanding of the practice by the practitioners; and improvement of the situation in which practice takes place (1986, p. 165). Indeed, they argue that action research can be emancipatory – releasing practitioners from 'the often unseen constraints of assumptions, habits, precedents, coercion and ideology' (Carr and Kemmis, 1986, p. 192). In this sense, action research can be seen as having a potentially 'critical' edge.

4.4   Critical research

The most common forms of critical scholarship are sociological, though there are also examples in psychology, history, politics and other disciplines. Critical research can be distinguished from other approaches in several ways. In the first place, it is far more wide-ranging, for it is based on the assumption that specific situations, practices and perspectives can only be understood in relation to their historical, economic, cultural and political contexts. Comparative and historical studies provide one form of this (e.g. Alexander, 2000; Altback and Kelly, 1986; Green, 1990). In its sociological form it rejects narrow forms of scientific,

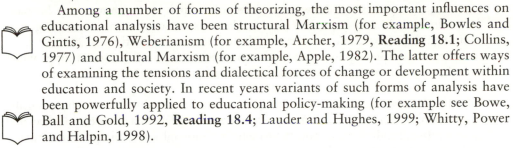

positivistic empiricism which tend to ignore such wide-ranging factors, and uses various forms of theorizing to try to make sense of social structures, their processes and development (e.g. Bernstein, 1975, 1996; Bourdieu and Passeron, 1977).

Among a number of forms of theorizing, the most important influences on educational analysis have been structural Marxism (for example, Bowles and Gintis, 1976), Weberianism (for example, Archer, 1979, **Reading 18.1**; Collins, 1977) and cultural Marxism (for example, Apple, 1982). The latter offers ways of examining the tensions and dialectical forces of change or development within education and society. In recent years variants of such forms of analysis have been powerfully applied to educational policy-making (for example see Bowe, Ball and Gold, 1992, **Reading 18.4**; Lauder and Hughes, 1999; Whitty, Power and Halpin, 1998).

4.5   Post-modern research

One of the most significant research developments in recent years has been the emergence of 'post-modernism'. The term itself challenges the seventeenth-century Enlightenment philosophy that society could be constantly improved through the application of 'scientific reason'. Indeed, such 'modernist' assumptions can be seen as underpinning each of the approaches to research that we have previously considered. From the post-modern perspective, they may be seen as rather conventional, lacking in insight or, indeed, reinforcing the status quo through the production of 'regimes of truth'.

Post-modernism highlights the consequences of social positioning and of the ways in which tacit forms of control become embedded in everyday life. A common research technique is the deconstruction of forms of 'discourse' – a concept deriving from the French philosopher, Derrida. This can be extremely revealing. It might show, for instance, how some social groups, such as girls or black pupils, are 'positioned' in classrooms as a result of taken-for-granted ways of thought, speech and interaction (for further explanation and an example of this in the case of race and racism, see Epstein, 1993, **Reading 15.7**). Analysis of this type has been used with particular effectiveness by feminist researchers such as Walkerdine (1988), Davies (1983) and Francis (1998). However, it is also effective at another level in analysing public policy and deconstructing the statements of politicians (e.g. Ball, 1994). In this scenario, policies presented with an appealing popular rationale may be shown to have underlying assumptions and effects which are more disturbing – the deconstruction of 'spin'?

Post-modernists have developed some particularly powerful ideas about how people view themselves. Conventionally, it has been thought that each individual develops a sense of 'self', of the person they are. Theorists such as Giddens (1991) suggest that, whilst this might have been a plausible assumption in stable societies, it is no longer tenable in the context of diversity, complexity and change in global societies today. In such circumstances, it is argued, many established and taken-for-granted social practices and ways of thinking have to be questioned – including the unitary view of self. The alternative position is to argue that people develop multiple views of self, 'multiple identities'. The global media, new technologies and communication systems, and the diverse cultural reference points which these enable, make it possible for people to join 'imagined communities', to develop a variety of personal narratives, and to present themselves in different ways in new situations. The influence of culture(s) is obviously crucial here, but it is reinforced by the ready availability in wealthy societies of the accoutrements of diverse lifestyles, shop by shop. Who would you like to be today? However, some roles, such as teaching, may be more constrained. Maclure suggests that teachers use identity as an organizing principle in their work, but this is not without many contradictions (2001).

Post-modernism thus offers both a number of powerful research approaches and many challenges to conventional ways of perceiving the social world.

In this section we have identified five major forms of research: the scientific, interpretive, action, critical and post-modern. Whilst such theoretical ideas may seem abstract, they are connected to whole philosophies, paradigms and ways of thinking that are of enormous richness and importance. From a scientific viewpoint, your teaching and the children's learning is measured and quantified. But from the interpretive position the feelings, perspectives and social relationships of the people in the classroom become key issues. On the other hand, the critical theorist observes the classroom and offers an analysis of the historical constraints and emancipatory possibilities of both your role and that of your pupils. And the post-modern perspective challenges your discourse and seeks to deconstruct power relationships between yourself and the children that you really had not noticed. Meanwhile, working in what Schon called the 'swampy lowland' of complex, professional practice, you devise an action research programme to directly improve your teaching and enhance the children's learning. This has enormous value, but it will have a lot more if you are also able to draw on the insights of other approaches and the accumulated knowledge of social science. This is the key role of the sections on *Key Readings* at the end of each chapter and, more particularly, of the *Notes for Further Reading* which we make available on **RTweb**.

CONCLUSION

This chapter has provided a brief introduction to some of the practical issues and techniques of undertaking classroom research as reflective teachers. We have also located such practice within other, more social scientific research approaches. Readers are advised to follow up other more detailed references on **RTweb** or elsewhere.

In particular, we would stress that 'doing research' is not just about collecting data. Indeed, the most important consideration is undoubtedly to conceptualize the issues and ask appropriate questions. The research process must be seen as a whole because initial assumptions will have significant implications for later findings. As indicated in Section 2, the enquiry process should be systematic, involving clearly demarcated stages from research design, identification of research questions, issues or hypotheses, to data collection, data analysis, drawing conclusions and finally, after professional reflection, planning new actions. The process of data analysis is a particularly important phase in which to demonstrate open-mindedness and objectivity.

As we have also suggested, reflective teachers need to be able to relate their findings to those of others and to consider results in the context of the current debates about educational issues. More specifically, performance data about their school, classroom or pupils may throw up particular issues for investigation or interpretation.

Part 2 of this book is designed to help to put such ideas into practice.

Key readings

The work of Lawrence Stenhouse provided a really important foundation for teacher research. For an excellent insight into his work, see:

Rudduck, J. and Hopkins, D. (eds) (1985)
Research as a Basis for Teaching: Readings from the Work of Lawrence Stenhouse.
London: Heinemann Educational Books.   📖 **Reading 3.1**

Good introductory guides to carrying out research activity include:

Blaxter, L., Hughes, C. and Tight, M. (1996)
How to Research.
Buckingham: Open University Press.

Hitchcock, G. and Hughes, D. (1996)
Research and the Teacher.
London: Routledge.

Denscombe, M. (1998)
The Good Research Guide for Small Scale Social Research Projects.
Buckingham: Open University Press.

Books that specifically support enquiries using classroom-based action research designs are:

Hopkins, D. (1986)
A Teacher's Guide to Classroom Research.
Milton Keynes: Open University Press.

Hustler, D., Cassidy, T. and Cuff, T. (eds) (1986)
Action Research in Schools and Classrooms.
London: Allen & Unwin.

McNiff, J. (1988)
Action Research: Principles and Practice.
London: Routledge.

An innovative book, relating research findings and activities to curriculum and classroom issues is:

Clipson-Boyles, S. (2000)
Putting Research into Practice in Primary Teaching and Learning.
London: David Fulton.

A clear description of small-scale case-study work, and an analysis of its strengths and weaknesses is:

Bassey, M. (1999)
Case Study Research in Educational Settings.
Buckingham: Open University Press.

Gathering data from children requires particular care. For this, see:

Christensen, P. and James, A. (eds) (2000)
Research with Children: Perspectives and Practices.
London: Falmer Press.

Finally, for more advanced insights into the work of professional educational researchers, see:

Pring, R. A. (2000)
Philosophy of Educational Research.
London: Continuum.

 Reading 3.2

Scott, D. and Usher, R. (1996)
Understanding Educational Research.
London: Routledge.

Robson, C. (1993)
Real World Research.
Oxford: Blackwell.

 Readings for Reflective Teaching (the companion volume) offers other closely associated work on the issues raised in this chapter. This includes work by authors such as:

Lawrence Stenhouse, Richard Pring, Michael Bassey and the Teacher Training Agency.

RTweb offers additional professional resources for this chapter. These may include *Notes for Further Reading, Reflective Activities,* useful *Web Links, Extension Texts* and *Download Facilities* for diagrams, figures, checklists, activities.

PART 2

BEING A REFLECTIVE TEACHER

CHAPTER 4

Social contexts. What are our circumstances?

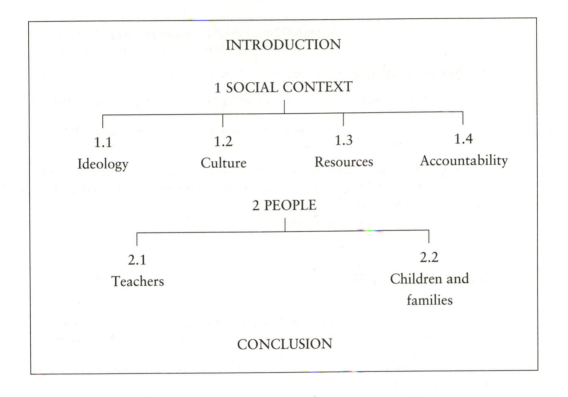

INTRODUCTION

1 SOCIAL CONTEXT

| 1.1 | 1.2 | 1.3 | 1.4 |
| Ideology | Culture | Resources | Accountability |

2 PEOPLE

| 2.1 | 2.2 |
| Teachers | Children and families |

CONCLUSION

Enhancing professional standards and competences

It is extremely difficult to develop high quality classroom practice without awareness of one's circumstances and those of one's pupils. This is important for decisions in the present, but also to enable adaption to the future – for we can be certain that educational provision and requirements will continue to change and develop throughout a professional career. In Scotland, each student teacher is therefore required to:

Demonstrate an understanding of the system in which he or she is working.
(Scottish Office, 1998, *Guidelines for Initial Teacher Education Courses in Scotland*, competence 3.2)

In Northern Ireland, the requirement is a little broader, to:

Demonstrate understanding of the relationship between the education system and other aspects of society.
(Department of Education for Northern Ireland, 1999, *The Teacher Education Partnership Handbook*, competence 1.13)

Teachers in England and Wales have a similar need to understand the cultural, social, political and historical context within which they make their professional contribution.

INTRODUCTION

This chapter provides a brief review of some of the contextual factors which are important for teachers. The specific challenges of teaching and learning are considered in detail in Part 2 of the book.

Figure 4.1 represents the way in which the relationships between these factors have been conceptualized in this book.

Of course, the influence of social context pervades everything that happens in schools and classrooms, and awareness of such issues is therefore an important contributing element of reflective teaching. This influence is felt at many levels – from the 'big picture' of national governments in Scotland, Wales, England, Northern Ireland and elsewhere, to the detail of community, school and family cultures and particular individual circumstances.

The second purpose of the chapter is to establish a theoretical model concerning the relationships of individuals and society. Indeed, the chapter is very deliberately in two parts. The first, 'social context', emphasizes the ideas, social structures and resources which *constrain* or *shape* action in various ways. The second part, 'people', is concerned with the various factors which, in some senses, *enable* action by individual teachers and children.

Of course, this argument can be applied to the education system of any country. However, for illustrative purposes, we have focused in this chapter on the various parts of the United Kingdom. The *Notes for Further Reading* on **RTweb** may contain sources concerning other countries and web links to

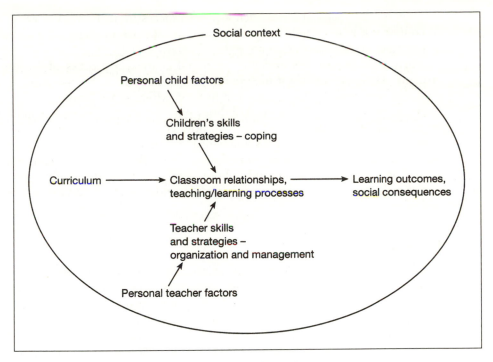

Figure 4.1 *Factors in classroom teaching and learning*

relevant organizations in each part of the UK are also provided.

We begin the chapter by introducing the theoretical framework.

1   SOCIAL CONTEXT

A particular theoretical position underpins this chapter and, indeed, the book as a whole. At its core is the conception of a dialectical relationship between society and individuals. This suggests the existence of a constant interplay of social forces and individual actions. On the one hand, the decisions and actions which people make and take in their lives are constrained by social structures and by the historical processes which brought about such structures. On the other hand, each individual has a unique sense of self, derived from his or her personal history or biography. Individuals have a degree of free will in acting and in developing understandings with others. Sets of these understandings, which endure over time, form the basis of cultures. Such understandings can also lead to challenges to established social structures and thus to future changes.

For example, there are differences between various social groups in terms of power, wealth, status and opportunities (Goldthorpe, 1987; Halsey, 1986; Reid 2000). However, individuals, each with their own background and sense of self, will react to such factors in a variety of ways. Some in powerful positions might wish to close ranks and defend themselves by suggesting that their position is inherited by right or earned by merit. Some among those who are less fortunate may accept the social order or even aspire to success in its terms. Others may try to contest it for, of course, to be able to question existing social arrangements is a fundamental right in our democratic societies.

There is, thus, an ebb and flow in social change, a process of tension and struggle. There is a constant interaction between action and constraint, voluntarism and determinism, biography and history (Mills, 1959, **Reading 4.1**).

A reflective teacher has responsibilities within this process which should not be avoided. With this in mind, we will now consider four aspects of the social context which are particularly significant for practice in primary schools: ideology, culture, resources and accountability. The influence of each can be traced at national, regional, local and school levels so that, although such issues sometimes seem distant, they affect children and teachers in classrooms in very real ways.

1.1   Ideology

A dictionary definition of ideology states that it means a 'way of thinking'. However, particular sets of ideas are often used, consciously or unconsciously, to promote and legitimize the interests of specific groups of people. Indeed, if a particular way of thinking about a society is dominant at any point in time, it is likely to be an important influence on education and on teachers' actions. It may produce a particular curriculum emphasis and even begin to frame the ways in which teachers think about their work and relate with children.

For instance, in the United States of America of the 1950s and the Cold War, anti-communist feeling was so great that it not only led to the now discredited inquisitions of the McCarthy Committee but also to a range of nationalistic practices in schools, re-interpretations of history and pressures to compete with the 'enemy', particularly after the 1957 launch of the Russian *Sputnik* satellite. Similarly, in the USSR and Eastern Block countries, before the revolutionary changes which swept Eastern Europe in 1989, pupils were taught highly selective views of history, of the values and achievements of their societies. They too were encouraged to compete, particularly to sustain exceptional international achievements in areas such as science and sport. In both cases, despite widely differing circumstances, it can be seen that the ideologies of key political elites interacted with the 'common-sense thinking' of the wider population to create particular ideological climates (see the work of Gramsci, 1978, for an analysis of such hegemonic phenomena). Although the influence of these ideological periods was enormous, they passed.

The specific ideologies that influence primary education also come and go. For instance, the 1960's and 1970's professional ideology of child-centredness (Alexander, 1984) was gradually supplanted by new ideas. Indeed, the educational policies of successive Conservative governments from 1979 to 1997 were based on the influence of 'New Right' ideologies and pressure groups such as the Hillgate Group and the Campaign for Real Education. Members of these groups argued that educational standards should be raised by exposing schools to market forces. They thus advocated more parental choice and school accountability. Another belief was that basic literacy skills should be taught traditionally, together with key elements of British history and culture. In the 1980s and early 1990s such ideas were taken up by many in the media and there were repeated 'moral panics'

(Cohen, 1972) in which public concern was orchestrated, for instance, over issues such as reading, spelling, 'failing schools', Shakespeare and teaching methods.

In the post-war years, civil servants and educationalists had tended to moderate such politicial activity, when it (relatively infrequently) occurred. This in itself was a reflection of the influence of policy-making professionals' own ideologies and 'assumptive world' (McPherson and Raab, 1988). However, they were unable to assert such influence in the late 1980s and 1990s, and there was a considerable struggle for control between politicians, civil servants and professionals over education policy (Ball, 1990; Bowe, Ball and Gold, 1992, **Reading 18.4**). By the mid 1990s, it was absolutely clear that the politicians had prevailed. There were successive re-organizations at the Department of Education in England, a reduction in the scale and independence of Her Majesty's Inspectors in favour of the new OFSTED inspection regime, creation of new bodies in England for curriculum and assessment and dismissal of the protests of teacher professional associations (see Pollard *et al.*, 1994, **Reading 18.5**). The climate of public opinion thus created also appears to have influenced New Labour policies when they came to power in 1997. Indeed, the emphasis on high standards of performance intensified. However, new concerns were introduced in relation to educational access and enhancing opportunities, particularly in deprived inner-city areas and estates. New Labour continued and built on these new, centralized forms of political power, whilst gradually tilting policies and resource allocation to support their city electorates.

Some historians have argued (for example, Simon, 1985, 1992) that such developments represent attempts to make the education system more effective as a means of 'social control'. Indeed, authors such as Althusser (1971) saw education systems within capitalist societies as forms of an 'ideological state apparatus' which are designed for precisely this purpose. On the other hand, sociologists such as Collins (1977), Kogan (1978) and Archer (1979, **Reading 18.1**) have argued that educational policies and provision are the product of competing interest groups and that control and power is more diffuse. In any event, years of legislation in England by both Conservative and Labour governments radically changed what had previously been a very decentralized system, based on the relative autonomy of local education authorities. Centres of control and accountability were restructured. As the National Literacy and Numeracy Strategies demonstrate, teachers in England are now routinely required to respond to the direction of central government, and dramatic innovation and diversity by local authorities is a phenomenon of the past. This is not quite the same story in Scotland, Northern Ireland or Wales, where devolution has enabled the centralist tendencies of the English system to be significantly moderated. No ideology is all-powerful, and countervailing ideas emerge over time, based on their own power bases and social movements. The Parliament in Scotland now ensures that education policy will not be dominated by an English ideology, and the National Assembly for Wales and the Northern Ireland Assembly, with more limited powers, act to interpret primary legislation and to develop their own new policy initiatives. However, all such measures simply reflect *different* sets of beliefs and power relations. In Wales, for instance, the *Curriculum Cymreig* and the compulsory teaching and learning of the Welsh language are particularly distinctive. In 2001, publication of school league tables of results was scrapped in Northern Ireland and Wales, and both also declined to require new teachers to take skills tests. Meanwhile, Scotland continued with what is, in principle, a non-statutory 5 to 14 Curriculum including environmental studies, integrated expressive arts and relatively light-touch assessment. Whilst the implication of significant professional autonomy in Scotland may be something of an illusion in reality, it was only the English government that started promoting 'city academies' run by private companies. The relationships between the four major parts of the UK have always been complex and, of course, they continue to evolve. Whilst such complexity has increased since devolution, it is reassuring that the basic educational issues to be tackled remain much the same. If possible, reflective teachers should try to develop their understanding at this enduring level.

In summary, we can note that the dominant patterns of thinking about primary-school practice, and much else, have thus changed considerably since the 1960s, and will change again. Awareness of the concept of ideology makes it more likely that reflective teachers will be able to evaluate the values or interests that may lie behind government proposals. It is also worth remembering that societies and dominant ideologies are never static. At some point in time, critique and experience lead to re-evaluation, counter-proposals, development and change (Bowe, Ball and Gold, 1992, **Reading 18.4**). There will be no end to this dialectical story.

Nor however, should we forget that no one, including ourselves, is immune to the influences of ideologies. For instance, professional ideologies are always likely to remain strong among teachers – they represent commitments, ideals *and* interests. Reflective teachers should be open-minded enough to constructively critique their own beliefs, as well as those of others.

1.2 Culture

Cultures can be seen as sets of shared perspectives. They often develop from collective activity and from the creative responses of groups to situations. Furthermore, cultures endure over time and thus represent sets of ideas, perspectives, values and practices into which individuals are likely to be socialized. The playground cultures of children provide an example here. In one sense, children in friendship groups develop unique and particular ways of perceiving school life. Indeed, they use these as a means of understanding school and coping with it (Clarricoates, 1987; Davies, 1982, **Reading 5.4**; Pollard, 1987b). Yet at the same time, continuities in children's culture, from generation to generation, provide a context which young children absorb (Opie and Opie, 1959; Sluckin, 1981). Of course, particular manifestations of child culture are now strongly influenced by films, television, toys, publishing and other commercial activities, but they are still only played out through children's collective agency.

The community within the school provides another cultural context. This will influence and be influenced by the perspectives of parents, children and teachers. However, few communities can be characterized as single, united entities. Among the many divisions which may exist are those relating to ethnicity, language, religion, social class, gender, sexuality and to political or personal values. The existence of such cultural diversity is particularly important in many inner-city schools and reflective teachers are likely to explore the relationship between cultures in young peoples' homes, communities and school very carefully indeed

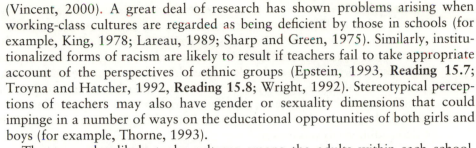

(Vincent, 2000). A great deal of research has shown problems arising when working-class cultures are regarded as being deficient by those in schools (for example, King, 1978; Lareau, 1989; Sharp and Green, 1975). Similarly, institutionalized forms of racism are likely to result if teachers fail to take appropriate account of the perspectives of ethnic groups (Epstein, 1993, **Reading 15.7**; Troyna and Hatcher, 1992, **Reading 15.8**; Wright, 1992). Stereotypical perceptions of teachers may also have gender or sexuality dimensions that could impinge in a number of ways on the educational opportunities of both girls and boys (for example, Thorne, 1993).

There are also likely to be cultures among the adults within each school. Those that are particularly important for teachers are the professional ones which develop out of the staff-room – that backstage area where tensions are released, feelings are shared and understandings about school life are developed. This is the territory of the classroom teacher, and the resulting teacher cultures usually provide a source of solidarity and sympathy when facing the daily pressures of classrooms (Southworth *et al.*, 1989, **Reading 17.2**). While colleagues may be stimulating and supportive of experimentation, they can also become protective of existing practices and inhibit innovation, (Pollard, 1987a; Sedgwick, 1988).

On a broader front, there are national and regional cultures, with wide differences across Europe (Thomas, 1989, **Reading 4.2**) and, say, between the worlds of rural Wales or Norfolk, and urban Glasgow or London. Indeed, the ways of life, assumptions and priorities of different parts of the UK have always been important to life in schools.

Devolution has had a particularly significant effect as cultural differences become reflected in education policies. From 1999, with the establishment of the Scottish Parliament, the National Assembly for Wales and the Northern Ireland Assembly, previously diverse and complex UK arrangements have been simplified to enable a high degree of political autonomy in each home country. Scotland and Northern Ireland took responsibility for legislation for education and training within their territories, and Wales took executive control for the implementation of shared English–Welsh legislation. There are many similarities between the four systems (Raffe *et al.*, 1999) with the same broad institutional structure of schools and many other arrangements. On the other hand, there are also many notable differences. Of particular note is the role of the Welsh language and the *Curriculum Cymreig* in asserting a strong Welsh identity. In Scotland, education has been seen as 'lying at the heart of Scottish identity' (Paterson, 1998), with teachers as significant cultural leaders. Perhaps this explains why Scottish education has not been substantially challenged from London over the past 20 years. Indeed, the 5 to 14 Curriculum reveals little of the influence of New Right thinking that was so influential in England. Rather, its origins can be traced back to the child-centred ideas of *Primary Education in Scotland* (SED, 1965), and a concern with the balance and coherence of the curriculum was retained long after these had been sacrificed in England on the alter of basic skills (see Adams, 1999). In Northern Ireland, where selective secondary education has been retained (though this is now under review), the degree of partnership and professional co-ordination for initial teacher education and the early years of professional development is distinctive (DENI, 1999). Whilst the influence of the churches remains an enduring feature of education in

Northern Ireland, an exciting new review promises considerable innovation, perhaps from 2003, in both curriculum and assessment (CCEA, 1999). There are thus both important differences and enduring similarities across the UK. Institutional arrangements are likely to become increasingly distinct, and particular educational priorities are evident in each territory. On the other hand, there is little doubt that the four parts of the UK are interdependent, now developing though some kind of synergy of comparison as each home nation asserts its cultural identity. And, of course, the regions of England may not be far behind in demanding devolved powers.

Cultures have a huge impact on learning and behaviour, as is being progressively demonstrated by the rapidly developing field of 'cultural psychology' (Bruner, 1986, 1990, **Reading 7.8**; Mercer, 1992, **Reading 7.9**; Pollard and Triggs, 2000, **Reading 7.11**; see also Chapter 7). For instance, Wertsch (1991) argues that the thinking of all learners is dependent on the 'cultural tools' that are available to them. These concepts and artefacts frame and mediate understanding and thus shape development. They will thus certainly have a direct impact on school performance. Similarly new learning may affect, or even change, the sense of identity of individuals, and such changes may or may not feel viable to them within their home culture. For instance, a classic study (Jackson and Marsden, 1962) showed the unease of working class boys on being sent out of their communities to a grammar school, and similar problems may affect the performance of children from minority ethnic groups today. It has been argued that organizations like schools can helpfully be seen as 'communities of practice' (Lave and Wenger, 1991) which evolve and maintain strong norms of behaviour and thought. New members must learn how to conduct themselves and there may be a process of 'cognitive apprenticeship' (Rogoff, 1990) as new understanding is acquired. However, depending on the social, cultural and economic background of a new pupil or teacher, such induction may or may not be comfortable. Cultures can thus be exclusive as well as inclusive, particularly when organizations feel the need to assert a narrow range of goals. Sadly, exclusion from school has become a significant issue in recent years.

There is thus a sense in which cultures can both enable and constrain learning. Indeed, they are likely to afford different opportunities for particular individuals and groups. In the case of school cultures, it should be remembered that they develop in response to particular conditions – many of which they are unlikely to control. One crucial factor here is the availability and nature of resources, and it is to this issue that we now turn.

1.3   Resources

Adequate resources are essential in education and we will distinguish four types here: people, buildings, equipment and materials. In both quality and quantity, these resources have an impact on what it is possible to do in schools and classrooms.

Many people are involved in the life of a successful school and, for this reason, collaboration and teamwork are needed, irrespective of status. Apart from the head and the teaching staff, there are many others, such as cleaners, dinner supervisors, cooks, secretaries, classroom ancillaries and caretakers, who all have very important supportive parts to play. However, it is arguably the case that, from the educational point of view, the number, quality and range of expertise of classroom teachers are major factors in determining what is done and what it is possible to do in schools. Teachers themselves are the most important resource. Where school governors and others make staff appointments, they have a particular responsibility to provide a teaching team with an appropriate balance of curricular expertise and teaching skill. This is far from easy, for schools are not funded on the basis of curriculum needs but on the basis of age-weighted pupil numbers. A very consistent feeling from teachers is that class size is a major factor in determining educational practice and there is much research which supports this proposition (e.g. Glass, 1982; Pate-Bain *et al.*, 1992, **Reading 10.3**). However, recent years have seen a welcome increase in the employment of classroom assistants and a gradual decrease in pupil–teacher ratios in primary schools.

Buildings are also an important influence on what goes on in schools. At its most obvious, buildings constrain decisions about numbers and types of classes because of the number and nature of the classrooms which are available. This often affects class sizes and forms of curriculum and teaching organization. The quality of the school environment will also be influenced by aesthetic considerations, and schools vary considerably in terms of the degree of consideration that is given to this issue. To their credit, an early action of the New Labour government of 1997 was to fund improvements in many school staff-rooms. Adequate maintenance of school buildings is recognized as being important and appropriate budget allocations have only recently become possible. Reflective teachers are likely to be concerned about the quality of the learning environment within their school and will aim to maximize the learning potential of the buildings and space which they have available. In one sense, buildings have an obvious fixed quality and are a source of constraint; on the other hand, it is surprising what uses and activities creative imaginations can produce.

Equipment is very significant because it is often through the use of equipment that young children are able to get appropriate learning experiences in school. This ranges from hall and playground requirements to the instruments for music-making, the artefacts for historical work and the wide-ranging resource needs of modern science, maths and English curricula. The most challenging form of equipment for schools to maintain relates to information technology. This has been a fast-moving field in terms of both hardware and software, and variation in provision between schools is often considerable. However, very significant government funding schemes are making a major impact.

Materials are the bread-and-butter consumables of a school, such as paper, pencils, creative and artistic materials. The quality of learning experiences will be directly affected by such provision. However, budgeting for them is often not easy, parental support is sometimes called for.

Since the (1988) Education Reform Act, all schools in England and Wales have had 'locally managed' budgets. Income is distributed annually from each LEA or direct from central government, on the basis of a formula (for some of the issues here, see Byrne, 1992; Hewton, 1986; Kingdom, 1991). This formula allocates a certain amount for each pupil on roll, plus certain other amounts in respect of social disadvantage, special educational needs or school size. Expenditure is the responsibility of the headteacher and governors. However, school managers often have relatively small sums to spend at their discretion, once fixed costs are taken out of the overall budget. For instance, the salaries of teachers and other staff often amount to around 75 per cent of the budget, followed by costs of building maintenance and school running costs. Only a relatively small percentage is left for books and materials.

There are, however, some significant national resources that are accessible to all schools, particularly in relation to information technology. The National Grid for Learning is formed by the interconnection of learning networks and education services, and is delivered via the internet. Associated funds are available for training and there is continuing work from various agencies to provide software and other forms of support through the medium of information and communications technology (ICT).

All resources have to be paid for and, on a national basis, education is a significant expense. For instance, the annual education expenditure of public authorities in 2001–2 was 43.5 billion, which is a little over 5 per cent of the UK Gross Domestic Product (though, we might note, a lower percentage than many other EU countries). Almost half of this was spent at local government level, and education is by far the largest item in council budgets (about 70 per cent in some cases, of which the most significant item is teachers' salaries). However, there is a significant centralizing trend in England in the funding of approved projects through applications to the DfES Standards Fund, or lottery sources such as the New Opportunities Fund, rather than via councils. Such payments have risen from 1 per cent of education spending in 1995–6 to over 6 per cent in 2000–1. Whilst English ministers seem to like this technique for exerting control, it has not been used with the same enthusiasm elsewhere in the UK.

The key factor in school budgets remains the number of pupils on roll, and each school's position in the quasi-market for pupil enrolments in its area is thus crucial to its resource base – hence the pressure for performance in formal assessments and in developing a positive local reputation. In many areas, some schools flourish whilst others may face gradually declining resources (see Dale, 1996). Further resource differences emerge due to the fact that a considerable contribution to total school incomes can be made by parental fundraising and through links with commercial companies which bring in donations or sponsorship. Such activities can produce very significant annual funds and these tend to increase social divisiveness because of wide differences in the distribution of wealth and incomes within local areas and between different regions of the country.

While resources structure the material conditions in which teachers work, the actions which they might take are also likely to be influenced by the degree of autonomy which they feel they have. For this reason, we now focus on the issue of accountability.

1.4 Accountability

Teachers in the public education system are paid, through national and local taxation systems, to provide a professional service. However, the degree of accountability and external control to which they have been subject has varied historically.

In the first part of the nineteenth century, the 'payment by results' system of the late 1800s, although superseded, still left a legacy in the form of imposed performance requirements in reading, writing and arithmetic. Handbooks of suggestions for good practice were published regularly, as guidelines, but were not enforceable. However, from the 1920s teachers began to develop greater professional autonomy and in this they benefited from the acquiescence of successive governments (Lawn and Ozga, 1986). In particular, the independence of headteachers within their schools, and of class teachers within their class-rooms, emerged to become established principles. After the Second World War, as professional confidence grew, this independence extended into the curriculum: so much so that, in 1960, it was described by Lord Eccles, Minister for Education, as a 'secret garden' into which central government was not expected to intrude. Such confidence was probably at a high point in the early 1970s.

Since then, the changing ideological, economic and political climate has resulted in teachers coming under increasing pressure: first, to increase their 'accountability'; and second, to demonstrate competent performance against centrally defined criteria. These developments were initially presented as a necessary reduction in the influence of the 'producers' (seen as teacher unions, administrators and theorists). This was supposed to enable educational provision to be shaped by the 'consumers' (seen as parents and industry, though with little direct reference to children and young people themselves) (Lawton, 1995). Later, the justification was in terms of applying modern personnel and performance management systems so that nationally prescribed curricula and pedagogies could be delivered, for instance, as set out through the Literacy and Numeracy Strategies.

Some of the products of these trends can now be seen, and the example of England is particularly vivid (Barber, 2001, **Reading 17.4**).

The specification of a National Curriculum, with associated assessment and pedagogic requirements, has been brought about through a series of initiatives following the Education Reform Act (1988). In England, successive government agencies were established to implement this transformation – the most recent of which is the Qualifications and Curriculum Authority (QCA). Together with other initiatives, such as the National Literacy and Numeracy Strategies and the DfES's Standards and Performance Unit, curriculum, assessment procedures and teaching approaches are tightly specified, and the resulting pupil performances are monitored. Information from both standardized and teacher assessment of pupils must now be published to parents, together with written, annual reports. These results, and other indicators such as school attendance and exclusion figures, are used to judge the effectiveness of schools.

The most powerful form of public accountability in England remains the OFSTED inspection system. OFSTED was formed in 1992 when Her Majesty's Inspectorate, previously independent for over 150 years, was scaled down and reorganized. OFSTED contracts teams of inspectors to make a structured report on every individual school in a regular cycle (see Chapter 17). Comparative data from schools serving similar socio-economic communities and baseline data from the school being inspected are used to evaluate levels of performance and improvement. The strongest signal of concern available to OFSTED is that a school be placed in 'special measures'. This means that it is deemed to have been failing to meet expected performance standards under the present management. Support or even an alternative leadership team may be provided.

With education now such a high profile public service, the media are vigilant in finding stories. Local press often offer the benign 'good news' variety, but teachers, schools or LEAs who are deemed to be under-performing have also become a regular feature for local, regional and national media. Such 'naming and shaming' is extremely distressing for those involved.

At the institutional level, governing bodies, including representatives of teachers, parents, industry and the community, are legally responsible for many aspects of their schools, including the budget, buildings, staffing, curriculum and standards of performance. Whilst governors are not expected to take detailed decisions about the day-to-day running of the school, they do have responsibility for setting policy frameworks covering the major aspects of school life. Governors must monitor the effectiveness of school management, participate in staff appointment and dispute procedures, ensure that value for money is provided, and present an annual report to parents.

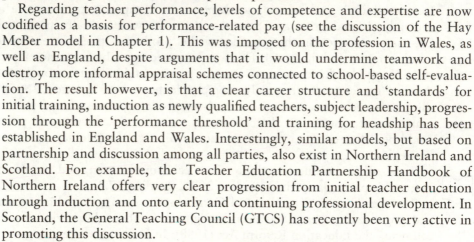

Regarding teacher performance, levels of competence and expertise are now codified as a basis for performance-related pay (see the discussion of the Hay McBer model in Chapter 1). This was imposed on the profession in Wales, as well as England, despite arguments that it would undermine teamwork and destroy more informal appraisal schemes connected to school-based self-evaluation. The result however, is that a clear career structure and 'standards' for initial training, induction as newly qualified teachers, subject leadership, progression through the 'performance threshold' and training for headship has been established in England and Wales. Interestingly, similar models, but based on partnership and discussion among all parties, also exist in Northern Ireland and Scotland. For example, the Teacher Education Partnership Handbook of Northern Ireland offers very clear progression from initial teacher education through induction and onto early and continuing professional development. In Scotland, the General Teaching Council (GTCS) has recently been very active in promoting this discussion.

Accountability can be seen as a crucial aspect of social context because it highlights legal requirements and shapes teacher decision-making. The concept of market competition 'forcing up standards' was crucial to the measures introduced by Conservative governments, and these ideas had enormous implications for teachers' work-experience (see Menter *et al.*, 1996). Underlying the requirements of New Labour administrations is the proposition that 'support' to education should be combined with high levels of 'challenge' to produce a 'framework for continuous improvement' (Barber 2000). This is likely to remain an area of much flux and considerable contest, particularly between the government and teacher unions.

The issue of accountability crystallizes many issues concerning the relationship between education and society. Should it be a relatively autonomous system or should it be under tight forms of control? Should teachers simply carry out centrally determined instructions, or should they use professional judgement? What, indeed, is the role of local democratic institutions in this? The history of our education system provides many fascinating instances of attempts to reconcile such dilemmas (Silver, 1980) and there are plenty of related current issues which a reflective teacher might consider. In particular, though, and following the dialectical model of social change which we discussed at the beginning of this chapter (**Reading 4.1**), the issues of accountability, autonomy and control pose questions of a personal nature for reflective teachers. How should each individual act? To whom do you feel you should be accountable – to children, parents, colleagues, your headteacher, local or national government, the media, inspectors, or yourself?

2 PEOPLE

Within the dialectical model, which conceptualizes the constant interaction of social structures and individuals, personal factors are the counterpart of social context. For instance, classroom life can be seen as being created by teachers and children as they respond to the situations in which they find themselves. Thus, as well as understanding something of the factors affecting the social context of schooling, we also need to consider how teachers and children respond. We begin by focusing on teachers.

2.1 Teachers

Teachers are people who happen to hold a particular position in schools. No apologies are made for asserting this simple fact, for it has enormous implications as we will see further in Chapter 5. Each person is unique, with particular cultural and material experiences making up his or her 'biography' (Sikes, Measor and Woods, 1985). This provides the seed bed for their sense of 'self' and influences their personality and perspectives (Mead, 1934). The development of each person continues throughout life, but early formative experiences remain important. Indeed, because personal qualities, such as having the capacity to empathize and having the confidence to project and assert oneself, are so important in teaching, much of what particular teachers will be able to achieve in their classrooms will be influenced by them. Of even greater importance is the capacity to know oneself. We all have strengths and weaknesses and most

teachers would agree that classroom life tends to reveal these fairly quickly (Nias, 1989, **Reading 5.1**). Reflective teaching is therefore, a great deal to do with facing such features of ourselves in a constructive and objective manner and in a way which incorporates a continuous capacity to change and develop.

Teachers, as people, have opinions, perspectives, attitudes, values and beliefs. This particularly human attribute of being able to review the relationship of 'what is' and 'what ought to be' is one which teachers often manifest when considering their aims and examining their educational values and philosophies. While there has always been a good deal of idealism in the thinking of teachers of young children, there has also always been a concern with tactical realism. Indeed, a very important factor which influences teachers' perceptions in the classroom is that the teacher has to 'cope', personally as well as professionally, with the classroom situation (Hargreaves, 1978a; Pollard, 1982; Woods, 1990). For this reason, we would suggest that a fundamental element of classroom coping, or survival, is very deeply personal, for it involves teachers, with a particular image of their self, acting in the very challenging situation which classrooms represent. In this, it is important to remember that what it is possible to do in classrooms is constrained by the basic facts of large numbers of children, limited resources, compulsory attendance, a legally defined National Curriculum and other external expectations which exist about what should and should not take place. The 'social work' role of teachers in supporting children and parents in some communities is also considerable (Webb and Vulliamy 2002, **Reading 4.3**)

In such circumstances, teachers face acute dilemmas between their personal and professional concerns and the practical possibilities (Berlak and Berlak, 1981, **Reading 1.3**). They are forced to juggle with their priorities as they manage the stress which is often involved (Cole and Walker, 1989; Dunham, 1992) and as they come to terms with classroom situations.

In recent years considerable attention has been paid to providing stronger continuity in professional development, so that the situation of a trainee, newly qualified teacher, established teacher, advanced skills teacher and headteacher is now very well defined. This may offer a sense of continuity for a career professional, and is certainly enabling government to provide more systematic forms of support and direction (DfEE, 2000).

The final set of personal factors about teachers to which attention will be drawn relates to their position as employees. The first aspect of this is that teachers are workers and have legitimate legal, contractual and economic interests to maintain, protect and develop (Lawn and Grace, 1987; Lawn and Ozga, 1981). The notion of 'directed time', in reference to the 1265 hours per year for which teachers in England and Wales are contracted, has now been combined with criteria for performance measurement and salary awards. The effect is that teachers are under increasing pressure to undertake activities which are additional to basic classroom teaching. These may include attendance at staff planning meetings and parents' evenings, and extra-curricular activities such as sport, clubs, choirs, orchestras and drama productions, or even evidence-based research as a form of continuing professional development (DfEE, 2001a). Given such activity, a PricewaterhouseCoopers survey of working hours in 2001 found that primary teachers in England actually worked 2174 hours per year – far in excess of their contractual obligation. Such efforts may not be sustainable, and it seems clear that a better balance has to be struck between educational expectations and what it is reasonable to ask of people who happen to earn their living from teaching. It should never be forgotten that teachers also have their own personal lives outside the classroom and their own independent identities – however challenged these may be by work and the complexities of modern society (Maclure, 2000). Many teachers have family responsibilities, as well as other interests which may be important to their own personal development (Acker, 1989; Bell, 1995; Evetts, 1990; Thomas, 1995).

2.2   Children and families

As with the personal factors associated with teachers, the most important point to make about children is that they are thinking, rational individuals (Corsaro, 1997; James, Jenks and Prout, 1998). Each one of the many millions of school pupils in the UK has a unique 'biography', and the ways in which they feel about themselves, and present themselves in school, will be influenced by their understandings of previous cultural, social and material experience in their families and elsewhere (Bruner, 1986). Through their compulsory education, from age 5 to 16, most children develop a relatively clear sense of their identity as learners

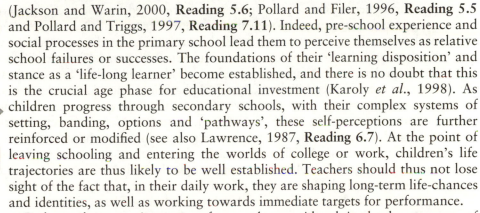

(Jackson and Warin, 2000, **Reading 5.6**; Pollard and Filer, 1996, **Reading 5.5** and Pollard and Triggs, 1997, **Reading 7.11**). Indeed, pre-school experience and social processes in the primary school lead them to perceive themselves as relative school failures or successes. The foundations of their 'learning disposition' and stance as a 'life-long learner' become established, and there is no doubt that this is the crucial age phase for educational investment (Karoly *et al.*, 1998). As children progress through secondary schools, with their complex systems of setting, banding, options and 'pathways', these self-perceptions are further reinforced or modified (see also Lawrence, 1987, **Reading 6.7**). At the point of leaving schooling and entering the worlds of college or work, children's life trajectories are thus likely to be well established. Teachers should thus not lose sight of the fact that, in their daily work, they are shaping long-term life-chances and identities, as well as working towards immediate targets for performance.

Perhaps the most important fact to be considered is the huge range of attributes and experiences that children may bring to school. Factors, such as sex, social class, race, language development, learning styles, health and types of parental support, are hugely complex in their effects (Maden, 1999, **Reading 15.1**). Indeed, although broad but important generalizations about patterns of advantage and disadvantage can be made (Halsey, Heath and Ridge, 1980; Osborn, Butler and Morris, 1984; Rutter and Madge, 1976), it is foolish to generalize in specific terms about their ultimate consequences. This caution is made even more necessary if it is acknowledged that factors in children's backgrounds can influence, but not determine, consequences. Nevertheless, children are faced by many challenges in the modern world (see Pollard and Triggs, **Reading 4.4**). For instance, the Institute for Fiscal Studies (1995) reported that 3.7 million children in the UK were growing up in families living on, or below, the poverty line (being dependent on Income Support benefits or with a household income below this level). A report by the Joseph Rowntree Foundation (Middleton, 2000) showed that income inequality widened rapidly from 1983 to 1999, with the lowest paid being worse off in both absolute and relative terms. Their 1998 report (Howarth *et al.*) recorded that over 8 million people in the UK are in households where disposable income, after housing costs, is less than 40 per cent of average income. The family circumstances in which children develop are becoming increasingly diverse, with UK marriages at their lowest number since the 1920s (Central Statistical Office, 1995), and poverty is particularly associated with one-parent families. Other factors also have important impacts, such as the growing diversity of cultures and social groups in our societies and the multiple influences of new forms of youth culture and mass media. Black children are substantially over represented among the 10–15,000 children excluded from school each year and, of course, those excluded often generate personal respect through strong alternative (but non-educational) identities.

However, coming between children's backgrounds, biographies and experiences and their educational development is the whole issue of how pupils actually respond to their circumstances and, indeed, of how teachers provide for them. Like teachers, children have to learn to cope and survive in classroom situations in which they may well feel insecure (Jackson, 1968, **Reading 6.2**). Children's culture and the support of a peer group are considerable resources in this. However, such cultural responses by children can also pose dilemmas in class when children try to satisfy personal interests by attempting to please both their peers and their teacher. Creative strategies are called for and these may cover a range from conformity through negotiation to rejection. Once again then, we wish to consider the importance of the subjectivity of the perspectives which teachers and children develop as they interact. Such perspectives are likely to be a great influence on the motivation which children feel and on the ways in which learning is approached (Pollard, 1987b, Pollard and Filer, 1996, **Reading 5.5**).

Above all, though, we must never forget that children are placed in the role of 'pupils' for only part of each day. It is no wonder that families, friends, relationships, television, film, computer games, music, fashion, sport, etc., are important to them. A reflective teacher, therefore, must aim to work with an understanding of the culture of young people. Indeed, it is very unwise to try to do otherwise and, if connections can be made, then pupil culture can itself provide an excellent motivational hook into schoolwork.

Parents and carers can play a particularly important role in supporting children and their learning. They are often thought of as supplementary teachers, with an advantageous 1:1 teaching ratio, and this has certainly been proved to be effective in supporting the development of early literacy. Indeed, work with parents and carers is an increasingly significant element of the work of early-years' teachers. Perhaps the most important role for parents and carers today is in providing a source of stable emotional support for each child as he or she encounters new challenges in school. Reay has provided a fascinating analysis of this as a form of 'emotional capital' (2000, **Reading 4.5**). Schools are increasingly pressured places, and there is a need for someone to really nurture the developing child from day to day, year to year. It is not necessary to be well-off financially to do this, indeed, the most valuable contributions are probably time, patience, understanding and affection. There is also an increasing understanding that all families and communities, including those that may seem disadvantaged, have

http://www.rtweb.info

'funds of knowledge' that should be tapped to enhance children's learning (Moll and Greenberg, 1990). Social circumstances do, however, radically affect participation (Reay, 1998; Vincent, 1996, 2000). If processes for supportive knowledge exchange between such parents and teachers could be established, the potential for enhancing children's learning is enormous (Hughes and Pollard, 2000). However, working with children's parents is by no means easy, for it may require teachers to open themselves up professionally. It is a suitable challenge for a reflective teacher.

CONCLUSION

The intention in this chapter has been to discuss the relationship between society as a whole and the people who are centrally involved in education. This is because school practices and classroom actions are influenced by the social circumstances within which they occur. It has also been argued that individuals can, and will, have effects on future social changes, though the degree of influence ebbs and flows at different phases of history.

A theoretical framework of this sort is important for reflective teachers. The provision of high-quality education is enhanced when social awareness is developed as well as high levels of teaching skills, and when individual responsibilities for professional actions are taken seriously.

This fundamental belief in the commitment, quality and role of teachers underpins the book. At a time when central control over education has been tightened, the analysis remains optimistic. High-quality education is not possible without the committed professionalism of teachers. To a great extent, this depends on personal commitment and the extent to which we identify with the professional role. This is a major theme of the next chapter.

Key readings

These suggestions concentrate on the theoretical framework which has been introduced, rather than on the topics through which it has been illustrated. The latter are all covered in more detail elsewhere in the book, and can be accessed via the Index.

On the theoretical framework which has been introduced, with its juxtaposition of social context and individuals, two classic books may be helpful. Chapter 1 of Mills and Chapters 4 and 5 of Berger are particularly relevant.

Berger, P. L. (1963)
Invitation to Sociology: a Humanistic Perspective.
New York: Doubleday.

Mills, C. W. (1959)
The Sociological Imagination.
Oxford: Oxford University Press.   Reading 4.1

For a readable analysis of British society, which illustrates aspects of this framework, see:

Halsey, A. H. (1986)
Change in British Society.
Oxford: Oxford University Press.

The best book to read to understand New Labour's approach to education was written by Michael Barber, a close adviser to the Prime Minister, Tony Blair:

Barber, M. (1996)
The Learning Game: Arguments for an Education Revolution.
London: Gollancz.

📖 **Reading 17.4**

Coffey offers a more specific analysis of education, showing how national policy changes impact on schools, identities and biographies:

Coffey, A. (2001)
Education and Social Change.
Buckingham: Open University Press.

Distinctions in each part of the UK are reviewed in:

Gearon, L. (2001)
Education in the United Kingdom: Structures and Organisation.
London: David Fulton.

Updated basic information is available from the annual review of Britain from the Office of National Statistics:

Office for National Statistics (annually)
Britain: The Official Yearbook of the United Kingdom.
London: The Stationery Office.

The issues are applied to primary education in:

Richards, C. and Taylor, P. H. (eds) (1998)
How Shall We School Our Children? Primary Education and its Future.
London: Falmer.

Richards, C. (ed.) (2001)
Changing English Primary Education: Retrospect and Prospect.
Stoke-on-Trent: Trentham.

Two classic case-studies of primary schools which specifically attempt to trace links between individual actions and the wider social context are:

Pollard, A. (1985)
The Social World of the Primary School.
London: Cassell.

📖 **Reading 6.4**

Sharp, R. and Green, A. (1975)
Education and Social Control.
London: Routledge and Kegan Paul.

Three very different illustrations of the uses of the basic framework are also provided by:

Connell, R. W., Ashden, D. J., Kessler, S. and Dowsett, G. W. (1982)
Making the Difference: Schools, Families and Social Division.
Sydney: Allen and Unwin.

Humphries, S. (1982)
Hooligans or Rebels?
Oxford: Blackwell.

Grace, G. (1978)
Teachers, Ideology and Control.
London: Routledge and Kegan Paul.

Connell *et al.* provide a comparative perspective with an analysis of school processes within Australian society. Humphries is based on oral histories and analyses the education of working-class children, whilst Grace is an historical study of the development of the teaching profession.

 Readings for Reflective Teaching (the companion volume) offers other closely associated work on the issues raised in this chapter. This includes work by authors such as:

C. Wright Mills, Norman Thomas, Rosemary Webb, Graham Vulliamy, Andrew Pollard, Pat Triggs and Diane Reay.

 RTweb offers additional professional resources for this chapter. These may include *Notes for Further Reading*, supplementary *Reflective Activities*, useful *Web Links*, *Extension Texts* and *Download Facilities* for diagrams, figures, checklists, activities.

CHAPTER 5

Values and identity. Who are we?

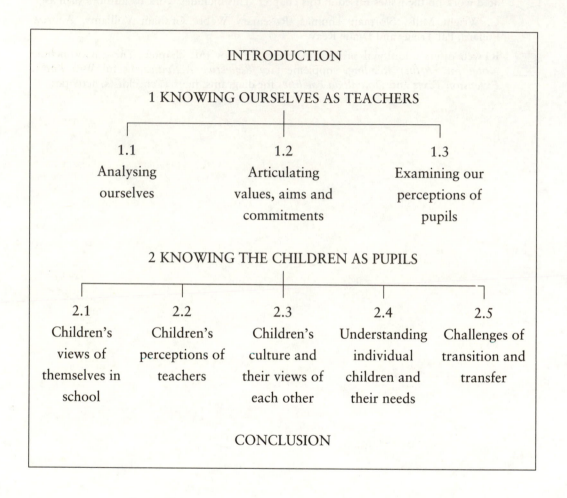

INTRODUCTION

1 KNOWING OURSELVES AS TEACHERS

1.1
Analysing ourselves

1.2
Articulating values, aims and commitments

1.3
Examining our perceptions of pupils

2 KNOWING THE CHILDREN AS PUPILS

2.1
Children's views of themselves in school

2.2
Children's perceptions of teachers

2.3
Children's culture and their views of each other

2.4
Understanding individual children and their needs

2.5
Challenges of transition and transfer

CONCLUSION

Enhancing professional standards and competences

Primary-school teaching tends to attract people who care about their profession, and care about the children with whom they work. This is true across the UK, for instance with proud traditions of service in Scotland and Wales. In Northern Ireland the commitment is reflected in a core statement of 'professional values' that each new teacher is expected to have. He or she should:

- like and care for children, and seek to promote the development of the whole child
- be enthusiastic about teaching and committed to the value of the education process
- believe in the promotion of equal opportunities
- possess high professional standards.

(Northern Ireland Department of Education, 1999,
The Teacher Education Partnership Handbook, core criteria 2.1)

In England, a similar, but subtly different, set of value standards has been identified. Teachers should:

- have high expectations of all pupils, respect their social, cultural, linguistic, religious and ethnic backgrounds, and be committed to raising their educational achievement
- treat pupils with consistency, respect and consideration, and have concern for their development as learners.

(TTA 2002, Standards for the Award of QTS, standards 1.1 and 1.2)

This is a considerable advance from the expectations in England of 1846 (see Chapter 1, Figure 1.3), which illustrates how things change and develop over time. This chapter will help you think through your own value commitments and your understanding of, and empathy for, young children.

INTRODUCTION

This chapter is concerned with the teachers and children in classroom life and with the feelings and perceptions they hold in relation to themselves and others. A key issue is that of their 'identities' as unique individuals and how they relate these identities to the roles that they must fulfil in classrooms.

In the first section of this chapter we focus on ourselves as teachers and pay particular attention to three central issues: the qualities of ourselves as unique individuals; our strengths and weaknesses in taking on the role of teacher; and the values and commitments which we hold. The second section focuses on understanding children and young people as pupils.

There are nine **Reflective Activities** within this chapter, but many more can be found on **RTweb**.

1   KNOWING OURSELVES AS TEACHERS

In considering ourselves as teachers, the first step is to consider the person we are. We could do this in terms of social, cultural and educational background, experience and qualifications, position, interests and personality. Such factors make up our 'personal biography' and together they can be seen as contributing to the development, within each of us, of a unique sense of 'self': a conception of the person we are. Social psychologists argue that this sense of self is particularly important because of the way in which it influences our perspectives, strategies and actions (Rosenberg, 1989; Secord and Backman, 1964). This is as true for teachers and young people in classrooms as it is for anyone else (Hargreaves, 1972; Kohl, 1986; Nias, 1989). Each individual is thus seen as having a 'self-image' which is based on a personal understanding of the characteristics which he or she possesses and on an awareness of how others see his or her 'self' (Hall and Hall, 1988). Individuals may also have a sense of an 'ideal-self', that is, of the characteristics which they may wish to develop and of the type of person which they might want to become. An individual's self-esteem is, essentially, an indicator of the difference between their self-image and their ideal-self.

The concept of ideal-self introduces the question of values, aims and commitments which individuals hold and to which they aspire. This is important because individuals in society, including teachers and pupils, actively interpret their situation in terms of their values, aims and commitments. Furthermore, teachers' values have considerable social significance because of the responsibilities of their professional position. Thus reflective teachers need to consider their own values carefully and be aware of any implications. In some circumstances, these could be very radical, as Paulo Freire demonstrated (Freire, 1999, **Reading 18.2**).

This brings us to a second set of factors which are to do with the 'roles' which are occupied by a teacher – or by a pupil too. Whilst teachers and pupils do not simply act out particular ascribed roles, it is certainly the case that expectations have developed about the sort of things that each should do. These expectations come from many sources: for example, headteachers, parents, governors, school inspectors, government and the media. Unfortunately expectations are frequently inconsistent. Thus teachers and pupils have to interpret these pressures and make their own judgements about the most appropriate actions.

Finally, more recent work in the field of educational studies has brought a new and more dynamic perspective to bear on the process of looking at teacher and pupil identity. This work suggests that we all inhabit multiple 'subject positions', and that our identities are fluid and fragmented, and are negotiated in social, political and cultural contexts through our interactions and relationships with others (Maclure, 2000.) Such a 'post-modern' perspective leads us to challenge simplistic, inflexible and externally imposed notions of teacher or pupil identity, for example, by asking what it *means* to be 'male' or 'Black', (Blair, Holland and Sheldon, 1995; Griffiths, 1995; Maclure, 2001; Marshall, 1994; Wexler *et al.*, 1992).

Few teachers, however committed, can hope to fulfil all their aims if the context in which they work is not supportive. For instance, some parents may have one set of educational priorities: staff may take up another value position. The established practices of the school may not support the particular styles of teaching which a teacher would wish to adopt. Staff may disagree with some aspects of government policy; the resources needed may not be available. For reasons such as these, teachers must continually adapt: they must know themselves and the situations in which they work, and they must be able to make astute strategic judgements as they seek to achieve personal and professional fulfilment and to resolve the dilemmas posed by idealism and pragmatism.

1.1 Analysing ourselves

Studies such as those of Huberman (1993), Goodson (1992), Thomas (1995) and Nias (1989, **Reading 5.1**) have shown that most people enter the profession with a strong sense of personal identity and of personal values. For instance, Nias reported that this sense of self was so strong that many teachers saw themselves as 'persons-in-teaching' rather than as 'teachers' as such. Clearly, if this is so, then the openness and willingness to change and develop, which is implied by the notion of reflective teaching, is dependent on the qualities and degree of confidence of each teacher's sense of self and the relationship of 'self' to 'role'. One issue of particular interest is that of achieving personal fulfilment from teaching. This seems to be most likely when there is a congruence between each teacher's personal sense of self and the ways in which they are expected to present their self in school – their public display.

This work raises a number of important points, particularly the need to develop self-knowledge. Easen (1985) has provided a useful framework for developing such understanding. He suggests that we can distinguish between a set of characteristics which we see as being part of ourselves (as representing our self-image) in contrast to a set of attributes which other people attribute to us on the basis of observation and interaction with us. There is also an unknown area of potential for self-development.

Using a model of this sort, one can distinguish between the following:

- our public display: aspects of ourselves which we project and others also see presented

- our blind spots: aspects of ourselves which others see but we do not recognize

- our dreamer spots: aspects of ourselves which we know are there, or would like to be there, but of which others are unaware

- our untapped reservoir: our unknown potential, of which we are also unaware.

These aspects are indicated in Figure 5.1. Gaining self-knowledge is not something which one can simply 'do' and complete in a single activity. It is something which develops over time, as a conscious process which goes on throughout life. As reflective teachers we will be aware of how much our biographies affect what we think and do (see Maclure, 2000). It is helpful and interesting to recall experiences at home and at school which you feel were significant – exchanging memories with a colleague is a good way to do this. However in Reflective Activity 5.1 our main purpose is to draw attention to a different aspect of self-awareness.

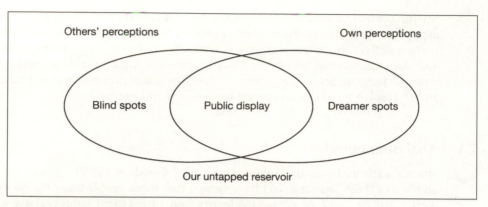

Figure 5.1 *Seen and unseen aspects of 'self'*

Reflective activity 5.1

Aim: To analyse dimensions of our 'selves'

Evidence and reflection: Think of specific and memorable incidents in which you were centrally involved. Try to identify the most prominent characteristics of your 'self' which they reveal. It may be helpful to situate your reflection (e.g. as a 'parent', as a 'child', as a 'pupil', as a 'trainee', as a 'teacher').

Try to identify:

1. Dreamer spots . . .   1.
    (parts you would like to develop)   2.
                                         3.

2. Blind spots . . .   1.
    (parts you do not often face up to) 2.
                                         3.

3. Public display . . .   1.
    (parts you publicly present)   2.
                                         3.

4. Untapped reservoir . . .   1.
    (parts you think might be there)   2.
                                         3.

It would probably be beneficial to do this exercise with a friend. It could help you to deepen your understandings, share and explain your perceptions, whilst providing mutual support.

Extension: Clearly, the challenge of being a reflective teacher is intimately bound up with reflection on such personal issues. It is about replacing blind spots with insights, about developing dreams and ideals into realities, about tapping potential and facilitating learning.

However, it is necessary to consider the fact that developing such self-awareness can involve a process of self-discovery which may, at times, be threatening and painful. The work of Carl Rogers (1961, 1969, 1980) is useful here. Rogers writes as a psychotherapist who has developed what he calls a 'person-centred' approach to his work. His central argument is that:

> individuals have within themselves vast resources for self-understanding and for altering their self-concepts, basic attitudes and self-directed behaviour.
>
> (1980, p. 115)

In addition to the focus on inner self-development, Rogers also suggests that personal development is facilitated by genuine acceptance by others. This has great relevance for professional and personal development in teaching. In particular, it points to the importance of working collaboratively with colleagues and developing open, trusting relationships. Such relationships should not only provide an alternative source of insights into our own practice but should also provide the support to face and deal with whatever issues may be raised. Recent work in the field of school effectiveness identifies the importance of schools developing cultures in which teachers are supported in taking risks, changing their practices and growing in effectiveness, creating 'learning communities' in which teachers are also learners (Hopkins, Ainscow and West, 1994; MacBeath and Mortimore, 2001, **Reading 17.1**, Southworth, Nias and Campbell, 1992, **Reading 17.2**; MacGilchrist, Myers and Read, 1997; Nixon, 1996).

1.2 Articulating values, aims and commitments

In beginning to consider our personal sense of values and how, when and where they arise, it is important to establish a basic point: our perspectives and viewpoints influence what we do both inside and outside the classroom. The values we hold are frequently evident in our behaviours, and thus, in our teaching.

Identifying values and aims is difficult, and so, too, is trying to identify what to look for in the learning environments we create and inhabit, which could tell us whether we are putting our aims into practice. The reflective teacher needs both to identify values, aims and commitments *and* to consider indicators of their actual implementation. Only then will we be able to judge whether what we do really matches what we say we believe.

One important step is to see that our own individual beliefs reflect our social position, previous experience and historical location. This is one reason why beliefs can be so difficult to change, since there can be significant material and cultural foundations to them, or edifices built upon them. Indeed, beliefs can often appear to be representations of 'objective truths', or 'natural facts', rather than socially constructed perspectives. One useful way forward can be to group such beliefs and to link them to educational ideologies (see Chapter 4, Section 1.1). These value positions and ideological perspectives can be labelled in many different ways – itself a challenging activity for a reflective teacher. We have identified seven positions below which we feel are, or have been, particularly important.

Social democracy. This is characterized by an egalitarian value-position and a focus on the potential of education as an instrument of gradual social change.

This was a prevalent ideology in the post-war years and, for a period, seemed to have a degree of all-party support in the UK.

Liberal romanticism. An example of this is the highly individualistic, 'child-centred' view of education focusing on the unique development of each child, a view which values diversity and individual difference. This is the ideology which was endorsed by the Plowden Report (CACE, 1967), and which underpinned the Free School Movement.

Traditional educational conservatism. A perspective that emphasizes, the transmission of established social values, knowledge and culture through a subject-oriented approach and which also has a particular emphasis on upholding 'standards'. This was the explicit ideology of the Black Papers (e.g. Cox and Boyson, 1975; Cox and Dyson, 1969) and was an important element of the thinking of the 1970s and 1980s [e.g. Hillgate, 1987; Scruton, 1986]. This ultimately led to the Education Reform Act (1988), the National Curriculum, and new forms of assessment and testing.

Economic pragmatism. An instrumental approach focusing on the individual's acquisition of useful skills. The term 'vocationalism' is sometimes used where the emphasis shifts, perhaps at times of high unemployment, to directing individuals to acquire skills economically useful to society. In England this approach is evident in recent debates concerning the need for basic skills and the National Literacy and Numeracy strategies, the reformation of the Post-16 Curriculum, and development of vocational education.

Social radicalism. An approach which is based on a commitment to develop education as a means of combating inequalities in society and promoting social justice. Proponents support positive action regarding such issues as sexism, racism, homophobia, social class, disability, rights and the distribution of power and wealth (Arnot and Weiler, 1993; Gilborn, 1995). Some 1980s' policies of the Inner London Education Authority, before it was disbanded, reflected this approach and the commitments, if not the actions, are embedded in UK laws (e.g. Race Relations Act, 1976; Sex Discrimination Act, 1975; Disability Discrimination Act, 1996) and international conventions (e.g. United Nations Declaration on Human Rights, 1948; Convention on the Rights of the Child, 1989).

Neo-liberal conservatism. A set of beliefs, going back to Adam Smith, about the efficiency of free-market forces in allocating resources and raising standards in the provision of goods and services (No Turning Back Group of MPs, 1986; Sexton, 1987, 1988); Chubb and Moe, 1990). As O'Keefe (1988) put it: 'If you do not like the groceries at one supermarket, try another.' These ideas have been very influential in the 1990s' restructuring of education in countries such as New Zealand, Australia and the United States of America, as well as in the UK (Bridges and McLaughlin, 1994; Gewirtz, Ball and Bowe, 1995).

New Labourism. An attempt, initiated by Tony Blair in the mid-1990s, to set a new social democratic agenda for the Labour Party, and aimed to distance new policies both from previous Labour Party commitments and from the neo-liberal conservatism of John Major's government. Characterized by 'toughness' regarding the quality and performance of public services, but also by a strong commitment to inclusion, this approach led to unexpected endorsement of private enterprise in public services (for an interim review, see Fielding, 2001).

Such educational ideologies are often not expressed or experienced in their 'pure' form. Indeed, the multiplicity of voices attempting to influence national educational policy has the potential to make it harder for teachers and school communities to clarify their own value positions. However, reflective teachers should aim to develop their own clearly defined personal perspective as a guide to everyday action and practical policies.

Reflective activity 5.2

Aim: To identify general aims which you hold for your pupils' learning.

Evidence and reflection: List your 'top three' aims, and number them in order of importance.

Extension: How do your aims relate to your 'value-position'? How do your aims compare with your colleagues? What are the implications of any similarity or difference?

To investigate our value-positions in greater depth the work of Eisner and Vallance (1974) is helpful. They distinguish three main dimensions upon which varied value-positions are held. They suggest these are best represented as continua:

individual ⟵⟶ society

(i.e. whether education should be geared to meet individuals' needs and demands, rather than to educational provision being planned to meet the needs of society)

values ⟵⟶ skills

(i.e. whether education should focus on developing individuals' sense of values in a moral and ethical context, or on developing their skills and competencies)

adaptive ⟵⟶ reconstructive

(i.e. whether education should prepare individuals to fit into the present society, or should equip them to change and develop it)

By identifying these three dimensions, it may be possible to clarify where each of us stands regarding our value-positions. For example, a trainee might place herself at the 'individual' extreme of the first dimension, tend towards the 'skills' extreme of the second dimension and feel most comfortable with the 'adaptive' extreme of the third dimension. Such a person would, therefore, be committed to an educational system which aimed at developing individuals with the skills and competencies to fit into the given present society. She would feel less ethical concern for the needs of society as a whole or desire to consider the possibilities and processes of change.

The importance of identifying our value-positions is threefold. First, it can help us to assess whether we are consistent, both in what we, as individuals,

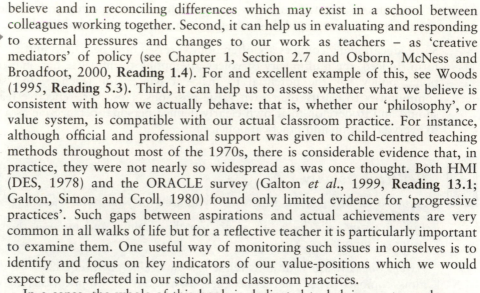

believe and in reconciling differences which may exist in a school between colleagues working together. Second, it can help us in evaluating and responding to external pressures and changes to our work as teachers – as 'creative mediators' of policy (see Chapter 1, Section 2.7 and Osborn, McNess and Broadfoot, 2000, **Reading 1.4**). For and excellent example of this, see Woods (1995, **Reading 5.3**). Third, it can help us to assess whether what we believe is consistent with how we actually behave: that is, whether our 'philosophy', or value system, is compatible with our actual classroom practice. For instance, although official and professional support was given to child-centred teaching methods throughout most of the 1970s, there is considerable evidence that, in practice, they were not nearly so widespread as was once thought. Both HMI (DES, 1978) and the ORACLE survey (Galton *et al.*, 1999, **Reading 13.1**; Galton, Simon and Croll, 1980) found only limited evidence for 'progressive practices'. Such gaps between aspirations and actual achievements are very common in all walks of life but for a reflective teacher it is particularly important to examine them. One useful way of monitoring such issues in ourselves is to identify and focus on key indicators of our value-positions which we would expect to be reflected in our school and classroom practices.

In a sense, the whole of this book is dedicated to helping us to analyse our own behaviour and its consequences in the light of our own beliefs. We may get help from the General Teaching Councils in our part of the UK, such as the Scottish GTC which has protected professional values since its foundation in 1966. In the end, however, there are many personal decisions to be made. It is helpful, too, to be aware of the ways in which classroom experiences actually shape our thinking as teachers. For example, Cortazzi (1990, **Reading 5.2**) identified a number of very grounded polar opposites, which are quite chastening.

1.3   Examining our perceptions of pupils

Just as it was important to understand what we expect of ourselves as 'teachers', so, too, it is important to understand what we expect of 'pupils'.

All of us are likely to have preconceptions and prejudices about what children should be like as pupils. For instance, it has been found that teachers are affected by children's sex, race or social class and even by their names (Meighan, 1981). If, as teachers, we hold such preconceptions, it can result in treating children in different ways, according to these preconceptions. Children then tend to respond differently, which reinforces our original preconceptions. Such labelling, or stereotyping, can lead to a phenomenon known as a 'self-fulfilling prophecy' and could result in considerable social injustices (Brophy and Good, 1974; Nash, 1976; Sharp and Green, 1975), particularly if it emerges in official assessment (Filer, 2000; Filer and Pollard, 2000). The reflective teacher, therefore, needs to question the bases for any differential treatment of the children in the class. This means examining the evidence upon which we base our conceptions of individual children. We need to try and ensure that opinions are based on impartial assessment, systematic and careful observation and discussions, rather than on prejudiced or haphazard impressions (see also Chapter 15 and **Reading 6.6**).

Teachers do, of course, have to develop ways of understanding, organizing and grouping children in order to respond effectively to their educational needs. Within the classroom however, this should be done with regard for the purposes of each particular situation or learning activity. An inflexible form of classroom organization is almost bound to disadvantage some children unnecessarily.

Reflective activity 5.3

Aim: To understand our perceptions of 'pupils'.

Evidence and reflection: First, without referring to the register or any lists, write down the names of the children in your class. Note which order you have listed them in and which names you found hard to remember. What does the order tell you about which children are more memorable than others, and for what reasons?

Second, use your complete class-list to generate the 'personal constructs' which you employ. To do this, look at each adjacent pair of names and write down the word that shows how those two pupils are most alike. Then write down another word which shows how they are most different.

When you have done this with each pair, review the characteristics that you have identified. What does this suggest to you about the characteristics by which you distinguish children? What additional qualities do the children have which these constructs do not seem to reflect and which perhaps you do not use? (See also Chapter 3, Section 3.24.)

Extension: Consider, perhaps with a colleague, the results of this activity and note any patterns that might exist: for example whether some of your ideas relate more to boys than girls, or to children from different class/race/religious backgrounds. There may also be a variety of constructs that relate to such things as academic ability, physical attributes or behaviour towards teachers or other children.

---

2 | KNOWING THE CHILDREN AS PUPILS

Developing an understanding of the children as pupils requires that a reflective teacher should empathize with what it is like to be a 'pupil' at school as well as develop personal knowledge of and rapport with individual children. This is a foundation for establishing good behaviour and a learning atmosphere in the classroom. It is also, of course, really important in maintaining inclusion. This is particularly important in the modern context when the pressure for 'performance' is severe. Less able children can feel rejected in such circumstances, but a sensitive teacher can find ways of building their self respect and making them feel valued.

2.1 Children's views of themselves in school

The way that children think of themselves in school will directly influence their approach to learning, their 'learning disposition' (Claxton, 1999, **Reading 7.7**; Katz, 1995). Some may be highly anxious and continually undervalue themselves. Others may seem over-confident and extremely resilient. Some may be very well aware of their own strengths and weaknesses whilst others may seem to have relatively naive views of themselves. Children may be gregarious, or loners, or they may be lonely. For instance, Pollard (1996) and Pollard and Filer (1999, **Reading 5.5**) traced the home, playground and classroom experiences of a small group of children through their primary-school careers. They argued that such experiences contribute to a sense of identity and thence to confidence and achievement in learning. Figure 5.2 provides a summary for one of the children in their study for a seven-year period from the ages of 5 to 11. Data from Reception, Year 3 and Year 6 are shown, indicating William's progression from 'nice but silly' to 'jester' and 'rebel'. His sense of humour is conveyed in a drawing from Year 2 (see Figure 5.3).

Reflective activity 5.4

Aim: To consider the influence of relationships in home, playground and classroom on the sense of identity and learning of a child.

Evidence and reflection: Select a child on whom to focus. Draw up a matrix, similar to that used by Pollard (1996), but for an appropriate period. Use records, observation and discussion to gradually complete each cell of the matrix. This may take some time and enquiry to do appropriately.

Extension: Consider your matrix as a whole. How is the child's view of his/ her self influenced by others? How does his/her view of self influence the approach taken to learning? Are there any specific implications for providing for this child or overall conclusions for understanding children more generally?

Reflective Activity 5.5 suggests a quick way of gathering evidence about the feelings of a whole class.

Reflective activity 5.5

Aim: To identify how children feel about themselves in a school context.

Evidence and reflection: Children can be asked to complete 'Me at School' sheets (Mortimore *et al.*, 1986). They should be completed by each child individually and can be administered to a whole class simultaneously. Each item can be read by the teacher in turn. Children should put a cross in the box which is 'most true for me'.

The children's responses will give an indication of their overall feelings about themselves at school and the items can be scored and aggregated. Scoring is from one to five for items 1, 3, 5, 6, 7 and 9. It is from five to one for items 2, 4, 8, 10 and 11. If an item is missed, code 0. If a more specific analysis is required then the following groups of items can be identified:

- 3, 7 and 10 relate to relationships with other children
- 1, 2 and 8 relate to anxiety
- 4, 5 and 9 relate to learning
- 6 and 11 relate to behaviour.

ME AT SCHOOL

MY NAME _____

TODAY'S DATE _____

	Always	Usually	Sometimes	Usually	Always	
1. I am happy and contented.	☐	☐	☐	☐	☐	I am unhappy nervous or worried
2. I find it difficult when I am put in new situations or meet new people	☐	☐	☐	☐	☐	I find it easy when I am put in new situations or meet new people
3. I am easygoing and it takes a lot to make me lose my temper	☐	☐	☐	☐	☐	I am irritable and quarrelsome
4. I find it hard to concentrate on work and I am easily distracted	☐	☐	☐	☐	☐	I can concentrate on my work and I am not easily distracted
5. I am keen to learn and I am interested in finding out about things	☐	☐	☐	☐	☐	I am not very interested in learning or finding out about things
6. I am well behaved and I do what my teacher tells me to do	☐	☐	☐	☐	☐	I am naughty and I don't do what my teacher tells me to do
7. I am helpful and kind to other children	☐	☐	☐	☐	☐	I bully or am spiteful towards other children
8. I'd rather be on my own than be with other children	☐	☐	☐	☐	☐	I'd rather be with other children than be on my own
9. I keep going if work is hard and I like to try and find the answer to difficult problems	☐	☐	☐	☐	☐	I give up easily if work is hard and I don't like trying to find the answer to difficult problems
10. Other children think I am unkind and spiteful	☐	☐	☐	☐	☐	Other children think I am kind and helpful
11. My teacher thinks I am naughty and don't do as I'm told	☐	☐	☐	☐	☐	My teacher thinks I am well behaved and I do as I am told

FAMILY RELATIONSHIPS	PEER GROUP RELATIONSHIPS	TEACHER RELATIONSHIPS	IDENTITY	CAREER
Reception: Mrs Powell				
William has a sister Abigail who is three years younger.	William's parents worry that he may be vulnerable to peer pressure.	Structural position: among the oldest few. Ma & Eng ½ way down class.	Confidence high, though not predictably so.	Considerable ability and enthusiams contrasted with frequently minimalistic approach to tasks and withdrawal.
His parents have strong Christian convictions.	He is popular and willing to lead or follow others.	Entered school full of confidence.	Popular with adults and children.	Strives for autonomy in teacher–pupil relationship.
Parents try to avoid putting pressure to succeed on children.	Some clashes with best friend Richard. Both are 'strong personalities' their teacher says.	'Played' for the first term with no concentration on work.	Teachers sees him as 'Nice', 'Silly', 'A bit tough', 'Strong willed'.	Concerned to avoid trouble with his teacher.
Mother taught William to read before school.	Picks up definite ideas about appropriate gender behaviour at school.	Minimalist approach to writing and rushes through artistic–creative tasks.	Difficult to discipline.	Attains status in the peer group.
He sometimes withdraws from situations he does not grasp immediately.	Likes to get the class laughing.	Doesn't see why anyone should tell him what to do.	Likes to create laughter in the classroom.	
			Consciously beginning to shape and articulate a positive self-image as a pupil.	

Figure 5.2 *Factors and processes in William's approach to learning from 5 to 11 years old*

FAMILY RELATIONSHIPS	PEER GROUP RELATIONSHIPS	TEACHER RELATIONSHIPS	IDENTITY	CAREER
Year 3: Mr Brown				
At home, can be critical of school organization and teacher strategies.	William openly acknowledges girls as friends again.	Structural position: age ½ way down class. Ma, Sci, Eng, in top ⅓ of class.	William is seen as 'ideas man' by teachers.	William's communicator –negotiator identity seen by his teacher as integral to the learning process.
Some concern and loss of sleep over tests. Parents coach to reduce anxiety.	William and friends describe selves as 'The Terrible Two' and 'Jesters'.	Mr Brown enjoys his company and sees him as lively and enthusiastic.	*Social* identity enhances his academic identity.	Thus, as in Year 2, social skills were harnessed for the benefit of learning.
Likes to relate to older boys as a matter of status.	Has a reputation for being exclusive in his friendships. Peers say 'they think they are the Smart Guys'.	Works with Daniel noisily, likes to articulate problems.	Says his teacher regards him as 'best-working boy'.	Ready to challenge authority.
Style conscious.		Challenges teacher with ideas 'Why don't we.'	'Jesters'.	Has a strong sense of his future.
Abigail starts school.			Williams group 'think they are the Smart Guys'.	

Figure 5.2 (continued)

FAMILY RELATIONSHIPS	PEER GROUP RELATIONSHIPS	TEACHER RELATIONSHIPS	IDENTITY	CAREER
Year 3: *Mrs Chard*				
Takes part in youth orchestra concert but expected to give up the violin.	William is back with his familiar year group.	Structural position: age ½ way down class. Ma & Sci ⅓ down the class, Eng well within top ⅓.	Seen by his teacher as something of a noisy nuisance, 'likes to come out as one of the top dogs'. Also 'fun', 'popular' and talented in the use of language and in his writing.	William could not achieve teacher esteem through either of his customary strategies in this class.
Challenges fairness of school rules at home.	Long-standing rivalries and resentments among high-achieving competitive pupils become publicly aired in classroom.	Has an 'abrasive' relationship with Mrs Chard who thinks he talks too much, lacks concentration and does not like being noticed.		Easy, negotiative relationships with teachers gradually degenerate into critical opposition.
Pushing hard at the boundaries at home.	William and friends think Mrs Chard favours girls and is sexist.	William withdraws co-operation from teacher when he feels unjustly treated. 'Gives of his best when he feels like it'.	Social identity no longer enhances his academic identity.	
Mother says William is friend-oriented more than family-oriented.	William's group dub themselves 'The Rebels'.		William and his friends redefine their group as 'The Rebels'.	William and friends condemn 'mismanagement' of school systems of reward, to which they still look for prestige.
Being his parents has always entailed constant negotiation.				

Figure 5.2 (continued)

Figure 5.3 *William's drawing of his Year 2 classroom*

A central strategy in the development of positive self-concepts among the children in school lies in encouraging individuals to identify qualities within themselves which they can value (Pollard and Filer, 1999, **Reading 5.5**; Moyles, 1994; Maylor, 1995, **Reading 5.7**). It is important to provide opportunities where a wide range of qualities can be appreciated. In classrooms where competitive achievement is greatly emphasized, some children may quickly come to regard themselves unfavourably, or else learn to resent and oppose the values and the teacher. It is, however, possible to create a climate where many different qualities are valued and where children are encouraged to challenge themselves to improve their own individual performance. In this way the dignity of the individual child

can be protected and individual effort and engagement rewarded. (These ideas are extended in Chapter 6, Section 3.)

One of the ways of establishing such a climate is to encourage children to evaluate their own work and to set their own personal goals.

2.2 Children's perceptions of teachers

If we are trying to negotiate a positive working relationship with children, it is important to know how each of the individuals involved in the relationship views the others. It is, therefore, important to know how children perceive their teachers.

A considerable amount of evidence has been collected in relation to children's views of teachers (Blishen, 1969; Makins, 1969; Meighan, 1978; Pollard *et al.*, 2000) and trainees (Cooper and Hyland, 2000). Much of the evidence suggests that children like teachers who 'make them learn'. They expect teachers to teach, by which they seem to mean to take initiatives, to be in control and to provide interesting activities. On the other hand, they also like teachers who are prepared to be flexible, to respond to the different interests of the individuals in the class and to provide some scope for pupil choice. Children dislike teachers who have favourites or who are unpredictable in their moods. Most children like a teacher who can sometimes 'have a laugh'. Overall, it seems that children like teachers who are firm, flexible, fair and fun.

Reflective activity 5.6

Aim: To find out children's criteria for a 'good teacher'.

Evidence and reflection: Hold a discussion (with the whole class, or in small groups which can then report back to the whole class) on what makes a 'good teacher'. Perhaps the discussion could be couched in terms of suggestions for a trainee on how to become a good teacher. Discussions with children on such a topic must obviously be handled very carefully and only with the agreement of any teachers who are involved.

Extension: Such information can be interesting in two ways:

● It reveals something of the children's expectations of what it is to be a good 'teacher'.

● It can contribute to reflection on our own effectiveness as teachers and in implementing our values, aims and commitments. It could also lead to a reconsideration of those values, aims and commitments.

2.3   Children's culture and their views of each other

So far the focus has been on the teacher, the child and their mutual perceptions. However, it is most important to remember that, although the teacher is a central figure, classrooms are a meeting place for many children – indeed, Jackson (1968, **Reading 6.2**) referred to 'the crowd' as being a salient feature of classroom life. How children learn to cope with being one of a crowd and how they relate to each other is of consequence. This can affect how well the children settle in the class socially, and, in turn, may affect their learning. There is, thus, a social dimension to classroom life.

Children's culture has been described by Davies (1982, p. 33) as the result of children 'constructing their own reality with each other' and 'making sense of and developing strategies to cope with the adult world' (**Reading 5.4**). It thus reflects the children's collective perspectives and actions, many of which can be interpreted as defensive responses to children's relative dependence on adults.

Children's play is, therefore, an important means by which they can identify with each other, establish themselves as members of a group, try out different roles and begin to develop independence and responsibility. Young children often make friends with those who are immediately accessible and with whom they share common experiences (Rubin, 1980). Typically, their friends are children who live close by, who are in their class or who are the children of their parents' friends. When peer groups begin to form, each individual is likely to have to establish their membership of the group in a number of ways. For example, each member may be expected to contribute and conform to the norms which are shared by the group: for example, liking similar games, toys and TV programmes; supporting the same football team or pop group; liking the same fashions. Group members will also be expected to be loyal to each other, 'stand up for their mates', play together and share things.

A further feature of children's culture is status. As children try to establish their individual identities among their peers each will be valued in particular ways. Sometimes this value will be based on prowess in the playground: for example in skipping, football, fighting. In addition, the identity which children develop through their school-work and their relationships with parents, siblings and teachers may influence the way children are perceived by their peers. Where this is the case, there are clear implications for us as teachers. This process of differentiation of children, in terms of their status with both teachers and with other children, affects their own self-image. The process starts during the early years at school and has been found to increase during children's school lives (Breakwell, 1986; Pollard, 1996). It may lead to a polarization of pro-school and anti-school cultures (Lacey, 1970). Hence, the status and self-image of the children have significant consequences for the children's development during their school years – and these can last into their adult lives.

Teachers may wish to know something of the patterns of children's friendships in order to use this information to sustain a positive learning atmosphere and so that friendships can be considered when deciding on grouping arrangements in classrooms (**Reading 10.5**).

For reasons of this sort, trying to establish the friendship patterns within the classroom may be of particular interest. Many teachers feel that they 'know' their class well and several friendship groupings may be clearly identifiable.

Nevertheless, friendship is very complex, and with younger children may be highly fluid. Constructing a sociogram, as described in Chapter 3, can capture some of this complexity.

Friendships can be a source of much pain and distress. It is also easy to fail to notice things, such as that an outgoing child may actually lack a particular friend of his or her own. Sociometric analysis can help in developing this sort of awareness and sensitivity but there are other ways. For instance, Sluckin (1981) spent many hours watching children in their playgrounds. He observed their 'playground code' which encompassed things such as ways of behaving, establishing status and resolving disputes. Playground observation, in a consciously focused way could be valuable in understanding such issues (see also Blatchford, 1989).

One particular issue which could be watched for is that of bullying (Elliott, 1992; Tattum and Lane, 1989). This is an unacceptable aspect of child culture and often reflects both its tendency to emphasize conformity and its concern with status, as well as, frequently, the relative insecurity of the perpetrators. Thus children who are different in some way – new to a school, overweight, or possibly have an unusual accent or simply a different culture – are picked on physically and verbally and are excluded by other children as their unacceptability for cultural membership is asserted or as a pecking order is maintained. In one of its worst forms this can degenerate into overt racism.

Adult intervention must be firm but sensitive to the realities of the social situation. All children need to have friends, to play with and feel accepted by others. The teacher's task is therefore to stop the bullying whilst facilitating the entry of the 'victim' into an appropriate niche within the child culture.

2.4 Understanding individual children and their needs

Just as we looked at personal and personality factors in the teacher, so a similar kind of 'biographical' knowledge about each child is valuable in understanding them as individual people and as learners. This can be seen through a longitudinal study of children's learning and careers through primary school (Pollard and Filer, 1996 and 1999; Pollard *et al.*, 2000, **Readings 5.5** and **7.11**). These books provide very detailed case studies of individual pupils as they develop through their primary school, and document the ways in which family, friends and relationships with successive teachers influence learning progress and the emergent identity of each child (see Figure 5.2). (For a different case, see also **Reading 5.7**.) Awareness of such factors and processes is crucial to maintaining inclusion, for there is little doubt that children experience problems and may fall out of the system when they feel personally misunderstood or unable to cope.

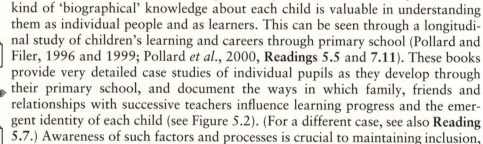

Many schools collect basic information about each child's medical history and educational progress, but such records, although sometimes helpful, rarely convey an impression of the 'whole child'. As a move in this direction, profiles, portfolios or 'records of achievement' used to be commonplace in schools. Increasingly, however, such forms of record tend to focus on each child's progress and targets achieved in different subject areas, supplemented perhaps with examples of their work at different ages. However, they may be enhanced by including information about hobbies and interests, abilities and tastes and materials which reflect each child's social attitudes, behaviour, out of school achievements and family context. Perhaps each child could also help in decisions about what to include.

Such records may provide an excellent starting point for understanding each child, in terms of their material, social and cultural circumstances as well as their development in school. They thus provide a context for understanding children. However, such records cannot replace the awareness which will come from personal contacts with children and their parents.

Reflective activity 5.7

Aim: To construct a biographical perspective of a child.

Evidence and reflection:

1. Present open-ended opportunities where a child can write, draw, talk or otherwise communicate about herself or himself. Discussions about friends, experiences, family or about favourite books or TV characters can be revealing. Make notes.

2. Observe and take notes on the child's general behaviour in the play-ground and in the classroom. Consider how they interact with other children and how they tackle learning tasks.

3. Take informal opportunities to talk with and get to know the child. Allow an intuitive understanding to develop, and let this complement and interact with the other information you record.

4. If possible, discuss the child with parents and other teachers. Make notes.

5. Summarize your key understandings and your areas of uncertainty. Consider the child's strengths and areas of need.

Follow-up: Accumulating such information can take time and will only develop gradually. Nevertheless, it could provide a valuable profile of the specific and unique characteristics of an individual. Then it is necessary to consider what implications it has for shaping the educational provision that is appropriate for the child.

It is often argued that the 'needs' of the learner should be seen as the starting-point for teaching and learning policies. However, the notion of appropriate needs is a very problematic one, since it begs questions about prior aims, and judgements about what is worthwhile (Barrow, 1984; Dearden, 1968). Nevertheless, it may be valuable for us as reflective teachers to articulate what we see as the basic 'needs' of every child which we commit ourselves to trying to meet. Maslow (1954) identified three classes of needs:

- primary needs . . . for food, sleep and shelter
- emotional needs . . . for love and security
- social needs . . . for acceptance by peers.

This is not dissimilar from those suggested by Kellmer-Pringle (1974) who identified four basic types of needs for young children:

- the need for love and security
- the need for new experiences
- the need for praise and recognition
- the need for responsibility.

Within each of these general areas, it would be possible to identify many further needs. This could be attempted in the specific context of one's class, though one would have to be careful to guard against adversely labelling the children in the process (see Woodhead, 1997).

Reflective activity 5.8

Aim: To identify some needs of a selected number of children in one's class and to establish an order of priority.

Evidence and reflection: List the children's names and beside each name record your judgement of that child's key needs.

Extension:

1. Consider which criteria you used in deciding 'key' needs. Was your choice based on the fact that you value certain needs more than others and believe them to be of greater importance in themselves?

2. Examine the needs that you have listed and see if any pattern exists across the class which could form a common basis for planning activities.

3. Identify needs which are specific to individual children and consider how you could make provision for them.

2.5   Challenges of transition and transfer

Children are perhaps most routinely vulnerable, and in need of particular support from teachers and others, at times of transition and transfer. Transition denotes movement from class to class within a school, whilst transfer is used to describe the more major move between institutions. In either case, however, many children move from the relative security of a situation in which they feel well established to one of relative uncertainty. Starting school and end of Key Stage transfers may be particularly traumatic, and there is cumulative evidence from OFSTED and others (e.g. Rudduck, Chaplain and Wallace, 1996) of a significant drop in pupil performance in the early years of secondary education – which the National Key Stage 3 Strategy is designed to address. With increasing amounts of mobility, children are also required to change their schools more often than in the past.

Many schools do a wonderful job in facilitating transition and transfer. Transition is easiest, for pupils are likely to 'go up' with their classmates and have good knowledge of their future teacher. Continuity in curriculum, assessment and teaching methods has also increased considerably with the introduction of national requirements and whole-school strategies.

Transfer is more difficult because there is movement across institutional environments, cultures and practices. These may be quite different, but most schools have developed effective ways of providing information, orienting and inducting new pupils (see, for instance, Nichols and Gardner, 1999). However, it has been suggested that schools have not paid sufficient attention to continuity of academic progress. Previous attainment is usually underestimated, with the result that new pupils may become bored and demotivated, and this is a major focus of the Key Stage 3 Strategy.

However, the issues are complicated, for it is certainly the case that performance is affected by circumstances. Thus a child's capability at home may not be forthcoming when she enters her Reception class, just as pupils' attainment in primary school may not be matched by their first efforts in secondary. Relationships and feelings do affect performance and learning. So what is going on here, and what can be done about it?

To answer this question, we revert to first principles. As we saw in Section 2.1, when children move through schooling they develop an identity, a view of themselves as a learner and as a person. As Pollard and Filer (1999) showed, pupil identity evolves over time, reflecting the influence of significant others such as friends, parents, siblings, teachers and the situations to which the child has had to adapt. Each child has to develop a viable identity in the context of school life, and because the demands of parents, school friends and teachers are not always consistent, this is sometimes quite a feat. Transfers are traumatic because they disrupt these settlements, and threaten identity. This was a core argument of Measor and Woods (1984) and has been revisited by Jackson and Warin (2000, **Reading** 5.6) and Lucey and Reay (2000) in the cases of initial school entry and transfer to secondary. A major point which they make is that anxieties result from disruption of an established process of identity construction, so that new means of self-constuction must be found. Strong, culturally established forms of sense-making then tend to be drawn on, of which gender has been found to be particularly salient. As Jackson and Warin put it, 'people rely on gender to cope with the unfamiliar' (p. 387). Clearly, there are implications here for other forms of identification, by social class, ethnicity or religious affiliation, for example.

Transition and transfer are thus only partly about organizational matters, curriculum continuity and progression, important though these are. They also concern each child's attempts to develop a viable identity, and to feel at ease in the new situation. They are unlikely to learn effectively until this condition is met, which leads us on, in the next chapter, to considering the issue of relationships.

It is worth commenting here on the particular circumstances of children of migrant families. As Maylor (1995, **Reading 5.7**) shows, the challenge to identify may be particularly stark and uncompromising. Refugee children and those from other migrant families are likely to need particular support from their teachers.

CONCLUSION

The process of reflecting on our aims and commitments as teachers should help us in developing a realistic personal perspective. If the many unconscious influences on our teaching can be made explicit, it is easier to identify where we are being most successful and where perhaps our aims and our practice don't match as well as they might. It is also possible, by trying to make the implicit explicit, to be more aware of how we get to know children and of the evidence upon which we base our understanding. Furthermore, by becoming more aware of the children's perceptions of us as teachers, of their culture and of their perspectives on themselves and each other, we are more likely to be able to take account of their needs when planning and making provision for classroom activities, or the major challenges of transitions and transfers.

Key readings

An accessible and insightful introduction to the importance of considering the 'self' of teachers and children remains:

Hargreaves, D. H. (1972)
Interpersonal Relationships and Education.
London: Routledge.

The following books offer particularly sensitive accounts of the challenges which are posed for primary-school teachers who take their values and their professional commitment seriously:

Evans, L. (1998)
Teacher Morale, Job Satisfaction and Motivation.
London: Paul Chapman.

Nias, J. (1989a)
Primary Teachers Talking: a Study of Teaching at Work.
London: Routledge.

📖 **Reading 5.1**

Troman, G. and Woods, P. (2000)
Primary Teachers' Stress.
London: Routledge.

On questions of aims, values and commitments, there are a number of distinctive philosophical analyses. For example:

Barrow, R. and Woods, R. (1988)
An Introduction to Philosophy of Education.
London: Routledge.

The most recent research on primary teachers' aims and sense of professional responsibility is reported in:

Osborn, M., McNess, E. and Broadfoot, P. (2000b)
What Teachers' Say. Changing Policy and Practice in Primary Education.
London: Continuum.   📖 **Reading 1.4**

There are a number of interesting books on children's culture, friendships and perspectives. Davies offers a classic study from Australia, Pollard's contributors argue the case for taking children's perspectives seriously whilst Woods provides an excellent overview of the field:

Davies, B. (1982)
Life in the Classroom and Playground.
London: Routledge and Kegan Paul.   📖 **Reading 5.4**

Pollard, A. (ed.) (1987)
Children and their Primary Schools: A New Perspective.
London: Falmer.

Woods, P. (1990)
The Happiest Days? How Pupils Cope with School.
London: Falmer.

For detailed case-studies of children's developing identities and careers through primary school, see:

Pollard, A. and Filer, A. (1999)
The Social World of Pupil Career: Strategic Biographies through Primary School.
London: Cassell.   📖 **Reading 5.5**

Other interesting books which focus on specific issues are:

Sluckin, A. (1981)
Growing Up in the Playground.
London: Routledge and Kegan Paul.

Mayell, B. (1994)
Negotiating Health: Children at Home and Primary School.
London: Cassell.

Connelly, P. (1998)
Racism, Gender and Identities of Young Children.
London: Routledge.

Francis, B. (1998)
Power Plays: Primary School Children's Construction of Gender, Power and Adult Work.
Stoke-on-Trent: Trentham.

A classic approach to children's 'needs' is:

Kellmer-Pringle, M, (1974)
The Needs of Children.
London: Hutchinson.

 Readings for Reflective Teaching (the companion volume) also offers other closely associated work on the issues raised in this chapter. This includes work by authors such as:

Jennifer Nias, Martin Cortazzi, Peter Woods, Bronwyn Davies, Andrew Pollard, Ann Filer, Carolyn Jackson, Joanna Warin and Uvanney Maylor.

 RTweb offers additional professional resources for this chapter. These may include *Notes for Further Reading*, *Reflective Activities*, useful *Web Links*, *Extension Texts* and *Download Facilities* for diagrams, figures, checklists, activities.

CHAPTER 6

Relationships. How are we getting on together?

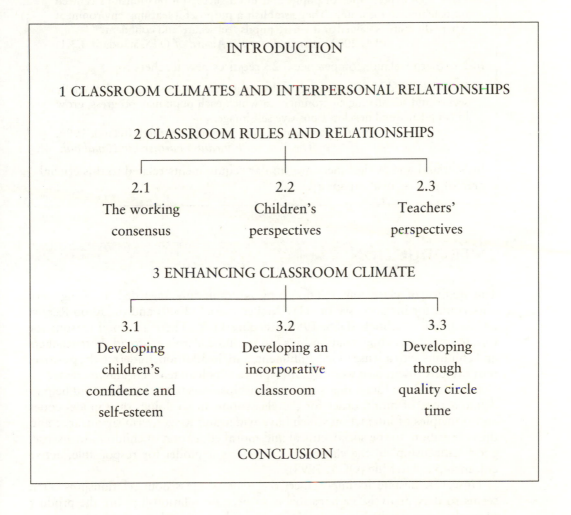

INTRODUCTION

1 CLASSROOM CLIMATES AND INTERPERSONAL RELATIONSHIPS

2 CLASSROOM RULES AND RELATIONSHIPS

2.1
The working
consensus

2.2
Children's
perspectives

2.3
Teachers'
perspectives

3 ENHANCING CLASSROOM CLIMATE

3.1
Developing
children's
confidence and
self-esteem

3.2
Developing an
incorporative
classroom

3.3
Developing
through
quality circle
time

CONCLUSION

Enhancing professional standards and competences

Understanding and mutually respectful relationships underpin classroom order, help to create an effective learning environment and offer a great deal of personal enjoyment for teachers and children alike. This virtuous circle has been, and will continue to be, one of the pleasures of teaching.

For example, in England, trainees must demonstrate that they:

Have high expectations of pupils and build successful relationships centred on teaching and learning. They establish a purposeful learning environment where diversity is valued and where pupils feel secure and confident.
(TTA, 2002, *Standards for the Award of QTS*, standard 3.3.1)

In Northern Ireland, competence 3.23 requires new teachers to:

Establish good classroom rapport by providing a pleasant, psychologially secure and stimulating environment in which each pupil may progress, grow in confidence and develop a positive self-image.
(Department of Education for Northern Ireland, 1999,
The Teacher Education Partnership Handbook)

In Scotland and Wales, there are similar requirements related to this crucial area of professional capability.

INTRODUCTION

The quality of classroom relationships is commonly regarded as being very important, for instance, see the Hay McBer model (2000) and the Elton Report on discipline in schools (DES, 1989, **Reading 11.8**). There are good reasons for this, for good classroom relationships can facilitate learning, provide both teachers and children with a sense of self-fulfilment, and, in addition, underpin the positive, purposefully disciplined working atmosphere which all teachers aim to create.

Nor should we forget that such relationships reflect certain values and help to define a type of moral order for the classroom. In so doing, they model codes and principles of interaction which have wider and longer-term significance and thus contribute to the social, ethical and moral education of children. In a sense, good 'citizenship' in the classroom can act as a model for responsible, active citizenship in later life (QCA, 1998).

However, despite its importance, the issue of classroom relationships often seems to defy analysis. Perhaps this is so because relationships are the product of such very particular, complex and subtle personal interactions between teachers and children. Despite such inherent difficulties, the issue is of such significance that reflective teachers are likely to have it almost constantly in mind and this chapter sets out a framework for consideration of the issue.

This chapter is structured in three main parts. It is particularly concerned with the importance of the mutual awareness of classroom rules, with the monitoring of children's perspectives and with developing positive and incorporative classroom strategies. It also addresses the issue of our own feelings towards children. The chapter begins, in a more general way, by considering some of the insights on classroom climates and interpersonal relationships which have been developed by social-psychologists.

RTweb offers many additional *Reflective Activities* for this chapter, as well as *Notes for Further Reading*.

1 CLASSROOM CLIMATES AND INTERPERSONAL RELATIONSHIPS

The influence of classroom environments on teachers and children has been a research topic for many years. One obvious question which emerged was how to define the 'environment'. Withall (1949) answered this by highlighting the 'socio-emotional climate' as being particularly significant (**Reading 6.1**). Indeed, he attempted to measure it by classifying various types of teacher statement – learner supportive, problem structuring, neutral, directive, reproving and teacher self-supportive. Understanding of the topic moved on when researchers began to define classroom environment in terms of the perception of teachers and children, rather than relying on outside observers (see Moos, 1979; Walberg, 1979). Further developments in this field have been comprehensively reviewed by Fraser (1986). He also provides a way for teachers to investigate the climate in their own classrooms with the 'My Classroom Inventory' (Fraser and Fisher, 1984; see Reflective Activity 6.1). This can give direct and structured feedback on children's feelings about classroom life which could be obtained, for example, at the beginning and end of a school year. The use of instruments, such as the 'My Class Inventory', can provide a helpful description of children's collective feelings and thus go some way towards representing the classroom climate. However, such techniques arguably fail to grasp either the subtleties of the interpersonal relationships to which many primary school teachers aspire, or the dynamic complexity of teacher–pupil interaction.

Reflective activity 6.1

Aim: To 'measure' overall classroom environment at a particular point of time.

Method: Each child will need a copy of the inventory below. As a class (or in a group) the children should be asked to circle the answer which 'best describes what their classroom is like'. The items could be read out in turn for children to give a simultaneous, but individual, response. Scoring of answers can be done using the teacher's column. 'Yes' scores 3 and 'No' scores 1 except where reversed scoring is indicated (R). Omitted or indecipherable answers are scored 2.

There are five scales, made up by adding various items, as follows:

Satisfaction (S)	Items 1, 6, 11, 16, 21
Friction (F)	Items 2, 7, 12, 17, 22
Competitiveness (CM)	Items 3, 8, 13, 18, 23
Difficulty (D)	Items 4, 9, 14, 19, 24
Cohesiveness (CH)	Items 5, 10, 15, 20, 25

Follow-up: Mean scores for each scale will provide some indication of the quality of the overall classroom climate and may raise issues for further consideration. (It should be noted that the inventory reproduced here is a short form of a longer inventory and is not a statistically reliable measure of the feelings of individuals.)

NAME _____

SCHOOL _____

CLASS _____

Remember you are describing your *actual* classroom	Circle your answer	For teacher's use
1. The pupils enjoy their school work in my class	Yes No	
2. Children are always fighting with each other	Yes No	
3. Children often race to see who can finish first	Yes No	
4. In our class the work is hard to do	Yes No	
5. In my class everybody is my friend	Yes No	
6. Some pupils are not happy in class	Yes No	R
7. Some of the children in our class are mean	Yes No	
8. Most children want their work to be better than their friend's work	Yes No	
9. Most children can do their schoolwork without help	Yes No	R
10. Some people in my class are not my friends	Yes No	R
11. Children seem to like the class	Yes No	
12. Many children in our class like to fight	Yes No	
13. Some pupils feel bad when they don't do as well as the others	Yes No	
14. Only the smart pupils can do their work	Yes No	
15. All pupils in my class are close friends	Yes No	
16. Some of the pupils don't like the class	Yes No	R
17. Certain pupils always want to have their own way	Yes No	
18. Some pupils always try to do their work better than the others	Yes No	
19. Schoolwork is hard to do	Yes No	
20. All of the pupils in my class like one another	Yes No	
21. The class is fun	Yes No	
22. Children in our class fight a lot	Yes No	
23. A few children in my class want to be first all of the time	Yes No	
24. Most of the pupils in my class know how to do their work	Yes No	R

Enduring insights on the foundations of good relationships are provided by the work of Rogers (1961, 1969, 1980) on counselling. He suggests that three basic qualities are required if a warm, 'person-centred' relationship is to be established – acceptance, genuineness and empathy. If we apply this to teaching, it might suggest that acceptance involves acknowledging and receiving children 'as they are'; genuineness implies that such acceptance is real and heart-felt; whilst empathy suggest that a teacher is able to appreciate what classroom events feel like to children. Rogers introduced the challenging idea of providing 'unconditional positive regard' for his clients and perhaps this can also provide an ideal for what teachers should offer children. Good relationships are, according to Rogers, founded on understanding and on 'giving'.

Rogers' three qualities have much in common with the three key attitudes of the reflective teacher, discussed in Chapter 1. Being able to demonstrate acceptance and genuinely empathize requires 'open-mindedness' and a 'wholehearted' commitment to the children. It also necessitates 'responsibility' when considering the long-term consequences of our feelings and actions. However, this analysis is not really adequate as a guide to classroom relationships because additional factors are involved. For a number of reasons, the warmth and positive regard which teachers may wish to offer their class can rarely be completely 'unconditional'. In the first place, we are constrained by our responsibility for ensuring that the children learn adequately and appropriately. Second, the fact that teachers are likely to be responsible for relatively large numbers of children means that the challenges of class management and discipline must always condition our actions. Third, the fact that we ourselves have feelings, concerns and interests in the classroom means that we, too, need to feel the benefit of a degree of acceptance, genuineness and empathy if we are to give of our best.

Good relationships in classrooms must then be based on each teacher having earned the respect of the children by demonstrating empathy and understanding *and* by establishing a framework of order and authority (Woods, 1988, **Reading 6.3**). It is a finely judged balance between two necessary elements.

If, as reflective teachers, we are to take full account of the interpersonal climate in our classrooms, we need a form of analysis which recognizes this subtlety. It needs to recognize both the importance of interpersonal understandings and the inevitable power relationships between teachers and children. One such form of analysis, we suggest, is offered by adopting an interpretive approach and, in particular, by using the concept of a 'working consensus'.

2   CLASSROOM RULES AND RELATIONSHIPS

Classroom order and discipline, as the Elton Report (DES, 1989, **Reading 11.8**) repeatedly emphasized, is most constructively based on good relationships and a sense of community. The concept of 'working consensus' (Hargreaves, 1972) helps us to identify the factors involved in the dynamic relationships between teacher and children.

2.1   The working consensus

A working consensus is based on a recognition of the legitimate interests of other people and on a mutual exchange of dignity between the teacher and the children in a class. Embedded in this is a tacit recognition of the coping needs of the other and a shared understanding that the 'self' of the other will not be unduly threatened in the classroom (Pollard, 1985, **Reading 6.4**). Over time, a good classroom relationship builds upon a store of shared experiences, jokes, anecdotes, etc., which serve to ground classroom experiences (Gallas, 1994). This is often enhanced by situations in which normal constraints are relaxed a little (but not too much). For instance, educational visits, special shared events, working with the children on physical tasks or projects that are important to them, talking with them in the playground – or anything else that affirms their identity and breaks down something of the formality of teacher–pupil roles.

In a classroom, both teachers and children have the capacity to make life very difficult for each other and a pragmatic basis for negotiation thus exists. However, a positive relationship, or working consensus, will not just appear. To a very great extent, the development and nature of this relationship will depend on initiatives made by teachers, as they try to establish rules and understandings of the way they would like things to be in their classrooms.

Children expect such initiatives from teachers and they are less likely to challenge their teacher's authority to take them, as long as the teacher acts competently and in ways which children regard as 'fair' (see also Robertson, 1996). However, it is also the case that, through negotiating the working consensus, the children recognize the greater power of the teacher. As they do so they also expect that the teacher's power will be partially circumscribed by the understandings which they jointly create within the classroom. Hopefully, these teacher initiatives will be based on appropriate principles and values. One consequence of this is that teacher-pupil behaviours tend to mesh together (see Galton *et al.*, 1999, **Reading 6.5**).

Understandings and 'rules' develop in classrooms about a great many things. These might include, for example, rules about noise levels, standards of work, movement, interpersonal relationships. The first few weeks of contact with a class – the period of 'initial encounters' (Ball, 1981b) – is a particularly important opportunity during which a teacher can take initiatives and introduce routines and expectations (Hamilton, 1977). This is often a 'honeymoon period' when teachers attempt to establish their requirements and the children opt to play a waiting game. However, both the 'rules' and the teacher's capacity to enforce them are normally tested by the children before long, for children usually want to find out 'how far they can go' and 'what the teacher is like' when pressed.

As a working consensus is negotiated, both overt and tacit rules are produced. These are normally accepted by the majority of the class and become taken for granted. Awareness of tacit rules is particularly important for a trainee teacher who is likely to be working with children who have already established a set of understandings with their normal class teacher. Two things have to be done: the first is to find out what the rules are; the second is to check that when attempting to enforce and act within them, trainee teachers are doing so in ways which will be regarded as 'fair'. This is essential if teachers are to establish the legitimacy of their actions in the eyes of the children. The concept of 'fairness' is vitally

important in establishing a working consensus. Because of this, reflective teachers need to develop a variety of ways of monitoring children's perspectives and the criteria by which they make judgements about teachers. For this reason, a number of possible techniques are suggested below.

Reflective activity 6.2

Aim: To identify the overt and tacit content of classroom rules.

Evidence and reflection: Asking the children is an obvious first step. With care, this can be done either in discussion or might be introduced as a written activity. Young children might be asked to make up stories about 'naughty children' at school and to explain things that they might have done or 'should have done'. Children usually enjoy such activities, and they may make it possible to increase awareness of tacit rules.

Extension: A further way to gather information on tacit rules is to study the patterns which exist in what people do. Observation, using a notebook to record such patterns, is one possibility. A more explicit method is to record the events which lead to children being reminded of 'the way we do things here' or to being 'told off'. These could be noted during observation, or a video recording could be made of a session for later analysis.

Follow-up: Knowing the overt and tacit content of rules in a classroom makes it easier to evaluate social situations accurately, to act with the competence of a 'member' and to use such rules in achieving goals. Thoughtful discussions and observations thus provide a foundation for combining good relationships and effective classroom management.

To be unaware of classroom rules and understandings is likely to produce a negative response from the children, because actions which they regard as incompetent or unfair will almost inevitably be made.

Reflective activity 6.3

Aim: To check that we are acting in ways which are regarded as being 'fair'.

Evidence and reflection: Again, the only really valid source of information on this is the children. Whilst it is possible to discuss the issue openly with them or to approach it through story or drama, it is probably less contentious and as satisfactory to watch and note their responses to teacher actions. This should be a continuous process for teachers who are sensitive to the way their children feel about school, but it is worthwhile to focus on the issue from time to time. Both verbal and non-verbal behaviour could be noted and interpreted – the groans and the expressions of pleasure, the grimaces and the smiles. From such information, and from the awareness to be gained from such an activity, it should be possible to analyse classroom actions in terms of the classification which is discussed below.

One obvious but important point to note here is that not all the children will feel the same about teacher actions. This requires careful consideration (see Chapter 10, Section 3).

Extension: The feedback which this activity should produce, could contribute to the smooth running of the classroom and to the maintenance of the working consensus. If rules which were previously established are being broken by a new teacher, then the children are likely to become resentful. If classroom rules are not being maintained and enforced by the teacher, then the children may well consider the teacher to be 'soft' and may try some 'playing-up' for 'a laugh' at his or her expense.

In addition to the content and legitimacy of classroom rules, on which practical activities have been suggested, there are several other aspects of rules which can also be productively considered. In particular, the 'strength' and the 'consistency' of rules can be identified.

The strength of rules indicates the extent to which situations or events are 'framed' by expectations. This concept is referred to as 'rule-frame' (Pollard, 1980). It relates to the way in which action is constrained by understandings of appropriate behaviour which are developed for particular situations. For instance, one might compare the strong rule-frame which often exists in a hushed library, with the weak rule-frame which often exists in classrooms during wet dinner-breaks. For some purposes, such as during the introduction to a teaching session, one might want the rule-frame to be strong thus ensuring tight control and attention. On other occasions, such as during an indoor play-time, a weak rule-frame may be perfectly acceptable and may allow children considerable choice. Situations of difficulty often arise where a strong rule-frame is expected

Teacher acts				Child acts
Unilateral	Within working consensus			Unilateral
Non-legitimate censure	Legitimate routine censure	Conformity	Legitimate routine deviance	Non-legitimate rule-framed disorder

Figure 6.1 *A classification of types of teacher and child classroom action*

by a teacher but children act as if the rule-frame is weak. If this happens, a teacher has to act quickly to clarify and define the situation and to re-establish the rules in play.

Teachers can influence the degree of rule-frame by their actions, statements and movements. For example, an active, purposeful entry to a classroom is a clear signal that a teacher wants to get attention and one which will normally tighten the frame immediately. Conversely, acting rather casually, or withdrawing into conversation with a visiting adult, will usually cause the rule-frame to weaken and may result in children relaxing in their approach to activities.

The ability of a teacher to manage the strength of rule-frame has a great deal to do with classroom discipline. In particular, skilful management provides a means of pre-empting serious difficulties through giving clear expectations about acceptable behaviour. By its very nature, though, the development of such understandings cannot be rushed and frequently needs to be reviewed explicitly by teachers and children.

The degree of consistency with which rules are maintained provides an underlying structure for learning sessions. Conversely, teacher inconsistency tends to reduce the integrity of the working consensus and the sense of fairness on which it is based. This, in turn, can lead to a variety of subsequent control difficulties.

Relationships between teacher and children, which derive from a working consensus, have important implications for discipline and control. Figure 6.1 provides a simple model which may help us to reflect on the types of action which teachers and children may make in classrooms when a working consensus exists. The most important distinction is between actions which are bounded by the understandings of the working consensus and those which are not. Five basic 'types of action' can be identified.

Non-legitimate censure. This is the type of teacher action which children dislike and cannot understand. It often occurs when a teacher loses his or her temper or feels under great pressure. The effect of such actions is that the children feel attacked and unable to cope. They perceive teacher power being used without justification. Such actions lie outside the bounds of the working consensus and are likely to lead to a breakdown in relationships.

Routine censure. This is the typical teacher response to children's routine deviance – a mild reprimand. It will be regarded by the children as legitimate, in so far as such a reprimand will not threaten the dignity of a child nor be employed inappropriately. Censures of this type are within the bounds of the working consensus.

Conformity. These actions, by teachers or children are 'as expected'. They are according to the tacit conventions and agreements of the working consensus.

Routine deviance. This is the type of mischief or petty misdemeanour which is accepted as being part of the normal behaviour of children. Talking too loudly, 'having a laugh' and working slowly are examples. Such activities are partly expected by teachers and are not normally intended by children as a threat. They are thus within the bounds of the working consensus.

Non-legitimate, rule-framed disorder. This is a type of child action which teachers dislike and find hard to understand. It often occurs when a child or a group of children feels unable to cope with a classroom situation and thus seek to disrupt it. They are particularly prone to do this if they perceive themselves to have been treated 'unfairly' or feel that their dignity has been attacked. Action of this type usually reflects the cultural rules of peer groups and can be used to build up a type of 'solidarity' or an alternative source of positive self-esteem.

Many of the suggested activities below are designed to assist in the analysis of classroom relationships, using this basic classification. The central argument in what follows is that 'good relationships' are based on the existence of a negotiated sense of acceptability and fairness which teachers and children share. It is therefore important to begin with considering various ways of understanding children's perspectives.

2.2 Children's perspectives

Teaching can only be regarded as successful if the learners are learning. Generally speaking, for this to be achieved, the learners have to be motivated and achieve a sense of self-fulfilment through their classroom activities. They have to be involved in the process of learning and they have to appreciate that the effort which is required of them is worthwhile. It is thus very valuable to collect data from children on the subject of how they feel about the classroom activities in which they are required to engage. This information supplies a basic type of feedback on children's motivation and can be set alongside other diagnostic information about their learning achievements and difficulties.

The method suggested below involves direct comparison between classroom activities in different areas of the curriculum. Such comparisons are useful because they often highlight hidden issues. Worryingly for instance, evidence gathered by Pollard and Triggs (2000, **Reading 7.11**) suggests that pupils' learning engagement was undermined by the introduction of the National Curriculum in England.

Another important aspect of children's perspectives is their views on their own teacher – already introduced, in a general way, in Chapter 4. This is a fairly well researched issue and enquiry into it can yield good summary data on the way children feel about the quality of relationships and education in their classroom. Obviously, for professional and ethical reasons, teachers should only collect such information in their own classroom, or with the permission of other people who may be concerned. Research has consistently shown that children like teachers who are kind, consistent, efficient at organizing and teaching,

Reflective activity 6.4

Aim: To gather information on how children feel about curricular activities which they undertake in school.

Evidence and reflection: One method, suitable for children for whom writing is not difficult, is simply to ask them to write a comparison of two activities which you choose. It may be worth structuring this at the beginning by getting the children to make notes under headings such as the ones below:

	Good things	Bad things
Activity 1		
Activity 2		

An alternative method would be to carry out a similar exercise verbally. There is no reason why even very young children cannot participate in discussions about the activities which they like and dislike. Fairly open questions might be used, such as, 'Can you tell me about the things that you like doing best at school?' and 'Can you tell me about the things which you don't like doing?'. These, if followed up sensitively by further enquiries to obtain reasons (and the results recorded), should soon show up the children's criteria and patterns in their opinions about your provision. The recording is important, for when there is no record to analyse it is very easy to fail to fully appreciate the messages one may be being offered.

Extension: This activity should yield data of considerable importance for future planning and provision, and should be analysed to identify any patterns in the children's perspectives. If some children seem to be poorly motivated, to lack interest or to dispute the value of an activity, then the situation must be reconsidered and remedial measures taken.

patient, fair and who have a sense of humour. They dislike teachers who are domineering, boring, unkind, unpredictable and unfair. Strict/soft are two common constructs which children use, with 'strict but fair' often being positively valued. 'Softness' is usually regarded as a sign of weakness.

Predictability is also usually important and children are often expert interpreters of the 'moods' of their teachers. Indeed, more generally, children's feedback to their teachers has been found to be both relatively accurate and reliable.

2.3 Teachers' perspectives

So far a number of suggestions have been made about how a teacher can take account of the perspectives, feelings and position of children. Now it is time to change the focus onto ourselves as teachers for, as was discussed in Chapter 5, the self-image of a teacher is just as important to maintain as the self-image of the child. Good teaching has never been easy, for to some extent it has always meant placing the learner's needs before the teacher's. However, classroom relationships are a very special and subtle phenomenon. On the one hand, the nature of the working consensus is related to disciplinary issues and problems which are likely to confront the teacher. On the other hand, the quality of the relationships can, potentially, provide a continuous source of personal pleasure and self-fulfilment for a teacher.

If our own feelings as teachers are also an important factor in maintaining a positive working consensus, then ways of monitoring our feelings may be useful. Reflective Activity 6.5 suggests keeping a personal diary. This has been used by classroom researchers over many years (Dadds, 1995) and is a tried and tested way of reflexively taking stock of life as it unfolds.

Reflective activity 6.5

Aim: To monitor and place in perspective our own feelings on classroom relationships.

Evidence and reflection: Probably the best way to do this is by keeping a diary. This does not have to be an elaborate, time-consuming one, but simply a personal statement of how things have gone and of how we felt.

The major focus of the diary in this case will obviously be on relationships. It is very common for such reflections to focus in more detail on particular disciplinary issues or on interaction with specific individuals. It should be written professionally, with awareness of ethical issues and the feelings of other classroom participants.

Diary-keeping tends to heighten awareness and, at the same time, it supplies a document which can be of great value in reviewing events.

Extension: Once a diary has been kept for a fortnight or so, you might set aside some time to read it carefully and to reflect upon it with a view to drawing reasonably balanced conclusions regarding yourself and your planning of future policies in the classroom. It would be better still to discuss the issues which are raised with a colleague or friend.

3 ENHANCING CLASSROOM CLIMATE

So far in this chapter we have argued that the nature of classroom climate and the quality of interpersonal relationships are fundamental to establishing a positive learning environment. Having identified ways of improving our understanding of both teachers' and children's perspectives of these issues, it is now time to consider ways of enhancing other aspects of the learning environment.

3.1 Developing children's confidence and self-esteem

Children often feel vulnerable in classrooms, particularly because of their teacher's power to control and evaluate. This affects how children experience school and their openness to new learning. Indeed, it is often suggested that

children only learn effectively if their self-esteem is positive. A considerable responsibility is thus placed on teachers to reflect on how they use their power and on how this use affects children.

 There are two basic aspects of this. First there is the positive aspect of how teachers use their power constructively to encourage, to reinforce appropriate child actions and to enhance self-esteem (Lawrence, 1987, **Reading 6.7**). Indeed, the importance of maintaining 'high expectation' of children cannot be overemphasized (Gipps and MacGilchrist, 1999, **Reading 6.6**). Secondly, however, there is the potential for the destructive use of such power. The second issue thus concerns the manner in which teachers act when 'rules' are broken. This can be negative and damaging, but skilful and aware teachers will aim to make any necessary disciplinary points yet still preserve the dignity of each child. Activities are suggested below to monitor each of these aspects, starting with 'being positive'.

'Being positive' involves constant attempts to build on success. The point is to offer suitable challenges and then to make maximum use of the children's achievements to generate still more. This policy assumes that each child will have some successes. Sometimes a child's successes may be difficult to identify. Such difficulties often reveal more about the inability of an adult to understand and diagnose what a child is experiencing. As the psychologist Adler argued many years ago (Adler, 1927), irrespective of the baseline position, there is always an associated level of challenge – a target for learning achievement – which is appropriate and which can be the subject of genuine praise. It may range from correctly forming a letter of the alphabet to producing a vivid story; from sustaining concentration in story-time to helping another child to understand a lesson; from eating a pea to finishing off the meal; from joining in sporting activities to breaking a school record, etc. The appropriateness of the achievement is a matter for a teacher to judge, but the aim should be to encourage all children to accept challenges and achieve successes (Merrett and Wheldall, 1990, **Reading 11.7**; see also Chapter 9, Section 3.2 on lesson planning for differentiation).

This brings us to 'avoiding destructive action'. This is the second aspect of the teacher's use of power – the way in which control is used. On this issue, we want to focus on the dangers of 'flash-points' in classrooms – situations in which teachers 'lose their head' and start to act unilaterally. All teachers would probably agree that a class of children has to be under control if purposeful and productive activities are to take place. However, a teacher's power can be exercised in many ways. In most situations teachers try to be calm, firm and fair – they act within the bounds of the working consensus and use various types of legitimate 'routine censure' to maintain discipline.

Unfortunately, there is a well-documented tendency for teachers to reprimand children over-personally when telling them off in the heat of the moment, rather than focusing positively on the activity in which they should have engaged. The effect of this can be that the children may feel attacked and humiliated so that, rather than conforming more, the children 'want to get back at' the teacher who has 'picked on' them 'unfairly'. Here, the problem is that the teacher's action is 'unilateral' and lies outside the understandings of the working consensus. The normally recommended way of enforcing authority whilst at the same time protecting the self-esteem of each child is to focus on the action of the children for condemnation rather than on the children themselves (Hargreaves, Hestor and Mellor, 1975; Robertson, 1996). Reprimand can then be firmly given, but the self-image of each child is left relatively intact. Each child can then conform

with dignity if he or she so wishes, and the incident is contained within the bounds of the working consensus. This will be discussed further in Chapters 10 and 11 where we focus on classroom management and on further aspects of discipline and behaviour.

Thus, reflective teachers are likely to attempt to use their power positively and constructively, and they will be particularly aware of the potential damage to relationships which can be done by over-hasty reactions to some classroom crises.

A further type of reflection on relationships concerns the degree of involvement by children, which brings us to the notion of what we have called the 'incorporative classroom'.

3.2 Developing an incorporative classroom

An 'incorporative classroom' is one which is consciously designed to enable each child to act as a full participant in class activities and also to feel themselves to be a valued member of the class. This is what most teachers would wish but there is plenty of evidence that, in the context of curriculum pressures, large class-sizes and the requirements of many assessment procedures, it is difficult to achieve.

One feature which often causes problems is that there are variations in both the quantity and quality of teacher attention that is given to different categories of children. Sadly, this is a clear example of variations in expectation (Gipps and MacGilchrist, 1999, **Reading 6.6**). There are four fairly obvious categories around which such variations have often been found – ability (e.g. Bossert, 1979; Mortimore *et al.*, 1988), gender (e.g. Clarricoates, 1978, 1981), race (e.g. Giles, 1977; Tizard *et al.*, 1988) and social class (e.g. Rist, 1970; Sharp and Green, 1975; see also Chapter 13 on inclusion). Age could also be an important factor particularly in mixed-age or vertically grouped classes. In addition, it is necessary to analyse and to be aware of the responses to school life of individual children, for they each respond in particular ways. It is very understandable if teachers tend to deal first with children whose needs press most or whose actions necessitate an immediate response. However, the problem which then arises is that some other children may be consistently passed over. We may have to accept that the needs of all the children in a class cannot be satisfied simultaneously by any teacher. Croll and Moses (2000, **Reading 10.6**) provide a challenging analysis of this in relation to children with special educational needs, but we have a responsibility to ensure that teacher effort is distributed equitably.

Classes also vary in the degree to which differences between children and their abilities are valued. Such differences between people must inevitably exist (see Pollard, 1987a, **Reading 15.2**), but a contrast can be drawn between classes in which the strengths and weaknesses of each child are recognized and in which the particular level of achievement of each child is accepted as a starting-point, and classes in which specific qualities or abilities are regarded as being of more value than others in absolute terms. Sadly, in the case of the latter, the stress is often on levels of attainment rather than on the effort which children may have made. Indeed, relative attainments become institutionalized through inflexible 'ability' grouping systems; the ethos becomes competitive rather than co-operative; and the success of some children is made possible only at the cost of the relative failure of others. The overall effect is to marginalize and exclude some children whilst the work of others is praised and regarded as setting a standard to which other children should aspire. This can have very negative consequences for children's perceptions of themselves as learners (Dweck, 1986, 1999, **Reading 7.6**).

Quality of work and standards of achievement are crucially important considerations, but there are also many other factors to bear in mind. For instance, we would suggest that an incorporative classroom will produce better classroom relationships and more understanding and respect for others than one which emphasizes the particular success of a few. Such issues are particularly significant when specific assessment knowledge is gathered. In the United Kingdom the outcomes of both teacher assessment and national testing now produce relatively formalized 'results' and must be handled very carefully if they are not to threaten the self-esteem of lower-achieving children. Of course, children who are less academically successful may have considerable other strengths and achievements and these can be recognized and celebrated.

Thus, there are some central questions about how children are valued which should be answered by a reflective teacher. Among them are those which are suggested in Reflective Activity 6.6 below. This time they takes the form of a checklist.

Reflective activity 6.6

Aim: To consider the degree to which the classroom is structured and run so that each of the children can identify with class activities and feel secure in tackling new learning challenges.

Evidence and reflection: There are many indicators which might be considered. For instance:

1. Are children helped to learn to respect each other? Does any unnecessary and divisive competition take place? Which is emphasized most, the achievement of children or the learning efforts that are made?

2. How flexible and responsive are classroom organizational groupings? Do they reflect the diversity of children's capabilities?

3. In decisions about the curriculum, are the interests of each of the children recognized and given appropriate attention? Is the children's previous experience drawn on as National Curriculum requirements are adapted?

4. How are the products of the class represented – in classroom displays, in assemblies, in more public situations? Are there some children whose work features more often, and others whose work is seen less often?

5. How wide-ranging are the pupil achievements which are valued? Does every child experience at least some success to reinforce their self-belief and commitment to learning? Is formal assessment activity and its reporting handled sensitively?

Extension: Having completed your review, what can you do to increase the sense of inclusion of all pupils? How could you develop the classroom climate to increase children's confidence as learners?

Overall then, teachers wishing to sustain an incorporative classroom will set out to provide opportunities for children to feel valued, to 'join in' and to believe in themselves as learners. At the same time they will attempt to eliminate any routines or practices which would undercut such aims by accentuating the relative weaknesses of some children (Prutzman, 1978; Putnam, 1992; see also Clegg and Billington, 1994, **Reading 10.2**; Moyles, 1997, **Reading 10.1**).

3.3 Developing through quality circle time

One of the most influential approaches to enhancing classroom climate in recent years has been through the development of 'circle time'. A firm priority on the development of positive interpersonal relationships is combined with imaginative processes and activities to offer a 'listening system' in which children can speak frankly with themselves, each other and their teachers (Mosley, 1996). The core goal is the enhancement of children's self-confidence and esteem.

'Circle Time' is intended to provide a class of children with a regular time, structured by secure, mutually respectful ground rules, in which they can openly share their perspectives and opinions. Games and exercises are used to foster a sense of the class as a community, to negotiate rules and understandings, resolve difficulties and establish boundaries. 'Bubble Time' operates in a similar way, but for individuals in dialogue with their teachers, and 'Think Books' open up a written form of communication. The core activity of circle time has been augmented with systems of 'Golden Rules', incentives and sanctions and a broadening of the approach across the school and beyond (see Figure 6.2).

This approach has been popular when tried in schools and, although it takes some time to establish, it can operate as an important form of quality enhancement – based, very significantly, on real participation and negotiation with children. Where it works well, there is a good deal of evidence that this enhances the pleasure and morale of staff.

We need to note however that, as with any other heavily promoted 'programme' of proposals concerning teaching, relationships or learning, things can

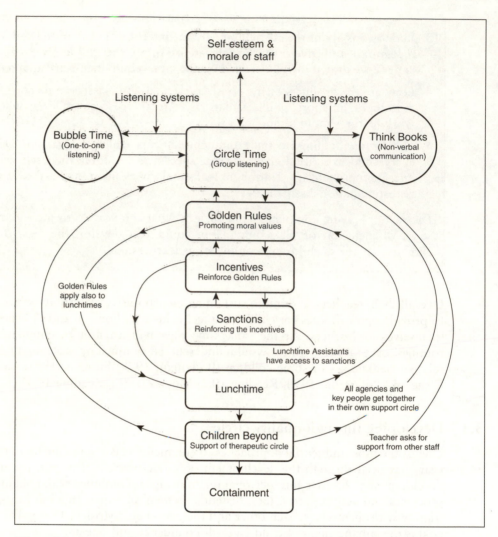

Figure 6.2 *A model for whole-school quality circle time (Mosley, 1998)*

also be less positive in some circumstances. For instance, there may be ethical issues in the encouragement of some forms of 'sharing' and disclosure, and the effects of circle time can include routinized banality and divisiveness as well as collective problem-solving and affirmation (see Housego and Burns, 1994). Used thoughtfully however, this is an effective strategy for building an inclusive classroom culture.

CONCLUSION

Apart from increasing the happiness and educational achievement of individual children, teachers who are attentive to the particular needs of individuals and develop good relationships with the class as a whole are likely to find that they encounter fewer disruptive incidents. Perhaps, too, an expectation of being caring towards each other may spread among the children and be of longer-term benefit for society more generally. An inclusive, incorporative classroom will also support the development of positive dispositions towards learning itself, and thus contribute to long-term educational performance.

Good relationships are thus intimately connected to classroom discipline and effective teaching. Preventative of trouble, foundational for learning, and pleasurable to participate in, classroom relationships that are going well are a considerable source of teacher fulfilment.

Finally, we should note that there are sometimes children with whom more specific efforts to develop good relationships may need to be made. Such cases might include particularly able children who may become bored; children who find school-work difficult and may become frustrated; children who have special educational needs; children who are new to the class or school; and children who have been upset by events in their lives over which they have little control, such as a bereavement, a break-up of their parents' marriage, parental unemployment or even sexual or physical abuse. Such children need very sensitive and empathic attention and they may need special help to express their feelings, to put them in perspective, to realize that their teacher and others care about them and to feel that they have tangible and appropriate targets to strive for in their lives. Such care may enable a child to take control of the situation, with the support of their teacher, to the extent that this is possible. However, teachers should guard against being amateur therapists. Child psychologists and social workers are available and they should be invited to give advice if circumstances require their help.

A good link here, would be to Chapter 11, which deals with behaviour and classroom management. Of course, these issues are closely related to the quality of classroom relationships.

Key readings

For Withall's classic study on 'socio-emotional climate', see:

Withall, J. (1949)
'The development of a technique for the measurement of social-emotional climate in classrooms',
Journal of Experimental Education 17, 347–61.   Reading 6.1

One of a number of classic books by Carl Rogers on 'person-centred' theory is:

Rogers, C. (1969)
Freedom to Learn.
New York: Merrill.

More general overviews of research on classroom relationships are provided by:

Rogers, C. and Kutnick, P. (1990)
The Social Psychology of the Primary School.
London: Routledge.

The interpretive approach to classroom relationships which has informed much of this chapter, is discussed in detail in:

Pollard, A. (1985)
The Social World of the Primary School.
London: Cassell.   Reading 6.4

The 'art' of maintaining relationships while teaching is described by:

Woods, P. and Jeffrey, B. (1996)
Teachable Moments: the Art of Teaching in Primary Schools.
Buckingham: Open University Press.   📖 **Reading 6.3**

On children's confidence and self-esteem the books below provide a conceptual overview, a research review and practical ideas, respectively:

Lawrence, D. (1987)
Enhancing Self-esteem in the Classroom.
London: Paul Chapman.   📖 **Reading 6.7**

Cranfield, J. and Wells, H. (1976)
100 Ways to Enhance Self-concept in the Classroom.
Englewood Cliffs, NJ: Prentice-Hall.

Other constructive and stimulating books which will support the development of classroom relationships are:

MacGrath, M. (2000)
The Art of Peaceful Teaching in the Primary School: Improving Behaviour and Preserving Motivation.
London: David Fulton.

Humphreys, T. (1995)
A Different Kind of Teacher.
London: Cassell.

Putnam, J. and Burke, J. B. (1992)
Organising and Managing Classroom Learning Communities.
New York: McGraw Hill.

Ingram, J. and Worrall, N. (1993)
Teacher–Child Partnership: The Negotiating Classroom.
London: David Fulton.

A book specifically on supporting children's learning at these times of great pressure on performance, is:

Decker, S., Kirby, S., Greenwood, A. and Moore, D. (1999)
Taking Children Seriously.
London: Continuum.

The importance of interpersonal relationships in classrooms and schools is repeatedly asserted in:

DES (1989)
Discipline in Schools.
Report of the Committee of Enquiry chaired by Lord Elton.
London: HMSO.   📖 **Reading 11.8**

For suggestions of other books on classroom discipline, see Chapter 11.

📖 **Readings for Reflective Teaching** (the companion volume) offers other closely associated work on the issues raised in this chapter. This includes work by authors such as:

John Withall, W. Lewis, Philip Jackson, Peter Woods, Andrew Pollard, Maurice Galton, Linda Hargreaves, Chris Comber, Debbie Wall, Anthony Pell, Caroline Gipps, Barbara MacGilchrist and Denis Lawrence.

 RTweb offers additional professional resources for this chapter. These may include *Notes for Further Reading*, supplementary *Reflective Activities*, *Web Links*, *Extension Texts* and *Download Facilities* for diagrams, figures, checklists, activities.

CHAPTER 7

Learning. How can we understand children's development?

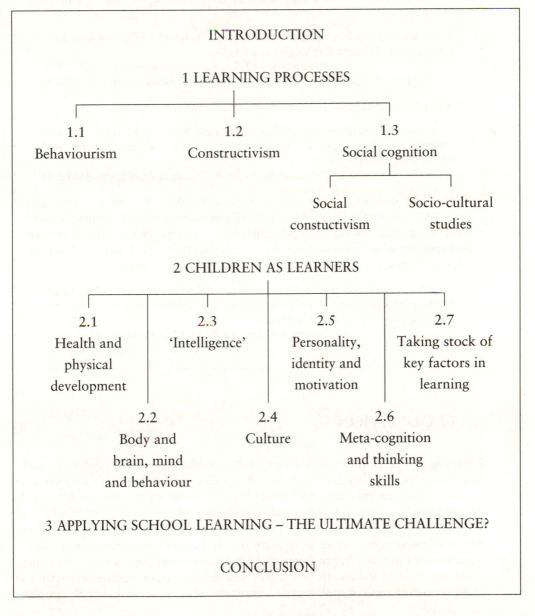

INTRODUCTION

1 LEARNING PROCESSES

1.1
Behaviourism

1.2
Constructivism

1.3
Social cognition

Social
constuctivism

Socio-cultural
studies

2 CHILDREN AS LEARNERS

2.1
Health and
physical
development

2.3
'Intelligence'

2.5
Personality,
identity and
motivation

2.7
Taking stock of
key factors in
learning

2.2
Body and
brain, mind
and behaviour

2.4
Culture

2.6
Meta-cognition
and thinking
skills

3 APPLYING SCHOOL LEARNING – THE ULTIMATE CHALLENGE?

CONCLUSION

Enhancing professional standards and competences

During a teaching career, the detail of required curricular priorities (like governments) will come and go, but the ways in which children learn are much more enduring. Some argue that this fact has been neglected in some countries, in favour of an emphasis on the teaching of subject knowledge. Clearly, some sort of balance is needed.

For example, the first competences in Northern Ireland's framework state that the trainee teacher must:

demonstrate knowledge of child development, spiritual, moral, intellectual, physical, social and emotional, and an understanding of how it can be promoted;

demonstrate knowledge of the various ways in which children learn, both generally and in particular subject contexts.

> (Department of Education for Northern Ireland, 1999,
> *The Teacher Education Partnership Handbook*, competences 1.1 and 1.3)

The twelfth standard in the English requirements states:

Trainees must demonstrate that they understand how pupils' learning can be affected by their physical, intellectual, linguistic, social, cultural and emotional development.

> (TTA, 2002, *Standards for the Award of QTS*, standard 2.4)

Many educationalists draw attention to the *interaction* of teaching and learning, and would argue that children's development and learning should be given higher priority in the English requirements. However, the present requirement in Wales is very similar – although a review is expected. At the time of writing, Scotland requires that student teachers must:

be able to justify what is taught from knowledge and understanding of the learning process, curriculum issues, child development in general and the needs of his or her pupils in particular.

> (Scottish Office, 1998, *Guidelines for Initial Teacher
> Education in Scotland*, competence 1.6)

INTRODUCTION

Learning can be considered as the process by which knowledge, concepts, skills and attitudes are acquired, understood, applied and extended. Children also discover their feelings towards themselves, towards each other and towards learning itself. Learning is thus partly a cognitive process, and partly social and affective. A reflective professional has two major concerns – there is a short-term focus on pupil performance in relation to curriculum tasks, but there is also a longer-term responsibility to foster each child's personal confidence as a learner.

At the level of the curriculum task, there must be both engagement with the child's existing understanding and support for its *extension*, hence the importance of formative, diagnostic assessment (see Chapter 14) and of each teacher's subject knowledge (see Chapter 8). Pupil learning should thus not be confused, as it so often is, with mere task completion. Indeed, in routinized work children may finish a task 'correctly' but have learned nothing new. They may also learn things which the teacher did not intend and which could cause them problems later, e.g. incorrect spellings or letter-formation skills, or inefficient subtraction procedures. As we shall see, high-quality instruction is thus very important in effective, progressive enhancement of performance.

A more enduring professional responsibility arises as children's immediate classroom experiences accumulate into longer-term feelings and beliefs. For instance, whilst successful learning may result in confidence, pleasure and a sense of achievement, persistent failure may lead to low self-esteem, apathy, avoidence or aggression. Here we are dealing with the cumulative formation of the person as a learner, with each child's sense of themselves and of their capacities – their 'learning identity'. Facilitating such holistic development is an extremely rewarding aspect of teaching in primary schools, but it is no indulgence. Indeed, the complex, fast-moving nature of modern economies and societies demands that future citizens are adaptable, confident 'lifelong learners' (DfEE, 1998a). In their teaching in the present, primary-school teachers thus contribute to the foundations of our collective future – as well as to the personal well-being of their pupils.

The two themes of task-focused learning and cumulative personal learning interact throughout this chapter. We begin by reviewing three key theories of *learning processes* (behaviourism, constructivism and social constructivism) and consider how they have influenced classroom practice. The second part of the chapter moves the focus diretly to *children as learners*. Here we consider the influence of factors such as health and physical development, the brain, 'intelligence', culture, personality, motivation and thinking skills before providing an integrative review of key factors in learning. The chapter concludes with a challenge to face the difficulties of *applying* school learning in authentic, 'real-world' situations. The issues raised in this chapter are taken up again in Chapter 9 in relation to planning a curriculum that matches cognitive and motivational aspects of school tasks to pupils' learning needs. It is relevant to almost every other chapter too – classroom relationships, behaviour, communication, assessment, social differences, etc.

A specific word about the role of language and communication in learning and teaching is appropriate here for there is probably no more significant factor. Indeed, that is the reason why two whole chapters of this book are devoted to it (Chapters 12 and 13). In this chapter we have let the issue permeate as a recurring theme.

The *Notes for Further Reading* on **RTweb** are likely to be particularly useful for this chapter.

1 LEARNING PROCESSES

Learning is a highly complex aspect of human activity and one which, even now, is not fully understood. Of course, humans learned for many thousands of years

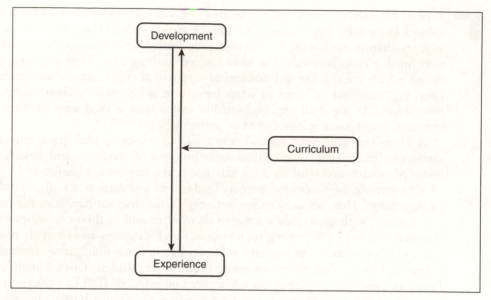

Figure 7.1 *Development, experience and curriculum (after Blyth, 1984)*

before anyone thought that a 'curriculum' and 'schooling' were necessary – and it is worth keeping our own role as professional educators in perspective! At its simplest, learning can be seen as the product of a continuous interaction between *development* and *experience* through life (Blyth, 1984) (see Figure 7.1). Seen in this way, the delivery of the specific curriculum required by society in any particular historical time and place pales into insignificance. Nevertheless, learning can be more or less effective, and the professional teacher's job is to understand the process as well as possible and to offer children the benefit of that understanding.

For centuries, philosophers and psychologists have worked to analyse learning and such enquiries will undoubtedly continue. The result is that there are many alternative theories which attempt to describe the process. We have simplified this complex field by identifying just three theories of learning which have been of particular influence on teaching and learning in primary schools.

1.1 Behaviourism

This theory suggests that living creatures, animal or human, learn by building up associations or 'bonds' between their experience, their thinking and their behaviour. Thus as long ago as 1911, Thorndike expressed both the 'law of effect':

> The greater the satisfaction or discomfort, the greater the strengthening or weakening of the bond

and the 'law of exercise':

> The probability of a response occuring in a given situation increases with the number of times that response has occurred in that situation in the past.

Thorndike was confident and claimed that these 'laws' emerged clearly from 'every series of experiments on animal learning and in the entire history of the management of human affairs' (Thorndike, 1911, p. 244).

A variety of versions of behaviourism were developed and provided the dominant perspective on learning until the 1960s. Perhaps the most significant of these later psychologists was Skinner (e.g. 1968, see **Reading 7.1**) who, through his work with animals, developed a sophisticated theory of the role in learning of stimulus, response, reinforcement and consequence.

The influence of behaviourist theory in education has been immense because, in the early part of the century, it provided the foundations of work on a 'science of teaching' based on whole-class, didactic approaches through which knowledge and skills were to be taught. The 'law of effect' was reflected in elaborate systems and rituals for the reinforcement of correct pupil responses. The 'law of exercise' was reflected in an emphasis on practice and drill.

Behaviourist learning theory casts the learner in a relatively passive role, leaving the selection, pacing and evaluation of learning activity to the teacher. Subject expertise can thus be transmitted in a coherent, ordered and logical way, and control of the class tends to be tight – because, the children are often required to listen. There is a problem though in whether such teaching actually connects with the learner's existing understanding.

Teaching which has been influenced by behaviourism can been seen in all primary schools. The importance of reinforcing children's work and effort is well established, and reflects the work of Skinner (e.g. 1953) in demonstrating the failure of punishment as a means of supporting learning. The use of practice tasks is also widespread (Bennett *et al.*, 1984), particularly for teaching aspects of the core curriculum such as numerical computation, spelling and writing, and this type of work reflects the influence of the 'law of exercise'. The use of teacher-controlled explanation and of question-and-answer routines are important parts of any teacher's pedagogic repertoire. They will be found, for instance, in school assemblies, when new topics are being introduced and when taking stock of achievements. The idea of building progressive steps in learning (e.g. Gagné, 1965) is, of course, directly reflected in the organization of the National Curriculum of the UK and other countries into 'levels'. Behaviourism has also been influential in work with children with behavioural difficulties, achieving significant successes through reinforcement of appropriate actions (Wheldall, 1991).

Figure 7.2 represents the roles of children and adult in behaviourist-influenced teaching and learning processes.

Some particular points could be noted. First, there is a high degree of adult control in the process; deciding on the subject matter, providing instruction, pacing the lesson, correcting, assessing and reinforcing pupil responses. In principle, this makes it relatively easy for teacher expositions and explanations to be logical, coherent, linear and progressive as subject matter or skills are introduced to the pupils. However, there are also some difficulties in teaching in this way. The most important is the question of connecting with the existing understanding of children. In this respect, the strength of subject exposition can also be a weakness if a child does not recognize subject divisions as being relevant to daily experiences (see Chapter 8, Section 2.2). Such a mismatch can reduce motivation and achievement as the child cannot use the knowledge which

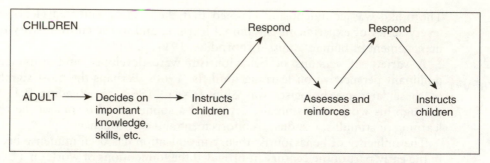

Figure 7.2 *A behaviourist model of roles in the teaching–learning process*

is offered to build a meaningful understanding. In such circumstances, learning tends to be superficial and fragmented. This problem may be made acute when large groups are taught because it is very hard for a teacher to 'pitch' the lesson appropriately for all learners.

The influence of behaviourism has been greatest on what are commonly termed 'traditional' teaching methods, and particularly those associated with whole-class, subject-based teaching. Careful programmes of reinforcement have also been found to be appropriate and effective for some children with special educational needs and emotional or behavioural difficulties. However, behaviourism can be oversimplified as a 'training' model and it is unfortunate that the value which it does have, when used appropriately, tends to be generalized by non-educationalists. Perhaps this is because of its association with tight discipline and strong subject teaching. However, as we have seen, these can also be weaknesses. The responsibility of teachers is to interact with children so that they actually learn, not simply to expose them to subject matter and drill.

Teaching methods based on behaviourism must, therefore, be fit for their purpose.

1.2 Constructivism

This theory suggests that people learn through an interaction between thinking and experience, and through the sequential development of more complex cognitive structures. The most influential constructivist theorist was Piaget (e.g. 1926, 1950, 1961; see **Reading 7.2**) whose ultimate goal was to create a 'genetic epistemology' – an understanding of the origin of knowledge derived from research into the interaction between people and their environment.

In Piaget's account, when children encounter a new experience they both 'accommodate' their existing thinking to it and 'assimilate' aspects of the experience. In so doing they move beyond one state of mental 'equilibration' and restructure their thoughts to create another. Gradually then, children come to construct more detailed, complex and accurate understandings of the phenomena they experience.

Piaget proposed that there are characteristic stages in the successive development of these mental structures, stages which are distinctive because of the type of cognitive 'operation' with which children process their experience. These stages are:

http://www.rtweb.info

- the sensori-motor stage (approximately birth–2 years)
- the pre-operational stage (approximately 2–7 years)
- the concrete operations stage (approximately 7–12 years)
- the formal operations stage (approximately 12 years onwards).

In each of the first three stages the role of the child's direct experience is deemed to be crucial. It is only in the formal operations stage that abstract thinking is believed possible. In the sensori-motor and pre-operational stages children are thought to be relatively individualistic and unable to work with others for long. Children are believed to behave rather like 'active scientists', enquiring, exploring and discovering as their curiosity and interests lead them to successive experiences. Play and practical experimentation has a crucial role in the assimilation process at each stage (Piaget, 1951) – a point that is particularly well understood by early childhood educators (Moyles, 1994; Parker-Rees, 1999, **Reading 7.4**; Curriculum and Assessment Authority for Wales, 1996, **Reading 9.3**).

The influence of constructivist theory in primary education was considerable following the report of the Plowden Committee (CACE, 1967, **Reading 8.3**) in which it was suggested that:

> Piaget's explanation appears to fit the observed facts of children's learning more satisfactorily than any other. It is in accord with what is generally regarded as the most effective primary school practice, as it has been worked out empirically.
>
> (CACE, 1967, para. 522)

'Child-centred' teaching approaches, based on interpretations of Piaget's work, were adopted with enormous commitment by many teachers in the late 1960s and 1970s. Great imagination and care was put into providing varied and stimulating classroom environments from which children could derive challenging experiences (e.g. Marsh, 1970). Sophisticated forms of classroom organization, such as the 'integrated day' (Brown and Precious, 1968; Walton, 1971) were introduced and developed to manage the problem of providing individual children with appropriate direct learning experiences. Despite these efforts, empirical research showed that constructivist methods were not greatly reflected in the actual practice of teachers of older primary children, (Galton, Simon and Croll, 1980). Constructivism has always been particularly influential in work with younger pupils with whom the benefits of working from children's interests, from play and from practical experience are relatively clear-cut (Anning, 1991; Dowling, 1992; Moyles, 1994; 1995, **Reading 10.1**). However, Piaget's work has influenced important work on the development of thinking skills and 'cognitive acceleration' in science and maths across the age range (Adey and Shayer, 1994).

There have been a number of criticisms of Piaget's work, particularly because of the way in which seeing children's development in sequential structured stages can lead to under estimation of their capacities. Psychologists, such as Donaldson (1978) and Tizard and Hughes (1984), have demonstrated that children's intellectual abilities are far greater than those reported by Piaget. Such findings emerge when children are observed in situations that are meaningful to them. In such circumstances they have also shown considerably more social competence at young ages than Piaget's theory allows (Dunn, 1988; Siegler, 1997). From a different perspective, sociologists such as Walkerdine (1983, 1988) have argued

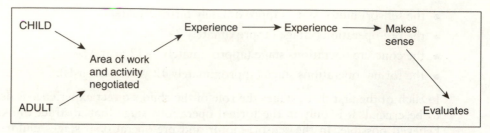

Figure 7.3 *A constructivist model of roles in the teaching–learning process*

that Piaget's stages became part of child-centred ideology and a means through which teachers classify, compare and, thus, control children. Critics have also suggested that this form of constructivism over-emphasizes self-discovery by the individual and ignores the social context in which learning takes place. In so doing, the potential of teachers, other adults and other children to support each child's learning is underestimated.

Constructivist learning theory, as adapted by educationalists, casts the learner in a very active and independent role, leaving much of the selection, pacing and evaluation of the activity to the child to negotiate. There is considerable emphasis on pupil interests and some compromise on the specifics of curriculum coverage. In its place, there tends to be more emphasis on learning concepts and skills through work on pupil-chosen topics.

Teaching which has been influenced by constructivism can be seen in all schools. It is reflected in the provision of a rich, varied and stimulating environment, in individualized work and creative arts, the use of practical apparatus, the role of play and imagination in media such as sand, water and clay, as well as in simulated play-contexts such as the 'home corner'. It may also be reflected in exercises and tests of 'readiness' for new stages of reading, or in direct Piagetian tests of young children for one-to-one correspondence and conservation of number. Above all, though, the influence of constructivism is reflected in the ways in which primary-school teachers relate with children. Perhaps this is an unintended legacy, but the nature of constructivism, with its close identification with the learner, provides many opportunities for primary school teachers to share in children's fascination and excitement when encountering new and meaningful experiences.

Figure 7.3 represents the roles of child and adult in constructivist-influenced teaching and learning processes.

Note here the *negotiation* of pupil activity and the emphasis placed on direct experience in learning. Together, these have the enormous strength, in principle, of creating high levels of pupil motivation and engagement. In the right circumstances, creativity and other forms of pupil achievement can reach exceptional levels of excellence. However, coverage of a particular curriculum is hard to monitor and the diversity of individual pupil interests tends to produce relatively complex forms of classroom organization as a range of activities is provided. Research shows that teachers then tend to be drawn into managing this complex environment rather than teaching itself.

As with behaviourist approaches, professional judgements about 'fitness for purpose' will guide decisions about the use of teaching methods based on constructivism.

1.3   Social cognition

This perspective on learning takes two main forms. On the one hand, it draws attention to the language and forms of understanding that are embedded in particular contexts and social practices – and sees these as important 'cultural resources' that are available to a learner from that setting. Studies with this emphasis are often referred to as *socio-cultural*. On the other hand, it draws attention to the key role of experienced participants in inducting less competent learners, and in 'mediating', 'scaffolding' and extending their understanding. Studies with this emphasis are known as *social constructivist*, because they retain the constructivist concern with learner activity, but also recognize the significance of social processes.

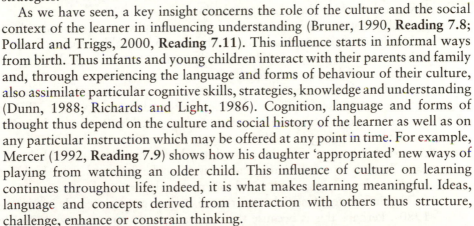

We might say then, that theories of social cognition affirm the importance of recognizing and building on pupils' family and community knowledge, whilst also emphasizing the role of teaching and instruction in extending such knowledge. The seminal writer on this approach was Vygotsky (1962, 1978, **Reading 7.3**) whose publications in Russian actually date from the 1930s. The increasing availability of Vygotsky's work in English coincided with reappraisals of the strengths and weaknesses of Piagetian theory. Psychologists such as Bruner (1986), Wood (1988) and Wertsch (1985) have been able to demonstrate the considerable relevance of Vygotsky's work to modern education. This complemented empirical work by other child psychologists, and curriculum-development initiatives by subject specialists, and has led to the incorporation of such work into national strategies.

As we have seen, a key insight concerns the role of the culture and the social context of the learner in influencing understanding (Bruner, 1990, **Reading 7.8**; Pollard and Triggs, 2000, **Reading 7.11**). This influence starts in informal ways from birth. Thus infants and young children interact with their parents and family and, through experiencing the language and forms of behaviour of their culture, also assimilate particular cognitive skills, strategies, knowledge and understanding (Dunn, 1988; Richards and Light, 1986). Cognition, language and forms of thought thus depend on the culture and social history of the learner as well as on any particular instruction which may be offered at any point in time. For example, Mercer (1992, **Reading 7.9**) shows how his daughter 'appropriated' new ways of playing from watching an older child. This influence of culture on learning continues throughout life; indeed, it is what makes learning meaningful. Ideas, language and concepts derived from interaction with others thus structure, challenge, enhance or constrain thinking.

An extremely practical conclusion from this is that teachers must engage with children's existing cultural and conceptual understandings (and misunderstandings) before attempting further instruction. To quote a recent US review: 'if initial understanding is not engaged, students may fail to grasp new information and concepts, or may learn for the purposes of the test, but fail to transfer the learning to new situations' (National Research Council, 1999, p. 25). As we will see later in this chapter, this argument for 'deep' and 'connected' learning is also linked to learner identity. Does the learner feel comfortable with new, school knowledge? Can they incorporate it and feel supported by the significant others in their lives (such as parents or their peers), or do they experience apathy or even disapproval?

The second major aspect of social cognition on which we will focus concerns

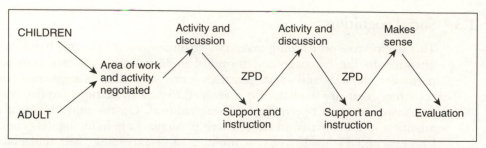

Figure 7.4 *A social constructivist model of roles in the teaching–learning process*

the social constructivist mediation of understanding by more knowledgeable others. This is best illustrated through Vygotsky's concept of the 'zone of proximal development' (the ZPD) (1978, **Reading 7.3**). This is:

> the distance between the actual developmental level (of the child) as determined through problem solving and the level of potential development as determined through problem solving under adult guidance or in collaboration with more capable peers.

(Vygotsky, 1978, p. 86)

The ZPD concerns each child's potential to 'make sense'. Given a child's present state of understanding, what developments can occur if the child is given appropriate assistance by more capable others? If support is appropriate and meaningful, then, it is argued, the understanding of children can be extended far beyond that which they could reach alone.

Such assistance in learning can come in many ways. It may take the form of an explanation by or discussion with a knowledgeable teacher; it may reflect debate among a group of children as they strive to solve a problem or complete a task; it might come from discussion with a parent or from watching a particular television programme. In each case, the intervention functions to extend and to 'scaffold' the child's understanding across their ZPD for that particular issue. An appropriate analogy, suggested by Bruner, is that of building a house. Scaffolding is needed to support the process as the house is gradually constructed from its foundations – but when it has been assembled and all the parts have been secured the scaffolding can be removed. The building – the child's understanding – will stand independently.

The influence of social constructivism has grown steadily since the early 1980s. Perhaps this is because the approach seems to recognize both the needs of learners to construct their own, meaningful understandings and the strength of teaching itself. Indeed, a key to the approach lies in specifying constructive relationships between these factors. As Tharp and Gallimore (1988) suggest learning can be seen as 'assisted performance'.

Figure 7.4, elaborated from Rowland (1987), represents the roles of children and adults in social constructivist teaching and learning processes. Negotiation, focused perhaps on a national curriculum topic, is followed by activity and discussion by children. However, the teacher then makes a constructive intervention to provide support and instruction – a role which Rowland named as that of the 'reflective agent'. This draws attention to the fact that any intervention must be appropriate. It must connect with the understandings and purposes of the learners so that their thinking is extended. If this is to happen, teachers need to draw on both their subject knowledge and their understanding of children in general and of their class in particular. They must make an accurate judgement themselves about the most appropriate form of input. In this, various techniques of formative assessment (see Chapter 14, Section 1.3) are likely to be helpful. If such judgements are astute then the input could take the children's thinking forward, across the ZPD and beyond the level of understanding which they would have reached alone. Clearly there could be successive cycles of this process.

The influence of social constructivist ideas is implicit in much of the documentation of the National Curriculum, the National Literacy and Numeracy Strategies in England and, for the last decade, these ideas have progressively underpinned the work of curriculum associations and teacher-based curriculum innovation in all subjects. The role of language and of discussion is paramount in learning in each area.

Reflective activity 7.1

Aim: To consider the influence and strengths of behaviourist, constructivist and social constructivist psychology when applied to children's learning and primary school practice.

Evidence and reflection: Review a selection of major learning situations and teaching methods, which your class has experienced during a school day.

Note each learning situation, each teaching approach and then consider the psychological rationale for its use.

Learning situation	Teaching approach used	Psychological rationale for the teaching approach

Consider if you are drawing effectively on the strengths of each approach. Does this activity have any implications for the repertoire of teaching strategies that you use?

Extension: Consider the influence, strengths and weaknesses of each learning theory on teaching and learning in your school. Are the teaching approaches used 'fit for their purpose'?

Summary

Figure 7.5 provides a very simple summary of some key points in the previous discussions of teacher–learner interaction. We return to broader socio-cultural factors in Section 2.4 of this chapter.

So far in this chapter we have considered three major theoretical influences on learning and teaching processes in primary schools. We now move on, in Part 2, to think more specifically about *children as learners* and factors which influence individual differences in learning.

2 | CHILDREN AS LEARNERS

Two key themes of this chapter, the concern for pupils' task performance and the longer-term responsibility to foster each child's self-confidence as a learner, will feature strongly in the discussions below. We need to explore the interconnections between the two and consider if we can create virtuous, mutually reinforcing relationships between them. However, we begin by focusing on children's health and physical development.

2.1 Health and physical development

Children's health and stage of physical development are crucial to their wellbeing and capacity to learn (Hugdahl, 1995). The pioneering work of Tanner at the London Institute for Child Health (see Tanner, 1978) was influential in demonstrating patterns of normal development in children and it was on the basis of such work that mass-screening procedures were introduced into the United Kingdom. Carried out in schools by visiting medical staff, measures such as height and weight are still used as indicators of child health – thus enabling problems to be identified and help offered if necessary.

Indeed, health has always been strongly associated with social conditions (Rutter and Madge, 1976; Wilkinson, 1986) and perhaps it has been the general rise in average standards of living since the 1970s which has reduced the prominence of the issue. However, in the final decades of the twentieth century, UK poverty levels for those out of work steadily worsened and the health of children in poor families was badly affected (Joseph Rowntree Foundation, 2000). Health across the UK as a whole remains an issue of considerable concern to government (Secretary of State for Health, 1999). See also Maden, 1999, **Reading 15.1**.

Children develop physically at very different rates and such differences can affect both children's capacity for new learning and their self-confidence. Differential rates of development should therefore be carefully considered by teachers, particularly if national curriculum and assessment procedures make little explicit allowance for such variations (Maude, 2001). In this context, there is concern that children may sometimes be required to do things, such as controlling a pencil, before they are sufficiently physically developed. Indeed, levels of attainment may reflect present development rather than long-term capability, and this is a vital distinction.

	Behaviourism in classrooms	Constructivism in classrooms	Social constructivism in classrooms
Image of learner	* Passive * Individual * Extrinsically motivated	* Active * Individual * Intrinsically motivated	* Active * Social * Socially motivated
Images of teaching and learning	* Teacher transmits knowledge and skills * Learning depends on teaching and systematic reinforcement of correct behaviours	* Teacher gives child opportunity to construct knowledge and skills gradually through experience * Learning can be independent of teaching	* Knowledge and skills are constructed gradually through experience, interaction and adult support * Learning comes through the interdependence of teacher and children
Characteristic child activities	* Class listening to an adult * Class working on an exercise	* Individuals making, experimenting, playing or otherwise doing something	* Class, group or individual discussion with an adult or other child/ren * Group problem-solving
Some characteristics	* Draws directly on existing subject knowledge in a logical, linear manner * When matched to existing understanding, can be a fast and effective way to learn	* Uses direct experience and allows child to explore in their own way at their own pace * Can build confidence and practical, insightful understanding	* Encourages collaboration and language development * By structuring challenges can clarify thinking and extend meaningful understanding
Some issues	* May not connect with existing understanding and may thus lead to superficiality * Difficult to motivate all children in class * Difficult to adapt structure of subject matter to varied pupil needs	* Has significant resource and organisational implications * Management of classroom often dominates actual teaching * Anticipates motivation and responsible autonomy from children	* Requires an appropriate, learning-oriented classroom climate * Requires a high level of adult judgement, knowledge and skill * Anticipates language, reasoning and social capability from children

Figure 7.5 *Some features of behaviourist, constructivist and social constructivist models of learning in primary-school classrooms*

Modern family lifestyles have also produced concerns about the diet and lack of physical exercise of many children (Gold, 2000). The general view is that children consume too much fat and sugar and that the exercise which they get is not sufficiently sustained to ensure healthy development of muscles and heart. Environmental issues such as toxicity in cities and the rapid development of child allergies are obviously additional concerns.

What, too, do children think of their own health and health care at home and school? Mayall (1994) researched this question in London and found that children were both aware of many important health issues and capable of taking more responsibility than they were normally offered by adults. Those bodies had minds of their own, and wanted to be consulted!

Reflective activity 7.2

Aim: To evaluate the exercise taken by children in your class.

Evidence and reflection: We suggest that a simple daily record sheet is developed such as the one below.

The task for the children could be:

If you had any exercise at these times, please write in what you did.

After getting up
Getting to school
First lesson
Playtime
Second lesson
Dinner time
Third lesson
Story-time
Getting home
At home before tea
At home after tea

This could be completed retrospectively by each child for one week, perhaps at the start of each day regarding the day before.

Extension: Analyse your results. You should be able to see patterns in the type, amount and timing of activities. Perhaps there will be differences between boys and girls, or between children with gardens at home and those without. Do you judge that the amount of exercise is sufficient for healthy physical growth at the age of your children?

2.2 Body and brain, mind and behaviour

The work of biologists and neurologists has attracted much attention in recent years and new knowledge is beginning to affect our understanding of human development and its implications for teaching (Dowling, 1999; Greenfield, 1997). On the one hand, we have the extraordinary mapping of human DNA and some 30,000 genes from which each of our species is formed. Scientists now

race to document the proteins within the body, which are arguably even more significant (see Morange, 2001). However, the implicit biological determinism of the concept of the 'selfish gene' (Dawkins, 1978) has developed into more wide-ranging socio-biological analyses which demonstrate the interaction of *genes* and *culture* (for an influential text, see Wilson and Lumsden, 1981) From the educational point of view, we must therefore accept the contribution of genetic variation whilst also affirming our responsibility with parents and others for helping each child to fulfil his or her potential in the context of specific social, cultural and economic opportunities. However, before exploring this further, we need to understand a little more about the brain itself. The brain has three key biological elements:

- *the reptilian system*: a deep, core element that monitors basic survival needs, such as hunger, thirst, temperature, light, threat and risk
- *the limbic system*: associated with emotions and long term memory
- *the neocortex*: located at the top of the brain, associated with more advanced mental functions and split into two hemispheres.

Learning is not effective if core survival needs are not met and, whilst this is particularly true for babies, it is a factor at any age – thus, for instance, justifying the provision of school breakfasts for young children in some communities and the establishment of stable and emotionally secure classroom climates.

Within the neocortex, parts of the left hemisphere have been found to control analytic capacities such as language, logic, pattern recognition and reflective thought; whilst much of the right hemisphere is associated with more intuitive and representational capabilities such as visualization, imagination, rhyme, rhythm and expression. There is a danger however, in over-simplification of what is actually a complex, interacting cognitive system (Hellige, 1993).

Trillions of networks of neural cells are interconnected within the brain by 'synapses', and it is the number and complexity of these that affect the brain's capacity. There are two ways in which synapses are added to the brain – in part determined by biology, and in part by each child's experiences. First, in the early stages of development, the brain over-produces synapses but then selectively prunes out those which are not used. As Bransford, Brown and Cocking, put it (1999, p. 104):

> the nervous system sets up a large number of connections. Experience then plays on these networks, selecting appropriate connections and removing inappropriate ones. What remains is a refined form that constitutes the sensory and cognitive bases for later phases of development.

The second way in which synapses are added is actually *driven* by experience, when additions occur as a biological consolidation of new learning. This process of adaption and development is known as 'plasticity', and operates throughout life. Such processes have enormous implications for teaching.

There is no doubt at all then, that children's mental capacities (or our own) are the product of the interaction of biological and environmental factors. In this context, it is helpful to distinguish between 'brain' (as a biological organ), 'mind' (the personal meanings which become embodied within a brain) and 'behaviour' (actions taken on the basis of thoughts and feelings). Of course, the mind strongly reflects the influence of culture. As leading neuroscientist, Colin Blakemore (2000) wrote: 'if our behaviour were determined by our genes, we should be stuck in the world of the very first of our species who appeared some 100,000 years ago. But the extraordinary capacity of the brain to modify itself on the basis of its own experiences has fuelled a different form of evolution, the evolution of mind and culture.'

So how do we get the best out of children as learners? One answer to this has been provided by those promoting forms of 'accelerated learning' (e.g. Smith, 1998). This offers a 'big picture' of factors involved in 'brain-based methods for accelerating motivation and achievement'. In particular, it aims to enable teachers to access the implications of recent research so that this can be drawn into classroom practice. The approach tries to be holistic, as can be seen from the 'memory map' introducing a key model of learning in Figure 7.6, and it leads to a wide range of recommendations. However, caution is necessary, because much scientific knowledge on the brain is not yet sufficiently robust to underpin the conclusions that are sometimes drawn for practice.

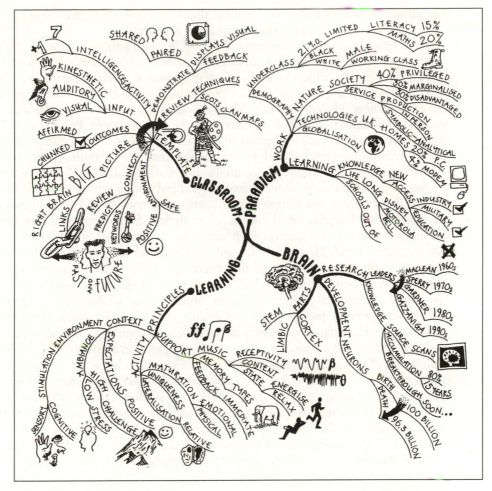

Figure 7.6 *Memory map introducing a model of learning (from Smith, 1998)*

2.3 'Intelligence'

Teachers meet the specific needs of children by knowing them well. It is thus right and proper that concepts to describe the attributes of pupils should exist. However, such concepts should be accurate, discriminating and capable of impartial application. Notions of 'intelligence' have a long history but, given what we now know about the capacity of people to develop themselves, there are also serious dangers of stereotyping and inappropriate generalization.

Although the validity and measurement of the concept of intelligence has been in dispute among psychologists for many years, the idea was once taken for granted and has passed into our culture to denote a generalized form of ability. It is part of our language and it influences our ways of thinking about children. For instance, parents often talk about their children in terms of 'brightness' or 'cleverness', and teachers routinely describe children and classroom groupings in terms of 'ability'. The concept of intelligence is important too because it is often used in the rhetoric of politicians and the media when they communicate with the public. It is thus routinely assumed that there *is* both a generalized trait of intelligence and that it is possible to measure it objectively.

Of course, such beliefs underpinned the UK use in the 1950s and 1960s of intelligence tests, at eleven-plus, to select children for secondary education. Belief in the context-free, objectivity of such testing was severely undercut by studies at the time such as those by Simon (1953) and Squibb (1973). Indeed, research in areas where eleven-plus is still used, such as in Northern Ireland, has continued to show the lack of objectivity of the measurement. For instance, Egan and Bunting (1991) recorded gains of 30 to 40 per cent for a coached group of eleven-year-olds compared with an uncoached group. The results showed clearly that children can be taught to do intelligence tests and that it is not possible to identify or measure some context-free generalized ability with any confidence.

The debate about the notion of intelligence also continues. Psychologists such as Kline (1991) argue, on the basis of statistical factor-analysis, that general ability remains a valid concept to describe an amalgam of inherited attributes. On the other hand, Howe (1990) used experimental and biographical evidence from different cultures to argue that there are many types of ability and that generalized measures, such as IQ scores, are misleading. According to Howe, the origins of exceptional abilities lie in an interaction of intellectual, motivational and temperamental factors produced within a social and cultural context, and this may, itself, enhance or inhibit achievement. As he put it, 'faced with a new task, the chances of a person being successful depend on a myriad of contributing influences. These include the person's existing knowledge in relation to the particular task, existing cognitive skills, interest, motivation, attentiveness, self-confidence and sense of purpose, to mention only a few' (Howe, 1990, p. 221).

The idea that there are many forms of intelligent behaviour, and that these are influenced by the social context in which people act, is thus now largely accepted. A particularly developed form of this argument is that of Gardner (1985, **Reading 7.5**; 1999) who has suggested that there are 'multiple intelligences':

- *linguistic*: enables individuals to communicate and make sense of the world through language (e.g. as journalists, novelists and lawyers)

- *logical mathematical*: allows individuals to use and appreciate abstract relations (e.g. scientists, accountants, philosophers)

- *visual spatial*: makes it possible for people to visualize, transform and use spatial information (e.g. achitects, sculptors and mechanics)

- *bodily kinaesthetic*: e.g. enables people to use high levels of physical movement, control and expression (e.g. athletes, dancers and actors)

- *musical*: allows people to create, communicate and understand meanings made from sound (e.g. composers, singers, musicians)

- *interpersonal*: helps people to recognize and make distinctions about others' feelings and intentions and respond accordingly (e.g. teachers, politicians and sales people)

- *intrapersonal*: enables a capacity for a reflective understanding of others and oneself (e.g. therapists and some form of artists and religious leaders)

- *naturalist*: allows people to understand and develop the environment (e.g. farmers, gardeners and geologists).

Gardner's analysis is an advance over the notion that each person has a unified and fixed intellectual capacity. In particular, it has the direct implication for teachers that pupils should be offered diverse learning tasks which can tap into a wide range of abilities and 'intelligences'. An interesting, and influential, extension of this argument has been offered by Goleman with his concept of 'emotional intelligence' (1996, 1998). This draws particular attention to the feelings that are often associated with learning, and the ways in which these are managed. However, the concepts of multiple intelligences and emotional intelligence both risk giving the impression that capacities are fixed. As we have seen, neuroscientists suggest that the brain is 'plastic' and can be moulded and developed by new experiences and opportunities. Indeed, many stories of 'the teacher who changed my life' concern professionals who believed in a child's capability, and helped them to succeed in a new field of learning.

Research by Dweck over many years (e.g. 1986, 1999, **Reading 7.6**) has established the crucial importance of how children think about their own capability. Those who adopt an 'entity theory' of intelligence tend to believe that their personal capability is fixed, and that they either 'can' or 'cannot' succeed at the new challenges that they meet in school. For this reason, they may adopt a form of 'learned helplessness' and dependency to accomplish school life. However, those who adopt an 'incremental theory' of their capability believe that they are able to learn and improve. They are thus likely to be more highly motivated, have greater engagement and take risks, exhibit 'resilience' (Claxton, 1999, **Reading 7.7**) and act independently.

It is perhaps worth remembering some simple points about 'intelligence' and learning:

- the use of generalized terms such as intelligence, ability, etc. is imprecise, insecure and unreliable – but is often put to rhetorical use;

- there are many kinds of abilities and one challenge for teachers is to enrich their pupils' lives by identifying, developing and celebrating the diverse attributes of each child;

- whatever a child's present capabilities, a teacher *can* influence the quality of pupil learning experiences and *can* thus enhance future intellectual capacity.

Reflective activity 7.3

Aim: To monitor the use and abuse of concepts of 'intelligence'.

Evidence and reflection A simple method is proposed based on noticing, recording and studying any use of language which denotes generalized ability.

This could be done in a school, in discussion with governors, teachers, parents, non-teaching staff or children, from printed articles in newspapers and the educational press, from school or government documents, from the speeches of politicians. It will require active listening – becoming attuned to

> things which are said which are relevant – and the period of awareness may need to extend over a week or so.
>
> Whatever sources are chosen, the statements and the context in which these occur should be recorded in notes as accurately as possible.
>
> When you have a collection of statements, study them.
>
> Think about them in their context. For instance: Do they recognize the richness and diversity of children's present capabilities? What particular expectations about future attainment are implied?
>
> *Extension*: Try to monitor your own use of language. Be explicitly aware of the words and concepts which you use. Distinguish between abilities and attainments. Try to satisfy the criteria of accuracy, discrimination and impartiality in your thinking about children's capacities and potential.

As we have seen, the influence of culture is profound. It impacts on pupils' interpretation of task performance and their views of themselves as learners – and thus merits our specific attention.

2.4 Culture

Of course, it has always been thought that home background, peer relationships, the cultures of different schools and, increasingly, the media influence how children learn. However, the development of social constructivist and socio-cultural psychology has led to a much greater understanding of the processes which are at work (Bruner, 1990, **Reading 7.8**) (Mercer, 1995, 1992, **Reading 7.9**, Pollard, 2000, **Reading 7.11**). (See also Section 1.3 of this chapter.)

We can identify three particularly significant cultural influences on learning:

Cultural resources and experiences. Learning is a process of 'making sense' and whatever is taken as being meaningful ('makes sense') will be strongly influenced by the culture, knowledge, values and ideas of social groups which the child has previously experienced. Such cultures provide an initial framework of understanding. Thus, each child's early learning will tend to elaborate and extend the knowledge which is embedded in their experienced culture. Sometimes this is talked about as 'situated learning' (Lave and Wenger, 1991).

The mediation of language. Language is the medium of thinking and learning and is created, transmitted and sustained through interaction with other people within the cultures of different social settings. These settings influence the range of 'languages' we use – the register, styles, dialects, etc. Language also embodies the 'cultural tools' through which new experiences are 'mediated' and interpreted as learners become inducted into the knowledge of their

communities (Wertsch 1985, 1991). Sometimes this is know as 'cognitive apprenticeship' (Rogoff, 1990). See also Chapter 13.

Learning disposition. The approach to learning adopted by each child is crucial to educational outcomes. Will a child be open or closed to experience and support, will they be confident or fearful, willing to take risks or defensive? What is their self-belief, their 'identity' as a learner? Can they overcome setbacks, and will they become a 'lifelong learner'? The origins of disposition and learner identity lie in early childhood and reflect the learning cultures which each child has experienced (Claxton, 1999, **Reading 7.7**; Pollard and Filer, 1996, **Reading 5.5**), yet schools continue the process as the first formal institution which most children experience in a sustained way.

The major sources of such cultural influence are commonly seen as family and community, peers, the school and the media. We will consider each in turn.

Family and community. Family background has been recognized as being of crucial significance in educational achievement for many years. This occurs not just in material ways, depending on the wealth and income of families, nor simply because of ownership or otherwise of overt forms of 'cultural capital' (Bourdieu and Passeron, 1977) or 'social capital' (Coleman, 1988), which are often associated with high-status groups in society. The most significant issues for school learning concern what the culture of the family and community provides in terms of a framework of existing understanding, a language for further development and the child's disposition regarding learning. Relationships with siblings are likely to be important but, in most cases by far the most significant influence for young children will be with their mother or carer. Reay (2000, **Reading 4.5**) has coined the term 'emotional capital' to identify the essential, emotional underpinning of learning, which is largely provided through maternal nurturing. Of course, with high rates of divorce and single-parenthood in modern society, family forms are now very diverse and additionally families are themselves part of culturally diverse communities. Children's cultural circumstances can thus vary widely, even within the same class of pupils.

Peers at school. As we saw in Chapter 4, peer group culture is important to children as a way of both enjoying and adapting to school life (Davies, 1982, **Reading 5.4**). As children get older, the culture of boys and girls tends to become more distinctive and the culture of the playground also starts to mirror both academic achievement within school and social factors outside the school such as social class and ethnicity. Such differentiation is particularly important to gendered patterns in motivation and learning disposition (Murphy, 2001, **Reading 15.6**). Some peer cultures favour school attainment and are likely to reinforce teacher efforts to engender a positive approach to learning. Other peer cultures derive meaning from alternative values, and children who are influenced by such cultures may approach school with minimal or even oppositional expectations. Such children will still be constructing understanding, but it may not be the type of understanding for which teachers would have aimed.

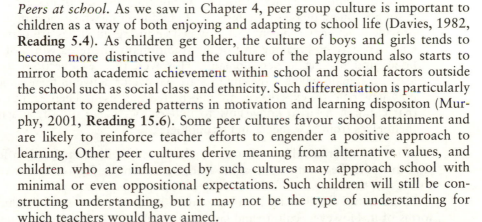

The school. Schools each have their own unique culture, a point which we shall elaborate in Chapter 17. Such cultures are created by those who work in the school and those who are associated with it. A school culture must be seen as a learning context which is at least as important as the bricks and mortar, books and equipment which make up the material environment of a school (see, for instance, Southworth, Nias and Campbell, 1992, **Reading 17.2**). Again, we have to ask how this culture influences the framework for understanding which is offered to the children, the language in which teaching and learning is transacted and the stance which pupils adopt. For instance, are children encouraged to take risks in their learning? Is a positive learning disposition engendered through the symbolic rituals and events of the school, the assemblies and demonstrations of 'good work'? What criteria about standards of school-work are communicated? What are the underlying assumptions about learning and knowledge within the school – and how do these impact on the children? It is also important to recognize that the school culture will not necessarily have the same meaning for all those who work and study in the institution. For instance, some teachers may feel that the cultural milieu inhibits the kind of teaching approach they favour, whereas other teachers may find it enabling and supportive. A further factor is the existence of subcultures within the school. Although looked at from the 'outside', so to speak, schools have their own distinctive culture, on closer inspection this can be seen to be made up of a number of separate cultural groupings amongst staff and pupils each of which has a different relationship to the official dominant culture. This heterogeneity is often reflected in classroom practice, and gives rise to a unique 'ethos' in each classroom.

The media and new technologies. The influence of the media is a controversial topic. Some feel that, whilst book reading seems in relative decline, young children watch many hours of television each week and their play and lifestyles are influenced by advertizing, soap-operas and other forms of popular media, including, for some, the internet. Whilst contradictory research findings abound, many teachers and parents believe that the influence is noticeable. Certainly, young people may identify with particular 'imagined communities' (Anderson, 1991), perhaps from television programmes, or adopt particular forms of consumption or behaviour associated with popular music or computer games. However, as Buckingham (2000) has argued, this is simply a new phase in the history of childhood in which electronic media provide a new environment within which enduring questions are played out. Children may be breaking free of the traditionally sheltered world of 'child-hood' and playing in new domains. However, the key questions for their learning remain whether the children are passive or active in their stance and how new cultural experiences are interpreted and used. There is little doubt that children need to know how to understand, make use of, and protect themselves from new media and technologies.

Clearly, the nature of these influences on each child will dramatically affect the way in which he or she approaches learning at school. Reflective Activity 7.4 focuses on this issue.

In summary, children are both reproduced by their culture, and produce new forms of it. However, culture and language always mediate thought, interpreta-

Reflective activity 7.4

Aim: To map the influence of culture on the learning of a pupil.

Evidence and reflection: This activity is directly based on the text of Section 2.4. It provides an opportunity to review the range of influences on a child and their capacity as a learner. Begin by drawing up a table, as below, on a large sheet of paper.

	Cultural resources and experiences	The mediation of language	Learning disposition
The influence of family and community			
The influence of peers and friends at school			
The influence of the school			
The influence of the media and of new communication technologies			

Think of a child whom you know well. Consider the way culture and experiences influence the child's understanding, the language he or she uses and the learning disposition he or she adopts. Complete each cell of the table, far as you can, to map what you know about the sources of influence on that child.

If you have time it would be valuable to talk to the pupil and others – parents, peers and teachers – to improve the quality of your data.

Extension: Repeat this exercise with different pupils, or compare the results of similar activities by colleagues. What insights are produced by comparisons of children of different sex, ethnicity, religion, social class, attainment? You can see some examples of this sort of analysis in the final chapters of Pollard and Filer (1996, 1999).

tion and learning. Thus success or failure through curriculum tasks and short-term performance is given particular significance by the cultural interpretations that are made of it (Filer and Pollard, 2000, **Reading 14.7**). In these ways, culture both structures learning attainment and shapes the self-belief of the learner. What then, are the consequences for the personality, identity and motivation of the child?

2.5 Personality, identity and motivation

Psychologists' understanding of personality has, according to Hampson (1988), derived from three contributory strands of analysis. The first is the *lay perspective* – the understandings which are implicit in common-sense thinking of most of us about other people. This is evident in literature and in everyday action. It is a means by which people are able to anticipate the actions of others – ideas about the character and likely actions of others are used for both the prediction and explanation of behaviour.

Such understandings have influenced the second strand of analysis – that of *trait theorists*. Their work reflects a concerted attempt to identify personality dimensions and to objectively measure the resulting cognitive and learning styles. Among the most frequently identified dimensions of cognitive style are impulsivity/reflexivity (Kagan, 1964) and extroversion/introversion (Eysenck, 1969). Such early work has been synthesised by Riding and Rayner (1998) into two orthogonal families – wholist/analytic and verbal/imager. Other accounts identify more general learning styles such as the concrete/abstract/sequential/random offered by Butler (1998) and the visual/auditory/tactile of Sarasin (1999). However, whilst this approach is important in recognizing patterns of individual difference, it is not straightforward to translate it into specific classroom provision. Further, we need to be wary of inappropriately limiting the expectations that we make of children. Perhaps, in other circumstances, they would sometimes surprise us?

A third strand of personality analysis has become prominent in recent years, and Hampson calls this the *self perspective*. This approach sees the development of personality in close association with that of self-image and identity. Crucially, it draws attention to the capacity of humans to reflect on themselves, to take account of the views of others and to develop. The social context in which children grow up, their culture, interaction and experiences with significant people in their lives, is thus seen as being very important in influencing their views of self and consequent patterns of action.

A key aspect of this concerns the meaning which learning has for a child. In one sense, such motivation issues can be seen as being technical and related to specific tasks. Certainly, when children fail to see any purpose or meaning in an

activity it is unlikely to be productive – however well-intended and carefully planned. Sadly, as we saw in Chapter 4, a very common perception of children regarding schools is that lessons are 'boring' and, for this reason, engendering

enthusiasm often requires sensitivity, flexibility, spontaneity and imagination from the teacher. The nature of this challenge is represented in Figure 7.7, which plots the relationship between new learning challenges and existing skills, knowledge and understanding. If too great a challenge is set for a child, then the situation of risk may produce withdrawal. Conversely, if the challenge is too little, then boredom and mischief may ensue. Targeting the effective learning

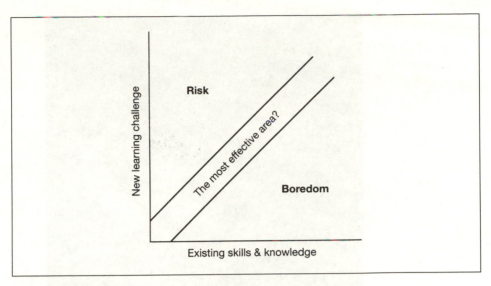

Figure 7.7 *Risk, boredom and motivation*

area in which the child will be highly motivated requires considerable skill and knowledge of both the subject matter and the child. Of course, motivation can stem from a wider range of factors too, from 'intrinsic' and 'extrinsic' interest, to a fear of receiving negative sanctions.

However, the most enduring form of motivation is connected to the evolving identity of each person and to their 'framework of meaningfulness' (US National Research Council, 1999). For example, Pollard and Filer (1999) tracked a cohort of English children through the seven years of their primary schooling, documenting their 'strategic biographies' as they adapted to successive teachers and classrooms. In some settings, particular children felt affirmed as they developed new skills, appropriated new knowledge and fulfilled their learning identities *through* the school curriculum. Other settings were less conducive to such processes and children felt little personal connection to the curriculum. It became something that was done to them, that they had to endure, rather than an activity through which they could experience personal development and understanding. Pollard and Triggs (2000, **Reading 7.11**) argued that learning in such circumstances tends to be superficial, and retained only to pass a test, please a teacher or satisfy some other short-term goal. Deep, enduring learning only occurs when new knowledge connects meaningfully with the personal narratives through which we make sense of life.

We also need to remember that learning can be emotionally challenging, and is certainly not simply cognitive and rational. Frijda (2001) suggests that emotions are subjective responses to events that are important to individuals. Positive or negative emotions reflect the affirmation or threat to previous understandings and 'meaning structures', or indeed the affirmation or threat that an activity poses for a child's personal identity, self-esteem or social status. As children sometimes say, whilst it can be 'embarrassing' to succeed, it is often humiliating to fail. Learning can thus be stressful at both the micro level of the task, but also at a more enduring, personal level (Lazarus, 1991, 1999).

One way of overcoming this two-pronged challenge is to become more effective at 'learning how to learn', and it is to this powerful set of ideas that we now turn.

2.6   Meta-cognition and thinking skills

We have considered some major factors which are likely to produce patterns in children's approaches to school tasks. The interplay of such factors is, however, extremely complex and will never be entirely predictable. Furthermore, children have the crucial capacity to reflect on their own thinking processes and to develop new strategies. This capacity for self-awareness regarding one's own mental powers is called 'meta-cognition' (Flavell, 1970, 1979). It has received strong endorsement and extension in recent years through the refinement of practical ways of developing 'thinking skills' (Fisher, 1999; McGuinness, 1999).

Meta-cognition is a particularly important capacity once children start to attend schools. Prior to this, at home, learning is largely self-directed and thinking tends to be embedded in immediate personal experience (Donaldson,

1978); at school, the agenda for learning increasingly becomes directed by teachers. Thinking is challenged to become more disciplined and deliberate; tasks are set, problems posed and instructions given; criteria for success and failure become more overt. The result of all this is that a new degree of self-control is required and, in order to achieve this self-control, new forms of reflective self-awareness become essential.

Play and 'playfulness' make a significant contribution to the development of learning capacity. This is particularly important for young children, as with many other animal species. Indeed, Bruner's classic paper on 'the nature and uses of immaturity' (1972) argued that a prolonged immaturity was positively associated with the development of playfulness and learning capacity. Play is thus a crucial aspect of human intellectual ability. Parker-Rees (1999, **Reading 7.4**) has built on this analysis, suggesting that playfulness, whilst vital for young children, is also important at all ages and is a foundation of creativity, imagination and problem-solving. Perhaps playfulness should be a criterion for becoming a teacher?

Another significant influence in the development of this field was Vygotsky, the social constructivist psychologist (see Section 1.3). He believed that learners, in working to understand and cross their 'zones of proximal development', could be supported by their own disciplined and reflective thinking, in addition to the assistance offered by more capable adults and peers. He called this 'self-regulation'. School instruction serves a particular purpose here in raising aware-ness and challenge, and from this higher order thought is developed. Tharp and Gallimore (1988, **Reading 13.2**) provide a particularly good illustration of this, with their four-stage theory of 'assisted performance'.

The meta-cognitive capacity of children has been a flourishing area of work amongst psychologists for many years (e.g. Robinson, 1983; Scardamalia and Bereiter, 1983; Wood, 1988; Yussen, 1985). Perhaps the most accessible account is that of Nisbet and Shucksmith (1986) who advocate the identification and development of six 'learning strategies' (see Checklist).

Other development projects by innovative practitioners have foregrounded

---

Checklist 7.1

Asking questions	establishing aims and parameters of a task, discovering audience, relating a task to previous work.
Planning	deciding on tactics and time schedules, reduction of task into manageable components, identification of necessary skills.
Monitoring	continuing attempt to match efforts, solutions and discoveries to initial purposes.
Checking	preliminary assessment of performance and results.
Revising	re-drafting or setting revised goals.
Self-testing	final self-assessment of results and performance on task.

Checklist 7.1 *Classroom strategies for developing thinking about learning*

more substantive thinking skills (such as information processing, reasoning, enquiry, creative thinking and evaluation), and considered whether they can be taught directly to enhance curriculum work. For instance, Feuerstein's *Incremental Enrichment* (IE) programme (1980) has been effective for over 40 years, and Lipman's *Philosophy for Children* (1980) has been influential in the UK through the work of Fisher (1990, 1999). CASE (Cognitive Acceleration through Science Education; Adey and Shayer, 1994) has been successfully adapted for primary children and for mathematical learning (CAME). Such work is also perfectly possible with very young children. For example, the High/Scope nursery programme (Hohmann, Banet and Weikart, 1979) uses a plan–do–review cycle as the basis of classroom activities. At each stage children are supported in thinking about their own learning and performance. As McGuinness (1999) put it in her DfEE review:

> There is a need to be explicit about what we mean by better forms of thinking. If students are to become better thinkers – to learn meaningfully, to think flexibly and to make reasoned judgements – then they must be taught explicitly how to do it.
>
> (DfEE, 1999, p. 3)

Such approaches have now been affirmed in the official endorsement of 'thinking skills', for instance in the preface of the English 'Curriculum 2000'.

2.7   Taking stock of key factors in learning

This section offers a simple summary of the key factors that affect learning and motivation (see Figure 7.8). Our understanding has moved a long way beyond simple behaviourist and constructivist models, though there is much more to discover. We now know that the most effective, deep, long-term learning is meaningful and conceptual. This is hugely important for teaching, and Reflective Activity 7.5 encourages you to apply these insights to children in your class.

Reflective activity 7.5

Aim: To review what is known about factors affecting learner engagement, and to apply this understanding to children in our class.

Evidence and reflection: Try to take stock of the issues that have been raised in this chapter. Although they are complex, they directly affect individuals such as the children in our classes.

Consider a boy and a girl with contrasting motivation towards learning. Using the structure provided by Figure 7.8, make notes on the factors which, in your opinion, affect their engagement with learning. Record physical and circumstantial factors, personal factors, forms of social support, and the quality of tasks and challenges which they typically meet in school.

Does such a review help in understanding and making better provision for such children?

Extension: To what extent have such factors affected your own engagement as a learner through your educational career? Over time, could you use this understanding to develop your personal learning effectiveness?

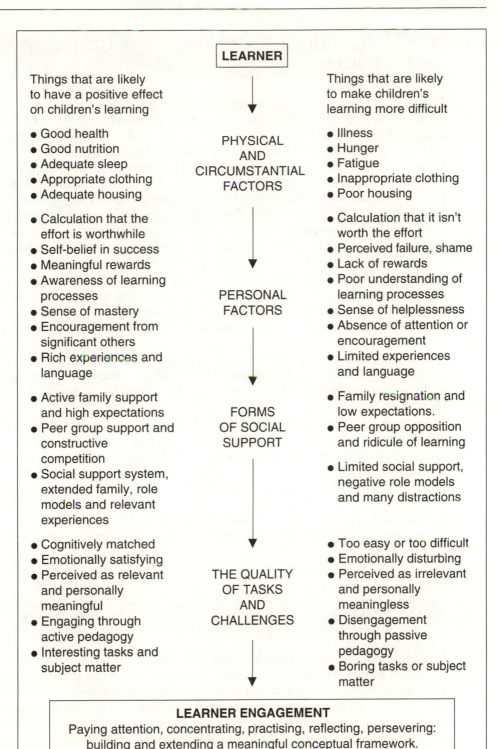

Figure 7.8 *Factors affecting learner engagement (adapted from US National Research Council, 1999)*

3 APPLYING SCHOOL LEARNING – THE ULTIMATE CHALLENGE?

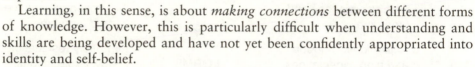

We conclude this chapter by drawing attention to a major problem of school learning – in the 'real world' outside, it is hard to actually *apply* the knowledge that has been learned. This seems to be because of the very different frames of reference that structure thinking in the different settings. Routine activities at home, parks, shops or street are accomplished using a quite different set of procedures and forms of knowledge than the procedurally constrained require- ments of school. Whilst the former tend to be pragmatic and informal, the latter are formal and are often assessed. The result, sadly, is that children often find it hard to make connections between their learning in these two worlds. For instance, Hughes *et al.* (2000, **Reading 7.10**) documented the gap between the abstract, formal knowledge of National Curriculum mathematics in primary classrooms, and the authentic contexts in which it might have been applied (but often remained unused). Similar findings exist across the curriculum, from doing geography tasks in school, to getting lost when travelling; and from doing well in the Literacy Hour, to being unable to write a real letter about something important.

Learning, in this sense, is about *making connections* between different forms of knowledge. However, this is particularly difficult when understanding and skills are being developed and have not yet been confidently appropriated into identity and self-belief.

From the teachers' perspective, we need to acknowledge that children prob- ably know a lot more than we think they know. If only we could tap into, and interconnect with, the funds of knowledge that are sustained in the social practices of their families and communities, then pupils' learning might become much more authentic, flexible and sustained.

We thus have yet another topic on which a reflective and aware teacher can be really effective – this time in encouraging children to think about what they know, how they know it, how it fits into their lives and how they can apply such knowledge in the future.

3 CONCLUSION

Learning is an immensely complex topic and this chapter has simply touched the surface of some of the many issues which are involved. In one sense, perhaps the provisional nature of our understanding is no bad thing, because, if we knew it all, then one of the greatest sources of fascination and fulfilment in teaching would be diminished. The vocation of teaching will certainly always include this element of intellectual challenge as teachers seek to understand what children understand, and then to provide appropriate support.

In this chapter we have reviewed three influential theories on children's learning and discussed some of the key issues which are involved. We then considered how physical and biological factors in the body and brain interact with the social and cultural factors of the broader society. Learning capability and motivation, we argued, must be addressed in terms of completing curricular tasks – but it should also be complemented by an understanding of the long-term process of developing a positive learner identity. Such self-understanding and belief, with its associated dispositions towards learning, are likely to be particularly enduring outcomes of primary education.

Whatever the strength of subject requirements and pressures for short-term attainment, teachers are thus likely to be most effective in supporting children's learning if they bear such insights in mind.

Key readings

Two excellent books on children's development, and the ways in which it influences learning are:

Smith, P. K., Cowie, H. and Blades, M. (1998)
Understanding Children's Development.
Oxford: Blackwell.

Meadows, S. (1992)
Children's Cognitive Development: The Development and Acquisition of Cognition in Childhood.
London: Routledge.

Through detailed case-studies, Pollard and Filer illustrate the significance of social influences on children's developing sense of identity as learners.

Pollard, A. and Filer, A. (1996)
The Social World of Children's Learning.
London: Cassell.   Reading 5.5

On learning itself, Howe offers a splendid account of psychological research and the ways in which it affects school life. Whitebread's collection provides expert coverage of a wide range of topics in relation to primary education specifically.

Howe, M. J. (1999)
A Teacher's Guide to the Psychology of Learning.
Oxford: Blackwell.

Whitebread, D. (ed.) (2000)
The Psychology of Teaching and Learning in the Primary School.
London: Routledge Falmer.

Psychological research from the United States has been very influential in recent years. Gardner's work established the idea of 'multiple intelligences' and Dweck has done brilliant work on motivation. Beyond this, there have been significant attempts to take stock and review everything that is known about learning and schooling. Bransford, Brown and Cocking's book is one outcome.

Gardner, H. (1985)
Frames of Mind: The Theory of Multiple Intelligences.
London: Paladin Books.   Reading 7.5

Dweck, C. (1999)
Self-theories: Their Role in Motivation, Personality and Development.
New York: Psychology Press.   Reading 7.6

Bransford, J. D., Brown, A. I. and Cocking, R. R. (eds) (2000)
How People Learn: Brain, Mind, Experience and School.
Washington, DC: National Academy Press.

Debate on the implications of the neurobiology of the brain is growing, though caution is appropriate in such a new field of research. For good introductions, see:

Dowling, J. (1999)
Neurons and Networks: an Introduction to Behavioural Neuroscience.
Cambridge, Mass.: Harvard University Press.

Greenfield, S. (ed.) (1996)
The Human Mind Explained.
London: Cassell.

Many argue that the significance of play and of imagination in learning is becoming seriously underestimated in these days of detailed curriculum prescription. For sources which assert its importance, for children's learning and beyond, see:

Moyles, J. R. (ed.) (1994)
The Excellence of Play.
Buckingham: Open University Press.   (see also **Reading 7.4**)

Sutton-Smith, B. (1998)
The Ambiguity of Play.
Cambridge, MA: Harvard University Press.

Among many interesting books on the development of meta-cognitive and thinking skills, see:

Fisher, R. (1998)
Teaching Thinking.
London: Cassell Education.

Readings for Reflective Teaching (the companion volume) offers other closely associated work on the issues raised in this chapter. This includes work by authors such as:

Burrhus Skinner, Jean Piaget, Lev Vygotsky, Rod Parker-Rees, Howard Gardner, Carol Dweck, Guy Claxton, Jerome Bruner, Neil Mercer, Martin Hughes, Charles Desforges, Christine Mitchell, Clive Carré, Andrew Pollard, and Pat Triggs.

RTweb offers additional professional resources for this chapter. These may include *Notes for Further Reading*, supplementary *Reflective Activities*, useful *Web Links*, *Extension Texts* and *Download Facilities* for diagrams, figures, checklists, activities.

CHAPTER 8

Curriculum. How do we develop knowledge and understanding?

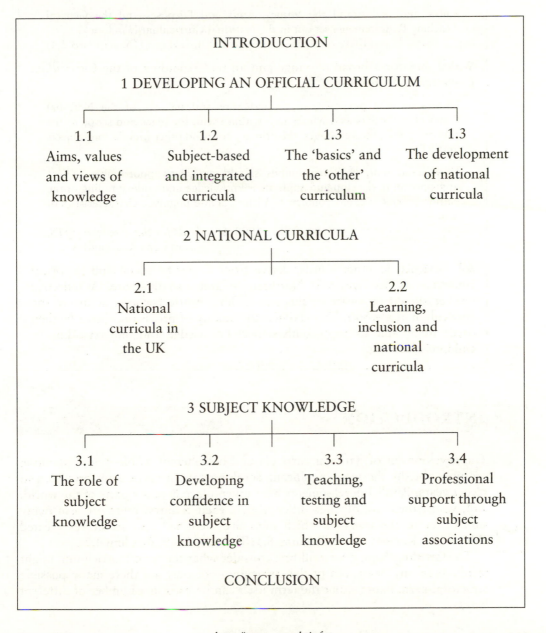

INTRODUCTION

1 DEVELOPING AN OFFICIAL CURRICULUM

1.1	1.2	1.3	1.3
Aims, values and views of knowledge	Subject-based and integrated curricula	The 'basics' and the 'other' curriculum	The development of national curricula

2 NATIONAL CURRICULA

2.1	2.2
National curricula in the UK	Learning, inclusion and national curricula

3 SUBJECT KNOWLEDGE

3.1	3.2	3.3	3.4
The role of subject knowledge	Developing confidence in subject knowledge	Teaching, testing and subject knowledge	Professional support through subject associations

CONCLUSION

Enhancing professional standards and competences

The aims and structure of the curriculum are of enormous importance, and in recent years have been given a great deal of emphasis and seen a great deal of change.

In England there are specific requirements for each phase. However, the overall requirement is for each qualified teacher to:

> Have secure knowledge of the subject(s) they are trained to teach (and areas of learning at Foundation Stage).
>> (TTA, 2002, *Standards for the Award of QTS*, standard 2.1)

> Know and understand the Values, Aims and Purposes and the General Teaching Requirements set out in the National Curriculum Handbook.
>> (TTA, 2002, *Standards for the Award of QTS*, standard 2.4)

Wales aims for a broad coverage and an understanding of the *Curriculum Cymreig*. Students must:

> Understand the purposes, scope, structure and balance of the National Curriculum Orders as a whole and, within them, the place and scope of the primary phase, the key stages, the primary core and other foundation subjects and RE.

> Understand that, in Wales, pupils should be given opportunities, where appropriate, to develop and apply their knowledge and understanding of the cultural, economic, environmental, historical and linguistic characteristics of Wales.
>> (Welsh Office, 1998, *Standards for the Award of QTS*, standards A: 1ii and A: 2a)

All curricula, in other words, derive from a specific social and historical context – as Scotland and Northern Ireland also illustrate. A reflective teacher should be aware of this and of how it affects the structure of the curriculum as a whole. To maximise the quality of provision, she or he then needs to be able to apply both subject knowledge and understanding of children's learning.

INTRODUCTION

The development of national curricula and of coherent whole-school planning are undoubtedly the most significant developments in curriculum provision in recent years. Parallel developments have taken place in many parts of the world, and, whilst there are obvious differences in each country, there are also many similarities in the ways in which aims are identified and structures created (Meyer and Kamens, 1992, **Reading 8.1**; Thomas, 1989, **Reading 4.2**).

To start this chapter, we will first consider what the term 'curriculum' might mean, as in any discussion of the curriculum not only are there many possible structural permutations, but the term itself can be used in a number of different ways.

The official curriculum. This can be defined as 'a planned course of study', i.e. an explicitly stated programme of learning, perhaps incorporating a national curriculum which has been endorsed by government. Such a course of study is likely to have three elements. First, there will be an intended curriculum content. This will have been consciously planned, but is unlikely to include a consideration of learning which may take place outside school. Second, the official curriculum will usually structure sequence and progression, thus framing the content and course of activities. Third, the planned course of study will be designed with the intention of challenging children appropriately and matching their learning needs. For an example of this, see the Curriculum and Assessment Authority for Wales 'Desirable outcomes for young children's learning' (**Reading 9.3**)

In England, Wales and Northern Ireland, the official curriculum is based on each national, statutory curriculum, the content of which must be included in the teaching programme. In Scotland, a national curriculum is presented as 'guidance' to schools only, though, in practice, this guidance is widely followed (subject to local adaption for environmental studies) (see SEED, 2000, **Reading 9.2**).

As has been indicated, however, in terms of the official curriculum as the 'planned course of study', the National Curriculum is only one, albeit central, element. The place of spiritual, moral, social and cultural education in both subject teaching and the wider life of a school is a key focus for school inspection throughout the UK. From the perspective of the '2000 version' of the National Curriculum in England and Wales (DfEE/QCA, 1999) personal, social and health education (PSHE) and education for citizenship are strongly promoted through non-statutory guidance. Schools across the UK need to consider the place of sex education in preparing policies, and religious education, whilst not a National Curriculum subject in England and Wales, is nevertheless statutory in these countries. Thus the official curriculum must be viewed as wider than the National Curriculum, and the 'whole curriculum' is wider still.

The hidden curriculum. The hidden curriculum consists of all that is learned during school activities which is not a designated part of the official curriculum. It is what is 'picked up' about such things as the role of the teacher and the role of the learner, about the status and relationships of each, about attitudes towards learning and to school. Children may also acquire ideas about the ways boys or girls 'should' behave, or about differences 'because' of being black or white, middle-class or working-class. Part of this comes from the way in which values are conveyed through the interaction and language which are associated with teaching and learning processes. The hidden curriculum is thus implicit within regular school procedures and curriculum materials, and can exert a powerful influence on pupils through the communication of the values of teachers and of the school. Indeed, though known as 'hidden' (because it is not 'official'), these issues may be extremely salient to children. In fact, it has been suggested by writers in this field (Jackson, 1968, **Reading 6.2**; Meighan, 1981) that the implicit messages conveyed through the hidden curriculum can have a profound effect on the self-image of children, upon their images of school and on their attitudes to other social groups. These have all been shown to have a direct impact on learning. Chapters 14 and 15 provide more extensive discussions of these issues.

The observed curriculum. This is the curriculum that can be seen to be taking place in the classroom. It may, of course, be very different from the intended official curriculum, especially where the bulk of that curriculum results from national or regional guidance. With respect to the statutory elements of the official curricula in England and Wales and in Northern Ireland, differences between this and the observed curriculum might be thought of as relating less to the underlying body of knowledge and skills being taught, and more to the effectiveness of different teaching strategies in promoting learning. It must be remembered however, that what can be seen in terms of subject content or activities is not the same thing as how the children feel about it, or what they learn through it. This leads to the next aspect of 'curriculum'.

The curriculum-as-experienced. This way of conceptualizing the curriculum identifies the parts of the curriculum, both official and hidden, which actually connect meaningfully with children. Whether officially anticipated or not, this is likely to reflect young children's developmental needs (see Katz, 1998, **Reading 8.4**). Arguably, it is only this curriculum-as-experienced that actually has an educational impact upon children.

Quite clearly then, the concept of the 'whole curriculum' is much wider than the official curriculum. It might, in fact, be envisaged as encompassing all the learning experiences, planned and unplanned, that the pupil encounters in a school. In this chapter, however, we focus mainly on the official curriculum. It is worth considering the whole of the following discussion in the light of **Reading 8.9**, in which Robin Alexander considers the nature of 'good primary practice'.

A *Compendium* of terms, organizations, ideas etc. is available on **RTweb** and may be particularly helpful for this chapter.

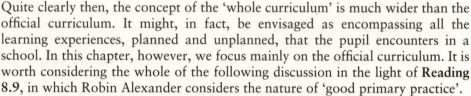

1   DEVELOPING AN OFFICIAL CURRICULUM

Historically, there have been two major alternative strategies for curricular planning within primary schools – by focusing on separate subjects or by planning forms of integration between subjects. The strengths of subject teaching, in terms of curricular progression, are also its potential weakness regarding overall coherence in pupil learning experiences. The reverse is also true, in that the coherence of integrated work can lead to fragmentation in understanding of particular subjects. Subject-based approaches have been, and remain, dominant in the secondary school tradition, whilst integrated approaches, using 'topics', were very significant in primary education in the UK from the time of the Plowden Report (CACE, 1967, **Reading 8.3**) until comparatively recently. As will be seen, however, subject-based national curricula almost invariably lead to a significantly diminished focus upon integrated work, particularly that drawing directly on the 'interests' of children.

Whatever approach is taken to the structure and organization of the curriculum, structures are usually underpinned by aims and values (Bernstein, 1971,

1996, **Reading 8.2**). The first paragraph of this chapter indicated that the connection is not always clear, or even, in some cases, there at all. Historical precedent and gradual pragmatic change to practice over time mean that contemporary curricula *can* obscure some key questions.

For instance:

- What are we hoping to achieve with this curriculum?
- Is our curriculum selection and organization consistent with our values and goals?
- Do our teaching and learning practices reflect these values and goals?

These simple questions bring into sharp focus the centrality of aims and values to the design and implementation of the curriculum, and it is to these that we now turn.

1.1 Aims, values and views of knowledge

We will focus primarily on the National Curriculum in England, though reference to the curricula of other countries of the UK appears throughout the text.

As a component of an official curriculum, let us start by considering the two broad aims for the school curriculum that appear in the English National Curriculum Handbook for 2000. It states:

> The school curriculum should aim to provide opportunities for all pupils to learn and to achieve.

> The school curriculum should aim to promote pupils' spiritual, moral, social and cultural development and prepare all pupils for the opportunities, responsibilities and experiences of adult life.

(DfEE/QCA, 1999)

Such aims are not exceptional in international terms (Taylor, 1990), though they are certainly the product of an enormous complexity of debate, interest and political activity both within and outside the teaching profession (Proctor, 1990).

> ### *Reflective activity 8.1*
>
> *Aim*: To examine statements of aims and values presented in national documentation.
>
> *Evidence and reflection*: Are aims and values stated within the national curriculum documentation at your disposal?
>
> If so, are the aims consistently supported by the stated underlying values? What 'vision' of an education system do you derive from reading these statements?
>
> If not, can you derive some of the core aims and values from an examination of the curriculum advice presented in the documentation?
>
> *Extension*: To what extent do the explicit or implicit aims and values reflect your own views of what should inform a structured national curriculum? Is there anything missing? Is there anything that shouldn't be there? Why?

They are, however, quite bland. It is only when combined with the statement of values devised by the National Forum for Values in Education and the Community (DfEE/QCA, 1999, pp. 147–9) that they might be seen as a 'coherent, humane vision by which schools can be guided' (Bramall and White, 2000). The preamble to the statement of values states 'schools and teachers can have confidence that there is general agreement in society upon these values'. They include statements about the self, relationships, society and the environment.

Whilst the national curricula of England and Wales present aims and values which could legitimate almost any form of curriculum organization, based upon almost any view of knowledge, they are clearly intended in this case to validate an education system that promotes a liberal, democratic society. The acid test is whether the structure and content of the curriculum are an appropriate vehicle for promoting the stated aims and values, or whether they are 'more like a piece of window dressing' (Bramall and White, 2000). We shall return to this when examining the structure and content of the curriculum for these countries. For a detailed consideration of the key question of 'whose values' underlie the process of curriculum construction, see Cairns, Gardner and Lawton (2000).

In other countries, different cultural imperatives tend to inform the stated aims and values of national curricula. In Northern Ireland and Scotland it is not a great surprise to find that they are similar to those for England and Wales, though in Scotland the 5 to 14 Curriculum is presented as non-statutory guidance (Scottish Executive, 2000b, **Reading 9.2**). In this guidance, aims and underlying values are elucidated to a greater extent than in England, Wales or Northern Ireland.

As briefly mentioned at the outset of this chapter, there seems to be, quite surprisingly, relatively limited diversity in curricular patterns around the world. In reviewing the work of Meyer and Kamens (1992, **Reading 8.1**), Ross (2001) points to developments in national curricula that have led to a position where 'local variations have been ironed out as a pattern of international conformity has prevailed' (p. 129). Ross indicates that national curricula across the world generally feature the following: one or more national languages; mathematics; science; some form of social science; and aesthetic education in some form, though this is less firmly established than the other four areas.

There are, however, notes of caution to be sounded with respect to the idea of homogeneity across countries. In his scholarly comparative study of the systems in operation in France, Russia, India, the USA and England, Alexander (2000) indicates that even the notion of what constitutes a school has a wide interpretation across countries. Galton (1998), meanwhile, referring to the 'tiger economies' of the Pacific Rim, notes the dangers inherent in imagining a simple transfer of educational policies from one country to another. He argues that another country's test scores can only be understood 'in terms of their social, economic and political contexts, and the associated value systems'. The message is that what looks the same may not be the same, and what seems transferable may in fact be inappropriate in another context.

Views of knowledge. Underpinning the aims of any national curricula are a set of understandings about the nature of knowledge. If we look at views of knowledge in a little detail, we find that there are four basic positions.

First, there are those who argue that different 'forms of knowledge' exist.

Forms of knowledge are thought to be distinguishable, philosophically, by the different ways of thinking and the different kinds of evidence which are employed in investigating them (Hirst, 1965; Peters, 1966). These different 'forms' are thought to be based on 'a priori' differences, i.e. logical and inherent differences. Such a view is referred to as 'rationalist' (Blenkin and Kelly, 1981) and is often used to legitimate curriculum subjects (see Wilson, 2000, **Reading 8.5**).

Second, there are those who argue that knowledge is achieved through individuals interacting with the environment and restructuring their understanding through their experiences. Hence, knowledge is the application of intellect to experience. Proponents of this view are sometimes termed 'empiricists' and it is evidenced in the writings of Dewey and Piaget (see also Chapter 7, Section 1.2, and **Reading 7.2**).

Third, a more sociological view suggests that knowledge can be constructed by groups of people, through their interactions with each other. Hence, they share their experiences and their perceptions of those experiences. In such an 'interactionist' approach people are seen as developing a common sense of 'reality' (Light and Littleton, 1999). This view has some resonance with the work on learning of Bruner and Vygotsky (see Chapter 7, Section 1.3 and **Readings 7.3 and 7.8**).

Finally, knowledge can be seen in the context of macro-social structures, and of historical forces, as being influenced by powerful social groups who define certain types of knowledge as being important or of high status. They may attempt to control access to certain forms of knowledge, particularly those associated with power (Young, 1971; Bernstein, 1971, **Reading 8.2**), but they may also try to insist on the exposure of pupils to other forms of knowledge which are deemed to be appropriate. We will call this view of school knowledge 'elitist'.

You might notice an overlap here with the philosophical approaches to research that were reviewed in Chapter 3, Section 4, p. 58.

Of course, these views of knowledge are not discrete and any one person's perspective may draw on several of them, or even on them all. However, the important point is that the different emphasis which is placed on particular views of knowledge tends to reflect social values, and these *can* influence the structure and content of the curriculum. For instance, during the 1990s the early National Curriculum of England and Wales was repeatedly criticized for reflecting elitist views. Ashcroft and Palacio (1995) provide a readable account of the establishment of the National Curriculum in England and Wales and demonstrate how those with political power promoted what they perceived to be 'important' areas of the curriculum.

When national curricula for the education of young people and future citizens are being developed, such debates are obviously very significant and often become political (see, for example, the Labour Party, 1994, **Reading 8.8**). Indeed, there may even be fears of state indoctrination. The outcome will certainly tend to reflect the balance of political power at the time of decision-making.

We will now consider some issues that have influenced the direction of 'the curriculum in practice' in the UK. As will be seen, sometimes underlying aims and values (officially stated or otherwise) have been at the heart of change; at other times they have not.

Reflective activity 8.2

Aim: To consider the influence of views of knowledge on a part of a national curriculum.

Evidence and reflection: This is a potentially large activity which needs to be scaled down and made specific. We suggest that you study the official, national documentation of a single subject – history or geography are often good choices.

Consider, how is knowledge viewed? Is it seen as an established body of subject content and skills to be transferred or as something to be created?

Extension: Is this view of knowledge consistent with the aims and values of the curriculum that you investigated in Reflective Activity 8.1?

1.2 Subject-based and integrated curricula

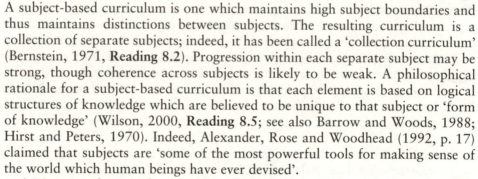

A subject-based curriculum is one which maintains high subject boundaries and thus maintains distinctions between subjects. The resulting curriculum is a collection of separate subjects; indeed, it has been called a 'collection curriculum' (Bernstein, 1971, **Reading 8.2**). Progression within each separate subject may be strong, though coherence across subjects is likely to be weak. A philosophical rationale for a subject-based curriculum is that each element is based on logical structures of knowledge which are believed to be unique to that subject or 'form of knowledge' (Wilson, 2000, **Reading 8.5**; see also Barrow and Woods, 1988; Hirst and Peters, 1970). Indeed, Alexander, Rose and Woodhead (1992, p. 17) claimed that subjects are 'some of the most powerful tools for making sense of the world which human beings have ever devised'.

An integrated curriculum, on the other hand, is one which draws on several subjects to construct a holistic and, it is hoped, meaningful focus for study. Different arguments for the desirability of an integrated curriculum have been offered. One suggests that the curriculum should draw on pupil experiences if effective learning is to take place. It is thus considered that the imposition of artificial subject boundaries may inhibit children's understanding. A second argument that underpins integrated curricular planning is that a higher priority can be given to generic processes, key skills and fundamental attitudes if the emphasis on particular subject knowledge is lessened. This is of particular relevance to early-years' education. Indeed Katz (1998, **Reading 8.4**) suggests that this is essential for a curriculum that recognizes children's developmental needs (see also ACCAC, 1996, **Reading 9.3**).

Historically, primary practice has been shaped by these two differing approaches to curriculum planning, subject and integrated (strongly contested by Alexander, 1992, **Reading 8.9**). However, in reality, it has drawn on both as professional judgement has been exercised. The subject-based approach is one that, in the past, has primarily appealed to traditionalists. Indeed, perhaps the origin of curriculum subjects can be found in the high status which is attributed to the formal, classical education of Public and Grammar Schools and to a belief that this is the only approach which will deliver competencies in basic subjects (Lawlor, 1988). At present, of course, arguments in favour of a subject based approach have held sway with respect to the introduction and subsequent revisions of the primary National Curriculum in both England and Wales and in Northern Ireland. Critics, however, retain some powerful arguments (see, for example, Dadds 2001, **Reading 9.4**), on the 'hurry along' curriculum.

1.3   The 'basics' and the 'other' curriculum

Whatever is said about the primary curriculum, the evidence from research shows that a 'two curricula syndrome' has been consistently a feature of practice. This argument was powerfully made by Alexander (1984, 1997) and was supported by the conclusions of Pollard *et al.* (1994) and Galton *et al.* (1999). The two curricula Alexander had in mind are that of the 'basics' (reading, writing and mathematics), and that of the rest – the 'other' curriculum. Alexander argued that the rhetoric of child-centred education, which was associated with an integrated form of curriculum organisation, prevented teachers from facing the fact that the basics in the curriculum have usually been taught in a relatively discrete and almost subject-based way. It is only with regard to other, less central, areas of the curriculum that attempts to establish integration have, historically, been made.

The notion of 'two curricula syndrome' was strongly emphasized in the devising of the National Curriculum in England and Wales. Whilst ten subjects were deemed to be 'foundation subjects', English, mathematics and science (and Welsh in Wales) became known as the 'core'. The primacy of English and mathematics has since been officially asserted within the curriculum of England with the introduction of the National Literacy Strategy (NLS) (DfEE, 1998b) and the National Numeracy Strategy (NNS) (DfEE, 1999). Parallel initiatives exist in Scotland, Wales and Northern Ireland, but these are much less prescriptive and are more variable between local education authorities.

Figure 8.1 shows Alexander's analysis of the major dimensions of the 'two curricula'. It shows how actual primary practice has often reflected the pragmatism and judgement of 'what works' (see also **Reading 8.9**). The result has been something of a necessary compromise, despite the impression that might sometimes be given by rhetoric from either side. The question that arises is whether such a compromise is still possible in the context of a statutory curriculum.

The focus on 'the basics' often impinges upon national and state government policy. As an example it is worth considering two key initiatives in England – the Literacy and Numeracy strategies. Though neither of these initiatives is statutory, it is informative to note that OFSTED (1999, p. 24), in providing guidance for school inspection, state that inspectors should 'pay particular attention to competence in literacy and numeracy'. In reality, nearly all maintained schools now teach literacy and numeracy sessions, though how tightly these adhere to the guidance provided in the literacy and numeracy strategies (DfEE, 1998b; 1999) varies from school to school.

The impact of these initiatives in schools can hardly be over-stated. OFSTED's (2000a; 2000b) own analyses of the strategies note the 'major impact' that they have had on the teaching of English and mathematics, their reports having as a major focus pupil attainment as reflected in end of Key Stage assessment test

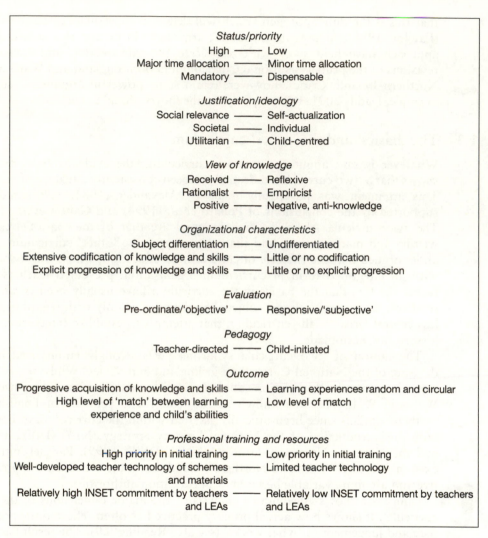

Status/priority

High	Low
Major time allocation	Minor time allocation
Mandatory	Dispensable

Justification/ideology

Social relevance	Self-actualization
Societal	Individual
Utilitarian	Child-centred

View of knowledge

Received	Reflexive
Rationalist	Empiricist
Positive	Negative, anti-knowledge

Organizational characteristics

Subject differentiation	Undifferentiated
Extensive codification of knowledge and skills	Little or no codification
Explicit progression of knowledge and skills	Little or no explicit progression

Evaluation

Pre-ordinate/'objective'	Responsive/'subjective'

Pedagogy

Teacher-directed	Child-initiated

Outcome

Progressive acquisition of knowledge and skills	Learning experiences random and circular
High level of 'match' between learning experience and child's abilities	Low level of match

Professional training and resources

High priority in initial training	Low priority in initial training
Well-developed teacher technology of schemes and materials	Limited teacher technology
Relatively high INSET commitment by teachers and LEAs	Relatively low INSET commitment by teachers and LEAs

Figure 8.1 *Dimensions for analysing the primary curriculum (from Alexander 1984, p. 76)*

results. This major impact extends, however, to curriculum organization and teaching and assessment strategies, and has had an effect on thinking about the place of 'the basics' within the primary curriculum. Studies such as that carried out by Anderson and Urquhart (2000) point to some effects of the Literacy Hour, highlighting teacher concerns about the marginalization of some English skills, the lack of coherence within the literacy hour itself, and the problems of maintaining a balanced curriculum. For instance, what should be the place of the arts (Robinson, 1999)? Do we just end up with superficiality and low motivation (Dadds, 2001, **Reading 9.4**)? Such criticisms must be weighed carefully against the stated benefits of such a focus on literacy and numeracy. Certainly, the introduction of the strategies brings into sharp focus the question of what constitutes appropriate curriculum content and classroom practice in two important areas of learning, and the focus on classroom practice has had implications for thinking about the presentation of the wider primary curriculum.

A further point that will be explored in more detail later relates back to the discussion on aims and values. Where there are clearly stated aims and values for the curriculum, one test of whether they are actually informing structure is to examine whether curriculum initiatives seem broadly to reflect them.

1.4   The development of national curricula

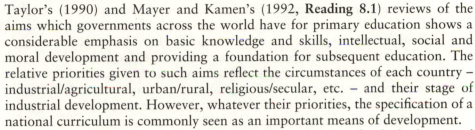

Taylor's (1990) and Mayer and Kamen's (1992, **Reading 8.1**) reviews of the aims which governments across the world have for primary education shows a considerable emphasis on basic knowledge and skills, intellectual, social and moral development and providing a foundation for subsequent education. The relative priorities given to such aims reflect the circumstances of each country – industrial/agricultural, urban/rural, religious/secular, etc. – and their stage of industrial development. However, whatever their priorities, the specification of a national curriculum is commonly seen as an important means of development.

For example, prior to the 1980s, English primary schools had enjoyed considerable autonomy in deciding both what should be taught and about teaching methods, but they were not considered to be contributing strongly to national economic development (Callaghan, 1976). Whilst there was considerable overlap in the content of the curriculum, this was combined with much diversity and variation in the quality of the education provided (HMI, 1978; House of Commons Select Committee on Education, 1986). Many schools were excellent, but the provision was very uneven across the country. This was a major reason given by educationalists arguing for curriculum reform to raise standards. There was a plethora of curriculum documents, from a number of public bodies, including *The School Curriculum* (DES, 1981), *A View of the Curriculum (DES, 1980)*, *Better Schools* (DES, 1985), *The Curriculum from 5–16* (HMI, 1985) and *Primary Practice* (Schools Council, 1983).

Whilst many agreed in principle with the proposal to create a national curriculum, some important questions were nevertheless raised. What exactly should a framework contain? Who should decide this and how often should it be reviewed? How detailed should the curriculum be and should it be advisory or compulsory? What implications would this have for an increase in central control and the subsequent possible reduction of the professional autonomy of the individual classroom teacher? What would be the likely effects on the balance between individually and socially determined goals, between personal freedom and professional responsibility? Would a national curriculum affect the career structure of the profession? What is 'good practice' anyway? (See Alexander, 1992, **Reading 8.9.**).

Driven particularly, as it was, by rationalist and elitist views of knowledge and by the influence on successive Conservative governments of a number of right-wing pressure groups (Ball, 1990; Lawlor, 1988), it is hardly surprising that the debate surrounding the introduction of the National Curriculum led, in due course, to highly specified subject-based curriculum orders (see Galton *et al.*, 1999, Chapter 1). Interestingly, the Labour Party of the time opposed such 'overprescription' (Labour Party, 1995, **Reading 8.8**). It is worth noting here that the National Curriculum can be seen as providing an expression of the view that the classification of knowledge is socially and historically determined. This was most powerfully argued in a collection of papers published in the early 1970s, *Knowledge and Control* (see also Bernstein, 1971, **Reading 8.2**; Young, 1971). From this perspective, what counts as knowledge is contested and the dominant view arises from the competing definitions that are offered by various groups in a society. It follows that the way knowledge is classified and valued will reflect the distribution of power within a society. The consequence is that what is valued by those with power in society can largely determine policy and practice.

When New Labour came to power in 1997 they retained almost all of the structures that the previous administration had introduced. However, the content of the curriculum was reviewed and new priorities such as citizenship, that 'fitted' with emerging value statements, were introduced. History suggests that national curricula are constantly being developed and amended by successive generations and governments. This is not surprising when the key role of education is shaping the future for children and the country. Reflective teachers need not only to learn to accommodate such transitions, but also to consider whether pragmatic changes made to the structure of a curriculum have an effect on the relevance of the stated aims and values of that curriculum.

For example, in the life of the National Curriculum in England, amongst numerous other changes, there has been a gradual separating out of a specific curriculum for the early years, arriving at the current Early Learning Goals and associated curriculum guidance for the 'Foundation Stage' (QCA/DfEE, 2000). The place of science as a 'core' subject has arguably been diluted with the intro-duction of the National Numeracy Strategy and the National Literacy Strategy, and the Key Stage 3 strategy has now extended these into this phase of schooling (e.g. DfEE, 2001). Interestingly, the introduction of these strategies has also led some primary schools to consider subject integration as a means of developing the foundation curriculum. The place of ICT has become central in all subject studies, the focus moving from learning about ICT to learning the value of using

ICT (Bonnett, McFarlane and Williams, 1999; Kennelwell, Parkinson and Tanner, 2000, **Reading 9.8**). The reflective teacher needs not only to learn to accommodate such transitions, but should be able to contribute to such change and consider the effect of changes on the overall aims and values of the curriculum.

2 | NATIONAL CURRICULA

2.1 National curricula in the UK

When reviewing the curricula of each of the four countries of the UK, the most notable thing is that they actually cover very similar broad areas of study (see Figure 8.2). However, this is done in interestingly different ways. In England and Wales, priority is given to English, mathematics and science (with, in Wales, Welsh). This asserts what is perceived as the overarching importance of these 'core' subjects. Whilst such core subjects are felt to be essential as basic skills for future learning and work, other 'foundation' subjects are seen as contributing to a broad and balanced curriculum. The same subject emphasis has been further

used to shape different forms of pupil assessment and reporting to parents (see Chapter 14).

Tradition 'subjects' remain extremely important in all UK curricula, but are particularly prominent in England and Wales (see Figure 8.2 for the basic stucture of their post-2000 curricula – the third version in ten years). The prominence of subjects reflects the continuing influence of a challenging report (Alexander, Rose and Woodhead, 1992) which argued that they enable transmission of a society's accumulated knowledge and support more rigour in teaching. The approach contests the extensive integration of humanities work that was once common in primary schools and challenges conservative notions of 'good practice' (see also Alexander, 1992, **Reading 8.9**). Echoes of that approach remain in Scotland where the 5 to 14 Curriculum remains formally 'non-statutory' and comprises five broad 'areas', plus five cross-curricular aspects, and highlights personal and social development as 'fundamental to the education of the whole child' (see also Scottish Executive, 2000, **Reading 9.2**). Nevertheless, in practice, conventional subjects and the press of external assessment and inspection produce strong expectations of conformity to the 'guidelines' (Adams, 1999). In Northern Ireland, new curriculum ideas are being developed (CCEA, 2000), and these are indicated in Figure 8.2. Specific objectives for this process of curriculum development include:

- clarifying aims, objectives and values
- clarifying generic skills
- improving relevance and enjoyment
- improving balance, coherence and flexibility at each Key Stage
- developing assessment mechanisms which better match curriculum aims.

It is proposed that 'the Key Stage 1 curriculum would focus mainly on the development of skills' and 'in the earliest years the focus should be on oracy, practical mathematics, personal development and learning through structured play' (CCEA, 2000, p. 24).

Whichever country you work or study in, the important thing to note is that curriculum arrangements are social constructions. Although they may seem 'set in stone', they actually do change over time and you are likely to see quite a few in the course of your career! They also, of course, reflect the culture, history and political context of their construction, with the *Curriculum Cymreig* of Wales providing a particular example of this (see, for instance, ACCAC, 1996, **Reading 9.3**).

The Education Reform Act 1988 introduced a clear structure for the education system in England and Wales. The main structural issues are indicated in Figure 8.3, though they have been modified to include the comparatively recent concept of a Foundation Stage of schooling.

The National Curriculum orders for England, Wales and Northern Ireland, though differing in numerous ways, share some common structures and terminology, which it is useful to outline here. We will then consider how this differs from the position in Scotland.

'Subject orders' for the core and foundation subjects are statutory and consist of 'programmes of study' and 'attainment targets'. Pupil attainment for each attainment target is described by 'levels of attainment' using 'level descriptions'. *Programmes of study* set out essential knowledge, skills and processes which need to be covered in each subject by pupils in each stage of schooling. These

England	Wales	Scotland	Northern Ireland
ENGLISH (and National Literacy Strategy)	**ENGLISH** (except in KS1 Welsh-medium classes)	Language	LITERACY
	WELSH (in Welsh-medium schools)		
MATHEMATICS (and National Numeracy Strategy)	**MATHEMATICS**	Mathematics	NUMERACY
SCIENCE	**SCIENCE**	Environmental Studies: Society, Science and Technology	THE WORLD ABOUT US (with identifiable strands at KS2 for Science and Technology, Geography and History)
DESIGN & TECHNOLOGY	DESIGN & TECHNOLOGY		
ICT	ICT		
HISTORY	HISTORY		
GEOGRAPHY	GEOGRAPHY		
ART & DESIGN	ART & DESIGN	Expressive Arts (including PE)	CREATIVITY (with identifiable strands at KS2 for Art and Design, Music and PE)
MUSIC	MUSIC		
PE	PE		
RE*	RE*	Religious and moral education (with personal and social development and health education)	PERSONAL DEVELOPMENT (personal understanding, personal health and living in the local and wider community)
Spiritual, moral, social and cultural development	Personal and social education		
Personal, social and health education, with citizenship			
Modern foreign languages may be taught at KS2	*Curriculum Cymreig:* the cultural, economic, environmental, historical and linguistic characteristics of Wales	*Cross-curricular aspects*: personal and social development, education for work; education for citizenship; the culture of Scotland; and ICT	
Thinking skills: information processing, reasoning, enquiry, creative thinking, evaluation			
Key skills: communication, application of number, information technology, working with others, improving own learning and performance, problem-solving	*Skill requirements:* communication, mathematical, information technology, problem-solving, creative		*Generic skills:* personal, interpersonal, thinking, learning, ICT and physical

(Key: **Bold** – core subject; UPPER CASE – statutory; * – a 'requirement', but not a subject)

Figure 8.2 *The national curricula for primary schools of England, Wales and Scotland (as of 2002–3) and proposals for Northern Ireland (for implementation from 2003–4)*

Age of pupils	Pupil year	Stage	School
3 4 5	Nursery/Reception	Foundation	Nursery/reception classes in school or separate
6 7	Year 1 Year 2	Key Stage 1	Infant school (or within a primary)
8 9 10 11	Year 3 Year 4 Year 5 Year 6	Key Stage 2	Junior school (or within a primary)
12 13 14	Year 7 Year 8 Year 9	Key Stage 3	Secondary school
15 16	Year 10 Year 11	Key Stage 4	Secondary school

Figure 8.3 *Age of pupil, school year and stage of schooling*

are minimum statutory entitlements. Programmes of study are intended to be used by schools in constructing schemes of work. *Attainment targets* are defined from within programmes of study to represent the knowledge, skills and understanding which pupils are expected to master as they progress through school. Attainment targets are used in assessment procedures. *Levels of attainment* identify points of knowledge, skill and understanding for each subject, against which pupil attainment can be assessed. Most pupils are expected to reach Level 2 at the age of seven, and Level 4 at the age of eleven. *Level descriptions* indicate the type, quality and range of work which a child 'characteristically should demonstrate' in a subject when they have reached a particular level.

As has been mentioned previously, the National Curriculum for Scotland is presented as guidance to schools, and though some structures and terminology are similar to those for the other UK countries, the tenor of the documentation tends to be more explanatory. For example, 'attainment targets' and 'levels of attainment' are defined, and characteristics underpinning the expected progression through and within the levels are made clear. Interestingly, it is suggested that the allocation of time within the curriculum is made on the basis of the five curriculum areas (see Figure 8.2), rather than on a subject basis.

As we have seen, the aims and values of a curriculum extend beyond the boundaries of subject learning. The second aim for the curriculum drawn from the National Curriculum handbook is that the curriculum should:

> . . . aim to promote pupils' spiritual, moral, social and cultural development and prepare all pupils for the opportunities, responsibilities and experiences of adult life.

The intention is that, through the permeating effect of the school ethos in action, as well as through direct teaching and example, pupils should 'develop principles for distinguishing between right and wrong . . . develop knowledge, understanding and appreciation of their own and different beliefs and cultures . . . (become) responsible and caring citizens . . . (and) understand their rights and responsibilities' (QCA, 1998a, p. 11). A tall order indeed, though one that most teachers accept as a central part of the role of a school. It is vigorously supported in the statements of underlying values related to the self, relationships, society and the environment that appear as part of the National Curriculum handbooks (QCA, 1998a, pp. 147–9).

The non-statutory guidelines for Personal, Social and Health Education (PSHE) and Citizenship (QCA, 1998a, pp. 136–41) are the parts of the National Curriculum that link most strongly with such stated aims and values (see Beck and Earl, 2000). As Bramall and White (2000) have argued, these aspects of the National Curriculum illustrate how values may influence content. On the other hand, statutory subject orders sometimes sit uncomfortably with the aims and values that are intended to inform them. Indeed, introductory paragraphs in the handbooks about the importance of each subject sometimes seem to have been written independently of the overall statements of aims and values. This is not to say that they have no merit, but simply that in any national curriculum there may still be work for a reflective teacher to do in developing real and applied consistency between values, aims, content and structure (Richards 1998, 1999, 2001).

2.2 Learning, inclusion and national curricula

A structured national curriculum would seem to provide numerous helpful features in support of children's learning. For example:

Objectives for each stage of children's education are clearly stated and provide a helpful clarification of what both children and teachers are expected to do. Research has consistently shown that the lack of clarity in teaching and learning objectives is a significant inhibitor of pupil progress.

Curriculum breadth and balance can be considered 'as a whole' (see Chapter 9), rather than simply in terms of the relationship between particular curriculum subjects.

Curriculum progression and continuity can be planned and monitored both from class to class and on transfer between schools (see also Chapter 9).

Training and professional development programmes for teachers can be tailored to known national curriculum needs (see Chapter 17).

Resources for the official series of teaching and learning programmes can be developed on a large scale and in an organized, cost-effective way.

Parents have the opportunity to know and understand what is being taught and may be able to support their children more effectively (see Chapter 17).

However, there is a dilemma for highly structured national curricula that can perhaps be encapsulated as follows. How can a specified curriculum, at one and the same time, address national concerns, set out a national framework for content and progression and yet remain flexible enough to draw on the interests, experiences, learning styles and physical and intellectual capabilities of individual children? Will this facilitate inclusion, or is there a risk that some pupils will feel excluded by the specified content? How, also, does innovation occur? The truth, of course, is that no national curriculum can meet all these objectives. There has to be a trade-off.

As we have seen, in the case of England, Wales and Northern Ireland, the legislation of recent years produced a much tighter specification of the curriculum in terms of both content and structure. Areas of study to be 'delivered' and assessed are specified in the programmes of study and attainment targets. To a large extent then, the curriculum for schools has be placed in a linear form within each subject – and this is, of course, backed up by formal assessment procedures.

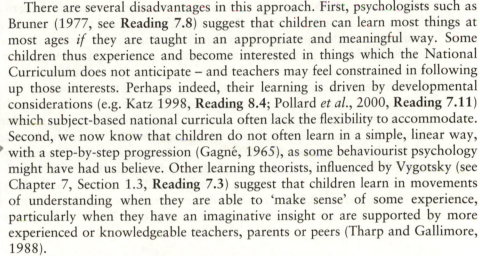

There are several disadvantages in this approach. First, psychologists such as Bruner (1977, see **Reading 7.8**) suggest that children can learn most things at most ages *if* they are taught in an appropriate and meaningful way. Some children thus experience and become interested in things which the National Curriculum does not anticipate – and teachers may feel constrained in following up those interests. Perhaps indeed, their learning is driven by developmental considerations (e.g. Katz 1998, **Reading 8.4**; Pollard *et al.*, 2000, **Reading 7.11**) which subject-based national curricula often lack the flexibility to accommodate. Second, we now know that children do not often learn in a simple, linear way, with a step-by-step progression (Gagné, 1965), as some behaviourist psychology might have had us believe. Other learning theorists, influenced by Vygotsky (see Chapter 7, Section 1.3, **Reading 7.3**) suggest that children learn in movements of understanding when they are able to 'make sense' of some experience, particularly when they have an imaginative insight or are supported by more experienced or knowledgeable teachers, parents or peers (Tharp and Gallimore, 1988).

Nor do philosophers affirm the existence of a logical and conceptual sequence of national curriculum knowledge. Indeed, their criticisms are combined with those of psychologists and applied even in the case of those subjects which are usually taken to embody progressive logic, such as mathematics (Brown, 1989; Ernest, 1991; Noss, Goldstein and Hoyles, 1989). Ernest's work makes the point particularly clearly. He writes:

> One of the greatest dangers in stipulating a statutory curriculum in mathematics at (several) levels of attainment is that it becomes a barrier which may deny a youngster access to higher concepts and skills when he or she is ready for them . . . The major flaw in this scheme (is) the mistaken assumption that children's learning in mathematics follows a fixed hierarchical pattern . . . This is nonsense.
> (Ernest, 1991, p. 50)

The over-riding message is perhaps that learning is not always predictable or linear, and any curriculum that diminishes the opportunity for teachers to respond to pupil needs is less likely to promote meaningful learning. Could the 'hurry along' curriculum actually inhibit learning? (Dadds, 2001, **Reading 9.4**). That is not to say, of course, that pupils cannot be taught successive stages of a pre-specified curriculum so that their performance rises – as has been demonstrated by the National Literacy and National Numeracy strategies in England.

But we should note here that important motivational issues have been raised and some research suggests that pupils' learning disposition and engagement may be undermined by this approach (Claxton, 1999, **Reading 7.7**; Pollard *et al.*, 2000, **Reading 7.11**). There is a risk then that tightly specified national curricula, backed by high-stakes assessment procedures, actually *produce* exclusion, with disengaged and disaffected children simply withdrawing in their minds and/or bodies.

At the classroom level the concept of 'negotiation' goes a long way in resolving this dilemma. Children are perfectly capable of accepting that there is nationally laid down curriculum coverage, but will welcome negotiation with their teacher about how it should be addressed and with what it should be augmented. Seen from a national level, negotiation may be perceived as producing an unacceptable degree of variation in pupil experience and learning, the eradication of which might be seen as one purpose of a national curriculum. Selley (1999), however, outlines clearly how such ideas of negotiation fit within a framework of 'constructivist' teaching. Here, teachers 'work collaboratively with the children so that the outcome is not only testable knowledge but mental growth, stability and power', and Selley shows how this need not be incompatible with the statutory remit provided by the National Curriculum.

Of course, some parents take the view that the National Curriculum in England is simply too restrictive and undermines independent learning and engagement with an appropriate range of experience. Over the last decade, Steiner schools and other alternative forms of education have become popular, despite having to rely on private funding. Education Otherwise, for children who are educated at home, has grown too. Indeed, Human Scale Education claims that that 150,000 British children were educated outside the school system in 2000, though the DfEE acknowledged only 25,000. In any event, the numbers of those rejecting formally structured state schooling is considerable.

Reflective activity 8.3

Aim: To experience children's capacity and inclination to search for understanding at young ages.

Evidence and reflection: Play with and talk to a young child with whom you have a good relationship. At an appropriate opportunity, develop a conversation about something in which they are interested. Note down the things which they say and ask, verbatim if you can, and consider what this shows you about their present understanding.

Think hard about some experience which you could offer the child to extend their thinking. Try it. Again, record and interpret the child's responses.

Extension: Consider the knowledge and understanding which the child has revealed and reached. Does this appear in the National Curriculum? If so, where? How appropriate does this seem? (For some examples of such conversations, see Tizard and Hughes, 1984).

3   SUBJECT KNOWLEDGE

3.1   The role of subject knowledge

Research evidence shows that most primary teachers in England and Wales welcomed the introduction of the National Curriculum (Osborn *et al.*, 2000) and very few now in post would want to work without it. There have, however, been consequences for teachers linked to the adjustment to more subject-based teaching and to an increasing definition of curriculum content. One of these consequences has been an increased expectation with respect to teachers' subject knowledge and the role that it should play.

Of course, there is no simple association between sound subject knowledge and effective teaching (Appleton, 1995). Indeed, teachers' subject knowledge is only one factor amongst many that contribute to effective teaching. Reconsider, for example, Figure 7.4 (from Chapter 7). This suggested that vital attributes of effective teaching includes understanding of how children learn and empathy with them. However, the model also illustrates the crucial instructional role of the teacher in explaining and scaffolding children's knowledge and understanding – and this is only possible where the teacher's own subject knowledge is secure. As Alexander, Rose and Woodhead put it:

> Subject knowledge is a critical factor at every point in the teaching process: in planning, assessing and diagnosing, task setting, questioning, explaining and giving feedback.
>
> (1992, para. 77)

Reflective teachers have to make judgements about the *appropriate* teaching of knowledge, concepts, skills and attitudes and there does seem to be something of a consensus that teachers with sound subject knowledge can do this more effectively. In science, for example, this consensus is strongly supported by Harlen (1996), Osborne and Simon (1996) and Watt (1996).

The most influential research-based support for this position was provided by Shulman (1986, **Reading 8.6**) who identified three sorts of subject knowledge.

- *Content knowledge* which refers to knowledge of the subject held by the teacher.

- *Pedagogic content knowledge* which refers to knowledge of how to use content knowledge for teaching purposes.

- *Curricular knowledge* which refers to knowledge of curriculum structures and materials, and how to use them effectively in classroom contexts.

For most teachers, curricular knowledge is much easier to acquire than content knowledge or even pedagogic subject knowledge. Indeed, some would argue that, whilst curricular knowledge can be obtained from text-books, resources and National Curriculum documentation, the acquisition of content *knowledge* calls for sustained study. Banks, Leach and Moon (1999) have reconceptualized and extended Shulman's model. They highlight curriculum-building processes that create new, grounded forms of 'school knowledge'.

Reflective activity 8.4

Aim: To assess our own feelings of competence in subject knowledge.

Evidence and reflection: For the Key Stage in which you teach (or in which you intend to teach) consider the curriculum, subject by subject. Note which parts you feel competent to teach and which parts you feel uncertain about.

Prioritize your needs for developing subject knowledge and competence.

Share your feelings with a colleague – perhaps you are being too self-critical, or too confident?

Extension: Consider the implications of your results. If you are a trainee teacher, what opportunities are there on your course for you to develop the subject knowledge that you need? If you are an experienced teacher, can you devise a practical programme for Continuing Professional Development? Can you find ways of co-operating with colleagues in reciprocal support? Have you checked official websites (e.g. DFES, TTA) for some of the support that may be available?

3.2 Developing confidence in subject knowledge

Primary teacher *confidence* in subject knowledge has always been a somewhat problematic area. This is despite the very real desire amongst teachers to develop their subject knowledge, demonstrated through, for example, participation in courses of Continuing Professional Development (Harland and Kinder, 1992; see Chapter 17). The scale of the challenge which the breadth and depth of knowledge of National Curriculum subjects poses for teachers undoubtedly caused many to doubt their capabilities (HMCI, 1998). The response to the 'subject knowledge issue' has been many faceted. Let us first consider two important responses from government.

Successive governments have used developments in teacher training and school inspection as a means to promote the development of teacher subject knowledge.

In Initial Teacher Training (ITT) subject knowledge requirements, particularly in the core subjects of the National Curriculum and in information and communications technology, have become increasingly demanding. From 1998 defined standards for the award of Qualified Teacher Status (DfEE, 1998c) included criteria for each of the above subjects that defined, in addition to pedagogical knowledge, teaching and assessment methods, a wide range of expectations with respect to content knowledge. Although these tight, atomistic criteria have been replaced by broader summary statements and a Handbook of guidance, there remains a problem in over-loading subject knowledge. Indeed, some have argued that the ITT curriculum is imbalanced, with insufficient time being spent on trainees' understanding of children's learning, both generally and in terms of particular subjects (see Chapter 7 for discussion of related topics). Further, as Shallcross *et al.* (2001) suggest, trainees can fail to see any clear relevance in their subject knowledge studies where there is no immediate link to their teaching in schools. Sound subject knowledge is thus perceived as a 'good thing', but as most relevant when acquired in preparation for teaching specific units of work.

A further ITT initiative that should be noted is the development of Key Stage 2/3 training courses. Here, the main intention appears to be to promote subject specialist teaching within primary schools, where most trainees on such courses find posts.

In the remit for school inspection, the Office for Standards in Education (OFSTED) consider how the quality of subject knowledge impinges on how well pupils are taught. Thus, the Handbook for Inspecting Primary and Nursery Schools (OFSTED, 1999, p. 46) states that, in determining their judgements, school inspectors should consider the extent to which teachers 'show good subject knowledge and understanding in the way they present their subject'. This is done not only through an analysis of classroom interactions – primarily the quality of questioning and exposition – but also through an examination of planning, interventions with pupils in the classroom, marking and target setting (which are looked at in more detail in Chapter 9, Section 3.2 and Chapter 14, Section 1.3). It is therefore an expectation within school inspection that teachers will demonstrate good subject knowledge.

In schools this heightened focus on subject knowledge has had some important effects and requires particular skills (see O'Hara and O'Hara, 2001, **Reading 8.7**). As was made apparent earlier, the primary school curriculum has, for many, increasingly been perceived as more manageable if taught in subject 'compartments'. Part of the reason for this is that schools have been concerned to ensure coverage of the statutory curriculum and this is seen as the clearest way of demonstrating coverage. Another consequence of this movement, however, has been to highlight the subject expertise of particular teachers. The traditional role of the subject co-ordinator may gradually become replaced by that of the subject specialist. In some schools this often subtle shift has been accompanied by a move to the teaching of more than one year group by the specialist, giving the management of some curriculum subjects a more 'secondary school feel'. In most cases 'the specialist' will be a generalist teacher with a class responsibility, but with a 'subject co-ordination' role (O'Hara and O'Hara, 2001, **Reading 8.7**).

Campbell (1996) noted that this move to teachers as specialists may empower some teachers, but that the danger is 'the valuing of the work of the generalist class teacher is being replaced by a concentration on the value of specialist subject expertise'. Thinking pragmatically for a moment, in most primary schools there will never be enough staff members to service a subject-based curriculum through specialist teaching. Any devaluing of the role of the generalist might thus be regarded with some concern. In addition, the implication that the generalist teacher might not be concerned with subject knowledge issues seems dubious to say the least. There are legitimate rationales for both approaches.

3.3 Teaching, testing and subject knowledge

The introduction of the National Curriculum preceded standardized testing at the ages of 7, 11 and 14. Though testing as part of overall assessment procedures is discussed in detail in Chapter 14, the influence of testing on curriculum teaching can be very considerable.

As early as 1996, only three years after the introduction of the pilot end of Key Stage assessment tests, (Brown *et al.*, p. 4) noted that in 31 Key Stage 2 classrooms surveyed:

- one third had changed from mixed-ability teaching to some form of setting
- one half had moved away from integrating subjects in cross-curricular combinations and towards subject-based teaching
- one quarter had decided to do more whole-class teaching
- just under half had introduced regular formal testing in Years 3, 4, 5 and 6.

So in a culture where the highest priority is given to the acquisition of strong end of Key Stage test results, 'high-stakes assessment', profound effects on the culture of teaching and learning can be identified.

Reflective activity 8.5

Aim: To consider the effects of national testing on teaching.

Evidence and reflection: If you are a trainee teacher, discuss with your mentor or an experienced teacher how they see the effects of the testing regime on their teaching. Have there been major changes in their teaching programme, their approach with the pupils, the ways in which groups are organized, etc.?

If you are an experienced teacher, discuss these issues with a colleague and decide which effects you feel have been positive and which seem to have been negative.

Extension: Such considerations lead directly to reflection on the real purposes of assessment. Should it be used formatively, to improve learning? Or summatively, to measure attainment? Can both goals be met? To follow-up these issues, you could turn directly to Chapter 14 where they are discussed at length. These are extremely important issues, given the incontrovertible evidence that high-stakes assessment distorts the curriculum. A broad and balanced curriculum can thus easily be narrowed.

Interestingly, Murphy *et al.* (2001), in looking at effective science teaching in Year 6 classrooms, confirm that *the* most commonly accepted measure of effectiveness used by schools, local education authorities (LEAs) and government is the level of end of Key Stage test results. They argue that in the quest for this 'Holy Grail' two effective teaching models can be identified. The first is a teacher who might be described as a social constructivist (Light and Littleton, 1999; see Chapter 7, Section 1.3), seeing the relationship between members of the class, including the teacher, as collaborative. Here, even though the curriculum may be subject-structured, subject boundaries are often crossed by the teacher's approach as s/he looks at ways of making learning meaningful to the pupil by connecting knowledge that is presented in authentic contexts. The best of such teachers get very high end of Key Stage test results and, if it is really going well,

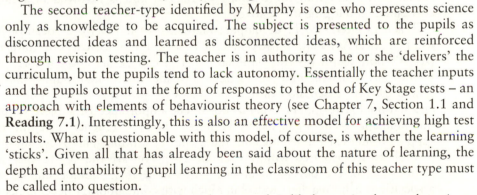

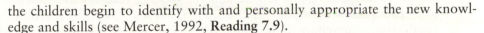

the children begin to identify with and personally appropriate the new knowledge and skills (see Mercer, 1992, **Reading 7.9**).

The second teacher-type identified by Murphy is one who represents science only as knowledge to be acquired. The subject is presented to the pupils as disconnected ideas and learned as disconnected ideas, which are reinforced through revision testing. The teacher is in authority as he or she 'delivers' the curriculum, but the pupils tend to lack autonomy. Essentially the teacher inputs and the pupils output in the form of responses to the end of Key Stage tests – an approach with elements of behaviourist theory (see Chapter 7, Section 1.1 and **Reading 7.1**). Interestingly, this is also an effective model for achieving high test results. What is questionable with this model, of course, is whether the learning 'sticks'. Given all that has already been said about the nature of learning, the depth and durability of pupil learning in the classroom of this teacher type must be called into question.

Further, the extent to which each approach is likely to stimulate and motivate pupils, and encourage them to see learning as important, must be a key consideration for any teacher. Most teachers, it will be realized, fall somewhere between the two ends of the continuum presented above, but it is clearly the responsibility of the reflective teacher to weigh these approaches in coming to a conclusion about an appropriate teaching methodology.

3.4 Professional support through subject associations

Despite the occasional problem of confidence, many teachers have worked hard to develop their subject knowledge. Some of the most exciting curriculum developments in recent years have come from subject-based initiatives, often resulting from networks of teachers meeting through national subject associations, or even international networks (perhaps accessed via the internet).

A steady stream of subject-related conferences, magazines, journals and books for teachers reflects the vigour and innovation of such associations. Here we present a brief review of the activities of just some, providing a flavour of the discussions of issues and sharing of expertise that take place through such groups.

Our first example, the Association for Science Education (ASE) provides a wide range of publications related to pedagogy, children's learning in science, assessment and subject knowledge. Bulletin boards allow professional dialogue between teachers, and between teachers and trainees. Membership of the association allows schools access to professional journals and to journals from linked associations – in the case of the ASE, these particularly consider health and safety issues. The opportunity to consider transition and progression across the Key Stages comes not only through such journals, but also through the annual nationwide and regular regional meetings.

The National Association for the Teaching of English (NATE) similarly aims to provide a national voice, in this case on key issues affecting English teaching. It encourages member participation in regional events, provides a newsletter and regular periodicals, access to a members area of their web site and an in-service programme. The annual conference of the association is a prestigious event that draws international interest. An important role of this, and other, subject associations is seeking and representing the views of teachers to national bodies, local education authorities, the DfES, OFSTED and QCA. In addition, NATE conducts research into the teaching of English and is involved in a range of curriculum development initiatives.

Teachers interested in developing mathematics have two associations – the Mathematical Association (MA) and the Association of Teachers of Mathematics (ATM). Both again provide national and regional events and support, publish periodicals, journals and newsletters, provide discounted publications, and encourage peer discussion on current issues to inform representations to local and national government organizations. The importance of subject support of this kind for teachers can hardly be over-estimated. Teachers give and receive support from their immediate colleagues with unstinting generosity, but it is still possible to feel isolated within a school when you are the key teacher who is responsible for the development of a curriculum area. Membership of subject associations helps teachers to feel in touch with contemporary developments and thus more confident in the assistance that they can provide to colleagues and to their school.

The Geographical Association (GA) has over 9000 members and is rightly proud of its influence on issues related to teaching and learning in Geography. It provides journals, books and other resources, curriculum advice, professional development and conferences. As with most associations it is a voluntary organization run by its members with a committee structure that encourages participation. Local involvement is strongly encouraged, and it is this opportunity for local networking on common issues that so attracts many members of this and other subject associations.

To end our examples (and here it is worth noting that references to other associations appear both at the end of this chapter and on **RTweb**) it is interesting to review a group that does not quite fit the subject association categorization, but which demonstrates the range of support that exists for the teacher. Micros and Primary Education (MAPE) is concerned with the effective use of ICT in primary schools, across subject boundaries. It provides publications, software, reviews, events and a web-site all serving this end, and as such is an invaluable resource for all teachers in primary schools.

Bramall and White (2000) point to how the agendas of subject associations offer a good fit with national agendas that emphasize subject-based curricula. This does not, however, invalidate their usefulness to teachers who may have broader concerns. Overall, in terms of innovation, application and specification of appropriate subject knowledge for primary schools, the subject associations offer rich resources on which to draw.

Phase-based associations are reviewed in Chapter 18, Section 3.

CONCLUSION

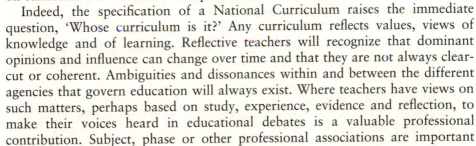

National curricula provide a significant means of attempting to fulfil national objectives and of attempting to provide coherence and progression in the learning of pupils. They also clarify the aims and role of teachers.

However, it is also worth highlighting the specific issue of inclusion/exclusion here. By the very act of setting out 'requirements', a 'framework' or a set of 'guidelines', the architects of national curricula prescribe particular content for teaching, study, learning and assessment. This material tends to cater for the majority, but must inevitably be more suitable and interesting for some children than for others. Children with particular special needs, or coming from particular backgrounds may not relate well to such curricula (see Chapter 9, Section 2.4 on curriculum relevance and Chapter 15 on social inclusion).

Indeed, the specification of a National Curriculum raises the immediate question, 'Whose curriculum is it?' Any curriculum reflects values, views of knowledge and of learning. Reflective teachers will recognize that dominant opinions and influence can change over time and that they are not always clear-cut or coherent. Ambiguities and dissonances within and between the different agencies that govern education will always exist. Where teachers have views on such matters, perhaps based on study, experience, evidence and reflection, to make their voices heard in educational debates is a valuable professional contribution. Subject, phase or other professional associations are important vehicles for this.

Nor should we forget the clarification with which we began this chapter. The official curriculum of any country is a very different thing from the whole curriculum, which includes the hidden curriculum, the observed curriculum and the curriculum-as-experienced by pupils. There is enormous scope for dilution, distortion, improvement, creativity, adaption and extension at every level of an education system (see Chapter 1, Section 2.7 and **Reading 1.4** on 'creative mediation').

In the next chapter we continue the focus on curriculum to attend to three major levels of curriculum planning – the whole school, the class programme and the lesson.

Key readings

An accessible history of the primary curriculum 1945–88 is provided by:

Cunningham, P. (1988)
Curriculum Change in the Primary School Since 1945: Dissemination of the Progressive Ideal.
London: Falmer.

An extremely helpful analysis of the debates and struggles around the establishment of the National Currriulum in England, raising important questions of democratic principle, is:

Ross, A. (1999)
Curriculum: Construction and Critique.
London: Routledge.

Alexander and his colleagues have continued to produce challenging analyses of primary education and primary teaching. These include:

Alexander R. J., Wilcocks, J., Kinder, K. and Nelson, N. (1995)
Versions of Primary Education.
London: Routledge.   📖 **Reading 8.9**

For an interesting philosophical overview of issues that are fundamental to the construction of the curriculum, see:

Bonnett, M. (1993)
Thinking and Understanding in the Primary School Curriculum.
London: Cassell.

An incisive review of the relationship between aims, values and structures in the National Curriculum for England is presented in:

Bramall, S. and White, J. (2000)
Will the New National Curriculum Live Up to its Aims?
(Impact policy discussion document No.6).
Ringwood: Philosophy of Education Society of Great Britain.

A wide-ranging comparative account of primary and elementary schooling in England, France, India, Russia and the United States, showing that we don't all do things the same way, is:

Alexander, R. (2000)
Culture and Pedagogy: International Comparisons in Primary Education.
Oxford: Blackwell.

Focusing on implementing a broadly constructivist approach in the classroom, Selley shows how, for the reflective teacher, this is compatible with highly structured national curricula. You might also want to consider how the curriculum is experienced by children:

Selley, N. (1999)
The Art of Constructivist Teaching in the Primary School.
London: David Fulton.

Pollard, A., Thiessen, D. and Filer, A. (eds) (1999)
Children and Their Curriculum: The Perspectives of Primary and Elementary School Pupils.
London: Falmer.

Shulman provided the classic text analysing key dimensions of subject knowledge, and the 'three wise men' (Alexander, Rose and Woodhead) reinforced a major change in policy when they asserted its importance:

Shulman, L. S. (1986)
'Those who understand: knowledge and growth in teaching',
Educational Researcher, **15**, 4–14.

Reading 8.6

Alexander, R., Rose, J. and Woodhead, C. (1992)
Curriculum Organisation and Classroom Practice in Primary Schools: a Discussion Paper.
London: Department of Education and Science.

Among many useful books on the role of subject knowledge in primary schools, and its implications for subject leadership, is:

Turner-Bisset, R. (2001)
Expert Teaching: Knowledge and Pedagogy to Lead the Profession.
London: David Fulton.

For a wonderful supply of subject ideas and innovation, see the regular flow of practical journals on various subjects for teachers in the UK. These include:

Teaching History and *Primary History* (The Historical Association)

Computer Education (Computer Users Group)

British Journal of Religious Education (Professional Council for Religious Education)

British Journal of Teaching Physical Education (Physical Education Association of the United Kingdom)

The Journal of Design and Technology Education (Design and Technology Association)

Reference to official web sites for UK countries that provide information about national curricula and links to subject knowledge, including ACCAC, QCA, NINE and LTScotland, can be found on **RTweb**.

Most specialist educational publishers also have useful series of books based on curriculum subjects for primary schools. For instance, in the UK see the catalogues of Continuum, Blackwell, David Fulton, Routledge, Falmer, Simon and Schuster, Open University Press, Paul Chapman Press, etc.

Readings for Reflective Teaching (the companion volume) offers other closely associated work on the issues raised in this chapter. This includes work by authors such as:

John Meyer, David Kamens, Basil Bernstein, the Plowden Committee, Lilian Katz, John Wilson, Lee Shulman, Lucy O'Hara, Mark O'Hara, the Labour Party and Robin Alexander.

RTweb offers additional professional resources for this chapter. These may include *Notes for Further Reading*, supplementary *Reflective Activities*, useful *Web Links*, *Extension Texts* and *Download Facilities* for diagrams, figures, checklists, activities.

CHAPTER 9

Planning. How are we implementing the curriculum?

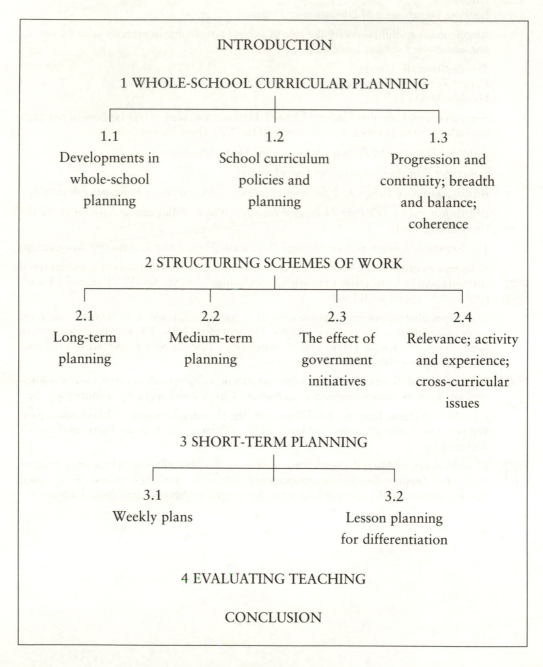

INTRODUCTION

1 WHOLE-SCHOOL CURRICULAR PLANNING

1.1
Developments in
whole-school
planning

1.2
School curriculum
policies and
planning

1.3
Progression and
continuity; breadth
and balance;
coherence

2 STRUCTURING SCHEMES OF WORK

2.1
Long-term
planning

2.2
Medium-term
planning

2.3
The effect of
government
initiatives

2.4
Relevance; activity
and experience;
cross-curricular
issues

3 SHORT-TERM PLANNING

3.1
Weekly plans

3.2
Lesson planning
for differentiation

4 EVALUATING TEACHING

CONCLUSION

Enhancing professional standards and competences

For hundreds of years, there has been controversy about the extent to which a curriculum should be based on socially approved subject knowledge or built up from the more direct experiences and interests of the pupils. Clearly, in practice, teachers will create some sort of inspired combination, but national requirements still differ in their emphasis.

In England, trainees must:

> set challenging teaching and learning objectives which are relevant to all pupils in their class. These must be based on knowledge of: the pupils; evidence of their past and current achievement; the expected standards of the relevant age range; the range and content of work relevant to that age range.

They must then:

> use these teaching and learning objectives to plan lessons and sequences of lessons, showing how they will assess pupils' learning, taking into account and supporting pupils' varying needs.
> (TTA, 2002, *Standards for the Award of QTS*, standard 3.1)

In Scotland, regarding competences relating to 'the subject and content of teaching', the student-teacher must:

> be able to justify what is taught from knowledge and understanding of the learning process, curriculum issues, child development in general and the needs of his or her pupils in particular.
> (Scottish Office, 1998, *Guidelines for Initial Teacher Education in Scotland*, competence 1.6)

However the dilemma is resolved (and requirements in Wales and Northern Ireland suggest slightly different solutions) imaginative but realistic curriculum planning is a very important teaching skill. If the children are highly motivated and engaged by the curriculum and the way it is presented to them, then other problems rapidly recede.

INTRODUCTION

This chapter has a three-level structure, focusing first on planning and implementing a curriculum for the whole school, then on the schemes of work of a single class, and finally on short-term planning and implementing particular teaching sessions. It thus moves through successive levels of detail, exactly in the way in which teachers or trainee teachers must when planning their teaching programme.

Lest this sound overly structured, we must once again affirm the uniquely enriching role of the creativity and imagination of individual teachers in providing high quality, responsive curriculum experiences for the pupils in their classes (Woods and Jeffrey, 1996, Moyles, 2001, **Reading 13.3**). Qualities of experience which may be produced – excitement, surprise, awe, spontaneity, concentration, humour, amazement, curiosity, expression, to name but a few – are enhanced by the dynamics of rapport and interaction between a teacher and his or her class. From the pupil's point of view, they are often what brings the curriculum 'alive'.

So, whilst attending to the necessary logic of planning within a National Curriculum framework (the *science* of curriculum planning?), we must not lose sight of the unpredictable and uniquely enriching human relationships through which it is manifest (the *art* of teaching?). Chapter 6, on classroom relationships, is particularly relevant here.

Reflective teachers are likely to aim to carefully address the structured aspects of curriculum provision, but with a view to this enabling them to interact with the children more empathically and responsively. When it comes to implementation, a *combination* of structure and responsiveness is likely to be most effective (see, for instance, **Reading 5.3** by Woods or **Reading 9.5** by Bennett). The key judgement, which only the teacher on the spot can make, is what particular combination and form of structure and response is most appropriate.

It is also important to say, at the outset, that whilst this chapter is concerned with the implementation of the curriculum within given national frameworks, there are alternative conceptions of the curriculum of which it is useful for the reflective teacher to be aware. Perhaps the most important is that of early childhood educators, such as Katz (1998, **Reading 8.4**), who argue that the developmental appropriateness of the curriculum is at least as important as rigorous plans for the delivery of subject matter. In Wales, 'desirable outcomes' for young children (ACCAC, 1996, **Reading 9.3**) convey this with flair and wholeheartedness. Eisner (1996) and Egan (1992) present further alternatives to the school reform route that has been taken in the UK in recent years.

Perhaps the most robust and concise statement of key principles in curricular planning is HMI's classic *The Curriculum from 5 to 16* (1985, **Reading 9.1**), and its logic underlies this chapter.

This chapter offers eight *Reflective Activities* designed to help with curriculum planning and implementation. **RTweb** offers many more.

1   WHOLE-SCHOOL CURRICULAR PLANNING

1.1   Developments in whole-school planning

Whole-school curriculum planning has become of enormous significance with the advent of national curricula and the concern for curriculum progression and coherence. Teachers' responsibility for selecting the curriculum at a classroom level has been reduced in favour of co-ordinated whole-school work, within a national framework. It is very important for trainee teachers to recognize this, for the implication is that any planning for work in classrooms *must* take account of the overall curriculum planning of the school (Boyd and Loyd, 1995).

In England and Wales, planning at a whole-school level seems to have gone through three phases. An *adaption phase* when the National Curriculum was new, characterized by the key strategy of 'mediation' of the initial, over-loaded and incoherent National Curriculum (Croll, 1996). Here, the programmes of study of the National Curriculum were grafted onto, and mapped against, existing practices. An *adoption phase* only became fully possible after 1995 with the availability of the revised National Curriculum following a holistic review (Dearing, 1993). With a 'moratorium' on further changes until 2000, it was possible for curriculum provision to become more embedded in schools. However, in more recent years an *extension phase* can be identified incorporating curricular initiatives such as the Literacy and Numeracy strategies and the Qualification and Curriculum Authority's Schemes of Work (DfEE, 1998b; 1999).

1.2 School curriculum policies and planning

Irrespective of national requirements, curriculum planning is likely to be influenced by the overall philosophy of the school. Good practice is to tie this in with the process of school improvement planning (see Chapter 17) and with consultations with school governors, who have legal responsibility for the school curriculum. In 1995, the now superseded School Curriculum and Assessment Authority provided very useful advice on curriculum planning across the primary school. This analysis of long-, medium- and short-term planning was taken up by OFSTED and still provides professionals with a clear review of the different levels of planning (SCAA, 1995, p. 10; OFSTED, 1999). Historically, an important decision in any consideration of the organization of the primary curriculum has been when to use an integrated or semi-integrated topic-based approach and when to plan by subjects. In the early years of the National Curriculum, Alexander, Rose and Woodhead (1992) challenged primary-school teams to confront this issue directly. As we saw in Chapter 8, the evolution of this debate has meant that planning by subjects – particularly at Key Stage 2 but also at Key Stage 1 – has become increasingly the norm as the National Curriculum (QCA, 1998a) has moved through successive phases of development and as curriculum initiatives have been introduced by government.

Figure 9.1 provides a model of the links between policies the subsequent levels of curriculum planning. We will consider these levels in more detail, after a brief consideration of policy statements and a definition of the term 'scheme of work'.

Curriculum policies

Policy statements are intended to act as a simple statement of purpose and framework for action, with regard both to curriculum subjects and to other aspects of the life of the school (e.g. special educational needs and equal opportunities). They need not be long but must be endorsed by school governors, with dates set for review by the governing body. Obviously they do need to reflect the overall school philosophy. Very often policy statements amount to single A4 sheets with simple, standard headings such as:

- Rationale
- Purposes
- Guidelines.

Policy statements provide for an input from governors without involving them in implementation detail.

Aims and values of the curriculum
Nationally derived, institutionally adopted and adapted by
the school.

⇓

Policies: subject, cross-subject and management-based
Providing purposes, rationale and broad guidelines.
Regular review by school staff and governors.

⇓

Long-term plans
Broad framework of curricular provision.
Coverage of curriculum subjects, review of 'blocked' and
'continuing' units of work.

⇓

Medium term plans
Detailing objectives, activities, assessment opportunities
and resource/health and safety considerations for termly/
half-termly units of work. Inclusion of cross-curricular
considerations.

⇓

Weekly plans
Providing an overview of the 'curriculum in action' across
curriculum subjects.

⇓

Lesson plans
Providing lesson objectives, procedures, differentiation
strategies and assessment criteria.

⇓

Assessment and evaluation
Feeding back into all levels of planning and informing
policy change.

Figure 9.1 *School philosophy, policies, schemes of work and teacher planning*

Schemes of work

Schemes of work can be thought of as encompassing the long-, medium- and short-term planning of a school (OFSTED, 1999). They should incorporate the programmes of study of the National Curriculum, and set out to describe how the curriculum should be taught by the staff team. Schemes of work may well draw on non-statutory guidance or other resources, and are frequently modified in the light of both experience and curriculum initiatives. A key intention is that well-structured schemes of work should give a clear view of how progression and continuity in learning is provided through the school.

It is recommended that each scheme of work, within the appropriate elements of long-, medium- and short-term planning, should address four basic issues:

- *What do we teach?* To outline knowledge, concepts, skills and attitudes to be developed, links between subjects and cross-curricular elements.

- *How do we teach?* To cover how the curriculum and learning processes are to be organized, units of work, learning activities and processes, forms of grouping to provide differentiation, resources needed, time allocations and opportunities for assessment.

- *When do we teach?* To address the issues of curriculum continuity and progression throughout appropriate key stages.

- *How do we know that children are learning?* Methods and plans for monitoring progress and attainment, and for setting future learning targets.

From these issues, a degree of consensus has emerged in recent years about key features of high-quality whole-school planning. Many of these originated in early work by HMI (DES, 1985a), and some have been heavily promoted in the UK by government. Principally these are:

- Progression and continuity
- Breadth and balance
- Coherence.

Others remain very significant in the judgement of many teachers, but have been less prominent in official documents. These include relevance, cross-curricular issues and the nature of activity/experience and are the focus of Section 2.4 in this chapter.

In Section 1.3 we will consider briefly the issues of progression; breadth, balance and continuity; and coherence. In Section 2 we will see how these features of planning relate to long-, medium- and short-term plans. Prior to this, however, a consideration of Reflective Activity 9.1 will provide practical examples that will form a basis for reflection throughout the chapter.

Reflective activity 9.1

Aim: To investigate the approach to whole-school curriculum planning in your school.

Evidence and reflection: Insights on this are likely to come from two main sources – documents and discussion. Begin by studying available policy statements and schemes of work – it *may* be sensible to do this for just one subject area. Then ask the headteacher if she or he could talk to you about how whole-school planning has taken the form which it does and how they see it evolving. Write a concise summary of the position.

Extension: Consider what the implications of the approach to whole-school planning are for you. How does it and will it impact on your plans for classroom teaching?

1.3 Progression and continuity; breadth and balance; coherence

The concepts reviewed in this section derive from HMI (DES, 1985a, **Reading 9.1**) which identified key issues in curriculum planning. In recent years, the English curriculum has narrowed and become increasingly subject based, with the result that concepts such as 'balance' and particularly 'relevance' seem less important (see also Section 2.4 of this chapter). This framework has however continued to be influential elsewhere in the UK. The Welsh Framework for the Whole Curriculum (CCW, 1991) was directly underpinned by such concepts, and Scotland's 5 to 14 Curriculum continues to offer considerably more breadth, balance and relevance than the English equivalent (see Scottish Executive, 2000a, **Reading 9.2**)

Progression and continuity. The concepts of progression and continuity in provision highlight the intended, cumulative outcomes which a planned curriculum is expected to produce: the expectation is that children should make progress in their learning, should build on and integrate their knowledge so that they deepen their understanding and skills.

The sequencing of tasks within the curriculum raises several issues depending, as we saw in Chapter 8, on our view of knowledge and our view of how children learn. At a classroom level, it is possible to be more specific and more flexibly responsive to the evolving understanding of the children we teach. Nevertheless, careful planning is an essential rock upon which such responsiveness can be built.

Breadth and balance. As we also saw in Chapter 8, the requirement that the curriculum in England and Wales should be broad and balanced is set out in the Education Reform Act, 1988. This can be interpreted in its widest sense, with reference to 'spiritual, moral, cultural, mental and physical development' and preparing pupils for 'the opportunities, responsibilities and experiences of adult life'. This suggests that breadth and balance in a pupil's learning experiences should not be seen reductively. Taken seriously, breadth and balance address holistic questions about educational provision. The statutory curriculum contributes an important part, but should not be seen as the whole educational experience.

Whilst acknowledging the above, the creation of national curricula usually involves the prioritizing of particular subject matter as more or less important. The 'core' and 'foundation' approach taken with the introduction of the National Curriculum for England and Wales is testament to this, and the introduction of the Literacy and Numeracy strategies (DfEE, 1998b; 1999) has clearly defined these as priorities within the curriculum. In an important sense, then, the current statutory curriculum of the primary school might be seen as very far from balanced.

> ### Reflective activity 9.2
>
> *Aim*: To evaluate an individual child's curricular experiences over one day.
>
> *Evidence and reflection*: Identify a child for detailed observation. Record the major curriculum activities in which he or she engages during this period. You might do this by briefly recording the following:
>
> Time activity started/ended
>
> Curriculum subject (English, History, etc.)
>
> Curriculum activity (reading, task completion, independent study, painting, etc.)
>
> *Extension*: What kind of breadth and balance exists in the observed curriculum of your target child? Is any action or curriculum adjustment necessary?

Coherence. Coherence refers to the extent to which the various parts of a planned curriculum actually relate meaningfully together. The opposite would be fragmentation.

Clearly this is an important issue if we conceive of learning as a process of 'making sense' (Haste, 1987), for that process calls for understanding at overall levels as well as in more detail. Indeed, Gestalt psychologists such as Koh and Lewin established the enormous significance which developing an over-arching understanding and frame of reference has on learning.

Coherence is often sought across subjects and this, of course, has been a prime goal of integrated curricula. However, coherence is also necessary, and is not assured, within *single* subjects. In this respect, as we saw in Chapter 8, it is likely to be associated with the extent of subject confidence and expertise of the teacher.

Some research has shown that people tend to enjoy and value learning more when they understand it as a whole. Rather than experience anxiety, or bewilderment from fragmented experiences, they feel more in control and are more willing to think independently and take risks. Whilst perceptions of incoherence can lead to feelings of frustration and strategies such as withdrawal, coherence leads to satisfaction and engagement. Coherence is only partially amenable to planning, for it derives its force from the sense, or otherwise, which the children make of the curriculum which is provided. Thus, whilst consideration of coherence at the planning stage is obviously important, we have chosen to focus Reflective Activity 9.3 on the actual *reception* of the curriculum by children. This data will bring us far greater awareness of the 'curriculum-as-experienced', allowing us to consider adaptations that may be appropriate.

Reflective activity 9.3

Aim: To investigate the coherence which a planned curriculum has for children.

Evidence and reflection: We suggest that the technique of concept mapping is ideal for gathering data on this issue (see Chapter 14, Section 2.3 and 2.4). You will have to focus the children's thoughts on a small area of the curriculum on which you have worked with your class or group. When they have identified the content, pay particular attention to the connections which they draw, or fail to draw, between the parts. Discuss this with them.

Extension: To what extent do you feel curriculum coherence was reflected in the attitudes and learning strategies of the children?

2 STRUCTURING SCHEMES OF WORK

2.1 Long-term planning

Long-term plans should provide a broad framework of curricular provision for each year of each key stage. For each year group they should specify the broad content to be taught, organize that content into manageable and coherent units of work and identify links between different aspects of curricular provision. They should allocate notional time to teach and assess work and should sequence work into three terms (see SCAA, 1995). Units of work are sometimes referred to as 'blocked' or 'continuing'. Blocked units occupy a particular time period (from a week to a term), whilst continuing units are ongoing (such as work associated with the first Science Attainment Target, Scientific Enquiry).

In providing an overview of coverage of the school curriculum, including the National Curriculum and religious education, long-term planning thus begins to address progression, breadth, balance, continuity and coherence, both within and between subjects. It is an essential stage in planning that forms a bridge between policy and practice.

Long-term plans are often presented as a collection of curriculum matrices. It should be noted, however, that the systematic appearance of such matrices can sometimes provide a poor representation of the reality of provision, particularly where there are overlaps and connections between subjects.

It is essential that the whole teaching staff of a school, led by senior management and subject specialists, is involved in revising long-term planning. Teacher trainees are unlikely to be centrally involved in such revisions, but should become familiar with schools' long-term plans as a means of 'placing' their own teaching in the context of their pupils' previous and planned future curricular experiences.

It should be noted here that the planning procedures and structures for the curriculum of the Foundation Stage are very different from those outlined in this section and in subsequent sections. An initial insight into this difference can be gleaned from even a cursory reading of *Curriculum Guidance for the Foundation*

Stage (QCA/DfEE, 2000). Perhaps the key distinction is between the planning *of* activities in Key Stages 1 and 2, and planning *for* a wide range of child-initiated activities in the Foundation Stage.

2.2 Medium-term planning

Medium-term plans are usually plans for each curriculum area that outline in detail what is to be achieved over a half term or term. Sometimes these plans will cover a shorter period (e.g. in the case of shorter discrete topics for younger children). They are the teacher's essential tool for explaining how the work to be undertaken during the term fits together and addresses the educational needs of the children in the class.

This level of planning is usually undertaken by class teachers, individually or in teaching teams, supported by subject specialists. It is updated, as with all planning, on the basis of the analysis of assessment data, teachers' views on the quality of activities and changes in school or year group organization. For each unit of work the medium-term plans will usually provide detail with respect to the following:

Class/subject details. Brief details are needed, stating the year group, Key Stage, the term in which the work will be carried out, and the subject/curriculum areas encompassed in the plan. Medium-term plans are invariably shared with the headteacher and a range of colleagues; these details allow them to quickly key-in to the nature of the document.

Learning objectives. Objectives express what we intend that the pupils learn in terms of skills, knowledge and understanding. They are the *essential* planning tool of the teacher, as without clear, concise objectives linked to specific activities, the teacher has little basis on which to define the purpose of a task clearly for the pupils, or assess pupil progress. Though it is not the only way, it is sometimes helpful to write objectives as 'Pupils should be able to . . .' statements, as this indicates, to some extent, intended outcomes. For example, in a session on material science for Year 2 pupils, objectives might be expressed as follows.

Pupils should be able to :
- use all appropriate senses in grouping a random 'rubbish bin' of materials – *skills*
- express the fact that some materials are shiny and may be grouped together – *knowledge*
- express an understanding of the reflective nature of shiny materials – *understanding.*

It should be noted that one learning objective may relate to a number of activities.

National curriculum links. Usually coded to indicate subject, section of the programme of study (see Chapter 8), paragraph and statement, the links show how long-term plans link to the teaching programme devised through medium-term planning.

Activities. This section indicates what the pupils will be doing in order to satisfy the objectives stated elsewhere in the medium-term plan. Only a very brief description of activities is required at this stage of planning, and it is important for teachers to consider whether activities are appropriately varied and therefore likely to maintain pupil interest. Bennett *et al*. (1984) analyse activities in five categories that remain useful in judging whether activities are appropriately varied:

- *Incremental*, where new learning is the key objective.
- *Practice*, where familiar ideas are rehearsed.
- *Restructuring*, where familiar materials and ideas are applied in considering new ways to look at familiar problems.
- *Enrichment*, where existing ideas are applied to new circumstances.
- *Revision*, where existing knowledge and concepts are reviewed.

At this stage of planning the teacher may wish to indicate how some activities are to be differentiated for different year groups or ability groups in the same class.

Caution is needed at this stage of planning over the number of tasks set for practice. What are pupils learning through such tasks, cognitively or affectively? Practice tasks may be useful in confirming knowledge or skills, but one needs to consider at what point such tasks might cease to increase confidence and instead cause frustration. In Bennett's study, the percentage of practice tasks was even higher when examined in terms of how the tasks were perceived and performed by the children. This was particularly so for high ability children, who were often set tasks intended as incremental or enrichment, but which, in fact, involved yet more practice.

Reflective activity 9.4

Aim: To consider the nature of activities in medium term plans.

Evidence and reflection: Consider the activities presented in two medium-term plans, either for your own class or for a specific age range; you may wish to use the QCA or other official schemes of work for this purpose. What is the balance of activity? Is there a preponderance of practice tasks? Are activities incremental in terms of pupil learning? Are the suggested activities likely to enthuse and motivate pupils?

Extension: Which activities would you replace, what with, and why?

Thus, in planning activities, a reflective teacher should consider that tasks of each type are probably necessary if learning is to develop positively and surely. As we saw in Chapters 7 and 8, increases in learning do not necessarily occur in a smooth, ever-upward fashion. If learning progresses in somewhat unpredictable developments of insight and understanding then occasional plateaus may also be experienced and needed. A reflective teacher needs to monitor activities closely to try to ensure the best balance between boredom from too easy tasks, frustration from tasks that are too hard, comfort from consolidation tasks and

excitement from tasks that are challenging but not too daunting. This theme is extended in discussing differentiation in lesson planning in Section 3.2.

Key assessment opportunities. At this stage it is only really appropriate, or possible, to consider broadly what might be assessed for particular activities – e.g. products of work, discussion responses – and whether there are to be specific tasks that are included for assessment and target setting purposes (see Chapter 14). Where it is clear that specific evidence will need to be collected and recorded, this should be noted. The teacher may wish to include reference to how previously indicated differentiated activities are to be assessed. Essentially, however, this is the point at which the key learning objectives for the unit of work are decided upon, and where some initial thought is given to assessing these objectives.

Resources/risk assessments. In a medium-term plan, only the main resources required for the unit of work should be indicated. It is particularly important to note those resources that need to be acquired from outside the school, such as library loans, museum artefacts, etc. Resources, in the form of equipment, apparatus, artefacts and media, are a means of deepening, enriching and broadening the curriculum through providing first-hand experiences. Artefacts can be brought into the classroom or children can be taken out on visits. Radio, television and multimedia information and communications technology (ICT) resources can play a role in providing vicarious first-hand experience. This at least allows each pupil to see and to indirectly experience other environments. In planning a classroom curriculum, then, some attention should be paid to the practical resource implications.

All resources call for particular skills from pupils if they are to be used successfully to develop learning. For example, children need to learn how to listen actively to explanations, to look carefully at objects or television, to read books actively and to set up investigations so that they can 'make knowledge their own' and develop strategies for learning. Different resources have particular implications for the curriculum-as-experienced and for the skills, attitudes, knowledge and concepts which are likely to be developed through them. Resources should thus be seen to support a curriculum rather than as a means by which it is selected (see Clegg and Billington, 1994, **Reading 10.2**).

With respect to health and safety, it is essential that all such issues are briefly noted at this stage of planning. This includes both issues for the teacher to note and explicit safety issues that will be raised with the pupils. Advice is available from professional organizations, particularly with respect to work in such curriculum subjects as science (Association for Science Education, 1994) and design and technology (NAAIDT, 1992).

Cross-curriculum considerations. In addition to these essentials, medium-term plans should also briefly refer to a range of whole- and cross-curricular issues that place the plan in a wider learning context. Where objectives and activities have an *explicit* link to pupils' spiritual, moral, social and cultural education then this should be indicated; for example, where work in history or geography allows a broader consideration of other cultures. Links with the non-statutory guidance on personal, social and health education, and on citizenship, should also be made clear at this point in planning. In addition, connections with medium-term plans for different subject areas should be shown. Increasingly, reference is made in medium-term planning to the key skills outlined in National Curriculum documentation (e.g. QCA, 1998b, p. 20–1).

Though ICT may well form the basis of a separate medium-term plan, the intention is that it should be 'used across the curriculum' (Ager, 2000; Bonnett, McFarlane and Williams, 1999). As such, specific reference to the use of ICT in enhancing learning in specific subject areas must be included in the relevant medium-term plans. Such references should include a note of appropriate National Curriculum ICT statements.

2.3   The effect of government initiatives

In the context of the curriculum in England, the non-statutory Literacy and Numeracy strategies and the Qualification and Curriculum Authority's Schemes of Work (DfEE, 1998b; 1999, and onwards) are of central importance. They provide an example of how additions to national curricula can extend the centralized control of the day-to-day school curriculum by governments. This is not to say that such non-statutory initiatives are necessarily unhelpful, though Davies and Edwards (2001) refer to the work of Stenhouse (1983) to pose the question of whether the literacy and numeracy hours 'could be seen as the pedagogical equivalents of painting by numbers' (p. 137). The scope for the imposition of such initiatives is, however, undoubtedly greater in the context of the operation of national curricula.

Within the Literacy Strategy, work at the word, sentence and text level is defined for each term for each year group. Training material for teachers recommends an approach to medium-term planning that uses the rigidly defined material in the Literacy folder to develop continuous and blocked units of work for phonics, vocabulary and spelling; grammar and punctuation; comprehension and composition; and texts. Here, the reflective teacher needs to be imaginative in developing contexts for the work in literacy, and in using texts in such a way that appropriate links can be made to work in other subjects of the curriculum. Advice proliferates about ways to use subject texts in the Literacy Hour, and how to promote literacy objectives through work in a range of subjects (e.g. Parkin and Lewis, 1998).

The Numeracy Strategy features a rather different approach. Key objectives and a teaching programme for each year group are defined, and these are supported by supplements of examples for different year groups that include objectives, possible activities and suggested outcomes. In many schools this material is reorganized so that it is coherent for the purposes and circumstances of the school (e.g. taking into account mixed-age classes) and is used as the medium-term planning for mathematics. This is possible both because of the level of detail included in the Numeracy Strategy folder, and because the strategy is a 'framework for teaching mathematics from Reception to Year 6'. It includes the whole curriculum for mathematics, in contrast to the Literacy Strategy, which leaves significant areas of English still to be incorporated into planning.

Perhaps one of the most significant features of these initiatives in preparing medium-term plans for other subjects has been the amount of curriculum time that they absorb. In the context of the National Curriculum, trying to satisfy the demands of curriculum coverage and the time demands of the Literacy and Numeracy 'hours' has meant that teachers have had to be creative in ensuring an appropriate mix of activity types both within and across subjects. As Galton *et al.* (1999, p. 181) point out, 'the current requirements to devote nearly half of the week to mathematics and language, while at the same time providing adequate coverage of the remainder of the curriculum, including the arts, sharpens the dilemma experienced by headteachers' (see also **Reading 13.1**).

> ### Reflective activity 9.5
>
> *Aim*: To review medium-term planning for literacy and numeracy.
>
> *Evidence and reflection*: Compare the medium-term planning for literacy and numeracy in one class with the same level of planning for the other curriculum subjects in the same class. Are there features of planning in literacy, numeracy or the other curriculum subjects that are unique? Are there features of planning in one of these areas that really should be incorporated into the medium-term planning for the other areas?
>
> *Extension*: Established teachers should bring any issues raised by this review process to the attention of the whole staff for consideration. Trainee teachers should discuss their conclusions with their school mentor.

In Section 1.2, some key features of whole-school planning were referred to, and progression, breadth, balance, continuity, and coherence have been given some consideration. In the light of the above discussion, it is now appropriate to consider relevance, activity/experience, and cross-curricular issues.

2.4 Relevance; activity and experience; cross-curricular issues

Of vital importance in the selection of content is 'relevance'. Here, the term is used to emphasize the importance of the curriculum making connections, in meaningful ways, with pupils' previous experiences. In a way then, it has resonances with child-centred ideas and this is, perhaps, why it was derided by some right-wing groups and was absent from government documentation in the early years of the English National Curriculum – though it remained a serious consideration elsewhere in the UK. This concern is now becoming more prominent again, for there is no doubt whatsoever that children learn most effectively when they understand the purposes and context of the tasks and challenges with which they are faced (see also Chapter 8, Section 2.2 on inclusion, and Chapter 7, Section 2.5 on motivation). Of course, relevance also refers to that which is 'useful' and has an instrumental, practical function. It can be used in a short-term or a long-term context. However it is used, it relates to meaningfulness and 'worthwhileness', from the learner's point of view.

When a pupil complains that an activity is 'pointless', is 'boring' or that they 'don't see what it's for', then the curriculum is failing to satisfy the criterion of relevance. Motivation may fall and with it may go concentration, commitment and quality (see Pollard *et al.*, 2000, **Reading 7.11**). The standard of work is thus likely to decrease unless the teacher can justify the activity and bolster motivation. Indeed, even when an activity could have great relevance, this may not have been explained to or appreciated by the children. One long-running finding regarding teaching has been that, very often, pupils have not known why they are doing an activity.

Reflective activity 9.6

Aim: To explore the extent to which sharing learning objectives, and making connections between work in different subjects, influences feelings of relevance for the pupil.

Evidence and reflection: The simple method here is to ask the pupils.

Having taught a lesson, or seen one taught (pupils will often 'open up' more to someone who is not their own teacher), select a small group of children – ask them some or all of the following:

- What was the lesson mainly about?
- What did they think that they were supposed to be learning?
- Do they see any connections with other work that they have done in the same subject?
- Do they see any connections with work that they have done in other subjects?
- Did they enjoy the lesson?

Extension: Review what you have learned about the pupils' views. Share your findings with the class teacher if they were not 'your' pupils. What are the implications for the future?

The key consideration here is the value of incorporating practical activities and first-hand experience into the teaching programme. The value of such experiences has been taken to lie in the opportunity it provides for children to interact directly with learning apparatus, real materials and events in their lives. As we saw in Chapter 7, such an emphasis is again founded on psychology and on a view of learning as the product of interaction between teaching and experience. For instance, in infant classes an enormous amount of language, mathematics, art and science development can be derived from children's play in media such as sand, water and clay. Older children benefit from more structured direct experiences, such as carrying out fair tests and investigations in science, field work in geography and investigation of artefacts in history (see Hunter and Scheirer, 1988). All children also benefit from being able to make connections between their experiences out of school and those within it, hence the importance of home–school partnerships.

Use of the children's immediate environment for providing experiences is practical but may need monitoring, for it has been suggested that over-dependence on the locality might result in limiting the children to that environment and thus in creating a rather parochial curriculum. On the other hand, it can be argued that children may be able to relate meaningfully to an environment with which they can identify. They can be helped to examine it more closely, to value what they have around them, and then be helped to move from the familiar to the unfamiliar.

In any event, the incorporation of activity and direct experience, in proportions and ways which are appropriate to the age of the pupils, is an essential part of any curriculum provision. If this is ever doubted, try asking the pupils. One of the most consistent findings in pupil interviews is the liking for 'doing something interesting', which does not mean activities like the almost universally condemned 'writing'.

With respect to cross-curricular issues, a little has already been said about indicating appropriate subject links between medium-term plans. Wider than this, however, the topic takes us directly back to the debate about the value of focusing a curriculum on transferable skills and attitudes – a 'process oriented' curriculum. In terms of the National Curriculum, this debate has been placed in sharp focus by the developing emphasis on 'key skills' and 'thinking skills', with key skills defined as communication, application of number, information technology, working with others, improving own learning/performance and problem-solving, and thinking skills defined as information-processing skills, reasoning skills, enquiry skills and evaluation skills (QCA, 1998b, p. 20–2). Although subject-based curricula tend to narrow cross-curricular potential, the need to consider how such skills are developed through the curriculum as a whole presents clear challenges and opportunities for schools.

 Work where subject boundaries are sometimes broken down has exciting potential, for pupils are very often interested by cross-curricular themes (see for example, Siraj-Blatchford and Siraj-Blatchford, 1995; Webb, 1996). Indeed, this has been the foundation of 'topic work' approaches to curriculum planning to which reference was made in Chapter 8. With the current statutory influences on the structure of the curriculum, however, there are problems as well as possibilities in such work (Holden and Smith, 1992), including the risk that too great an emphasis on cross-curricular themes and links may produce an impractical and over-crowded curriculum (Campbell and Neill, 1992).

Looking rather more deeply, however, and referring back to the arguments in Chapter 8 that considered deriving the curriculum from its aims and values, it is clear that some elements of the National Curriculum are intended both to be the focus of specific teaching and also to inform and pervade the subject curriculum. Reflective Activity 9.7 asks you to consider this from the perspective of PSHE and Citizenship.

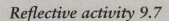

Reflective activity 9.7

Aim: To explore the extent to which themes linked to PSHE and Citizenship pervade the planning of the curriculum.

Evidence and reflection: Talk to a school colleague about your mutual understanding of how non-statutory guidance on PSHE and Citizenship should influence the school curriculum; if you are a trainee teacher, you might devise an interview schedule for a *willing* experienced teacher so that you can explore these ideas.

Extension: Compare the 'ideal' that has probably been arrived at through discussion with the practicality of what happens in the existing curriculum of the school. What are the differences? Why do they exist? Is it possible to move nearer to the 'ideal'?

3   SHORT-TERM PLANNING

3.1   Weekly plans

Increasingly, headteachers use weekly plans to gain an insight into the 'curriculum in action' in their schools. Where weekly plans are produced for each subject area, they tend to be quite brief, pulling information from the relevant medium-term plan and supplementing it with information concerning differentiation, grouping strategies, immediate resource implications, etc. Such plans are not a substitute for lesson plans – rather, the intention is that they should give an overview of the teaching programme in a class for a given week.

Teachers of younger children will find weekly planning particularly useful in considering the range and coherence of the experiences being offered, and in planning for staff to observe, support and extend children's play and other forms of learning.

Teaching of literacy and numeracy often receives particular attention in weekly plans. For experienced teachers, the combination of medium-term planning and these detailed weekly plans often provides enough detail for effective teaching and assessment. The trainee teacher, however, should use these levels of planning to produce lesson plans for each lesson, thereby developing and demonstrating a clear understanding of the core elements of a lesson – as outlined below.

3.2   Lesson planning for differentiation

Classroom learning sessions are central activities for teachers and learners. When devising lesson plans, reflective teachers will consider long- and medium-term plans, their classroom organizational strategies (including the use of colleagues), and practical considerations (such as the time-tabling of the hall). They will have some formative assessment information about their pupils so that specific objectives can be refined and differentiated. Against this background, a particular learning session can be planned effectively (Bennett 1992, **Reading 9.5**).

Of course, such plans provide a teacher with structure and security and it should not be forgotten that the resulting confidence can be used to be responsive to the children during the session. Good planning underpins *flexibility*.

Core elements of a lesson plan are likely to be:

Class and subject details. A short heading providing information about the class, grouping strategies, the date and duration of the lesson, and the subject/aspect being taught.

 Learning objectives. The importance of concise, clearly expressed objectives clearly linked to pupil tasks has been explored in Section 2.2. Here, it is important to note that too many objectives stated for any one lesson are likely to prevent a clear focus on the core learning that the teacher hopes will take place. The number of objectives should therefore be limited, and they should be shared with the pupils as one way of allowing them to be part of the process that is moving their learning forward.

National Curriculum (including, if appropriate, NLS/NNS) links. References should be transferred from medium-term planning, showing how the work to be undertaken links with the demands of the statutory curriculum.

Resources and safety. These factors should be defined in sufficient detail to ensure that all necessary resources can be acquired through operating a checklist system, and, more importantly, that the safety implications and associated teaching issues of a given activity are clearly defined.

Procedures. Here, the details of the lesson are concisely expressed. To indicate what might be included, it is worth asking the following questions about this section of any lesson plan:

- Are the pupil activities clearly expressed, giving sufficient detail for colleagues to follow?

- Is there a clear structure to the lesson? For example, is there a clear introductory and concluding section?

- Are the key teaching points apparent?

- Are key questions and vocabulary apparent, associated with appropriate points in the lesson?

- Is the teacher's role, and the role of supporting adults, clear for each part of the lesson?

- Are there opportunities for teacher modelling and scaffolding of pupil behaviours?

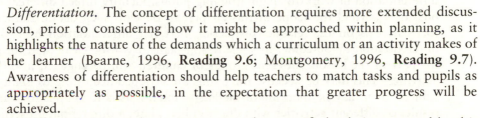

Differentiation. The concept of differentiation requires more extended discussion, prior to considering how it might be approached within planning, as it highlights the nature of the demands which a curriculum or an activity makes of the learner (Bearne, 1996, **Reading 9.6**; Montgomery, 1996, **Reading 9.7**). Awareness of differentiation should help teachers to match tasks and pupils as appropriately as possible, in the expectation that greater progress will be achieved.

Differentiation can be seen at a general or specific level. At a general level it relates to the appropriateness, or otherwise, of an activity for pupils with particular needs. Thus, for instance, the needs of young pupils are significantly different from those of older pupils and, for those at the Foundation Stage, their whole curriculum must be planned with this in mind (Anning, 1995; Hurst, 1992; QCA/DfEE, 2000). Similarly, the needs of pupils with special educational needs are very significant (Croll and Moses, 2000, **Reading 10.6**; Roaf and Bines, 1989, **Reading 15.5**). Those who are deemed 'gifted' may also need particular provision (Montgomery, 1996, **Reading 9.7**). Delivering a full National Curriculum in some circumstances is extremely difficult (Jones and Charlton, 1992) and through the statementing process (DFES, 2001) it may be necessary to 'disapply' parts of the curriculum where they are inappropriate.

At a more specific level, differentiation relates to the appropriateness, or otherwise, of particular tasks and activities. In investigating this match between pupil and learning task, four stages of analysis are implied:

- Understanding the perceptions and intentions of the teacher and the pupil
- Identifying the pupil's existing knowledge, concepts, skills and attitudes
- Observing the process by which the task is tackled
- Analysing and evaluating the product, or final outcome, of the task, so that future plans can be made.

A mismatch could occur at any (or all) of the stages. To take an example at the first stage, a teacher could set a task for a particular purpose, but, if it were not explained adequately then the pupil might misunderstand. Any task might be done 'wrongly', or it may be done 'blindly', i.e. without seeing the point of it. There could also be a mismatch at the second stage. The task may be too hard for a pupil because it requires certain knowledge or skill which they do not have. A mismatch at the third stage can be illustrated by a task which may be set with an instruction to use certain apparatus, or to present the outcome in a certain way. However, the apparatus may not be necessary and may actually confuse the pupil, or, the style of presentation may assume some skill which the pupil has not yet acquired.

Additional problems could also arise from a mismatch at the fourth stage. For instance, teachers often 'mark' the end product of children's learning. However, a high percentage of 'errors' cannot necessarily be assumed to relate to 'bad' work or 'poor' learning. Indeed, the 'errors' can be very important clues as to the learning that has taken place. In this respect they can be regarded as 'mis-cues' which indicate where misunderstandings may have occurred. (For more on evaluative issues, see Section 4 of this chapter and Chapter 14.)

At a practical level, differentiation strategies can be presented in lesson planning in various ways. In fact, Kerry and Kerry (1997), in discussing differentiation in work for high attaining pupils, identify fifteen different methods. It is beyond the scope of this chapter to develop such detail. Rather, the focus here is on the 'classic' distinction between differentiation by task and differentiation by outcome. In some lesson plans it will be clear that, for all or for part of the lesson, different groups of children will be engaged in different activities. This may be because the pupils are grouped according to ability in a subject, or it may be that one of the lesson intentions is for pupils to share the results of different activities with one another. Here, a differentiation section of a lesson plan would make clear not only the groups and activities, but also whether there were any differentiated objectives linked to specific groups and tasks. Alternatively, the procedures section of the lesson plan might be expanded so that differentiated tasks could be incorporated.

In differentiating by outcome, one possible approach is to define outcomes in terms of 'All will . . . Most will . . . Some will . . .' For example, for a Year 2 science lesson:

- All will be able to set up the investigation so that a fair test can occur.
- Most will be able to understand why some of the ramp materials allow the car to move faster than others.
- Some will be able to fully interpret the class graph results, identifying from the graph the surfaces that give the most and the least frictional resistance.

Such differentiated outcomes would naturally refer back to the learning objectives of the lesson.

Experience will show that the neat distinction between differentiation by task and outcome is, in reality, often blurred. For example, 'All will . . . Most will . . . Some will . . .' is sometimes used to define progressive tasks that can be worked through; or as staging posts, that allow the teacher to assess progress with respect to a given activity. For the reflective teacher, whatever the method of differentiation decided upon, the vital importance of differentiating lessons is that it is the way in which the teacher can respond to the enormous diversity of ability in any class. It allows a tailoring of learning experiences to the learner as far as is possible given the constraints under which schools and teachers operate.

ICT opportunities. If the inclusion of ICT elements in the lesson is not obvious in sections related to procedures or differentiation, a separate part of the lesson plan should indicate how ICT is to be used. It is worth re-emphasizing here that ICT should only be used in a lesson where it is the best way to promote learning. ICT should never be used as a cosmetic 'add on' (Bonnett, McFarlane and Williams, 1999; Kennelwell, Parkinson and Tanner, 2000, **Reading 9.8**).

Assessment criteria/focus. The issue of assessment is considered in detail in Chapter 14, and the use of assessment for the purposes of evaluation and future planning is examined in Section 4 of this chapter. However, it is important to reflect briefly on the importance of stated assessment intentions in lesson planning.

Assessment forms a vital element of every stage of planning. Without assessment and the consequent re-evaluation of planning that results, it is true to say that effective teaching cannot be maintained. At the level of the lesson plan, it is important that the teacher notes anticipated outcomes for the lesson, so that in interacting with pupils and in marking work clear criteria for success with respect to lesson objectives are borne in mind. For example, a lesson objective might be:

Pupils should be able to understand the operation of subtraction and the related vocabulary.

Within the assessment criteria/focus section of the plan, what the teacher is looking for as evidence of progress/success with respect to the objective should be briefly defined. Importantly, for a given objective, the anticipated outcomes will be influenced by the age of the pupils, by previous assessments of their capabilities, and by the precise nature of the activity. Thus, this objective is likely to lead to very different anticipated outcomes in a Year 1, Year 2 or Year 3 class.

Often outcomes are expressed in the form of questions from the teacher to her/himself. For example, anticipated outcomes for the above objective might lead to the following questions in a Year 2 lesson plan:

Do the pupils demonstrate in their work that subtracting zero leaves a number unchanged?

In discussion, do they demonstrate an understanding of the terms 'take away' and 'find the difference between'?

Importantly, this thinking done at the planning stage allows the teacher to share with the pupils not only the broad lesson objectives but also the specific expectations of activity targets and outcomes. If pupil involvement in assessing their own work is desirable, and Chapter 14, Section 1 argues strongly that it is, then this is a powerful tool in helping teachers to develop self-assessment as part of the pupil learning process (Clarke, 2001; Muschamp, 1994, **Reading 14.5**).

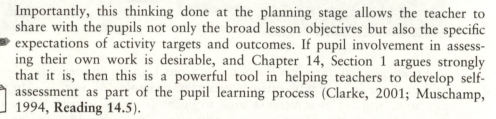

Reflective activity 9.8

Aim: To review existing lesson planning in the light of the above 'core elements'.

Evidence and reflection: For trainee teachers, we suggest that you select one lesson plan that you were responsible for creating (for this activity avoid using literacy and numeracy lesson plans that are linked to a school's existing weekly planning for these areas). Review the plan in the light of the 'core elements' defined in Section 3.2. Bearing in mind that lesson plans cannot be over-long, to what extent does your plan reflect adequate inclusion of these elements? What might be done to improve this specific plan, or the next plan in the teaching sequence?

Experienced teachers will agree that planning becomes more streamlined with experience. From an OFSTED perspective, however, clearly stated objectives, differentiation strategies and assessable outcomes remain key features that are looked for in any plan. Review some lesson plans over at least three curriculum areas. Are these features clear in your planning?

Extension: Compare your planning with that of another trainee or with another teacher in a different teaching team in your school. What are the similarities and differences? How might both sets of planning be improved?

Supporting adults. Whether it is a Learning Support Assistant (LSA), a volunteer parent or any one of a range of other adults who may be supporting work in the classroom, if such vital support is available to the teacher then the effectiveness of its use depends on careful planning. It is likely that the teacher will share the nature of lesson activities with any supporting adult, and make it clear which pupil or pupils should be the focus of their attention. However, it is also vital to share the learning intentions for an activity if the supporting adult is to play a full part in promoting learning (see Chapter 10, Section 2.3 and **Reading 10.7** for much fuller accounts of the effective use of adult learning support). Some teachers do this verbally, but many have a book to which supporting adults can refer that defines the lesson learning intentions, the activity and their role.

In a lesson plan it is important the teacher has briefly reviewed these issues. As with all sections of lesson plans, it is sometimes helpful to think 'how intelligible would this be to another teacher?'

4   EVALUATING TEACHING

Planning is not static. It is best seen as organic, in the sense that all plans, at whatever level, should be open to modification and change dependent upon their success in aiding the development of learning in the classroom. Specifically, long-term plans must be open enough to allow for interpretation in medium-term planning, and medium-term plans must allow for appropriate interpretation in short-term planning.

A reflective teacher is one who clearly understands the intimate links between the processes of planning, teaching and assessment (see Figure 1.5, Chapter 1 and Bennett, 1992, **Reading 9.5**). Thus, in considering the evaluation of lessons, it is possible to highlight many of the features of this cycle. The following questions are suggested by Scott-Baumann, Bloomfield and Roughton (1997) as a guide:

- What happened?
- What effect did it have?
- Why did it happen?
- How can I make sense of it?
- How could it be different?
- How might I (we) have behaved differently?
- What would I do next time?

Essentially, some of these questions focus more directly on the learner, whilst others focus primarily on the teacher. The teacher uses a range of evidence in assessing learning (see Chapter 14, Section 1), with the intention of ascertaining the next learning step for the groups and individuals in the class. Some evidence will be derived from discussion, questioning and observation and other evidence will result from an examination of pupils' work. In making formative assessments (Torrance and Pryor, 1998), brief lesson evaluations can form the basis of target-setting for future work for individuals. Hayes (1999) proposes that individual target setting, based upon pupil's ongoing classroom work, should be based on four principles:

- It must be specific
- It must be realistic
- It must take account of time factors
- It must be manageable.

Several ideas will be important from this discussion. First, the overall purpose of planning is to help in the process of developing pupil learning. Second, that planning must be open to modification and change on the basis of pupil responses. Finally, and as a result of these two ideas, we might note that it is unlikely that any 'authoritative' planning structure can specify content that will be equally appropriate for, say, all Year 5 pupils. A key task for the reflective teacher, therefore, is to regard planning as an aid to effective teaching that must be critically evaluated and flexibly interpreted at all times.

CONCLUSION

Curriculum planning is a highly skilled activity underpinned by understanding of key principles (HMI, 1985, **Reading 9.1**). It requires awareness of curriculum requirements at national level, of whole-school policies and team decisions and, not least, of the needs and interests of children. Subject expertise must then be combined with sound practical organization to deliver an interesting and appropriately challenging set of learning experiences. In the hands of a skilled and sensitive teacher, structure and purpose will be tempered by flexibility and intuition, and enriched by imagination and excitement.

Having completed our discussion of the principles of curriculum planning, a good link from this point would be to go directly to Chapter 14 on assessment. There is a lot of material there to support ongoing, formative classroom assessment as part of routine teaching. However, we have opted to trace our way there via other key elements of teaching – classroom organization, behaviour, communication, language and teaching strategies.

Key readings

For an official account of how planning, and all other aspects of the life and management of the school may be considered within a school inspection process, see:

OFSTED (1999)
Handbook for Inspecting Primary and Nursery Schools.
London: HMSO.

Providing an overview of the general principles of constructivist learning and teaching, Ager demonstrates how the idea of pupils' participation in their own learning need not be incompatible with working within the context of a National Curriculum:

Ager, R. (2000)
The Art of Information and Communications Technology for Teachers.
London: Fulton.

Drawing on the work of a range of authors, Bearne grapples with the difficult concepts and practicalities that inform differentiation practice within schools. Simpson offers an analysis of the implications for learning of different forms of differentiation:

Bearne, E. (ed.) (1996)
Differentiation and Diversity in the Primary School.
London: Routledge.   **Reading 9.6**

Simpson, M. (1997)
'Developing differentiation practices: meeting the needs of pupils and teachers',
The Curriculum Journal, 8 (1), 85–104.

Looking broadly across interrelated aspect of the primary teacher's role, Hayes includes useful material on planning and links this firmly to the cycle of planning, teaching and assessment:

Hayes, D. (1999)
Foundations of Primary Teaching.
London: Fulton.

In a thought-provoking chapter, Davies and Edwards consider the growing tendency for the government in England to exert control over pedagogy in order to deliver 'standards':

Davies, M. and Edwards, G. (2001)
'Will the curriculum caterpillar ever learn to fly?', in Collins, J., Insley, K., and Soler, J. (eds) *Developing Pedagogy*. London: Paul Chapman.

For a comprehensive whole-curriculum framework that makes constructive use of the concepts of breadth, balance, coherence, continuity and progression:

DES (1985a)
The Curriculum from 5 to 16.
HMI, Curriculum Matters Series.
London: HMSO.   **Reading 9.1**

For stimulating views on the principles that underpin curriculum planning and design, emphasizing radical alternatives to the school reform routes of recent years and stressing the engagement of children in learning, see:

Egan, K. (1988)
An Alternative Approach to Teaching and the Curriculum: Teaching as Storytelling.
London: Routledge.

Eisner, E. (1996)
Cognition and Curriculum Reconsidered.
London: Paul Chapman.

Readings for Reflective Teaching (the companion volume) offers other closely associated work on the issues raised in this chapter. This includes work by authors such as:

HMI, Scottish Executive, Curriculum and Assessment Authority for Wales, Marion Dadds, Neville Bennett, Eve Bearne, Diane Montgomery, Steve Kennelwell, John Parkinson and Howard Tanner.

RTweb offers additional professional resources for this chapter. These may include *Notes for Further Reading*, supplementary *Reflective Activities*, useful *Web Links*, *Extension Texts* and *Download Facilities* for diagrams, figures, checklists, activities.

CHAPTER 10

Organization. How are we managing the classroom?

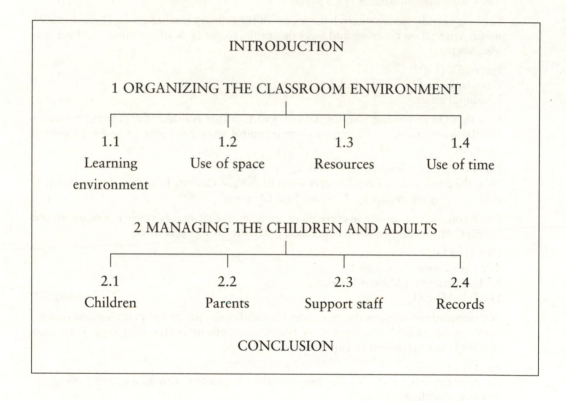

INTRODUCTION

1 ORGANIZING THE CLASSROOM ENVIRONMENT

1.1	1.2	1.3	1.4
Learning environment	Use of space	Resources	Use of time

2 MANAGING THE CHILDREN AND ADULTS

2.1	2.2	2.3	2.4
Children	Parents	Support staff	Records

CONCLUSION

Enhancing professional standards and competences

In this chapter you will find material which is related to a fairly common set of requirements in each part of the UK. For example, in Northern Ireland suggestions include the following. Student teachers should:

> Deploy a range of strategies to create and maintain a purposeful, orderly, safe and appropriate environment for learning. Manage play and activity-based learning when appropriate. Manage space effectively though awareness of a variety of classroom layouts.

> Be able to prepare appropriate learning material for pupils and make use of available resources. Manage his or her own time and that of the pupils effectively.

> Teach in whole-class, group, pair or individual modes as appropriate for particular learning experiences. Relate effectively with parents. Make effective use of non-teaching staff.
> (Northern Ireland Department of Education, *The Teacher Education Partnership Handbook*, competences 3.8, 3.9, 3.20, 3.22, 3.27, 3.28, 3.29, 5.7)

Inclusion is an important issue (see Chapter 15) and the English requirement states that those awarded QTS must demonstrate that they can:

> Take account of the varying interests, experiences and achievements of boys and girls, and pupils from different cultural and ethnic groups, to help pupils make good progress.
> (TTA, 2002, *Standards for the Award of QTS*, standard 3.3.6)

Whatever the ways in which classroom organization is described at particular points in time, it is intrinsic to effective teaching.

INTRODUCTION

Effective classroom management and organization is vital in implementing plans for learning. By this, we mean the way in which the classroom and class is structured in order to facilitate teaching and learning. For such teaching and learning to succeed, classroom organization and management strategies must relate to values, aims, requirements and curriculum plans as a whole and also to practical circumstances.

If an appropriate coherence can be achieved, then the teacher and the children should benefit from having a common framework within which to work. The strength of such a framework will derive from its internal consistency: (the mutual reinforcement of its elements), and its legitimacy (the negotiated agreement between the teacher and the children). This is strongly connected to the issue of developing good classroom relationships (see Chapter 6). Because of the interdependent nature of classroom elements it is important to remember that change made in one aspect is likely to affect others.

Having a clearly organized and managed classroom should not be taken to imply rigidity, for if the rules and routines of the classroom are clear and agreed, good organization can increase freedom for the teacher to teach and the learner to learn. In particular, it should give the teacher more time to diagnose children's learning difficulties; to design appropriate learning objectives; and to *teach* rather than having to spend time on 'housekeeping' aspects of routine classroom life (Hastings and Wood, 2001; Pollard *et al.*, 1994). One particularly memorable image of this has been offered by Campbell and Neill (1992) with their concept of 'evaporated time' – time lost to organizational trivia. They found that it took up about 10 per cent of all classroom time: the equivalent of one afternoon a week!

This chapter is organized in two parts. The first part considers how to organize and manage the classroom environment in terms of space, resources and time. The second part focuses on the management of children and adults to support learning. It concludes with a discussion of how records may be organized and used (see also Chapter 14, Section 4.1).

The *Reflective Activities* in this chapter are supplemented by others on **RTweb**.

1 ORGANIZING THE CLASSROOM ENVIRONMENT

1.1 Learning environment

Research by ecological psychologists (Bronfenbrenner, 1979; Gump, 1987; Pointon and Kershner, 2000) has suggested the importance of the quality of the environment and the fact that it can influence behaviour. Such research reinforces the view, which is commonly expressed by practitioners, that the environment in a primary-school classroom should be aesthetically pleasing; should stimulate children's interest; should set high standards in the display and presentation of children's work; and should be created in such a way that it is practical to maintain (Clegg and Billington, 1994, **Reading 10.2**; Cooper *et al.*, 1996). Moyles (1995, **Reading 10.1**) extends these concerns further to include issues such as 'rights, responsibilities and rules' (see Chapter 6).

Reflective teachers may also aim to structure the environment so that opportunities are taken to reinforce their overall purposes. They should be able to develop their classroom environment by considering the questions in Checklist 10.1

1.2 Use of space

The way a teaching space is organized has considerable impact on the kind of teaching that can happen, the attitude of the learners and the quality of learning. Space in a classroom is always limited; yet what space there is must be utilized in such a way that the wide-ranging activities which form essential elements of the primary-school curriculum can occur without major disruptions. For example, initiatives such as the National Literacy Strategy require rapid shifts between whole-class teaching and group work, with associated implications for

Checklist 10.1

Aim: To examine the classroom environment.

1. *Design*. What are the main design features of the room and how do they affect its aesthetic feel?

2. *Possibilities*. What are the possibilities for display (in two and in three dimensions) on walls, on windows, on flat surfaces, off the ceiling? What are the possibilities for plants or animals? Is work displayed in a variety of media? Is it mobile or static?

3. *Purposes*. Do the displays stimulate and inform? Do they provide opportunities for children to interact with them, for example, by posing questions; inviting their participation in a quiz or problem-solving challenge; offering alternative viewpoints to consider; encouraging the children to touch/smell/taste as well as look and listen? Further, do displays only show finished products or do they also reveal processes, which might be used for discussion, sharing problems, giving mutual support and advice?

4. *Quality*. Is the standard of mounting, writing and display such that it shows that the children's work is valued? Does it provide a model which children may apply to their own work?

5. *Practicality*. Is the classroom environment as practical as it can be to maintain? How often is it necessary to change displays? Do the children mount their own displays? Can children help with classroom jobs such as watering plants and feeding pets?

seating arrangements in the classroom. The possible introduction of interactive whiteboards and personal laptop computers in classrooms also creates different demands on classroom space (see for example the introduction to McFarlane, 1997. Organizing space requires a considerable amount of thought. A first step is to produce a planning tool, such as a classroom plan (see Reflective Activity 10.1), with which the existing constraints and the possibilities of the room and furniture can be explored.

Reflective activity 10.1

Aim: To produce a classroom plan.

Evidence and reflection: A simple plan should be made of the fixed points in the classroom – walls, windows, doors, sinks, pegs, etc. If squared paper is used, it is relatively easy to produce a plan to scale.

Major existing items of furniture should be represented on card and to the same scale as the classroom plan.

The 'furniture cards' can be moved around on the plan to experiment with different classroom layouts.

Extension: Careful analysis is needed of the space requirements of each classroom activity and of each activity in relation to the others. So, for example, it is important to note if creative artwork or relatively noisy activities will interfere with quieter ones. Also, consider the relationship of activity areas and the accessibility of the resources for each activity. Finally, it is necessary to relate the location of the activities to the likely movement of the children, so that crowding or bottle-necks can be anticipated. This may need to be done on a session-by-session basis, and by first considering the most commonly occurring sessions. The children can help in this activity, and thereby become more aware of the need for careful use of space.

1.3   Resources

A good supply of appropriate resources is essential, given the importance of direct experience and practical work to children's learning. In some ways, this aspect of organization is a straightforward matter, but it also requires careful thought and attention to detail. For instance, it is all too easy to discover that the clay has dried out or the paint is not mixed, when a group of children come to use them. Moreover, the rapid development of ICT in classrooms also involves teachers making decisions about the location and management of computer hardware as well as about access to software (Bonnett, McFarlane and Williams, 1999; Kennelwell, Parkinson and Tanner, 2000, **Reading 9.8**). Decisions also have to be made about the availability and use of internet access and printing resources. There is growing evidence (Selwyn and Bullon, 2000) that organizational and management features of the classroom determine the levels of use of ICT by children. In some situations a minority of children dominate what is still seen as a scarce resource in the classroom.

Four possible criteria which might be considered when organizing resources are:

- *Appropriateness.* What resources are needed to support the learning processes which are expected to take place?
- *Availability.* What resources are available? What is in the classroom, the school, the community, businesses, libraries, museums, resource centres? Are there cost, time or transport factors to be considered?
- *Storage.* How are classroom resources stored? Which should be under teacher control? Which should be openly available to the children? Are they clearly labelled and safely stored?
- *Maintenance.* What maintenance is required? Is there a system for seeing that this is done? In the case of ICT where is the expertise and technical support located and how can this be accessed?

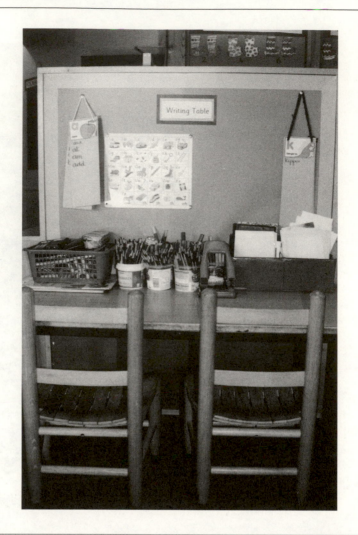

Reflective activity 10.2

Aim: To plan the resources to support specific learning activities.

Evidence and reflection: Identify the aim for each activity, then consider the resources which are required, using the four criteria listed in Section 1.3 as a starting point:

Activity:

Aim:

Resources required:

Appropriateness:

Availability:

Storage:

Maintenance:

Extension: Analysing the need and use of resources in this fashion could lead to their more rational and practical deployment. Can you produce a programme for immediate action and another for further development?

1.4   Use of time

The way in which time is used in a classroom is very important. Studies such as those of Campbell and Neill (1992) show that the notion of the time available for teaching needs careful analysis. The average hours of work of the infant school teachers whom Campbell and Neill studied in 1992 were as given in Figure 10.1.

A great deal of effort thus goes into the creation of 'teaching time'. However, as we have already commented, Campbell and Neill show that almost 10 per cent is lost as 'evaporated time' in the classroom-management activities which are necessary to create teaching and learning opportunities. Children have to get books out, change, move locations, tidy up, etc.

Looking at this issue in terms of pupil time, Bennett (1979) has related pupil progress not only to the time which is actually made available for 'curriculum activity' but also to the pupil time spent in 'active learning'. 'Active learning', as opposed to just 'busy work', is a qualitative category not just a quantitative one. 'Active learning' is linked to further factors such as motivation, stimulus and concentration. There is evidence to suggest that, in order to maintain 'active' learning, appropriate variety in activities is needed (e.g. Kounin, 1970, **Reading 11.6**). However, even quantitatively, findings from the PACE and Oracle studies (Pollard *et al.*, 1994; Osborn, 2000; Galton *et al.*, 1999, **Reading 13.1**), showed considerable variations between different classrooms in the proportions of pupil time with high levels of engagement. Overall, Key Stage 1 children were task-engaged for about 60 per cent of classroom time, distracted for about 20 per

Category	Hours per week	Percentage of total time
Teaching	18.0	34
Preparation	14.5	28
Administration	13.6	26
Professional development	7.2	14
Other activities	3.8	7
Total	**52.4**	**100**

(Note: The sum of hours is slightly smaller than the parts because of overlapping of categories)

Figure 10.1 *Hours of work per week by Key Stage 1 teachers*

cent of the time and organizing themselves or being organized for the remaining 20 per cent. There is also evidence (Selwyn and Bullon, 2000) of teachers using computers as 'pacifiers' rather than as a stimulating medium for developing problem solving skills, especially in early-years' classrooms.

Thus we have three aspects to consider in the use of time:

- the time available for curriculum activity
- the time spent in active learning
- the stimulus and variety in activities over time.

The first of these, time available for curriculum activity, is the remaining time in each teaching/learning session, once it has properly started, excluding interruptions and up to 'tidying up' time. This is relatively easy to audit, and there may be national requirements to be considered. Maximizing time available for curriculum activity was, of course, one of the stated intentions of the National Numeracy Strategy and National Literacy Strategy. Only time will tell the result of these initiatives. All that is necessary to establish the time available for curriculum activity is to use a notebook and a watch to record the actual time available for curriculum activity throughout a school day.

The time available for curriculum activity is clearly related to a number of organizational strategies. The most obvious of these concerns are the routine procedures which are developed, for example, those which help to avoid queues and bottle-necks. These help to manage the pressure which might otherwise be placed on the teacher by the children and they contribute to producing a positive, structured classroom environment. Reflective Activity 10.3 may be helpful in enabling you to improve your classroom procedures and thus increase the time available for curriculum activities.

Reflective activity 10.3

Aim: To evaluate procedures for routine activities of the school day with a view to maximizing time for teaching and learning.

Evidence and reflection: Use this list as a starting point for considering the routines that affect your lessons. Amend the list to match your situation. Consider possible improvements. Identify any aspects of organization you can deal with in advance of the lesson. Can you improve your own routines? Are you planning far enough ahead or practising crisis management? Can you actively involve pupils, giving them routine responsibility for specific aspects of lesson organization?

Purpose of procedure	Procedure	Evaluation of procedure	Possible improvement
Entering in the morning Completing the register			

http://www.rtweb.info

Collecting dinner money			
Managing playtime			
Managing dinner-time			
Ensuring health and safety			
Moving to and from assembly			
Changing for PE			
Going to the toilet			
Tidying up			
Exiting at the end of the day			

Extension: Teachers build up a wonderful repertoire of strategies for these organizational matters. A good extension would be to share and exchange ideas with a 'critical friend' or with your mentor.

The second of the issues identified here is the time spent on active learning, which is affected by a wide range of factors. Thus, whilst the time spent on active learning can be assessed at any point, it may also be seen as providing summative information: a product of the overall organization, relationships and teaching which are provided for the children.

Reflective activity 10.4

Aim: To monitor an individual child to estimate active learning time.

Evidence and reflection: Watch a chosen child during a teaching/learning session. Judge the times at which:

1. The child is 'on task' (i.e. actively engaged in the given task and learning objectives)

2. The child is doing other necessary activities related to the task (e.g. sharpening pencils, fetching equipment)

3. The child is 'off task' (i.e. appears distracted or disengaged).

Calculate the total amounts of learning time in each category:

'On-task' time [   ]

'Task-management' time [   ]

'Off-task' time [   ]

Extension: Are there any changes in classroom organization or management strategies which could help to maximize active learning time?

Are there also children in your class who seem to spend significant amounts of time 'off task' but still manage to learn effectively? Is it helpful to distinguish between 'playfulness'and 'time-wasting'? For sophisticated studies of young children's 'involvement' in activities, see Laevers (1995) and the EEL project (Pascal and Bertram, 1997). For primary-school pupils' persuasive explanations about being distracted, see Pollard *et al.*, 2000, Chapter 9.

The third aspect of time is an organizational issue, the stimulus and variety of tasks over time, is one to which Kounin (1970, **Reading 11.6**) drew attention when arguing that teachers should avoid 'satiation' (i.e. letting the children get bored by monotonous activities) (see Section 2.5 of Chapter 7 for further discussion). It is very easy to fall into this trap through an over-reliance on published materials, such as work schemes, or through the setting of repetitive individualized activities even in terms of drill and practice software on computers. Resources in the form of schemes are convenient. They appear to offer a secure basis for implementing the curriculum in which progression has been systematically considered and they are often strongly marketed by publishers. However, over-reliance on schemes can have a narrowing effect on the curriculum and lead to satiation and boredom. Considerable amounts of child activity will inevitably be directed through print, there is a tendency to require written recording and a remorseless, hierarchical structure is often in-built. All these aspects impose a relatively de-personalized and technical control on children. Indeed, it has been argued that the preponderance of such routine activities in some schools may have consequences in terms of the reproduction of a docile workforce, rather than develop children whose creativity and critical thinking have been stirred (Bowles and Gintis, 1976; Apple, 1982; see Reflective Activity 10.5).

Reflective activity 10.5

Aim: To evaluate the stimulus and variety of learning objectives, tasks and activities.

Evidence and reflection: This evaluation could be carried out by an observer who focuses on a particular child for a day. All activities should be recorded in terms of their motivational appeal, explicit purpose and in terms of what the child was required to do (write, draw, listen, watch, move, sing, etc.).

Alternatively, tasks could be monitored, by the teacher, for a longer period.

Some questions which might be asked could include:

a) Is there a planned highlight for each day?

b) Are there long sequences of seatwork and/or writing?

c) Is there a reasonable degree of variety between active and passive tasks?

d) Is there a reasonable degree of variety between children working alone, in small groups, as a whole class?

Extension: Consider the findings from this exercise, and, preferably with a colleague, try to deduce the reasons for any patterns you identify. How do you evaluate the results? If you judge it appropriate, what could you do to increase the stimulus and variety of learning objectives, tasks and activities?

2   MANAGING THE CHILDREN AND ADULTS

The people in a classroom need to be organized and managed in ways which are most appropriate for supporting the learning activities which have been planned. Obviously this involves children but, in many classes, it also involves adults such as classroom assistants and other support staff. There is also an increasing degree of involvement by parents in classrooms. However we will begin by focusing on the children.

2.1   Children

Perhaps the most important decision we make is how we choose to organize children for teaching purposes. Our choices must be made with regard to both pedagogical and practical considerations and always with the over-riding principle of 'fitness for purpose' (Alexander, Rose and Woodhead, 1992). Pedagogical considerations include the general aims of the teacher as well as any particular learning objectives for the task and children. Practical factors include the number of children, the size of the room and the availability of resources – factors which will be discussed in more detail below. Many believe that class size is a vital factor in effective learning. Headteachers, governors, teachers and parents appear to be consistent in terms of wanting smaller classes (Bennett, 1994) and there have been many research studies which support their point of view (Glass, 1982; Hall and Nuttall, 2000; Pate-Bain *et al.*, 1992, **Reading 10.3**; Jamison, Johnson and Dickson, 1998). However, further research is needed because findings are not entirely consistent, perhaps because of the measurement of slightly different Rose andfactors. International examples are extremely instructive (Alexander, 2000). A key general issue seems to be the extent to which teaching methods are adapted to suit a particular class size, rather than simply extended from one situation to another.

In planning a lesson we make decisions about how we think our children will best learn what we want to teach. Here we set out the three basic organizational choices available to us – class work, individual work and group work – identifying the main characteristics of each and discuss the idea of 'match' between organization, activity and learning. For further discussion of issues related to organizing group work for learning see Chapter 13, Section 2.

Class work

This is the long-established form of organization for starting and ending a lesson, for giving out administrative instructions and introducing learning objectives, tasks and activities. It is also used for teaching specific concepts and knowledge, for demonstrating and for extending and reviewing work. As a consequence of the National Literacy Strategy and National Numeracy Strategy initiatives, the three-part lesson which begins and ends with whole-class discussions has become widespread throughout primary education.

Whole-class activity is generally assumed to be teacher centred but there is a continuum of teacher dominance even when the whole class is involved in the same activity. At one end of the scale is the situation where the teacher talks and the children listen, take notes or copy from the board. At the other, however, the teacher may plan to give control of the activity to the children who may 'teach' by, for example, reporting what they have learned, demonstrating the result of an activity, offering solutions for problem-solving, discussing alternative or conflicting ideas, and asking questions. These activities can create a sense of class identity and shared endeavour.

What all whole-class activities have in common is that for the most part the teacher remains the focus of control, probably with the support of chalkboard, overhead projector, 'Big Book' or other stimulus materials. These sessions can be highly interactive with a great deal of pupil participation (see, for example, Muijs and Reynolds, 2001, **Reading 13.4**; Perrot, 1982, **Reading 13.5**).

Using whole-class organizational procedures may give the teacher a chance to instruct the class more directly and economically. For instance, he or she may be able to stimulate children's thinking by sharing lesson objectives, exploring ideas, asking more 'probing' questions, modeling quality answers, and supporting review, assessment and reflection on their learning.

However, class work can challenge both the teacher and the listener. It is very difficult to match the instruction appropriately to each pupil's different needs. There is a tendency for teaching to be pitched at the 'middle', failing both to extend those capable of more and to meet the needs of low attainers. Whilst some believe that one of the strengths of whole-class teaching during the National Literacy Strategy and National Numeracy Strategy is that it 'pulls along' the less able, others recognize that engagement can be uneven, with some children 'opting out' even though they retain an apparent 'listening posture' (Cordon, 1999, 2000). Some children may be reluctant to face the risks involved in contributing to the whole class (Collins, 1996). The ability of listeners to remain focused on one speaker is limited and affected both by the listeners' motivation and the speaker's skill. There is evidence of teachers addressing questions only to children in a V-shaped wedge in the centre of the room, or to particular groups or individuals (Wragg, 1984, 2000). We explore some of these issues in more depth in Chapter 11.

Individual work

Children spend a great deal of time working individually. They may be learning via tasks which require them to work alone, perhaps from text-books, work-sheets, computers or other resources. They may be demonstrating the results of their learning in individual outcomes. Individual work is thought to be particularly useful for developing children's ability to work independently and autonomously.

Working individually may be the dominant mode in many lessons. Alternatively you may plan for children to work individually on specific tasks in or out of the classroom, including for homework. The amount of time spent working individually in any lesson may be a few minutes or an extended period.

This approach has its limitations. For example, a teacher who relies heavily on setting individual work in lessons may find that similar teaching points have to be explained on many separate occasions to different children. It is therefore particularly important to establish that children understand the aims and requirements of the set activity, before individual work begins. Individual work also often results in a lot of movement in the classroom, with either the teacher moving around the classroom seeing each pupil in turn, or children moving from their seats and queuing at the teacher's desk. This emphasis on working with each individual separately inevitably means that only a limited amount of time can be spent with any one pupil. In addition, it has been shown that most of this time is spent monitoring children's work, rather than in developing their understanding (Galton *et al.*, 1999; Galton, Simon and Crolly, 1980).

Group work

This is often recommended for developing social and language skills and as a means by which children can support, challenge and extend their learning together, for example, in searching CD-ROM encyclopaedias for information or through problem-solving or work on a creative task. Group work can provide teachers with opportunities to observe children's learning more closely and, through questioning or providing information, to support them as they move forward to new knowledge, skills or understanding. This approach draws particularly on social constructivist psychology (see Chapter 7 for a discussion of the theoretical understanding behind this approach).

'Groups' are likely to exist in some form in every classroom. However, their form and function may vary considerably (McNamara, 1994, **Reading 10.4**; Reason, 1993, **Reading 10.5**). Four main types of groups can be identified according to the purpose they are intended to serve:

- *Task groups.* The teacher decides on a group of children to work together on a particular task or learning objective. Indeed the teacher may have a group of children in mind when setting or allocating an activity, though the group may not normally sit or work together.

- *Teaching groups.* Groups can also be used for 'group teaching' purposes, where the teacher instructs children who are at the same stage, doing the same task, at the same time. This may be followed by the children working individually. Such a system can be an economical use of teacher instruction time and, possibly, of resources. The teaching may be directive or be based on a problem-solving activity where a task is designed to challenge children's learning in a particular way.

- *Seating groups.* This is a very common form of grouping, where a number of children sit together around a table, usually in a four or six. Such an arrangement is flexible. It allows children to work individually, to socialize when appropriate, and can be used as the basis for other forms of group work.

- *Collaborative groups.* This is a more-developed form of group work, where there is a shared group aim, work is done together and the outcome is a combined product – perhaps in the form of a model, story or problem solved. As a varient, the collaboration may lead to a number of different and differentiated outcomes from individuals or pairs. Although less teacher-centred than teaching groups, teachers may observe children and, as a result, plan to intervene to support learning. A variant of this is 'reciprocal teaching' where children work in pairs, one taking the role of 'teacher partner', offering evaluation, and feedback. It is particularly evident in subjects like PE, drama and languages which involve 'performance'. The teacher supports by intervening to develop the quality of the evaluation and feedback.

Although groups are very commonly found for task allocation, seating purposes and teaching purposes, relatively little collaborative group work has been found by observers (Galton *et al.*, 1999; Pollard *et al.*, 1994; Bennett and Dunne, 1992, see also **Reading 13.7**; Galton and Williamson, 1992). Teachers have identified a number of problems which they associate with group work and, therefore, consider to be disadvantages (Tann, 1981). First, many teachers appear concerned about motivating the children and helping them to recognize that being in a group is for the purposes of work rather than a chance to chat and just 'have fun'. Second, the monitoring of group work can pose problems, especially if the group is intended to work collaboratively on their own without a teacher. Third, the management of groups, in terms of such issues as who should be in the group, how many children and where they should work, may pose difficult dilemmas which have to be resolved. See Chapter 11 for further discussion of issues related to group work.

Group work most frequently fails where children do not have the necessary skills to work together effectively. Identifying criteria by which groups may be formed may help to clarify some of the key issues. Possible criteria may include:

- *Age groups.* These are occasionally used as a convenient way of grouping for some activities. They are much less useful as a basis for specific teaching points because of the inevitable spread of attainment interests and needs.

- *Attainment groups.* Groups based on attainment levels are useful for setting up specific and well-matched tasks. They are divisive if used as a permanent way of grouping.

- *Interest groups.* It is important to enable children with shared interests to work together from time to time. There may be particular advantages for the social cohesion of the class when children are of different attainment, sex, race, social class.

- *Friendship groups.* These are popular with children and provide opportunities for social development. Awareness of the needs of any isolate and marginal children is necessary, as is some attention to the possibility that friendship groups can set up divisive status hierarchies among the children, or reinforce stereotypes about gender, race or abilities.

As with decisions concerning the balance between different general strategies for organizing the children, if group work is to be used, professional judgement is necessary to achieve an appropriate balance in the use of particular types of groups. Each has a different purpose and specific potential and, therefore, each has its own justifiable place in the primary classroom (Reflective Activity 10.6; see also McNamara 1994, **Reading 10.4**).

Reflective activity 10.6

Aim: To decide the most appropriate type and size of grouping for the activities planned.

Evidence and reflection: We suggest that notes on the size of groupings are made on the most appropriate cell of a matrix of types such as the one given below:

Activity	Individual work	Whole-class work	Group work				
			Random grouping	Age grouping	Attainment grouping	Interest grouping	Friendship grouping
Investigative science activities							
Literacy Hour introduction							
Guided reading							
Data input using ICT							
Clay work							
Drama							

Extension: The benefit of this sort of analysis is in the increased sensitivity to the unique potential of each type of learning situation. It will support the development of professional judgement and should help in ensuring coherence between learning aims, social context and organizational strategies.

Having looked at how we organize the children in the classroom we now go onto consider how we as teachers can liaise and work with other adults in the classroom including other professionals, e.g. classroom assistants and support staff as well as volunteers such as parents and carers.

2.2   Parents

Parental involvement is particularly significant in work with young children and has a justifiably high profile in early-years work. As we saw in Chapter 7, children experience and make sense of the world as a whole, and parents and other carers offer crucial support in this. Parents also provide an important source of emotional support (Reay, 2000, **Reading 4.5**). However, it is still the case that less than half of British primary schools involve parents in the classroom. Of course, the 'Parent's Charter', introduced by a Conservative government in 1992, implied a more distant relationship with the parent simply as a 'consumer' of educational services.

Despite some well-documented educational benefits of the involvement of parents in classrooms (e.g. Wolfendale, 1989), there is also considerable scope for the wastage of their time and their talents, or for misunderstandings and anxieties to emerge. Perhaps three basic things need to be done. The first is to find time for adequate discussion with parents to find out what they have to offer and to help them relax in the school environment. The second is to think carefully about how parents can be most educationally productive when they are in the classroom. The third is to negotiate clear ground rules on issues such as classroom roles, confidentiality and access to the staff-room.

A wide range of patterns of parental involvement thus exist (Hughes *et al.*, 1994), but we will identify three:

- *Parents as consumers*: receiving the services of the school but maintaining a discrete separation of parent and teacher responsibilities (e.g. where involvement is through formal parents' evenings, and other 'managed' school events).

- *Parents as resources*: providing a range of help, for example, parental activity in support of the school, as in PTA fund-raising schemes, outside school time; parents working in school on non-educational activities, as in helping to duplicate, or mend books; parents involved with educational activities, as in helping children in the library, hearing reading; parents teaching with small groups (often withdrawn), as in cooking and sewing; parents teaching in the classroom, as in the art area, or with general learning activities.

- *Parents as partners*: recognized as a partner in each child's all-round development, e.g. discussing the curriculum and each child's response; supporting curriculum (e.g. reading), learning at home; supporting skill development (e.g. writing and other skills) at home; contributing as parent governors; having open access to the classroom and regular informal contacts with teachers.

It seems however, that both parents and teachers, and perhaps the children, have mixed feelings on the question of parental involvement in classrooms (Cullingford, 1985; Vincent, 1996). All the children in one study, for example, expressed strong views about the privacy of their home-life in relation to schools and teachers (Edwards and Alldred, 2000). On the other hand, some parents may feel anxious and uneasy about working in a school. This may be because of their own 'bad' experiences of school, or because they do not feel they have anything to offer the 'expert' teacher. Parents may be unsure about how to relate to children in the school situation, particularly if their own child is in the class to which they are attached. Because of this, parents are unlikely to take initiatives in the classroom unless these are suggested and endorsed by the teacher. Further, parents are often only available for short and specific periods of the day. They are volunteers and have many other responsibilities and do not always find it easy to fit into school routines especially if they want to be free to spend quality time with their children at the end of the school day. Other parents feel unwilling to participate in classroom activities for quite different reasons. Some would maintain that it is the teacher's job to do the teaching and that they should therefore be allowed to get on with it. Others may feel that if they tried to help the child, at home or at school, they may do things in different ways to the teacher's approach which might only confuse the child.

Although we have talked of 'parents', in practice, the vast majority of those involved in school-life are mothers who are concentrating their efforts on bringing up a family. Indeed, we are, in general, referring to fathers or mothers who are not committed during normal '9 to 5' working hours, for despite the interest of many, very few parents with full-time jobs have the opportunity to participate in classroom life.

There are also mixed feelings amongst teachers about parental involvement. Some welcome the opportunity to create a stronger partnership between home and school so that both can work together in the interests of the children. Others, however, feel vulnerable in case something goes wrong which could undermine their status in the eyes of the parents. Teachers are also aware that parental help can become a socially divisive factor, giving still greater advantages to the already advantaged middle-class children whose parents are most likely to participate in such schemes.

2.3 Support staff

The past decade has seen an enormous increase in the number of support staff in schools. By 2000, there were over 150,000 in England alone, with primary schools averaging five each. Nevertheless, it is easy to slip into the mistaken belief that the 'classroom assistants' are a homogeneous group. Indeed, in a recent paper Hancock (2001) reports that a stratified sample of assistants in three LEAs preferred the following titles: classroom assistant (63 per cent); special support (SEN) assistants (23 per cent); nursery nurse (12 per cent); specialist teacher assistant (STA) (2 per cent). In addition to differences in preferred title, Hancock also found that the role of support staff also varied enormously depending on a teacher's acceptance of co-working, and an assistant's skill and confidence. Some are purely 'assisting' as and when directed. Many are working autonomously and intuitively with some very pressing children's needs – very much in teacher-like ways. Some assistants are becoming involved in staff meetings and staff training, particularly since the introduction of the National Literacy Strategy and National Numeracy Strategy.

Many support staff are involved in 'teaching-related' activities. For instance, 76 per cent of teachers said assistants were involved in recording children's progress, 84 per cent of teachers said assistants contributed to the assessment of children's work. They are now heavily involved in the National Numeracy Strategy and National Literacy Strategy. Indeed, Hancock argues that many teachers have wisely decided to lean on assistants in order to cope with multiple government initiatives. Some head teachers in the study have said that their teachers could not now manage without their assistants. As support staff are a variously distributed resource an assistant's day and week can be quite fragmented – perhaps moving alternately between two classes during one Literacy Hour or working with up to six classes a week. Some head teachers are using assistants as a rapidly deployed resource – to back-up supply teachers in a demanding class, for short-term cover when a teacher needs to be out of class for a while or out of school for an afternoon or even a day. Hancock (2001) has also found evidence that all assistants, whatever their title, are very involved in working with children with learning and behaviour difficulties – often at the sharp end, and with some assistants feeling out of their depth given the nature of the responsibility.

Close liaison and mutual support between teaching and support staff would be one measure of a reflective teacher's classroom. In studies of 'room management', for example, it is suggested that the quality of classroom teaching is very greatly enhanced if all the adults in a classroom plan together so that they understand and carry out specific activities in a co-ordinated and coherent fashion (Thomas, 1992, **Reading 10.7**). Adult partnership in the classroom means making careful organizational provision to use the time and talents of parents and support staff to the full. Reflective Activity 10.7 identifies some of the issues reflective teachers are likely to consider when preparing to work with parents and support staff in the classroom.

Reflective activity 10.7

Aim: To prepare for having parents or support staff working in the classroom.

Evidence and reflection: A pro forma, such as the one below, could be used to prepare for a session with parental or ancillary involvement, to monitor it and to get the parents' feedback.

Initial discussion with parent/support staff

Parent/support staff's feeling about involvement ....

Parent/support staff's contribution on offer ....

Parent/support staff availability ....

Any anticipated problems ....

Planning activities and objectives for sessions

1) ....

2) ....

3) ....

4) ....

Agreed contribution for parent/support staff ....

The session in action

Notes ....

Follow-up discussions

Notes ....

Extension: It is unlikely that this activity would be carried out for every session involving parents or support-staff assistants but it is very valuable when starting off a new partnership for classroom work. It is also useful on an occasional basis to heighten awareness and to check that benefits are being maximized.

2.4   Records

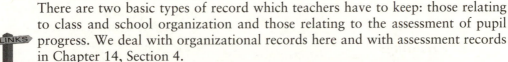

There are two basic types of record which teachers have to keep: those relating to class and school organization and those relating to the assessment of pupil progress. We deal with organizational records here and with assessment records in Chapter 14, Section 4.

By organizational records we simply mean those records that are necessary to ensure the smooth running of the school and classroom. These range from the attendance and dinner registers, which are extremely important to the administration of the school, to such things as records of group membership for various activities, timetables for use of shared school facilities such as the hall, and records of resource maintenance or loan periods.

Records of classroom organization are also essential for the smooth day-to-day running of the class. Whatever system of record keeping is chosen it is important that it is quick and easy for teachers and children to use. Teacher care and ingenuity has been enormous over many years, in attempts to develop smoothly operating and manageable ways of resolving the fundamental dilemma: how do you motivate and develop individual children whilst managing a class of many children? How, then, are learning objectives made clear, and how are tasks and activities delivered to, or chosen by, children?

Where specific literacy or numeracy strategies are followed, some aspects of classroom organization may be relatively constrained. However, for more flexible areas of curricular work, many other approaches are possible. For instance, a teacher may devise a number of tasks which the children may do on a rotation basis. The tasks may be displayed as a constant reminder in either pictorial codes or writing. Older children may extend this and negotiate with the teacher on a range of tasks that need to be completed over the period of a whole week, and which can be chosen in an order which is most satisfactory and meaningful to them. Even very young children can be encouraged to take some responsibility in deciding the tasks and in planning when and how they should be completed. This has been demonstrated by the High Scope nursery project (Hohmann, Banet and Weikart, 1979), where children are asked to 'plan', 'do' and then 'review' their activities.

Organizational procedures for homework are equally important. There may be a school-wide system involving, for example, a homework diary kept by children and seen by parents. It is vital, as part of establishing your expectations of children, to keep track of homework. Has it been done? Has it been given in on time?

CONCLUSION

In this chapter we have discussed some of the key aspects of organizational planning and the need for consistency between them. We have also emphasized the importance of coherence between classroom organization and educational aims. This can only be achieved through the exercise of professional judgement by reflective teachers who have the knowledge, skill and confidence to draw on a range of forms of classroom organization and thus maximize 'fitness for purpose'.

It is now time to turn to the issue of managing the implementation of those plans in action.

Key readings

As all practising educationalist know, circumstances vary in different classrooms and professional judgement has to be applied to select appropriate forms of classroom organization for the purposes which the teacher has in mind.

For insights into the complexities, challenges and opportunities presented by the need for teachers to meet the competencies in the *4/98 Standards in Planning, Teaching and Classroom Management* in England, see:

Hayes, D. (1999)
Planning, Teaching and Class Management in Primary Schools: Meeting the Standards.
London: Fulton.

For principled and practical guidance on classroom organization, see:

McNamara, D. (1994)
Classroom Pedagogy and Primary Practice.
London: Routledge.   Reading 10.4

Dean, J. (1991)
Organizing Learning in the Primary School Classroom
London: Routledge.

For a review of research, and a classic overview of pedagogy in primary education, see:

Galton, M. (1989)
Teaching in the Primary School.
London: David Fulton.   Reading 13.1

For a balanced approach to classroom organization, particularly with younger children, see:

Moyles, J. (1992)
Organising for Learning in the Primary Classroom: A Balanced Approach to Classroom Organisation.
Buckingham: Open University Press.   Reading 10.1

Drawing on the experience of student-teachers, mentors and children, the following is an excellent introduction to the principles and practice of classroom display:

Cooper, H., Simco, N., Hegarty, P. and Hegarty, P. (1996)
Display in the Classroom: Principles, Practice and Theory.
London: Fulton.

For practical suggestions as to how ICT may be incorporated into teaching across the curriculum, see:

McFarlane, A. (ed.) (1997)
Information Technology and Authentic Learning: Realising the Potential of Computers in the Primary Classroom.
London: Routledge.   See also **Reading 9.8**

For a practical introduction to organizing, running and evaluating effective group work, see:

Galton, M. and Williamson, J. (1992)
Groupwork in the Primary Classroom.
London: Routledge.   **Readings 10.5, 13.7 and 13.8**

The following is an excellent case study of development of parental involvement in one school over seven years:

Edwards, V. and Redfern, A. (1988)
Parental Participation in Primary Education.
London: Routledge.

For an overview of research, legislation and practice with regard to the support, management and staff development needs of classroom assistants and others in school, see:

Balshaw, M. H. (1999)
Help in the Classroom.
London: Fulton.   See also **Reading 10.7**

For a practical handbook containing information for support assistants and teachers, see:

Fox, G. (1998)
A Handbook for Learning Support Assistants: Teachers and Assistants Working Together.
London: Fulton.

Ideas for record-keeping appear in many different 'subject' based books and are influenced by the assessment requirements of the national curriculum. However, for a wide range of suggested ways for 'keeping track' see:

Johnson, G., Hill, B. and Turnstall, P. (1992)
Primary Records of Achievement.
London: Hodder and Stoughton.

Most specialist educational publishers also have useful series of books based on classroom organization in primary schools. For instance, in the UK see the catalogues of Continuum, RoutledgeFalmer, David Fulton, Simon and Schuster, Open University Press, Paul Chapman Press, etc.

Readings for Reflective Teaching (the companion volume) offers other closely associated work on the issues raised in this chapter. This includes work by authors such as:

Janet Moyles, David Clegg, Shirley Billington, Helen Pate-Bain, Charles Achilles, Jayne Boyd-Zaharias, Bernard McKenna, David McNamara, Rea Reason, Paul Croll, Di Moses and Gary Thomas.

 RTweb offers additional professional resources for this chapter. These may include *Notes for Further Reading*, supplementary *Reflective Activities*, useful *Web Links*, *Extension Texts* and *Download Facilities* for diagrams, figures, checklists, activities.

CHAPTER 11

Behaviour. How are we managing the class?

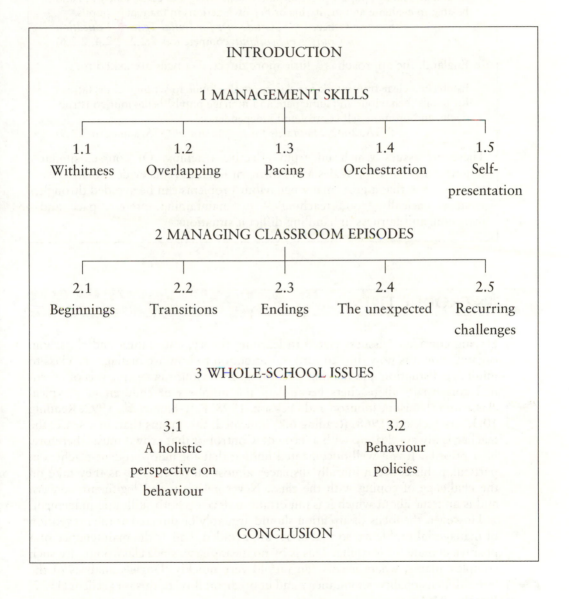

INTRODUCTION

1 MANAGEMENT SKILLS

| 1.1 | 1.2 | 1.3 | 1.4 | 1.5 |
| Withitness | Overlapping | Pacing | Orchestration | Self-presentation |

2 MANAGING CLASSROOM EPISODES

| 2.1 | 2.2 | 2.3 | 2.4 | 2.5 |
| Beginnings | Transitions | Endings | The unexpected | Recurring challenges |

3 WHOLE-SCHOOL ISSUES

| 3.1 | 3.2 |
| A holistic perspective on behaviour | Behaviour policies |

CONCLUSION

Enhancing professional standards and competences

Scottish requirements emphasize a positive approach to behaviour management. Student teachers must:

> Demonstrate that he or she knows about and is able to apply the principles and practices which underlie good discipline and promote positive behaviour.

> Be able to manage pupil behaviour fairly, sensitively and consistently . . . and be able to evaluate and justify his or her own actions in managing pupils.
> (Scottish Office, 1998, *Guidelines for Initial Teacher Education Courses in Scotland*, competences 2.2.2, 2.2.4, 2.2.6)

In England, the approach is a little more direct. Trainees are asked to:

> Establish a clear framework for classroom discipline to set high expectations for pupils' behaviour and anticipate and manage pupils' behaviour constructively, and promote self-control and independence.
> (TTA, 2002, *Standards for the Award of QTS*, standard 3.3.9)

These are issues which underpin effective teaching. Of course, similar requirements exist for Wales and Northern Ireland. As is evident below, we take the view that a great many behaviour problems can be avoided through what is basically 'good teaching' – by maintaining interest, pace and inclusion, and fairness in handling difficult situations.

INTRODUCTION

Having considered issues related to learning theory, curriculum and classroom organization it is now time to turn our attention to how we manage the class to minimize disruption and maximize learning. Behaviour management is of perennial concern to all teachers because of the numbers of children in a typical classroom (Jamison, Johnson and Dickson, 1998, Pate-Bain *et al.*, 1992, **Reading 10.3**). As Jackson (1968, **Reading 6.2**) indicated, this means that, in a sense, the teacher is always dealing with a 'crowd'. Control of that crowd must, therefore, be a priority. It is a well-documented finding that for many student-teachers in particular this concern initially displaces almost all other aims as they take on the challenge of coping with the class. Nevertheless, it is a legitimate concern and is an issue about which it is important to develop both skills and judgement.

However, the focus of attention should arguably be directed at the prevention of managerial problems, so that crises are avoided, and at the maintenance of a positive climate for learning. This is by no means easy, since classrooms are such complex places, where events can unfold very quickly. Doyle's analysis of the 'multidimensionality, simultaneity and unpredictability' of this is excellent (1977, **Reading 11.1**).

Given the multidimensionality of the classroom it is all too easy for classroom management objectives to take precedence over learning requirements. Moreover, even where teachers have control of the classroom, pupils may remain unclear about the aims of learning tasks set for them. As Galton (1989, **Reading 11.2**), suggests, the consequence is a sense of ambiguity and risk, which then undermines the quality of children's engagement with learning. Holt (1982, **Reading 11.3**) makes this idea more controversial by suggesting that pupils 'learn to be stupid' in schools. They do this when teachers' requirements for conformity with managerial rules, structure and order over-ride the pupils' need for understanding and engagement in high-quality learning tasks. The vital message of such work is that classroom management is an absolutely necessary means to an end – but it is not the end itself.

Before starting work in a new school reflective teachers will ensure that they know and understand something about the ethos and values of the school they are about to join. At the very minimum they will ask to see copies of the school's behaviour policies and talk with senior managers and other staff about how those policies are put into practice. Following behavioural guidelines laid down in the school's policy is an important step towards ensuring that all the staff in a school adopt a coherent and consistent approach to behaviour. Consequently, we begin this chapter with a checklist of some questions you might want to consider as you move into a new school. Think about these as you work through the activities in this chapter.

Checklist 11.1

Aim: To find out about a school's policies and practices with regard to behaviour management.

The answers to the following questions should be found by studying the schools behaviour policies and through talking to senior managers and other staff.

- What are the school's values?
- What principles are derived from these?
- What procedures are in place to help staff to apply these principles?
- How could I reflect these principles in my classroom organization?
- What do these principles suggest in terms of my personal organization (e.g. timing, pacing, rules, routines, etc.)?
- What are the implicit and explicit school and classroom rules?
- How can I apply these in my classroom?
- What are the set routines that should guide behaviour when pupils move about the school?
- Where and in what way should I ask for support when things go wrong?
- What reinforcements and sanctions are accepted?
- When was the policy written, when will it be revised and what input could I have to this process?

Add other questions to the list as they occur to you.

This chapter has been structured in three sections. Having introduced the idea that whole-school policies are central to effective behaviour-management we begin by focusing on some key classroom-management skills which impact on individual teachers. The second section then considers some of the most regularly occurring classroom episodes which require management. The chapter concludes with an overview of whole-school behaviour and management issues.

RTweb offers additional activities for this chapter.

1   MANAGEMENT SKILLS

This section builds on the work on curriculum planning and on preparing for a teaching session which was discussed in Chapter 9. Having considered how a learning session might be planned with appropriate differentiation, etc. (Chapter 9, Section 3.2), we will now look at five important management skills which relate to the maintenance and development of such sessions in action: 'withitness', 'overlapping', 'pacing', 'orchestration' and 'self-presentation'. Many of the issues in this and the following section on managing classroom episodes are also addressed in **Readings 11.4** and **11.6**.

1.1   Withitness

This is a term coined by Kounin (1970, **Reading 11.6**) to describe the capacity to be aware of the wide variety of things which are simultaneously going on in a classroom. This is a constant challenge for any teacher and can be a particular strain for a new teacher until this skill is acquired.

Teachers who are 'withit' are said to 'have eyes in the back of their head'. They are able to anticipate and to see where help is needed. They are able to nip trouble in the bud. They are skilful at scanning the class whilst helping individuals, and they position themselves accordingly. They are alert; they can pre-empt disturbance; and they can act fast. They can sense the way a class is responding and can act to maintain a positive atmosphere.

1.2   Overlapping

This is another of Kounin's terms and describes the skill of being able to do more than one thing at the same time. This is similar to the popular term 'multi-tasking'. Most teachers work under such pressure that they have to think about and do more than one thing at a time. Decisions have to be made very rapidly. It has been calculated that over a thousand interpersonal exchanges a day typically take place between each teacher and the children in their care. Frequently scanning the class, even whilst helping one individual, should enable the teacher to anticipate and intervene at the first signs of trouble. As Kounin (**Reading 11.6**) points out, if children perceive that the teacher is 'withit' enough to know what is going on then they are more likely to remain on task and achieve the appropriate learning objectives.

1.3 Pacing

Pacing a teaching–learning session is another important skill. Pacing involves making appropriate judgements about the timing and phasing of the organization, manner and content of sessions. At the simplest level, there is the practical judgement to be made about the organization of the session. Decisions have to be made about when to begin and end an activity and how much time to leave for tidying up or a plenary discussion. It is very easy to get involved in activities, forget about the clock and suddenly to find that it is playtime. More complex educational judgements are necessary in relation to learning activities and the various phases of a typical session. For example, the motivation generated at the start of an activity has to be sustained throughout. There may also be a need for 'incubation' and 'developmental' phases in which children think about the activities, explore ideas and then tackle tasks. From time to time there may be a need for a 'restructuring phase' where objectives and procedures may need to be clarified further. Finally, there may be a 'review phase' for reinforcing good effort or for reflecting on overall progress. (For more detailed discussion on the pacing of content delivery, questions and answers, etc., see Chapter 13, Sections 1.1 and 1.2.)

In England, the National Literacy Strategy and National Numeracy Strategy potentially impose a strict lesson structure on both teachers and learners. Nevertheless, where scope for flexibility exists, judgements about pacing remain vitally important. They depend crucially on being sensitive to how children are responding to activities. If they are immersed and productively engaged then one might decide to extend a phase or run the activity into the next session. If the children seem to be becoming bored, frustrated or listless then it is usually wise to retain the initiative, to restructure or review the activity or to move on to something new. If the children are becoming too 'high', excited and distracted, then it may be useful to review and maybe redirect them into an activity which calms them down by re-channelling their energies. As will be discussed in the next section, working with a class of individuals may involve being able to respond to many, if not all, of their responses at the same time. You might like to reflect in the consequence of a prescribed lesson structure on the pace of lessons.

1.4 Orchestration

Here we are using the term 'orchestration' to refer to the way in which a teacher works with the whole class rather like a conductor controls an orchestra or a stand-up comedian 'plays' an audience. Whether the teacher is adopting whole-class, individual or group teaching strategies, part of their job is to maximize the time that all the individuals in the class are on task and paying attention. Involving all the children in the learning activities of a classroom involves developing the sensitivity to be able to 'read' how individual children are responding and to be able to anticipate the most effective way of maintaining interest or re-engaging attention. This will differ from individual to individual and in different contexts. Bored, listless behaviour might be engendered because a task is too easy or too difficult (see Chapter 9 on differentiation). On the other hand some children may be highly motivated by an activity which others find tedious and dull. In all cases the teacher has to be aware of everything that is happening in their classroom and be prepared to act accordingly. This may involve a differentiated response in which some children are allowed to continue with what they are doing whilst a new focus is found for others. Certainly, teachers have to be aware of a range of ways of motivating all the individuals in the class.

1.5   Self-presentation

Another set of management skills which we have identified is related to self-presentation, for how to 'present' oneself to children is also a matter for skill and judgement. Teachers who are able to project themselves so that children expect them to be 'in charge' have a valuable ability. There is a very large element of self-confidence in this and student-teachers, in particular, may sometimes find it difficult to enact the change from the student role to the teacher role. Perhaps this is not surprising for a huge change in rights and responsibilities is involved. The first essential, then, is to believe in oneself as a teacher.

A second range of issues concerned with self-presentation is more skill based. Here non-verbal cues are important. Self-presentation relates to such things as gesture, posture, movement, position in the room, facial expression, etc. These will be actively interpreted by children. The intended impression might be one of sureness, of confidence and competence. The reflective teacher will need to consider how non-verbal cues can help to convey such attributes.

A further very important skill is voice control. A teacher's use of voice can be highly sophisticated and effective. Changing the pitch, volume, projection and the intensity of meaning can communicate different aspects about self. If anyone's voice is to be used in this way then it will require some training and time to develop. Teachers, like singers and actors, can learn to use their diaphragm to project a 'chest voice', to breathe more deeply and speak more slowly so that their voice and their message is carried more effectively. Developing voice control is also an important asset in telling and reading stories, which may involve having to present many different characters. In the first instance it may be a good idea to try out different 'voices' – privately, and far enough away from others that a 'big' voice does not disturb anyone else! Although tape-recorders never seem flattering, recording a practice story-telling can be a useful way of seeing how much your appropriate voice variety is developing.

A fourth and more general area of skill which is involved in how teachers present and project themselves is that of 'acting' – as though on a stage. In this sense it is the ability to convey what we mean by 'being a teacher', so that expectations are clear and relationships can be negotiated. Acting is also an enormous strength for teachers for one other particular reason. When one is acting one is partially detached from the role. It is possible to observe oneself, to analyse, reflect and plan. Acting, in other words, is controlled behaviour which is partially distanced from self. In the situations of vulnerability which sometimes arise in classrooms this can be a great asset.

The skills which we have been reviewing above need to be put in a context. They are simply skills and have no substantive content or merit in their own right. A self-confident performer who lacks purpose and gets practical matters

wrong (for example has ill-defined objectives, mixes up children's names, plans sessions badly, loses books, acts unfairly, etc.) will not be able to manage a class. A teacher has to be competent as well as skilled and must understand the ends of education as well as the means.

Reflective activity 11.1

Aim: To gather data about one's management skills and judgement.

Evidence and reflection: Ask a colleague to observe a session which you take and to make notes on the way in which you manage the children. They could watch out for examples of appropriate withitness, overlapping, pacing, orchestration and self-presentation (or chances missed). Discuss the session together afterwards.

Alternatively, set up a video camera to record a session which you take. Analyse the playback in terms of the criteria above.

If there is a danger that you are becoming too negative about your management skills and judgements then adopt the 3 to 1 rule. This rule states that you can only identify one negative thing after you have identified three positives. When you run out of positives you have to stop. (This strategy also works with children who have been asked to evaluate their own work or that of others.)

Extension: Such analysis should increase self-awareness of management skills. Try to identify possible improvements which could be made. These can be practised and worked on.

2 MANAGING CLASSROOM EPISODES

'Flow' is an important summary criterion which can be used to describe classroom management. By 'flow' we mean the degree of continuity and coherence which is achieved in a learning session. It implies a steady, continuous movement in a particular direction. The suggestion is thus that we should work with the children to develop a coherent sense of purpose within our classes; organize our classrooms in ways which are consistent with those purposes; and manage the children, phases and events so that learning objectives are cumulatively reinforced. Consistency and reinforcement of desirable behaviours can be important here, as Merrett and Wheldall (1990, **Reading 11.7**) have emphasized. We would suggest that, if this can be done, then energy, interest and enthusiasm for learning is likely to be focused productively.

In this section we discuss five issues which pose particular management challenges to the flow of sessions. We discuss 'beginnings' of sessions; 'transitions' between phases of sessions or between sessions themselves; and the 'endings' of sessions. We also consider strategies for dealing with 'the unexpected' and 'recurring challenges'.

2.1 Beginnings

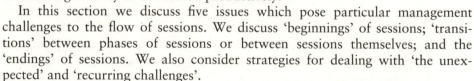

The beginning of a session is often seen as important because of the way in which it sets a tone. Simple strategies such as being in the classroom to receive the children help to establish that you are receiving them on your territory and, by implication, on your terms (Laslett and Smith, 1992, **Reading 11.4**).

The next important goal is usually to introduce and interest the children in the planned activities; to provide them with a clear indication of the learning objectives of the session, a clear understanding of what they are expected to do; and to structure the activity in practical, organizational terms. See Reflective Activity 11.2.

Reflective activity 11.2

Aim: To evaluate the beginning of a session and to consider areas for improvement.

Evidence and reflection: Video a session you have taught or observe someone else's lesson. Consider what happened in terms of the following questions.

- How did the teacher attract the children's attention?
- How did the teacher keep the children's attention?
- How did the teacher maximise the conditions for listening?
- What did the teacher use as a stimulus at the start of the lesson?
- How effective was this stimulus?
- What else might the teacher have done?
- Were the instructions to the class clear?
- Do the children know why they are doing this activity?
- Do the children know what they are going to learn from it?
- Do the children know if any follow up is expected?
- Do the children know on what criteria their work is to be assessed?
- Do the children know how this activity links with other work they have done or will do next?

Extension: What specific actions could be taken for improvement? What general skills need to be worked on?

2.2   Transitions

Transitions are a regular cause of control difficulties, particularly for trainee teachers. This often arises when expectations about behaviour concerning one activity have to be left behind and those of the new one have yet to be established. In these circumstances, a skilled teacher is likely to plan carefully, take an initiative early and structure the transition carefully.

For example, it would be a challenging prospect if a whole range of creative, artistic activities were in full flow when the children suddenly had to get changed for a physical education session in the hall. We would suggest that it is important to break down a transition such as this into three discrete stages. The skill lies in first, anticipating problems before they arise (e.g. Why has the PE lesson come as such a surprise in the first place? What might happen as a consequence of the change in activities?); second, in pre-structuring the next phase; and finally in interesting the children in the next phase so that they are drawn through to it. These principles apply to any transition.

Reflective activity 11.3

Aim: To monitor periods of transition in your own teaching.

Evidence and reflection: Consider a transition phase in your own teaching in the light of the following questions.

- Did you give an early warning of the transition?

- Did you give clear instructions for leaving existing work?

- Did you give the children clear instructions for the transition and for any movement that was necessary?

- Did you arouse the children's interest in the next phase?

Extension: Reviewing your performance as a whole, what are the major points for improvement? Do you see these as technical, as personal, or as associated with other factors? What might you try next time?

2.3   Endings

Ending a session is a further management issue and four aspects will be reviewed. The first is a very practical one. At the end of any session equipment must be put away and the classroom must be tidied up ready for future sessions. The second aspect relates to discipline and control. Children can sometimes get a little 'high' at the end of a session when they look forward excitedly to whatever follows. This, combined with the chores of tidying up, can require a degree of awareness and firmness from the teacher. The procedures that are called for here are similar to those for transitions.

The two other aspects involved in ending sessions have more explicit and positive educational potential. One of these concerns the excellent opportunities which arise, for example in the plenary of a literacy lesson, for reviewing educational progress and achievements, for reinforcing good work and for contextualizing activities which have been completed. This is complemented by the opportunities that also arise for asserting the membership of the class as a communal group. Shared experiences, team-work and co-operation can be celebrated and reinforced through the enjoyment of poetry, singing, games, stories, etc. Moreover, there are lots of very productive opportunities at the ends of sessions and even an odd space of unexpected time, perhaps waiting for a bell, which can be used constructively.

Overall, a carefully thought-out and well-executed ending to a session will contribute to the flow of activities by providing an ordered exit, by reinforcing learning and by building up the sense of 'belonging' within the class as a whole.

Reflective activity 11.4

Aim: To monitor the end of a session and identify areas for improvement.

Evidence and reflection: Reflect back on a session you taught recently in the light of the following questions.

- Did you give early warning of the end of the session?
- Did you give clear instructions for tidying up?
- Did you reinforce those instructions and monitor the tidying up?
- Did you take opportunities to reinforce the educational achievements, efforts and progress made?
- Did you take opportunities to build up the sense of the class as a community?
- Did you praise the children for what they did well?
- Did you provide for an ordered exit from the room?
- How might you respond differently in future?

Extension: You could very usefully ask a mentor or an experienced colleague to observe your session and offer specific comments. Before you do, highlight the particular issues on which you want feedback. This might also be a good moment to do some reading about the principles of class management. Kounin (1970, see **Reading 11.6**) remains a classic.

2.4 The unexpected

As Doyle (**Reading 11.1**) identified, unpredictability is one of the most salient features of the classroom for trainee teachers. It is difficult to predict children's reactions to questions or how they will respond to specific activities. Similarly, it is difficult to predict how long it will take for a class to complete an activity. These are skills which are acquired over time and with experience. However, in any classroom there is the continuous possibility of internal and external interruptions, for example there may be changes in the normal schedule or a potential breakdown in equipment. Skilled teachers learn to plan ahead, to anticipate potential difficulties and have a range of strategies for dealing with the unexpected. In this section we consider how teachers might deal with the unexpected in terms of both learning outcomes and 'crises'.

In line with a social constructivist approach to learning, teachers are encouraged to ask open-ended questions which can be interpreted and answered in a number of different ways (see Chapter 7, Section 1.3 and Chapter 13, Section 1.2 for further discussion). As appropriate answers are not predetermined, teachers may be surprised by the children's responses. Where the answer is unexpected the teacher then faces the dilemma of wanting to acknowledge the legitimacy of the response without being drawn too far away from the teaching point being made. Consider, for example, the following situation. A teacher introduces her class of seven-year-olds to the subject of soil erosion and, assuming that the class are following her discussion, asks how grass might help to control this process. Unfortunately, several members of the class remember an earlier lesson about the oxygen cycle and want to discuss the idea that grass is important to humans because it releases oxygen into the atmosphere. As a skilled practitioner the teacher affirms the children for remembering the previous lesson before returning to her original topic. Being able to handle the unexpected in a way which reinforces children's prior learning and yet remains true to the original learning objective is the mark of a skilled teacher. (Note also the role of teacher knowledge in making this possible, as discussed in Chapter 8, Section 3.)

On a more practical level, a classroom 'crisis' is a clear example of the unexpected. Crises can come in many forms, from a child being sick or cutting a finger, to children (or perhaps a parent) challenging the teacher's authority and judgement. Despite the wide-ranging issues which are raised, there are three fairly simple principles which can be applied from the classroom-management point of view.

The first principle is to minimize the disturbance. Neither a child who is ill or hurt, nor a parent or child who is upset, can be given the attention which they require by a teacher who has continuing classroom responsibilities. Help from the school secretary, an ancillary helper, or the head teacher should be called in either to deal with the problem or to relieve the class teacher so that they can deal with it. In this way disturbance to the classroom flow can be minimized and those in need of undivided attention can receive it. The school should have an identified procedure for how to handle crises. Of course, a student-teacher usually has a full-time teacher upon whom to call.

The second principle for handling a crisis is to maximize reassurance. Children can be upset when something unexpected happens and it may well be appropriate to reassert the security of their classroom routines and expectations. A degree of caution in the choice of activities for a suitable period might therefore be wise.

The third principle which is appropriate when a crisis arises concerns oneself and pausing for sufficient thought before making a judgement on how to act. Obviously, this depends on what has happened and some events require immediate action. However, if it is possible to gain time to think about the issues outside the heat of the moment, then it may produce more authoritative and constructive decisions.

Reflective activity 11.5

Aim: To monitor responses to a classroom crisis.

Evidence and reflection: After a crisis has arisen, a diary-type account of it and of how it was handled could be written. This might describe the event, and also reflect the feelings which were experienced as the events unfolded. It might be valuable to encourage children to record and talk about a similar account and reflection after the event, so that you can gain an insight into why they behaved as they did.

The following questions might be asked:

- Did you minimize disturbance?

- Did you maximize reassurance?

- Did you make appropriate judgements on how to act?

Extension: Having examined your actions and the children's responses to the crisis it would probably be helpful to discuss the event and the accounts with a friend or colleague. An interesting reading would be David Tripp (1993) on 'critical incidents'.

2.5 Recurring challenges

Although, hopefully, crises will be rare, there may be other sorts of behavioural problems which can upset the 'flow' of a session. In this section we present them in terms of recurring challenges which even the most experienced teacher may have to deal with. However, by constant monitoring and being 'withit', it is usually possible to anticipate undesirable behaviour which threatens the negotiated relationships of the working consensus (see Chapter 6, Section 2.1) and to 'nip it in the bud'. Nevertheless, difficulties are bound to occur from time to time and prudent teachers are likely to want to think through possible strategies in advance so that they can act confidently in managing such situations.

In terms of dealing with behavioural problems the most effective strategy is, without doubt, to try to prevent them from happening in the first place. Certainly, the incidence of inappropriate behaviour is likely to be significantly reduced by following some fundamental principles (see Checklist 11.2).

Unfortunately, whilst these strategies may significantly reduce the incidents of misbehaviour they are unlikely to eliminate it altogether. Consequently, a prudent teacher will plan ahead and develop a range of strategies for dealing with inappropriate behaviour.

The first strategy for dealing with misbehaviour might be to ignore it, especially if it has only happened once or you consider it to be a minor infringement of the classroom rules. Picking up on each and every infringement may be time consuming and detract from the educative content of the session. A more positive strategy might be to reward someone who is on task and behaving appropriately.

If the infringement is more serious or is repeated it would be appropriate to

Checklist 11.2

Aim: To pre-empt general misbehaviour and to reduce incidents of inappropriate behaviour.

1. Be clear about general class rules and what constitutes acceptable behaviour.

2. 'Catch' children being good and reward appropriate behaviour.

3. Have clear learning objectives and make sure the children understand these.

4. Explain the activity or task clearly and be sure that everyone knows what to do and how to do it.

5. Show approval of appropriate work and reward effort.

6. Be supportive of any problems encountered.

7. Be consistent.

---

consider the strategies listed below. Suggestions are offered for five progressive stages. The emphasis should remain on prevention, and you should bear in mind that, whilst the 1997 Education Act enables teachers to restrain pupils with 'such force as is reasonable in the circumstances', corporal punishment in any form is illegal.

1. If inappropriate behaviour only occurs once and seems inconsequential:
   - Note it, and wait to see if it builds; or
   - Indicate that you have noticed and disapprove of the behaviour, but take no action.

2. If repeated:
   - Make sustained eye contact, use non-verbal gestures.
   - Move towards the child.
   - Invite the child to participate – ask a question or encourage a comment, direct focus on work.

3. If persistent, in addition to the responses above:
   - Name the child firmly and positively.
   - Move to the child.
   - Stop the action.
   - Find out the facts if the situation is ambiguous; avoid jumping to conclusions.
   - Briefly identify the inappropriate behaviour, comment on the *behaviour* (not the child), avoid implying disapproval of the individual, keep voice low, avoid nagging/lecturing, don't confuse respect and fear.
   - Clearly state the desired behaviour, and expect a compliant response.
   - If necessary, isolate the child – avoid a contagious spread, a public clash and an 'audience' which can provoke 'showing-off'.
   - Focus on the principle individual involved; don't be drawn into discussion with a group; followers will conform if you control the leader.

- Deal with the situation as quickly and neatly as possible; don't be drawn into long arguments; don't let the situation distract your attention from the rest of the class and the goals of your lesson.

4. If punishment is judged to be necessary:
   - Don't threaten disciplinary action too soon.
   - Be sure it is appropriate and that you can carry it through.
   - Avoid indiscriminate punishment of class or group.

5. Closure/after the event:
   - Take everyone involved to one side – preserve their dignity, avoid 'supporters' chipping in.
   - Encourage the child to identify what had been wrong, thus sharing responsibility.
   - Try to be fair; if necessary apologize.
   - Invite the child to draw up a 'contract' of what the child and the teacher will do and with which tangible rewards.
   - Modify behaviour by withdrawal of privileges and by providing opportunities to earn praise.
   - Conclude with peace-terms clear to all parties.

Other, major ongoing problems can also exist in any classroom. These may be associated with an individual child who has particular difficulties. In such instances, it is important to record and analyse the behaviour and try to identify the possible causes before any positive action can be taken. In keeping a diary of events one might record the conditions, characteristics and consequences of the behaviour and thus produce an evidence-base for action.

> ## Checklist 11.3
>
> *Aim*: To record incidents of ongoing 'problem' behaviour.
>
> *Conditions*: When exactly does the disruption occur?
>
> - Is it random or regular?
> - Is it always the same child?
> - Is it always regarding the same task?
> - Is it always with the same teacher?
>
> *Characteristics*: What exactly happens?
>
> - Is it a verbal reaction?
> - Is it a physical reaction?
>
> *Consequences*: What are the effects?
>
> - On the child, the teacher?
> - On the class, the school?
> - Do they join in, ignore, retaliate?

Such major, persistent problems are best discussed with other colleagues and a common strategy worked out in line with the school's behaviour policy. This might also involve the parents and the whole class, if necessary, so that a consistent approach can be adopted.

Whether a problem is associated with an individual child or most of the class, a consistent approach is essential and would, hopefully, provide security for the children as well as support for the teacher. It must be remembered that children respond to situations and experiences. We, as teachers, structure such experiences. Thus, if children respond problematically, we must reflect on the experiences that we provide rather than simply trying to apportion blame elsewhere. Teachers can be 'provocative' or 'insulative' (Hargreaves, Hester and Mellor, 1975, **Reading 11.5**). Which are you?

3　WHOLE-SCHOOL ISSUES

3.1　A holistic perspective on behaviour

Good behaviour and order in classrooms and schools are the products of a great many factors and influences. When they break down though, there tends to be an almost instinctive, but over-simplified, response to 'sort out the troublemakers'. This can even occur at a national level. For instance, in March 1988 a Committee of Enquiry, chaired by Lord Elton, was set up in the United Kingdom following a media outcry over reports of teachers being physically attacked by pupils and about 'indiscipline in schools today'. Wisely, however, the Elton Committee took a balanced and wide-ranging view of the issues involved and this is reflected in their report (DES, 1989, **Reading 11.8**). As the Elton Report stated:

> The behaviour of pupils in a school is influenced by every aspect of the way in which it is run and how it relates to the community it serves. It is the combination of all these factors which gives a school its character and identity. Together, they can produce an orderly and successful school in a difficult catchment area; equally, they can produce an unsuccessful school in what should be much easier circumstances.
>
> (DES, 1989, p. 8)

The report went on to emphasize the importance of having clearly stated boundaries of acceptable behaviour, of teachers responding promptly and firmly to those who test boundaries, of motivating pupils to learn, of providing a stimulating and appropriately differentiated curriculum, of managing groups skilfully, of creating a positive school atmosphere based on a sense of community and shared values, of achieving the highest possible degree of consensus about standards of behaviour among staff, pupils and parents, of promoting values of mutual respect, self-discipline and social responsibility. Furthermore, it drew attention to the role of governors, local education authorities, training organizations and government in supporting teachers.

The holistic approach of the Elton Committee is well founded and the issues to which they drew attention are considered thoroughly in the chapters of this book. School and classroom misbehaviour should, above all, be pre-empted where purposeful communities of people exist; with teachers acting sensitively, skilfully and authoritatively to maintain the values, rules, expectations and activities which provide an infrastructure for order and meaning.

Of course, primary schools are generally seen as being relatively successful in developing and maintaining good behaviour and in providing a constructive atmosphere for learning. 'In 1997/1998 behaviour of pupils was judged to be good in 80 per cent of schools and unsatisfactory in only 2 per cent' (OFSTED, 1999, p. 60).

However, there is no place for complacency and it must be recognized, in particular, that many of the skills which lead to competence in classroom management can only be developed through extensive practice with children in classrooms. In doing this it is advisable for the trainee teacher to move gradually from working with small groups, to larger groups and on to taking the whole class. The support and advice of an experienced mentor or colleague is likely to be invaluable.

The Elton Report includes a statement of eleven 'principles of classroom management' (DES, 1989, p. 71) which reflect much good sense and experience. We include them in Checklist 11.4, in the form of questions for use in planning, undertaking and reflecting on classroom practice.

Checklist 11.4

Aim: To reflect on classroom management and discipline using the Elton Report's 'principles of classroom management'.

Do I:

- Know my pupils as individuals – names, personalities, interests, friends?
- Plan and organize both the classroom and the lesson to keep pupils interested and minimize the opportunities for disruption – furniture layout, pupil grouping, matching of work, pacing lessons, enthusiasm, humour?
- Involve pupils in establishing the rules for classroom behaviour and routinely reinforce why they are necessary?
- Act flexibly to take advantage of unexpected events rather than being thrown by them?
- Continually observe or 'scan' the behaviour of the class?
- Remain aware of, and control, my own behaviour, including stance and tone of voice?
- Model the standards of courtesy that I expect from pupils?
- Emphasize the positive, including praise for good behaviour as well as good work?
- Make sparing and consistent use of reprimands – being firm not aggressive, targetting the right pupil, using private not public reprimands, being fair and consistent, avoiding sarcasm and idle threats?
- Make sparing and consistent use of punishments – avoiding whole-group punishment and pupil humiliation which breed resentment?
- Analyse my own classroom management performance and learn from it?

As the Elton Committee concluded, the final point about reflection on one's practice is 'the most important message of all'.

3.2 Behaviour policies

The Elton Report (DES, 1989, **Reading 11.8**) confirmed that the features and processes of a school could influence pupils' behaviour and that significant improvements in behaviour could be achieved through institutional change. Schools also have a legal responsibility to state and pursue policies designed to promote good behaviour and discipline.

It is recommended that schools see the writing of a behaviour policy as an opportunity for all those who will be affected – governors, managers, teaching staff, ancillary staff, pupils, parents and the wider community – to discuss the components of the policy in terms of practice, organization and ethos. Such an inclusive approach to the development of policy should help to ensure that it reflects a consensus view and that 'ownership' of the final policy is maximized. Despite individual differences there are likely to be some common areas or issues. These include:

1. Statement of ethos/principles
2. Roles and responsibilities
3. Procedures and practice
4. Outline of rules and expectations
5. Outline of rewards for good behaviour
6. Outline of consequences of undesired behaviour
7. Relationship with other policies
8. Working with parents
9. Working with outside agencies
10. Outline of development, monitoring and evaluation.

A school's policy should relate to its aims and 'mission statements' and reflect the general school ethos. The following checklist should help in the evaluation of a behaviour policy.

Checklist 11.5

Aim: According to the Birmingham City Council Education Department (1998) a school's behaviour policy should:

- Be concise and avoid unnecessary bureaucracy
- Be easy to understand by all
- Be 'owned' by the whole school
- While retaining flexibility, provide positive direction and support for teachers from the earliest point of concern
- Provide a positive environment for parental involvement
- Involve pupils and parents in its development and evaluation
- Inform and be informed by classroom practice
- Codify practice in the school
- Plan for monitoring, evaluation and change
- Provide a balance between the needs of the majority and the individual child
- Have clear intentions, aims and objectives for development and success.

However, behaviour policies alone are not the answer. Implicit in the development of positive attitudes is the notion that schools will function as a community that actively encourages all members of that community to value and respect each other. Moreover, the inter-relationship of the behaviour policy with other policies such as those on equal opportunities, special educational needs, anti-bullying, and, more importantly, the relationship of policy to practice, organization and ethos is more likely to produce a climate of good behaviour and effective learning. Once established, a positive climate can seem virtually self-sustaining as new entrants are inducted, though interpersonal skills, respect, judgement and fairness will remain its foundation.

CONCLUSION

This chapter has examined aspects of behaviour management which help to establish and sustain conditions for successful learning. These questions of management are matters of great concern to teachers, as are the questions of teachers and children learning to cope with each other and with learning situations. Most of us soon become more familiar and gradually grow in confidence and competence with such challenges. Direct experience is irreplaceable in developing competence, but there is also much to be said for sharing ideas, problems and successes through discussion with colleagues.

 Managing collaborative group work can be particularly challenging and is discussed at length in Chapter 10, Section 2 and Chapter 13, Section 2. Many of the issues considered in this chapter also relate closely to the content of Chapter 6, on classroom relationships.

Key readings

For powerful beliefs and practical strategies to enhance the personal development and self-esteem of teachers, see:

Hook, P. and Vass, A. (2001)
Confident Classroom Leadership.
London: David Fulton.

Another concise discussion of the major issues, and with a good section on teacher stress and how to cope with it is provided by:

Laslett, R. and Smith, C. (1992)
Effective Classroom Management: a Teacher's Guide.
London: Routledge.   Reading 11.4

For a book which provides many insights on classroom management, and which has become a classic, see:

Kounin, J. S. (1970)
Discipline and Group Management in Classrooms.
New York: Holt Rhinehart and Winston.   Reading 11.6

For help in identifying the patterns of difficulty which occur in particular classrooms, see:

Robertson, J. (1996)
Effective Classroom Control: Understanding Teacher–Pupil Relationships.
London: Hodder and Stoughton.

Watkins, C. (2000)
Managing Classroom Behaviour: from Research to Diagnosis.
London: Institute of Education Publishers.

It is crucial to hold on to management issues in the context of broader educational objectives. On this, see:

Putnam, J. and Burke, J. B. (1992)
Organising and Managing Classroom Learning Communities.
New York: McGraw Hill.

For a philosophical account see:

Straughan, R. (1988)
Can We Teach Children to be Good? Basic Issues in Moral, Personal and Social Education.
Buckingham: Open University Press.

Sound advice deriving from an empirical study of the issues may be found in:

Wragg, E. C. (1993)
Class Management.
London: Routledge.

As we have seen, the Elton Report is well worth consulting:

DES (1989)
Discipline in Schools
Report of the Committee of Enquiry chaired by Lord Elton.
London: HMSO.   📖 **Reading 11.8**

For helpful and practical approaches to improving whole-school and classroom behaviour, see:

Watkins, C. and Wanger, C. (2000)
Improving School Behaviour.
London: Paul Chapman.

Munn, P., Johnstone, M., and Chalmers, V. (1992)
Effective Discipline in Primary Schools and Classrooms.
London: Paul Chapman Publishing.

Most specialist educational publishers also have useful books based on managing behaviour. For instance, in the UK see the catalogues of Continuum, RoutledgeFalmer, David Fulton, Simon and Schuster, Open University Press, Paul Chapman Press, etc.

 Readings for Reflective Teaching (the companion volume) offers other closely associated work on the issues raised in this chapter. This includes work by authors such as:

Walter Doyle, Maurice Galton, John Holt, Robert Laslett, Colin Smith, David Harvreaves, Stephen Hestor, Frank Mellor, Jacob Kounin, Frank Merrett, Kevin Wheldall and Lord Elton.

 RTweb offers additional professional resources for this chapter. These may include *Notes for Further Reading*, supplementary *Reflective Activities*, useful *Web Links*, *Extension Texts* and *Download Facilities* for diagrams, figures, checklists, activities.

CHAPTER 12

Communication. What are its classroom characteristics?

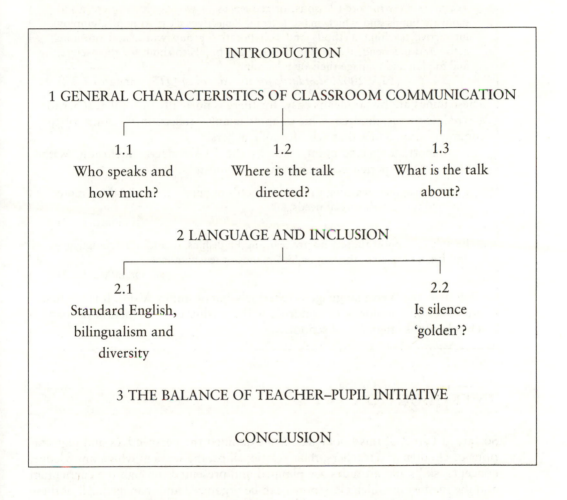

INTRODUCTION

1 GENERAL CHARACTERISTICS OF CLASSROOM COMMUNICATION

1.1	1.2	1.3
Who speaks and how much?	Where is the talk directed?	What is the talk about?

2 LANGUAGE AND INCLUSION

2.1	2.2
Standard English, bilingualism and diversity	Is silence 'golden'?

3 THE BALANCE OF TEACHER–PUPIL INITIATIVE

CONCLUSION

Enhancing professional standards and competences

Communication is, and will always be, at the heart of teaching. In Scotland, 'communication' heads a whole section of specific compentences (Scottish Office, 1998, *Guidelines for Initial Teacher Education Courses in Scotland*, section 2.1). However, in England, a more general approach is taken. Trainees must demonstrate that they can:

> Teach clearly structured lessons, or sequences of work, which interest and motivate pupils and which make learning objectives clear to pupils, employ interactive teaching methods and collaborative group work, and promote active and independent learning that enables pupils to think for themselves, and to plan and manage their own learning.
>
> (TTA, 2002, *Standards for the Award of QTS*, standards 3.3.3)

These things are by no means easy, for there is normally just one teacher for a whole class of children. This chapter enables reflection on some of the communication issues that arise for all teachers.

An important specific point made by the TTA concerns inclusion. With the help of an experienced teacher, students must:

> Differentiate their teaching to meet the needs of pupils, including those more able and those with special needs.
>
> (standard 3.3.4)

> Be able to support those who are learning English as an additional language, and begin to analyse the language demands of teaching tasks.
>
> (standard 3.3.5)

Of course, the Welsh language is extremely important in Wales. It is the first language for a minority of children, is the medium of instruction in many schools and is taught in all schools.

INTRODUCTION

So far, in Part 2 of this book, we have examined the perspectives and expectations of children and teachers, their relationships, the ways in which knowledge, concepts, skills and attitudes are planned and presented through the curriculum and the manner in which classrooms can be organized and managed. All of these aspects facilitate the learning that we hope will be taking place in the classroom. It is now time to turn directly to teaching processes. In this chapter, we focus on the major features of classroom communication. In Chapter 13, this is extended to consider the explicit use of language to develop instructional teaching strategies.

 A central task of teaching is to make new knowledge, skills and conceptual frameworks available to pupils and this takes us back to the theories of learning reviewed in Chapter 7. There we suggest that learning involves using language to engage with and order experience so that new patterns of thinking and new ways of understanding and representing reality are developed (Wells, 1987,

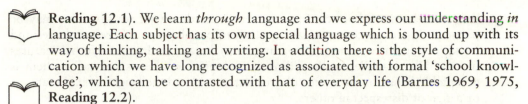

Reading 12.1). We learn *through* language and we express our understanding *in* language. Each subject has its own special language which is bound up with its way of thinking, talking and writing. In addition there is the style of communication which we have long recognized as associated with formal 'school knowledge', which can be contrasted with that of everyday life (Barnes 1969, 1975, **Reading 12.2**).

In accepting the centrality of language, this chapter focuses on the nature of spoken communication, and specifically on the characteristics of classroom communication. Section 1 reviews who speaks, how much, to whom and about what. Section 2 addresses issues associated with standard English, linguistic diversity and inclusion. Finally, Section 3 offers a way of analysing the balance of pupil–teacher initiative in classroom activity.

Language and communication are very complex. *Notes for Further Reading* or **RTweb** may therefore be particularly helpful for this chapter.

1   GENERAL CHARACTERISTICS OF CLASSROOM COMMUNICATION

A constant dilemma for teachers is how to select teaching strategies which enable pupils to learn well and teachers to 'cover' their syllabus. Embedded in that dilemma are a number of questions. How effective is teaching by telling? Can we do it better? How much can pupils learn from speaking to each other? Talking is important, but how do we know if it's the right kind of talk? How can we make discussion work better? How good are we at asking questions? Is whole-class discussion valuable? What's the best way to set up small group discussion? It is no accident that all these questions involve communication. Sharpening our awareness of classroom communication and interaction will help us to resolve the dilemma and make best use of the time available.

Communicating is a complicated business and it is not surprising that it frequently goes wrong. In the rapidity of encoding and decoding processes, there are endless possibilities for misunderstanding. Of course, language skills are fundamental but, since communication involves people, it requires social skills as well. In addition, since communication is usually focused on some meaningful topic, it calls for appropriate cognitive capacities – knowing something about the subject under consideration and being able to think about and process what we want to communicate to others and what they are trying to communicate to us. Nor can we forget the attitudes of the participants, the relationship between them, and the context itself, for these add another layer of meanings to the encounter.

Para-verbal and non-verbal features of oral language contribute to the effectiveness of how we communicate. Apart from what we say, a great deal is conveyed by how we say it. Thus, tone of voice, pace, pitch and how we project our voice are all part of the communication process. In addition, there are non-verbal aspects such as looks and gestures, and the ways in which we move, which accompany what we say. These can sometimes extend our meanings but they can also sometimes confuse or even contradict what we say. This may be particularly true in communication between people from different cultures and backgrounds where different meanings may be ascribed to non-verbal features of talk. For example, looking directly at someone when speaking to them is acceptable behaviour in some cultures but considered the height of bad manners or a sign of disrespect in others.

In classroom situations, teachers and pupils will act as both speakers and listeners. Hence, if classroom communication and learning are to be assured, all the participants need to have knowledge, skills and attitudes which are appropriate to both speaking and listening in schools. This cannot be assumed. When we examine classroom interaction closely a number of characteristics can be identified. These can provide important clues to the views of learning being expressed as well as the nature and quality of the teaching–learning processes being observed.

1.1   Who speaks and how much?

As identified in Chapters 10 and 11, classrooms are busy places in which, typically, individual teachers work with relatively large groups of children. In their desire to maximize learning opportunities and, at the same time, maintain order and organize the classroom it is not surprising that research shows that teachers do the majority of speaking in the classroom. A classic research study carried out in America indicated that, in the teaching sessions observed, two-thirds of the time was spent in talk and two-thirds of that talking was done by the teacher (Flanders, 1970). The picture was of a predominantly teacher-dominated situation. Since then investigations in British primary schools have shown similar figures (Bennett *et al.*, 1984; Galton *et al.*, 1980; Galton *et al.*, 1999).

The 'transmission' model, a situation in which teachers do the majority of the speaking and the role of children is to listen and to occasionally answer teacher-directed questions runs counter to a socially constructed view of learning as identified in Chapter 7. As we will discuss in Chapter 13 a wider range of teaching strategies have been developed and implemented over the years. However, teacher direction of talk and activities in classrooms remains at the core of practice. Indeed, many argue that the implementation of the National Literacy Strategy and National Numeracy Strategy has led to an increase in teacher-directed talk and a reduction of pupil-directed small-group discussion (e.g. Cordon, 2000; Haworth, 2001; Mroz, Smith and Hardman, 2000). Taking a socially constructed view of learning, these authors would argue that the further ligitimization of teacher-directed whole-class talk is seriously detrimental to learning. See Chapter 13 for a further discussion of these issues?

The diagram below (Barnes, 1975, **Reading 12.2**), was developed as a hypothesis about the relationship between styles of communication and views of learning and knowledge. The original is regarded as a seminal text in the field of language and learning. According to Barnes, if a teacher sees knowledge as content (as existing, prescribed subject matter which pupils are required to accept), then the communication will be mainly transmission and assessment will also predominate. As a consequence, pupils' talk will be presentational and there will be little opportunity to revise or re-draft writing. The resulting learn-

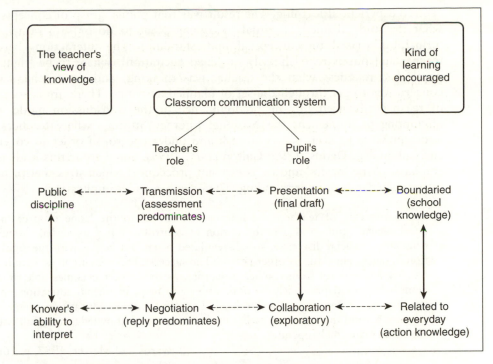

Figure 12.1 *Relationships of knowledge, communication and learning*

ing will be 'school knowledge' where what is 'known' is useful for answering teacher's questions, but it may be quickly forgotten and may have little or no impact on the learner's personal understanding and life outside school. However, if the teacher takes a social constructivist view and sees knowledge as existing in the learner's ability to interpret, then communication will be interactive, and there will be negotiation between the teacher's knowledge and the pupils' knowledge. Talk and writing will be collaborative and exploratory, and will support the struggle to understand as new knowledge is related to the learner's 'action knowledge'. There are clear resonances here with the contrasting views of learning which were reviewed in Chapter 7. As you look at Figure 12.1 you might consider: What are your own views of knowledge? How far are your views reflected in the curriculum you teach and the pedagogies you adopt?

Particularly in the light of the questions above, it is important to recognize that to advocate interpretation does not mean that teachers should never tell pupils things or present knowledge directly. Rather, it implies that transmission should be part of patterns of communication which are fundamentally designed to allow pupils to negotiate their own way into new knowledge and understanding. Equally, communication systems that appear pupil-centred sometimes turn out to be simply more subtle forms of transmission. For instance, a study involving analysis of teacher–pupil interaction in group work (Edwards and Mercer, 1987, **Reading 12.3**) showed teachers maintaining tight control over the activity and the discourse, even while overtly espousing the principle of pupil-centred experiential learning. The result was that pupils' grasp of concepts was what the study defined as 'ritual' (knowing what to do or say) rather than 'principled' (based on conceptual understanding). The interactions between teacher and pupils relied heavily on 'cued elicitation' (where to be 'right' the pupils had to guess what the teacher was thinking) and the teacher's main concern was to get through the set of planned activities. There are echoes here of reasons advanced for the predominance of the transmission mode when attempting to implement the National Literacy Strategy where teachers feel under pressure to keep pupils on-task and under control in order to cover the curriculum (e.g. Dadds, 1999; Galton *et al.*, 1999). Some argue this leads to an emphasis of the 'basics' and to assessment procedures which stress performance rather than depth of understanding. The issue has wider implications.

> The asymmetry of teacher and learner is essential to the 'zone of proximal development', and so also is the notion of control . . . Just as verbal thought originates as social discourse, so self-regulated behaviour begins with the regulation of one's behaviour by other people. The successful process involves a gradual handover of control from teacher to learner, as the learner becomes able to do alone what could previously be done only with help. In formal education, this part of the process is seldom realised. For most pupils, education remains a mystery beyond their control, rather than a resource of knowledge and skill with which they can freely operate.
>
> (Edwards and Mercer, 1987, p. 168)

Here and now, such paradoxes and dilemmas are even more evident. A rapidly changing society may require pupils to learn to be flexible, adaptable, multiskilled problem-solvers who can apply learning in new situations. At the same time there is increased emphasis on narrowly defined qualifications, examination success, 'standards' and statistical comparison of results – all linked explicitly or by inference to economic and moral revival. In addition, the National Curriculum is expressed in subjects and underpinned by the idea of cultural transmission. In making choices about classroom communication teachers are thus balancing a number of potentially conflicting demands, and the decisions they make about 'who does the talking' will inevitably reflect their values, beliefs and responses to some of these unresolved dilemmas.

To begin to reflect on classroom communication, a reflective teacher is likely to want to collect data rather than rely on impressions. Tape recording can be a useful technique for collecting certain kinds of data on classroom talk (see Chapter 3, Section 3.19). An alternative way of collecting information about particular aspects of teacher talk is to devise appropriate checklists. These can be helpful both as a guide when preparing a session, or as a framework within which to reflect afterwards. A third approach is to devise an observation schedule which focuses on specific categories of behaviour. For example, four categories could be used, such as when the teacher asks a question, explains a task, manages the situation or disciplines a pupil (questioning, explanation, management, discipline). Each time one of these behaviours is noted it can be 'marked up' using a tally system: see Chapter 3, Section 3.6. In the next Activity you are asked to record a lesson or part of a lesson, to reflect on who speaks and how much and to consider what that might reveal about the teacher's views of knowledge and learning.

Reflective activity 12.1

Aim: To investigate who speaks and how much during a lesson. You may want to gather data on your own teaching or that of another teacher.

Evidence and reflection: We recommend that you begin with a tape recording of a lesson but if this is not possible you might consider one of the other methods mentioned above and supported on the web.

Now consider:

- How much speaking is there?
- Who is doing the speaking?
- Which pupils speak?
- When does the teacher speak?
- When do the pupils speak?

Information of this kind can highlight the pattern of talk in a classroom. It can often reveal aspects which surprise us, because it is so difficult to be aware of how much we talk, to whom and when, whilst we are engrossed in the process of teaching itself.

Extension: Having identified the pattern of talk we need to decide whether what we do is consistent with our aims. You might like to see if you can change the way you teach in the light of what you have learned in this activity. You could also use a similar approach to investigate different aspects of classroom interaction, e.g. teacher–pupil interaction in group work; pupil–pupil interaction, generally or in small group work. You will find suggestions for other observations in subsequent Reflective Activities in this chapter.

1.2 Where is the talk directed?

The findings of one large investigation into classroom talk, the ORACLE research, showed that approximately 80 per cent of teachers' time, in Key Stage 2 classrooms, was spent in talk between the teacher and children – 56 per cent with individuals, 15 per cent with the whole class, 7 per cent with groups (Galton, Simon and Croll, 1980). In a more recent study (Galton *et al.*, 1999, p. 84) found that 'for the typical pupil, 75 per cent of all pupil–teacher exchanges are experienced as a member of the class, exactly as they were twenty years ago'. Interestingly, a similar large project, the PACE research, found that in Key Stage 1 classrooms, the proportion of whole-class work was twice as high, with a lower figure for individual work (Pollard *et al.*, 2000).

Apart from the size of the 'audience' with whom a teacher is communicating, it is also significant to consider how the teacher's time is distributed between the children; between girls and boys, and between children of different abilities or different needs. Some research suggests that boys often receive a greater share of a teacher's attention – both positive and negative (Spender and Sarah, 1980; Swann, 1994; Swann and Graddol, 1994), and that children of different ethnic origins receive different types of attention (Biggs and Edwards, 1994). The impact of including children with special needs has also been studied (Croll and Moses, 1985, 2000, **Reading 10.6**).

Given that much of the interaction in a classroom is teacher-controlled it is useful to consider how the teacher's time is distributed between whole class, individuals and groups. There is plenty of evidence that, in the context of curriculum pressures, large class sizes and the demands of assessment, parity of attention is difficult to achieve. One feature which often causes problems is that there are variations in both the quantity and quality of teacher attention which is given to different categories of pupils.

There are a number of obvious categories around which such variations have often been found, such as ability, gender, ethnicity and social class. The impact of integrating pupils with special needs also has to be considered. In busy classrooms, it is very understandable that teachers tend to deal first with pupils who demand attention either because they have acute needs or because their actions necessitate an immediate response. However, there is a potential danger that some other pupils may be consistently passed over as they move from class to class (Collins, 1996, **Reading 12.6**). Whilst the needs of all the pupils in a class cannot be satisfied simultaneously by any teacher, we do have a responsibility to ensure that teacher effort is distributed equitably.

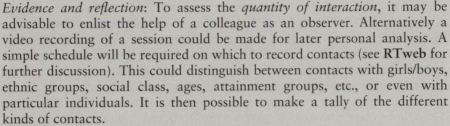

Reflective activity 12.2

Aim: To identify possible patterns in the quantity and quality of teacher–child contacts.

Evidence and reflection: To assess the *quantity of interaction*, it may be advisable to enlist the help of a colleague as an observer. Alternatively a video recording of a session could be made for later personal analysis. A simple schedule will be required on which to record contacts (see **RTweb** for further discussion). This could distinguish between contacts with girls/boys, ethnic groups, social class, ages, attainment groups, etc., or even with particular individuals. It is then possible to make a tally of the different kinds of contacts.

Decisions about whether to try to record all contacts or whether to adopt a time sampling techniques will have to be taken (see Chapter 3, section 3). If the latter is chosen, some practice is essential for the observer. It is also possible to focus on an individual child and to monitor the contacts with just that child. It may be interesting to note pupil-initiated interaction with the teacher.

To assess the *quality of contacts* requires a different approach. By quality we have in mind (Rogers, 1980) the 'genuineness, acceptance and empathy' that is conveyed through the contact, in combination with, and the cognitive 'match' of task to pupil (Bennett *et al.*, 1984). Subjective interpretations are more likely to play a dominant part in this analysis, so it is probably helpful to use a video or for an observer to make field-notes concerning the nature of contacts made. It would be particularly useful if time could be made for discussion with the teacher and pupils after the session.

Extension: You might want to share your observations with a friend or colleague. How do you interpret what you have found? How will it affect your planning and your teaching?

1.3 What is the talk about?

Teacher talk in the classroom can be divided into three categories: talk related to learning (e.g. exploratory talk, exposition, questioning); administrative talk to ensure the management of tasks and activities; and disciplinary talk concerned with managing behaviour and maintaining control. In this way teachers have control of the material to be learned and the way in which talk is conducted. This is 'controlling not just negatively, as a traffic policeman does to avoid collisions, but also positively, to enhance the purposes of education' (Cazden, 1988, p. 3). The balance of time given to different kinds of teacher talk in a lesson indicates the quality of the learning taking place. Similarly, some researchers suggest that the use of indirect speech acts, i.e. statements whose real meanings are different from their surface meaning, e.g. 'would you like to sit down', rather than direct requests 'now sit down' are a mark of superior teaching (Manke, 1997). Advocates of the use of indirect speech acts argue that they are a way of protecting personal dignity. However, for indirect speech acts to work effectively there has to be a shared understanding between teachers and pupils as to what is regarded as being an appropriate response. As Edwards and Mercer identify (1987, p. 241, **Reading 12.3**) 'the relation of power and control to the creation of joint understandings is both problematic and of great importance'.

The ORACLE study showed that the highest percentage of teacher talk in Key Stage 2 classrooms was generally devoted to supervizing tasks set – rather than to talking about the substantive content of those tasks (Galton, Simon and Croll, 1980). Most of this talk was in the form of statements of fact. Very little time indeed was spent in asking questions which required children to think for themselves in any kind of open-ended, problem-solving capacity. In general, teacher talk seemed to be largely concerned with the smooth running and management of the classroom and the practice of engaging the children in challenging discussion was rare. There is also evidence that the endorsement of whole class teaching as part of the National Literacy Strategy and National Numeracy Strategy 'appears to have had little effect in providing opportunities for pupils to question or explore ideas to help them develop their own thinking' (Mroz, Smith and Hardman, 2000). In infant classrooms such talk is also likely to concern the shaping of pupil behaviour as the children learn various aspects of the pupil role (Willes, 1983).

As reflective teachers it is particularly important to consider the significance of teacher talk – processes which can be seen in the development work of the National Oracy Project (Norman, 1990) and the Language In the National Curriculum project (LINC) (Carter, 1990; DES, 1990–1). For example, why are there such high proportions of teacher talk in classrooms? What might be the effects of teacher talk on pupils? What impressions might they gain about learning and about their own role in the learning process? What kinds of attitudes towards learning might pupils acquire? What types of learning are likely to take place?

Reflective activity 12.3

Aim: To identify patterns in the purpose of teacher contacts with pupils.

Evidence and reflection: We suggest the development of a schedule which lists different kinds of contact. This should be in terms of descriptive and visible actions (so that the amount of inference is low) and which do not overlap (so that the categories are exclusive). For example, you could try classifying teacher contacts with pupils using categories such as: 'instructional', 'managerial', 'social' and 'other'. Data might then be collected by time sampling or a tally (see **RTweb** for further discussion). The results could then be analysed to try to identify any different patterns of contact based on gender, ethnicity, class, attainments, achievement or personalities.

Extension: You might want to consider looking at pupil-initiated contacts, or at pupil–pupil interaction in a similar way.

http://www.rtweb.info

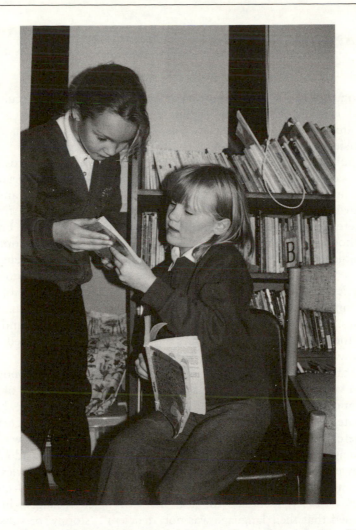

Of interest too is the kind of talk involved in pupil–pupil interaction. How much of pupils' talk is learning related and 'on task'? How much is social, and might be deemed to be 'off task'? Of on-task talk, how much is related to managing the task (fetching equipment, sharpening pencils, rubbing out) and how much to carrying out the work and developing understanding? Some sorts of activities – cutting out, colouring in, routine procedures – seem to precipitate social talk. As one Year 9 pupil explained, 'I can colour in and talk at the same time.' What should our reaction be to this?

Looking at what talk is about leads us also to consider the issue of the specialized language of each subject. Most noticeably this concerns technical terms and specialist vocabulary. We need to think about how teachers introduce and use these in their expositions and interactions. Equally, observations of pupil talk will help us to consider whether they are taking on the language of the subject as part of their conceptual development (as a significant act of ownership which is the basis for further thinking) or whether they are using terms as 'labels' with no real understanding.

2 LANGUAGE AND INCLUSION

2.1 Standard English, bilingualism and diversity

Language is one of the most significant manifestations of culture and identity, and is thus of enormous significance for the self-respect of individuals and groups, and for the majority and many minorities within the UK. We will consider three main issues. First, we have the explicit, dominant belief in the importance of 'standard English' and established, high-status forms of speech. Indeed, in some respects, particularly in England, this has been strengthened by the introduction of national literacy targets, common standards for school provision and arguments about entitlements to be realized through schooling. There is an important debate here about whether standard English is an elitist orthodoxy, or an entitlement. Second, we have the development of national languages within the UK, particularly Welsh in Wales, Gaelic in Scotland and Irish in Northern Ireland. The case of Welsh as a medium of instruction is particularly important. Third, there is the crucial significance of the rich diversity of cultures and languages within the UK generally, particularly in our larger cities. This, of course, is connected to growth in migration and multiculturalism as the global economy becomes increasingly interconnected. Nor can we be unaware of the problem of racism.

Standard English, once associated with 'classic' BBC pronounciation, syntax and vocabulary, has by no means conceded to the diversity of culture and style of modern society. Indeed, the formal prescription of the National Literacy Strategy in England shows just how strong conceptions of 'correctness' still are. There is also, it is argued, an entitlement issue in being aware of and able to manage this dominant form of language, even if few may adopt it as their own. However, we have known for some time that different styles of language are not necessarily less effective forms of communication. Indeed, early work by Labov (1973) identified the grammars of Black teenagers in New York and argued that their language was not 'deficient', 'sloppy' or substandard. Rather, he suggested that their grammars were 'different' and just as regularly rule-bound as more socially accepted forms of standard English. In contemporary times, we also find that new cultural styles are associated with highly sophisti-cated non-standard language forms as a matter of choice. Outside school con-texts, there has been a change in the social acceptability of different styles of language. This has meant that the notion of 'appropriateness' has increasingly come to be used (i.e. that different kinds of language are suitable for different purposes, audiences and situations). This is a contrast to the notion of 'accu-racy' as an absolute standard to be used to judge all language situations (see Stubbs and Hillier, 1983; Davies, 2000, **Reading 12.4** for further discussion of this issue). In a further twist, we also have plentiful evidence of standard English which is spoken with a regional or other accent – though some accents still have higher status than others. Within classroom contexts, a dilemma has to be faced. First, one might believe in the importance of accepting a pupil's language, whatever its form, because that affirms the child, strengthens their self-image and supports inclusion. On the other hand, it can be argued that children need and have an entitlement to learn more standard forms of English, and that to fail to teach them is to limit their life-chances. The use of non-standard English, for instance by pupils from working-class communities, has long had negative social consequences of a discriminatory nature. Reflective teachers will want to maximize both their entitlements and their inclusion. Creative teaching strategies may provide ways forward. For instance, children may be encouraged to engage in role-play in which they can 'pretend' to talk in standard English without feeling that they have to abandon their own forms of language.

Bilingualism in the UK is associated with two main circumstances. The situation of the indigenous Celtic populations, with languages such as Welsh, Gaelic, Irish, Manx and even Cornish, is rather different from those of newer cultures and communities in the UK, whose origins usually lie in immigration either to support our economy and public services, or as political refugees.

Following many centuries in which use of Celtic languages has been eroded, their role in affirming identity has become more fully recognized in recent years. This has become particularly significant in Wales, where there are major populations, particularly in the North and West, for whom Welsh is their first language. The Welsh Language Act of 1993 established significant statutory bilingual rights and the *equity* of Welsh and English. Welsh is the language of instruction in over a fifth of Welsh schools, is taught alongside English in all Welsh primary schools, and is used extensively in politics, business and everyday life throughout the country. Whilst Wales does not have a National Literacy Strategy in the English mould, it is developing a National Languages Strategy. Offering support to the European Year of Languages, Jane Davidson, Welsh Assembly Minister for Education said: 'Welsh is a wonderful language and everyone should take the time to learn it. Our success as a nation depends on lifelong learning and I want to encourage everyone to take up the opportunities available to them – opportunities like learning Welsh' (July 2001). Bilingualism then, is seen as a national strength, and a crucial element of identity (Baker and Jones, 1998; Blackledge, 1994; Jones and Ghuman, 1995). In this, the role of the education system in affirming and teaching the Welsh language, alongside English, is seen as immensely valuable – and most teachers in Wales also feel that the prominence of Welsh culture and language enriches the curriculum and the educational experiences of their pupils.

Minority ethnic communities in the UK face rather different circumstances, but they too would value a constructive and appreciative approach of this sort. The extent of diversity is considerable. For instance, a 1987 language census in London (ILEA, 1987) found that no less that 172 different languages were spoken by school pupils. Some of such languages have been mapped in terms of the geolinguistic areas from which they are derived (Alladina and Edwards, 1991) and this is shown in Figure 12.2.

Language varieties used within a society with a single dominant language, such as English, reflect far more than simply an alternative means of communication (Pinsent, 1992). As we have seen, language is intimately connected to cultural identity, to concepts and to patterns of thought. It is thus both educationally essential and a legitimate right to expect formal education systems to recognize and build on existing language capabilities. Additionally, the needs of children for whom English is an additional language (EAL) need specific recognition.

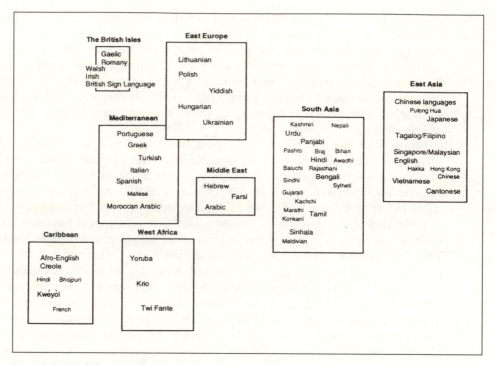

Figure 12.2 *Geolinguistic areas of languages spoken in Britain*

Unfortunately, the life experiences of many minority ethnic groups in Britain have, with some notable exceptions, been associated with various degrees of economic and social disadvantage. Despite many years of peaceful coexistence, attempts to affirm identity risk aggressive responses by some indigenous groups, whether powerful or powerless, that may feel threatened. Increased votes for the implicitly racist British National Party in the national election of 2001 and riots in Bradford and Burnley, are examples of this phenomenon. As Pattanayak has so clearly expressed it:

> As the identity of the various oppressed groups is threatened, identity assertion movements ensue ... Ethnicity, which in the literature is variously expressed as assertion of cultures, communal upsurges, revival of religions, voices and movements of marginalised peoples ... hurts the power elites ... Britain is on the crossroads. It can take an isolationist stance in relation to its internal cultural environment ... The second road would be working together with cultural harmony for the betterment of the country. The choice is between mediocrity and creativity.
>
> (Pattanayak, 1991, p. x)

Teachers have a particularly important and sensitive role to play here, where they can. The danger is that the constant pressure for performance in targets for English reflect a monolingual conception of our culture and social circumstances. As Atkinson (2000) has powerfully argued: 'the National Literacy Strategy is a tool through which the "literate" can be defined as "English" and the "English" as "literate", thus preserving a long held image of cultural superiority.' Whatever the circumstances, we would suggest that reflective teachers should work to affirm the positive value of minority languages and cultures, wherever they teach. This means affirming and building on the bilingual capacities of pupils, and there are many practical examples of how this can be done (e.g. Blackledge, 1994, **Reading 12.5**; Edwards, 1998; Gravelle, 2000; Gregory, 1996; Wrigley, 2000).

Reflective activity 12.4

Aim: To highlight some of our own responses to language varieties.

Evidence and reflection: Use your results on this provocative rating scale for discussion with the views of colleagues.

	I tend to agree			I tend to disagree
1. Dialects are ungrammatical forms of English	1 2	3	4 5	
2. Pupils should speak standard English at all times in school, including in the playground	1 2	3	4 5	
3. Dropping your 'H's is sloppy, and creates a bad impression	1 2	3	4 5	
4. Poor grammar and spelling should be corrected at all times	1 2	3	4 5	
5. All pupils should learn to appreciate Shakespeare	1 2	3	4 5	
6. In general, middle-class pupils speak better than working-class pupils	1 2	3	4 5	
7. Children's home language is not the concern of their teacher	1 2	3	4 5	
8. It is confusing for pupils to speak two languages in school	1 2	3	4 5	
9. The most important task for all pupils in Britain is to learn good English	1 2	3	4 5	
10. We should not use expressions like 'black mark' as they illustrate racist language	1 2	3	4 5	
11. Cultural identity is one thing, but learning to read is another	1 2	3	4 5	

Extension: The exercise above should produce some interesting discussion, but actual knowledge and understanding of these issues is another thing. Among speakers of majority languages, the most common state is one of relative ignorance regarding language varieties and the cultures and social circumstances of different social groups. Key Readings for this chapter may provide some ideas.

2.2   Is silence 'golden'?

Traditionally, quiet classrooms have been regarded by many as being synonymous with well-controlled classrooms in which children are thought to be working hard and focusing on the learning tasks in hand. However, we believe that for reflective teachers, quiet compliant behaviour does not necessarily equate with a commitment to learning. Observations suggest that quiet children might be, 'playing truant in mind whilst present in body' (Young, 1984, p. 12). Although they complete the bare minimum of work they appear to have little interest or investment in the outcome. 'They conform, and even play the system, but many do not allow the knowledge presented to them to make any deep impact upon their view of reality' (Barnes and Douglas, 1979, p. 17).

 As we have made clear in this chapter (see also Chapters 7 and 13) spoken language is central to children's cognitive and emotional development. It is by talking that children develop their perceptions of themselves and their world. Moreover, it is by talking with children, and listening to what they have to say, that teachers assess and support children's learning. When children are quiet and do not participate in classroom discussions it is extremely difficult for teachers to assess the extent and depth of their understanding or to support further learning. This problem is compounded by the fact that children who are quiet often find it very difficult to ask for help from the teacher even when they are experiencing serious difficulties. As we have said earlier in this chapter, the teacher usually determines the content and style of classroom discussions. Consequently, there may be few opportunities for children to raise their own issues or to voice things in their own terms. In addition, whole-class or large-group discussions are difficult contexts for some children when they have to compete for the teacher's attention. In these contexts some pupils also fear the responses of their peers who may not be supportive.

Teachers face a double bind in trying to encourage reluctant pupils to speak. Drawing attention to such pupils or their behaviour increases feelings of embarrassment but the alternative is to ignore the pupils and deny them opportunities to practice learning through talk.

Based on the above, we would argue that silence is not golden. Rather it is an indication of a lack of active participation on the part of the pupils. From a social constructivist view of learning we believe that for pupils to be successful and make the most of the learning opportunities offered it is important that they become active participants in the discourse of the classroom. Children who are unable or unwilling to talk freely to their teacher are at an acute disadvantage when compared with their more vocal peers. Whilst it is relatively easy to identify the emotional and behavioural difficulties of loud, potentially aggressive pupils, the special educational needs of quiet withdrawn pupils can be easily overlooked.

The following checklist identifies some of the ways in which habitually quiet non-participatory behaviour should be regarded as potentially detrimental to learning. Can you add others to this list?

Checklist 12.1

Quiet non-participatory behaviour may be detrimental to learning because it:

- Prevents children from learning to express themselves (learning to talk)
- Prevents children from asking questions and making the learning their own (learning through talk)
- Prevents children from an active exploration of the subject being learned
- Prevents teachers from finding out what children know and thus monitor and support learning
- Reinforces stereotypes. Girls, especially those with moderate learning difficulties, are more likely to exhibit quiet passive behaviour in the classroom than other groups of children
- Renders children invisible and can reinforce poor self-images
- Can be linked with social isolation and can make pupils vulnerable to bullying
- Can, in a minority of cases, mask serious emotional trauma such as bereavement, abuse, family separation, etc.

Reflective activity 12.5

Aims: To identify pupils who exhibit quiet non-participatory behaviour during your lesson.

Evidence and reflection: Given the nature of the behaviour you are trying to observe it may be necessary to video a lesson and watch it carefully several times to identify those who do not participate. You might want to reflect back on a video recording which you produced for a previous activity.

As you watch the video try to notice:

- Pupils who do not volunteer to speak or answer questions.
- Pupils who avoid being chosen to speak, perhaps by only putting up their hand as someone else is chosen to answer.
- Pupils who seem embarrassed if they feel that they have become the centre of attention.
- Pupils who always provide monosyllabic answers or who refuse to speak at all.

What did the teacher do? Did it help and if so in what way?

Extension: Having identified pupils who might exhibit quiet behaviour, what might you do to encourage their active participation in future? How might you ensure that you continue to notice and monitor those pupils who do not demand your attention?

Drawing on longitudinal research, which involved detailed analysis of classroom observations in primary and secondary schools (Collins, 1996, **Reading 12.6**), we would identify the following as potentially useful strategies in encouraging all children to participate in whole-class and large-group discussions.

Checklist 12.2

In order to encourage pupil participation we would suggest:

- Emphasizing the value of talk and making it the medium for learning rather than the precursor to the 'real' work of writing

- Rejecting whole-class teacher-directed talk in favour of small-group child-centred talk

- Identifying the rules of discussion and making them explicit to the pupils

- Increasing feelings of security by establishing friendship groups or 'talk partners' and using them as the basis for all initial discussions

- Providing activities which encourage collaboration

- Allow pupils opportunities to consider what they want to say before calling on them to speak in front of large groups

- Working with the pupils to devise ways of assessing talk and providing opportunities for pupils to reflect on what makes for effective talk

Which of these strategies do you use? Which might you use in future?

---

3   THE BALANCE OF TEACHER–PUPIL INITIATIVE

We conclude this chapter with reference to a technique which was designed to look at literacy learning across the curriculum (Webster, Beveridge and Reid, 1996, **Reading 12.7**) but which can be applied to teaching and learning processes as a whole. The model which is set out in Figure 12.3 can be used to highlight particular characteristics and qualities of interaction between teachers and learners.

The teacher axis runs vertically and represents the degree of *teacher activity* in the learning interaction ('high' to 'low'). A learner axis runs horizontally and represents the degree of *learner initiative* (from 'high' to 'low'). The model thus plots two key variables in any teaching and learning interaction. These combine to give four distinctive 'quadrants of interaction' – teacher-driven, resource-driven, child-driven and learning-driven. In the latter, for instance, high levels of teacher activity are combined with high levels of child initiative.

Characteristic forms of practice are described for each quadrant in Figure 12.3, which clearly echoes back to Chapter 7 on learning. The model could be used to consider the repertoire of teaching strategies that we use. Of course, these should be 'fit for their purpose' for any particular age group. However, we might expect that in Foundation Stage, there might be a generally higher

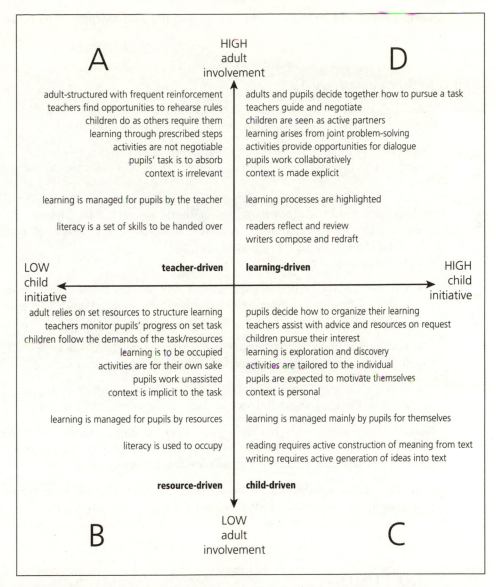

Figure 12.3 *A model of adult–child interaction in classrooms*

emphasis on child initiative and building from children's interests and experiences. At Key Stage 3, pupil initiative tends to be lower and there is often a higher use of resource-based activities.

In an empirical study using the framework (Webster, Beveridge and Reid, 1996, **Reading 12.7**), a comparison was drawn between the quadrant from which teachers thought they derived their pedagogy and what they were actually observed to do in the complex realities of their lessons. Of course, teacher and pupil talk is, with observed behaviour, a clear source of evidence on matters of this sort. Using this type of representation allows teachers to examine and develop beliefs and practices concerning teaching and learning – to reflect on their practice.

Reflective activity 12.6

Aim: To consider the qualities of interaction in a lesson, by reflecting on differences between a lesson plan and the lesson as actually taught.

Evidence and reflection: First, you will need to produce a full lesson plan, setting out your educational objectives and teaching strategies (see Chapter 9).

Then you need to teach the lesson, and collect some evidence about it. Perhaps you could use some of the methods suggested in Chapter 3, or elsewhere in this book. Having gathered some data, take stock of it and produce a clear description of what happened.

The third stage is more analytical:

- On two sheets of blank paper, draw two copies of the basic four-quadrant framework (the skeleton without the writing) given in Figure 12.3.

- Using your first copy, analyse your initial lesson objectives by recording the key activities you intended in the appropriate quadrant.

- Using your second copy, analyse your evidence about what happened by describing what actually took place in the appropriate quadrant.

Consider any differences between your two versions. What might these indicate to you about the dilemmas faced by teachers and the struggle for control over learning which takes place in classrooms?

Extension: How would you evaluate your findings? What strategies might you develop to shift pupils' initiative into a 'higher' quadrant?

CONCLUSION

This chapter has raised a large number of issues relating to the characteristics of classroom communication. Communication has been viewed as a key component of classroom life and therefore as an important influence on the learning which might take place. Building on this discussion we now need to reflect specifically on the way we use language in our teaching. This is the subject of Chapter 13.

Key readings

As accessible introductions to the importance of communication in the primary classroom and the relationship between language and understanding, the following have become classics amongst both practitioners and academics:

Edwards, D. and Mercer, N. (1987)
Common Knowledge: the Development of Understanding in Classrooms.
London: Methuen. **Reading 12.3**

Wells, G. (1987)
The Meaning Makers: Children Learning Language and Using Language to Learn.
London: Hodder and Stoughton. **Reading 12.1**

For insights into how we use language to think and get things done, the following draws on real-life language use within and beyond the classroom:

Mercer, N. (2000)
Words and Minds: How We Use Language to Think Together.
London: Routledge.

To make the points about the centrality of language and imagination in a different and very engaging way, see:

Paley, G. V. (1981)
Wally's Stories.
Cambridge, MA: Harvard University Press.

For a celebration of research that draws on the experience of teachers and pupils to emphasize the centrality of talk for learning, see:

Norman, K. (ed.) (1992)
Thinking Voices: the Work of the National Oracy Project.
London: Hodder and Stoughton.

Written in response to the implementation of the National Literacy Strategy, the following offers a range of practical strategies aimed at ensuring that literacy is taught in a vibrant and stimulating way through interactive discourse and effective questioning:

Cordon, R. (2000)
Literacy and Learning Through Talk: Strategies for the Primary Classroom.
Buckingham: Open University Press.

For a brilliantly principled but very practical guide to young bilinguals learning to read, see:

Gregory, E. (1996)
Making Sense of a New World: Learning to Read in a Second Language.
London: Paul Chapman. See also **Reading 12.5**

Addressing the needs of bilingual learners across the curriculum is considered in:

Gravelle, M. (ed.) (2000)
Planning for Bilingual Learners: an Inclusive Curriculum.
Stoke-on-Trent: Trentham.

For a consideration of strategies to recognize and meet the social, emotional and educational needs of the quieter children in the classroom, see:

Collins, J. (1996)
The Quiet Child.
London: Cassell. **Reading 12.6**

For an excellent introduction to the methods of recording and analysing classroom talk, see:

Edwards, A. D. and Westgate, D. P. G. (1994)
Investigating Classroom Talk.
London: Falmer. **Reading 12.7**

Webster, A., Beveridge, M. and Reid, M. (1996)
Managing the Literacy Curriculum.
London: Routledge.

Most specialist educational publishers also have useful series of books based on communication in schools. For instance, in the UK see the catalogues of Continuum, RoutledgeFalmer, David Fulton, Simon and Schuster, Open University Press, Paul Chapman Press, etc.

Readings for Reflective Teaching (the companion volume) offers other closely associated work on the issues raised in this chapter. This includes work by authors such as:

Gordon Wells, Douglas Barnes, Derek Edwards, Neil Mercer, Chris Davies, Adrian Blackledge, Janet Collins, Alec Webster, Mike Beveridge and Malcolm Reid.

RTweb offers additional professional resources for this chapter. These may include *Notes for Further Reading*, supplementary *Reflective Activities*, useful *Web Links*, *Extension Texts* and *Download Facilities* for diagrams, figures, checklists, activities.

CHAPTER 13

Teaching. How are we developing our strategies?

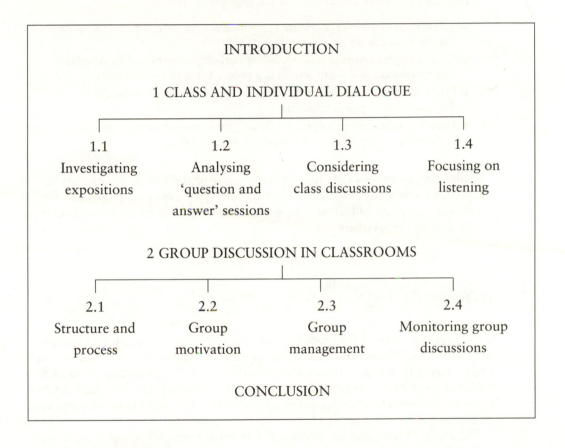

INTRODUCTION

1 CLASS AND INDIVIDUAL DIALOGUE

1.1	1.2	1.3	1.4
Investigating expositions	Analysing 'question and answer' sessions	Considering class discussions	Focusing on listening

2 GROUP DISCUSSION IN CLASSROOMS

2.1	2.2	2.3	2.4
Structure and process	Group motivation	Group management	Monitoring group discussions

CONCLUSION

Enhancing professional standards and competences

This chapter focuses on core teaching strategies, for whole-class, individual and group work. These are crucial for all teachers. For instance, although under consideration for revision, the present Welsh *Standards for the Award of QTS* provide a clear set of requirements.

Trainees should be able to use teaching methods which sustain the momentum of pupils' work and keep all pupils engaged through:

- Stimulating intellectual curiousity, communicating enthusiasm and fostering and maintaining pupils' motivation
- Structuring information well, including outlining content and aims, signalling transitions, and summarising key points as the lesson progresses
- Effective questioning which matches the pace and direction of the lesson and ensures that pupils take part
- Listening carefully to pupils, analysing their responses and responding constructively in order to take pupils' learning forward.

(standard B: k)

Similar requirements exists for the other parts of the UK, but with varying degrees of specificity. However, explanation, questioning and dialogue for different groupings of learners require a range of generic strategies and skills from teachers everywhere.

INTRODUCTION

In the previous chapter we looked at the characteristics of classroom communication. In that chapter we discussed aspects of whole-class discussions and teacher-directed talk. In particular we identified how the implementation of the National Literacy Strategy and the National Numeracy Strategy had further legitimized whole-class teaching. We also reiterated the importance of pupil talk for learning.

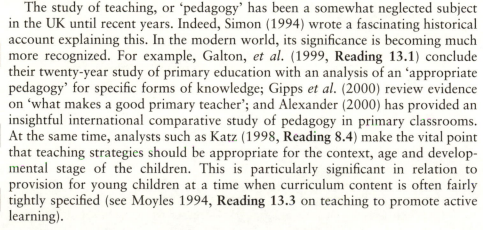

The study of teaching, or 'pedagogy' has been a somewhat neglected subject in the UK until recent years. Indeed, Simon (1994) wrote a fascinating historical account explaining this. In the modern world, its significance is becoming much more recognized. For example, Galton, *et al.* (1999, **Reading 13.1**) conclude their twenty-year study of primary education with an analysis of an 'appropriate pedagogy' for specific forms of knowledge; Gipps *et al.* (2000) review evidence on 'what makes a good primary teacher'; and Alexander (2000) has provided an insightful international comparative study of pedagogy in primary classrooms. At the same time, analysts such as Katz (1998, **Reading 8.4**) make the vital point that teaching strategies should be appropriate for the context, age and developmental stage of the children. This is particularly significant in relation to provision for young children at a time when curriculum content is often fairly tightly specified (see Moyles 1994, **Reading 13.3** on teaching to promote active learning).

In the present chapter we particularly focus on the ways in which we use *language* for teaching and learning. Section 1 focuses on dialogue with whole classes and individual learners. Section 2 looks specifically at aspects of small group discussion.

RTweb offers additional *Reflective Activities* designed to enhance your teaching.

1   CLASS AND INDIVIDUAL DIALOGUE

We have identified four common types of oral classroom communication. As you read about them you might want to consider the extent to which these may occur in whole-class, individual or small group discussions. The four types of talk are:

- *Expositions*: where the speaker describes, informs, instructs, or explains directly.

- *Question-and-answer exchanges*: frequently for testing and checking purposes, where there is often one right answer, (i.e. a 'closed' situation); also to encourage thinking, speculation, to develop understanding.

- *Discussions*: or exploratory talk where the participants explore ideas and feelings together, (i.e. an 'open' situation). This could involve interpretation and speculation where participants apply a principle to a case, use evidence, find overarching principles or formulate hypotheses.

- *Listening*: where the receiver hears and responds to the speech of other people.

Each of these situations has features in common as well as features which are unique to itself. For example, since every communicative situation is at least a two-way process, we need to consider the speakers as well as the listeners. In 'exposition' or 'direct instruction' (Muijs and Reynolds, 2001, **Reading 13.4**) the listeners may not participate verbally very much. Direct instruction has become a very significant teaching approach in recent years with the introduction of national literary and numeracy strategies. Muijs and Reynolds suggest that there are five key conditions that make it effective: clearly structured lessons; clearly structured presentations; pacing; modelling; and the use of conceptual mapping. The latter links back to the work of Galton *et al.* (2000, **Reading 13.1**) on the forms of knowledge to be learned. There are potential problems though, if pupils are cast in passive roles and fail to engage with the curriculum. Indeed, the teacher must be aawre of the childen and watch for signs of understanding or otherwise, so that adjustments can be made.

All forms of classroom interaction, in fact, call for particular types of awareness about the rules of communication. In order to participate productively, the rules must be clear and each participant must understand and accept those rules. Learning to speak and to listen are thus very important skills. Neither skill can be considered 'passive', for they both take place through interaction. Moreover, it is important to remember that the rules of communication in classrooms are significantly different from the rules of communication in other contexts. There is evidence, for example, that even very young children modify their talk to conform to teacher expectations and ask significantly fewer 'curiosity' type questions in school than at home (Tizard and Hughes, 1984). However, we also know that young children are more likely to ask such questions after periods of more 'open' conversation in classrooms.

We now turn to examine the first of the four main types of oral communication that we find in the classroom – exposition.

1.1 Investigating expositions

For an effective teaching session it is necessary both to stimulate your pupils' interest and to provide structure for the subsequent activities. These requirements are just as pertinent for whole-class sessions as for group or individual work. Expositions, therefore, are a very common aspect of any teacher's talk. Indeed, as we mentioned in Chapter 12, the three-part lesson advocated by the National Literacy Strategy and the National Numeracy Strategy increases the amount of teacher exposition and direct instruction (e.g. Mroz, Smith and Hardman, 2000). Although less commonly required of pupils, from time to time especially during plenary sessions, they may be asked to make a formal report back on an activity or a prepared presentation. In any such situation the opening 'moves' are particularly important in setting the tone of the session.

A number of different aspects of exposition might be considered:

1. Getting attention.
2. Motivating the listeners.
3. Orientating, so that expectations about the session are clear.
4. Constructing and delivering the exposition itself.

 The first three of these aspects have already been discussed in Chapter 10, as part of our consideration of classroom management. Here, therefore, we suggest some checks (Checklist 13.1) to help to focus our attention on the fourth aspect of expositions – constructing and delivering the exposition itself.

Reflective activity 13.1

Aim: To observe and consider exposition as a teaching strategy.

 Evidence and reflection: Use Checklist 13.1 to structure your observation and analysis of teaching by exposition. You may be observing another teacher or asking a colleague to observe you. It may be possible to do some self evaluation by means of an audio (or video) recording (see Chapter 3, Section 3.14 and 3.19 and Reflective Activity 12.1). What do you see as the strengths and weaknesses of this approach?

Extension: What are the implications for your teaching on what you have discovered? It may be helpful to talk with your mentor about this or share your analysis with a colleague who has also undertaken a similar observation.

> ## Checklist 13.1
>
> *Aim*: To examine how an exposition is structured and delivered.
>
> Are the instructions, directions, descriptions and explanations clear, concise and coherent?
>
> Has the speaker:
>
> - Planned what is going to be said?
> - Stated the outline structure of the exposition? ('advance organizers' e.g. 'We are going to find out . . .')
> - Selected the key points: identified and made explicit the relevance of each and their relationship to each other? ('There are four things we need to think about . . . because . . .')
> - Sequenced key points appropriately?
>
> When the speaker plans and delivers the exposition have they:
>
> - Used short, simple sentences: explained specialist vocabulary if it needs to be used, given concrete examples or asked the listeners to generate their own?
> - Signalled when a new point is made? ('Now let's look at . . .', 'The third thing to look out for is . . .')
> - Summarized key points (or got the listeners to summarize)?
> - Sought feedback to check understanding (at each point if necessary)?
>
> When the speaker delivers the exposition:
>
> - Is eye contact sustained, to hold attention and give interim feedback? How might this be achieved when working with large groups?
> - Is an interesting, lively and varied tone of voice used?
> - Is the pace varied for emphasis and interest?
> - Does encouraging orderly participation vary the exposition?
> - Are pauses used to structure each part of the exposition?
> - Are appropriate examples, objects or pictures used to illustrate the main points?
> - Are appropriate judgements made regarding the level of cognitive demand, size of conceptual steps, and length of the concentration span required?
> - Is a written or illustrated record of key points provided as a guide, if listeners need memory aids?

1.2 Analysing 'question and answer' sessions

Questions can be used for a wide range of purposes and they can be seen as a vital tool for teaching and learning. It is a powerful way of 'scaffolding' children's understanding and raising their performance (see Tharp and Galli-more, 1998, **Reading 13.2**). The way in which teachers can use questions to improve the quality of children's thinking and the extent of their participation is discussed in Perrot (1982, **Reading 13.5**). Asking questions can provide teachers with immediate feedback on how participants are thinking and on what they know and it accounts for a high proportion of teacher talk. Question and answer techniques are therefore seen as an essential means of helping us to understand learning processes. Listening to the 'answers', and not pre-judging them, is an important way of learning about a learner.

Particular aspects concerning questions which might be reviewed are:

- the purpose, or function, of questions
- the form in which questions are asked
- the ways in which responses are handled.

Each of these aspects is now considered in further detail.

The purpose, or function, of questions

Questions can be grouped in many different ways. However, two main categories commonly occur. The first is psycho-social questions: those which centre on relationships between pupils or between a teacher and the pupils. The second category is 'pedagogic' questions: those which relate to more specifically educational concerns, and to the teaching and learning of skills, attitudes, concepts and knowledge.

In addition, questions are frequently designated 'open' or 'closed'. A closed question has a specific answer; an open question can be answered in a variety of ways. Advice to teachers sometimes appears to suggest that it is always better to ask open rather than closed questions. For instance, we might distinguish between 'do you know?' questions, and more inclusive 'do you think?' questions. However, rather than adopt an inflexible prescription, it is more useful to be clear about why questions are being asked, as well as how we think we are using them to develop thinking and support learning. There are situations where closing down the questioning is a very useful strategy, perhaps for instance during recapping work or within an interactive sequence if it becomes necessary to re-establish focus or assert control.

As Perrot suggests (1982, **Reading 13.5**), it may be more profitable to think of questions in terms of the level of demand on pupils' thinking. Lower-order questions do not require pupils to go beyond recall of information previously taught or already known. Answers are 'right' or 'wrong'. Higher-order questions require pupils to apply, reorganize, extend, evaluate, analyse information in some way. In this context it is important to consider the level of thinking indicated by a pupil's *answer*. A 'lower-order' question may produce a 'higher-order' answer and vice versa.

Checklist 13.2 offers a framework for considering different kinds of questions in relation to purposes.

The form in which questions are asked

Among the most important issues associated with classroom questioning techniques is the form in which the question is posed in relation to its purpose. The

---

Checklist 13.2

Aim: To provide a framework for analysing classroom questions. See how many uses of classroom questions you can spot in your school.

Purposes of psycho-social questions:

- *to encourage* shy members to integrate by participating (e.g. 'Jan, you've got a little kitten too, haven't you?')

- *to show interest* in and value for group members (e.g. 'You had a good idea, Norita. Will you tell us?')

- *to develop respect* for each others' views (e.g. 'What do you think you would have done?')

- *to assert control* (e.g. 'Wayne, what are you up to?')

- *to implement routines and procedures* (e.g. 'Ahmed, what did I tell you to do next?')

Purposes of pedagogical questions:

1. Closed questions (low level cognitive demand):

- *to recall information* – for testing, consideration or feedback (e.g. 'Where is Ethiopia?')

- *to give an on-the-spot solution* (application of known rule to new variables) (e.g. 'What is 28 divided by 4?')

- *to encourage analysis* – by describing, comparing or classifying (e.g. 'What's the difference between . . .?')

2. Open questions (high-level cognitive demand):

- *to explore information and ideas* with no set 'answer' (reasoning/interpreting, hypothesizing/speculating, imagining/inventing) (e.g. 'How do you think the hero would feel if . . .?')

- *to encourage synthesis* of information and ideas by focusing on contradictions, discrepancies, different sources of evidence (e.g. 'What do you think really happened . . .?')

- *to encourage evaluations, decision-making, and judgements* (e.g. 'Would it be fair if . . .?')

- *to encourage the transfer of ideas* and application of knowledge (e.g. 'How is what we've found out useful . . .?')

---

form of a question can have very diverse effects. For example, a teacher wants to encourage an evaluative response to personal reading and asks a 'higher order', 'open' question.

Q. 'Did you like the book?'
A. 'Yes/No'.

How could you reformulate this question to avoid this kind of monosyllabic answer?

In a testing situation what kind of information about what a pupil knows are we getting from this question and answer?

Q. 'Has potato got starch in it?'
A. 'Yes/No'.

Another form is the 'direct' question, which is short and simple in construction and has a single specified focus. For instance,

Q. 'How did the Vikings make their boats?'

to which the answer may be lengthy though straightforward and factual, or

Q. 'What makes a good book?'

to which the answer may also be lengthy but consisting of opinions and ideas which may be complex to articulate.

Very different effects might result from using a 'direct' question compared to one which invites a monosyllabic response. A reflective teacher would need to consider whether such a form would be appropriate if the aim was to encourage exploration, evaluation or to focus contributions on a particular suggestion.

A third form of question is the 'indirect' question. This is a long, composite question which may include a number of different leads. Again, such a question can be very useful in some situations but inappropriate in others. For example, 'indirect' questions can offer a number of different suggestions which might help in opening out a discussion and in providing a range of possible leads to explore. It would be less suitable in a testing situation, as the focus of the question would be relatively unclear. It could also be confusing to a pupil who found it hard to take everything in and who therefore got lost.

This highlights the need to formulate questions matched to pupils' learning needs. This requires reflective teachers to think about appropriate language and about the sequencing of questions to promote thinking which will lead to the development of understanding or the acquisition of knowledge (Tharp and Gallimore, 1998, **Reading 13.2**). These questions need to pick up on the child's interests, conceptions and misconceptions. Analysis of lessons observed by Brown and Edmundson (1984) provides a very useful diagrammatic representation of some typical sequences (Figure 13.1).

In effective questioning sequences, teachers hold in mind the key questions for the learning they have planned. Around these they ask related questions which they formulate based on their professional judgement of pupils' needs, prior knowledge and understanding. It is possible to plan these sequences (four or five questions) but as important is the questioning that arises from careful listening to pupils' responses. Where the teacher is too concerned to lead pupils towards a predetermined answer it is easy to miss hearing important clues to how understanding (or misunderstanding) is developing.

The ways in which responses are handled

The third aspect of questioning, that of the ways in which responses are handled, is important to consider because it is the means by which feedback is offered to

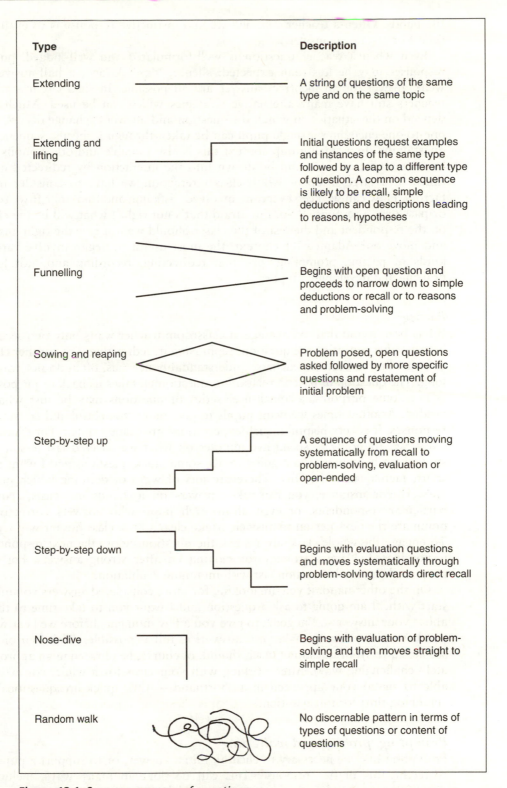

Type		Description
Extending		A string of questions of the same type and on the same topic
Extending and lifting		Initial questions request examples and instances of the same type followed by a leap to a different type of question. A common sequence is likely to be recall, simple deductions and descriptions leading to reasons, hypotheses
Funnelling		Begins with open question and proceeds to narrow down to simple deductions or recall or to reasons and problem-solving
Sowing and reaping		Problem posed, open questions asked followed by more specific questions and restatement of initial problem
Step-by-step up		A sequence of questions moving systematically from recall to problem-solving, evaluation or open-ended
Step-by-step down		Begins with evaluation questions and moves systematically through problem-solving towards direct recall
Nose-dive		Begins with evaluation of problem-solving and then moves straight to simple recall
Random walk		No discernable pattern in terms of types of questions or content of questions

Figure 13.1 *Some sequences of questions*

the pupils. Often a teacher's immediate and instinctive response is to evaluate, repeat or restate an answer.

Even when a teacher question is well-formulated and well-judged, pupils' responses may be less than expected: silence, 'don't know', a half-answer, a weak answer, or an incorrect answer are all possible. In such circumstances, teachers still have many alternative strategies which can be used. Much will depend on the situation in which the question-and-answer exchange occurs. In a one-to-one encounter a single pupil can be taken through a specific sequence of questioning. In a small group context this is also possible and other pupils can be encouraged to listen and be drawn into the interaction by redirected questions. In a large-group or whole-class interaction we have to consider more factors. How can we keep everyone involved, listening and thinking? If we reject or pass over a response ('No, I'm afraid that's not right') what will be the effect on the respondent and the rest of the class? Should we just give the right answer and move on? Adapted for context, the most useful strategies involve various kinds of pacing, prompting, probing, redirecting, recording and, not least, praising and developing rapport.

Pacing

It has been found that, on average, a classroom teacher waits only two seconds before either repeating the question, rephrasing it, redirecting it to another child, or extending it. Student-teachers, understandably nervous, often do not wait so long. The question of pace in relation to questioning takes us back to purpose.

For some purposes, a 'quick-fire' series of questions may be just what is needed. At other times we want pupils to give more thoughtful and considered responses. It is very helpful if such expectations are made explicit. For example, 'Now we are going to spend five minutes on what we covered last lesson and studied for homework. I am going to ask some quick questions and I want very short, factual answers. OK?' There are lots of ways of deciding which pupils answer. For instance, you can take answers on a 'hands up' basis, request particular respondents, or even allow each pupil who answers correctly to nominate the next person to answer. Make clear to the class how it will work. To engage the whole class, always ask the question before the next respondent is nominated. Have a strategy for moving on after wrong answers. For this purpose, keep the interaction fast with minimum evaluation.

On the other hand, if you are looking for more considered answers you might start with, 'I am going to ask a question and I want you to take time to think about your answer so I'm going to give you a few moments before we hear what you have to say. Try to make your answers as full as possible.' Wait four or five seconds after your question (which should, of course, be phrased in an appropriately challenging way). After working with your class for a while, you will be able to signal your approach in a shorthand – 'OK, quick-fire questions' or 'Thinking time for this question.'

Prompting, probing and redirecting

Prompting may be necessary to elicit an initial answer, or to support a pupil in correcting his or her response. This can be done in many ways, including simplifying, closer focusing, taking the pupil back to known material, giving hints or clues, asking leading questions, accepting what is right and prompting for a more complete answer.

Probing questions are designed to help pupils give fuller answers, to clarify their thinking, to take their thinking further or to direct problem-solving activities. There are a number of possible formulations, for example: 'Can you say that in another way?', 'Can you say a bit more about that?', 'Could you give us an example?', 'Can you say why you think that?', 'Is that always the case?', 'I'm not sure I understand. Can you make it clearer?', 'Does this remind you of anything we found when we were studying . . .?'

Redirecting questions to other pupils can be a productive way of probing and keeping the class or group involved in the thinking. For example: 'Can anyone else help?', 'Can we accept that answer?', 'How does that fit with your idea, Susan?', 'You've nearly got it. Can anyone else explain the last step?', 'Does that help us with this . . .?', 'Can we think of a better way to put that?'

Recording

Another approach allows you to accumulate a range of responses to a question and to avoid evaluating individual answers. In this case you hold a string of answers (by recording on a chalkboard, an overhead projector or by repeating aloud) for general consideration and discussion. In the same way you can build up a teaching sequence, such as solving a mathematical challenge, restructuring or analysing an investigation, considering 'for' and 'against'. Recording answers allows thinking to be held for more careful consideration and evaluation. In the same way recapping or summarizing responses is helpful in keeping thinking focused.

Praising and developing rapport

As always, remember the value of encouragement and praise: 'That's a new point', 'We could use that idea', 'Simon knows something about this', 'I hadn't thought of that. Well done', 'You've nearly got it . . .'

Additionally, there is much value in encouraging pupils to formulate and ask questions for themselves and each other. Nor do you lose face by acknowledging that you don't always get it right, 'That wasn't a very good question, let's try another one.' Indeed, question and answer sessions are an important form of classroom interaction for the development of rapport. They have an evaluative element and, as relatively overt and public, they are potentially threatening to pupils. Respectful interaction, perhaps even with a little humour, is likely to be greatly appreciated.

Reflective Activities 13.2 and 13.3 suggest ways of examining question-and-answer sessions with regard to asking questions and handling responses. In addition these activities invite you to consider the management of such sessions particularly in connection with the distribution of questions/responses between boys and girls and pupils of different attainment. Also of interest are the patterns of participation in a session, whether pupils volunteer or are nominated. It is useful to note the context, e.g. one-to-one, group, whole-class.

The discussion above has focused primarily on teacher-led direct instruction (Muijs and Reynolds, 2001, **Reading 13.4**). It has been well established by research over the years that teacher-led question-and-answer exchanges are a dominant feature of primary school classroom communications (Edwards and

Reflective activity 13.2

Aim: To investigate teacher questions within question-and-answer exchanges.

Evidence and reflection: Either tape record a suitable teaching session, or, by agreement, observe a colleague. Choose three five-minute periods in the teaching session (e.g. beginning/middle/end) and write down the questions the teacher asks during each period.

It may also be possible to code the audience to whom the questions were addressed, (e.g. B= boy, Bg = group of boys, G = girl, Gg = group of girls, Mg = mixed group, C = class).

The questions could be classified using the pedagogic or psycho-social categories from Checklist 13.2.

Extension: Classifying questions should highlight the variety and level of the cognitive demands that were made. It is then possible to consider whether what we do matches our intentions and, if not, what changes could be made.

If the audience has been noted, it is also possible to analyse the distribution of questions and to consider any implications.

The activity could be repeated to analyse pupil's questions.

Reflective activity 13.3

Aim: To investigate teachers' handling of pupil's responses within question-and-answer exchanges.

Evidence and reflection: Choose three five-minute periods during a teaching session, (beginning/middle/end) and record how the teacher handles pupil responses during each period.

The responses can be related to the use of pausing, prompting and probing discussed above. Remember that the use of these strategies should be matched to the teacher's purpose.

Extension: Analysing the data may help reflection upon the teacher's intentions, and whether they were fulfilled. It may also illuminate the extent to which pupil responses are 'heard' and engaged with by teachers. What effects can be identified resulting from the ways in which pupil responses were handled?

Westgate, 1994; Osborn *et al.*, 2000). As you may have identified for yourself, one of the weaknesses of teacher-directed talk is that the pupil's role in these discourse processes is often one of respondent, where the skill of the exercise could be more related to 'guessing what the teacher wants to hear' rather than to the pursuit of personal understanding. Pupils ask very few questions in school (Beck, 1998; Dillon, 1988; Wood, 1986).

As we have discussed earlier, a social constructivist view of learning would advocate learners taking a more active role by initiating discussion, asking questions and making the learning their own. Strategies for organizing talk in ways that provide pupils with more space in which to initiate, extend and elaborate personal meanings are important. With this in mind we now move on to consider classroom discussions. As we have already suggested (see Chapter 12, Section 1) it is often difficult to engage, motivate and include a large groups of pupils in a single discussion. As you read, you might consider the extent to which you may be able to overcome this.

1.3 Considering class discussions

Discussion makes an absolutely fundamental contribution to learning. Its import-ance is well established for the development of very young children and Wells (1986, **Reading 12.1**) coined the attractive image of 'conversation as the reinven-tion of knowledge'. This is relevant for learners of all ages. Barnes (1977) refers to pupils 'talking themselves into understanding', a process which we will probably all recognize if we reflect on our own learning processes and the element of exchange, construction and interpretation which is involved. Of course the psychological theories of Vygotsky and Bruner are central to this (see Chapter 7, Section 1.3, **Readings 7.3** and **7.8**).

However, as we have already suggested, much so-called 'discussion' in schools takes the form of teacher-dominated transmission of pre-established knowledge. One common result of such tight teacher control is that pupils' engagement may become relatively routinized and ritualistic. According to Edwards and Mercer (1987, **Reading 12.3**), classroom discussions certainly function to 'establish joint understandings' and 'common knowledge' between teachers and pupils. They conclude that 'the basic process is one of introducing pupils into the conceptual world of the teacher. It is essentially a process of cognitive socialisation through language' (1987, p. 157). We might note however, that teacher perceptions should, and often do, change and evolve in relation to pupil responses. We are also learners.

Because of the imbalance of power in classrooms between pupils and teachers – important both for learning and control – pupils normally do what the teacher has decided. Thus the idealized conception of the handover of control from teacher to self-directed learner is seldom realized, even in higher education. Whilst such teacher control is appropriate for some purposes, a genuine class discussion must start with some attempt to elicit opinions and knowledge from the pupils, to treat these views seriously and to explore their consequences. It is also productive to make the purposes of such activity explicit for pupils in terms of learning goals. What kind of questions would you ask to begin this process? How could you encourage pupils to ask questions based on their own prior knowledge and experiences?

To be clear about distinctions between the various forms and purposes of discussion is particularly important for teachers. At the beginning of a session a teacher may wish to find out what pupils already know about the topic on which he or she wishes to focus. This 'elicitation' may be achieved through open questioning. The elicitation may call for factual knowledge or opinions. If the pupils are to become genuinely engaged than the teacher must be prepared to wait a while for answers and must resist the temptation to provide the answers themself. Where the information that is elicited from pupils is also examined, interrogated and interpreted, then the episode becomes a more open-ended 'exploration'. It is the latter, exploratory, situation which can be identified as a discussion. In addition to asking questions, reflective teachers also consider how they might use the pupils' own questions effectively in the discussion.

The content of what is discussed may vary considerably and may include what is believed to be factual knowledge, opinions, speculation, hypotheses, etc. It is the manner in which the content is treated rather than the content itself which is the distinguishing factor between elicitation and exploration. The teacher's role is to structure learning activity which involves discussion and to ensure that pupils develop the associated skills which make the process possible and effective (Phillips, 1985, **Reading 13.6**). We deal with this in more detail in Section 2 of this chapter, when we focus specifically on group work.

✓ *Checklist 13.3*

Aim: To examine discussion skills.

A reflective teacher may find it useful to consider some of the following questions:

1. Do the participants take turns or do they frequently talk over each other or interrupt?

   Do they invite contributions, redirect contributions for further comments, give encouragement?

   Do they listen to each other? Are they willing to learn from each other (i.e. respond and react to each other's contributions)?

   Do they indulge in 'parallel' talk (i.e. continue their own line of thinking)?

   Does conflict emerge or is harmony maintained?

   Is conflict positively handled?
   - by modifying statements, rather than just reasserting them?
   - by examining assumptions, rather than leaving them implicit?
   - by explaining/accounting for claims?

2. Do participants elaborate their contributions?
   - by giving details of events, people, feelings?
   - by providing reasons, explanations, examples?

   Do they extend ideas?
   - by asking for specific information?
   - by asking for clarification?

   Do they explore suggestions?
   - by asking for alternatives?
   - by speculating, imagining and hypothesizing?

   Do they evaluate?
   - by pooling ideas and suspending judgement before making choices?

Discussion can also be distinguished from debate in terms of both aims and style. Discussion aims to explore and is relatively loose and informal in style, whilst debate aims to persuade and is more tightly and formally structured. The recognition of the importance of such oral forms is given, for example, in the national curricula of England and Wales. They refer to discussion skills as well as to argumentation in both oral and written form.

1.4   Focusing on listening

If communication is a two-way process, we have dwelt long enough on the speaker, or 'initiator'. It is also necessary for teachers and pupils to be competent listeners, or 'receivers'. However, we have already noted how the position of 'initiator' is usually taken by the teacher and that the role of 'receiver' is more often than not assigned to the pupils.

It is possible to identify different types of listening situations within classrooms, which serve specific purposes and impose particular demands. These purposes can be categorized in the following way:

- *Interactive listening*: such as during a discussion, where the role of speaker and listener changes rapidly. In such circumstances, where participants need to exercise 'bidding' skills, for example, by raising a hand; sitting more upright and forwards; or by starting to move their lips. Some individuals will not have acquired any such skills and thus find it very hard to draw attention to the fact that they want to join in. Others may find it hard to notice tentative moves by group members and therefore may not 'let others in'. An effective way to teach these skills is to involve children in role-playing discussions, with exaggerated conversational 'vices'.

- *Reactive listening*: where listeners follow an exposition. For example, a set of instructions may be given which pupils are then expected to act upon, or an extended input of information may be provided, which the listeners are expected to be able to 'take in', possibly 'take notes' on, and then respond to. In reactive and interactive listening, the emphasis is on following the meaning of the speakers. Differences are often in the degree of formality and the status of the speaker *vis-à-vis* listeners.

- *Discriminative listening*: where listeners have to discriminate between and identify sounds rather than meaning. For example, phonic sounds for spelling or reading purposes, or environmental/musical sounds.

- *Appreciative listening*: where listeners listen for aesthetic pleasure, perhaps to musical or environmental sounds. For example, to the rhythm or sounds of words in poems and stories; or to other languages or accents.

It is useful to distinguish between these different types of listening so that we can be aware of the demands we make upon ourselves and the pupils. For example, how often do we allow appreciative listening, requiring perhaps a receptive level of listening? Do we convey how we want the pupil to listen actively in such a situation? How often do we demand extended attention, in a reactive situation, so that we hear someone out, follow a line of argument, consider a large amount of information, before moving into discussions?

Reflective activity 13.4

Aim: To analyse listening demands in the lesson.

Evidence and reflection: During a session or series of lessons try to note down how much time a teacher or pupils spend:

1. On each of the four types of listening mentioned above.
2. In each of the four contexts indicated below.

The results could be recorded on a matrix for each session/series.

Types of listening (purposes)	Contexts of listening			
	Where (informal to formal)	To whom (known to unknown)	What (familiar to unfamiliar)	For how long
Interactive				
Reactive				
Discriminative				
Appreciative				

Extension: Having collected the data, it is then possible to consider the range of listening experience pupils encounter. Is there a particular kind of listening which is important in your subject? How much attention is given specifically to assessing the level of listening skill pupils have and to how these might be developed? Are you making assumptions about pupils' listening skills which are not realistic?

It could be interesting to collect data on listening across the curriculum by undertaking this activity for one class through a day.

Reflective activity 13.5

Aim: To appraise the listening skills of individuals.

Evidence and reflection: Record, or observe, a range of individuals (including the teacher) during a normal teaching–learning session in a classroom.

Note the types of listening called for and the contexts. Also, note any child's behaviour that might indicate that they heard, understood or responded. For example, did they look at the speaker, or look around; appear to agree, answer questions, offer suggestions; show awareness of others' needs, take turns?

> *Extension*: By watching individuals closely, it may be possible to pinpoint more precisely any difficulty a child might have, and whether it is specific to certain types of listening or contexts.

As reflective teachers, we may want to be aware of the different demands that each type of listening makes. We also need to consider how many different listening contexts are experienced and how this might affect our listening and that of our pupils (Dickson, 1981).

2   GROUP DISCUSSION IN CLASSROOMS

Prior to the introduction of the National Literacy and National Numeracy strategies, a great deal of emphasis had been placed on the use of group work in classrooms. This was based on the knowledge that it is a very common means of working in the adult world. Indeed, the success of the human species itself has been attributed to the capacity to co-operate (Schmuck, 1985). However, there is increasing evidence to suggest that while social groupings continue to be commonplace in many primary classrooms, genuine group work remains relatively rare (Galton *et al.*, 1999) even during the middle section of the Literacy Hour (Cordon, 2000).

Group work also, of course, fits well within the social constructivist model of learning, which we considered in Chapter 7, Section 1.3, and this potential has been exploited in a number of excellent studies of classroom group work (see for example, Bennett and Dunne, 1992, **Reading 13.7**; Galton and Williamson, 1992). Vygotskian ideas emphasize the importance and meaningfulness of the social context in which the learner acts. Co-operative classroom group work, at its best, can provide a particularly good context for pupil learning. However, clarity of goals, the appropriateness of the task and the composition of the group have been found to be particularly significant. Bennett and Dunne (1992) for instance, offer an illustration of a teaching cycle for a group task on co-operatively producing a plan for a story. This is based on the five key elements, or phases, in the teaching cycle which had been identified in Bennett and Dunne's research.

Despite many of the positive outcomes which can emerge from such collaborative, learner-centred contexts, large classes with a wide range of pupil abilities, personalities, aptitudes and experiences pose severe challenges to any teacher. Indeed, the most consistent finding from the research is that, despite the commitment to this form of classroom practice, it is very difficult to implement consistently. From the point of view of a reflective teacher, a number of issues arise. These relate to:

- Structure and process
- Motivation and inclusion
- Management
- Monitoring.

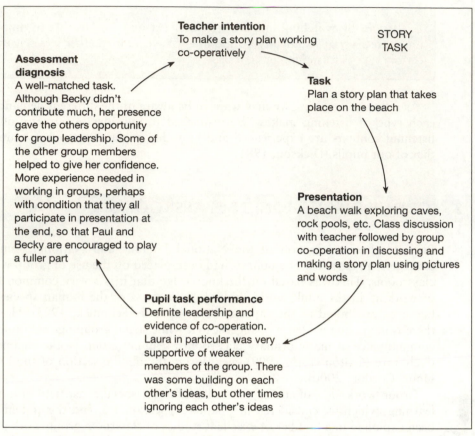

Figure 13.2 *A teaching cycle for an illustrative group task (Bennett and Dunne, 1992)*

2.1   Structure and process

There are many formulations of structures and processes for this kind of learning. The model we offer here is based on the one used in the Avon Collaborative Learning Project (Avon County Council, 1993). The structure described was designed to encourage collaborative groupwork in which discussion would play a major part.

The structure comprises four explicit and sequential stages: preparation, planning, action and review (see Figure 13.3).

During the preparation and planning stages, decisions and ideas could be recorded by a designated scribe – a standard pro-forma might be useful in the early stages of working in this way. Groups can also be encouraged to select one member to act as observer of the group process and report back findings at the review stage.

Group work often fails where pupils do not recognize talk as an important contribution to their learning; do not share a clear appreciation of the goal; or when they lack necessary skills to accomplish the task to their own satisfaction. In addition to understanding the cognitive task to be completed, learners also need to know how to work within a group context. All the participants also

need to understand the ground rules of effective discussion in group work and have the confidence and skills to be willing and able to participate. These are complex and difficult issues for many, and reflective teachers should aim to structure the group activity in such a way as to ensure everyone understands what is expected of them and can make their contribution without fear of ridicule or humiliation. As we discussed in Chapter 12, Section 2.2, situations in which individuals can work together over time with people they trust in 'friendships groups' or with 'talk partners' can help to create a suitably secure environment for less confident or quiet learners.

Even in the best organized group activities, learning may be superficial if the talk is not developing thinking. However, research has shown how, with appropriate guidance, Key Stage 1 and 2 pupils can become very skilled discussants in collaborative group work situations (Collins, 1996; Hughes and Westgate, 1998; Pollard *et al.*, 2000). Many examples of classroom initiatives can also be found in the work of the National Oracy Project (Norman, 1990).

It is also useful to recognize the kinds of group roles which participants might adopt which affect the dynamics of the group: leaders and followers, or jokers, inquisitors, non-participants, obstructionists and many other 'characters' might emerge.

An implicit aim of collaborative group work is the development of skills of interaction which foster collaboration, encourage respect for individuals and the contribution they make, support the development and articulation of ideas and minimize conflict. These include active listening, taking turns, communicating clearly and concisely, being aware of the effect of one's actions on other individuals, encouraging others, nurturing not criticizing ideas, tolerating opposition, creating enthusiasm. Checklist 13.4 may be useful for shaping observation of these interactive skills.

Preparation	Planning
Clarify the purpose and aims of the task in hand; identify the outcomes required, set standards for the task outcome.	Identify and assemble relevant facts and skills; decide what has to be done; translate this into a detailed action plan.
During this stage pupils consider questions such as:	During this stage pupils consider questions such as:
Why are we doing this task? *What are we trying to learn?* *What will we end up with when it is finished?* *What will it look like? Who is it for?* *How will we know if we have a successful outcome?* *How will we know if we have learned what we set out to?*	*What do we know already?* *What ideas do we have?* *What do we need to know?* *What resources do we have already?* *What resources will we need?* *What could each of us do that might help?* *How long have we got to complete this task?* *Who will do what?* *When should we do it?*
Review	**Action**
Review learning. The review can be concerned with the achievement of the task, the quality of the outcome, the success of the process.	Put the plan into action as a team. Build, stage-by-stage, on previous planning and preparation to meet the collective goals.
Task review questions might include:	During this stage pupils consider questions such as:
Have we achieved what we set out to? *Have we met the standards we set ourselves?* *What have we learned about the content of the task?*	*Are we doing what we planned to do?* *How are we doing for time/targets?* *Do we need to check/discuss what we have done so far?* *Are we using our collective skills most effectively?*
Process review questions might include:	
What has gone well? *What problems occurred? How could we avoid these in future?* *What have individuals done that helped?* *When did the group make progress and why?* *How could we co-operate better next time?*	

Figure 13.3 *Stages in collaborative group-work*

Checklist 13.4

Aim: To examine communicative and interpersonal skills in group work.

A reflective teacher may find it useful to consider some of the following questions:

1. Do the participants take turns or do they frequently talk over each other or interrupt?

   Do they invite contributions, redirect contributions for further comments, give encouragement?

   Do they listen to each other? Are they willing to learn from each other (i.e. respond and react to each other's contributions)?

   Do they indulge in 'parallel' talk (i.e. continue their own line of thinking)?

   Does conflict emerge or is harmony maintained?

   Is conflict positively handled?
   - by modifying statements, rather than just reasserting them?
   - by examining assumptions, rather than leaving them implicit?
   - by explaining/accounting for claims?

2. Do participants elaborate their contributions?
   - by giving details of events, people, feelings?
   - by providing reasons, explanations, examples?

   Do they extend ideas?
   - by asking for specific information?
   - by asking for clarification?

   Do they explore suggestions?
   - by asking for alternatives?
   - by speculating, imagining and hypothesizing?

   Do they evaluate?
   - by pooling ideas and suspending judgement before making choices?

Reflective activity 13.6

Aim: To analyse the dynamics of group interaction and consider how we could and should influence the dynamics of the group interaction.

Evidence and reflection: Tape (or video) a group discussion. General features can be monitored on the following schedule. Additional detailed analysis can be carried out using Checklist 13.4.

Group characteristics	Comments
1. Composition of the group (e.g. size, sex, ability)	
2. Seating arrangement (draw diagram)	
3. Was there a leader, or scribe?	
4. Was this challenged?	
5. Did anyone not participate? (How did the others respond?)	
6. In what ways did the group collaborate?	
7. Was help needed/requested?	
8. What intervention was given?	
9. In what ways was the task successful?	
10. Did the group feel satisfied?	

Extension: Information gained from such schedules can help in the analysis of group interaction. It can help in understanding the roles of the members and whether these change if the composition of the group changes. Devising our own schedule can make us more aware of what we are aiming at. It also provides a framework for action to develop the potential of the group.

Based on what you have observed what might you do in future to influence the dynamics of group interaction?

Given the importance of making the ground rules of talk explicit to pupils, reflective teachers might consider involving pupils in their own evaluation of their participation in group work. The following evaluation sheet is a version of one devised with a group of Key Stage 2 pupils. Self-assessment of this kind can reveal real insights into pupils' perceptions of themselves and their participation in small group activities. This may be especially true when the pupils devise their own schedule after some experience of participating in and discussing group work with others.

Checklist 13.5

Aim: To involve pupils in the self-assessment of their own participation in group activities.

Question	Score
How well did I try to include others?	1 2 3 4 5
How well did I listen to other people's ideas?	1 2 3 4 5
How well did I express my feelings?	1 2 3 4 5
How well did I share my feeling?	1 2 3 4 5
How well did I show respect for other people's ideas and feelings?	1 2 3 4 5
Did I ask questions?	1 2 3 4 5
Did I use an appropriate level of voice?	1 2 3 4 5
Did I disagree with others without putting them down?	1 2 3 4 5

In my opinion today's discussion was ....

I think I was ....

Next time I would like to ....

2.2 Group motivation

Perhaps the most important contributory factor to successful group work is the nature of the task itself, with both social and cognitive aspects (Bennett and Dunne, 1992, **Reading 13.7**). It is important to decide whether a task could just as effectively be done by an individual or whether there is a genuine need for a group. This, of course, depends on the purpose of the task and on the way it is presented.

It has long been established that the teacher's presence often inhibits pupils and prevents them from putting the issues in their own language and focusing on questions which they want to raise. Instead, in the presence of a teacher pupils engage in a game of 'guess what's in the teacher's mind': they therefore try to anticipate correct answers rather than raise questions or explore issues. A teacher's presence can close down previously productive discussion (Collins, 1996, **Reading 12.6**). In the National Literacy Strategy and National Numeracy Strategy pupils are expected to work without a teacher present for part of the lesson and to take responsibility for their own learning. However, without a clear perception of the nature of the task and the purpose of the activity, teacherless small-group activity can become a time for 'chat and mucking about', rather than for 'discussion and work'. However, it has to be recognized that some off-task discussion might be educationally advantageous. This is especially true where it allows pupils to draw on their previous experiences and make connections with their prior knowledge.

Collaborative group work provides a unique context for pupils in which they can learn and demonstrate new social skills. The composition of such groups is critical (see Chapter 10) and is more important than just attainment. Sometimes friendship groupings can be successful, but not if friendship is more highly prized by the members than critical exploration which might reveal friendship differences. Interest groupings might be useful, but not where personalities might clash destructively. A teacher therefore needs to be very alert to the social groupings within the class in terms of gender, race, etc., and to the placement of shy or less popular children and with regard to the possible interaction of different personalities. Reflective teachers will be sensitive to the needs of all children especially those who are anxious about speaking to people they do not know well or who find it difficult to form and sustain relationships with others. Devising strategies which make it possible for all children to participate in group discussions should be a part of every teacher's lesson planning.

2.3 Group management

Group size and type are particularly important factors in management, but so too is the overall classroom context in which groups work. Many (see for example, Bennett and Dunne, 1992, **Reading 13.7**; Biott and Eason, 1994, **Reading 13.8**), advocate that co-operative groups are also involved in whole-class activities and that they report back to the whole class. This provides a sense of purpose and accountability within the culture of the class as a whole.

For a discussion of the sorts of groups which are possible in the classroom, see Chapter 10, Section 2.1. Whatever size, type or composition of group is chosen, the success or otherwise of the activities which follow cannot be absolutely predicted. There are no consistent research findings but teachers are wise to attend carefully to the personalities and attainment of the children whom they select to work together. It is also crucial that the task, and its parameters, is clearly presented.

2.4 Monitoring group discussions

Several phases have been identified in successful group work which can be used as a framework in monitoring progress. First, children need to be encouraged to spend time orientating themselves to the other members of the group. They need time to listen to each other and to explore the demands and boundaries of the particular task. Second, during the development phase, the participants must learn to share ideas and extend suggestions and give time for the ideas to incubate. Although the number of contributions at this stage may be an indication of exploration and collaboration, it is the nature of the interactions which is of greatest importance to the quality of discussion. In the third, conclusion phase, the quality of group interaction, together with the quality of the ideas themselves, should be evident. This should be apparent if a final 'product' is shared with the rest of the class.

A major component of developing discussion skills is encouraging the participants to monitor themselves. While the more socially and linguistically competent children may well 'pick things up', and therefore learn to discuss by discussing, children with less meta-cognitive awareness (see Chapter 7, Section

2.6) may benefit from more specific support. Hence, discussion about discussing can make an important contribution to developing co-operation. At the end of a discussion, a group can be asked if it thought it had been a 'good' discussion and if so, what had made it good. The children could be encouraged to consider their discussion and identify useful strategies using their own terms. These can then be compared to those in Checklist 13.5.

Teachers can do a number of things to help develop constructive group work and discussion. For example, by praising those strategies which children use, they can motivate children to want to contribute. Role-play in which children have been given secret roles (interrupt a lot, always agree, don't listen to them, say nothing, say lots) can highlight key issues, whist also introducing an element of fun. It is important too that the classroom is managed so that opportunities for discussion can be supported. Finally, teachers need to monitor discussions with the children and to record their progress and problems.

CONCLUSION

This chapter has built on the ideas raised in Chapter 12 and has considered how we use language in our teaching to support pupil learning. We have approached the issue teaching strategies in a relatively technical way. However, there are important links back to Chapter 6 on classroom relationships, for teaching strategies certainly contribute to the climate of the classroom and its 'moral order'. Additionally, there are links to Chapter 5, and the processes and experiences that contribute to each child's evolving sense of personal identity. How can we promote the 'active learning' of pupils (Moyles, 2001, **Reading 13.3**)? Classroom teaching can enable and develop positive learner identities – but it can also constrain and undermine confidence. Such processes underlie classroom life and justify the sense of moral responsibility that many teachers feel. Pollard *et al.* (2000, **Reading 7.11**) developed an analysis of this as part of their evaluation of the impact of the Education Reform Act in England. Coming from a related direction, Osler and Starkey (1998, **Reading 13.9**) draw attention to the 'human rights' of children (such as 'dignity', 'participation', 'inclusivity') and their implications for teaching.

It is now time to consider the assessment of learning and how reflective teachers might analyse and respond to it. This is the subject of Chapter 14.

Key readings

Teachers communicate both information and values to their pupils almost exclusively through the medium of language. Using transcripts of lessons to illustrate the key points, the following offers classic and salutary reflection on language use in classrooms:

Barnes, D., Britton, J. and Rosen, H. (1986)
Language, the Learner and the School.
Harmonsworth: Penguin.

For practical and principled strategies for encouraging autonomous learning, as well as positive self-esteem, through discussion, see:

Marlowe, B. A. and Page, M. L. (1998)
Creating and Sustaining the Constructivist Classroom.
London: Sage.

Barnes, R. (1999)
Positive Teaching, Positive Learning.
London: Routledge.

An excellent review of evidence about instruction methods is:

Muijs, D. and Reynolds, D. (2001)
Effective Teaching: Evidence and Practice.
London: Paul Chapman.   📖 **Reading 13.4**

For a discussion of language use across the curriculum and specifically in literacy and numeracy lessons, see:

Edwards, S. (1999)
Speaking and Listening for All.
London: David Fulton.

Bearne, E. (ed.) (1998)
Use of Language Across the Primary Curriculum.
London: Routledge.

For work on explaining and questioning skills, see:

Wragg, T. and Brown, G. (1993)
Explaining.
London: Routledge.

Brown, G. and Wragg, T. (1993)
Questioning.
London: Routledge.

For a brief, research-based and highly accessible introduction to issues of gender difference in classroom interactions and a consideration of the ways in which schools might perpetuate behavioural differences between males and females, see:

Howe, C. (1997)
Gender and Classroom Interaction: a Research Review.
Edinburgh: SCRE.

For a discussion of the importance of group work in primary classrooms, strategies for how to introduce it as well as ways to evaluate it, see:

Bennett, N. and Dunne, E. (1992)
Managing Classroom Groups.
Hemel Hempstead: Simon and Schuster.   📖 **Reading 13.7**

Galton, M. and Williamson, J. (1992)
Groupwork in the Primary Classroom.
London: Routledge.

Fascinating work on young children's thinking is provided in:

Hart, N. and Martello, J. (eds) (1996)
Listening to Children Think: Exploring Talk in the Early Years.
London: Hodder and Stoughton.

For a thought-provoking, practical and highly accessible guide to the use of ICT to provide rich interactive learning environments, see:

Cook, D. and Finlayson, H. (1999)
Interactive Children, Communicative Teaching: ICT and Classroom Teaching.
Buckingham: Open University Press.

Most specialist educational publishers also have useful series of books on teaching. For instance, in the UK see the catalogues of Continuum, RoutledgeFalmer, David Fulton, Simon and Schuster, Open University Press, Paul Chapman Press, etc.

Readings for Reflective Teaching (the companion volume) offers other closely associated work on the issues raised in this chapter. This includes work by authors such as:

Maurice Galton, Linda Hargreaves, Chris Comber, Debbie Wall, Anthony Pell, Roland Thorp, Ronald Gallimore, Janet Moyles, Daniel Muijs, David Reynolds, Elizabeth Perrot, Terry Phillips, Neville Bennett, Elizabeth Dunne, Colin Biott, Patrick Eason, Audrey Osler and Hugh Starkey.

RTweb offers additional professional resources for this chapter. These may include *Notes for Further Reading*, supplementary *Reflective Activities*, useful *Web Links*, *Extension Texts* and *Download Facilities* for diagrams, figures, checklists, activities.

CHAPTER 14

Assessment. How are we monitoring learning and performance?

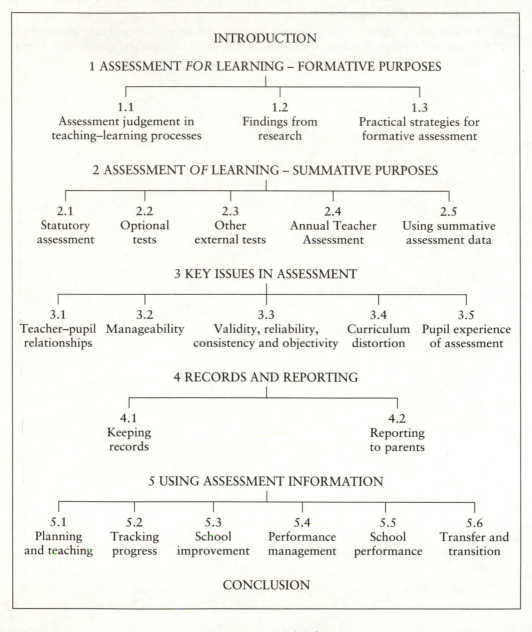

INTRODUCTION

1 ASSESSMENT *FOR* LEARNING – FORMATIVE PURPOSES

1.1
Assessment judgement in
teaching–learning processes

1.2
Findings from
research

1.3
Practical strategies for
formative assessment

2 ASSESSMENT *OF* LEARNING – SUMMATIVE PURPOSES

2.1
Statutory
assessment

2.2
Optional
tests

2.3
Other
external tests

2.4
Annual Teacher
Assessment

2.5
Using summative
assessment data

3 KEY ISSUES IN ASSESSMENT

3.1
Teacher–pupil
relationships

3.2
Manageability

3.3
Validity, reliability,
consistency and objectivity

3.4
Curriculum
distortion

3.5
Pupil experience
of assessment

4 RECORDS AND REPORTING

4.1
Keeping
records

4.2
Reporting
to parents

5 USING ASSESSMENT INFORMATION

5.1
Planning
and teaching

5.2
Tracking
progress

5.3
School
improvement

5.4
Performance
management

5.5
School
performance

5.6
Transfer and
transition

CONCLUSION

Enhancing professional standards and competences

This chapter will contribute to satisfaction of professional requirements for assessment in each part of the UK. For example, in England, the TTA requires that those awarded Qualified Teacher Status can:

Make appropriate use of a range of monitoring and assessment strategies to evaluate pupils' progress towards planned learning objectives, and use this information to improve their own planning and teaching.

Monitor and assess as they teach to give immediate and constructive feedback to support pupils as they learn.

Involve pupils in reflecting on, evaluating and improving their own performance.

Record pupils' progress and achievements systematically to provide evidence of the range of their work, progress and attainment over time. They use this to help pupils review their own progress, and to inform planning.

(TTA, 2002, *Standards for the Award of QTS,*
standards 3.2.1, 3.2.2, 3.2.6)

There are differences of detail in Scotland, Northern Ireland and Wales, but core issues concerning assessment are impervious to time and place. The role of the professional teacher is to use assessment constructively, and to be aware of its power to distort both curriculum and learning.

INTRODUCTION

In recent years and in most parts of the world, assessment has become more and more important in education. This has occurred for two reasons.

The first, and by far the most significant, has been the concern of governments to introduce ways of 'measuring' educational outputs. In the United Kingdom in the early 1990s this was seen as a means of enabling parents to compare schools so that they could choose where to send their children, with the assumption that the operation of an 'educational market' raises standards. Labour governments from 1997 have continued to place great emphasis on standards of literacy and numeracy, as measured by testing. They have put pressure on all schools to perform well, within a context of diversity of types of schools, and 'earned autonomy' for schools judged to be successful. The use of output-assessment data, in the way required by these arguments, is known as 'summative'.

The second reason for the growth in interest in assessment derives from the increasing realization of the value of continuous assessment in informing teaching and improving learning. An influential review of research by Black and Wiliam (1998, 1998c) emphasizes the potential of assessment used in this way to raise standards. As a course of study or a lesson progresses, a teacher gathers evidence of pupil responses and adjusts the learning programme to meet pupil needs. Teachers are thus able to engage more directly and accurately with the development of the learner's thinking and understanding. Pupils themselves are involved in the processes of assessment and learning through reflecting on their own progress and responding to feedback. The use of process-assessment data, as required by these arguments, is known as 'formative'.

The basic difference in purpose produces serious tensions between these two forms of assessment – for instance, comparison *vs* support, product *vs* process, government *vs* professional control. Many assessment experts suggest that the effectiveness of one form of assessment is likely to have the unfortunate effect of undermining the effectiveness of the other (see Harlen *et al.*, 1992, **Reading 14.1** for an important discussion of the purposes of assessment). In particular, when summative testing is emphasized, there is a tendency for teaching to be narrowly directed towards whatever the tests measure. A broad and balanced curriculum is thus distorted (e.g. Gipps, 1990, Broadfoot *et al.*, 1991). Others commentators feel that the two major forms of assessment can be mutually supportive – formative assessment supports the process of learning, summative assessment measures the result.

Another way of viewing the purposes of assessment is to consider the people assisted or informed by the information.

- Assessment helps *children* learn by providing them with feedback so they know what they have achieved and how they can improve; enabling them to judge and take responsibility for their own learning; providing encouragement; and helping to develop the skills of lifelong learning.

- Assessment helps *teachers* by providing them with information about children's learning so they can adjust their teaching; inform their planning; set appropriate targets; and evaluate the effectiveness of their teaching.

- Assessment helps others by providing information about attainment and progress which informs *parents*; enables the *next teacher* and/or school to build on previous learning; informs school improvement planning, helps evaluate the effectiveness of earlier developments, feeds into target setting, and contributes to performance management, all of which are the concerns of *school leaders*.

Whatever purpose is to be served by assessment, there are some fundamental principles which should influence practice. The Association of Assessment Inspectors and Advisers (AAIA) has produced a set of principles to guide all assessment, recording and reporting, as well as principles relating to each aspect of assessment.

How children feel about their learning is a key factor in their success. Children's motivation and self-esteem are very vulnerable and responsive to the processes and outcomes of assessment (see also Chapter 9, Section 3.2 on differentiation). Both can be enhanced by assessment, but all too often they are damaged, often unintentionally. The pupil experience of assessment is considered in more detail in Section 3.5, but the effects of assessment practice on children's motivation and self-esteem need to be continually borne in mind.

Whenever teachers are engaged with assessment, they should be reflecting upon purposes and principles, as well as the impact of their practice on children's motivation and self-esteem.

This chapter is organized in five parts. We begin by considering the interrelationship of teaching, learning and assessment, and the very positive forms of

Assessment, recording and reporting should:

- offer all pupils an opportunity to show what they know, understand and can do

- help pupils to understand what they can do and what they need to develop

- recognise that the National Curriculum does not encompass all learning; there is the wider curriculum and pupils' personal and social development

- be based on a considered view of what learning should be assessed in each subject or area of experience

- relate to shared learning objectives

- advance the learning process

- enable teachers to plan more effectively

- help parents to be involved in their children's progress

- provide schools with information to evaluate work and set suitable targets.

Figure 14.1 *Fundamental principles for assessment, recording and reporting (AAIA, 1998)*

support to learning which can derive from formative assessment. In Section 2 we concentrate on summative assessment, before reviewing some of the key issues in assessment in Section 3. Section 4 concerns records and reporting, while Section 5 looks at the use of assessment information.

The *Compendium* in **RTweb** may be particularly helpful for the technical aspects of this chapter.

1 ASSESSMENT *FOR* LEARNING – FORMATIVE PURPOSES

1.1 Assessment judgement in teaching–learning processes

We have repeatedly drawn attention in this book to the role of judgement in determining appropriate teacher actions, and this is of paramount importance in the flow of teaching–learning processes. The social constructivist model reviewed in Chapter 7, Section 1.3, conceives of teachers analysing pupil skill and understanding, in the course of an activity or task, so that appropriate information, questions, explanations or advice can be offered. A teacher acts, we suggested, as a 'reflective agent' who makes accurate judgements, provides an appropriate teaching input and thereby scaffolds the child's understanding across what Vygotsky called the 'zone of proximal development'. Children's knowledge and understanding is thus extended, by appropriate teaching, to levels which could not have been attained without the teacher intervention.

Notwithstanding the need for subject knowledge (see Chapter 8, Section 3) and a repertoire of teaching skills (Chapter 12), this process is fundamentally dependent on the quality of the teacher's formative assessment. Without that, an intervention could easily be inappropriate and confuse the child's attempt to construct a meaningful understanding – and evidence from Bennett *et al.* (1984) has shown just how common this is. This, then, is the direct link between assessment and learning in modern primary-school practice. Without it, no teacher can hope to support children's learning appropriately.

It is worth looking at the various stages of this process in more detail and we represent it, schematically, in Figure 14.2 (derived from National Primary Centre (SW), 1991). Five phases of a teaching programme are distinguished in this model. They build, progressively, from children's existing knowledge, understanding and skill and, at each point, the role of teacher assessment is emphasised.

Such a model is helpful in highlighting the significance of formative assessment. Continuous assessment is the crucial means through which a teacher 'connects' with the pupils' thinking, and is thus able to extend, challenge and reinforce it as appropriate.

1.2 Findings from research

Many recent developments in formative assessment, also known as assessment for learning, have been prompted or endorsed by the work of the Assessment Reform Group, an offshoot of the British Educational Research Association. Black and Wiliam (1998) conducted an extensive survey of research literature in order to answer the following questions:

- Is there evidence that improving formative assessment raises standards?
- Is there evidence that there is room for improvement?
- Is there evidence about how to improve formative assessment?

The answer to all three questions is 'Yes'.

	PURPOSES		POSSIBLE PROCESSES
ORIENTATION	Arousing children's interest and curiosity	Ensures that the children are focused on the topic and are motivated	Introducing Explaining Discussing
ELICITATION/ STRUCTURING	Helping children to find out and clarify what they think	Enables the teacher to assess pupil understanding in order to plan appropriate next steps	Questioning Discussing Predicting
INTERVENTION/ RESTRUCTURING	Encouraging children to test, develop, extend or replace their ideas or skills	Provides opportunities for children to engage, actively, in learning tasks Enables the teacher to observe pupil behaviour and, by assessing their skill and understanding, to make appropriate teaching interventions	Practising Observing Measuring Recording Speculating
REVIEW	Helping children to evaluate the significance and value of what they have done	Offers a chance for pupils to take stock of their learning and for the teacher to guide them in consolidating their understanding Provides an opportunity for the teacher to assess new learning and to consider next steps	Recording Discussing Explaining Hypothesizing Reporting Evaluating
APPLICATION	Helping children to relate what they have learned to their everyday lives	Enables the children to locate new learning meaningfully in the wider context of their lives Provides an opportunity for the teacher to reinforce and consolidate key points	Relating to experience Discussing Interpreting

Figure 14.2 *Phases of teaching, learning and assessment*

Reflective activity 14.1

Aim: To study key phases of a teaching session.

Evidence and reflection: Plan to teach a session involving some new learning to a group of children. As you plan, think about the five phases which are identified in Figure 14.1 and about the role of assessment. Consider how best to orientate the children, how to elicit and then make use of what they already know, etc. Having thought about the possibilities, be prepared to respond to their input.

Prepare for obtaining a record of what happens. For instance, you could set up a video or ask a colleague to observe you. In the case of the latter, try to get your colleague to make detailed notes on what is said by both you and the children.

Teach the session.

Analyse what happened. Were the five phases apparent and helpful? What opportunities for assessment occurred? Were they used to maximize the quality and appropriateness of the teacher input?

Extension: This is primarily an activity for awareness raising. We suggest you try it from time to time, mulling over the results and considering ways in which you could apply the insights about your teaching which you obtain.

Formative assessment can produce substantial learning gains for all learners, with (the previously) lower attainers improving even more than the others. This means that the spread of attainment is reduced whilst attainment is raised overall. The formative assessment processes which lead to these improved performances also equip pupils for taking responsibility for their learning. The Assessment Reform Group (ARG, 1999, p. 2) summarize the findings by saying that:

> The important message now confronting the educational community is that assessment which is explicitly designed to promote learning is the single most powerful tool we have for both raising standards and empowering lifelong learning.

Black and Wiliam present the evidence about how to improve formative assessment in five points.

> Feedback to any pupil should be about the particular qualities of his or her work, with advice on what he or she can do to improve, and should avoid comparisons with other pupils.
>
> (Black and Wiliam, 1998, p. 9)

This point emphasizes the importance of self-esteem and motivation for successful learning, and reminds us to focus comments upon the actual work, rather than the pupil. Rewards, such as gold stars, or grades, tend to result in children trying to find ways to obtain the rewards themselves, rather than thinking about their actual learning needs. Time and energy can be spent looking for clues to the 'right answer', and many are reluctant to try for fear of failure.

> For formative assessment to be productive, pupils should be trained in self-assessment so that they can understand the main purposes of their learning and thereby grasp what they need to do to achieve.
>
> (Black and Wiliam, 1998, p. 10)

Self-assessment is concerned with thinking about your own performance in relation to clearly stated objectives. It is not, as some have interpreted self-assessment, checking your work against an answer sheet. A word not to be overlooked in the quotation is 'trained'. Self-assessment is a skill, which like any other skill needs coaching and practice. Black and Wiliam say that the necessity for pupils to have an overview of their targets for learning, and for them to think and talk about their learning means that 'self-assessment by pupils, far from being a luxury, is in fact an essential component of formative assessment' (Black and Wiliam, 1998, p. 10).

> Opportunities for pupils to express their understanding should be designed into any piece of teaching, for this will initiate the interaction whereby formative assessment aids learning.
>
> The dialogue between pupils and a teacher should be thoughtful, reflective, focused to evoke and explore understanding, and conducted so that all pupils have an opportunity to think and to express their ideas.
>
> (Black and Wiliam, 1998, pp. 11, 12)

These points reinforce the importance of classroom practices which really enable children to demonstrate their understanding, and enable teachers to develop real insights into children's thinking. Sometimes the tasks we set mean that it is possible for children to get the right answers for the wrong reasons, and without carefully designed and conducted questioning and discussion these misconceptions may remain undetected, and so become a bar to later learning.

> Tests and homework exercises can be an invaluable aid to learning, but the exercises must be clear and relevant to learning aims. The feedback on them should give each pupil guidance on how to improve, and each must be given opportunity and help to work at the improvement.
>
> (Black and Wiliam, 1998, p. 13)

Just as oral questioning can provide teachers with rich assessment information, so too can written questions, provided they are carefully constructed. Devising questions and tasks which give real insights into children's understanding can be difficult, and whenever possible teachers should work together to collect and share good questions. Black and Wiliam's review of research showed that the quality of feedback is a crucial element in effective formative assessment. Feedback improves learning when it gives specific information on strengths and weaknesses of the work in relation to the learning objectives, and provides guidance on how to improve (Burrell and Bupp, 2000, **Reading 14.3**). Marks reduce the effectiveness of any comments given. In order to really learn from the comments, pupils need time to put into practice the suggestions for improvement. This has implications for the lesson planning (for example, building in time for children to respond to the teacher's comments), and for the timing of assessments linked to a unit of work. A test given at the end of a block with no time for proper follow-up will be useless for formative purposes: a review activity three-quarters of the way through may be more supportive of learning.

One of the very important conclusions drawn by Black and Wiliam is that implementing the changes which research suggests will have such dramatic effects on pupil performance will not be easy in practice. This is because they challenge fundamental beliefs held by some teachers, firstly about the nature of learning, and secondly about the potential of all pupils to learn. The approaches to formative assessment described above indicate a change in the roles and relationships of teachers and pupils, and the reflective teacher will realize that these are not easily or quickly achieved. Nevertheless, persistent teachers find that the rewards are enormous.

1.3 Practical strategies for formative assessment

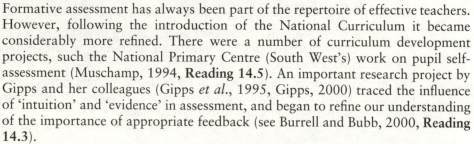

Formative assessment has always been part of the repertoire of effective teachers. However, following the introduction of the National Curriculum it became considerably more refined. There were a number of curriculum development projects, such the National Primary Centre (South West's) work on pupil self-assessment (Muschamp, 1994, **Reading 14.5**). An important research project by Gipps and her colleagues (Gipps *et al.*, 1995, Gipps, 2000) traced the influence of 'intuition' and 'evidence' in assessment, and began to refine our understanding of the importance of appropriate feedback (see Burrell and Bubb, 2000, **Reading 14.3**).

Many teachers, advisers, consultants and lecturers continue to work hard at translating research findings on the value of formative assessment into the practicalities of classroom practice, and the quantity and quality of experience and evidence grows daily. For example, Shirley Clarke has taken the findings of Gipps, Black and Wiliam, and through extensive work with many primary school teachers has developed practical guidance (Clarke, 1998, 2001).

She identifies six major strategies and, although many of these interrelate, a logical sequence can be identified. We review the major points of each below:

Adjusting teaching to take account of learning

- Plans should be regarded as guides not strait jackets.

- Short- and medium-term plans need to be adapted to match pupils' needs, bearing in mind longer-term plans and objectives.

- Finding out about pupils' knowledge, skills and understanding before starting a topic enables any necessary adjustments to the plans to be made so that learning is more effective.

- Short-term plans should be regarded as working documents, and if they are annotated they also become records.

Sharing learning objectives

- There should be an expectation, on the part of children and teachers, that the learning objective for every lesson will be made clear, in language that is appropriate for the children.

- Learning objectives can be made explicit by a statement (for example, 'By the end of the lesson we will have learnt . . .'), or in the form of a question (for example, 'How can we double numbers?').

- Write up the learning objective so that it is on view throughout the lesson.
- Separate the objective from instructions about the activity.
- Sharing learning objectives is more effective if success criteria are also clarified; children can be invited to help create the success criteria by asking them "How will we know we have achieved this?" Teachers can model quality by showing or demonstrating aspects of what it is that is being aimed for.
- Explaining how the learning objective 'fits into the world' helps children construct understanding and appreciate the relevance of their learning.
- Asking children to repeat the learning objective helps establish it in their minds.
- Refer to the learning objective throughout and at the end of the lesson.

Questioning to support learning
- Use a variety of questions for specific purposes, for example, to engage interest, to ascertain current knowledge, to gain insight into children's understanding, or to check learning.
- Questions, particularly those designed to probe thinking, are best planned in advance. Teachers should be encourage to share questions to build up a bank of particularly effective questions.
- Use strategies in the classroom so that all pupils are thinking all the time.
- Apart from rapid recall questions, time is needed for children to think and to answer, and for teachers to think and respond.
- Encourage pupils to critique questions – the teacher's, their own and other children's.

Self-assessment
- It is a thinking and talking activity, not a writing one.
- Self-assessment is a skill, and children, of whatever age, need to be *trained* in self-assessment. This can be done for example through modelling responses.
- Self-assessment should be related to the learning objective, success criteria and any exemplification.
- A variety of approaches avoids boredom or unthinking responses.
- Self-assessment must be related to the task, not the learner. For example, '*What* did you find hard, and why?' not '*Who* found it hard?'

Feedback and marking
- It should be provided as promptly as possibly, and ideally orally.
- Feedback needs to include information about success in relation to the learning objective and success criteria, and the next steps.
- Comments about improvement should provide specific advice on ways to 'close the gap' between the current performance and what is aimed for.
- Comparison with others should be avoided, but comparison with previous work should be encouraged.

- Children must be able to read and understand teachers' marking and comments.

- Comments and codes relating to the learning objective (which children know mean for example 'At this point you have achieved the learning objective and success criteria') should be used, rather than symbols or rewards which act as grades.

- Provide time for pupils to read and respond to marking.

- Inform parents about the marking and feedback policy.

Individual target setting

- Appropriate targets should be decided with the pupil, on the basis of their work, and key learning objectives.

- Targets should be as 'SMART' as possible: Specific (exactly what needs to be done); Measurable (it will be clear whether or not they have been reached); Achievable; Relevant; and Timebound (they can be achieved within two to six weeks, depending on the child).

- National Curriculum levels should not be added to individual targets for pupils as they take the emphasis away from the specifics of what the pupil needs to do. They may also encourage unhelpful comparison with other pupils.

- Targets are most effective if they are visible, for example by being written on a card, or a flap which can open out from the cover of a book.

- Establish a rolling programme of setting and reviewing targets with children so that the process is manageable.

Whilst many people are adopting formative assessment strategies, the reflective teacher will be continually monitoring the detail of the way in which they are being implemented, and considering the effect the practice is having on the children. Unfortunately, it is all too easy to slip into doing things which one thinks are supporting assessment for learning, but in actual fact are having a detrimental effect. For example, if the teacher clearly states the learning objective at the beginning of the lesson, but just before the children start work reminds them 'To remember your spellings, punctuation, paragraphs, best handwriting and those descriptive words we used last week' the children have far too many things to attend to, and the point of the lesson may well be lost. Similarly, the positive support to learning given by 'comment only' marking may be totally undermined if the teacher adds a smiley face. Children will probably just look to see whether they have got a smiley face or not (a short-hand for 'was my work good or bad?'), and ignore the teacher's comment. Smiley faces and other devices such as stickers may possibly have a place if the children are always clear exactly which task related achievement they were for, but the reflective teacher will be alert to the way children are interpreting smiley faces and stickers, and the actual effect they are having, whatever the original intention.

Reflective activity 14.2

Aim: To develop the use of assessment for learning practices in the classroom.

Evidence and reflection: Think about a class you are working with, and the practical strategies for formative assessment listed in Section 2.2. Are there any which are particularly well developed? Which area would it be sensible to concentrate upon (bearing in mind the logical sequence of the strategies)?

Decide which strategy you are going to work on, and use the main points listed and any supporting resources you can access to think about and plan your development. You may need to talk to other people first, for example the class teacher (if you are a trainee) or the headteacher (if you plan to deviate from an agreed marking policy).

Put your plans into operation (remembering that this is not a 'quick fix'), be alert to the effect that they are having, and reflect upon the impact particularly upon children's learning, their involvement, motivation and self-esteem.

Extension: Find other people who are also working on formative assessment strategies and share ideas and findings with them. Move your development into other areas of the curriculum; extend the strategies you use.

2 ASSESSMENT OF LEARNING – SUMMATIVE PURPOSES

Assessment *of* learning is a phrase used for summative assessment, as assessment *for* learning is used for formative assessment. Since the introduction of the National Curriculum there has been a huge increase in the amount of formal assessment, often through testing, which is undertaken in primary schools.

2.1 Statutory assessment

In England, there are statutory requirements for assessment on entry to primary education (baseline assessment) and at the ends of Key Stages 1, 2 and 3. A new assessment for the Foundation Stage begins in the academic year 2002/3. This will assess children's progress and achievements at the end of the stage and in relation to the Early Learning Goals. It will be known as the Foundation Stage Profile.

Baseline assessment covers aspects of language and literacy, mathematics, and personal and social development. It is normally carried out through observation in the course of normal classroom activities. Baseline assessment has two major purposes:

- To identify children's learning needs to inform planning
- To enable future progress to be measured.

	Teacher Assessment	Tasks or tests
Entry to primary education (baseline assessment)	Language and literacy Mathematics Personal and social development	
End of Key Stage 1	English (but Welsh in Welsh-speaking schools) Mathematics	English (but Welsh in Welsh-speaking schools) Mathematics
End of Key Stage 2	English (but Welsh in Welsh-speaking schools) Mathematics Science	English (but Welsh in Welsh-speaking schools) Mathematics Science

Figure 14.3 *Statutory assessment in England and Wales, 2001*

In England and Wales, end of Key Stage National Curriculum assessment is carried out through tests or tasks, and Teacher Assessment, and applies to English, mathematics and science. At the end of Key Stage 1 there are a variety of tests and tasks designed for children working at different levels. The lowest attaining pupils at Key Stage 2 are assessed through Teacher Assessment alone. The Key Stage 1 tests and tasks are marked by the teachers, with Local Education Authorities undertaking audit to ensure consistency of administration and marking. The Key Stage 2 tests are marked externally.

For end of Key Stage Teacher Assessment the teacher makes judgements for each child in the form of a level for each attainment target in English, mathematics and science; an overall subject level in mathematics and science is also calculated.

The Qualifications and Curriculum Authority spells out the relationship between Teacher Assessment and tests and tasks:

> Teacher assessment is an essential part of the national curriculum assessment and reporting arrangements. The results from teacher assessment are reported alongside the task and test results. Both have equal status and provide complementary information about children's attainment. The tests and tasks provide a standard 'snapshot' of attainment at the end of the key stage, while teacher assessment, carried out as part of teaching and learning in the classroom, covers the full range and scope of the programmes of study, and takes account of evidence of achievement in a range of contexts, including that gained through discussion and observation.
>
> (QCA, 2000, p. 8)

Despite the assurance from QCA that Teacher Assessment and tests and tasks are of equal status, they are not treated as such. The requirement for Local Education Authorities to publish Key Stage 2 Teacher Assessment results along-

http://www.rtweb.info

side test results was dropped in 1999, although many LEAs continue to publish both. The media concentrate upon test results alone, and test results tend to be given greater prominence than Teacher Assessment in evaluating schools, for example by OFSTED.

In Scotland 5 to 14 national testing arrangements are based on advice from the Scottish Executive Education Department (SEED) and are not statutory. They are currently given at five levels of the curriculum in Maths, Reading and Writing. A pupil is tested when his/her teacher deems it appropriate, with most pupils expected to move on from one level to the next at roughly two-year intervals (Scottish Executive, 2001). In Northern Ireland teachers currently choose from a wide selection of units to confirm their classroom assessments of pupils in English, mathematics and also Irish in Irish-speaking schools. However, the guidelines in both Scotland and Northern Ireland are, at the time of writing, under review.

2.2 Optional tests

QCA has developed optional tests in English and mathematics for use with children at the end of Years 3, 4 and 5 to help schools in monitoring progress during Key Stage 2. Their format is based on the Key Stage 2 tests, and this change in style from Key Stage 1 assessment may be one of the reasons for the apparent dip in performance of some children at the end of Year 3. Unlike the end of Key Stage 2 tests, optional tests are marked by the teachers of the pupils being tested. This activity itself gives teachers an insight into the statutory assessment process, helps them become more familiar with standards, and provides them with detailed information about each child's performance, well beyond that provided by the actual mark. In Wales, ACCAC have also produced optional assessment materials which cover most subjects of the curriculum in Key Stage 2.

2.3 Other external tests

A variety of other externally produced tests are used routinely by schools, although in some cases the reasons for doing so should be questioned. A recent unpublished survey undertaken by the Research Team at QCA revealed that despite arguments about there being 'too much testing' in schools, people are electing to do more testing than is required. A number of reasons for using additional tests are given, and some, such as the diagnosis of specific reading difficulties, may be laudable.

However, much more serious than the over-use of tests, is the false confidence put in their results. Black talks of the 'very limited reliability of external tests, which command a degree of confidence which they do not deserve' (Black and Wiliam, 1998a, p. 158), an issue which is not well understood by either teachers or educational administrators (see also Wiliam, 2001). Similarly, Filer and Pollard (Filer and Pollard, 2000, **Reading 14.7**) have published a critique of supposedly 'objective' assessment practices, showing how they depend on the contexts and social practices in which performance, judgement and interpretation of judgement are produced, and so are vulnerable to bias and distortion.

2.4 Annual Teacher Assessment

Another way in which schools keep track of children's progress is by using Teacher Assessment at the end of each year. Judgements are made in the same way as at the end of a Key Stage: by making a 'best fit' judgement against the level descriptions for each attainment target. Since one National Curriculum level represents, on average, two years' progress, teachers sometimes refine the judgement by giving grades as well as levels (for example, 3c, 3b, 3a). The c, b, a grading mirrors the grades used in some of the Key Stage 1 tests and tasks, and reflects the checking against adjacent levels that a teacher does when making a rounded judgement according to the QCA guidance. For example, a judgement might be: '3c: level 3 is the best fit description, but I also checked level 2 as the child is working at that level in some respects in this particular attainment target'.

Although making an annual Teacher Assessment can be very useful, as with all forms of assessment there are some cautions to be considered. Firstly, the level descriptions were written to be used at the end of a Key Stage, and refer to the complete programme of study for that Key Stage. If they are used part way through a Key Stage the appropriate programme of study will not have been completed. Secondly, a refinement of a Teacher Assessment grade into, for example, 3c, may help in tracking progress more precisely, but it provides very little information about what the pupil actually understands and is able to do.

2.5 Using summative assessment data

Summative assessment data, whether from tests or annual Teacher Assessment, assist schools in tracking the progress of individuals, groups and the whole cohort. They are essential in providing the information to support whole-school target setting, and to track progress towards targets. Pupil performance data also has a role to play in providing the evidence for teachers' performance management (see Chapter 17, Section 3.3). Analysis of assessment information provides important information for teachers to use in adjusting their planning. These aspects of the use of assessment information are considered in more detail in Section 5 of the present chapter.

---

3 KEY ISSUES IN ASSESSMENT

The introduction of assessment procedures tends to cause anxiety. For instance, in the United Kingdom, of all the diverse features of the recent educational reforms, the assessment requirements have been of particular concern to teachers of young children.

Of course, we should not forget that assessment happens informally, and quite naturally, all the time in relationships with people. Whenever people meet, judgements are made and expectations developed. During interactions, knowledge of each other may be reinforced, refined or changed. These new understandings are then brought to the next encounter.

Such processes enable people to build reciprocal expectations, to develop close relationships and to become aware of needs. Sensitivity to others, empathy and understanding are thus founded, one way or another, on naturally occurring forms of assessment.

However, there is a world of difference between this naturally occurring interpersonal awareness and assessment procedures which are required by national governments and are intended to be formally institutionalized in schools, detailed in league tables and made available to the press. The potential destructive power of such a system is immense, and in this section we consider some of the main issues which are raised.

3.1 Teacher–pupil relationships

There is concern that assessment procedures, particularly tests, may intrude upon or even destroy the warm interpersonal relationships which have characterized primary practice for so many years (see Chapter 6). As a teacher said to one of us:

> Relationships with the children is the key. If you get on well with them, discipline problems don't emerge and you get more done. I also think they learn better in a secure environment and I certainly get more personal satisfaction from being with them – in fact, for me, it's what is really rewarding about teaching.

The fear is that, if badly handled, formal assessment may introduce tension and suspicion into teacher–child relationships, for few people feel comfortable when being assessed. More common is a sense of vulnerability, of exposure, of scrutiny and of threat.

Early research on the impact of assessment in England and Wales (Gipps *et al.*, 1991, Pollard *et al.*, 1994) suggested that teacher skill and commitment can minimize this potentially divisive effect. Nevertheless, the issue of how children feel about assessment and how this influences their relationships with their teacher is so important that it must be kept under review.

> ### Reflective activity 14.3
>
> *Aim*: To obtain direct evidence of children's feelings about routine assessment.
>
> *Evidence and reflection*: We suggest that you work with a group of children from your class and discuss with them examples of some assessments which you have made. Perhaps you could use some written work that has been produced and look at any comments and corrections which you made. How do the children feel about your responses?
>
> You could also self-consciously monitor your verbal feedback to children during a teaching session. Listen to your comments, observe the children's faces. How do they seem to respond? Are they delighted, wary, confused, anxious, angry, resigned?
>
> *Extension*: What ways of protecting children's dignity can you develop, whilst still providing appropriate assessment feedback to them? Could you negotiate with the children to establish criteria by which their work will be evaluated? (See 'sharing learning objectives' in Section 1.3)

3.2   Manageability

An assessment issue which teachers are keenly aware of every day is manageability. It is simply not physically possible to gather, record, analyse and report assessment evidence of everything that children learn.

Assessment needs to be planned so that it is manageable, and so that over time significant evidence is obtained for each child across the broad curriculum. In looking at any unit of work reflective teachers, in conjunction with subject leaders, will be considering which are the key learning objectives that should be a focus for assessment, taking into account their importance for supporting future learning, and whatever other opportunities may exist for assessing them.

Nor is it necessary to record the outcome of every assessment made:

> Decisions about how to mark work and record progress are professional matters for schools to consider in the context of the needs of their children. In retaining evidence and keeping records, schools should be guided by what is both manageable and useful in planning future work. OFSTED inspectors will not require more detailed records.

> (QCA, 2000, p. 7)

There is a tendency with assessment to continue to add to practice, but to be reluctant to drop any established routines. A particular area where a critical review of practice could lead to a decision to do less is in the use of external tests. Whilst non-statutory optional tests can be very useful in tracking progress through Key Stage 2, schools are often surprised when they realize just how many other tests they are also doing, and the limited use they make of the information produced (see Section 2.3).

Another route to manageability in assessment is to ensure that wherever possible any particular practice fulfils multiple functions. For example, annotated plans become records, as do children's books when comments within them are related to clear learning objectives.

3.3   Validity, reliability, consistency and objectivity

Validity and reliability are technical terms of immense importance. Do assessments actually represent what they purport to measure (validity)? Can the procedures be implemented in ways which ensure consistency in assessments across the country and from year to year (reliability)? In addressing the latter question regarding end of Key Stage Teacher Assessment, the term 'consistency' has also been used.

Opinions and evidence about the validity and reliability of any assessment system are crucial to its long-term credibility. If high standards on both criteria are not met, then criticism is likely to follow. Where validity is low, assessments will be regarded as partial, limited and crude because of the factors which they ignore or cannot measure. Where reliability is low, assessments will be regarded as inconsistent, unfair and unreliable because of the variation in the procedures by which the assessment results were produced.

The quest for validity tends to lead in the direction of assessment procedures which are designed for normal classroom circumstances, covering a wide curriculum and using a range of assessment techniques. In the specialist literature, this is known as 'authentic assessment'. However, the drive for reliability tends to suggest simplification in both assessment procedures and in the range of the curriculum to be assessed, so that there is more chance of comparability being attained. The result of this is likely to be greater use of methods which can be tightly controlled, such as pencil and paper testing, or tests using ICT.

When National Curriculum assessment was first introduced, the balance in the dilemma between validity and reliability was more in favour of validity, with authentic classroom tasks being used to assess seven-year-olds. However, they were found to be both unmanageable and to have considerable problems of reliability (Shorrocks, 1991; Whetton, 1991). In 1992, the assessment procedures were simplified and tightened, to introduce a greater element of testing. Although many teachers protested at the more limited view of the curriculum which these narrow procedures implied, evaluative evidence again showed that there were reliability problems across schools and LEAs (Pollard *et al.*, 1994). After the Dearing Review, assessment procedures for English and mathematics were simplified and tightened further, an external 'audit' procedure was introduced and attempts to introduce standard assessment in science were dropped. At Key Stage 2, when national assessment was introduced in 1994, pencil and paper tests were used immediately, and the testing arrangements have since been further refined, all the time with a view to enhancing reliability.

One of the consequences of a heavy concentration on reliability in testing is that we tend to measure, and thus value, that which is easy to measure. It is more difficult to assess application, understanding and practical aspects of a subject (the Attainment Targets 1 in mathematics, science and English) through a written timed test, and since end of Key Stage Teacher Assessment (TA) is not given the same prominence as test results, these aspects tend to become devalued.

There is a similar story regarding Teacher Assessment. In the early 1990s, the role of teacher assessment in informing the teaching–learning process was emphasized. As the Task Group on Assessment and Testing (TGAT) put it, such assessment evidence was to 'feed forward' and enable teachers to meet pupil needs more precisely. The profession endorsed this view wholeheartedly, and a great deal of work was done in schools and LEAs to develop the approach (see for example, Muschamp, 1993, **Reading 14.5**, on a process involving pupils directly). Soon however, teacher assessment activities became directed almost exclusively as a means of assessing and reporting pupil attainment against National Curriculum levels. Rather than draw out the potential contribution to teaching and learning, the School Curriculum and Assessment Authority (the government agency at the time) emphasized the need to 'define the standard' of National Curriculum levels and 'the benefits of consistency' for reporting purposes. For instance:

> Consistency in assessment helps to ensure that, when judgements are made against the standards in the revised National Curriculum, there is fairness for pupils across classes, schools and key stages.

> (SCAA, 1995, p. 5)

The trend during the 1990s was thus in the same direction for both National Curriculum tests and Teacher Assessment, with the formative role of assessment in informing teaching being gradually eroded by the priority given to the production of summative assessment information.

Statutory assessment arrangements have continued to be tightened in a drive to improve reliability so that the performance of pupils and schools can be monitored. However, this is likely to continue to reduce validity. The results may become more precise and comparable, but they may also become narrower, less meaningful and less helpful to teachers in informing future teaching.

Drummond (1993, **Reading 14.6**) has published an extremely insightful critique of such narrow forms of assessment. Working in particular with young children, she insists that assessment data is not some form of objective 'evidence', but requires interpretation to make sense of it in terms of a teacher's understanding of the child. Pollard and Filer (2000, **Reading 14.7**), building on a two-school comparison of pupils' assessment experiences throughout their primary schooling, demonstrate that 'objectivity' is a myth. Pupil performance is crucially affected by the context of its production and social and cultural factors have considerable influence over its interpretation, meaning and consequence.

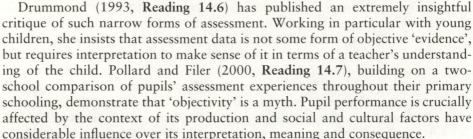

Reflective activity 14.4

Aim: To highlight the dilemma between validity and reliability.

Evidence and reflection: Focus on a specific objective for pupil attainment, for instance, one of those associated with children's mathematical understanding and computational competence with number. Consider how the competence and understanding of pupils across the country could be assessed with regard to the selected objective. Focus this, perhaps by imagining some individual children whom you know in different schools, or by discussion with teachers or student teachers working in different schools.

Do you think your assessment method could reflect what is really involved in understanding and competence (validity), and yet be administered in standard and consistent ways by teachers wherever or whoever they are (reliability)?

Extension: Consider any test materials with which you are familiar. How do you feel that the test-designers have tried to resolve the validity/reliability dilemma? What compromises have they made? Do you think it is possible to devise assessment with high validity and high reliability for all subjects?

3.4   Curriculum distortion

The tension between validity and reliability is so endemic that it is unlikely that a complete solution will ever be found. Where assessment is used formatively, to inform the teaching–learning process, this is of less significance because the information can still be used constructively within each school. However, where assessments are used summatively, and published with the claim that they reflect pupil and school performance, then the stakes become high, both for pupils and schools. In these circumstances there is a well-documented tendency for teachers and pupils to 'work to the test' (Broadfoot *et al.*, 1991). The result is likely to be a narrowing of the curriculum and, whilst standards in the tested areas of the curriculum may rise, a reduction in overall standards across the broader curriculum may occur.

Concern is justified by the experience of the United States of America, where a great deal of testing has been used for many years (Corbett and Wilson, 1991; Rottenberg and Smith, 1990; Shepard, 1987). As Rottenberg and Smith comment:

> As the stakes become higher, in that more hangs on the results, teaching becomes more 'test-like', such that testing tends to result in the substitution of means for ends.

It is interesting to note that determined moves have been made in the United States to move away from 'high-stakes testing' (such as end of Key Stage tests with league tables) towards formative, authentic testing (Resnick and Resnick, 1991), but these are not easy to sustain in the face of public pressure for 'performance measurement'. Northern Ireland and Wales have, however, recently given up publications of some test results, which is a move to reduced distorting effects.

Reflective activity 14.5

Aim: To investigate the danger that high-stakes assessment distorts curriculum provision.

Evidence and reflection: Talk to several teachers about the assessments which they carry out and, in particular, about those which have to be reported publicly. Ask them about any concerns which they may have. Enquire if it has been necessary to change curriculum provision to ensure that the children can perform respectably on publicly reported tests. Ask if public reporting of assessment results broadens, narrows or makes no difference to the curriculum which they provide.

Extension: You could reflect on a potentially very significant dilemma here. The National Curriculum sets broad curriculum targets, whilst national assessment procedures test only a narrow range. Does one undermine the other?

3.5 Pupil experience of assessment

We have already discussed the potential threat which increased assessment activity could pose to the quality of teacher–pupil relationships, the dangers of stress and of a narrowing curriculum as teachers 'teach to the test'. Many teachers have feared that such effects will eventually be felt by children in a worsening of the quality of their education experiences and an undermining of the self-confidence of less successful pupils.

Evidence on the short-term impact of new assessment procedures in the United Kingdom was somewhat inconsistent. The early phases of the introduction of assessment procedures in England and Wales brought enormous protests from teachers, many of whom provided illustrations of distressed children (Torrance, 1991). However, more representative samples of teacher opinion did not show the same level of concern (Pollard *et al.*, 1994). Worries from parents were very strong in Scotland, but were relatively small in England and Wales (Hughes, Wikeley and Nash, 1994). Evidence from children themselves on their experience of National Curriculum testing mostly shows that many of them enjoyed it (Pollard *et al.*, 1994). Indeed, in many classrooms the *early* assessment procedures seemed to have broadened the curriculum, such was its power, and to have been well received by children.

The longer-term picture appears to have begun to change as testing procedures have been narrowed and tightened by government agencies. Evidence of classroom practice suggests that teaching programmes are being attuned more closely to assessment requirements and this will limit the scope for some children to demonstrate their capabilities (see Chapter 7, Section 2.5). Similarly, there are dangers of stigma emerging from the overt form of some assessment procedures and categoric nature of the results. In such situations, some children may simply opt out – 'I'll be a nothing', as one child put it (Reay and Wiliam, 1999). The ways in which assessment results influence the expectations which teachers have of pupils, pupils have of each other, and pupils have of themselves are not yet fully researched. However, the PACE project (Pollard *et al.*, 2000, **Reading 7.11**), the largest independent study of the implementation of the National Curriculum and assessment into England, suggested that pupil motivation, engagement and zest for learning were being adversely affected by the 'hurry along curriculum' (Dadds, 2001, **Reading 9.4**) and the extent of its assessment. Despite the rise in measured standards, a significant number of children were showing signs of developing negative dispositions towards learning itself (Claxton, 1999; Dweck, 1999). As we will see in Chapter 15, it is likely that the socially differentiating effect of formal assessment will be reinforced by pupils' cultural responses, and the situation may polarize further (see **Reading 15.2**).

There is little doubt that national assessment procedures will have long-term effects on pupils. Perhaps these will be seen as positive, in that the quality of teaching and learning will be enhanced. Reflective teachers though, will want, prudently, to watch for effects which could both damage the self-image and self-confidence of pupils and have other divisive effects.

4   RECORDS AND REPORTING

4.1   Keeping records

This discussion complements that in Chapter 10, Section 2.4 on how records may be *organized*.

It is not necessary, and it would be impossible, to record the outcomes of all the assessment that is carried out. Decisions are needed, therefore, about *what* should be recorded, and *how* it should be recorded.

The first question, about *what* needs to be recorded, relates to the purpose of the assessment and recording. In England and Wales, the basic legal requirement is that individualized records of attainment in each National Curriculum subject must be kept for each pupil. This requirement could be met by simply keeping a copy of all annual reports to parents, but this would not be found sufficient to support children's learning, nor would it satisfy the expectations of school inspectors and others. Within any school there will be a number of different records, each with their own specific purpose, but taken together a whole school's records should be used:

- to help the teacher plan the next steps in teaching and learning
- to show what a child knows, understands and can do, and the progress that he or she has made
- to help children see the progress they are making
- to provide information for setting targets at all levels – individual, group and cohort targets
- to inform discussions with parents, and end-of-year reports
- to provide accurate information about a child's attainment, progress and learning needs that can be passed on to the next teacher or school
- to assist with end-of-year and statutory end of Key Stage Teacher Assessments
- to inform subject co-ordinators of any changes required to medium-term plans and schemes of work
- to evaluate the effectiveness of teaching
- to identify issues for the school improvement plan.

(Swaffield, 2000)

The second question, about *how* information should be recorded, is mostly about manageability and the use of records. It is useful to think of the range of forms that records can take: see Figure 14.4.

Along with whatever recording systems the school decides upon, individual classroom teachers, and trainee teachers, can keep whatever personal records they wish, but they will be required to contribute to the whole-school system. As one of a series of booklets promoting the effective use of assessment information in Welsh schools, ACCAC has produced guidance for headteachers, subject leaders/heads of departments and teachers on Recording Key Stages 1–3 (ACCAC, 2000).

It should be remembered that in most countries there are moves towards increasing access to records. For instance, in England and Wales teachers can keep personal records of their own, but any record which may be seen by or transferred to other teachers or other professionals must be made available to parents on request. This can help teachers develop the habit of recording in a positive form – e.g. 'Sally is beginning to participate in group story sessions', rather than: 'Sally often interrupts story sessions'. The issue reflects general ethical concerns about the central accumulation and recording of information about individuals – whether it is medical information, financial, criminal or anything else. Indeed, most of us would probably want to know what was being kept on us and many people take the view that this is a legitimate right. Continuous awareness of the possible audiences for teacher-created records is thus necessary. Schools should consider the implications of the requirements of the Data Protection Act, 1998, for information contained in children's educational records.

Annotated plans	Turn short term plans into working documents, recording what has actually been taught, and 'next steps' to be fed into the planning for the next lesson or following week
Children's work and books in different subjects	These show attainment and progress over time, particularly in specific subjects. They are even more useful as records if the learning objective is noted at the top of a piece of work, or incorporated into the teacher's comments
Children's target cards	Individual target cards are a record of specific learning needs. Dates when targets are achieved show attainment and progress
Teacher's mark book/record file	Mark books or record files can be customized in a whole variety of ways to suit the teacher, different subjects, and various groupings of children. Recording specific learning objectives increases their usefulness
Children's self-assessment	Children may occasionally record some aspects of their self-assessment, but self-assessment is above all a thinking activity, and an emphasis on recording too often detracts from this
Unit records	When work has been taught in units (such as in the QCA schemes of work), the attainment of children can be recorded in three groups, matching the learning objectives that you would expect all, most, or some of the children to achieve
Information technology	IT is being used increasingly and is a very powerful tool. Large amounts of assessment data can be stored, analysed, displayed, transferred and reported. As with all assessment and recording, it is essential that IT systems used are manageable and useful, that numbers are treated with the caution they deserve, and that data relates to and informs learning and teaching
Individual portfolios	Whilst these may be highly valued by children, teachers and parents, the time involved needs to be found and justified. As a whole school practice, they have been criticised, but they remain important in understanding individuals. Targeted use may be most appropriate
School portfolios	Annotated examples of work and observations which demonstrate standards agreed by teachers. These complement other forms of records, and are useful for sharing with others (children, parents, inspectors) and for reference by teachers
Work samples	Regularly collected samples of work, often representing three broad bands of attainment, serving as a record of the type and level of work produced, and useful for monitoring
Individual Education Plans	IEPs are records of targets and progress for individual children
Teachers' day books and personal notes	Teachers' own personal notes. A notebook may be particularly important for early years' teachers becausy much of the evidence of children's achievements may be ephemeral – behaviour or comments, rather than recorded 'work'. The habit of jotting down these observations may be difficult to acquire, especially for student teachers who may be pre-occupied with management issues. Time has to be planned for observation of children

Figure 14.4 *Forms of records*

> ### Reflective activity 14.6
>
> *Aim*: To identify information about the children which it is important for you, as their teacher, to know and record.
>
> *Evidence and reflection*: Make notes, under the following headings, of:
>
> 1. What information do you think is important for you to know about children in your class?
> 2. Why is it important?
> 3. How would you use it?
> 4. How would you record it?
> 5. How would you check on the objectivity and fairness of your records?
> 6. Who has a right of access to your records?
>
> *Extension*: Asking such basic questions could provide a check on the keeping of records. Any information which is not demonstrably useful to teaching, manageable, consistent with school policy and ethically sound should be reviewed.

4.2 Reporting to parents

The ways in which primary-school teachers report children's progress to parents are influenced by two seemingly contradictory sets of expectations.

The first makes the assumption that parents are *partners*, with teachers, in supporting the learning of each child (Wolfendale, 1992). Parents may thus be routinely invited into school, parent–teacher discussions are likely to be wide-ranging and include consideration of the processes and progress of the pupil – perhaps illustrated by reference to the child's work.

The second expectation is based on an image of parents as *consumers* of education, having contracted with the school for the provision of educational services to their child (Chubb and Moe, 1990; Johnson, 1990). They thus require a report of outcomes, through which the school can be held accountable for pupil progress.

Needless to say, most schools make provision which reflects elements of both these approaches. This is not surprising, for, whilst the partnership model is professionally acknowledged as contributing very constructively to pupil learning, the consumer model is increasingly underwritten by legal requirements.

For instance, in England and Wales annual reports to parents are required to include:

- comments on general progress
- details of arrangements for a parent–teacher discussion of the report
- particulars of progress on each subject or area of learning, highlighting strengths and weaknesses.

The partnership aspect is most clearly demonstrated by the inclusion within reports of targets for the future, and of advice about specific ways in which parents can help.

However, more detail is required in reporting the achievements of seven-year-olds and eleven-year-olds at the end of each Key Stage, including:

- National Curriculum assessment levels, and a commentary about what the results show about the child's progress
- comparative information about the attainment of all other pupils in the school at the end of the Key Stage
- national comparative information (as supplied by the DfES).

Such specification reflects an emphasis on standards in basic skills. However, in the requirement for comparative information to be provided, national requirements feed the 'consumer' model of education.

It is by no means certain how this tension between partnership and consumerist models of parent–school relationships will develop. Whilst the consumer model is projected centrally, local influences on primary schools seem very resilient. For instance, a research project (Hughes, Wikeley and Nash, 1994) reported that the proximity of the local school was the most important factor in influencing parental choice of primary school. In characterizing a 'good school', the first ten factors which parents looked for were, in order of frequency:

- relationships between parents, teachers and children
- the staff
- the atmosphere
- the ethos of the school
- good discipline
- wide-ranging education offered
- the headteacher
- development of the whole child
- academic results
- good resources.

This is an instructive list, with academic results listed in ninth position. It may be that many parents of young children understand the importance of the conditions in which pupil learning takes place and are concerned about the wider social and developmental aims of primary education. One of the most explicit ways of manifesting the partnership model will be through the processes which a school adopts in reporting pupil achievements to parents.

Reflective activity 14.7

Aim: To develop an informative and constructive procedure for reporting to parents.

Evidence and reflection: This activity must be tailored to circumstances. Discuss with appropriate colleagues the aims and scope of a reporting exercise. If you are a student teacher, you might want to limit it to reflect a project which you have completed, or build it into an end-of-term open day.

Consider the following questions:

How can you best provide information to parents?

How can you involve the children?

How can you elicit information and support from parents?

Extension: Evaluate your reporting procedure. Did you find consumerist or partnership expectations from parents? How did the children benefit? What will you do when your next opportunity arises?

5 | USING ASSESSMENT INFORMATION

An enormous amount of time, energy and money is expended on assessment, yet pupils' learning is only improved if assessment information is actually used, rather than simply collected. As is suggested in this chapter, assessment information can and should be used in a wide variety of ways, by different people, and for different purposes.

5.1 Planning and teaching

 In the constructivist model (see Chapter 7, Section 1.2) the key to learning is building on current knowledge, so at the start of any unit of work teachers need to use assessment information to match their teaching to the children's knowledge, skills and understanding. One of the purposes of baseline assessment, carried out when children first enter school, is to enable the teacher to plan appropriately for the children. Once children have been at school for some time, information about their current attainment should be available from records but, especially if it is some time since related work was addressed, recorded information should be supplemented by up-to-date information gleaned, for example, from questioning or concept mapping. The reflective teacher will also want to take heed of how previous groups of children have responded to a particular unit of work, and adapt established plans accordingly.

When teaching any lesson, teachers will constantly be using assessment information formatively to adapt their teaching depending on the children's responses. At the end of each lesson they will be noting, probably on the plans themselves or in their day book, things that need to be taken account of in the next lesson. These may apply to all or just some of the children, and could be about the need to reinforce a particular concept, or omit a planned activity since the learning objective it was designed to support is already well grasped. Towards the end of a unit the teacher may devise a particular assessment activity focusing on the key learning objectives for that unit, and will use the last period of time to extend the work or review those objectives, as the need is demonstrated. After a unit of work has been completed, notes will again be made to inform both the future teaching of that unit to other groups of children, and the future teaching of related units to the same group of children.

5.2 Tracking progress

Assessment data, particularly in the form of levels and grades, enable the progress of individuals and groups of children to be tracked fairly easily. This information becomes even richer when compared with previous progress, with progress in other subjects, with other children in the same class and school, and with national expectations. Comparisons become even more meaningful when value-added measures are used rather than attainment (for example, looking at the improvement from Year 2 to Year 6, and comparing Key Stage 2 results with those of other children who got the same Key Stage 1 results, rather than simply looking at the Year 6 results in isolation).

It is important to remember that despite their apparent attractiveness, numbers are a very blunt instrument when trying to represent progress. Concerns about reliability have been raised earlier in this chapter (see Section 3.3), and the difference between two levels in a test is just one mark.

Assessment information other than levels and grades can enable progress to be tracked. When expectations are set for a unit of work in terms of what all, most or some of the children should attain (as is the case in the QCA schemes of work), these can be used to see how children are performing over a period of time in relation to these expectations.

5.3 School improvement

End of key stage assessment data are used in increasingly sophisticated ways, and the 'Autumn Package' produced annually by the DfES for schools in England is one way of doing this, which encourages schools to look at their results and use them to plan school improvement. The Autumn Package is based upon a five-stage cycle, and is a framework which is also used by many local authorities providing similar support for schools in their areas.

The most important stage in the cycle is 'taking action and reviewing progress' as this is the only one that actually makes any difference to learning. Obviously the previous stages are important for ensuring that it is the most appropriate action which is taken, but all too often so much time and effort is spent in detailed analysis at the earlier stages that there is little energy left for actually implementing action.

The Autumn Package and the associated school-specific document known as the 'Panda' (Performance and Assessment) report which is provided by OFSTED have tended to be the preserve of the headteacher, with classroom teachers having little knowledge of them, and therefore making little use of them. Whilst teachers shouldn't spend hours and hours on data analysis, all teachers should find them a stimulus for reflection. English, mathematics and science subject leaders in particular should be familiar with data and analysis.

5.4 Performance management

Performance management has been the spur for many teachers to come to grips with the Autumn Package. This is due to the requirement for teacher objectives to cover pupil progress, and for pupil progress data to be one set of evidence presented for threshold assessment. 'Pupil progress objectives' as referred to in

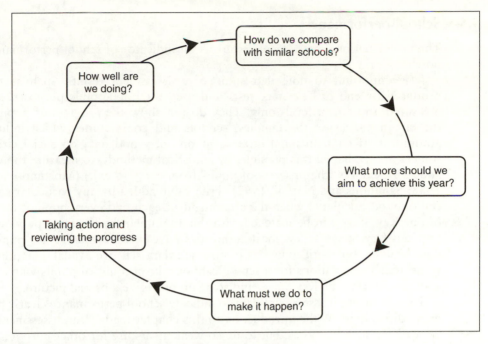

Figure 14.5 *Five-stage cycle for school improvement*

performance management, are essentially end of year targets for pupil attainment, perhaps expressed in the form 'End of Year 3: 50 per cent of pupils achieving learning objectives indicating emerging skills within Level 3 for reading and writing, and 15 per cent working securely within Level 3.' End of year targets such as this need to be set by considering the children's prior attainment, end of Key Stage targets, and associated factors such as additional support that may be available.

Assessment information has many parts to play within performance management, including:

- helping to set appropriate pupil progress objectives
- aiding learning and teaching so that those objectives can be met or exceeded
- helping to monitor progress towards the objectives
- judging the extent to which the objectives have been met or exceeded.

Reflective teachers will be aware of the complex issues surrounding assessment and pupil progress, for example those referred to in Section 3, as well as the ways in which assessment can support learning, which were discussed in Section 1, and so will be in an informed position to engage with performance management arrangements.

See Chapter 17, Section 3, for a broader discussion of continuing professional development and the role of performance management.

5.5   School performance

The use of national assessment results as an indicator of school performance is now the norm.

It is important to note that summative assessment results, such as those produced by end of Key Stage tests and used for league table purposes, show measured attainment levels only. They do not show the *progress* of pupils, or the circumstances of the families, schools and communities which influence attainment. If data on pupil attainment on entry and data on social circumstances are available, it is possible, by statistical methods, to measure the value added by schools (the *progress* of pupils from entry to exit) (Mortimore *et al.*, 1988; Sammons and Nuttall, 1992). True value added by any particular school can only be calculated when the attainment of each and every pupil at the end of one Key Stage can be matched with the attainment by the same pupil at the previous Key Stage. A few local authorities have this information for pupils in their schools, but until individually matched data sets are available nationally, value-added calculations for a school cannot take account of pupils who arrive and leave during the Key Stage, and so again only give a partial picture.

The use of pupil assessment data to indicate school performance clearly poses many difficulties. As the introduction to this chapter made clear, assessment can be used for such purposes, but to do so weakens its use for other purposes (see also Harlen *et al.*, 1992, **Reading 14.1**).

5.6   Transfer and transition

Assessment information has a very important role in effective transfer (when pupils move from one school to another) and transition (moving from one class to another within the same school). In order that the next teacher and/or school can extend each pupil's present attainment, building on strengths and addressing weaknesses, it is vital that key pieces of information from the present teacher's knowledge are passed on in a manageable way and at times when the information can be used effectively. This is a notoriously difficult area, and LEAs, central bodies and software firms, among others, devise and refine procedures, paper forms and software solutions. However, successful transfer and transition goes far beyond the mere passing on of assessment information. In particular, the value of informal, but principled, professional conversation between past and future teachers at times of transition and transfer is extremely valuable in

bringing documentary information to life. The move from primary to secondary school is addressed by Sutton (2000) and is more fully discussed in Chapter 5, Section 2.5.

CONCLUSION

Assessment has been, and remains, a controversial issue in education. It is a fast-moving area in policy terms and receives much media attention. As we have seen, professional practice tends to be shaped by the assessment purposes which have been given priority. In recent years, summative performance measures for pupils and schools have been emphasized extremely strongly. However, the direct contribution of formative assessment, at the heart of the teaching–learning process, is beginning to be formally recognized and given support. Research suggests that it will be more important in enhancing pupils' commitment to learning and in achieving long-term educational quality.

Key readings

Black and Wiliam's influential review of research is summarized in:

Black. P. and Wiliam, D. (1998c)
Inside the Black Box: Raising Standards through Classroom Assessment.
London: King's College.

For practical guidance on developing assessment for learning practices as an integral part of learning and teaching in the primary classroom see:

Clarke, S. (2001)
Unlocking Formative Assessment: Practical Strategies for Enhancing Pupils' Learning in the Primary Classroom.
London: Hodder and Stoughton.   ☐ **Reading 14.4**

A highly readable, practically based and thought provoking book, which addresses some important aspects of assessment is:

Sutton, R. (1995)
Assessment for Learning.
Salford: RS Publications.

A range of contributors provides insights into a number of topics from baseline assessment to using assessment data for school improvement in:

Conner, C. (ed.) (1999)
Assessment in Action in the Primary School.
London: Falmer.

A book which explores how assessment is carried out and the consequences for children's learning is:

Torrance, H. and Pryor, J. (1998)
Investigating Formative Assessment: Teaching, Learning and Assessment in the Classroom.
Buckingham: Open University Press.

Through a comprehensive study of assessment in children's lives many unsettling issues are addressed in:

Filer, A. and Pollard, A. (2000)
The Social World of Pupil Assessment: Processes and Contexts of Primary Schooling.
London: Continuum.   ☐ **Reading 14.7**

A comprehensive and accessible introduction to many issues relating to assessment is provided by Black in:

Black, P. (1998)
Testing Friend or Foe? Theory and Practice of Assessment and Testing.
London: Falmer.   ☐ **Reading 14.2**

An excellent overview of issues to do with equity and assessment, drawing on research from around the world, is provided in:

Gipps, C. and Murphy, P. (1994)
A Fair Test? Assessment, Achievement, and Equity.
Buckingham: Open University Press.

Practical support for classroom teachers on recording, analysing and using assessment data is provided in a very accessible way in:

Pringle, M. and Cobb, T. (1999)
Making Pupil Data Powerful: A Guide for Classroom Teachers.
Stafford: Network Educational Press.

The statutory requirements for assessment and reporting are published annually in separate Key Stage booklets. Some guidance and exemplars are also contained in these booklets:

QCA (2000)
Assessment and Reporting Arrangements.
London: QCA.

A book which specifically addresses the assessment aspects of the National Standards for QTS status is:

Headington, R. (2000)
Monitoring, Assessment, Recording, Reporting and Accountability: Meeting the Standards.
London: David Fulton.

A journal entirely dedicated to assessment issues is:

Assessment in Education: Principles, Policy and Practice.

Many other journals carry articles relating to assessment.

 Readings for Reflective Teaching (the companion volume) offers other closely associated work on the issues raised in this chapter. This includes work by authors such as:

Wynne Harlen, Caroline Gipps, Patricia Broadfoot, Desmond Nuttall, Paul Black, Andrew Burrell, Sara Bubb, Shirley Clarke, Yolande Muschamp, Mary Jane Drummond, Ann Filer and Andrew Pollard.

 RTweb offers additional professional resources for this chapter, including *Web Links* to sites such as the Association of Assessment Inspectors and Advisers (www. aaia.org.uk), the Assessment Reform Group (www.assessment-reform-group.org.uk/), QCA (www.qca.org.uk) which has an area specifically focusing on assessment for learning (www.qca.org.uk/ca/5-14/afl/index.asp), and the DfES (www.dfes.gov.uk).

CHAPTER 15

Social inclusion. What are the consequences of classroom practices?

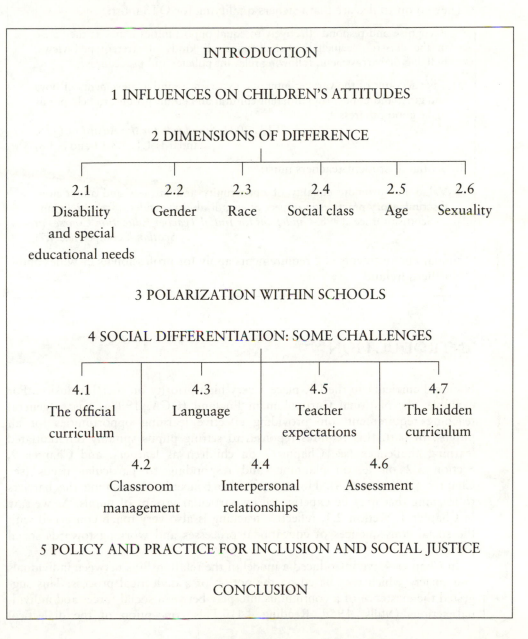

INTRODUCTION

1 INFLUENCES ON CHILDREN'S ATTITUDES

2 DIMENSIONS OF DIFFERENCE

2.1 Disability and special educational needs

2.2 Gender

2.3 Race

2.4 Social class

2.5 Age

2.6 Sexuality

3 POLARIZATION WITHIN SCHOOLS

4 SOCIAL DIFFERENTIATION: SOME CHALLENGES

4.1 The official curriculum

4.2 Classroom management

4.3 Language

4.4 Interpersonal relationships

4.5 Teacher expectations

4.6 Assessment

4.7 The hidden curriculum

5 POLICY AND PRACTICE FOR INCLUSION AND SOCIAL JUSTICE

CONCLUSION

Enhancing professional standards and competences

Inclusion and the provision of equal opportunities for learning is, and is likely to remain, a key issue in modern societies. Indeed, it is being taken very seriously within education across the UK. For example, the first value requirement suggested by the English TTA is that teachers must:

> Have high expectations of all pupils: respect their social, cultural, linguistic, religious and ethnic backgrounds, and be committed to raising their educational achievement.

They go on to declare that teachers qualifying for QTS must:

> Recognise and respond effectively to equal opportunities issues as they arise in the classroom, including challenging all kinds of strereotyped views, bullying or harrassment, following relevant policies and procedures.

> Take account of the varying interests, experiences and achievements of boys and girls, and pupils from different cultural and ethnic groups, to help pupils make good progress.
>
> (TTA, 2002, *Standards for the Award of QTS*, standards 1.1, 3.3.14 and 3.3.6)

In Scotland, student-teachers must:

> Value and promote equality of opportunity and fairness and adopt non-discriminatory practices in respect of age, disability, gender, race or religion.
> (Scottish Office, 1998, *Guidelines for Initial Teacher Education Courses in Scotland*, competence 4.7)

Similar commitments and requirements apply for professionals in Wales and Northern Ireland.

INTRODUCTION

National curricula in the UK place a very high priority on social inclusion. For example, the National Curriculum in England (QCA, 1998a) has a 'general teaching requirement' on 'providing effective learning opportunities for all pupils'. In part, this requires reponses to setting pupils suitably differentiated learning challenges (see Chapter 7 on children as learners, and Chapter 9, Section 3.2 on lesson planning) and responding to particular needs (see Chapter 5, Section 2.4). However, it also concerns overcoming the barriers to learning that may be experienced by particular groups of pupils. As we saw in Chapter 1, Section 2.1, reflective teaching is also very much concerned with the social consequences of educational processes and working towards social justice.

In Chapter 4, we introduced a model of the relationships between individuals and society which was based on the notion of a dialectical process. This suggested the existence of a continuous interplay between social forces and individual actions (Mills, 1959, **Reading 4.1**). This conception of the dialectical process of social change should cause us to look at our daily actions in the classroom and to consider their possible social implications. In this view, 'society' does not develop exclusively 'somewhere else' controlled by indeterminate powers – by 'them'. Future developments are partially in our own hands and we can make our own small, but unique, contribution. Indeed, many educationists argue (e.g. Carr and Hartnett, 1996) that one of the aims of education should be the creation of a more democratic and inclusive society. This position holds true despite arguments that the underlying factors in exclusion are structural, and that many are amplified by government policies (see Vulliamy, 2000).

To the credit of the teaching profession, there is considerable awareness of how opportunities can be unequal for some groups of children and how such inequalities can be tackled. It is recognized that the provision of social justice requires both careful reflection on the social consequences of routine classroom practices and the development of constructive whole-school policies. Concerned teachers will want to consider how to provide the best possible educational experiences for all children, including any groups that are particularly vulnerable to inequalities in provision (Maden, 1999, **Reading 15.1**). These teachers also aim to enable children to learn about important issues of equality and rights throughout society. They do this through the curriculum, in the choice of appropriate materials and pedagogies, as well as by promoting equal opportunities through staffing policies and practices.

These are perennial issues. In 1948 the Universal Declaration of Human Rights stated that education 'shall promote understanding, tolerance and friendship among all nations, racial or religious groups' (Article 26, p. 2). In England in the 1960s, the Plowden Report (1967) recognized the particular needs of children living in disadvantaged socio-economic conditions. In the intervening years, social justice issues have become more clearly understood and, as a result, concern has become more specifically focused. There was legislation, including a Race Relations Act (1976), a Sex Discrimination Act (1975) and the Education Act (1981) on Special Education. The Commission for Racial Equality and the Equal Opportunities Commission were created. Major reports have been published on the education of children from ethnic minority groups (Rampton, 1981; Swann, 1985) and on children with Special Educational Needs (Warnock, 1978). More recently, the Education Act (1993), the Children Act (1989) and the Education Reform Act (1988) the new Special Needs Code of Practice (DfES, 2001) all had implications for the provision of equal opportunities. Inspections also focus on the issue, and inspectors are required to evaluate how each school complies with relevant legislation and 'promotes equal access by all pupils to the full range of opportunities for achievement that the school provides,' (OFSTED, 1995, p. 106).

Within schools, facing issues of social inclusion and social justice remains a challenging process. To be successful, it almost always requires a spirit of co-operation, support and collective openness among all staff – teaching and non-teaching. Notwithstanding this, the issues remain just as real at the level of the individual classroom and there is much that even an individual reflective teacher can do to ensure that all the children feel included and have an equal opportunity to fulfil their potential.

This chapter is structured in five parts, beginning in Section 1 with consideration of factors that influence children's attitudes towards others. Section 2 considers some major dimensions of social difference – disability, gender, race, social class, age and sexuality. In Section 3, we offer a simple analytic framework concerned with differentiation and polarization within schools, which we hope will support future interpretation of experiences or requirements in this field (see also **Reading 15.2**). The chapter then reviews seven ways in which schools and classroom life can unwittingly affect social exclusion and differentiation, before concluding with a discussion on how to develop more affirming and inclusive classroom policies.

This chapter touches on a wide range of issues and the resources on **RTweb** will help in investigating them more deeply.

1   INFLUENCES ON CHILDREN'S ATTITUDES

Categorization is used by people to help them make sense of their lives. It is thus a natural, and necessary, process. Our concepts and categories reflect the cultures from which they have originated – they are 'cultural tools' (Wertsch, 1998) and, as such, they enable us to understand, think and realize our humanity in culturally 'intelligent' ways. However, a problem arises if such thinking perpetuates the inequalities that divide society or if it obstructs efforts to enhance social justice.

Of course, no child is born with innate prejudices but, from a very young age, all children learn and gather ideas from people and influences within their environment. Unfortunately, from the perspective of enhancing social justice across the whole of society, such socialization can sometimes be inappropriate. For instance, research has shown that racist and sexist prejudices can develop at very young ages, though it can also be appropriately challenged (Connelly, 1998). We review below some of the major factors that contribute to the formation of children's attitudes (see also Chapter 6, Section 2.2).

In Chapter 7, Section 2.4 we discussed the major sources of cultural influence on children. Here we look again at these influences but specifically focus on how these influences impact on children's attitudes to issues of variety and difference.

The Family. Adults' actions, words and deeds are living examples for young children. Through interpreting the social practices of significant others in their families, young children begin to assimilate the norms and values of their society. Children engage in a type of 'apprenticeship' as they learn how to behave as fully capable participants (Lave and Wenger, 1991; Rogoff, 1990). Of course, young children may not fully understand what they are learning, but they tend to follow established social conventions as they seek to develop positive identities with significant others such as parents, carers, grandparents, siblings and peers. The behaviour may display attitudes that are sexist and/or racist which, among other things, perpetuates inequalities. The behaviour and values of the family may also run counter to those supported in schools which many would argue, despite increased awareness of an increasingly diverse and multicultural society, continue to uphold predominantly white, middle-class values.

Reflective Activity 15.1 may help in exploring this issue by considering families and roles within families. Before doing this activity with children it would be revealing for you to reflect on the variety of 'families' you know about or can imagine. We believe that being aware of and tackling our own attitudes and prejudices is an important prerequisite to addressing them with children.

> ### Reflective activity 15.1
>
> *Aim*: To explore children's understanding of family practices and roles.
>
> *Evidence and reflection*: Ask the children to draw a house with a family in the house 'doing things that people in families do'.
>
> Individually or in groups encourage the children to explain their drawings. Have they drawn their own family? If not, how did they decide what to draw? What are different members of the family doing in the drawing? Why were those particular activities chosen for the picture? What might each member of the family be feeling? Discuss the variations in their drawings.
>
> Analyse the differences that emerge in the children's understandings of what constitutes a family. Perhaps you could discuss your conclusions with a colleague who has also done this activity.
>
> *Extension*: You might like to consider ways of discussing and exploring with the children the variety of families and family lifestyles in this country. You could start with your own family or the families of the children in the class, encouraging a positive view of variety and difference.

Peers at school. This is an enormous influence at school and as children grow older. When children work and play together they create a type of child society which mirrors many of the features of the adult world (see Chapter 5, Section 2.3, **Reading 5.4**). There are patterns in the friendship groups and status hierarchies which tend to evolve, and these often reflect the influence of gender, ethnicity, social class, age, attainment and physical abilities. The social structure which emerges within child culture has been found to reflect the initial differentiation by adults so that, put crudely, 'pro-school' and 'anti-school' pupil sub-cultures may form. Processes within peer culture can thus reinforce and multiply the effect of school-initiated differentiation, as we will see in Section 3 of this chapter.

The school. Of course, the school is also likely to influence a child's perspectives on the capabilities of their own and other social groups. For instance, a modelling of possibilities is provided by the presence, absence and roles of people of different ethnic groups, able-bodied and disabled people, women and men on the staff. Children will also be directly influenced by the information, values and attitudes which are conveyed through the curriculum, social practices and experiences which are provided within the classroom and school. Of particular importance are the values that are projected regarding diversity and the uniqueness of individuals. This is likely to be expressed most powerfully through symbolic events, such as assemblies, when the school community comes together as a whole under the leadership of the headteacher. The ways in which school and classroom life act as forms of 'social differentiation' is the subject of Section 4 of this chapter.

The media and new technologies. For many years, books have been the most influential carriers of culture. Their influence may have diminished, but much children's literature inevitably reflects the attitudes of its time towards ethnic groups, gender, social class, disability, etc. While older children may be more critical of such content, a young child has little on which to base discrimination.

We must therefore look closely at the reading material which is provided for children and at the hidden messages which it may convey (see also Chapter 8, Introduction). Classic children's literature might be discussed and interpreted, and many new authors are extremely inventive in challenging taken-for-granted assumptions.

There is now considerable evidence of the long television-viewing hours of children and of the growing impact of computer games and internet activities. As a result, concern has been raised over the power of electronic media to dispose people to be violent, to develop sexist or racist views, or simply to while time away, alone, in cyberspace. More optimistic opinion highlights the activity of users in processing information. However, while such media may not determine attitudes, they do structure and select the information that colours them. Indeed, it is interesting to note research which shows that, while younger children largely depend upon their parents for views and attitudes, older children place greater dependence on their peers, television and new communication media. A tendency also grows to recall those items that support opinions that have already formed.

The community. Each child and family, are members of wider communities. They belong to a racial group, they may follow a specific religion, and they are also likely to belong to a range of social groups. All these communities help to shape an individual's values, behaviour and sense of self. Once again these different views might be contradictory. It is possible for example that the values espoused by adults in the community may be significantly different from those supported by the youths in the same community. Similarly, the values of the family may be different from those of a specific religious leader. In addition, children may also assimilate attitudes which others understand as myths and stereotypes. If, for instance, the language that is used about Black people and/or women tends to be derogatory, then children may unwittingly absorb such prejudices as they become fully integrated into the community within which they live. For example, if a child sees Black people only in menial jobs or as sports people, dancers or musicians, then, unless he or she is shown otherwise, the child may think that these are the limits of their capabilities. If a child sees women only as mothers and in domestic roles, rather than in external positions of responsibility, then that is the expectation which the child may form. If people with a disability are always treated as being in need of help, then that is what a child is likely to believe. Fortunately, the reverse is also true, if children were to be brought up in a community in which people were not defined or limited by issues of race, gender, etc., then those children would regard equality as the norm.

2 DIMENSIONS OF DIFFERENCE

In this section we consider six dimensions in terms of which social differences, inequalities and rights have often been discussed: disability, gender, race, social class, age and sexuality. Clearly, such issues are both interconnected and highly permeable. Indeed, without exception, the experiences and life-course of each of us are simultaneously played out though their interaction. The challenge for a socially aware teacher is to spot possible injustices in children's experiences, and decide what to do about them. Is it possible, we might open-mindedly ask ourselves, that a perceived deficiency is merely a difference? And if we looked, what attributes might this difference reveal?

2.1 Disability and special educational needs

Understanding of disability as a question of rights and opportunities has grown in recent years as a result of people with disabilities articulating a strong voice and rejecting society's traditional views of the disabled as 'inadequate' or 'less than whole'. Under the enormous influence of what is known as a 'medical model', people in the past have been defined by their physical or mental impairments as 'abnormal', placed in institutions, segregated into separate schools, and often denied access to a full family life, to employment and to a voice. Increasingly this medical model, which views disability as an individual problem, is being rejected in favour of more enlightened views which see important elements of disability as constructed and created by society. In this view an individual is not disabled just by their inability to walk but by a society which constructs buildings which deny access to wheelchairs. A visually impaired child is not disabled by her loss of sight, but by the difficulty in providing braille and other aids in mainstream schools. A child with poor hearing is not excluded simply through his reception of sound, but by the inadequate provision of audio aids and sound-field systems in classrooms. Increasingly, disabled people have demanded the same rights as the able-bodied:

> Disabled people's own view of the situation is that whilst we may have medical conditions which hamper us and which may or may not need medical treatment, human knowledge, technology and collective resources are already such that our physical or mental impairments need not prevent us from being able to live perfectly good lives. It is society's unwillingness to employ these means to altering *itself* rather than *us*, which causes our disabilities.
>
> (Rieser and Mason, 1990)

In England, both the Warnock Report (1978) and the 1981 Education Act recommended that children with special educational needs should be integrated into mainstream schools, whenever possible. The 1981 Act, however, was 'enabling' legislation rather than being compulsory. Local Education Authorities were thus encouraged, but not legally obliged, to implement integration and no extra resources were made available by government to help achieve this. In 2000, there were still almost 100,000 children in English special schools. The Children Act of 1989 requires co-ordination of services and establishes children's interests as the top priority – but again no further resources are guaranteed. This is a significant issue. Whilst, in 2001, the proportion of pupils with formal 'statements' of special needs was only around 2 per cent of the primary-school population, 21 per cent of pupils were on the special needs register – a proportion that has been steadily rising. There is thus a significant problem of resources to provide the services that could satisfy the needs of all such children.

A new Special Educational Needs (SEN) Code of Practice (DfES, 2001) has set out guidance on policies and procedures aimed at enabling pupils with SEN to reach their full potential, to be included fully in their school communities and make a successful transition to adulthood. Amongst other directives the code states that:

- the special educational needs of children will normally be met in mainstream schools or settings
- the views of the child should be sought and taken into account
- those responsible for special educational provision should take into account the wishes of the child concerned, in the light of their age and understanding
- there is close co-operation between all the agencies concerned and a multi-disciplinary approach to the resolution of issues.

When thinking of a child in school, we first have to consider whether he or she has a recognized disability or special need and why. This is not always straight-forward. The definition of disabled children in the Children Act (1989) and the definition of disability in the Disability Discrimination Act (1995) are different from the definition of children with special educational needs in the Education Act (1996). Education legislation does not distinguish between special educational needs and disability. A child may fall within one, two or all of the definitions, and the expertise of SEN co-odinators and the educational psychological service is likely to be extremely helpful.

The next key question is whether any child who has a disability is restricted in access – physically or psychologically – to the education that is enjoyed by able-bodied children. If access is restricted then the child has been handicapped and the *right* of access to the National Curriculum has not been fulfilled (see Roaf and Bines, 1989, **Reading 15.5**).

2.2   Gender

There is a readily accepted scientific basis for recognizing two sexes. Clearly there are differences within the reproductive process and there is also evidence of genetic and neurobiological differences affecting innate behaviours and even brain functioning (Greenfield, 1997). Nevertheless a large number of differences which are conventionally associated with sex have been shown to be socially constructed through such processes as socialization, the pressure of expectation and the adoption of culturally ascribed roles and identities. As we saw in Section 1, the cultural tools and social practices of our societies are extremely resilient and tend to be reproduced from one generation to another. For instance, it is all too easy to think of occupations in which the workforce is predominantly of one sex or the other, but in fact there are few occupations that cannot be carried out equally by women and by men. Of course, things may be done differently, but most jobs can still be completed.

The term 'gender' is important because it describes the *social definition of sex roles* rather than the biological distinction itself. 'Sexism' is the operation of forces in society by which members of one sex get advantages over the other, because of and through their gender. It has been most commonly evident in the advantages men acquire over women. For instance, in primary teaching itself it is difficult, if not impossible, to explain the disproportionate number of men in headships and deputy headships without reference to processes of sexual discrimination (see De Lyon and Migniuolo, 1989; Weiner, 1990). However, it is also pertinent to note how few men are teachers in nursery and reception classes, and to reflect on the attitudes encountered by those men who do choose to work with this age range (Cameron, Moss and Owen, 1999).

Considering pupils, we need to remember that gender is an extremely important factor in any child's sense of identity. Most primary school-age children rely on single-sex friendship groups, which themselves articulate with the scripts of youth and adult cultures. Such differences are clearly not a problem in themselves – they are part of growing up to adulthood. However, patterns of discrimination between the sexes are a different matter. Enduring questions have included whether boys and girls are treated equally at school; whether school life contributes to restrictive or enabling gender socialization; and why it is that girls tend to perform slightly better than boys when in primary school (e.g. Davies, 1993; Delamont, 1990; Francis, 1998; Gipps and Murphy, 1994; Reay, 2001; Reynolds, 2001; Walkerdine, 1988). Such patterns in performance are not inevitable and the underlying processes that give rise to them may be challenged if principles of social justice are infringed (Murphy, 2001, **Reading 15.6**). On the other hand, it is also important not to inadvertently disadvantage one group in the act of trying to improve the performance of another.

2.3   Race

The word 'race' has a strong common-sense meaning in society. However biologists have shown that differences of external physical features which are most commonly associated with the idea of race, are relatively insignificant in terms of fundamental capacities. Humans are essentially enormously alike. However, cultures and social structures, compounded by differences of historical development such as the effect of colonization and geographical setting, can make a considerable difference to people's experience, thus leading to much variation amongst ethnic groups. This has produced a confusion, and in some cases a distortion, whereby race is wrongly understood to be a determining factor in intelligence and behaviour. From the belief in people having distinct racial origins, strongly felt ideas sometimes follow which separate people into 'us' and 'them'. It is then an easily taken, but false, step to define one set of people as 'superior' and another as 'inferior'.

To challenge the validity of ethnicity and race as factors in determining human capacities is not to deny the significance of racism as a cause of the unequal opportunities afforded to some children. Racism is the term that describes processes in society which affect people according to their identification as members of one ethnic group or another. Racism has a long history in the UK going back to the imperial past and beyond, and it has taken root in the discourse and structure of society. It has led to the development of fairly

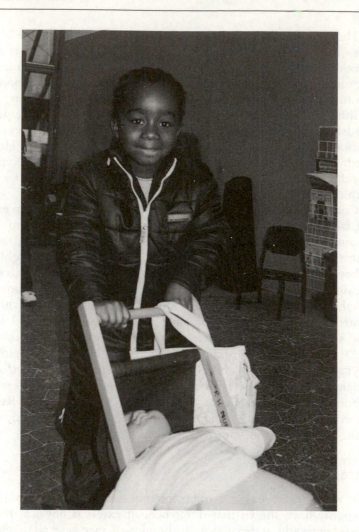

 widespread racial prejudice, which sometimes takes hold in the minds of certain individuals or groups, and may even be reflected within child culture (Connelly, 1999; Troyna and Hatcher, 1992, **Reading 15.8**). Such prejudices may be further amplified by the social, cultural, legal and political structures that have developed over time (see Epstein, 1993, **Reading 15.7** for further discussion of these issues). However, there is little doubt, for instance, from Connelly's study, that with sensitive guidance, even very young children are capable of thinking through the consequences of their attitudes and behaviour in relation to race, and understanding that certain things are wrong.

The population of the UK is multiracial. At the 1991 census there were 52 million White British, with all other ethnic minority groups (Black Caribbean, Black African, Indian, Pakistani, Bangladeshi, Chinese and others) amounting to 3 million, or just over 5 per cent of the total population, of whom almost half were born in Britain. The cold-blooded murder of Stephen Lawrence at a bus-stop and the subversion of justice that followed, showed that racism is still a significant problem. Indeed, despite the distinctive achievements of some, prejudiced behaviour associated with racism makes a significant contribution to the relative inequality that is experienced by Black people in society. Most Black people, for example of Caribbean origin, gain less in society in terms of employment, education, income, housing and wealth than their White peers. Education's multicultural teaching is a necessary contribution to the learning of each child, but hardly a sufficient response to deep-seated prejudices that still exist. Interestingly, Alibhai-Brown (2000) has argued that Britain should adopt a more modern, cosmopolitan approach which accepts the diverse contributions of different cultures and groups, past and present – including those White communities, rich or poor, which also feel excluded from significant aspects of modern society and which may harbour racism. Materials such as QCA's web-based *Respect for All* (QCA, 2000a), prepared following summer riots in Burnley, Oldham and Bradford, make a useful contribution. However, with immigration from Europe and asylum seekers rising, a more holistic review of curriculum, teaching and school organizations may be necessary. Is diversity really valued?

Some ethnic minority communities are strongly supportive of learning, but wish to preserve their own cultural traditions and beliefs. For instance, the recent growth of Muslim and other 'faith schools' in the UK may be seen as a recognition of cultural difference and a fulfilment of religious rights, though it is interesting that Church of England schools are also expanding in numbers.

2.4 Social class

Inequalities of wealth, income and material opportunities remain highly signifi-cant in determining life-chances (Reid, 1998). For instance, there has been no 'withering away of class' as a factor in the lived experience of citizens in the UK. Indeed, between 1977 and 2001 there was a consistent trend for the gap between the highest and lowest incomes to widen each year. This was caused by developments such as the shift to indirect taxation policies that disadvantaged those who must spend a large proportion of their income, changes in the labour market which adversely affected job security, the introduction of new technolo-gies, and competition from cheap labour sources overseas. One consequence was the fact that in 2000 there were 3.5 million children living in families on or below the 'poverty line' (Office for National Statistics, 2000). However, at the same time, many families were very well off and approximately 8 per cent of school-age children attended private schools.

Not all definitions of class are based on income, wealth or economic capital as such. For example, most teachers are not particularly wealthy, but teaching is certainly considered to be a 'middle class' occupation. Some definitions thus relate more to status and level of education than to material assets. A social class judgement may also be affected by a person's lifestyle – taste in clothes, food, music and art for example. Of course, in reality it is not possible to separate the factors of gender, race, ability, age, sexuality and social class. Nevertheless, some commentators, perhaps inspired by Marx, argue that social class is the most significant factor, providing the structural framework through which the others are played out.

The concepts of 'cultural capital' (Bourdieu and Passeron, 1977) and 'social capital' (Coleman, 1988) were developed to describe the knowledge, attitudes and experiences which socialization within a 'higher-class' family may offer, and which complements material wealth. One of their major insights on educational inequality is that students with more valuable social and cultural capital are likely to fare better in education than their otherwise comparable peers with less valuable social and cultural capital. Reay (2000, **Reading 4.5**) has also expanded this analysis to review the 'emotional capital' available to children – a key issue for effective learning. Resourceful parents may thus deploy their economic, cultural, social and emotional capital to support their children – for instance, by purchasing a private education, by developing a particularly close relationship with teachers at a maintained school, or by providing sensitive support during a period of stress or learning difficulty. Such strategies are manifestations of the process of 'social reproduction', in which one generation seeks to pass on the advantages of its social position to another (see Connell *et al.*, 1982; Pollard and Filer 2002). Many feel that one of the aims of education is to reduce inequality by providing access to valuable cultural capital which may not, for whatever reason, be available at home or in the local community. However, whilst a number of studies have identified cultural and social factors that contribute to educational inequality there is less knowledge as to the process whereby social and cultural resources are converted into educational advantage (Lareau, McNamara and Horvat, 1999).

Most teachers are aware of the effects of social context on children's learning and development. Indeed, pupil achievement tends to be closely related to social-class factors, as is particularly apparent from the publication of raw-score league tables of school results. Indeed, parental enrolment selections can create spirals of success and failure for schools, with tendencies for pupils to be moved out of inner-city schools to those in 'leafy suburbs' or out of town locations. Such problems have been understood for a very long time, though some lessons of the past seemed hard to learn (see Jackson, 1964).

Although children from poor homes tend not to do as well as children from wealthy homes, this is by no means inevitable, and there are always many exceptions. Indeed, it has been argued that there is potential for a significant improvement in the attainment of working-class children if the 'funds of knowledge' (Moll and Greenberg, 1990) within their families and communities were recognized and harnessed to support children's engagement with school curricula. Learning is, after all, not just about the simple acquisition of knowledge or skill, it is also about their appropriation within the personal identity of the learner. Since learning is thus inevitably connected to cultural identity (see Chapter 7, Section 1.3 and 2.4 and **Readings 7.8** and **7.9**), then social class is a crucial factor. If social justice and equality of opportunity are important, then this implies that curricular and educational processes should be accessible to children from all backgrounds. This is an enduring theme, but also provides an important principle to work towards.

2.5 Age

The Universal Declaration of Children's Rights establishes the principle that children and young people should not be discriminated against because of their age. However, whilst the use of the term 'ageism' is normally associated with the elderly, it is arguably as appropriate in respect of children's experience of growing up in an adult-dominated world. Research in the sociology of childhood has repeatedly demonstrated how children's perspectives, activities and rights are structured, ignored or constrained by adults (James, Jenks and Prout, 1998; Miller, 1997). Alternative conceptions of children as being either 'innocent' or 'evil' (Aries, 1962) can be found in popular culture (and public policy), with the associated adult responses of both protection and moralizing. Thus we lurch between indulging children and telling them off. In fact, younger people are much like older people. They are intelligent, strategic decision-makers, working with the knowledge and information they have available, and seeking to develop security and a meaningful identity in life. Within the limits of their development, experience and resources, they negotiate their circumstances and pursue their interests (for instance see Pollard and Filer, 1999, for an analysis of 'pupil careers').

Teachers have been accused of constraining children because of a misplaced adherence to Piaget's conception of 'stages of development' (Walkerdine, 1984, see also Chapter 7, Section 1.2). There is a risk that assumptions associated with National Curriculum 'levels' could have a similarly limiting effect. Whilst recognizing the imperatives of developmental processes and measured attainment, so many capabilities have now been demonstrated at very young ages that it is foolhardy to underestimate children in any way (see, for instance, Gopnik, Meltcoff and Kuhl, 1999; Mehler and Dupoux, 1994). A simple, but appropriate, position therefore is to say that children and young people should always be taken seriously as thinking decision-makers. They should be offered explanations, and talked with (not at) in ways that are appropriate to their understanding. Additionally of course, among the indivisible rights that applies to children is the right not to be punished physically (see Article 19 of the UN Convention on Children's Rights).

Such principles are not easy to put into practice, though suggestions will be found throughout this book (for instance, see Chapters 5 and 12 on understanding pupil perspectives, Chapter 6 on negotiating classroom relationships, and Chapter 14 on target setting with children and pupil self-assessment). Perhaps the biggest challenge however is to treat children equally in the course of such processes. It is all too easy to talk, listen and negotiate with articulate, well-behaved pupils whilst leaving less engaging children on the margins (see the discussion of 'goodies, jokers and gangs' later in this chapter). This will produce a differentiating effect within the classroom.

There is another sense in which children's age can lead to social differences. In the UK, children are required to begin formal education in the school year in which they become five years old, but there is wide local variation in admission policies. Thus some full cohorts start at the beginning of the year, other children are admitted at the beginning of the term in which their birthday falls, whilst the remainder must wait until after their fifth birthday. The accident of birth date, when combined with the start of the school year in September each year, produces age effects that can be traced through attainment in secondary school. In particular, children who are young in their year can suffer from low teacher expectations when immaturity is misinterpreted as a lack of ability. Of course, starting school early is not necessarily a positive benefit and the admission age for formal schooling is much higher in many parts of the world. For instance, in much of Scandinavia children start formal school at age seven or later because they are deemed to need more open, play-centred experiences as a basis for their early development. The introduction of the Foundation Stage in England could be seen as a move in this direction.

Once in school, children are usually managed as a class. However, many primary-school classes are made up of mixed year groups and maintaining high-quality learning experiences for children across the age range is a significant challenge. Nevertheless, this is clearly each child's right, and some countries do move children on the basis of attainment rather than age. However, see Chapter 9, Section 3.2 for suggestions on the UK solution, the differentiation of learning activities.

Overall therefore, we can see that age is a potentially significant dimension of inequality. Because of developmental processes, professional judgement on age appropriateness is essential, but the fundamental principle is to respect even young children's dignity and agency. An even bigger challenge is to do this equally for all children, irrespective of character, background and date of birth.

2.6 Sexuality

There is still considerable social stigma associated with open expressions of sexuality and most teachers are understandably hesitant about addressing such issues, especially with young children. Yet the recognition and acceptance of such differences may be extremely important to the provision of equal opportunities for some pupils – and also for some teachers and others in the school community. Indeed, the increasing openness of members of the lesbian and gay communities has generated more supportive recognition of them as minority groups.

With regard to education, there are several important issues to consider. First, what is the school experience of teachers who are lesbian or gay? Discrimination has been common in the past, obliging many to work under the continual stress of pretence and secrecy. Second, what provision should be made for children who come from families where one or more members are lesbian or gay? The relationship may be just as stable, loving or prone to breakdown as any heterosexual marriage. Do the ethos and curriculum of the school offer appropriate support to such children? Third, should primary school pupils be introduced to sexuality as an issue or not? There is likely to be awareness among many. For instance, we know that accusations of homosexuality are sometimes used among surprisingly young children to reinforce conformity to sex roles. An independent girl may be accused of being a 'lessie', or an affectionate, gentle boy may be labelled 'queer' or a 'poof'. The term 'gay' may be used to mean 'pathetic' or 'naff' – thanks to the South Park cartoon. The notorious 'Section 28', which became part of the Local Government Act (1986), prohibits the 'promotion' of homosexuality and exerts a strong influence on the teaching of this important subject. What place should discussion of sexuality have in a sex-education programme?

In Section 2 above, we have briefly introduced six dimensions which research shows may, in interaction, be associated with unequal experiences and life chances. These are enormously complex issues, and no teacher can shoulder full responsibility for them. However, we do have a responsibility to consider how our daily practice may affect such issues, and this could partially be achieved though a review of our expectations of particular children. This is suggested in Reflective Activity 15.2.

Reflective activity 15.2

Aim: To review the possible influence of common dimensions of inequality on our expectations of children.

Evidence and reflection: Think of yourself, a relatively-high-attaining and a relatively-low-attaining pupil in your class. Taking each applicable dimension in turn, think of how you and the children are affected by it, and make some brief notes.

	Yourself	A high-attaining pupil	A low-attaining pupil
Disability			
Gender			
Race			
Social class			
Age			
Sexuality			

Some cells will clearly have more significance than others, but try to relate each dimension to each person. Then think hard about the capabilities and the potential of each of the children. How are these enabled – or constrained – by the dimensions being considered?

Extension: Consider the implications of this activity. For instance, a very exciting and worthwhile thing to do is to identify and gradually build on the particular strengths and potential of children who may have been performing relatively poorly at school.

In the previous two sections, we have considered both common influences on children's attitudes and perceptions and six of the major dimensions around which significant differences are likely to be found within the cultures of the UK. Such factors affect children's experiences inside and outside school, and influence their concepts, knowledge and frameworks for making sense of the world. 'Society', 'the media', 'schooling' and much else, gradually contribute to each child's sense of himself or herself, and sense of difference from others. Such processes are often reinforced within schools by the interaction of teacher decisions and peer-group cultures, as is described in the next section of this chapter.

3 POLARIZATION WITHIN SCHOOLS

When children share a similar position in relation to school success or failure and regularly come together as a group, they begin to develop sub-cultures. For example, children who are regularly placed in different 'sets' or groups for particular activities, are likely to develop a sense of themselves as a group (Ireson and Hallam, 2001, **Reading 15.3**).

This is a very common social process. Indeed, whenever children (or people of any age, for that matter) regularly experience being 'differentiated' by organizations or in other circumstances, they tend to share their experiences and provide each other with mutual support. Such groups develop both friendships and their own perspectives – ways of thinking about themselves and ways of thinking about other people. As they bond together, the cultures of each group tend to be affirmed more strongly, particularly if there is rivalry or competition between groups. In school contexts, the latter process is termed 'polarization', for ironically, it involves a reinforcement of the initial differentiation as the children themselves respond to it. In a sense, it is a form of cultural coping strategy, developed in response to experience and circumstances. But it is a strategy that can easily make a poor situation worse.

There has been a series of studies of such processes within secondary schools (e.g. Ball, 1981a; Hargreaves, 1967; Lacey, 1970) which has shown how children interpret their experiences of differentiation. There are tendencies for them to identify with or against school, and children who feel that they are 'educational failures' may reject school values in order to protect their own pride and self-esteem. Similar processes may be found in primary-school contexts. Indeed, Pollard and Filer (1999) traced the 'school careers' of individual pupils and recorded the social influence of peer, family and teacher relationships as they form increasingly differentiated and unique identities. The danger, of course, is that such processes reinforce and deepen exclusion, thus creating a negative cycle of poor behaviour, under-performance, low self-esteem, and negative peer influence which is extremely difficult to break out of.

This analysis is summarized in Figure 15.1, and a more complete discussion is available in **Reading 15.2** and Pollard, 1987a.

Similar arguments have been developed in relation to gendered cultures within primary-school peer groups, and show the overlapping of such signifi-

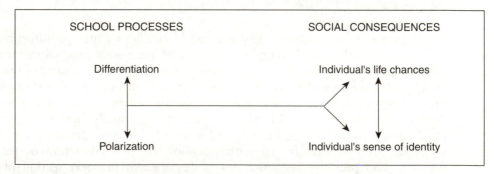

Figure 15.1 *Differentiation–polarization process and its consequences*

cant factors. For example, Reay's study (2001) of girls' friendship groups – 'Spice Girls', 'Nice Girls', 'Girlies' and 'Tomboys' – showed a very common range of responses to school circumstances, but highlighted the way this was overlain by cultures of femininity. As she put it, 'despite widely differentiated practices, all of the girls at various times acted in ways which bolstered boys' power at the expense of their own' (p. 153). Similarly, Reynolds (2001) showed how dominant ideas about masculinity shape boys dispositions to schooling, school-work and academic achievement. She found that, even in primary school, high-achieving boys felt the need to use 'disguise' to maintain an apparently masculine disdain for school-work, and also clearly wanted to differentiate themselves from girls. In such ways, pervasive cultural differences within our societies are reinforced by social processes within schools, classrooms and playgrounds.

Perhaps, differentiation and polarization processes are inevitable in schools, but this cannot diminish our responsibility as teachers for monitoring them and for acting to minimize divisive effects. Reflective Activity 15.3 offers a way of gaining some insights into the polarization of primary-school pupils within their peer culture.

Reflective activity 15.3

Aim: To explore children's perceptions of playground friendships.

Evidence and reflection: Watch the children at your school in the playground. Notice particularly how children use and occupy playground spaces and any significant actions or verbal exchanges between different groups of children. Make quick notes of your observations.

In the classroom, talk with the children about their friendship groups and their use of the playground. Ask them to draw a plan of the playground, marking areas in which they or others like to go or play, and noting the major activities that take place. Discuss the plans with the children in friendship groups. Take the opportunity to discuss how they feel about playing with different groups of children.

Make a note of the points that emerge. Do you begin to get a sense of the friendship groups that exist within the pupil culture of your school? What are their characteristic activities and attitudes to school?

Extension: Share your response to the activity with a colleague who has also done the activity. Can you see any patterns in terms of the major friendship groups and the attainment and attitudes to school of the children within them? Do some have higher status and others lower? How do the patterns in children's friendships relate to organizational differentation within the school?

A key connection is to try to relate the differentiating effect of teachers and schools to the polarizing processes that occur within child culture. The key processes lie in a chain as classroom differentiation is reinforced by polarization and then begins to affect self-image and self-esteem. The next effect is likely to be felt on attainment and, in due course, inclusion, exclusion and life-chances.

Lest readers feel overawed by the responsibilities outlined above, we should remember two realities. First, all children have different prior experiences and capabilities on entry to classrooms. Teachers cannot wave magic wands and make them all be equal in what they can achieve, though pupils do have equal rights to be supported in fulfilling their potential. Second, the differentiation of pupils to meet educational needs is both necessary and inevitable in classrooms. It is part of helping each child to fulfil their potential. And yet, that prime responsibility also brings a second responsibility, which is, wherever possible, to mitigate adverse social effects. In Section 4, we consider the nature of this challenge.

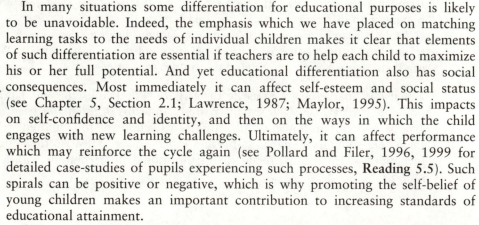

4   SOCIAL DIFFERENTIATION: SOME CHALLENGES

'Differentiation' is used here to refer to social processes which increase distinctions between children and which are largely under teacher or school control. There is a danger, of course, that these accumulate to undermine and 'exclude' some children.

At a whole-school level, a classic form of differentiation is 'streaming' which was commonplace in the 1960s but was found to be divisive (Barker-Lunn, 1970; Jackson, 1964). New forms of 'setting' for particular subjects have been developing in recent years and it remains to be seen if these will have unintended social effects, as seems likely (Ireson and Hallam, 2000, **Reading 15.3**). Within classroom settings, differentiation arises from such practices as the use of 'ability-based' groups, hierarchically organized schemes of work, 'star' systems for rewarding good behaviour, imbalances in the display of children's work, and from variations in teacher's perceptions of and relationships with children. We discussed similar issues from the perspective of lesson planning in Chapter 9.

In many situations some differentiation for educational purposes is likely to be unavoidable. Indeed, the emphasis which we have placed on matching learning tasks to the needs of individual children makes it clear that elements of such differentiation are essential if teachers are to help each child to maximize his or her full potential. And yet educational differentiation also has social consequences. Most immediately it can affect self-esteem and social status (see Chapter 5, Section 2.1; Lawrence, 1987; Maylor, 1995). This impacts on self-confidence and identity, and then on the ways in which the child engages with new learning challenges. Ultimately, it can affect performance which may reinforce the cycle again (see Pollard and Filer, 1996, 1999 for detailed case-studies of pupils experiencing such processes, **Reading 5.5**). Such spirals can be positive or negative, which is why promoting the self-belief of young children makes an important contribution to increasing standards of educational attainment.

The challenge of providing appropriate educational differentiation whilst avoiding inappropriate social differention may be particularly difficult when implementing new curriculum directives. For example, shortly after the imple-

mentation of the National Literacy Strategy in England, Smith and Whiteley (2000) found that the majority of primary teachers they surveyed felt that the Literacy Hour represented an inappropriate and poorly differentiated pedagogy. These teachers criticized the Literacy Hour because in their opinion;

- It was not suited to classes with children with a large range of abilities. It is very difficult to find tasks that are at the right level for all the children in the class. Several respondents commented that the higher-ability children gain the most.

- It was not suited equally to all year groups. One upper-junior teacher complained of the Literacy Hour's *'infant practices'*.

(Smith and Whitely, 2000, p. 37)

Worries about the difficulty of meeting the needs of all children during the Literacy Hour reinforce concerns about provision for children perceived to have SEN. An NFER pilot survey in 1998 found that children with SEN showed less improvement than their classmates (Sainsbury, 1998). Indeed, evidence of children being withdrawn from whole-class sessions (Jones, 1999) suggests a movement away from inclusive education that many will find ideologically disturbing. Hopefully, this situation will improve as teachers become more familiar with the Literacy Strategy and the material to be covered, and as adaptions are made to its requirements. Thorne (1993, **Reading 15.4**) makes particular suggestions for how to promote co-operation among children.

Almost all classroom practices thus touch on issues of social differentiation. It is part of life. It is not therefore surprising that this section reaches out across the book as a whole. The role of the reflective teacher, however, is to be socially aware, to minimize damage and maximize opportunities for all the children in his or her care. The analysis is elaborated from the discussion in Pollard (1987a, **Reading 15.2**).

4.1   The official curriculum – how inclusive is it?

The content of the curriculum, and the focus of books, resources and school activities, places value on what is taught and learned. The curriculum is thus a vital issue in the social reproduction of culture and values, as well as knowledge, skills and attitudes. As an aspect of differentiation, where the curriculum fails to affirm the experiences of particular social groups, then this very omission devalues them, just as inclusion could contribute to the development of self-confidence.

National curricula documents are very good at making overarching statements about the importance of inclusion in the curriculum. However, the reality is that they are forced to be selective in identifying curricular requirements, and they often fail to take valid account of the interests of minorities or the disaffected. This can increase exclusion. As we shall see (Section 4.6), assessment processes may then reinforce such differentiation, and make relative failures seem 'official'. Chapters 8 and 9 offer a full discussion of other curriculum issues.

4.2   Classroom management – can you bind them in?

This is a very important topic, an adequate treatment of which must recognize the classroom necessity for practical and effective systems, rules and strategies for managing the class and maintaining order. Such issues are the subject of Chapters 10 and 11 in both this book and in *Readings*.

However, the reality is that management and organization of the 'crowd' of children (Jackson, 1968, **Reading 6.2**) almost invariably rests on forms of social differentiation. Thus we have grouping systems, procedures for reward and punishment, routines for particular phases of the school day and a myriad of classroom rules (of both explicit and tacit types). Maintenance of such structures is a necessary part of a teacher's repertoire, but we must also recognize that they do tend to suit some children more than others. Thus we get different patterns of pupil response, ranging from forms of conformity through to negotiation and deviance.

From here it is not far to the introduction of classroom-management strategies based on comparison and competition: 'The Red Group is sitting up well. I wonder if the rest of you could do that too?', 'Who is ready to go out now?', 'Let's see who got that right.' In one sense, such interactions simply introduce the children to the realities of the modern world, but in another sense they can be seen as a form of the classic tactic of 'divide and rule' which the powerful have used to further their positions throughout history. Teachers are certainly in positions of power, and classrooms must be organized and managed effectively. The responsibility and challenge, however, is in using that power wisely and

with social awareness, in ways which do not undermine the confidence and opportunities of children who are less advantaged in school situations. Reflective Activity 6.5 suggests ways of reviewing the ways in which all children can identify with class activities within an incorporative classroom.

4.3   Language – does yours convey respect?

Language is a primary medium of social interaction and learning. It is thus of enormous importance, as we saw in Chapter 12. In Section 2.1 of Chapter 12, we raised the issue of linguistic diversity in all its forms. How do issues such as dialect, accent, vocabulary, grammar, bilingualism, and the use of standard English affect classroom processes (see also **Readings 12.4** and **12.5**)? Many years ago Bernstein suggested that there were two language codes – 'restricted' and 'elaborated' (1971). Since schools use forms of elaborated code, pupils who were reliant on more restricted codes, predominantly from working-class communities, were disadvantaged. However, many linguists following Labov (1973) have shown the sophistication of the diverse forms of language use which we have in modern societies, so that it is not possible to say that one is 'better' than another. A professional consensus has thus settled on the proposition that children should be prepared to use language appropriately, in relation to particular audiences and contexts. However, it is certainly the case that standard English is the highest status form of language in the UK and being taught to speak in this way has been enshrined as an entitlement in the curriculum. In many Welsh schools, Welsh is the language of instruction.

Within any classroom there will be children with very different levels of linguistic capability in relation to the four basic skills of speaking, listening, reading and writing in English. Attainment in most school subjects is likely to be closely related to these capabilities, but a reflective teacher would wish to monitor the extent to which the form of language used in the classroom helped, or hindered, fulfilment of the capabilities of each individual.

Language is particularly important as a way of making sense of experience, and one way in which this is done regarding people and relationships is through naming. In the playground domain of peer culture, names are often used to assert inclusion or exclusion between groups of children. This can be quite divisive, as the example of racist name calling illustrates (Connelly, 1999; Troyna and Hatcher, 1992, **Reading 15.8**). However, we as adults can also learn something from considering colloquial uses of language to name people.

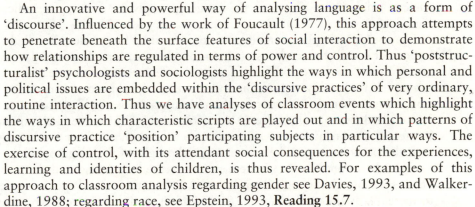

An innovative and powerful way of analysing language is as a form of 'discourse'. Influenced by the work of Foucault (1977), this approach attempts to penetrate beneath the surface features of social interaction to demonstrate how relationships are regulated in terms of power and control. Thus 'poststructuralist' psychologists and sociologists highlight the ways in which personal and political issues are embedded within the 'discursive practices' of very ordinary, routine interaction. Thus we have analyses of classroom events which highlight the ways in which characteristic scripts are played out and in which patterns of discursive practice 'position' participating subjects in particular ways. The exercise of control, with its attendant social consequences for the experiences, learning and identities of children, is thus revealed. For examples of this approach to classroom analysis regarding gender see Davies, 1993, and Walkerdine, 1988; regarding race, see Epstein, 1993, **Reading 15.7**.

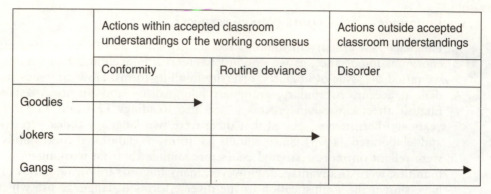

	Actions within accepted classroom understandings of the working consensus		Actions outside accepted classroom understandings
	Conformity	Routine deviance	Disorder
Goodies	——————————→		
Jokers	————————————————————→		
Gangs	——————————————————————————————————————→		

Figure 15.2 *Parameters of child behaviour*

4.4 Interpersonal relationships – are you fair, understanding *and* interesting?

We discussed classroom relationships at length in Chapter 6, Section 2.1 and suggested that teachers and children usually negotiate a 'working consensus' of accepted classroom understandings (see also **Reading 6.4**). This represents ways of 'getting along together', and from it emerges a range of tacit rules about behaviour and a sense of what is and is not 'fair'. We suggested that children's actions might range from conforming to rules, to engaging in routine deviance and mischief or, by stepping beyond this, to acting in unilateral and disorderly ways. These enduring patterns are indeed commonly found. For example, Pollard (1985) identified three types of friendship groups among eleven-year-olds. 'Goodies' were very conformist, fairly able but considered rather dull. 'Jokers' were able and liked to negotiate and 'have a laugh' with their teachers. 'Gang' group members were willing to disrupt classes, had low levels of academic achievement and were thought of as a nuisance. If we relate characteristic pupil actions to types of child friendship group, then we can analytically represent the range of likely behaviour, as indicated in Figure 15.2.

Figure 15.2 simplifies significant complexities, but it does highlight some important social consequences of classroom relationships. In particular, it draws attention to the issues of being fair and offering interesting learning opportunities. If the quality of both interpersonal relationships and curriculum provision is high, then the parameters of children's actions are likely to move to the left of the diagram and children's behaviour and inclusion are likely to improve. If interpersonal relationships are poor and curriculum provision is inappropriate, then the parameters are likely to move to the right of the diagram. The result is likely to be an increase in disruption, a decrease in learning and the growth of dissatisfaction with school. Overall, social differentiation and exclusion are likely to increase, as the teacher acts to deal with disruptive children – who may then become 'labelled' as such.

It is very easy and common to see causes of disruption as being exclusively to do with particular children. Reflection on the quality and pattern of relationships and of teacher actions in respect of the working consensus may provide another set of issues for consideration – issues, furthermore, which, to a great extent, are within our own control as teachers. For evidence of the role of the teacher in engendering or reducing disruption try observing a group of children working in different contexts with different teachers.

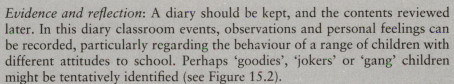

Reflective activity 15.4

Aim: To reflect on the quality and consequences of relationships between teacher and children, over several weeks.

Evidence and reflection: A diary should be kept, and the contents reviewed later. In this diary classroom events, observations and personal feelings can be recorded, particularly regarding the behaviour of a range of children with different attitudes to school. Perhaps 'goodies', 'jokers' or 'gang' children might be tentatively identified (see Figure 15.2).

Some weeks later, the diary should be reviewed. This will trigger personal recall of events and feelings, and enable you to construct a meaningful (and evidence-informed) story of how classroom relationships developed. Did the children's behaviour remain within the bounds of the working consensus that you had previously established with them – just a little mischief and other forms of routine deviance? Or were some pupils acting beyond these limits so that they actually challenged your authority – if so, which children and with whom? Could you feel the engagement of the class ebb and flow over the period? What helped them to become more settled? What disturbed them? Can you relate these patterns to the things that you did, or felt? How did these changes affect particular groups of children?

Extension: Perhaps an important influence on children's behaviour and application to work is the quality of our own energy, commitment and educational provision? If this seems to be true, then a reflective teacher may want to consider how the development of good relationships and a stimulating curriculum can pre-empt challenging behaviour and produce an inclusive, fulfilling classroom.

4.5 Teacher expectations – can you enhance the confidence of all?

The expectations of teachers for the children in their charge have long been recognized as contributing to children's achievements in school. The classic study of this, by Rosenthal and Jacobson (1968), suggested that a 'self-fulfilling prophecy' could be set up, in which children who were believed to be 'bright' would do well but, where negative expectations existed, then children would underperform. Indeed, although the ways in which teacher expectations influence pupil behaviour and attainment is highly complex, there is a broad consensus that high expectations can have a very positive effect (Gipps and MacGilchrist, 1999, **Reading 6.6**).

However, other research has shown differences in teachers' expectations of children from different social class backgrounds (e.g. Hartley, 1985; King, 1978; Sharp and Green, 1975). Similar issues have been raised in relation to gender

(Delamont, 1990) and race (Wright, 1992). This raises a very important issue for reflective teachers who will want to ensure that they do not unwittingly favour some children over others. Two particularly comprehensive studies of links between expectations, behaviour and performance were carried out in London and considered differences in terms of gender, social class, race, etc. (Mortimore *et al.*, 1988; Tizard *et al.*, 1988).

Whilst teachers should aim to raise their expectations and look for positive points for potential development in their pupils, there are also dangers from the existence of negative expectations. For instance, stereotyping is the attribution of particular characteristics to members of a group, and is often used negatively. Thus sex role stereotyping might be found, say, in an infant classroom with girls being encouraged to become 'teacher helpers'. Perhaps they might also play domestic roles in the 'home corner' while boys engage in more active play such as using construction equipment. Some research (e.g. Murphy, 2001, **Reading 15.6**) suggests that gendered play might be related to later differences in learning styles. However, as Walkerdine and other feminists have shown, girls in such situations can assert power through the adoption of an appropriate discourse (Walkerdine, 1981). Stereotyping should be avoided, but it is never absolute in its effects.

Bias is a further source of unequal treatment of pupils. It might refer to images and ideas in books and in other resources which suggest the superiority or inferiority of certain groups of people (see Chapter 8). However, educational procedures can also be biased in themselves. For example there has been a long-standing debate about bias in intelligence tests and such questions are recurring with regard to aspects of national assessment procedures. This debate has focused on class, gender and cultural bias at various times and is closely associated with the ways in which disadvantages can be 'institutionalized'. The institutionalization of disadvantage refers to situations in which social arrangements and procedures are established and taken for granted, despite the fact that they may systematically disadvantage a particular social group. Epstein has provided a particularly clear analysis of this with regard to racism (Epstein, 1993, **Reading 15.7**).

For a practical enquiry to try at this point, you could revisit Reflective Activity 5.3. This explores teacher perceptions of children in class and the possibility of patterned differences in the ways in which particular groups of children are viewed.

4.6 Assessment – can you minimise the risk of exclusion?

The evaluation of pupils has always been an endemic feature of classroom and school life (Jackson, 1968, **Reading 6.2**). After all, children attend school to learn. However, following the 1988 Education Reform Act, the significance of assessment in primary education has grown considerably (see Chapter 14). Whilst it once took place relatively informally using intuitive criteria, assessment has become increasingly 'categoric' and formal (Osborn *et al.*, 2000).

Children are aware of teacher judgements in many ways (Pollard *et al.*, 2000), and indeed, of where they personally stand in relation to them. Even in routine classroom life there are often relatively overt indicators of attainment and, despite the best efforts of teachers, children are often acutely aware of their position in reading-book systems, maths schemes or grouping systems. Pupils are also very aware of more subtle indicators of teacher assessment and disposition, for these are revealed through the quality of rapport or interaction that develops between the teacher and particular individuals. Some argue that because the Literacy and Numeracy strategies emphasize class teaching, where everyone works with the same material, this reduces the likelihood of children feeling that they are getting 'left behind'. However, as has already been discussed, whole-class teaching does raise the issue of how to meet different needs through differentiation. A number of strategies may be useful here, for example, by asking different pupils different types of questions.

In England and Wales, for the core subjects, National Curriculum Assessments (NCA) including Teacher Assessment (TA) are now required (see Chapter 14, Section 2). As explained in more detail in Chapter 14, children's attainment must be assessed against external criteria or 'levels' which are set out in the statutory orders for the subject. Whilst the NCA are assessed by a child's present attainment against specific criteria, teacher assessment for this purpose is based on judgements of which official 'level description' provides a 'best fit' with the pupil's attainment. This judgement is obviously vulnerable to the unintended influence of teacher expectations, stereotyping, etc. and variations in the assessment process itself. Indeed, with particular reference to contextual variations in performance, Filer (2000) has argued that assessments should be seen as social products rather than as 'objective' measures (see also Filer and Pollard, 2000, **Reading 14.7**).

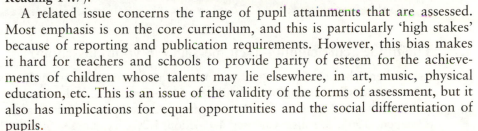

A related issue concerns the range of pupil attainments that are assessed. Most emphasis is on the core curriculum, and this is particularly 'high stakes' because of reporting and publication requirements. However, this bias makes it hard for teachers and schools to provide parity of esteem for the achievements of children whose talents may lie elsewhere, in art, music, physical education, etc. This is an issue of the validity of the forms of assessment, but it also has implications for equal opportunities and the social differentiation of pupils.

Social differentiation is connected to assessment processes because of the use that is made of assessment information, and also because of the social messages that are conveyed. For instance, assessments in reading or number work are often used as a basis for the allocation of pupils to groups. At a whole-school level, other ways of setting or targeting to match the intellectual challenge to each child are also developing rapidly. Placement of a child in a particular group or set will certainly be noted by parents and by other pupils, and the latter may well identify the 'bright ones' and 'thickos', with consequent implications for the self-image and social status of both groups. There is research evidence that the assessment process itself can place children under enormous pressure and can have a negative effect on children's perceptions of themselves and their peers. For example, in an article entitled evocatively 'I'll be a nothing', Reay and Wiliam (1999) identify the fact that many children are anxious and afraid during formal testing processes. This can reduce an individual's self-esteem and sense of agency. Moreover, high-attaining peers may become the subject of bullying as a consequence of good results.

Encouraging pupils to become involved in target setting and self-assessment (Chapter 14, Section 1.3 and **Readings 14.4** and **14.5**) are constructive ways of guiding each child to understand what is needed for future development and to recognize their own capacities. In particular, the involvement of each pupil in self-assessment is likely to make its implications less socially divisive and to bring new challenges within the control and understanding of the child.

> ### Reflective activity 15.5
>
> *Aim*: To investigate assessment results, their use and implications.
>
> *Evidence and reflection*: Consider a set of test, task and/or teacher assessment results for one subject, say English, for a year group. Are there any patterns in the scores in relation to gender, ethnicity, social class, age, special needs, etc.? Do you feel that the results provide a valid indicator of the full attainment of the children? Do the results give a clear indication as to what the children have achieved? What use is made of such results within the school? What meanings are inferred by other teachers and parents? How do pupils interpret the results when thinking about others, and when thinking about themselves?
>
>
>
> *Extension*: Try reading Armstrong (1989) and Drummond (1993, **Reading 14.6**) for suggestions about how important it is to use *valid* forms of assessment and to relate outcomes to children's learning needs.

4.7   The hidden curriculum – tacit messages in your classroom?

As teachers, the consequences of our actions are likely to show in the perspectives, attitudes and behaviour of children whom we teach. Indeed, to 'socialize' children into the 'values of society' has often been seen as part of a teacher's role (Dreeben, 1968, see also Chapter 4, Section 1.2, Chapter 18, Section 1, and Tate, 1997; Parsons, 1959). However, this often occurs relatively imperceptibly and unconsicously. There also needs to be some discussion as to the nature of the 'society' into which the children are to be socialized.

The concept of the 'hidden curriculum' offers a way of understanding such processes. As we saw in the introduction of Chapter 8, the hidden curriculum is defined as those tacit assumptions and practices which nevertheless convey messages and expectations to children. Some sociologists have suggested that the hidden curriculum is directly concerned with reproducing social conformity. For instance, Bowles and Gintis (1976) argued that some school processes tend to induce passivity and the acceptance of authority in combination with concern for the quantity and quality of work irrespective of purpose. There was said to be a 'correspondence' between the social relationships of workplaces and those of schools. The suggestion which follows is that, rather than becoming self-critical, flexible, life-long learners, children who attend such schools may come to accept future positions in society which 'seem appropriate' to their social class, gender, race, etc. Their future opportunities and rights as individuals might thus be narrowed by school practices. Dale (1977) suggested that such processes of social reproduction have always existed within the education system. How-

ever, whereas they were once relatively explicit in the official curriculum, in modern societies it is the 'form' of schooling which is important. This is part of the 'hidden curriculum'.

An example of this may be helpful. Pollard (1985) collected examples of teacher talk – instructions, comments, questions. They were analysed to reveal three clusters of values:

1. *Relating to productivity and efficiency at school work*
   Effort (e.g. Let's make a really big effort today.)
   Perseverance (e.g. Try a bit longer.)
   Neatness (e.g. That's a nice page.)
   Regularity (e.g. Is that your best work?)
   Speed (e.g. Has anyone finished yet?)

2. *Relating to behaviour and social relationships*
   Self-control (e.g. Stop being silly.)
   Obedience (e.g. Did you hear what I said?)

Politeness (e.g. That's not a very nice thing to do.)
Quietness (e.g. Silence, now.)
Truth (e.g. Let's have it straight now.)
Respect for authority (e.g. Hands up if you want something.)

3. *Relating to individualism and competitiveness*
Achievement (e.g. Have you got that right?)
Individualism (e.g. Do it yourself.)
Hierarchy (e.g. Who got ten out of ten?)
Self-reliance (e.g. Go and find out.)

The existence of such values in schools may seem to support the current social and economic system which sets out to achieve high levels of both economic productivity and of individual competition. Simultaneously, at the classroom level, such values may also support teachers' concerns with discipline and control. They thus may seem to 'make sense' at both levels.

We might note that the hidden curriculum of schooling is the very antithesis of the formal goals of producing articulate, independent, flexible, self-critical, life-long learners which have been promoted by politicians as being essential attributes for the twenty-first century. Ironically however, research suggests that one of the unintended consequences of the drive to raise attainment in the core subjects of English, mathematics and science is to compound the effects of the long-established hidden curriculum of schooling and to undermine pupils' learning engagement further (Pollard *et al.*, 2000).

The projection of values is inevitable in a classroom, but these should be carefully monitored as a necessary part of reflective practice.

5   POLICY AND PRACTICE FOR INCLUSION AND SOCIAL JUSTICE

In this chapter we have suggested a number of ways in which reflective teachers might monitor their practices in terms of social consequences and the provision of inclusion and equal opportunities. Such monitoring may also facilitate our own learning and professional development because of the increase in our understandings of classroom life.

Any of the forms of social differentiation, described in Section 4 above, could harm a child's sense of self-esteem and thus their learning. They influence self-confidence and engagement with educational experiences. Where children are adversely affected by several factors, effects are likely to be compounded and may lead to a sense of exclusion. A review of these possibilities is suggested in Reflective Activity 15.6. However, there can be difficulties here, for classroom life makes complex demands on teachers. Indeed, Doyle (1977, **Reading 11.1**) has suggested that, for trainee teachers, the complexity and need for rapid decision-making in classrooms can often be overwhelming. Ways of simplifying such complexities need to be found.

Reflective activity 15.6

Aim: To reflect on common forms of social differentiation and polarization.

Evidence and reflection: Review the issues raised in Sections 3 and 4, and read Pollard's article on 'social differentiation' in **Reading 15.2**. Seven aspects of classroom differentiation are raised, as is the multiplying effect of polarization within pupil culture. Consider each in turn as they may apply to your own classroom.

The official curriculum

Classroom organization and management

Language

Interpersonal relationships

Teacher expectations

Assessment

The hidden curriculum

Polarization within pupil culture

Choose **one** issue for particular attention, and target developments in your practice which you think will help you to provide more equal opportunities for your pupils. Try out your ideas for, say, a week. As you do this, identify the things which go well and consider how you were successful. Think about the things which did not go so well. Consider the difficulties you encounter and alternative approaches you could try.

Extension: You might like to consider the ways in which various forms of differentiation and polarization may interconnect. A specific focus helps to make development work manageable, but is likely to highlight other issues for further exploration. Pace classroom development work, reviewing and planning as you go.

We would suggest that one way of simplifying such complexities is to consciously try to develop classroom policies for social inclusion. As long-term targets, such policies can inform specific actions and support continuous development. Reflective teachers who have gathered evidence on their practices should be in a very good position to think through such policies and to take control of their own classroom actions. It is one more way of ensuring that the cyclical process of reflection, discussed in Chapter 1, Section 2.2, moves forward positively.

The list below provides some examples of issues about which long-term policies on inclusion might be framed, though obviously many others could be identified. In considering them, it is obviously important to consider the key dimensions of difference – disability and special needs, gender, race, social class, age and sexuality.

1. *Listening to children*. As part of the search for understanding the interactive nature of the teaching–learning process it is clearly important to gain access

to children's perceptions. This requires that we are open and receptive listeners and it may change our relationship with the children. Also, in encouraging children to explain their views they are also likely to begin to reflect themselves. This process may help the children to become more aware as learners and perhaps help them to develop independence and self-confidence. However, such developments are unlikely unless we consciously and consistently provide the conditions for children to talk and explain their points of view.

2. *Being positive.* It is very easy to respond negatively to children when under pressure. Perhaps taking a policy-decision to try to be encouraging, and to seek out good work and reinforce creativity, would provide a check and a guide when responding in potentially difficult situations.

3. *Encouraging co-operative relationships among children.* This is particularly important because of the effects which pupil culture can have. Barrie Thorne (1993, **Reading 15.4**) suggests a range of teacher strategies including using particular forms of grouping and task setting, facilitating equal access to activities and intervening to challenge stereotyping or inappropriate use of power.

4. *Acting 'fairly'.* This is a very suitable issue for a policy-decision bearing in mind the power of teachers as seen by children. It is a very important issue to children and simply calls for awareness of how they are likely to view a teacher's action *before* it is made. The role model offered by a teacher as she exercises her authority is certainly a very significant social consequence of classroom life.

CONCLUSION

Whatever forms of school or classroom practices are developed, there will be social consequences, because processes of social differentiation and polarization are impossible to avoid in school settings. A crucial issue thus concerns how to manage these social processes so that their most divisive effects are mitigated. At the same time, the promotion of social inclusion and social justice should be actively pursued through school policies, teaching of the curriculum and other classroom practices. They are difficult goals, but working towards them never-theless remains a continuing educational responsibility. Education may not be able to change society (Bernstein, 1970), but teachers should endeavour not to make society more fractured than it is already and should, if possible, try to ameliorate its divisive effects.

Despite a comprehensive awareness of the risks of exclusion and positive commitments regarding constructive classroom policies and social justice, it is clear that classroom teachers cannot act in isolation from the school in which they work and the society in which they live. For this reason we conclude the book by moving 'beyond the classroom' to consider the reflective teacher in the context of schools and society.

Key readings

There is an enormous amount of literature on social exclusion, differentiation, equal opportunities, etc., and this list is highly selective. Consulting **RTweb** will expand the choice.

We begin with two books of overall interest. For an insightful, value-led, yet practical account of developing equal opportunities practices in primary school classrooms, see:

Griffiths, M. and Davies, C. (1995)
In Fairness to Children.
London: David Fulton.

For a discussion of the ways in which children's social, moral and cultural development can be promoted through debate and a critical appraisal of citizenship with regard to issues of social inclusion, see:

Holden, C and Clough, N. (eds) (1988)
Children as Citizens: Education for Participation.
London: Jessica Kingsley.

Specific treatment of particular issues with regard to dimensions of difference is provided in books such as the following.

On disability and special educational needs, innovative perspectives are provided by:

Croll, P. and Moses, D. (2000)
Special Needs in the Primary School.
London: Cassell.

Reading 10.6

Thomas, G. and Loxley, A. (2001)
Deconstructing Special Education and Constructing Inclusion.
Buckingham: Open University Press.

On gender, Gallas and Francis provide two interesting books. Gallas quotes the children she teachers as a vehicle through which to explore the way in which they experience and understand issues of gender, race and power. Francis highlights the ways in which children make sense of their classroom (and other) experiences in ways that reinforce gender identities.

Gallas, K. (1998)
'*Sometimes I can be Anything': Power, Gender and Identity in a Primary Classroom.*
London: Teachers College Press.

Francis, B. (1998)
Power Plays: Primary School Children's Constructions of Gender, Power and Adult Work.
Stoke-on-Trent: Trentham.

On race, Connelly has produced a fascinating account of the perspectives and social relationships of young children, also incorporating a gender perspective. Nieto uses the experiences of teachers in creating multicultural classrooms and schools to discuss educational inequality and the influences of culture on learning. Troyna and Hatcher demonstrate how racism permeates.

Connelly, P. (1998)
Racism, Gender and Identities of Young Children: Social Relations in a Multi-ethnic, Inner-city Primary School.
London: Routledge.

Nieto, S. (1999)
The Light in their Eyes: Creating Multicultural Learning Communities.
London: Trentham.

Troyna, B. and Hatcher, R. (1992)
Racism in Children's Lives: a Study of Mainly White Primary Schools.
London: Routledge. 📖 **Reading 15.8**

On social class, the advantages and disadvantages reach well beyond the classroom. The most comprehensive account of the facts is by Reid. Many other books trace the implications in more personal terms. For example, see work by Reay, Plummer and many others.

Reid, I. (1998)
Class in Britain.
Cambridge: Polity.

Reay, D. (1998)
Class Work: Mother's Involvement in Children's Schooling.
London: University College Press. 📖 **Reading 4.5**

Plummer, G. (2000)
Failing Working Class Girls.
Stoke-on-Trent: Trentham.

Given the performance pressures of recent years, increasing numbers of schools have returned to the practice of grouping children by achievement. The following report reviews the research literature to attempt to assess the possible implications of this trend.

Sukhnandan, L. and Lee, B. (1998)
Streaming, Setting and Grouping by Ability: a Review of the Literature.
Slough: NFER.

An analysis of how national assessment requirements can actually reproduce social exclusion is:

Filer, A. and Pollard, A. (2000)
The Social World of Pupil Assessment.
London: Continuum. 📖 **Reading 14.7**

Most specialist educational publishers also have useful series of books based on social inclusion, equal opportunities and the sociology of education. For instance, in the UK see the catalogues of Continuum, RoutledgeFalmer, David Fulton, Simon and Schuster, Open University Press, Paul Chapman Press, etc.

 Readings for Reflective Teaching (the companion volume) offers other closely associated work on the issues raised in this chapter. This includes work by authors such as:

Margaret Maden, Andrew Pollard, Judith Ireson, Susan Hallam, Barrie Thorne, Caroline Roaf, Hazel Bines, Patricia Murphy, Debbie Epstein, Barry Troyna, Richard Hatcher.

 RTweb offers additional professional resources for this chapter. These may include *Notes for Further Reading*, supplementary *Reflective Activities*, useful *Web Links*, *Extension Texts* and *Download Facilities* for diagrams, figures, checklists, activities.

PART 3

BEYOND CLASSROOM REFLECTION

CHAPTER 16

Learning as a newly qualified teacher

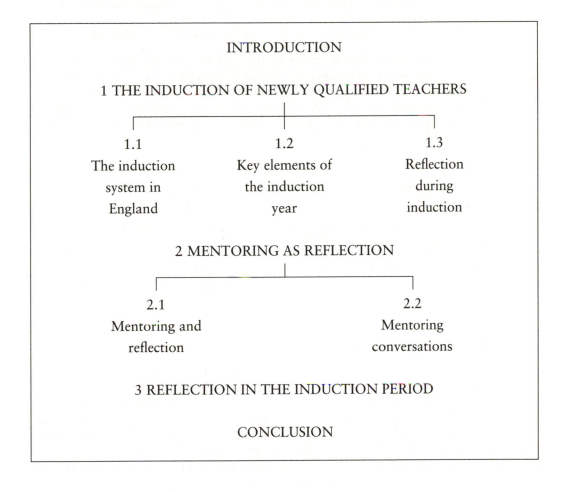

INTRODUCTION

1 THE INDUCTION OF NEWLY QUALIFIED TEACHERS

1.1	1.2	1.3
The induction system in England	Key elements of the induction year	Reflection during induction

2 MENTORING AS REFLECTION

2.1	2.2
Mentoring and reflection	Mentoring conversations

3 REFLECTION IN THE INDUCTION PERIOD

CONCLUSION

Enhancing professional standards and competences

This chapter relates to the process of induction and early professional development. It has been designed to support newly qualified teachers and mentors in maximizing learning and professional development in the first, formative year of teaching. As the TTA's statement of professional values puts it. Qualified teachers should:

> Have the motivation and ability to take increasing responsibility for their own professional development.
>
> (TTA, 2002, *Standards for the Award of QTS,* standard 1.7)

Very similar statements are made by the authorities in Scotland, Northern Ireland and Wales. The chapter does not directly address standards or competences, for example as identified in DfEE circular 0090/2000 and *Supporting New Teachers* (Wales, 2001). However, these address a familiar list of topics (covered elsewhere in this book), but at a slightly more advanced level:

- Planning, teaching and class management
- Making use of relevant information and specialist help
- Monitoring, assessment, recording, reporting and accountability
- Other professional requirements.

The chapter highlights support which initiates and enhances the career-long process of continuing professional development through reflective practice.

INTRODUCTION

In this chapter we focus on the role of reflection in the first year of teaching – the 'induction' period. The chapter will be of particular interest if you are a newly qualified teacher, or you are about to become one, or if you are an induction tutor. To get 'first things first' though, the most crucial question when starting a teaching career is to think about 'the sort of teacher you want to be', as Smith and Coldron (1998, **Reading 16.1**) put it. This issue also relates back to Chapter 5 on values and identity.

A key theme of the chapter concerns the role of an induction tutor (or mentor) in facilitating reflection in, on, and for, practice (Eraut, 1994, see also the discussion and readings associated with Chapter 2 on mentoring; Schon, 1983, **Reading 1.2**). The principles that are highlighted in this chapter apply in any context. However, we provide examples from the current national induction arrangements in England. The chapter is organized around three questions:

- What are the main characteristics of the induction period as it is currently defined?
- What is the relationship between mentoring and reflection?

- What is the role of the mentor in the development of reflective practice within induction?

The first section of the chapter outlines the main features of the current induction process as outlined in the national framework for induction for England (DfEE, 2000a). It relates this description to the historical development of induction arrangements in England and argues that current arrangements support particular forms of reflection. The main features of the induction process are reviewed, including the writing of individual development plans for NQTs, observations of teaching, post-observation discussions, meetings to review professional progress, and assessment meetings.

The second section reviews the generic literature highlighting links between mentoring and reflective practice. An important argument is that key elements of reflective activity are embedded in professional conversation.

Finally, the chapter focuses on the link between induction tutoring and reflective NQTs. Illustrated through the case of a newly qualified teacher (NQT), it is suggested that the induction tutor has a critical role in engaging with the NQT as a reflective agent to trigger reflective thinking and action. Mentoring conversations are particularly important.

1   THE INDUCTION OF NEWLY QUALIFIED TEACHERS

Whilst this chapter focuses on the current English system of induction, it is instructive to note that other areas of the UK, particularly Scotland and Northern Ireland, have developed arrangements that are distinctively and interestingly different.

For example, in Scotland the long-established General Teaching Council leads a strong commitment to professional induction and development for beginning teachers. This work is strongly supported by Local Education Authorities and schools. In Northern Ireland there is an integrated approach to initial teacher training, induction and the early years of professional development. This draws on a common framework of core criteria and competences which is applied across each stage. Foci for the competences include professional values, professional development, personal development, communication and relationships, and synthesis and application. It is interesting to note how the same set of competences is considered at the three main stages, but different elements are emphasized at each stage. For example, a competence statement relating to 'knowledge about children's learning' is something which should be addressed during initial teacher education, whilst 'knowledge of the education system and its interrelatedness' is something which will be considered mostly during induction. The stated aim of Northern Ireland's approach to teacher education is:

> To encourage beginning professionals to develop their critical, reflective practice in order to improve their teaching and the quality of pupils' learning.
>
> (DENI, 1999, p. 8)

This is interesting because of its explicit references to teacher *education* and *critical, reflective practice*. In England the notion of teacher education has almost universally been replaced by *training*. The system in Wales is under review, but has been considerably influenced by the English approach. (Please see **RTweb** for *Links* to government agencies in each part of the UK.)

1.1 The induction system in England

When the Labour government was elected to power in 1997 one of the key elements of its programme was reform of the education system. One aspect of this related to arrangements for the induction of new teachers. Indeed, the Teaching and Higher Education Act (1998) was quickly followed by DfEE circulars introducing radical new arrangements for the induction of NQTs.

Two key ideas underpin this policy development. The first is that NQTs have an entitlement to effective support and monitoring and access to professional development opportunities. The second is that in order to ensure high standards of entry to the profession, NQTs should be assessed against a predetermined list of national 'induction standards'. As the Teacher Training Agency put it:

> Structured support and guidance will be provided to all NQTs to help them develop as confident professionals. Induction will build on what new teachers have learned in meeting the Standards for the award of QTS, and will take account of the strengths and areas for development that are set out in the Career Entry Profile. NQTs will be assessed at the end of the induction year against a set of induction standards. These include a requirement to continue to meet the Standards for the Award of QTS and to progress further in specific areas.
>
> (TTA, 1999, p. 3)

Of course, the most important person in induction is the NQT. Indeed, there is a clearly defined expectation that induction activity should occur *with* NQTs, rather than being as something that is done *to* them (Bubb, 2001; Simco, 2000). This works particularly well when NQTs are willing to take responsibility for their own professional development, including devising targets, proposing actions and engaging in processes of self-assessment against these targets. This also creates an excellent potential context for reflection as in the arrangements the NQT is encouraged to engage with the whole process.

Other stakeholders also have important responsibilities within induction. For example, headteachers and governors have responsibilities to ensure that the employing school is able to provide a context for induction that enables systematic professional development to occur. Local Education Authorities normally act as the bodies that decide whether an NQT has satisfied the requirements of the induction period.

However, perhaps it is the induction tutor within each school who has the most crucial influence on the success, or otherwise, of the induction year. This person will be responsible for acting as mentor to facilitate professional development activities, to observe the NQT and to take part in the assessment process. Carroll and Simco (2001) identify a number of very specific responsibilities associated with the role:

- The induction tutor should have an appropriate knowledge/skills base. This includes key skills such as observation, conducting professional development tutorials and detailed knowledge of formal requirements. It follows that although an induction tutor would almost always be a very experienced

teacher, the skills of effective teaching are not the same as those of effective mentoring. A critical difference is that the mentoring role involves posing the right questions at the right time to facilitate professional development in a structured and systematic fashion.

- A second area of responsibility relates to assessment. Although it is the case that an induction tutor does not have sole responsibility for assessing the newly qualified teacher, they do have a very significant contribution to make. They will need to ensure that they understand the need for assessment to be valid, inclusive and evidence-based.

- The third major area of responsibility is related to entitlement. Here the induction tutor is responsible for ensuring that the newly qualified teacher has every opportunity to experience a professional development programme based on a rich diet of appropriate experiences and opportunities.

1.2 Key elements of the induction year

We can now consider six elements of the induction process, noting again that, whilst these relate to requirements in England, the principles behind each element are transferable to other settings.

The Career Entry Profile (CEP)

One of the aspects of induction which has been elusive for a large number of years has been the idea that there should be close linkage between initial teacher training (ITT) and induction. Indeed Evans (1978) reminds us that, as long ago as 1925, the Board of Education was grappling with this particular problem. Is it possible for individual professional development to be continuous in an explicit and defined way across the barrier which separates initial teacher training and induction? In 1999 the new regulatory framework suggested the use of a Career Entry Profile to contribute to a more seamless transition between ITT and induction (Kempe and Nicholson, 2000, **Reading 16.2**). The 2001 version of this (TTA, 2001) has three main sections, the first two of which are completed prior to the trainee leaving training and the third at the point of entry to the induction period. Section A asks for biographical and course details. Section B invites the trainee to identify up to four strengths and priorities for further professional development in relation to the standards for the award of QTS, and in Section C these are taken forwards to the induction year and used to frame objectives and a professional development plan. In this way personal strengths and weaknesses are clarified and the information is utilized to support professional development. It is arguable that this process will, inevitably, involve a strong element of reflective practice. Specifically the Career Entry Profile:

> Provides information, in relation to the Standards for the Award of QTS, about new teachers' strengths and areas for further professional development. It helps new teachers to set objectives for professional development and, with their induction tutors, to develop an action plan for induction.

> (TTA, 2001, p. 2)

The individual development plan

The process of completing the Career Entry Profile will enable the NQT to identify a series of professional objectives, recorded in Section C, which are then used to frame action (for example, creating a circumstance where the NQT can observe a colleague teaching the Numeracy Hour), success criteria (for example, an enhanced quality of the plenary in the NQT's teaching of numeracy) and target dates for achievement. In essence this process amounts to the creation of an individual development plan which can be used to facilitate a wide range of professional development activities – such as those suggested in this book. Also included here will be observation of other teachers in the NQT's school and beyond, attendance at LEA courses, opportunities for professional conversations with subject leaders within the school and collaborative teaching with colleagues. The principle here is that the identification of specific professional objectives and focused action taken in relation to these objectives will lead to identifiable professional development. To support this whole process NQTs have an entitlement to 10 per cent release time.

Professional review meetings

Built into the induction year arrangements are six professional review meetings where there is a process of professional conversation which explores the extent to which objectives recorded in Section C of the Career Entry Profile have been met in the light of the available evidence. The meeting will then go on to frame new objectives or revize existing objectives based on this review. The aim of this process is to ensure that the whole induction year centres on identifiable and specific targets and actions that lead to clear action and review. In a sense, these

meetings can be seen as focusing the cycle of reflective development, as described in Chapter 1 of this book.

Observation of NQTs' teaching

The process of observation and the professional discussions that surround it are a particularly rich context for the realization of reflective practice in the induction period. Indeed, with a pre-determined focus and a structured post-observation discussion, the induction tutor has an excellent opportunity to act as a reflective trigger. The regulations are very specific in regard to the amount of observation that is expected and the characteristics of the process of observation:

> The NQT should be observed teaching at least once in every six to eight week period . . . including in the first four weeks in post. Observations should focus on particular aspects of the NQT's teaching.
>
> (DfEE, 2000a, para. 47–8)

Observations of others' teaching

The idea that observation of experienced colleagues should be included in early professional development has been a familiar part of initial teacher training and induction for some time. However, the advent of the current arrangements for induction means that observation of others can be recast in a more specific way. Indeed, the Career Entry Profile requires the NQT to develop very clear and precise professional development targets and from these there will be a range of

different kinds of ensuing action. One such action may relate to the observation of other teachers and, because the target is potentially precise, so too should be the focus of the observation. For example, it is not very focused to make a general observation of a Year 6 teacher teaching a Literacy Hour and considering issues as and when they emerge – compared, say, with addressing teaching techniques within the plenary part of the Literacy Hour in relation to the consolidation of learning.

The assessment of the induction period

We have already mentioned that there are two elements to the induction period, support and monitoring, and assessment. Three assessment meetings are required in the induction period. Each meeting would normally be attended by the NQT, the induction tutor and the headteacher. The first of the three meetings has a focus on whether the NQT has consistently met the requirements for the award of QTS (i.e. the national standards for this) and here many induction tutors would collect and cite specific illustrative evidence. However, this assessment will have a much broader feel than that carried out at the end of initial teacher training. At the end of the second term there will be an assessment against the induction standards, which progress from the QTS standards and are fewer in number. In the third term there is a summative assessment against all the requirements of the induction period. Each assessment is recorded on a national pro-forma which invites comments in three key areas which relate to the standards headings: planning, teaching and class management; monitoring, assessing, recording, reporting and accountability; and other professional requirements. A very small minority of NQTs will fail to meet the requirements of the induction period and in these cases, subject to an appeals process, will be not be allowed to continue in employment in state schools.

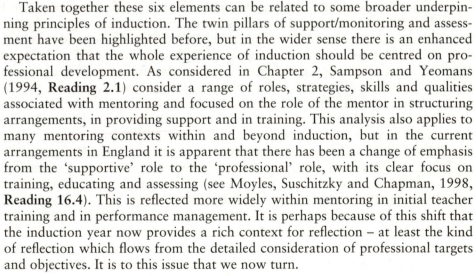

Taken together these six elements can be related to some broader underpinning principles of induction. The twin pillars of support/monitoring and assessment have been highlighted before, but in the wider sense there is an enhanced expectation that the whole experience of induction should be centred on professional development. As considered in Chapter 2, Sampson and Yeomans (1994, **Reading 2.1**) consider a range of roles, strategies, skills and qualities associated with mentoring and focused on the role of the mentor in structuring arrangements, in providing support and in training. This analysis also applies to many mentoring contexts within and beyond induction, but in the current arrangements in England it is apparent that there has been a change of emphasis from the 'supportive' role to the 'professional' role, with its clear focus on training, educating and assessing (see Moyles, Suschitzky and Chapman, 1998, **Reading 16.4**). This is reflected more widely within mentoring in initial teacher training and in performance management. It is perhaps because of this shift that the induction year now provides a rich context for reflection – at least the kind of reflection which flows from the detailed consideration of professional targets and objectives. It is to this issue that we now turn.

1.3 Reflection during induction

In the English context, the 1999 reforms for the induction of new teachers provide a strong context for a particular form of reflection. Individual pro-

fessional development has become systematized within a culture of mentoring. A structure has been created for individual professional development focused on the Career Entry Profile and the progressive refinement of individual action plans through specific objectives.

LINKS

In a sense, mentoring is becoming ubiquitous in supporting reflective professional activity. This includes performance management (see Chapter 17, Section 5.3), where every teacher from their second year of teaching engages in a continuous round of setting professional objectives, at least one of which must impact on pupils' learning; being observed teaching and receiving feedback from this observation; and reviewing professional objectives. Such cycles of focused professional development are, at least in theory, responsive to individual strengths and school priorities for development. A team leader is in place in each school to take forward these processes and one of the major attributes of this person is a range of mentoring skills and qualities. It is perhaps little wonder that the recent governmental framework for Continuing Professional Development (DfEE, 2001a) has at its centre a priority for developing mentoring and reflective skills, particularly for subject leaders. As the DfEE puts it:

> We want to encourage teachers, as reflective practitioners, to think about what they do well, to reflect on what they could share with colleagues, as well as identifying their own learning needs.
>
> (DfEE, 2001, para 22)

Of course, it is also the case that conceptions of 'reflection' change over the years. Previously prominent models supported teachers as relatively independent decision-makers in their classrooms, and highlighted consideration of aims, values, aspirations and philosophies. Whilst such issues remain important, a more limited form of reflection is emerging which is very sharply focused on fine-grain details of practice. This form of reflection is seen as a way to become more expert, *within* a nationally established framework of aims and values. Such developments can be related to McIntyre's (1993) definition of levels of reflection. He cites three levels. The technical level is concerned with 'the effective attainment of given goals' (p. 44) and in this respect there is a focus on what might be labelled the basic performance competences of learning to teach. A second level of reflection by contrast is termed practical reflection and is about the relationship of classroom practice to underpinning values and beliefs. The third level of reflection, the critical or emancipatory level, involves a process of looking beyond practice to become actively aware of the role of institutional and societal forces on teaching. It is arguable that the current arrangements for induction amount to an intensification of technical reflective practice at the expense of the other two levels of reflection.

In any event, the quality of reflective professional development will be very dependent on the relationship between individual NQTs and induction tutors, and on the understanding and skill that the induction tutor can offer. At best, he or she has a really exciting and constructive role in acting as a reflective trigger to the thinking and practice of the NQT.

Higher-education institutions can also play an important role in this, and their work with Local Education Authorities on induction and early professional development is highly valued in many parts of the UK. In this way, the infrastructure supporting early and continuous professional development is

reinforced and made more coherent. In such ways, we build the quality of the profession together. For case-studies of three new teachers – 'steady improvement', 'downhill progress' and 'rapid acceleration' – see Carré, 1993, **Reading 16.3.**

2 | MENTORING AS REFLECTION

We have argued that national arrangements for NQT induction, such as those introduced in England, provide a rich opportunity for the development of certain kinds of reflective practice, and we have drawn attention to the critically important role of the induction tutor as mentor.

We now explore the nature of this relationship between mentoring and reflection in a little more detail.

2.1 Mentoring and reflection

The relationship between mentoring and reflection is fundamentally important to the professional well-being of individual teachers.

Reflection is the process through which teachers become aware of the complexity of their work and are able to take actions which impact positively on this.

Mentoring provides a stimulus, drawing on accumulated professional knowledge and experience, which can help teachers to reflect with purpose and focus.

Taken together then, reflection and mentoring help to inform and build a culture of professional learning. There is an important synergy, which leads to the construction of a learning community in the school. These ideas were considered briefly in Chapter 1, Section 2.6 in relation to 'learning with colleagues', in Chapter 2, Section 2.2 where we considered the evolving role of the mentor as a 'model', 'trainer', 'critical friend' or 'assessor'. They are reinforced throughout this chapter in relation to the school as a whole.

Many argue that the processes involved in learning about teaching are fundamentally complex because classrooms themselves are complex and dynamic environments. Calderhead (1991, p. 53) suggests that 'learning to teach is different from other forms of learning in academic life' because the process involves being able to interpret and respond to complex classroom events with enormous rapidity. Some key characteristics of classroom environments were analysed by Doyle (1977, 1986, **Reading 11.1**). They are *multidimensional* in the sense that many events occur in the classroom at any one time. Indeed, each classroom is a crowded place in which many people with different preferences and abilities must use a restricted supply of resources to accomplish a broad range of social and personal objectives. Classrooms are also characterized by *simultaneity* where these events often occur at the same time and with multiple consequences. Further, classrooms are *unpredictable*, as it is not possible to state in advance whether or how a particular classroom activity will develop. Finally classrooms have a *history* in the sense that classroom participants will have an understanding of the current reality of that classroom based on all the experiences which have occurred previous to this.

The notion that classroom environments are complex and that professional learning within these environments is hence often problematic is underlined by the literature. The result is that professional learning can be slow. To get to grips with multidimensionality and simultaneity is immensely demanding. Calderhead and Shorrock concluded that 'learning to teach involves more than the mastery of a limited set of competences. It is a complex process. It is also a lengthy process, extending for most teachers well after their initial training' (1997, p. 194). Several years earlier, Desforges and Cockburn came to a similar conclusion suggesting that 'we have shown the job is more difficult than perhaps even teachers realise. We have demonstrated in detail how several constraining classroom forces operate in concert and how teachers' necessary management strategies exacerbate the problems of developing children's thinking' (1987, p. 155). Given this idea that classroom environments are complex and professional learning is slow, it is perhaps hardly surprising that in some countries induction is spread over several years. For example, in the State of Connecticut, the State Board has developed the BEST programme which provides a systematic approach to induction over a period of three years centred on the production of a professional development programme.

Learning to teach or developing existing understandings of teaching involves engaging in explicit ways with the dimensions of the fundamental complexity of classroom environments. Yet to do this is important if identifiable professional learning is to occur. In order to do this effectively we suggest that the mentoring role is critically important as it has the potential to provide the trigger for new professional behaviours.

2.2 Mentoring conversations

We have established that classrooms are complex social environments and that learning to teach in these environments is demanding. The knock-on effect is that, for many, the process of professional development will be slow and uneven. However, mentoring can provide really constructive support for professional learning.

Among the many possible forms of mentoring, are the following:

- Mentoring conversations where one teacher facilitates a discussion with another asking key questions that lead to the development of practice.

- Role modelling of good teaching for another to observe and utilize.

- Collaborative teaching involving a mentor and another teacher, each with defined roles within a lesson.

- Observation of teaching by a mentor and the provision of written feedback.

- Assessment of teaching by a mentor in either formative or summative contexts.

- Informal professional and/or personal support.

- Facilitating individual development plans for other teachers.

Many of these were considered in Chapter 2 but here we wish to focus on 'mentoring conversations' in particular detail. This follows Edwards and Collison (1996, **Reading 2.2**) who argued that new thinking is the essence of

professional development. This is hugely facilitated through professional conversations – and particularly those concerned with the critical review of practice. It
is through the process of questioning and seeking explanations for classroom
occurrences that new understandings form.

Sixsmith and Simco (1997) have extended this idea of the significance of
mentoring conversations and created a representation of how they may work in
practice. As a basis for this, they used Rowland's (1987) social constructivist
model which focuses on children's learning and the role of adult intervention
(see Chapter 7, Section 1.3 of this book). Sixsmith and Simco argue that there
are many parallels between the Rowland model and processes of mentoring
intervention.

Figure 16.1 shows the role of mentor as reflective agent, intervening skilfully
in a colleague's professional learning. In this model, the mentor and the teacher
who is being mentored (the mentee) negotiate the nature of the activity to be
taught. If the mentee is an NQT you can imagine that this may be based on a
professional objective which is recorded in the appropriate section of their
Career Entry Profile and this may take place before an observation. The children

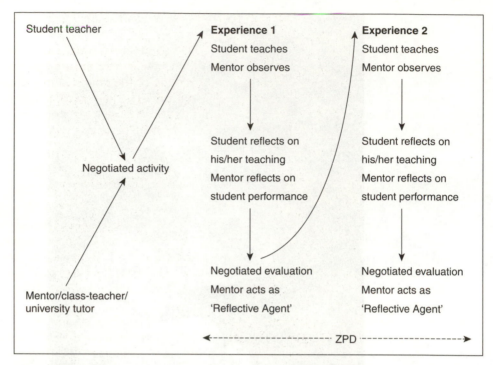

Figure 16.1 *Professional development through reflective mentoring (Sixsmith and Simco, 1997)*

then engage with the experience that has been planned and the mentor acts as observer. Following the observation the mentor and the mentee both reflect in different ways, the mentor preparing a written critique of the observation, the mentee writing an evaluative statement. However, both mentor and mentee focus on clearly specified professional development objectives. There is then a meeting between the mentor and the mentee to evaluate the lesson. It is at this point that the mentor takes on the role of reflective agent, bringing the professional knowledge associated with the mentoring role to assist the mentee in making sense of the lesson which is being evaluated. A particularly important element here is the approach to questioning the mentor adopts. Some kinds of questions – 'Why did you . . .?', 'Are there any alternatives?', 'What was the consequence of your doing . . .?', 'What was the impact on children's learning?' – are particularly important during the course of this conversation.

Through this process the mentor and the mentee also identify the potential learning for the latter. In this way, they effectively clarify the Zone of Proximal Development (ZPD) – or the gap between what the learner knows already and what they could learn with further support. This whole process leads to the children being re-engaged with a modified task and then a further period of evaluation which identifies the extent to which the mentee has maximized their potential and crossed the ZPD into new learning.

The fundamental premise underpinning this model is that high-quality mentoring conversations make a vital contribution to professional learning. With

http://www.rtweb.info

skilful intervention on the part of the mentor, new professional learning can be generated which has an impact on practice.

In summary then, this section has shown how mentoring and reflection interact. First, the complexity of the classroom environment must be recognized. The next stage is for there to be an understanding of the potential of mentoring conversations to lead to professional development. The key to reflection within the mentoring process lies in the fine-grain detail of these conversations, in the skills of the mentor and the receptivity of the mentee.

3 | REFLECTION IN THE INDUCTION PERIOD

In the previous section we considered the role of mentoring conversations in enhancing reflection. In this section we shall apply this generic notion of mentoring conversations to the role of the induction tutor. In particular, we will identify points in the induction period where conversations between the induction tutor and the NQT are likely to have particular significance in processes of professional learning.

We have already seen that the induction period in England involves a wide range of opportunities for mentoring. There is an expectation of classroom observation at least every half term, and the Career Entry Profile should frame induction through the setting of specific professional objectives. There should be three professional review meetings during the course of the year, and ample opportunities for informal dialogue. Of all these events it seems reasonable to suggest that the observations and the conversations following these, together with the professional review meetings, provide particularly rich contexts for reflective conversations between the NQT and the induction tutor.

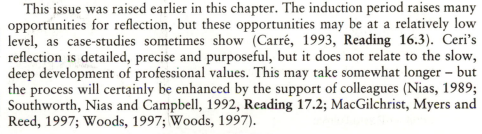 We will consider each of these in turn, using first a case-study to illustrate the former (see Figure 16.2).

This example illustrates many of the attributes of the Sixsmith and Simco (1997) model. There is a process of detailed professional dialogue, and this leads first to changed professional thinking and then to changed practice. In relation to *levels* of reflection (McIntyre, 1993), it is a clear example of technical reflection. Ceri has a goal which is stated in her CEP. The reflection which she undertakes is related to achieving that goal. There is very little reference to underpinning personal values. Indeed, the goal is more related to the values implicit within the education system. The plenary in the Numeracy Hour is framed nationally as a time when acquired learning is consolidated. Ceri's reflection does not question the appropriateness of this. It accepts the legitimacy of the national framework.

This issue was raised earlier in this chapter. The induction period raises many opportunities for reflection, but these opportunities may be at a relatively low level, as case-studies sometimes show (Carré, 1993, **Reading 16.3**). Ceri's reflection is detailed, precise and purposeful, but it does not relate to the slow, deep development of professional values. This may take somewhat longer – but the process will certainly be enhanced by the support of colleagues (Nias, 1989; Southworth, Nias and Campbell, 1992, **Reading 17.2**; MacGilchrist, Myers and Reed, 1997; Woods, 1997; Woods, 1997).

Ceri is an NQT in a suburban primary school in the north west of England, teaching a Year 2 class.

She is in the second term of her induction year and is working on a professional-development objective that she has recorded in her CEP. This is: 'to ensure that I manage the plenary in the Numeracy Hour so that there are opportunities to consolidate children's learning'. It has been decided that this objective will form a focus for the half-termly observation from Anne, the induction tutor.

Prior to the observation Anne and Ceri plan the plenary together by closely scripting the key parts.

During the observation Anne observes parts of all the lesson but focuses in depth on the plenary and notices that Ceri's questioning of the children does not always allow them the opportunity to express what they have learned (but does provide them with the opportunity to explain what they did).

During the post-observation tutorial, skilful questioning on Anne's part enables Ceri to realize this point of professional learning and they then plan the plenary for the next Numeracy Hour with this in mind. In particular, specific questions are planned.

Next time she teaches the Numeracy Hour, Ceri is able to implement her new understanding to good effect.

Figure 16.2 *Reflection and mentoring support during Ceri's induction year*

CONCLUSION

This chapter has interwoven the themes of induction, mentoring, reflection and professional learning. We suggest that, in a strong sense, a good induction system attempts to systematize professional reflection. We have explored the detail of reflective conversations through specific examples and illustrated a model for these. However, we also suggested that, whilst the requirements for the induction period may lead to opportunities for reflection, these opportunities may be mostly at the technical level. In particular, strict processes of objective setting, professional conversation and review may not extend to other issues such as professional values, quality of pupil experiences, social consequences or educational alternatives.

Nevertheless, such concerns can never be far away for any socially aware teacher – or for his or her colleagues in the school as a whole.

Key readings

There are several books which provide professionally oriented support for NQTs and prospective NQTs. See for example:

Bubb, S. (2001)
A Newly Qualified Teacher's Manual.
London: David Fulton.

Hayes, D. (2000)
The Handbook for Newly Qualified Teachers, Meeting the Standards in Primary and Middle Schools.
London: David Fulton.

Simco, N. (2000)
Succeeding in the Induction Year.
Exeter: Learning Matters.

Other texts have been prepared to offer induction tutors support in their work with NQTs. Both of the texts below offer clear practical advice on issues such as roles and responsibilities and, in addition, offer perspectives on policy initiatives within induction.

Bubb, S. (2000)
The Effective Induction of Newly Qualified Primary Teachers.
London: David Fulton.

Carroll, C. and Simco, N. (2001)
Succeeding as an Induction Tutor.
Exeter: Learning Matters.

Other books focus more strongly on policy and theoretical considerations. The two books below are particularly useful if you wish to consider alternative models of induction and both challenge effectively some underpinning assumptions about induction.

Bleach, K. (2001)
Inducting New Teachers.
Stoke-on-Trent: Trentham.

Tickle, L. (2000)
Teacher Induction: the Way Ahead.
London: Open University Press.

A range of professional development materials are regularly produced by national agencies, for instance the Teacher Training Agency, and by various professional associations.

 Readings for Reflective Teaching (the companion volume) offers other closely associated work on the issues raised in this chapter. This includes work by authors such as:

Robin Smith, John Coldron, Andy Kempe, Helen Nicholson, Clive Carré, Neil Simco, Janet Moyles, Wendy Suschitzly and Linda Chapman.

 RTweb offers additional professional resources for this chapter. These may include *Notes for Further Reading*, supplementary *Reflective Activities*, useful *Web Links*, *Extension Texts* and *Download Facilities* for diagrams, figures, checklists, activities.

CHAPTER 17

School improvement and continuing professional development

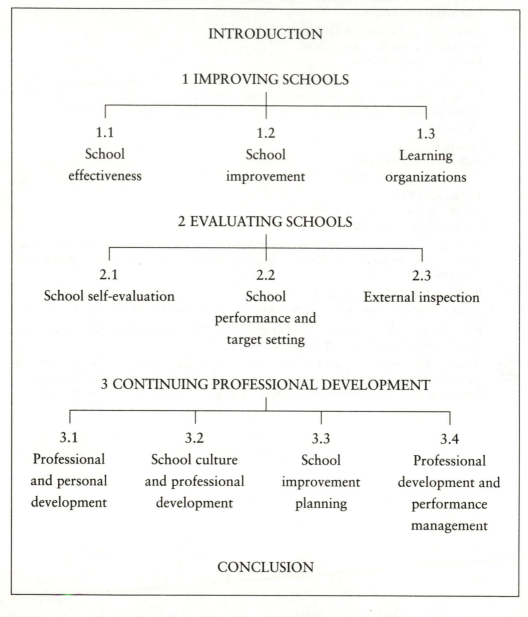

INTRODUCTION

1 IMPROVING SCHOOLS

1.1
School
effectiveness

1.2
School
improvement

1.3
Learning
organizations

2 EVALUATING SCHOOLS

2.1
School self-evaluation

2.2
School
performance and
target setting

2.3
External inspection

3 CONTINUING PROFESSIONAL DEVELOPMENT

3.1
Professional
and personal
development

3.2
School culture
and professional
development

3.3
School
improvement
planning

3.4
Professional
development and
performance
management

CONCLUSION

Enhancing professional standards and competences

The sense of professional fulfilment and quality of teaching performance of student, trainee and newly qualified teachers is always strongly influenced by the schools in which they work. This chapter thus helps in understanding these contexts, and the pressure for performance that schools are often under.

Training requirements in England and Scotland suggest that qualifying teachers should be able to:

Contribute to, and share responsibility in, the corporate life of schools.
(TTA, 2002, *Standards for the Award of QTS*, standard 1.5)

Demonstrate an awareness of his or her responsibilities for contributing to the ethos of the school, for example by promoting positive relationships between staff, pupils and parents.
(Scottish Office, *Guidelines for Initial Teacher Education in Courses in Scotland*, competence 3.4)

Of course, similar expecations have always been made of teachers in Wales and Northern Ireland.

INTRODUCTION

In this chapter we focus on the development of the whole school. However, this must itself be set in the wider policy context. Indeed, 'education, education, education' is the political mantra of our time, and the politicians' necessity is not only that standards are raised, but that they are seen and believed to be raised quickly.

There are many perspectives on how to develop high quality in schools, of which three are identified here. First, there are those who believe in various forms of school self-evaluation, quality management and review as internally driven processes. An alternative view is that competition, in a quasi-market for education where the provision of information enables 'consumers' and 'customers' to exercise the power of choice, drives up standards. Finally, there are those who emphasize external inspection, in which the work of a school is assessed against standardized national criteria. Despite their distinct origins, in recent years these approaches have begun to be combined. Thus, for example, a 1996 White Paper, *Competitiveness: Creating the Enterprise Centre of Europe*, identified the three elements as forms of 'quality assurance':

- self-assessment
- published information on performance
- external inspection.

Each of these approaches assumes that schools are essentially responsible, themselves, for the quality of their provision. Before the late 1980s, schools had been only semi-autonomous and were managed within the multi-layered structure of each Local Education Authority. However, during the 1990s there was an enormous increase in the significance of schools as free-standing and self-managed organizations. Legislation gradually moved state schools from the shelter of Local Education Authority support structures and their associated lines of accountability. By 2000, almost all schools had control of their budgets, policies and practices and were formally accountable, within frameworks externally imposed, to their own governors and parents.

A second Labour government, returned to power in 2001, continues to keep education central to its agenda, but with some subtle changes. The pressure remains, but the talk is of government working in partnership with schools, and the fostering of a self-critical, self-confident teaching force (Barber, 2001, **Reading 17.4**). Public–private partnerships are also becoming more and more common within education, whilst the range of different types of schools continues to grow. A primary school, for example, may be part of an Educational Action Zone, designated as a Beacon School, or apply for awards such as the Basic Skills Mark or Investors In People.

Pressure for schools to compete remains important, and this certainly impacts on educational standards in schools. However, it is by no means proven that all these effects will be positive. Indeed, as Dale (1996) and Gewirtz, Ball and Bowe (1995) have argued, the danger is that schools which are perceived to be 'good' draw pupils away from other local schools, thus causing financial difficulties and threatening a spiral of decline. This is already a problem in some major centres of population where middle-class pupils travel away from city schools to suburban or rural schools. Of course, these are essentially political issues, and this chapter is primarily focused on internal factors in school development. However, to consider these without an awareness of the wider context would be extremely misleading.

In this chapter we first look at work on school effectiveness, before moving to the related but more process-orientated school-improvement work. This leads us to explore the concept of the school as a learning organization, and then to consider various approaches to evaluating the work of schools. We conclude the chapter with a focus on continuing professional development.

The *Compendium* and *Notes for Further Reading* on **RTweb** will helpfully supplement these materials.

1   IMPROVING SCHOOLS

1.1 School effectiveness

Does it matter which school a child attends? What are the features of a school that make a difference? Defining the measures by which school effectiveness is judged is obviously significant. These are frequently related to pupil attainment, and recently more to the 'value added' between attainment when the pupil enters the school and subsequent results. An effective school has been described as 'one in which pupils progress further than might be expected from consideration of its intake' (Mortimore, 1991, p. 9).

Governments throughout the world have an active interest in school effectiveness. Indeed, there is a widespread desire to raise the achievement of pupils to strengthen international competitiveness, but this is also usually constrained by the costs of education. So an interest in effectiveness is also an interest in efficiency, or value for money.

Work on school effectiveness began thirty years ago in the United States with a concern for equality of educational opportunity. Research efforts were made to separate the impact of family background from that of the school, and to find out whether some schools were more effective than others. In the UK, the influential study *Fifteen Thousand Hours* (Rutter *et al.*, 1979), which detailed research on twelve London secondary schools, and its primary equivalent *School Matters: The Junior Years* (Mortimore *et al.*, 1988) indicated very clearly that the internal policies and practices of schools do influence educational effectiveness. From these and subsequent studies it has been possible to identify a generally agreed set of factors associated with school effectiveness. For instance, the following eleven 'key factors' derive from a review of school effectiveness research (Sammons, Hillman and Mortimore, 1995).

1. Effective headteachers are firm and purposeful, appoint effective teachers, create consensus and unity of purpose; they share and delegate responsibilities and involve all teachers in decision-making; they are 'leading professionals' with an understanding of classrooms and how teaching and learning can be improved.

2. In the school there must be 'shared vision and goals': necessary for lifting aspirations and creating consistency of practice through whole-school policies and contracts.

3. The 'learning environment' is attractive, orderly and encourages self-control among pupils; this is a prerequisite for a positive classroom ethos.

4. There is a clear priority focus on teaching and learning as the school's primary purpose. Four factors: time spent on learning, amount of homework, effective learning time, and learning time for different subjects are measures indicating the practical implementation of this focus.

5. Teaching is purposeful, well organized and clear about objectives, well prepared, appropriately paced and structured, and questioning focuses pupil attention.

6. There is a general culture which has high expectations of everyone: teachers, pupils and parents.

7. Better pupil outcomes follow from positive reinforcement, clear feedback, rewards and clear rules for behaviour. These are more successful than punishment or criticism.

8. Monitoring progress: keeps track of whether the school is meeting its targets and goals; maintains awareness of targets and goals among staff, pupils and parents; informs planning and teaching; sends clear messages to pupils that teachers are interested in their progress.

9. Giving pupils rights and responsibilities and enabling them to play an active role in the life of the school is important for raising self-esteem and encouraging children to take responsibility for their own learning.

10. Partnerships that encourage and foster parental support for learning have positive effects on achievement; successful schools make demands on parents as well as encouraging involvement.

11. Effective schools are 'learning organizations' where teachers and senior managers, as well as pupils, continue to be learners, improve their practice and keep up with change.

Of these, those factors that are concerned with the quality of teaching (factors 4 and 5) and expectations (factor 6) are most significant for fostering pupils' learning and progress. However, the other factors are important in that they provide the overall framework within which teachers and classrooms operate, enable the development of consistent goals and ensure that pupils' educational experiences are linked as they progress through the school. In reviewing the same list of eleven factors, MacGilchrist, Myers and Reed (1997) argue that the three essential core characteristics of an effective school are professional high-quality leadership and management (factor 1), a concentration on teaching and (pupil) learning (factor 4), and on developing the school as a learning organization (factor 11). MacGilchrist and her colleagues believe that these are of central importance, and that the remaining factors arise out of them.

The National Commission on Education (Education, 1996) identified a similar set of positive features in their detailed study of eleven schools which were effective despite being located in disadvantaged areas. They reported a 'can do better culture' and 'shared vision', together with leadership which was confident, positive, proactive and able to set strategic priorities. The most effective leadership enabled participation in the process of change by everyone in the school, including parents; encouraged shared leadership and teamwork; and developed unity of purpose and consistency of practice. An orderly and industrious climate for learning, clear policies on behaviour and discipline, high expectations of pupils expressed through curriculum planning, assessment and reporting, high levels of care for the physical environment (even where it was inadequate) were all identified as important. The follow-up study, *Success Against the Odds: Five Years On* (Maden, 2001) identifies the 'can do' culture as being particularly significant in the continued improvement of at least one school. The development through leadership of a critical mass of skilled and committed people was seen as important for sustaining improvement as opposed to a 'quick fix' which may not last.

The importance of internal school management and culture is confirmed by studies of the variations of school exam performance. For instance, Sammons, Hillman and Mortimore (1995) studied the GCSE results of 11,000 pupils from schools in Lancashire and inner London. Adjusting for pupils' home background and for attainment levels on entry to secondary school, they found that the schools can make a difference of as much as 10 per cent to GCSE marks – the equivalent of several grades. Interestingly, the study showed that some schools are more effective for low attainers than for high attainers (and vice versa); some for girls rather than for boys, and others for different ethnic groups. Similarly, school effectiveness often varies from year to year, and consistent improvement is hard to achieve. Where there was clear leadership and a shared whole-school emphasis on pupil learning, there was less variation in achievement among departments. In other schools it was harder for departments to be effective due to lack of overall leadership, shared goals and vision, poor expectations and inconsistent policies.

The differential effectiveness identified by Sammons, Hillman and Mortimore is extremely important. Very few schools, if any, are equally effective for all pupils all of the time. The large amounts of pupil-performance data, and sophisticated analyses made possible by powerful software, enable differential effectiveness to be identified, although all too often only data arising from the single source of test results are used. Perhaps the definition of 'effectiveness' should also be reconsidered, to include such as things as pupils' motivation and self-esteem. These are harder to measure, but insights can be gained through instruments such as pupil-attitude surveys or careful observation. For example, the Improving School Effectiveness project, which took place in Scotland and linked effectiveness and improvement, drew on a wide range of evidence, including pupils' perspectives (MacBeath and Mortimore, 2001, **Reading 17.1**). In England and Wales, the Effective Early Learning (EEL) project (Pascal and Bertram, 1997) has trained thousands of teachers in detailed classroom observation of pupil involvement, and provided a very impressive database on effective practice for young children.

Reflective activity 17.1

Aim: To reflect upon school effectiveness.

Evidence and reflection: How do you think school effectiveness should be characterized and measured? Using your definition of effectiveness, think about a school which you know well and consider the school's effectiveness for different groups of pupils (for example, boys and girls, higher and lower attainers, children from different ethnic and social backgrounds, and 'quiet' and attention-seeking children).

Extension: If it was difficult to come to firm conclusions about the school's effectiveness for all the pupils, consider what information would be needed to enable this, and how that information could be obtained. Which of the factors identified by Sammons, Hillman and Mortimore (1995) seem most closely related to your own emerging view of school effectiveness?

Studies of the characteristics of effective schools have been used to make assumptions about the characteristics of ineffective schools. Having identified factors associated with effective schools, the argument is that ineffective schools will be lacking those factors. However, this simplistic notion is challenged by reality: schools in difficulty have their own individual clustering of factors, as Myers (1996) found in her study. Indeed Reynolds (1995) has self-critically reviewed his own research, and has come to the conclusion that '. . . people like me have implicitly back-mapped the characteristics of the effective school on to the ineffective school, thinking that what the ineffective school has is the absence of things that make the effective school effective . . . We have, in short, only viewed failure as not being successful, not as failure' (p. 66–7).

Ideas about school effectiveness have played an important role in the formulation of education policy. For example, in England a 'School Effectiveness Unit' was set up within the DfEE in 1997; schools are required to set targets; and 'value added' league tables are being developed. However, identifying factors that indicate levels of school effectiveness does not, in itself, bring about school improvement. Correlation does not necessarily equal causation, and even if it did, knowing *what* are the factors of effective schools does not mean knowing *how* to establish those factors. Brighouse and Woods (1999) refer to school effectiveness as the 'nouns and adjectives of successful schooling' (p. 9) and contrast these with the 'verbs of successful schooling' (p. 11) which refer to the *process* of school improvement. This body of research has developed alongside and in conjunction with the measurement of effectiveness, and it is to this work that we now turn.

1.2 School improvement

The pressure is on for schools to show improvement within a context of more and more demanding expectations, regardless of difficulties such as the recruitment and retention of high-quality staff. Gray and colleagues (1999) offer a three-category framework for the way schools attempt to bring about improvement: tactics, strategies and capacity-building. An example of a tactical approach is concentrating on children considered to be on the borderline between National Curriculum Levels 3 and 4 in order to help them attain a Level 4 in end of Key Stage 2 tests. A strategic approach would be the focusing on a particular area of weakness throughout the school, for example writing, and the systematic evaluation and development of teaching approaches along with assessing, monitoring and tracking of pupils' progress in writing throughout the school. Both of these approaches may bring improved pupil performance in the short and medium term, but it is only the third approach, that of capacity-building, which leads to sustainable improvement.

The notion of capacity is central to the idea of school improvement, which has been defined by Hopkins, Ainscow and West (1994) as 'a distinct approach to educational change that enhances student outcomes as well as strengthening the school's capacity for managing change' (p. 3). MacBeath and Mortimore (2001, **Reading 17.1**) suggest using this definition to construct a two dimensional matrix (see Figure 17.1).

It is only schools which are high on both dimensions that are 'improving' schools. Those schools with high student outcome but low capacity for handling change could be thought of as schools which are becoming known as 'coasting' or under-achieving. However, those with high capacity for handling change but low student outcome could be considered to have improvement processes, even when these have not yet been realized in terms of student outcome.

MacBeath and Mortimore (2001) go on to say that 'the challenge of continuous improvement is to marry culture and structure. Structures without an underpinning culture of improvement are doomed to be ineffective. Strong cultures without sustaining structures will not survive from one generation to the next' (p. 18). We consider the concept of culture in relation to school development in more detail in Section 3.1.

MacGilchrist, Myers and Reed (1997) use the concept of *the intelligent school* as one which is able to maximize its improvement efforts by heeding some of the key messages that have emerged from the school improvement research. They

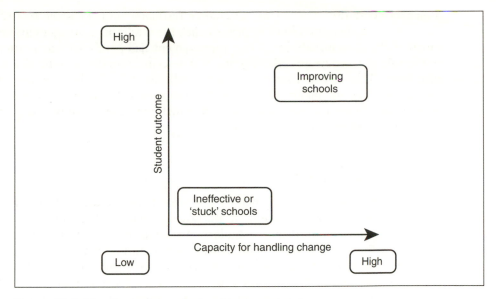

Figure 17.1 *The dimensions of school improvement*

identify six interrelated messages from the research which they believe are particularly helpful for schools (p. 9):

- change takes time
- a school's capacity for change will vary
- change is complex
- change needs to be well led and managed
- teachers need to be the main agents of change
- the pupils need to be the main focus for change.

Reflective activity 17.2

Aim: To consider the notion that teachers need to be the main agents of change.

Evidence and reflection: Think about a school that you know well, and recall two examples of change, one which could be considered to have gone well, and one which did not go well. To what extent were teachers the 'main agents of change' in each of the examples?

Extension: Do you agree with the assertion by Fullan (1991) that 'educational change depends on what teachers do and think. It's as simple and complex as that' (p. 117)? In what ways is it simple, and in what ways complex?

Teachers being the main agents of change resonates with Frost *et al.*'s (2000) concept of 'teacher-led school improvement'. Frost and his colleagues argue that much of the thinking about school improvement has paid insufficient attention to the role of teachers as active agents, and describe a model of 'reflective action planning'. They argue that the (teacher-led) 'model of school improvement enables teachers to make more of a difference in their schools by making a greater contribution to development work which will result in improved learning outcomes for their students' (p. 154).

1.3   Learning organizations

A learning organization, as defined by Leithwood and Aitken (1995) is 'a group of people who are pursuing common purposes (and individual purposes as well) with a collective commitment to regularly weighing the value of those purposes, modifying them when they make sense, and continuously developing more effective and efficient ways of accomplishing those purposes' (p. 41). Gray (2000) comments that this definition has obvious links with school improvement, and he emphasizes that schools 'must become committed to the idea of *continuous* improvement' (p. 236, emphasis in original).

The importance of organizational cultures has been asserted consistently. For example, Southworth *et al.*, (1989, **Reading 17.2**) produced a convincing account of how good staff relationships enhance school effectiveness. Rosenholz (1989) identified 'high consensus' schools in which principals and teachers appear to 'agree on the definitions of teaching', and in which 'their instructional goals occupy a place of high significance' (p. 206–8). She expressed this in ways which echo the concept of a 'learning organization':

> A spirit of continuous improvement seemed to hover school-wide, because no-one ever stopped learning to teach. It was assumed that improvement in teaching is a collective rather than an individual enterprise, and that analysis, evaluation and experimentation in concert with colleagues was a collective rather than individual enterprise.
>
> (Rosenholz, 1989, p. 73)

However, Rosenholz's model may seem somewhat idealistic and she herself drew attention to schools at the other end of the continuum. In such 'low consensus' schools there was no support for change or improvement; teachers were able to learn little from their colleagues and no one seemed to feel responsible for helping struggling teachers to improve; teachers experienced frustration, failure, tedium; they complained about the pupils and were self-defensive. Rosenholz described such schools as 'stuck', in contrast to the schools which are 'moving' forward. This typology has been further developed by Hopkins, Ainscow and West (1994) and by Stoll and Fink (1996) to a model in which schools are said to be 'moving, cruising, struggling, sinking or strolling'. In reality, just as no school is equally effective in all areas for all pupils, any one school may well display different trajectories and pace in different aspects of its provision and work. Reflective teachers find themselves in schools which could be characterized by any one or a combination of the labels, and the particular route to becoming a learning organization will be unique to each of them. As is apparent throughout this chapter, the process of building a collaborative culture is neither easy nor quick.

Senge's (1992) notion of 'organisational learning disabilities' has been drawn upon and developed by a number of writers (for example, MacBeath, 1998), and similar ideas are represented as 'blocks to improvement' which have been identified through work in schools. These include:

- teachers projecting their own deficiencies on to children or their communities
- teachers clinging to past practices
- defences built up against threatening messages from outside
- fear of failure
- seeing change as someone else's job
- hostile relationships among staff
- seeking safety in numbers (a ring-fenced mentality).

(MacBeath and Mortimore, 2001, p. 17)

> ### Reflective activity 17.3
>
> *Aim*: To reflect upon blocks to improvement
>
> *Evidence and reflection*: Consider the examples of blocks to improvement given by MacBeath and Mortimore. Do you recognize any of them in yourself or in teachers you know?
>
> *Extension*: Discuss with a colleague ways in which those blocks might be overcome. Try to put some of the suggestions into practice in relation to any blocks to improvement you recognized in yourself.

In a discussion of brakes and accelerators of school improvement, MacBeath and Myers (1998) suggest the following seven steps to be taken in sequence and over time en route to becoming a learning school:

- promote a learning climate
- identify the green shoots of growth
- identify the barriers
- share pedagogical leadership
- create intelligence from within
- use critical friends
- build resilient networks.

Any school which is, or seeks to become, a learning organization needs information about itself, and in the following section we explore different ways of evaluating schools.

2   EVALUATING SCHOOLS

When evaluating schools, many of the issues which relate to assessing pupils, and which we considered in Chapter 14, are pertinent. Is the evaluation valid, in that it evaluates what it claims to evaluate? Or are some measures taken as, perhaps not very good, proxies for others? Is the evaluation reliable, so that different evaluators come to the same conclusions? Teachers sometimes feel that a different team of inspectors would have made a different judgement. Different perspectives (for example those of pupils, parents and teachers) may well provide different views, and each need to be taken into account. Does the evaluation judge what we value (however hard it may be to 'measure'), or do we end up valuing what we assess because it is easy to measure? Results from National Curriculum tests may be easy to manipulate and compare, but do English and mathematics test results equate with all that we value about schools? What are the reference points by which schools are evaluated? Are there set criteria, are schools compared with each other, or with their own previous performance?

The context of school evaluation has changed dramatically in recent decades. The post-war period of relative autonomy and loose supervision by local educational authorities has been superseded by national frameworks of requirement, closely specified accountability systems, performance measurement and external inspection (Barber, 2001, **Reading 17.4**). The system is now more complex and reflective diagnosis that school teams generate and 'own' remains a vital driver of improvement.

2.1   School self-evaluation

If schools are to be effective, improve, and to become learning organizations, self-evaluation is essential. School self-evaluation is not a new idea, and to some extent all schools undertake an element of self-evaluation. Schools differ, though, in the ways they view self-evaluation, the prominence given and value attached to it, the purposes for which it is undertaken, the methods and data used, and the impact it has.

Pupil-performance data in the form of national assessment information, resources such as computer software and the English Autumn Package (see Chapter 14, Section 5.3), and requirements such as target setting, have led to one approach to evaluating schools. This is dealt with in Section 2.2. Quantitative performance data, plus qualitative data arising from classroom observations, are key features in the external evaluation of schools undertaken by Inspectors

from Estyn in Wales, HMI in Scotland, DENI in Northern Ireland and OFSTED in England. Such external inspection is the focus of Section 2.3. The OFSTED framework for inspection includes taking account of the school's own self-evaluation, and the OFSTED handbook includes guidance for schools on undertaking self-evaluation. This guidance encourages schools to use the same broad approach as the inspection regime itself, and has encouraged notions such as the headteacher being the school's resident inspector. Other, and somewhat different, approaches to school self-evaluation have also been developed, both in the UK and abroad, and are the focus of this section.

Whilst recognizing the value of pupil-performance data, and using them in increasingly sophisticated ways (for example looking at individual pupil inconsistencies across subjects), schools are also becoming aware of their shortcomings, and of the richness of information which is revealed by exploring the perceptions of pupils, parents and staff. Attitudinal data are typically gathered through questionnaires and interviews, but many other methods and instruments are available, for example, card sorting activities, diaries, and drawing. (A number of examples are given by MacBeath, 2000.)

One of the striking features of recent developments within school self-evaluation is the prominence given to what the pupils have to say. This does not seem a very revolutionary idea when one considers that their learning is the central purpose of schools, yet they are all too rarely listened to.

> Somehow educators have forgotten the important connection between teachers and students. We listen to outside experts to inform us, and, consequently, we overlook the treasures in our very own backyards: our students. Student perceptions are valuable to our practice because they are authentic sources; they personally experience our classrooms first hand . . . As teachers, we need to find ways to continually seek out those silent voices because they can teach us so much about learning and learners.
>
> (MacBeath and Mortimore, 2001, quoted in SooHoo, 1993, p. 389).

When pupils are listened to, though, they have much of great value to offer. For example, the Essex Primary School Improvement Project included group interviews to elicit pupils' perceptions. Actively seeking and making use of pupils' accounts was not part of the original plan of the project, but in the event '. . . primary pupil perception data . . . proved to be immensely powerful, perhaps the single most powerful, agent of change within a sophisticated school improvement programme'(Southworth and Lincoln, 1999).

Reflective activity 17.4

Aim: To explore the value of seeking pupils' views.

Evidence and reflection: Invite a small group of children to talk with you about one or more aspects of their learning and your teaching. For example, you could ask them about what helps them learn, what they think makes a good piece of work, or how they feel when you respond to their work. Reflect upon what they say. What has it added to your understanding of the situation? What are you going to do as a result?

Extension: How could you improve the process of seeking pupils' views? If it proves valuable, how can you make it a regular event?

Another feature of school self-evaluation is the role of the 'critical friend'. School self-evaluation as described above often uncovers information which, by its very nature of being powerful and revealing, is often quite salutary and sensitive. A highly skilled person, external to the school, can have a crucial part to play in helping a school to elicit, come to terms with, and use positively, school self-evaluation information.

2.2   School performance and target setting

National assessment results have increasingly been used as indicators of school performance. This began in England in the summer of 1992 when a number of newspapers published unofficial 'league tables' of secondary schools, based on GCSE results. For primary schools, LEAs are required to publish the Key Stage 2 test results, and these have been used by both national and local media to produce various forms of tables and lists. Initially LEAs were required to publish both test and Teacher Assessment results, but the requirement to publish Teacher Assessment data was later dropped, although many authorities continue to publish both since they provide different but complementary information.

The data published on schools show measured attainment levels only. If 'base-line' data of pupil attainment on entry are available, and these can be matched at individual pupil levels with attainment data at subsequent key points, it is possible to measure the progress of pupils whilst at a school. This progress information becomes much more powerful if it is compared with the progress of similar pupils from similar families in similar schools and communities. In this way factors which influence attainment can be taken into account, and the 'value added' (or difference from the attainment of pupils in similar contexts) calculated. Thus schools whose raw attainment data may appear to be very good may not be actually serving their pupils as well as schools with lower attainment, and vice versa. Although there are also issues surrounding value-added measures, many schools and LEAs are now engaging in these kinds of analyses.

The policies of the major political parties in the UK illustrate a gradual alignment in approaches to the use of raw data and value-added calculations. For most of the early 1990s, the Conservative Government advocated the simple use of raw data. This practice was criticized for failing to take account of pupil and school circumstances, and for fuelling the 'market' in education in misleading ways as it could lead to parents interpreting only raw results when choosing schools. In 1995 the Labour Party stated that:

> This process should not be used to develop a competitive market in education. The information should be used to lift and support schools, rather than to embarrass or denigrate them. The key way to raise standards is to set targets for pupils and schools and then set out the steps to achieve them.
>
> (Labour, 1995, p. 26–7)

Given the existence of performance data, the obvious next step is to plan improvements. In 1996, the concept of 'target setting' was endorsed for England by the DfEE who published a *Survey of Good Practice*, and since then the requirements, expectations and practice of target setting have become more and more deeply embedded. The Labour government that came to power in 1997 set national targets for 2002: the percentage of 11-year-olds reaching level 4 or above should be 80 per cent in English, and 75 per cent in mathematics. Each year, school Governing Bodies must set targets for the attainment of pupils; LEAs have the role of helping individual schools set realistic and challenging targets for their particular circumstances, which collectively reach or exceed the LEA's targets in their Education Development Plan. The LEA targets are checked and monitored by the DfES, with a view to meeting the national targets. The

Green Paper *Schools Building on Success* (DfEE, 2001c) says that these targets of 80 per cent and 75 per cent are 'staging posts on the way to even higher levels of performance' (p. 10).

Target setting for a whole year group, as required by statute, is informed by detailed performance data (as discussed in Chapter 14, Section 5). This is more and more frequently accompanied by a whole system of target setting at various levels within a school, from year group, through class and different groups (for example 'looked after' children), to individuals. It is through the plans and work for individuals and groups in a classroom that the school, LEA and, ultimately, national targets are met or not. Schools not only need to set targets and implement plans to attain them, but they also need to track progress towards targets, and reflect upon the actual performance levels in relation to the targets initially set. Performance data and associated commentaries are powerful tools for school improvement, and for providing information whether it be for use internally or externally. As well as playing a part in the setting of statutory targets, LEAs use performance, targets, and other indicators, to monitor and evaluate the schools in their authority.

Of course, performance and target-setting data are not the only sources of evidence that inform review and analysis in order to identify new targets for school improvement. An approach which puts a heavy emphasis on performance, but also considers other factors such as the quality of learning, teaching and leadership, is school inspection.

2.3   External inspection

In this section we first look at arrangements for external inspection of English schools before reflecting on some aspects of their impact.

A national school inspection system has existed from Victorian times and there is a long tradition of Her Majesty's Inspectors providing professional advice to government. Until 1993 this was achieved by HMI sampling schools for particular purposes and reviewing developments and quality in the system overall. For more specific information on standards of attainment, evidence had been provided by the 'Assessment of Performance Unit' (APU), which regularly tested a representative sample of pupils at different ages. Local Education Authority Advisers provided more immediate support and advice to schools.

In 1992, with a new emphasis on the provision of more specific information to parents about particular schools, the Education (Schools) Act established new procedures for the regular inspection of schools in England, to be co-ordinated by a new body, the Office for Standards in Education (OFSTED). A similar body, Estyn, inspects Welsh schools, while Her Majesty's Inspector of Schools, Scotland (HMIS) and the Inspectors of the Department of Education Northern Ireland (DENI) are responsible for schools in Scotland and Northern Ireland respectively. In England and Wales, the number of HMI was reduced and large numbers of new inspectors were trained. Teams of inspectors, led by a Registered Inspector (RgI), were then invited to bid for contracts to inspect particular schools (see Rose, 1995, for a rationale for the approach).

When OFSTED was first established, each school was inspected every four years, but a revised, differentiated, inspection system came into effect in 2000 whereby the most effective schools are offered less intensive, less frequent,

---

CONTEXT AND OVERVIEW
1. What sort of school is it?

OUTCOMES
2. How high are the standards?
2.1 What are the school's results and pupils' achievements?
2.2 What are pupils' attitudes, values and personal development?

QUALITY OF PROVISION
3. How well are pupils taught?
4. How good are the curricular and other opportunities offered to pupils?
5. How well does the school care for its pupils?
6. How well does the school work in partnership with parents?

EFFICIENCY AND EFFECTIVENESS OF MANAGEMENT
7. How well is the school led and managed?

ISSUES FOR THE SCHOOL
8. What should the school do to improve further?

Figure 17.2 *The structure of the OFSTED evaluation schedule and report*

inspections. These 'short inspections' are intended to be a 'light-touch' 'health check' of the school, sampling the school's work rather than inspecting and reporting fully on each subject. A short inspection in a primary school usually lasts two or three days, with a team of between two and five inspectors, whereas a full inspection lasts up to one week, and a large primary school may require seven or eight inspectors.

Short and full inspections have many common features. In both, inspectors are required to report on:

- the quality of the education provided by the school

- the education standards achieved in the school

- whether the financial resources made available to the school are managed efficiently

- the spiritual, moral, social and cultural development of pupils at the school.

Figure 17.2 shows the structure of both the evaluation schedule and the framework for the eventual report (OFSTED, 1999, p. 6). It highlights the distinction between the outcome *standards* achieved by the pupils, and the factors or provision which contribute to these outcomes, particularly the *quality of teaching*, and *leadership* and *management*.

In compiling their report, inspectors must assemble evidence for their judgements, some of which is available before the inspection. The school completes forms providing basic data about itself, making its own assessment of compliance with statutory requirements, and presenting its own self-evaluation in relation to the areas of its work which are to be inspected. The revised inspection system introduced in 2000 reduced the notice of an inspection which is given to schools to between six and ten weeks, and so headteachers are encouraged to keep an up-to-date self-evaluation document, a regularly up-dated reflection on the school, as a matter of good practice.

Some pre-inspection evidence is provided by OFSTED, in the form of *The Pre-Inspection Context and School Indicator* (PICSI). The PICSI report contains information about the school's results, trends, and how they compare with national averages and similar schools.

During the actual inspection, approximately 60 per cent of inspection time is devoted to observing lessons, having discussions with pupils and sampling pupils' work. Other forms of evidence are also used, although on short inspections inspectors are instructed to avoid undertaking too much documentary analysis. 'Schools should be judged primarily by their achievements, and on the effectiveness of their teaching, leadership and management in contributing to pupils' progress. Where a school is effective, there is little need to trawl through all the procedural documents' (OFSTED 1999, p. 137).

During every inspection the inspectors must consider whether the school is failing, or is likely to fail, to give its pupils an acceptable standard of education, and therefore requires special measures. If special measures are not required, inspectors have to consider whether the school has serious weaknesses or is under-achieving. In making judgements about all these three categories inspectors have set factors to consider and procedures to follow. The placing of a school in any of these categories leads to continued monitoring, and in the case of special measures, termly revisits by HMI.

Following an inspection visit, the inspection report is made publicly available and a summary is sent to parents. Governors must consider the report and produce an 'action plan' which sets out what it is going to do about the 'key issues for action' identified in the report.

Having considered the mechanics of inspection, what of its effects?

The inspection of schools, and OFSTED in particular, has been the focus of much criticism, not least because of its negative impact on the morale of teachers. Comments such as the following have been echoed in many schools:

> 'There was a lot of long-term illness, some never recovered, some have been off school ever since'; 'One teacher left shortly afterwards, it was not just this but OFSTED was the final straw'; 'Shortly after two staff went off with long-term sickness and have not returned. Both are first class teachers and got A1 reports but just couldn't cope with the stress.'
>
> (Lonsdale and Parsons, 1998, p. 121)

A survey of the chairs of governors and headteachers of primary schools conducted for OFSTED (MORI, 1998) found that nine out of ten felt that the inspection had been as stressful or more stressful than they had expected. Jeffrey and Woods (1998) conducted in-depth research in six contrasting primary schools that had all undergone inspections during the period 1995–7 and argue that the emotional responses of the teachers are best understood as illustrations of deprofessionalization against a background of managerialist reforms from government.

The inspection system in practice has seemed to emphasize the accountability function above the school-improvement function, and whilst the publication of inspection reports has generally been accepted, the reliability of their judgements has not (Richards, 2001, **Reading 17.5**). The 'name and shame' approach of the late 1990s caused particularly deep resentment. As was emphasized in Section 1 of this chapter, schools are complex places, and banner headlines such as 'the worst school in the country' can neither be a fair reflection of all aspects of a school nor do anything to help it improve.

The revised OFSTED inspection system (1999, effective from 2000) with its 'light touch' inspections for successful schools, and its encouragement of school self-evaluation (albeit in a form which closely resembles an OFSTED inspection), went some way to addressing some of the concerns. However, whilst HMCI has congratulated teachers for the improvement in the quality of teaching and wishes to find more valid indicators of school improvement, it is clear that 'rigour' will not be compromised (Tomlinson, 2001). Barber (2001, **Reading 17.4**), a key architect of Labour's policy initiations, sees new strategic balance in pressure and support, which will continue to raise standards.

3 CONTINUING PROFESSIONAL DEVELOPMENT

The concept of 'Continuing Professional Development (CPD) denotes the steady career-long process of learning and adaption which teachers are encouraged to undertake. This is intimately connected to personal development and career fulfilment, but this can only be fully realized in a school context with a favourable learning culture. The major manifestation of the school's ambition is reflected in its planning for school improvement, but continuing professional development is now strongly conditioned by performance management requirements. In this section, we address each of these issues.

3.1 Professional and personal development

As we indicated in Chapter 1, Section 1, reflective practice makes a significant contribution to such development of expertise. The self-conscious, skill-based emphasis of the trainee is replaced by the experimentation of newly qualified teachers, and then, after some years, is superseded by the almost intuitive judgement of the expert teacher. This progression was represented in Figure 1.1, with competence, confidence and expertise spiralling upwards through classroom-based self-evaluation, enquiry and reflective practice. Such teacher-controlled and evidence-informed processes are, as we saw, now strongly supported by the General Teaching Councils and government agencies in each part of the UK. This is a very welcome development.

Of course, from a government perspective, Continuing Professional Development is important to help teachers to accommodate to new initiatives and requirements. The teaching workforce is then able to fulfil its designated roles more effectively. There are new structures for ensuring high-quality induction provision and continuing opportunities for training of subject specialists and senior managers. These may take the form of school-initiated activities – which this book is explicitly designed to support. Alternatively, there may be external courses or personal research activities supported by LEAs or government agencies (such as Best Practice Research Scholarships in England), or accredited courses offered by higher education institutions. Regarding the latter, the Open University runs an excellent course on teaching in primary schools, and even the University of Cambridge now offers high quality part-time courses from Diploma level to PhD.

High-quality professional development activities certainly do enable teachers to build higher levels of expertise, and this is worthwhile in itself. However, professional development also normally offers a great deal of personal fulfilment too, both from processes of enquiry, training and study, and from the pleasure of accomplishment. This is particularly true if CPD is undertaken in a sustained way with like-minded colleagues, when mutual support and 'critical friendship' are easily available (see, for example, Dadds, 1995). The achievement of higher levels of understanding, deeper insight, additional skills or knowledge, etc. is thus in itself fulfilling. In favourable circumstances, such conscious knowledge gradually becomes embedded and thus enhances intuitive judgement, skills and expertise.

At its best, as Solomon and Tresman (1999, **Reading 17.3**) argue, continuing professional development also makes a connection with the 'self' and identity of the teacher. They see professionalism as a value-led activity in which the personal commitments of each teacher become entwined with their professional role. The self of the teacher is thus realized through professional development – and each person's unfolding biography become both a personal and professional narrative (see also Nias, 1989, **Reading 5.1**).

This ideal is greatly affected by the culture of the workplace. The ideal is a school in which the goals of each individual teacher can be realized through attainment of the school's goals and targets. Personal and institutional fulfilment are aligned. We discuss this issue further below.

3.2 School culture and professional development

A great deal is written about 'school culture' without problematizing the concept itself. From the sociological point of view, all sorts of normative assumptions are embedded within the idea. At its most developed, for instance by Southworth *et al.*, (1989, see **Reading 17.2**), the proposition is that individuals working in a school may identify personally and collectively with official goals and values – a 'culture of collaboration'. Fulfilment is thus achieved *through* institutional policies, practices and achievements. But to what degree can aims, understandings, conventions, habits and routines really be held collectively by a school-staff and fulfilled corporately though the organization? Arguably, the concept implies more consensus and commitment than is realistic in most situations.

Nevertheless, the idea of schools having a 'learning culture' is important as an ideal. To the extent that it is achieved, teachers will have the confidence to respond constructively to change; disagreement and debate will be possible because relationships are secure; individuals and groups will feel able to take risks; values and their relationship to school practices can be continuously considered; and both individuals and groups will feel collectively affirmed.

However attractive the ideal, a culture of collaboration may turn out to be more apparent than real. Hargreaves (1994) has suggested the idea of 'contrived collegiality' in which the management attempts to build collegiality but the hearts and minds of staff do not follow. A common factor that can impede the development of a collaborative culture is the existence of strong pre-existing group identities – sometimes referred to a 'balkanization'. Such separated cultures are particularly evident in secondary schools where there is a strong subject–department structure and identity, and they may produce concerns and struggles about territory in terms of time, space, resources, practices and procedures – but the same problem may occur in a primary-school setting. Another common problem is the situation which may be characterized as 'comfortable collaboration' where teachers work together in well established, warm and casual ways. There are many shared understandings, but not much questioning, enquiry or investigation of the status quo. Processes associated with systematic reflective practice are not in evidence (Levine and Eubanks, 1989).

Phenomena such as 'balkanized' cultures or 'comfortable collaboration' may be better understood in terms of micro-political analysis (Ball, 1987; Hoyle, 1986). In this form of analysis, school policies and practices are seen as temporary and negotiated products which reflect the existing balance of power and influence within a school. In a sense, they reflect an apparent consensus, which hides continuing conflicts concerning issues which are constantly being contested within ever-changing circumstances. The influence of any one individual at any given time will depend on their degree of status, power, charisma and authority. The role of both internal alliances and of other external factors, such as parental views and governor, LEA or government policies must also be recognized.

The most important player is likely to be the headteacher, who has both formal authority and a great deal of power. As Ball concludes, in one way or another this position is likely to be used to 'dominate' so that apparent agreement is achieved:

> I have tried to indicate the conflictual basis of the school as an organisation. Concomitantly, I have attempted to indicate that the control of school organisations, focused on the position and role of the headteacher, is significantly concerned with domination (the elimination or pre-emption of conflict). Thus domination is intended to achieve and maintain particular definitions of the school over and against alternative definitions.
>
> (Ball, 1987, p. 278)

Ball offers an interestingly provocative analysis of forms of participation in school decision-making (see Figure 17.3).

We are thus left with an image of school organizations as settings in which values, priorities and practices are contested by headteachers, management teams, departments, faculties and individuals. Sometimes such micro-political activity may be considerable, such as when a new headteacher arrives. There may also be periods of relative stability when 'comfortable collaboration' may exist for a while.

	Forms of participation	Responses to opposition	Strategies of control
Authoritarian	Prevents public access to voice	Stifle	Insulation, concealment and secrecy
Managerial	Formal committees, meetings and working parties	Channel and delay	Structuring, planning, control of agendas, time and context
Interpersonal	Informal chats and personal consultation and lobbying	Fragment and compromise	Private performances of persuasion
Adversarial	Public meetings and open debate	Confront	Public performances of persuasion

Figure 17.3 *Forms of participation in school decision–making*

Reflective activity 17.5

Aim: To consider micro-politics in schools.

Evidence and reflection: Thinking of a school in which you have worked, reflect on the various groups of staff and their perspectives and actions within the school. What relationships exist between these groups? Thinking of a significant incident or event, what variations were there in the responses of different individuals and groups? What strategies does the leadership team use in managing the different positions? To what extent do you feel that the culture of the school is affected by the influence which particular groups or individuals exert?

Extension: Consider the strategies of the headteacher in terms of Ball's forms of participation. To what extent is the headteacher authoritarian, managerial, interpersonal or adversarial?

During the 1990s, the growing emphasis on external accountability, school effectiveness, school development, target setting and inspection has meant that schools can no longer be considered as relatively closed and semi-autonomous institutions. Whether a school is best characterized in terms of its collaborative culture or its micro-politics makes little difference to the accountability and performance requirements which have to be met. The consequence of this structuring of external requirements, pressures and constraints is that schools are now *managed* in much more purposive and explicit ways than many were in the past. The major means of doing this are though target setting (addressed in

Section 2.2 of this chapter), and school improvement planning, to which we now turn.

3.3 School improvement planning

School improvement planning is a process of schools establishing priorities for development. These priorities are recorded in a school improvement (or 'development') plan, which is produced annually and, as part of the policy of encouraging individual school autonomy, such plans have been seen as enabling schools to become 'empowered' (Hargreaves and Hopkins, 1991). They are the prime means by which staff and governors can exercise coherent and forward-looking control over curriculum and school development. They also provide the context for the personal staff development of each individual teachers. School improvement plans are detailed for the coming year, and look ahead to the following two to five years in outline. Longer-term priorities are identified and sketched in, but in the knowledge that the further ahead they are, the more likely they are to be revised and amended.

Improvement plans generally include consideration of:

1. Aims and philosophy
2. A review of the previous year's plan
3. The present situation
    catchment and enrolment
    organization
    staffing
    curriculum provision
    resources
    achievements
4. Assessed needs and priorities for future development
    organizational development
    staff development
    curriculum development
    resource development
5. Success criteria and monitoring arrangements
6. How the assessed needs are to be met.

The last point is a significant one, for it brings the planning process up against practicalities – for instance, budgets. School budgeting should be 'curriculum-led' rather than be driven by financial considerations but this is not always possible. Nevertheless, in the words of HMCI (1992) development planning provides:

> A more rational and coherent framework in which to identify priorities, plan for change and allocate resources. In the best practice, development plans paid attention to teaching and learning, specified manageable time scales, and outlined arrangements for monitoring and evaluation.

> (HMCI, 1992, p. 20)

The whole-school development process is designed to lead to change and Miles (1986) identifies three overlapping stages in such innovation:

- Initiation – deciding to start, developing commitment, defining purposes and processes, appointing key people, making links with key issues for whole school explicit, guaranteeing support for involvement

- Implementation – the first cycle, a learning process; focus on co-ordination, adequate and sustained support in the form of INSET, supply cover; positive reinforcement. Skills and understanding are being acquired; groups of teachers may become self-governing as they move forward

- Institutionalization – development planning becomes part of the normal pattern of how the school does things; management arrangements have evolved to support further development and maintenance – they also are part of the pattern. The impact of development planning is seen in classroom practice and the innovation is no longer new.

Where there are a number of priorities and initiatives, developments are likely to overlap and interconnect, and each will have its own timescale. A coherent planning and development process will permeate the normal work of the school and, as Miles suggests, will eventually become encompassed in routine activity. Figure 17.4 illustrates this multi-level integration as a 'development cone'.

However, there are a number of reasons why some schools do not succeed with improvement planning. As with 'contrived collegiality', development can become a 'bolt-on' activity which happens procedurally but has no fundamental impact on the way the school works. Equally, it is possible to underestimate the need for the process to be managed, especially where this itself requires significant changes in established management practice. Associated with this is a failure to create the conditions under which change and innovation can happen; to be unaware, for example, of the distinctive nature of the three stages identified by Miles and of the different management and support required by each phase.

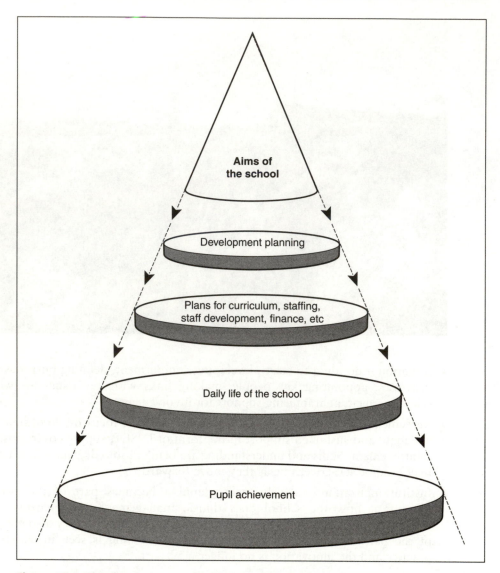

Figure 17.4 *The development planning cone (Hargreaves and Hopkins, 1991)*

Finally, it is possible to produce an improvement plan as a management document but give little or no thought to the processes by which it might be implemented.

Anning (1983) suggested that new headteachers attempting curriculum innovation face a course rather like that of the Grand National. The first jump, the improvement of the environment, and the second, that of producing new policy statements and curriculum guidelines, are accomplished smoothly. Beecher's Brook looms when it is realized that actual practice in the classroom may not be changing as fast and cannot be influenced by aesthetics and documents alone. This is a problem which faces everyone – for it is never easy to bring practice into line with ideals, let alone in the difficult circumstances which schools have faced in recent years. Indeed, many headteachers have found that the apparent ordered rationality of school improvement planning is disrupted by the turbulence of external events (Wallace, 1994), so that the whole process becomes something of a diversion from managing the 'real world'.

MacGilchrist *et al.* (1995) identified four types of school development plan. The 'rhetorical plan' (no sense of ownership by head or staff) the 'singular plan' (produced by the headteacher alone), the 'co-operative plan' (with partial involvement of teaching staff) and the 'corporate plan'. The latter was 'characterised by a united effort to improve . . . and a focus on teaching and learning' (p. 195). Of the four types, the rhetorical plan had a negative impact, while the corporate plan had 'a very significant positive impact on both the efficiency and the effectiveness of the school'.

Clearly, implementing a school improvement plan is far from easy, and is intimately connected with school culture, and management of the school's micro-politics.

3.4   Professional development and performance management

In management terms, continuing professional development (CPD) and performance management flow directly from, and feed into, school improvement planning. The process of planning school improvement may well identify areas that should be the focus for CPD and performance management. Conversely, teachers' training and development needs, whether identified through informal discussion or performance management, should become incorporated within the school improvement plan. In this section we consider continuing professional development and performance management and their relationship with reflective teaching.

A reflective teacher would find it hard to disagree with the reasons given by the DfEE (2001a) for encouraging continuing professional development:

- the demands on teaching are changing all the time. Becoming and remaining a good teacher, keeping knowledge of curriculum subjects up to date, and being able to make the most of new technology all require continuing professional development

- good professional development enables you to build the skills to enhance your career – whether that is in teaching, in education more widely, or beyond

- a strong professional culture in a school frequently makes it a much better place to work, with open, supportive relationships, and more enthusiastic, self-confident staff

- schools which offer teachers regular opportunities for professional development find it easier to attract and retain good staff

- we want pupils to develop enthusiasm for lifelong learning, since this is increasingly the key to success in adult life. That is more likely if they see their teachers involved in regular learning.

Nevertheless, there may well be other reasons that we would expect to see in such a list, such as finding out about and applying knowledge about how children learn, and keeping up to date with relevant research.

Professional development 'continues' in that it begins with initial teacher training, followed by the induction year (the focus of Chapter 16), and should carry on throughout a teaching career. Almost by definition, reflective teachers think about their own performance and progress and that of their pupils, and take responsibility for their own ongoing development. There are many routes to continuing professional development, including the traditional in-service training courses, ranging from stand-alone half-day courses to extended programmes lasting two or more years and leading to a Masters degree. Courses have an important place in CPD provision, but many more varied opportunities also exist. In England, a number of these are funded directly by the DfES. These include:

- extra CPD for teachers in their second and third years of teaching, building on the induction year
- professional bursaries for teachers in Education Action Zones and Excellence in Cities, which can be spent on any professional development activity of the teacher's choice
- Best Practice Research Scholarships which fund teachers to do sharply focused research into key areas of classroom practice
- opportunities to undertake short study visits or exchanges to learn from excellent practice in other countries
- sabbaticals, lasting up to six weeks in total, for any developmental activity that will benefit the teacher, their school and their pupils.

These approaches to CPD provide opportunities for individual teachers to pursue personal areas of interest, within the context of school improvement. Teachers who habitually reflect upon their own practice and the learning that goes on in their classrooms will undoubtedly be aware of questions and issues which they want to investigate. Investors In People, Beacon schools, Advanced Skills Teachers and standards for teachers with subject and specialist leadership responsibilities illustrate other schemes through which the DfES in England has sought to promote CPD and broaden its impact. Perhaps one of the most potentially powerful forms of CPD is peer observation which, when undertaken in a mutually respectful, enquiring way, with adequate time for preparation and follow-up discussion, can be professionally affirming and an excellent learning experience, for both the observed and the observer.

Whatever the particular combination of CPD activities in which an individual teacher engages, it is essential that a record is kept. This should go beyond logging the dates and titles of courses attended (although many teachers have had cause to regret not keeping even this most basic information as a matter of course). It should include reflections on such things as the content of the course and the process of learning, skills developed, implications for teaching and impact on children's learning. The National Record of Achievement, and its successor the Progress File (which has a version called 'Broadening Horizons' specially designed for adults) are recognized formats for recording, reflecting upon, planning and supporting personal and professional development. Other formats for 'personal portfolios' are of course also possible, for example Frost (1997) provides practical guidance for maintaining a portfolio. A reflective journal, an approach which is explored for example by Mary Louise Holly in her book *Writing to Grow* (Holly, 1989), is both a particular kind of record and at the same time a form of CPD in itself.

New systems of 'performance management' have been introduced into England and Wales. Whilst teacher associations argued that such systems are intrusive, inflexible, insulting and should definitely not be linked to salary payments, government bodies insisted that regular discussions of performance can support CPD by identifying individual teachers' development needs and linking them to the goals of the school. Performance management thus replaced previous 'teacher appraisal' schemes which had been inconsistently implemented since the early 1990s. A number of reasons for their demise can be identified, including the provision of time to do the appraisal properly and resources to follow-up on agreed development targets. Teachers were also concerned about the possible use of appraisal information in determining redundancies or promotions. A collation of evidence (TTA/OFSTED, 1996) concluded that appraisal processes were making very little impact on needs of the school as a whole. The report concluded:

> There is a need to set sharper targets, better linked to classroom practice and school management.
>
> (1996, p. 11)

Performance management goes some way to addressing some of the concerns about the 1990s appraisal scheme: for example, there are much more explicit links with classroom management. However, the English version certainly does not address teachers' concerns about the use of appraisal information – quite the reverse in fact. As the DfEE stated:

> The outcomes of performance review will be used to inform pay decisions, for example for awarding double performance increments for outstanding performance up to the performance threshold, and for awarding discretionary performance pay points above the threshold, for Advanced Skills Teachers and teachers in the leadership group. Information from performance reviews will provide evidence for assessment at the performance threshold.
>
> (DfEE, 2000b, p. 12)

Regarding the process of performance management, this is seen in the English scheme as an ongoing cycle, not an event. The cycle involves three stages:

- *planning*: team leaders discuss and record priorities and objectives with each of the teachers in their team. They discuss how progress will be monitored
- *monitoring*: the teacher and team leader keep progress under review throughout the cycle, taking any supportive action needed
- *review*: the teacher and the team leader review achievements over the year and evaluate the teacher's overall performance taking account of progress against objectives.

It is expected that each teacher will have between three and six objectives for every cycle. Some of these objectives must relate to pupil progress, and to ways of developing and improving teachers' professional practice. Objectives should be challenging but realistically achievable, and it is in everybody's interest to ensure that they are, and that the objectives set can be reviewed unambiguously. Teachers who continually reflect upon their pupils' learning and their own professional practice are well prepared to negotiate objectives which strike that delicate but crucial balance between challenge and realism.

Continuing professional development is thus a core professional activity. It makes a vital contribution to performance management processes, but should not be reduced to or limited by them. It can also make a vital contribution to personal fulfilment.

Career development and performance management are among the areas on which the General Teaching Councils are often required to provide advice. The GTCs in England and Wales were established in 1998, whereas the GTC for Scotland, the first professional council for teaching in the UK, has been operating since 1966. The form of a GTC for Northern Ireland is under discussion (see **RTweb** for *Links* to these and other organizations).

CONCLUSION

In this chapter, we began by looking at the policy context within which schools work before reviewing the main findings of school-effectiveness research, and the processes and factors associated with school improvement. Ideas connected with learning organizations were specifically related to schools, and different approaches to evaluating schools considered. Continuing professional development and performance management and their role in linking reflective teaching and school improvement were discussed.

Understanding such factors is important for a reflective teacher, for personal and classroom performance is enabled or constrained by circumstances. Nor should teachers think passively in such situations, for our schools are largely what we make of them. And in respect of continuing professional development, the case for taking personal responsibility is even stronger.

In the final chapter we move beyond the school to consider reflective teaching and society.

Key readings

The classic and outstanding guide to educational reform, recently revised and expanded is:

Fullan, M. (2001)
The New Meaning of Educational Change.
3rd edition.
London: Routledge Falmer.

A practical and easily read book which draws together the inter-related areas of research on school effectiveness, school improvement, teaching and learning, is:

MacGilchrist, B., Myers, K. and Reed, J. (1997)
The Intelligent School.
London: Paul Chapman.

Equally accessible and useful, and drawing particularly on their experience in Birmingham, is:

Brighouse, T. and Woods, D. (1999)
How to Improve Your School.
London: Routledge.

A sustained critique of school effectiveness and school improvement is offered through a collection of wide-ranging chapters in:

Slee, R. and Weiner, G. with Tomlinson, S. (eds) (1998)
School Effectiveness for Whom? Challenges to the School Effectiveness and School Improvement Movements.
London: Falmer Press.

The case for school self-evaluation and a step-by-step guide are included in:

MacBeath, J. (1999)
Schools Must Speak For Themselves: the Case for School Self-Evaluation.
London: Routledge.

A critical but constructive view of inspection, incorporating international and historical perspectives as well as questions to prompt reflection at the end of each chapter, is:

Learmonth, J. (2000)
Inspection: What's In It For Schools?
London: Routledge Falmer.

Planning a strategy for school improvement is the focus of MacGilchrist *et al.*'s book:

MacGilchrist, B., Mortimore, P., Savage, J. and Beresford, C. (1995)
Planning Matters: the Impact of Development Planning in Primary Schools.
London: Paul Chapman.

For an engaging example of how the continuing professional development of a reflective teacher can influence her workplace, see:

Dadds. M. (1995)
Passionate Enquiry and School Development: a Story about Teacher Action Research.
London: Falmer Press.

Two important studies from the National Commission on Education set out how schools in disadvantaged areas can be effective and whether improvement can be maintained:

National Commission on Education (1995)
Success Against the Odds.
London: Routledge.

Maden, M. (ed.) (2001)
Success Against the Odds – Five Years On: Revisiting Effective Schools in Disadvantaged Areas.
London: Routledge Falmer.

Finally, a principled polemic on how teachers and headteachers should work together to make change happen, is:

Fullan, M. and Hargreaves, A. (1992)
What's Worth Fighting for in Your School? Working Together for School Improvement.
Buckingham: Open University Press.

Articles relating to school development can be found in many journals such as:

Educational Leadership
Educational Management and Administration
The Head's Legal Guide
Improving Schools
Journal of In-Service Education
Management in Education

Managing Schools Today
Professional Development Today
Research in Education (SCRE Newsletter)
School Leadership and Management
School Effectiveness and Improvement
Teacher Development

 Readings for Reflective Teaching (the companion volume) offers other closely associated work on the issues raised in this chapter. This includes work by authors such as:

John MacBeath, Peter Mortimore, Geoff Southworth, Jennifer Nias, Penny Campbell, Joan Solomon, Sue Tresman, Michael Barber and Colin Richards.

 RTweb offers additional professional resources for this chapter. These may include *Notes for Further Reading, Reflective Activities*, useful *Web Links, Extension Texts* and *Download Facilities* for diagrams, figures, checklists, activities.

CHAPTER 18

Reflective teaching and society

INTRODUCTION

1 EDUCATION AND SOCIETY

2 CLASSSROOM TEACHING AND SOCIETY

3 REFLECTIVE TEACHING AND THE DEMOCRATIC PROCESS

CONCLUSION

Enhancing professional standards and competencies

This chapter addresses some issues that, at this particular point in history, receive little emphasis in national requirements for teacher education. Could it be that governments deem the issues raised to be too significant for teachers to consider?

Historically, however, there is a strong tradition of civic responsibility among teachers in all parts of the UK, and the contribution to public life of thinking, socially aware professional educators has been very strong in Scotland, Wales, Northern Ireland and England. It clearly cannot be inappropriate for teachers to reflect on the role that education plays in society as a whole.

In England, the TTA requires those awarded Qualified Teacher Status to demonstrate that they understand and uphold the professional code of the General Teaching Council. This includes a requirement to:

Demonstrate and promote the positive values, attitudes and behaviour that they expect from their pupils.
(TTA, *Standards for the Award of Qualified Teacher Status*, standard 1.3)

An example of such expectations would be *citizenship*, which teachers are now asked by the New Labour Government to gradually introduce to children. This is an excellent development for a democracy. However, we believe that awareness of citizenship and the broader role of the profession in our society is just as appropriate for teachers (see also Chapter 1 on the attributes of reflective teaching). Learning about the social and political context in which teachers work, locally, nationally or internationally, should not be excluded from teacher education programmes by the narrowness of standards or competence requirements.

INTRODUCTION

In many parts of this book we have considered the internal workings of classrooms and schools with just occasional references to the social, economic, cultural and political contexts within which they are located. While this may be necessary for a practice-oriented book of this sort, a reflective teacher will also certainly be aware of the ways in which educational processes are influenced by, and contribute to, wider social forces, processes and relationships (Archer, 1979, **Reading 18.1**). In Chapter 4, we introduced the idea of social development being based on a dialectical process, as individuals respond to and act within the situations in which they find themselves. Actions in the present are thus influenced by the past, but they also contribute to new social arrangements for the future. All teachers, as individuals, are members of society and we hope that reflective teachers will be particularly capable of acting in society to initiate and foster morally and ethically sound developments.

There are three sections in this chapter. The first discusses the relationship between education and society and reviews the theoretical framework referred to above. The second considers the classroom responsibilities of a socially aware and reflective teacher and discusses the formation of classroom policies. The final section focuses on the actions that a reflective teacher could take as a citizen in trying to influence democratic processes of decision-making by local, regional and national governments.

RTweb offers resources in *Web Links*, the *Compendium* and *Notes for Further Reading* that will help with this .

1   EDUCATION AND SOCIETY

Two major questions have to be faced with regard to the relationship between education and society. The first is, 'What should an education system be designed to do?' The second is, 'What can actually be achieved through education?' We will address these in turn and draw out the implications for reflective teachers.

Education has very often been seen as a means of influencing the development of societies, and we will identify three central areas of purpose. These are:

- wealth creation through preparation for economic production
- cultural production and reproduction
- developing social justice and individual rights.

Wealth creation. One educational priority is certainly likely to be wealth creation. For instance in the latter part of the industrial revolution in Great Britain, an important part of the argument for the establishment of an elementary school system was that it should provide a workforce which was more skilled and thus more economically productive. The idea became the linchpin of 'human capital' theory in the 1960s, (Schultz, 1961) and many new nations, influenced by analyses such as Rostow's *The Stages of Economic Growth* (1962), put scarce resources into their education systems. The economics of education is still a flourishing area of policy and research (Aldcroft, 1992). In Britain, the links between education and economic productivity are constantly being drawn by the government, with particular attention to the standard of basic skills achieved in schools and to the proportion of young people acquiring advanced knowledge and skills in higher education. In 1997, this link between education and the economic well-being of society was reinforced further by the New Labour administration which in the first paragraph of its central education policy document stated:

> Our goal is a society in which everyone is well educated and able to learn throughout life. Britain's economic prosperity and social cohesion both depend on that goal.

> (DfEE, 1997, p. 9)

This theme is carried forward into the rationale for additional education reforms post-2001. The focus of these is in secondary education, but the DfEE has been quick to explain the link between previous under-performance by that sector and economic considerations:

Parental expectations of secondary schools were generally low, particularly in regions with plentiful unskilled 'jobs for life'. Throughout the economy the demand for skills and qualifications and all type of further and higher education was also far lower than today.

(DfEE, 2001c, p. 4)

One of the drivers of this concern was the many international comparisons that were made in the 1990s between pupil achievement in Britain and that in other countries – most notably those in the Pacific Rim (e.g. Reynolds and Farrell, 1996). A major assumption behind this OFSTED-commissioned study was that Britain's future prosperity was related to pupil achievement and, in this crucial area, Britain was lagging behind other economically achieving countries. The consequence was that there should be a movement towards a pedagogy of 'interactive whole class teaching', for this appeared to be the pedagogy which was contributing to pupil success and educational achievement in countries such as Singapore and Taiwan. Educational achievement would in turn lead to economic prosperity and the maintenance of national status and global competitiveness. On the other hand, Galton (1998) proposed a note of caution. As he put it:

Anyone who had spent periods of time in these Pacific Rim countries, or who had read recent policy documents from their Ministries of Education, would have been struck by an interesting paradox. At the very time when our politicians are urging primary teachers to adopt the methods of these successful Asian teachers, the latter are being urged to become more like their English colleagues. Countries such as Singapore and Hong Kong are looking to increase the proportion of co-operative group work within the curriculum and to achieve a greater degree of critical thinking.

(Galton, 1998, p. 3)

An interesting point for debate concerns which pedagogic approach is *really* related to long-term economic success.

Cultural reproduction. Alternatively, there are those who would highlight the 'function' of education in the production and reproduction of a national culture. Again there were elements of the nineteenth-century British experience that illustrate this. For instance, the arguments and influence of Arnold (1889) helped to define the traditional classical curriculum that remains influential today. Indeed, study of Shakespeare and key episodes in English history was insisted upon in the initial construction of the National Curriculum. Even so, some remain concerned about the erosion of national identity in modern society (Tate, 1997).

A particularly clear example of cultural production is that of the USA through much of the twentieth century where the education system was required to 'assimilate' and 'integrate' successive groups of new immigrants into an 'American culture'. The education system was seen as a vital part of the 'melting pot'. Of course, a highly questionable assumption here was that there was a single American culture, but the notion of the existence of a set of 'central values' was important in this period of the development of the USA. There are thus costs in the use of education to develop or assert a national culture, and these costs are usually borne by minority or less powerful groups. The historical case of the education provided in the colonies of the British Empire provides a particularly graphic example of this last point (Mangan, 1993).

However, use of an education system for the production of a sense of shared national identity is common in many parts of the world, particularly where independent or democratic states have been established relatively recently. Of course, other forms of political structure can also be supported by education. Thus, we currently have many emergent forms of regional identity within the nations that make up the European Union. Education plays a part in producing and reproducing culture at each of these levels. For example, the people of Wales preserve an important part of their culture through the teaching of Welsh in their schools, but, at the same time, their education system inducts Welsh children into the culture of the United Kingdom and Europe. Another educational priority can thus be an integrative one, relating to the production or reproduction of 'culture' within political structures.

Social justice. Contributing to social justice is a third central purpose which is often identified for education systems. This concern was very much at the forefront of thinking in the production of the 1944 Education Act in the UK and also in the subsequent introduction of comprehensive schools. It has been an important element of policy in the USA and features prominently in the educational goals which are set by many countries in Europe and across the world (for a European example, see the 1985 Memorandum of the Council of Europe, 1985). One critical point to make is that 'equality of opportunity' and the meritocratic ideal, which often lie behind policies on this issue, are concepts which are vulnerable to rhetoric. Paulo Freire was internationally recognized for his advocacy of education for social justice, for a 'pedagogy of the oppressed' (**Reading 18.2**), and often insisted on the need to face the structural inequalities of wealth, status and power which exist. If such issues are glossed, then the promotion of social justice through education policy is very unlikely to be successful.

The concern for social justice through education can partly be seen as a desire to ensure that there is an acceptable and legitimated system for allocating jobs in democratic societies and for facilitating social mobility. However, there are more individualized and fundamental concerns which are perhaps more relevant to reflective teaching. A very clear exposition of such issues is contained in the Universal Declaration of Human Rights (United Nations, 1948). Article 1 of the Declaration states that:

> All human beings are born free and equal in dignity and rights. They are endowed with reason and conscience.

These rights are to be enjoyed, according to Article 2:

> Without distinction of any kind, such as race, colour, sex, language, religion, political or other opinion, national or social origin, property, birth or other status.

There then follow many articles dealing with rights and fundamental freedoms of movement, thought, religion, assembly, political participation, work, leisure, and an adequate standard of living. Article 26 deals with education and asserts that:

Education shall be directed to the full development of the human personality and the strengthening of respect for human rights and fundamental freedoms. It shall promote understanding, tolerance and friendship among all nations, racial and religious groups.

Education was expected to have a crucial role in the dissemination of the UN Declaration across the world, for it was to be 'displayed, read and expanded principally in schools and other educational institutions' in all member states. Needless to say, the achievement of social justice and individual rights for all citizens remains a noble and appropriate goal, but one which will probably always be with us, for it is optimistic to think that educational provision alone can overcome structural inequalities in society. Indeed the necessity of adopting a United Nations Convention on the Rights of the Child in 1989, underlines that fact. The Human Rights Act 1998 is the most significant recent UK legislation. This incorporates the European Convention on Human Rights into British law.

Education policies and systems can thus be designed to emphasize economic production, cultural production or reproduction, social justice or individual rights. Whilst such goals are not necessarily conflicting, various tensions and dilemmas are often posed. One obvious issue concerns the rights of minority groups to maintain an independent culture and sense of identity within a majority culture. Another is the dilemma between the demands of individual development and those of economic production. We have raised these issues in Chapter 4 and argued that a reflective teacher should make informed and responsible judgements about them (see also **Reading 1.5**). The ways in which action might follow will be discussed further below.

We now move on to the second question: 'What can actually be achieved through education?'

There has been a long running debate on this topic. Some people, such as Coleman, Coser and Powell (1966), Jenks *et al.* (1972), and Bowles and Gintis (1976), have argued that education can make little difference to social development. Although coming to the issue from different theoretical perspectives, they argue that educational processes reflect and reproduce major features of existing society, particularly with regard to distinctions related to social class. The suggestion is that relationships of power, wealth, status and ideology are such that education should be seen as a part of the dominant social system, rather than as an autonomous force within it.

Others, such as Berger and Luckman (1967), may be seen as taking a more idealistic theoretical position. They argue that, since our sense of reality is 'socially constructed' by people as they interact together, there is, therefore, scope for individuals to make an independent impact on the course of future social development. For a tangible example, the consequences of the Human Rights' agreements could be considered within schools and classrooms, as suggested by Osler and Starkey (1996, **Reading 13.9**). Thus there *is* potential for education to influence change. What we have here are the competing positions of those who believe in social determinism ranged against those who believe in individual voluntarism. As we have already seen, education is very often expected to bring about social and economic developments and it is an area which tends to attract idealists. However, we also have to recognize that the major structural features of societies are extremely resistant to change. What is needed then is a

theoretical position which recognizes the importance of action and of constraint. Such a position would accept that education has a degree of relative autonomy and would thus legitimate action by individuals to contribute to future social development.

Such a theoretical framework is provided by what we call the dialectic of the individual and society (see Chapter 4 and, in particular, **Reading 4.1**). As Berlak and Berlak (1981, **Reading 1.3**) put it:

> Conscious creative activity is limited by prevailing social arrangements, but human actions and institutional forms are not mere reflections of them.
>
> (1981, p. 121)

The clear implication is that people can make their own impact and history but must do so in whatever circumstances they find themselves. If this theoretical framework is adopted, social developments can be seen as the product of processes of struggle and contest between different individuals and groups in society. Such processes are ones in which education must, inevitably, play a part.

Our answer to the question of what education can actually achieve must thus be based on a guarded and realistic optimism. The dialectical model of the influence of individuals and social structures recognizes constraints but asserts that action remains possible (see Chapter 4 and **Reading 4.1**). This places a considerable responsibility on a reflective teacher whose professional work is both shaped by, and contributes to, society.

2 | CLASSROOM TEACHING AND SOCIETY

As we have seen, one implication of the adoption of a dialectical model of the relationship between individuals and society is that it highlights the possible consequences, for the 'macro' world of society, of actions, experiences and processes which take place in the 'micro' world of the classroom. In Chapter 1, we raised this issue with the assertion that 'reflective teaching implies an active concern with aims and consequences as well as with technical efficiency' and we must pick up the themes again here. One of the most important issues concerns the influence of a reflective teacher's own value commitments.

In Chapter 1, Section 2.1, we argued that reflective teachers should accept democratically determined decisions but should act both as responsible professionals and as autonomous citizens to contribute to such decision-making processes. We also suggested that attitudes of 'open-mindedness' and 'responsibility' are essential attributes. Open-mindedness involves a willingness to consider evidence and argument from whatever source it comes. It is thus the antithesis of closure and of habituated or ideological thinking. For example, we would suggest that there is a link between these attributes and the revisions to the National Curriculum implemented in England in 2000. Curriculum 2000 provides a framework for PSHE and citizenship in Key Stages 1 and 2.

> PSHE and citizenship help to give pupils the knowledge, skills and understanding they need to lead confident, healthy, independent lives and to become informally active, responsible citizens . . . They also find out about the main political and social institutions that affect their lives and about their responsibilities, rights and duties as individuals and members of communities.
>
> (DfEE and QCA, 1999, p. 136)

There is at least a rhetorical sense in which children are encouraged through the formal curriculum to engage with the social processes that underpin society. Through 'Development Education' they may also be introduced to global issues. It is also interesting to note the advent of citizenship as a formal National Curriculum subject in Key Stages 3 and 4 and the issuing of non-statutory guidance for Personal, Social and Health Education and Citizenship in Key Stages 1 and 2 (QCA, 1998). The rationale for this relates to the development of children's responsibilities in a liberal democracy.

There is also a relationship between the inauguration of citizenship within the National Curriculum and the development of Human Rights' legislation. In a recommendation to all member states of the European Union, the Council of Ministers reaffirmed the understandings embodied in the United Nations' Universal Declaration of Human Rights and the European Convention of Human Rights. The Council suggested that study in schools should 'lead to an understanding of, and sympathy for, the concepts of justice, equality, freedom, peace, dignity, rights and democracy,' (Council of Europe, 1985). Hugh Starkie (1987) claims that the United Nations' Declaration is accepted as a worldwide moral standard and that fundamental freedoms are what make effective political democracies possible. Importantly, since 1998, the principles underlying these declarations have been incorporated into the UK's Human Rights Act. These are seen as being fundamental to democratic societies and all schools, including those for young children, are encouraged to introduce them to their pupils and to develop their understanding (Osler and Starkey, 1996, **Reading 13.9**). Additionally, the adoption of the UN Convention on the Rights of the Child (1989) has considerable significance for practice in schools (**Reading 13.9**). Beck (1998) reminds us of the enormous influence of Marshall's 1950 classic, *Citizenship and Social Class* (1992). In particular, Marshall set out a number of freedoms – entitlement to welfare, free education and health – which he saw as the essence of the social element of citizenship. The formal incorporation of citizenship within the National Curriculum demonstrates the importance that is attached to pupils learning how to engage with social and political processes, and it can also be seen as placing responsibilities on teachers to model this within their professional lives.

Yet, the political context of recent years suggests that there are some tensions and contradictions. For instance, in England, at the same time as Curriculum 2000 is explicitly encouraging awareness and active engagement with the political systems which underpin our democratic society, the professional work of teachers continues to be structured centrally, with strong pressures, inspection procedures and sanctions to ensure *compliance*. Unfortunately, successive governments have not treated teachers as active, thinking, value-driven professionals with whom partnerships to develop the educational system should be created. At times indeed, teachers have been cast as the core 'problem' (HMCI, 1995). This point is illustrated by evidence from the Primary Assessment Curriculum and Experience (PACE) project, which explored the impact of the introduction of the National Curriculum. A major conclusion was that changes in curriculum, assessment and pedagogy were mishandled in many ways because of the lack of sincere attempts to work with teachers (Osborn *et al.*, 2000; Pollard *et al.*, 2000, see **Reading 18.5**). Since 1997, Labour governments maintained these attitudes, with the result being that, by 2001, there was considerable professional disengagement, with retirement, recruitment and very serious retention problems.

We can thus see that the relationship between teacher and society in England has dramatically changed since the inception of the National Curriculum. From a position of some public esteem and professional recognition, could the role of the teacher now simply be cast as being to comply with centrally defined frameworks? Perhaps not, but as Simco (2000) argues, there is a danger that acceptance of such compliance could eventually lead to the teaching profession retreating from consideration of aims, values and associated pedagogies. This would be deeply damaging, for engagement with underpinning values remains essential to the moral foundations of teaching as a professional vocation. Nor should we ever forget how policy is actually created, and the influence that remains with teachers. As Bowe and Ball with Gold (1992, **Reading 18.4**) argue, policy is not formed solely through political struggles and through the construction of legislation and official documents. Its operational reality is formed in the 'context of practice' – where it is often re-formulated and 'mediated' through the application of professional judgement (see also Osborn, McNess and Broadfoot, 2000, **Reading 1.4**).

Whilst, Scotland, Northern Ireland and Wales develop in increasingly distinctive ways, perhaps there are also some countervailing developments in England too, such as the new place of Citizenship within Curriculum 2000. There may also be grounds for optimism as the Labour government begins its second term of office with a major commitment to public services. Indeed, the TTA's 2002 standards for initial teacher training have an enhanced (though still limited) place for professional values, and it is important to understand the role which the General Teaching Council for England and other professional associations could have on providing teachers with an independent voice.

The basic truth is that, whatever a government may attempt to determine, there are some endemic issues in education that cannot be avoided. These include questions of individual dignity, equality and freedom, and the influence of sexism, racism and other forms of discrimination based on social class, age, disability or sexual orientation. These are issues upon which, we would argue, children have rights that socially responsible teachers should not compromise. We take this to constitute a 'bottom line', a value commitment to the fundamental rights of citizens in a democratic society and a necessary underpinning for reflective professionality.

3 REFLECTIVE TEACHING AND THE DEMOCRATIC PROCESS

In Chapter 1 we suggested that, in addition to professional responsibilities to implement democratically determined decisions, teachers as citizens also have responsibilities to act to influence the nature of such decisions. Teachers have rights and it is perfectly reasonable that they should be active in contributing to the formation of public policy. In terms of Bowe, Ball and Gold's model (1992, **Reading 18.4**), this is about teacher engagement in the 'context of influence'. The role, as White (1978) suggested, is close to that of the activist and the methods to be utilized are those which have been well developed in recent years by a variety of pressure groups. There are six basic elements of successful pressure group activity:

1. Demystifying the democratic process
2. Identifying decision-makers
3. Preparing the case
4. Forming alliances
5. Managing the media
6. Lobbying decision-makers
7. Following up.

Such techniques have been evident in UK debates about the curriculum in primary schools where lobbying of Members of Parliament has taken place. For instance, members of the National Association for Primary Education were encouraged to write to MPs and the views of the association were made clear to Education Ministers and to the House of Commons Select Committee on Primary Education. The techniques have also been deployed on more general educational issues such as cut-backs in educational expenditure in the 1980s and early 1990s, the growth of the private sector, the abolition of corporal punishment in schools and the introduction of formal assessment for young children. Some national educational pressure groups and phase-based associations have been influential for particular periods. These include CASE (the Campaign for the Advancement of State Education), ECEF (the Early Childhood Education Forum), NCNE (the National Campaign for Nursery Education), NAPE (the National Association for Primary Education), NAME (the National Anti-racist Movement in Education), NaPTEC (the National Primary Teacher Education Conference), NPT (the National Primary Trust), and TACTYC (Training, Advancement and Cooperation in Teaching Young Children). Professional associations such as the NUT, NAS/UWT and ATL are also active, though the most influential in recent years have been the headteacher associations of NAHT and SHA.

The ATL has been active in creating position statements on a wide range of educational issues relating to the teaching profession. One area in which it has taken an interest is the induction of newly qualified teachers (NQTs). Here it has both commissioned research into the experiences of NQTs and published guidelines (Moyles, Suschitzky and Chapman, 1998, **Reading 16.4**). Interestingly, as the title implies, the guide is not only about compliance with a nationally prescribed system, but also encourages NQTs to ask questions about the circumstances of the induction year. One section entitled 'Induction: bridge or barrier?' asks the reader to engage with critical questions such as 'What kind of induction does an NQT need?'

In addition to the education pressure groups and professional associations, there is a third type of research-led educational organization. For example, the Association for the Study of Primary Education (ASPE) is a national body whose main remit is to promote thinking and research about primary education, including the development of alternative perspectives to the status quo and the representation of these. ASPE funds small-scale research, holds an annual national conference and is involved in various regional events. It seeks to have some influence on the development of education policy through its activities. Likewise in recent years the Philosophy of Education Society of Great Britain has published six pamphlets on a range of educational issues, the stated purpose of which is to bring philosophical perspectives to bear on the development of policy in education. One of these pamphlets is focused on Curriculum 2000 (Bramall and White, 2000). In it the authors suggest that Curriculum 2000 is unique in providing a statement of educational aims, purposes and a rationale. However, they also argue that these aims have more radical consequences for the curriculum than is actually delivered. The most significant group is the British Educational Research Association (BERA) to which most active researchers in the UK belong. This organization has considerable resources and is able to set up policy-related initiatives, research reviews, seminars and other events. It convenes a large national conference at the start of each Autumn term, and regularly issues press briefings on its activities. Many

of the associations reviewed above have websites. See **RTweb** for links. The internet also opens up interesting new opportunities for campaigning. For instance, take a look at www.timetoteach.org.uk. This site was established by a former primary headteacher, Sue Palmer, to challenge the imposition of an overprescriptive curriculum in England.

Pressure-group activity and collective action by individuals can thus both bring about new policy priorities and lead to a reappraisal of existing policies. This is an essential feature of democratic decision-making and we would suggest that reflective teachers have both the right and responsibility to contribute to such processes. Reflective Activity 18.1 suggests learning about these processes by studying in depth a single example of political activity and decision-making.

Reflective activity 18.1

Aim: To investigate processes of political activity and decision making with regard to an educational issue.

Evidence and reflection: A necessary basic strategy here is to focus on one issue and to trace the debates in the media and elsewhere. This could helpfully be undertaken with colleagues so that the workload is shared. The issue could be local or national.

Newspapers provide useful sources of easily retrievable information. Some, such as *The Times*, publish an index and this is particularly helpful.

Having gathered a variety of statements about the issue in question, an attempt should be made to classify them so that the competing positions are identified. From this point, it may be possible to gather policy statements directly from the participants, by letter, discussion, interview or library search.

Finally, the decision-point can be studied. Were the public arguments influential? What interests seem to have prevailed when decisions were taken?

Extension: Having studied an example of political influence on decision-making it is worth taking stock of what has been learned. Did you feel that the debate reflected appropriate educational concerns? Could educationalists have made more constructive contributions?

We are conscious, though, that this is a book which is primarily designed to support student-teachers during periods of school-based work and that activities to influence wider policies may seem inappropriate. We include them because such activity is a logical consequence of taking reflective teaching seriously and because some preparation for such activity is perfectly possible before taking up a full-time teaching post. One of the most important aspects of this is to demystify the democratic process itself and we will make various suggestions on this and with regard to the six elements of pressure-group activity which we have identified. These might be followed up by small groups of students or teachers, perhaps by taking an educational issue as a case-study, or indeed, by facing a real current issue.

Demystifying the democratic process

There is a tendency to regard decision-making as something done by 'them' – an ill-defined, distant and amorphous body. In fact, decisions in democracies are taken by elected representatives. The connection between the ordinary citizen and decision-makers can thus be much more close, direct and personal.

Some possible ways forward here include visiting a relevant meeting of your local or regional council, assembly or parliament. For example, council committee meetings are normally open to the public and attendance at an Education Committee meeting is likely to be very interesting to reflective teachers. Alternatively, you could write to or make an appointment with your local elected representative. Discuss their views on educational issues and get them to explain the constraints and pressures within which they serve. Or, even more locally, you could ask to attend a meeting of the governing body of your school. Note who the governors are and enquire about their powers in relation to the affairs of your school. Consider the potential for partnership between teachers and governors.

Identifying decision-makers

Lists of MPs, Assembly Members and Councillors are normally available in local libraries, official offices and on the internet. It is then necessary to identify those who have a particular interest in education and those who have a particular degree of influence over decisions. A list of members of the education committee on a council or of members of the House of Commons with an interest in education will be helpful. The names of school governors will be available in your school.

It is also often appropriate to identify the leaders of political groups and those who speak on education issues. In addition, the chair of the Finance Committee on a local council or Treasury Ministers in the House of Commons are likely to be worth identifying – depending, of course, on the issue under consideration.

A further group to identify is the education officers and civil servants who advise decision-makers and implement many decisions. Chief education officers, for instance, can be extremely influential.

Preparing the case

It is essential to prepare a case well. This requires at least three things:

- appropriate factual information about the issue
- good educational arguments in support of whatever is being advocated
- an understanding of the interests and concerns of those whom it is hoped to influence.

A great deal of factual information can be gathered from the internet by visiting the websites of national, regional or local government agencies. For instance, the DfES website is highly regarded and not only provides much information but normally offers excellent links to other sites in the UK. At the time of writing these include QCA, TTA, OFSTED, DENI, CCEA, ACCAC, SEED, LTScotland, BECTA, etc. However, since these often change, for more continuity, try standard government addresses, such as 'www.wales.gov.uk'. Other sorts of information can be collected through discussion with those people who may be involved locally with the issue under consideration. Sources within your school should be one starting-point. Newspapers also offer a regular source of reports and comment on educational developments and can be monitored for relevant material. If possible, it is worth checking key facts from a number of sources.

To develop coherent educational arguments, the research literature is an important resource (see the suggestions at the end of Chapter 3). Almost all significant educational topics have been researched at some time, and there is much to learn from the experience of others. Of course, one would certainly wish to discuss the issues under consideration with colleagues, and to build a really secure understanding.

Regarding the interests of those whom one wishes to influence, a good place to start is with any published policy statements or manifestos. This could be followed up by discussion and by making judgements regarding the pressures and constraints that they face.

Forming alliances

Representative democracy is designed as a system which links decision-making with the views of a majority. It follows that the most successful type of campaigning is likely to be one which is broadly based – one which is produced by an alliance of interested parties bringing concerted pressure to bear on policy-makers.

Reflective teachers may thus wish to act with others if and when they wish to influence public policy. Obvious places to look for allies are other colleagues, perhaps through professional associations, trade-union links or the General Teaching Council; parents, and the importance of parental support cannot be overestimated; other workers in the public services; local community and interest groups who may be directly or indirectly affected by the issues under consideration; and existing national pressure groups such as those listed earlier in this section.

Managing the media

Important issues here include clarifying, very clearly indeed, your key message; carrying out a review of the types of media which might be interested in educational issues (press, radio, television, etc.); holding discussions with people who have had experience of managing publicity to learn from them; carrying out an analysis of the types of stories or news that each media outlet is likely to be interested in and, crucially, of the ways in which they are likely to handle educational issues; considering the timing constraints that appropriate media outlets face; holding discussions with selected journalists to get first-hand knowledge of their concerns; preparing press releases and considering suitable images for photographic or filming purposes; identifying and supporting a spokesperson for press follow-up.

Lobbying decision-makers

There are any number of possibilities here ranging from discrete lobbying, discussion, letter writing by individuals, through to petitions, media campaigns and demonstrations. However, it is important to remember that not many politicians enjoy being forced to change course, but most are open to persuasion if they have not previously taken up a hard, public position. An interesting English example relates to the introduction of skills tests in literacy and numeracy required for the award of QTS. In the summer of 2001, there was widespread lobbying of senior TTA officials and Government Ministers by individual trainees, their representatives and ITT providers. The issue was concerned with a widespread belief that the skills tests were unfair in that to fail four times led to all other successes in working towards QTS being nullified. QTS could not be awarded. The new Secretary of State for Education, Estelle Morris, bowed to this substantial lobbying and allowed trainees unlimited attempts to pass the tests.

Following up

There is no mystery here. If agreement for changes in policy or practice is reached, it is simply necessary to check that the agreement is enacted. One might, for instance, be alert to the possibility of policies being 'watered down' as attention moves onto new issues.

CONCLUSION

Education is inevitably concerned not just with 'what is' but also with what 'ought to be' (Kogan, 1978) (for example, teachers' struggling to convey an educational vision, see **Reading 18.5**). We hope that this book will help teachers and student-teachers to develop not only the necessary skills of teaching but also the awareness and commitment which will ensure the positive nature of their contribution to the education service in the future.

Key readings

Many of the books suggested as further reading for Chapters 1 and 4 will also be relevant here.

On the structural relationships between education and society, with fascinating comparative and historical dimensions, see:

Archer, M. (1979)
The Social Origins of Educational Systems.
London: Sage.

For a major work offering international comparisons of primary-education systems and their relationships to the culture, economy and political systems of their societies, see:

Alexander, R. (2000)
Culture and Pedagogy: International Comparisons in Primary Education.
Oxford: Blackwell.

The development of recent New Labour education policy in England can be seen quite transparently within:

Barber, M. (1996)
The Learning Game: Arguments for an Education Revolution.
London: Gollancz.

For a penetrating analysis of how education policy is created and has been used to control teachers, see:

Ball, S. J. (1994)
Education Reform: a Critical and Post-Structural Approach.
Buckingham: Open University Press.

Dramatic changes in primary-school practice as a result of changes in public policy, with considerable implications for the present, are recorded in the final outputs from the PACE project in:

Osborn, M., McNess, E. and Broadfoot, P. (2000)
What Teachers Do.
London: Continuum.

Pollard, A. and Triggs, P. (2000)
What Pupils Say.
London: Continuum.

Stenhouse continues to have much to teach us on the role of the teacher in a democracy:

Stenhouse, L. (1983)
Authority, Education and Emancipation.
London: Heinemann.

One more general way of following up many of these issues would be through the use of textbooks in sociology or the sociology of education. The most up-to-date specialist text is:

Meighan, R. and Siraj-Blatchford, I. (1997)
A Sociology of Educating.
London: Cassell.

The United Nations Convention on Children's Rights is an important international statement. For an excellent account of both it and its implications for the UK, see:

Newell, P. (1991)
The UN Convention and Children's Rights in the UK.
London: National Children's Bureau.

For a child-focused account and more general guidance on Human Rights education see:

Alderson, P. (2000)
Young Children's Rights.
London: Jessica Kingsley.

Starkey, H. (1991)
The Challenge of Human Rights Education.
London: Cassell.

Action by reflective teachers within the democratic process calls for some knowledge of political structures and processes. For excellent introductions, see:

Kingdom, J. (1991)
Government and Politics in Britain.
Oxford: Polity Press.

 Readings for Reflective Teaching (the companion volume) also offers other closely associated work on the issues raised in this chapter. This includes work by authors such as:

Margaret Archer, Paulo Freire, Council of Europe, Richard Bowe, Stephen Ball, Ann Gold, Andrew Pollard, Patricia Broadfoot, Paul Croll, Marilyn Osborn and Dorothy Abbott.

 RTweb offers additional professional resources for this chapter. These may include *Notes for Further Reading, Reflective Activities,* useful *Web Links, Extension Texts* and *Download Facilities* for diagrams, figures, checklists, activities.

BIBLIOGRAPHY

AAIA (Association for Advisers and Inspectors of Assessment) (1998) *Fundamental Principles for Assessment, Recording and Reporting*. London: AAIA.

ACCAC (Curriculum and Assessment Authority for Wales) (1996) *Desirable Outcomes for Children's Learning before Compulsory School Age*. Cardiff: ACCAC.

ACCAC (2000) *Making Effective Use of Assessment Information Recording at Key Stages 1–3*. Cardiff: ACCAC.

Acker, S. (1989) *Teachers, Gender and Careers*. London: Falmer.

Adams, F. (1999) 5–14: Origins, development and implementation, in Bryce, T. G. K. and Humes, W. M. (eds) *Scottish Education*. Edinburgh: Edinburgh University Press.

Adey, P. and Shayer, M. (1994) *Really Raising Standards: Cognitive Intervention and Academic Achievement*. London: Routledge.

Adler, A. (1927) *The Practice and Theory of Individual Psychology*. New York: Harcourt.

Ager, R. (2000) *The Art of Information and Communications Technology for Teachers*. London: Fulton.

Aldcroft, D. H. (1992) *Education, Training and Economic Performance, 1994–1990*. Manchester: Manchester University Press.

Alderson, P. (2000) *Young Children's Rights*. London: Jessica Kingsley.

Alexander, R. J. (1984) *Primary Teaching*. London: Holt, Rinehart and Winston.

Alexander, R. J. (1997) *Policy and Practice in Primary Education: Local Initiative, National Agenda*. London: Routledge.

Alexander, R. J. (2000) *Culture and Pedagogy: International Comparisons in Primary Education*. Oxford: Blackwell.

Alexander, R. J., Rose, J. and Woodhead, C. (1992) *Curriculum Organisation and Classroom Practice in Primary Schools: a Discussion Paper*. London: Department of Education and Science.

Alexander R. J., Wilcocks, J., Kinder, K. and Nelson, N. (1995) *Versions of Primary Education*. London: Routledge.

Alibhai-Brown, Y. (2000) *Who Do We Think We Are? Imagining the New Britain*. London: Allen Lane.

Alladina, S. and Edwards, V. (eds) (1991) *Multilingualism in the British Isles*. London: Longman.

Altback, P. G. and Kelly, G. P. (eds) (1986) *New Approaches to Comparative Education*. Chicago: University of Chicago Press.

Althusser, L. (1971) Ideology and the ideological state apparatus, in Cosin, B. R. (ed.) *Education, Structure and Society*. Harmondsworth: Penguin.

Anderson, B. (1991) *Imagined Communities: Reflections on the Origin and Spread of Nationalism*. London: Verso.

Anderson, H. and Urquhart, I. (2000) *A Timely Change? Hourwatch: Case Studies of Teachers' Experiences of the Literacy Hour*. Royston: UKRA.

Anning, A. (1983) The three year itch. *Times Educational Supplement*, 24 June.

Anning, A. (1991) *The First Years at School, Education 4 to 8*. Buckingham: Open University Press.

Anning, A. (ed.) (1995) *A National Curriculum for the Early Years*. Buckingham: Open University Press.

Apple, M. (1982) *Cultural and Economic Reproduction in Education*. London: Routledge and Kegan Paul.

Appleton, K. (1995) 'Student teachers' confidence to teach science: is more scientific knowledge necessary to improve self-confidence?' *International Journal of Science Education*, **17**(3), 367–9.

Archer, M. (1979) *The Social Origins of Educational Systems*. London: Sage Publications.

Aries, P. (1962) *Centuries of Childhood*. Harmondsworth: Penguin.

Armstrong, M. (1980) *Closely Observed Children: the Diary of a Primary Classroom*. London: Writers and Readers.

Armstrong, M. (1989) 'Another way of looking'. *Forum*, **33**(1), 181–8.

Arnold, M. (1889) *Reports on Elementary Schools 1852–1882*. London: Macmillan.

Arnot, M. and Barton, L. (eds) (1992) *Voicing Concerns: Sociological Perspectives on Contemporary Education Reforms*. Wallingford: Triangle.

Arnot, M. and Weiler, K. (1993) *Feminism and Social Justice for Education*. London: Falmer.

Ashcroft, K. and Palacio, D. (1995) *The Primary Teacher's Guide to the New National Curriculum*. London: Falmer.

Assessment Reform Group (1999) *Beyond the Black Box*. Cambridge: Cambridge University School of Education.

Association for Science Education (1994) *Safety in Science for Primary School*. Hatfield: ASE.

Atkinson, E. (2001) The National Literacy Strategy as cultural performance: some reflections on the meaning(s) of literacy in English primary classrooms. Paper presented at the BERA conference. September.

Atkinson, T. and Claxton, G. (eds) (2000) *The Intuitive Practitioner: on the Value of Not Always Knowing What One is Doing*. Buckingham: Open University Press.

Avon County Council (1993) *Collaborative Learning in Primary Schools*. Bristol: Avon County Council.

Baker, C. R. and Jones, S. P. (1998) *Encyclopedia of Bilingualism and Bilingual Education*. Clevedon: Multilingual Matters.

Ball, S. (1981a) *Beachside Comprehensive*. Cambridge: Cambridge University Press.

Ball, S. (1981b) Initial encounters in the classroom and the process of establishment, in Woods, P. F. (ed.) *Pupil Strategies*. London: Croom Helm.

Ball, S. (1987) *Micropolitics of the School: Towards a Theory of School Organisation*. London: Routledge.

Ball, S. (1990) *Politics and Policy Making in Education: Explorations in Policy Sociology*. London: Routledge.

Ball, S. (1994) *Education Reform: a Critical and Post-Structural Approach*. Buckingham: Open University Press.

Balshaw, M. H. (1999) *Help in the Classroom*. London: Fulton.

Banks, F., Leach, J. and Moon, B. (1999) New understandings of teachers' pedagogic knowledge, in Leach, J. and Banks, F. (eds) *Learners and Pedagogy*. London: Paul Chapman.

Barber, M. (1996) *The Learning Game: Arguments for an Education Revolution*. London: Gollancz.

Barber, M. (2000) 'The very big picture', *Improving Schools,* **3**(2), 5–17.

Barber, M. (2001) 'A new context for accountability and inspection.' *Education Review*, **14**(2), 4–8.

Barker-Lunn, J. C. (1970) *Streaming in the Primary School*. Slough: NFER.

Barnes, B. (1977) *Interests and the Growth of Knowledge*. London: Routledge and Kegan Paul.

Barnes, D. (1975) *From Communication to Curriculum*. London: Penguin Books.

Barnes, D., Britton, J. and Rosen, H. (1986) *Language, the Learner and the School* (3rd edition) (1st edition 1969). Harmondsworth: Penguin.

Barnes, R. (1999) *Positive Teaching, Positive Learning*. London: Routledge.

Barrow, R. (1984) *Giving Teaching Back to Teachers*. Brighton: Wheatsheaf.

Barrow, R. and Woods, R. (1988) *An Introduction to Philosophy of Education*. London: Routledge.

Bassey, M. (1995) *Creating Education through Research*. Newark: Kirtlington Moor Press and BERA.

Bassey, M. (1998) *Use of Language Across the Primary Curriculum* London: Routledge.

Bassey, M. (1999) *Case Study Research in Educational Settings*. Buckingham: Open University Press.

Bearne, E. (ed.) (1996) *Differentiation and Diversity in the Primary School*. London: Routledge.

Bearne, E. (ed.) (1998) *Use of Language Across the Primary Curriculum*. London: Routledge.

Beck, J. (1998) *Morality and Citizenship in Education*. London: Cassell.

Beck, J. and Earl, M. (eds) (2000) *Key Issues in Secondary Education*. London: Cassell.

Beck, T. A. (1998) 'Are there any questions? One teacher's view of students and their questions in a fourth grade classroom', *Teaching and Teacher Education*, **14**(8), 871–86.

Bell, J. (1987) *Doing Your Research Project: a Guide for First-Time Researchers in Education and Social Science*. Buckingham: Open University Press.

Bell, J. (ed.) (1995) *Teachers Talk about Teaching*. Buckingham: Open University Press.

Bennett, K. and Kastor, T. (1988) *Analysing Children's Language*. Oxford: Blackwell.

Bennett, N. (1979) Recent research on teaching: a dream, a belief and a model, in Bennett, N. and MacNamara, D. (eds) *Focus on Teaching*. London: Longman.

Bennett, N. (1994) *Class Size in Primary Schools: Perceptions of Headteachers, Chairs of Governors, Teachers and Parents*. Birmingham: NAS/UWT.

Bennett, N., Desforges, C., Cockburn, A. and Wilkinson, B. (1984) *The Quality of Pupil Learning Experiences*. London: Lawrence Erlbaum.

Bennett, N. and Dunne, E. (1992) *Managing Classroom Groups*. Hemel Hempstead: Simon and Schuster.

BERA (2001) 'Report on Methodological Seminar on Hay McBer Enquiry into Teacher Effectiveness', *Research Intelligence*, July.

Berger, P. L. (1963) *Invitation to Sociology: a Humanistic Perspective*. New York: Doubleday.

Berger, P. L. and Luckman, T. (1967) *The Social Construction of Reality*. New York: Doubleday.

Berlak, A. and Berlak, H. (1981) *Dilemmas of Schooling*. London: Methuen.

Bernstein, B. (1970) 'Education cannot compensate for society', *New Society*, 387, 344–7.

Bernstein, B. (1971) On the classification and framing of educational knowledge, in Young, M. F. D. (ed.) *Knowledge and Control*. London: Collier-Macmillan.

Bernstein, B. (1975) *Class, Codes and Control: Towards a Theory of Educational Transmission*. London: Routledge and Kegan Paul.

Bernstein, B. (1996) *Pedagogy, Symbolic Control and Identity: Theory, Research, Critique*. London: Taylor and Francis.

Biggs, A. P. and Edwards, V. (1994) I treat them all the same: Teacher–pupil talk in multiethnic classrooms, in Graddol, D., Maybin, J. and Stierer, B. (eds) *Researching Language and Literacy in the Social Context*. Clevedon: Multilingual Matters.

Biott, C. and Nias, J. (1992) *Working and Learning Together for Change*. Buckingham: Open University Press.

Black, P. (1998) *Testing Friend or Foe? Theory and Practice of Assessment and Testing*. London: Falmer.

Black, P. and Wiliam, D. (1998a) 'Assessment and classroom learning', *Assessment in Education*, 5(1), 7–74.

Black, P. and Wiliam, D. (1998b) *Inside the Black Box: Raising Standards through Classroom Assessment*. London: King's College.

Blackledge, A. (ed.) (1994) *Teaching Bilingual Children*. Stoke-on-Trent: Trentham.

Blair, M., Holland, J. and Sheldon, S. (eds) (1995) *Identity and Diversity: Gender and the Experience of Education*. Clevedon: Multilingual Matters.

Blakemore, C. (2000) It Makes You Think. *Independent on Sunday*. London.

Blatchford, P. (1989) *Playtime in the Primary School: Problems and Improvements*. London: Routledge.

Blaxter, L., Hughes, C. and Tight, M. (1996) *How to Research*. Buckingham: Open University Press.

Bleach, K. (2001) *Inducting New Teachers*. Stoke-on-Trent: Trentham.

Blenkin, G. M. and Kelly, A. V. (1981) *The Primary Curriculum*. London: Harper and Row.

Blishen, E. (1969) *The School that I'd Like*. Harmondsworth: Penguin.

Blyth, A. (1984) *Development, Experience and Curriculum in Primary Education*. London: Croom Helm.

Bolster, A. (1983) 'Towards a more effective model of research on teaching', *Harvard Educational Review*, 53(3), 294–308.

Bonnett, M. (1993) *Thinking and Understanding in the Primary School Curriculum*. London: Cassell.

Bonnett, M., McFarlane, A. and Williams, J. (1999) 'ICT in subject teaching: an opportunity for curriculum renewal, *The Currriculum Journal*, 10(3), 345–59.

Bossert, S. T. (1979) *Tasks and Social Relationships in Classrooms*. Cambridge: Cambridge University Press.

Bourdieu, P. and Passeron, J. C. (1977) *Reproduction in Education, Society and Culture*. London: Sage.

Bowe, R., Ball, S. and Gold, A. (1992) *Reforming Education and Changing Schools*. London: Routledge.

Bowles, S. and Gintis, H. (1976) *Schooling in Capitalist America*. London: Routledge.

Boyd, C. and Loyd, P. (1995) The school context for curriculum change, in Ashcroft, K. and Palacio, D. (eds) *The Primary Teacher's Guide to the New National Curriculum*. London: Falmer.

Bramall, S. and White, J. (2000) *Will the New National Curriculum Live Up to its Aims?* Ringwood: Philosophy of Education Society of Great Britain.

Bransford, J. D., Brown, A. I. and Cocking, R. R. (1999) *How People Learn: Brain, Mind, Experience and School*. Washington, DC: National Research Council.

Breakwell, G. (1986) *Coping with Threatened Identities*. London: Methuen.

Bridges, D. and McLaughlin, T. (eds) (1994) *Education and the Market Place*. London: Falmer.

Brighouse, T. and Woods, D. (1999) *How to Improve Your School*. London: Routledge.

Broadfoot, P., Abbott, D., Croll, P., Osborn, M., Pollard, A. and Towler, L. (1991) 'Implementing National Assessment: issues for primary teachers', *Cambridge Journal of Education*, 21(2), 153–68.

Bronfenbrenner, U. (1979) *The Ecology of Human Development: Experiments by Nature and Design*. Cambridge, MA.: Harvard University Press.

Brophy, J. E. and Good, T. L. (1974) *Teacher–Student Relationships*. New York: Cassell.

Brown, G. and Edmundson, R. (1984) Asking questions, in Wragg, E. C. (ed.) *Classroom Teaching Skills*. London: Croom Helm.

Brown, G. and Wragg, T. (1993) *Questioning*. London: Routledge.

Brown, M. (1989) 'Graded assessment and learning hierarchies: an alternative view', *British Educational Research Journal*, 15(2), 121–8.

Brown, M. E. and Precious, G. N. (1968) *The Integrated Day in the Primary School*. London: Ward Lock Educational.

Brown, M., Taggart, B., McCullum, B. and Gipps, C. (1996) 'The impact of Key Stage 2 tests', *Education 3–13*, 24(3), 3–7.

Brown, S. and McIntyre (1992) *Making Sense of Teaching*. Buckingham: Open University Press.

Bruner, J. S. (1972) 'The nature and uses of immaturity', *American Psychologist*, 27, 1–28.

Bruner, J. S. (1977) *The Process of Instruction*. Cambridge, MA: Harvard University Press.

Bruner, J. S. (1986) *Actual Minds, Possible Worlds*. Cambridge, MA: Harvard University Press.

Bruner, J. S. (1990) *Acts of Meaning*. Cambridge, MA: Harvard University Press.

Bubb, S. (2000) *The Effective Induction of Newly Qualified Primary Teachers*. London: David Fulton.

Bubb, S. (2001) *A Newly Qualified Teacher's Manual*. London: David Fulton.

Buckingham, D. (2000) *After the Death of Childhood: Growing up in the Age of Electronic Media*. Cambridge: Polity.

Burgess, R. G. (1984) *In the Field: an Introduction to Field Research*. London: Batsford.

Burrell, A. and Bubb, S. (2000) 'Teacher feedback in the reception class: associations with pupils' positive adjustments to school', *Education 3–13*, 28(3), 58–64.

Butler, K. A. (1998) *Learning and Teaching Style: In Theory and Practice*. Columbia: Learner's Dimension.

Byrne, T. (1992) *Local Government in Britain*. London: Penguin.

CACE (Central Advisory Council on Education) (1967) *Children and their Primary Schools* (Plowden Report). London: HMSO.

Cairns, J., Gardner, R. and Lawton, D. (eds) (2000) *Values and the Curriculum*. London: Woburn.

Calderhead, J. (1988a) 'Learning from introductory school experience', *Journal of Education for Teaching*, 4(1), 75–83.

Calderhead, J. (1988b) *Teachers' Professional Learning*. London: Falmer.

Calderhead, J. (1991) The nature and growth of knowledge in student teaching. *Teaching and Teacher Education*, 7(5/6), pp. 531–5.

Calderhead, J. and Shorrock, S. B. (1997) *Understanding Teacher Education*. London: Falmer.

Callaghan, J. (1976) 'Towards a national debate', *Education*, 148(17), 332–3.

Cameron, C., Moss, P. and Owen, C. (1999) *Men in the Nursery: Gender and Caring Work*. London: Paul Chapman.

Campbell, A. and Kane, I. (1998) *School-based Teacher Education: Tales from a Fictional Primary School*. London: David Fulton.

Campbell, J. (1996) Professionalism in the Primary School. ASPE conference paper, London: ASPE.

Campbell, J. and Neill, S. R. St J. (1992) *Teacher Time and Curriculum Manageability at Key Stage 1*. London: AMMA.

Carr, W. and Hartnett, A. (1996) *Education and the Struggle for Democracy: the Politics of Educational Ideas*. Buckingham: Open University Press.

Carr, W. and Kemmis, S. (1986) *Becoming Critical: Knowing Through Action Research*. London: Falmer.

Carroll, C. and Simco, N. (2001) *Succeeding as an Induction Tutor*. Exeter: Learning Matters.

Carter, R. E. (1990) *Knowledge About Language and the National Curriculum*. London: Hodder and Stoughton.

Cattell, R. B. and Kline, P. (1977) *The Scientific Analysis of Personality and Motivation*. London: Academic Press.

Cazden, C. B. (1988) *Classroom Discourse: the Language of Teaching and Learning*. Portsmouth: Heinemann.

CCEA (1999) *Developing the Northern Ireland Curriculum to Meet the Needs of Young People, Society and the Economy in the Twenty-first Century*. Belfast: Northern Ireland Council for the Curriculum, Examinations and Assessment.

CCEA (2000) *Proposals for Changes in the Northern Ireland Curriculum Framework*. Belfast: Northern Ireland Council for the Curriculum, Examinations and Assessment.

CCW (Curriculum Council for Wales) (1991) *The Whole Curriculum in Wales*. Cardiff: CCW.

Central Statistical Office (1995) *Population Trends 80*. London: HMSO.

Christensen, P. and James, A. (eds) (2000) *Research with Children: Perspectives and Practices*. London: Falmer Press.

Chubb, T. E. and Moe, T. M. (1990) *Politics, Markets, and America's Schools*. Washington, DC: Brookings.

Clandinin, D. J. (1986) *Classroom Practice: Teacher Images in Action*. London: Falmer Press.

Clarke, S. (1998) *Targeting Assessment in the Primary Classroom*. London: Hodder and Stoughton.

Clarke, S. (2001) *Unlocking Formative Assessment: Practical Strategies for Enhancing Pupils' Learning in the Primary Classroom*. London: Hodder and Stoughton.

Clarricoates, K. (1978) 'Dinosaurs in the classroom – a re-examination of some aspects of the 'hidden' curriculum in primary schools', *Women's Studies International Quarterly*, **1**, 353–64.

Clarricoates, K. (1981) 'The experience of patriarchal schooling', *Interchange*, **12**(2/3), 185–205.

Clarricoates, K. (1987) Child culture at school: a clash between gendered worlds?, in Pollard, A. (ed.) *Children and Their Primary Schools*. London: Falmer.

Claxton, G. (1999) *Wise Up: the Challenge of Lifelong Learning*. London: Bloomsbury.

Clegg, D. and Billington, S. (1994) *The Effective Primary Classroom: Management and Organisation of Teaching and Learning*. London: David Fulton.

Clipson-Boyles, S. (2000) *Putting Research into Practice in Primary Teaching and Learning*. London: David Fulton.

Coffey, A. (2001) *Education and Social Change*. Buckingham: Open University Press.

Cohen, S. (1972) *Folk Devils and Moral Panics*. Oxford: Martin Robinson.

Cole, M. and Walker, S. E. (1989) *Teaching and Stress*. Buckingham: Open University Press.

Coleman, J. S. (1988) 'Social capital in the creation of human capital', *American Journal of Sociology*, **94** (Supplement), 595–120.

Coleman, J. S., Coser, L. A. and Powell, W. W. (1966) *Equality of Educational Opportunity*. Washington, DC: US Government Printing Office.

Collins, J. (1996) *The Quiet Child*. London: Cassell.

Collins, R. (1977) 'Some comparative principles of educational stratification', *Higher Education Review*, **47**(1), 1–27.

Connecticut State Department of Education (2000) *Support Teacher Handbook: BEST Program*. Hartford: Connecticut State Department of Education.

Connell, R. W., Ashden, D. J., Kessler, S. and Dowsett, G. W. (1982) *Making the Difference: Schools, Families and Social Division*. Sidney: Allen and Unwin.

Connelly, P. (1998) *Racism, Gender and Identities of Young Children: Social Relations in a Multi-Ethnic, Inner-City Primary School*. London: Routledge.

Conner, C. (ed.) (1999) *Assessment in Action in the Primary School*. London: Falmer.

Cook, D. and Finlayson, H. (1999) *Interactive Children, Communicative Teaching: ICT and Classroom Teaching*. Buckingham: Open University Press.

Cooper, H. and Hyland, R. (eds) (2000) *Children's Perceptions of Learning with Trainee Teachers.* London: Routledge.

Cooper, H., Simco, N., Hegarty, P. and Hegarty, P. (1996) *Display in the Classroom: Principles, Practice and Theory.* London: David Fulton.

Corbett, H. D. and Wilson, B. L. (1991) Unintended and unwelcome: the local impact of state testing, in Niblett, G. W. and Fink, W. T. A. (eds) *Testing, Reform and Rebellion.* New York: Ablex Publishing Corporation.

Cordon, R. (1999) 'Shameful neglect: speaking, listening and literacy', *Forum*, 41(3), 104–6.

Cordon, R. (2000) *Literacy and Learning through Talk: Strategies for the Primary Classroom.* Buckingham: Open University Press.

Corsaro, W. (1997) *The Sociology of Childhood.* Thousand Oaks, CA: Pine Forge Press.

Cortazzi, M. (1990) *Primary Teaching How it is: a Narrative Account.* London: David Fulton.

Council of Europe (1985) *Teaching and Learning about Human Rights in Schools, Recommendation No. R (85) 7 of the Committee of Ministers.* Strasbourg: Council of Europe.

Cox, C. B. and Boyson, R. (eds) (1975) *Black Paper 1975.* London: Dent.

Cox, C. B. and Dyson, A. E. (eds) (1969) *Fight for Education, A Black Paper.* London: Critical Quarterly Society.

Cranfield, J. and Wells, H. (1976) *100 Ways to Enhance Self-concept in the Classroom*, Englewood Cliffs, NJ: Prentice-Hall.

Croll, P. (1986) *Systematic Classroom Observation.* London: Falmer.

Croll, P. (1996) *Teachers, Pupils and Primary Schooling: Continuity and Change.* London: Cassell.

Croll, P. and Moses, D. (1985) *One in Five: the Assessment and Incidence of Special Educational Needs* London: Routledge and Kegan Paul.

Croll, P. and Moses, D. (2000) *Special Needs in the Primary School.* London: Cassell.

Cullingford, C. (1985) Expectations of parents, teachers, children, in Cullingford, C. (ed.) *Parents, Teachers and Schools.* London: Robert Royce Ltd.

Cunningham, P. (1988) *Curriculum Change in the Primary School Since 1945: Dissemination of the Progressive Ideal.* London: Falmer.

Curriculum Council for Wales (1991) *The Whole Curriculum in Wales.* Cardiff: CCW.

Dadds, M. (1995) *Passionate Enquiry and School Development: a Story about Teacher Action Research.* London: Falmer.

Dadds, M. (1999) 'Teachers' values and the Literacy Hour', *Cambridge Journal of Education*, 29(1), 7–19.

Dadds, M. (2001) 'The politics of pedagogy', *Teachers and Teaching: Theory and Practice*, 7(1), 43–58.

Dale, R. (1977) Implications of the rediscovery of the hidden curriculum, in Gleedson, D. (ed.) *Identity and Structure.* Driffield: Nafferton.

Dale, R. (1996) Mechanisms of differentiation between schools: The four 'M's'. *Readings for Reflective Teaching in the Primary School.* London: Cassell.

Davies, B. (1982) *Life in the Classroom and Playground.* London: Routledge and Kegan Paul.

Davies, B. (1993) *Shards of Glass: Children Reading and Writing Beyond Gendered Identities.* Sydney: Allen and Unwin.

Davies, L. (1983) Gender, resistance and power, in Walker, S. and Barton, L. (eds) *Gender, Class and Education.* Lewes: Falmer.

Davies, M. and Edwards, G. (2001) Will the curriculum caterpillar ever learn to fly?, in Collins, J., Insley, K. and Soler, J. (eds) *Developing Pedagogy.* London: Paul Chapman.

Dawkins, R. (1978) *The Selfish Gene.* London: Granada.

Dean, J. (1991) *Organizing Learning in the Primary School Classroom.* London: Routledge.

Dearden, R. F. (1968) *The Philosophy of the Primary Education.* London: Routledge and Kegan Paul.

Dearing, R. (1993) *The National Curriculum and its Assessment: Final Report.* London: School Curriculum and Assessment Authority.

Decker, S., Kirby, S., Greenwood, A. and Moore, D. (1999) *Taking Children Seriously.* London: Continuum.

Delamont, S. (1990) *Interaction in the Classroom.* London: Routledge.

Delanty, G. (1987) *Social Science: Beyond Constructivism and Realism.* Buckingham: Open University Press.

De Lyon, H. and Migniuolo, F. (1989) *Women Teachers, Issues and Experiences.* Buckingham: Open University Press.

DENI (Department of Education for Northern Ireland) (1999) *The Teacher Education Partnership Handbook.* Belfast: DENI.

Denscombe, M. (1998) *The Good Research Guide for Small-scale Social Research Projects.* Buckingham: Open University Press.

DES (Department of Education and Science) (1978) *Primary Education In England: a Survey by HMI.* London: HMSO.

DES (1978) *Report of the Committee of Enquiry into the Education of Handicapped Children and Young People* (The Warnock Report). London: HMSO.

DES (1980) *A View of the Curriculum.* London: HMSO.

DES (1981) *Curriculum 11 to 16: a Review of Progress.* London: HMSO.

DES (1981a) *West Indian Children in Our Schools* (The Rampton Report). London: HMSO.

DES (1985) *Better Schools, a Summary.* London: HMSO.

DES (1985a) *The Curriculum from 5 to 16. Curriculum Matters 2, an HMI Series.* London: HMSO.

DES (1985b) *Education for All: Report of the Committee of Enquiry on the Education of Children from Ethnic Minority Groups* (The Swann Report). London: HMSO.

DES (1989) *Discipline in Schools, Report of the Committee of Enquiry, chaired by Lord Elton.* London: HMSO.

DES (1990–1) *Language in the National Curriculum (LINK) Materials for Professional Development.* London: HMSO.

Desforges, C. and Cockburn, A. (1987) *Understanding the Mathematics Teacher.* Lewes: Falmer.

Dewey, J. (1916) *Democracy and Education.* New York: Free Press.

Dewey, J. (1933) *How We Think: a Restatement of the Relation of Reflective Thinking to the Educative Process.* Chicago: Henry Regnery.

DfEE (Department for Education and Employment) (1997) *Excellence in Schools*. London: HMSO.

DfEE (1998) *The Learning Age: a Renaissance for a New Britain*. London: DfEE.

DfEE (1998a) *Teachers: Meeting the Challenge of Change*. London: DfEE.

DfEE (1998b) *The National Literacy Strategy: Framework for Teaching*. London: HMSO.

DfEE (1998c) *Teaching: High Status, High Standards. Requirements for Courses in Initial Teacher Training*. London: DfEE.

DfEE (1998d) *Requirement for Courses of Initial Teacher Training*. (Circular 4/98). London: TTA.

DfEE (1999) *The National Numercy Strategy: Framework for Teaching Mathematics from Reception to Year 6*. London: HMSO.

DfEE (2000) *Professional Development: Support for Teaching and Learning*. London: DFEE.

DfEE (2000a) *The Induction Period for Newly Qualified Teachers*. (Circular 0090/2000). London: DfEE.

DfEE (2000b) *Performance Management for Schools*. London: DfEE.

DfEE (2001) *Key Stage 3 National Strategy: Literacy across the Curriculum*. London: HMSO.

DfEE (2001a) *Continuing Professional Development*. Nottingham: DfEE.

DfEE (2001b) *Learning and Teaching: a Strategy for Professional Development*. London: DfEE.

DfEE (2001c) *Schools Building on Success: Raising Standards, Promoting Diversity, Achieving Results*. London: DfEE.

DfES (Department for Education and Skills) (2001) *Special Educational Needs: Code of Practice*. London: DfES.

DfES (2001b) *Code of Practice on the Identification and Assessment of Special Education Needs* London: DfES.

Dickson, W. P. (ed.) (1981) *Children's Oral Communication Skills*. New York: Academic Press.

Dillon, J. (1983) 'Problem solving and findings', *Journal of Creative Behaviour*, 16(2), 97–111.

Dillon, J. T. (1988) *Questioning and Teaching: a Manual of Practice*. New York: Teachers' College Press.

Donaldson, M. (1978) *Children's Minds*. London: Fontana.

Dowling, M. (1992) *Education 3–5*. London: Paul Chapman.

Dowling, M. (1999) *Neurons and Networks: an Introduction to Behavioural Neuroscience*. Cambridge, MA: Harvard University Press.

Doyle, W. (1977) 'Learning the classroom environment: an ecological analysis', *Journal of Teacher Education*, 28(6), 51–4.

Doyle, W. (1986) Classroom organisation and management, in Wittrock, M. (ed.) *Third Handbook of Research on Teaching*. New York: Macmillan.

Dreeben, R. (1968) *On What is Learned in School*. Cambridge, MA: Harvard University Press.

Drummond, M. J. (1993) *Assessing Children's Learning*. London: Cassell.

Dunham, J. (1992) *Stress in Teaching*. London: Routledge.

Dunn, J. (1988) *The Beginnings of Social Understanding*. Oxford: Blackwell.

Dweck, C. (1986) 'Motivational processes affecting learning', *American Psychology*, **41**, 1040–8.

Dweck, C. (1999) *Self-Theories: Their Role in Motivation, Personality and Development*. Philadelphia: Psychology Press.

Easen, P. (1985) *Making School-centred INSET Work*. London: Croom Helm.

Edwards, A. and Collison, J. (1996) *Mentoring and Developing Practice in Primary Schools: Supporting Student–Teacher Learning in Schools*. Buckingham: Open University Press.

Edwards, A. D. and Westgate, D. P. G. (1994) *Investigating Classroom Talk*. London: Falmer.

Edwards, D. and Mercer, N. (1987) *Common Knowledge: the Development of Understanding in Classrooms*. London: Methuen.

Edwards, R. and Alldred, P. (2000) 'Children's understanding of home-school relations', *Education 3–13*, **28**(3), 41–5.

Edwards, S. (1999) *Speaking and Listening for All*. London: David Fulton.

Edwards, V. (1998) *The Power of Babel: Teaching and Learning in Multilingual Classrooms*. Stoke-on-Trent: Trentham.

Edwards V. and Redfern A. (1988) *Parental Participation in Primary Education*. London: Routledge.

Egan, K. (1988) *An Alternative Approach to Teaching and the Curriculum: Teaching as Storytelling*. London: Routledge.

Egan, K. (1992) *Imagination in Teaching and Learning: Ages 8–15*. London: Routledge.

Egan, M. and Bunting, B. (1991) 'The effects of coaching on eleven-plus scores', *British Journal of Educational Psychology*, **61**(1), 85–91.

Eisenhart, M., Behm, L. and Riomagnano, L. (1991) 'Learning to teach: developing expertise of rite of passage', *Journal of Education for Teaching*, 7(1), 51–71.

Eisner, E. W. (1979) *The Educational Imagination*. New York: Macmillan.

Eisner, E. W. and Vallance, E. (eds) (1974) *Competing Conceptions of the Curriculum*. Berkeley: McCutchan.

Elbaz, F. (1983) *Teacher Thinking: a Study of Practical Knowledge*. London: Croom Helm.

Elliott, J. (1991) *Action Research for Educational Change*. Buckingham: Open University Press.

Elliott, J. and Adelman, C. (1973) 'Reflecting where the action is; the design of the Ford Teaching Project', *Education for Teaching*, 9(2).

Elliott, M. (1992) *Bullying: a Practical Guide to Coping for Schools*. London: Longman.

Epstein, D. (1993) *Changing Classroom Cultures: Anti-Racism, Politics and Schools*. Stoke-on-Trent: Trentham Books.

Eraut, M. (1994) *Developing Professional Knowledge and Competence*. London: Falmer.

Ernest, P. (1991) *The Philosophy of Mathematics Education*. London: Falmer.

Evans, L. (1998) *Teacher Morale, Job Satisfaction and Motivation*. London: Paul Chapman.

Evans, N. (1978) *Beginning Teaching in Professional Partnership*. London: Cassell.

Evetts, J. (1990) *Women in Primary Teaching: Career, Contexts and Strategy*. London: Routledge.

Eysenck, H. J. and Cookson, C. D. (1969) 'Personality in primary school children: ability and achievement', *British Journal of Educational Psychology*, **39**(2), 109–22.

Feuerstein, R., Hoffman, M. and Miller, R. (1980) *Instrumental Enrichment: an Intervention for Cognitive Modifiability*. Baltimore, MD.: University Park Press.

Fielding, M. (ed.) (2001) *Taking Education Really Seriously: Four Years of Hard Labour*. London: RoutledgeFalmer.

Filer, A. (ed.) (2000) *Assessment: Social Process and Social Product*. London: Falmer.

Filer, A. and Pollard, A. (2000) *The Social World of Pupil Assessment: Processes and Contexts of Primary Schooling*. London: Continuum.

Fisher, R. (1990) *Teaching Children to Think*. Oxford: Blackwell.

Fisher, R. (1998) *Teaching Thinking*. London: Continuum.

Flanders, N. (1970) *Analysing Teaching Behaviour*. Reading, MA: Addison-Wesley.

Flavell, J. H. (1970) Developmental studies of mediated memory, in Reese, H. W. and Lipsett, L. P. (eds) *Advances in Child Development and Behaviour*. New York: Academic Press.

Flavell, J. H. (1979) 'Metacognition and cognitive monitoring', *American Psychologist*, **34**(10), 906–11.

Foucault, M. (1977) *Discipline and Punish: the Birth of the Prison*. London: Peregrine Books.

Fox, G. (1998) *A Handbook for Learning Support Assistants: Teachers and Assistants Working Together*. London: Fulton.

Francis, B. (1998) *Power Plays: Primary School Children's Constructions of Gender, Power and Adult Work*. Stoke-on-Trent: Trentham.

Fraser, B. J. (1986) *Classroom Environment*. London: Croom Helm.

Fraser, B. J. and Fisher, D. L. (1984) *Assessment of Classroom Psychosocial Environment: Workshop Manual*. Bentley: Western Australia Institute of Technology.

Frater, G. (1999) 'National initiatives for literacy: two cheers', *Education 3–13*, **27**(1), 3–11.

Freire, P. (1999) *Pedagogy of the Oppressed*. London: Continuum.

Frijda, N. H. (2001) The laws of emotion, in Parrott, G. W. (ed.) *Emotions in Social Psychology*. Hove: Psychology Press.

Frost, D. (1997) *Reflective Action Planning for Teachers: a Guide to Teacher-Led School and Professional Development*. London: David Fulton.

Frost, D., Durrant, J., Head, M. and Holden, G. (2000) *Teacher-Led School Improvement*. London: RoutledgeFalmer.

Fullan, M. (1991) *The New Meaning of Educational Change*. London: Cassell.

Fullan, M. and Hargreaves, A. (1992) *What's Worth Fighting for in Your School? Working Together for School Improvement*. Buckingham: Open University Press.

Furlong, J. and Maynard, T. (1995) *Mentoring Student Teachers: the Growth of Professional Knowledge*. London: Routledge.

Furlong, J., Barton, L., Miles, S., Whiting, C. and Whitty, G. (2000) *Teacher Education in Transition: Reforming Professionalism?* Buckingham: Open University Press.

Furlong, J., Wilkin, M., Maynard, T. and Miles, S. (1994) *The Active Mentoring Programme*. Cambridge: George Pearson.

Gagné, R. M. (1965) *The Conditions of Learning*. New York: Holt, Rinehart and Winston.

Gallas, K. (1994) *The Languages of Learning: How Children Talk, Write, Dance, Draw and Sing their Understanding of the World*. New York: Teachers' College Press.

Gallas, K. (1998) '*Sometimes I can be Anything*': *Power, Gender and Identity in a Primary Classroom*. London: Teachers' College Press.

Galton, M. (1989) *Teaching in the Primary School*. London: David Fulton.

Galton, M. (1998) 'Comparative education and educational reform: beware of prophets returning from the Far East', *Education 3 to 13*, **26**(2), 3–8.

Galton, M., Hargreaves, L., Comber, C., Wall, D. and Pell, A. (1999) *Inside the Primary Classroom: Twenty Years on*. London: Routledge.

Galton, M., Simon, B. and Croll, P. (1980) *Inside the Primary Classroom*. London: Routledge and Kegan Paul.

Galton, M. and Williamson, J. (1992) *Groupwork in the Primary Classroom*. London: Routledge.

Gardner, H. (1985) *Frames of Mind: The Theory of Multiple Intelligence*. London: Paladin Books.

Gardner, H. (1999) *Intelligence Reframed: Multiple Intelligences for the Twenty-first Century*. New York: Basic Books.

Gearon, L. (2001) *Education in the United Kingdom: Structures and Organisation*. London: David Fulton.

Gerwitz, S., Ball, S. J. and Bowe, R. (1995) *Markets, Choice and Equity in Education*. Buckingham: Open University Press.

Giddens, A. (1991) *Modernity and Self Identity*. Cambridge: Polity Press.

Gilborn, P. (1995) *Racism and Anti-Racism in Real Schools*. Buckingham: Open University Press.

Giles, R. H. (1977) *The West Indian Experience in British Schools*. London: Heinemann.

Gipps, C. (1990) *Assessment, A Teachers' Guide to the Issues*. London: Hodder and Stoughton.

Gipps, C., Brown, M., McCallum, B. and McManus, S. (1995) *Intuition or Evidence? Teachers and National Assessment of Seven-year-olds*. Buckingham: Open University Press.

Gipps, C. and MacGilchrist, B. (1999) Primary school learners, in Mortimore, P. (ed.) *Understanding Pedagogy and its Impact on Learning*. London: Paul Chapman.

Gipps, C., McCullum, B. and Hargreaves, E. (2000) *What Makes a Good Primary Teacher? Expert Classroom Strategies*. London: RoutledgeFalmer.

Gipps, C., McCullum, B., McAllister, S. and Brown, M. (1991) National assessment at seven: some emerging themes, in Gipps, C. (ed.) *Developing Assessment for the National Curriculum*. London: Kogan Page.

Gipps, C. and Murphy, P. (1994) *A Fair Test? Assessment, Achievement and Equity*. Buckingham: Open University Press.

Glaser, B. and Strauss, A. (1967) *The Discovery of Grounded Theory*. Chicago: Aldine.

Glass, G. V. (1982) *School Class Size, Research and Policy*. Beverley Hills, CA: Sage.

Glass, G. V. (1982a) Culture, context and the appropriation of knowledge, in Light, P. and Butterworth, G. (eds), *Context and Cognition: Ways of Learning and Knowing*. Hemel Hempstead: Harvester Wheatsheaf.

Gold, K. (2000) 'The Food Deserts', *Times Eucational Supplement*. London: TES.

Goldthorpe, J. H. (1987) *Social Mobility and Class Structure in Modern Britain*. Oxford: Oxford University Press.

Goleman, D. (1996) *Emotional Intelligence: Why it Can Matter More than IQ*. London: Bloomsbury.

Goleman, D. (1998) *Working with Emotional Intelligence*. London: Bloomsbury.

Goodson, I. (1992) *Studying Teachers' Lives*. London: Routledge.

Gopnik, A., Meltzoff, A. N. and Kuhl, P. K. (1999) *How Babies Think*. London: Weidenfeld and Nicholson.

Grace, G. (1978) *Teachers, Ideology and Control*. London: Routledge and Kegan Paul.

Gramsci, A. (1978) *Selections from Political Writings*. London: Lawrence and Wishart.

Gravelle, M. (ed.) (2000) *Planning for Bilingual Learners: an Inclusive Curriculum*. Stoke-on-Trent: Trentham.

Gray, J. (2000) 'How schools learn: common concerns and common responses', *Research Papers in Education*, **15**(3), 235–9.

Gray, J., Hopkins, D., Reynolds, D., Wilcox, B., Farrell, S., and Jesson, D. (1999) *Improving Schools: Performance and Potential*. Buckingham: Open University Press.

Green, A. (1990) *Education and State Formation*. London: Macmillan.

Greenfield, S. (ed.) (1996) *The Human Mind Explained*. London: Cassell.

Greenfield, S. (1997) *The Human Brain: a Guided Tour*. London: Weidenfeld and Nicolson.

Gregory, E. (1996) *Making Sense of a New World: Learning to Read in a Second Language*. London: Paul Chapman.

Griffiths, M. (1995) *Feminism and the Self: the Web of Identity*. London: David Fulton.

Griffiths, M. and Davies, C. (1995) *In Fairness to Children*. London, David Fulton.

Grugeon, E. and Woods, P. (1990) *Educating All: Multicultural Perspectives in the Primary School*. London: Routledge.

Gump, P. V. (1987) School and classroom environments, in: Stokols, D. and Altman, I. (eds) *Handbook of Environmental Psychology*. New York: Wiley.

Hall, E. and Hall, C. (1988) *Human Relations in Education*. London: Routledge.

Hall, K. and Nuttall, W. (2000) 'Class size and pedagogy: how might infant teachers in England respond to class size changes?' *Education 3–13*, **28**(3), 52–7.

Hallam, S. (2000) *Truancy: Can Schools Improve Attendance?* London: Institute of Education.

Halpin, D. (2001) 'Hope, utopianism and educational management', *Cambridge Journal of Education*, **31**(1), 103–18.

Halsey, A. H. (1986) *Change in British Society*. Oxford: Oxford University Press.

Halsey, A. H., Heath, A. F. and Ridge, J. M. (1980) *Origins and Destinations: Family, Class and Education in Modern Britain*. Oxford: Clarendon Press.

Hamilton, D. (1977) *In Search of Structure*. Edinburgh: Scottish Council for Research in Education.

Hammersley, M. and Atkinson, P. (1983) *Ethnography: Principles into Practice*. London: Tavistock.

Hampson, S. E. (1988) *The Construction of Personality: An Introduction*. London: Routledge.

Hancock, R. (2001) *Classroom Assistants in the Primary School: Employment and Deployment*. Buckingham: Open University Press.

Hargreaves, A. (1978a) The significance of classroom coping strategies, in Barton, L. and Meighan, R. (eds) *Sociological Interpretations of Schooling and Classrooms*. Driffield: Nafferton.

Hargreaves, A. (1994) *Changing Teachers, Changing Times: Teachers' Work and Culture in the Postmodern Age*. London: Cassell.

Hargreaves, D. H. (1967) *Social Relations in a Secondary School*. London: Routledge.

Hargreaves, D. H. (1972) *Interpersonal Relationships and Education*. London: Routledge.

Hargreaves, D. H. (1978b) Whatever happened to symbolic interactionism?, in Barton, L. and Meighan, R. (eds) *Schools, Pupils and Deviance*. Driffield: Nafferton.

Hargreaves, D. H., Hestor, S. K. and Mellor, F. J. (1975) *Deviance in Classrooms*. London: Routledge and Kegan Paul.

Hargreaves, D. H. and Hopkins, D. (1991) *The Empowered School: the Management and Practice of Development Planning*. London: Cassell.

Harland, J. and Kinder, K. (1992) *Mathematics and Science Courses for Primary Teachers: Lessons for the Future*. Slough: NFER.

Harlen, W. (1996) Primary teachers' understanding in science and its impact on the classroom. *BERA annual conference*. September.

Harlen, W., Gipps, C., Broadfoot, P. and Nuttall, D. (1992) 'Assessment and the improvement of education', *Curriculum Journal*, 3(3), 217–25.

Hart, N. and Martello, J. (eds) (1996) *Listening to Children Think: Exploring Talk in the Early Years*. London: Hodder and Stoughton.

Hartley, D. (1985) *Understanding the Primary School*. London: Croom Helm.

Haste, H. (1987) Growing into rules, in Bruner, J. S. and Haste, H. (eds) *Making Sense: the Child's Construction of the World*. London: Metheun.

Hastings, N. and Wood, C. K. (2001) *Re-organising Primary Classroom Learning*. Buckingham: Open University Press.

Haviland, J. (1988) *Take Care, Mr Baker!* London: Fourth Estate.

Haworth, A. (2001) 'The re-positioning of oracy: a millennium project', *Cambridge Journal of Education*, 31(1), 11–23.

Hay McBer Consultancy (2000) *Research into Teacher Effectiveness: a Model of Teacher Effectiveness*. London: DfEE.

Hayes, D. (1999) *Foundations of Primary Teaching*. London: David Fulton.

Hayes, D. (1999a) *Planning, Teaching and Class Management in Primary Schools: Meeting the Standards*. London: David Fulton.

Hayes, D. (2000), *The Handbook for Newly Qualified Teachers, Meeting the Standards in Primary and Middle Schools*. London, David Fulton.

Headington, R. (2000) *Monitoring, Assessment, Recording, Reporting and Accountability: Meeting the Standards*. London: David Fulton.

Hellige, J. B. (1993) *Hemispheric Asymmetry: What's Left and What's Left*. Cambridge, MA: Harvard University Press.

Hewton, E. (1986) *Education in Recession: Crisis in County Hall and Classroom*. London: Allen and Unwin.

Hextall, I., Lawn, M., Menter, I., Sidgwick, S. and Walker, S. (1991) 'Imaginative projects: arguments for a new teacher education', *Evaluation and Research*, 5(1, 2), 79–95.

Hillgate Group (1987) *The Reform of British Education*. London: Hillgate Group.

Hirst, P. H. (1965) Liberal education and the nature of knowledge, in Archambault, R. (ed.) *Philosophical Analysis and Education*. London: Routledge and Kegan Paul.

Hirst, P. H. and Peters, R. S. (1970) *The Logic of Education*. London: Routledge and Kegan Paul.

Hitchcock, G. and Hughes, D. (1996) *Research and the Teacher: a Qualitative Introduction to School-based Research* (2nd edition). London: Routledge.

HMCI (Her Majesty's Chief Inspector of Schools) (1992) *Education in England. 1990–91: Annual Report*. London: DES.

HMCI (1995) *The Annual Report of Her Majesty's Chief Inspector of Schools*. London: HMSO.

HMCI (1998) *The Annual Report of Her Majesty's Chief Inspector of Schools in England. Standards and Quality in Education 1996–1997*. London: The Stationery Office.

HMI (1978) *Primary Education in England: A Survey by HMI*. London: HMSO.

HMI (1985) *The Curriculum from 5 to 16: Curriculum Matters Series*. London: HMSO.

Hohmann, M., Banet, B. and Weikart, D. (1979) *Young Children in Action*. Ypsilanti, MI: High Scope Educational Research Foundation.

Holden, C. and Clough, N. (eds) (1998) *Children as Citizens: Education for Participation*. London: Jessica Kingsley.

Holden, C. and Smith, L. (1992) 'Economic and industrial understanding in primary education: problems and possibilities', *Education and Training*, 34(3), 11–14.

Holly, M. L. (1989) *Writing to Grow: Keeping a Personal–Professional Journal*. Portsmouth, NH: Heinemann.

Holt, J. (1982) *How Children Fail*. London: Penguin.

Hook, P. and Vass, A. (2001) *Confident Classroom Leadership*. London: David Fulton.

Hopkins, D. (1986) *A Teachers' Guide to Classroom Research* (2nd edition). Milton Keynes: Open University Press.

Hopkins, D., Ainscow, M. and West, M. (1994) *School Improvement in an Era of Change*. London: Cassell.

House of Commons Select Committee on Education (1986) *Achievement in Primary Schools*. London: HMSO.

Housego, E. and Burns, C. (1994) 'Are you sitting too comfortably? A critical look at 'Circle Time' in primary classrooms', *Educational Psychology in Practice*, **15**(1), 23–9.

Howarth, C., Kenway, P., Palmer G. and Street, K. (1998) *Monitoring Poverty and Social Exclusion: Labour's Inheritance*. York: Joseph Rowntree Foundation.

Howe, C. (1997) *Gender and Classroom Interaction: A Research Review*, Edinburgh: SCRE.

Howe, M. J. A. (1990) *The Origins of Exceptional Abilities*. London: Blackwell.

Howe, M. J. A. (1999) *A Teacher's Guide to the Psychology of Learning*. Oxford: Blackwell.

Hoyle, E. (1986) *The Politics of School Management*. Sevenoaks: Hodder and Stoughton.

Huberman, M. (1993) *The Lives of Teachers*. London: Cassell.

Hugdahl, K. (1995) *Psychophysiology: the Mind–Body Perspective*. Cambridge, MA: Harvard University Press.

Hughes, M., Desforges, C., Mitchell, C. and Carre, C. (2000) *Numeracy and Beyond: Applying Mathematics in the Primary School*. Buckingham: Open University Press.

Hughes, M. and Pollard, A. (2000) Home–school knowledge exchange and transformation in primary education. *ESRC Project L139251078*. Bristol: University of Bristol.

Hughes, M. and Westgate, D. (1998) 'Possible enabling strategies in teacher-led talk with young pupils', *Language and Education*, **12**(3), 174–91.

Hughes, M., Wikeley, F. and Nash, T. (1994) *Parents and Their Children's Schools*. Oxford: Blackwell.

Humphries, S. (1982) *Hooligans or Rebels?* Oxford: Blackwell.

Humphreys, T. (1995) *A Different Kind of Teacher*. London: Cassell.

Hunter, R. and Scheirer, E. A. (1988) *The Organic Classroom: Organizing for Learning 7 to 12*. London: Falmer.

Hurst, V. (1992) *Planning for Early Learning: the First Five Years*. London: Paul Chapman.

Hustler, D., Cassidy, T. and Cuff, T. (eds) (1986) *Action Research in Schools and Classrooms*. London: Allen and Unwin.

ILEA (1987) *Language Courses*. London: ILEA Research and Statistics.

Ingram, J. and Worrall, N. (1993) *Teacher–Child Partnership: The Negotiating Classroom*. London: David Fulton.

Institute of Fiscal Studies (1995) *Low-Income Statistics: Low-Income Families, 1989–92*. London: HMSO.

Ireson, J. and Hallam, S. (2001) *Ability Grouping in Education*. London: Paul Chapman.

Jackson, B. (1964) *Streaming: an Education System in Miniature*. London: Routledge and Kegan Paul.

Jackson, B. and Marsden, D. (1962) *Education and the Working Class*. London: Ark.

Jackson, C. and Warin, J. (2000) 'The importance of gender as an aspect of identity at key transition points in compulsory education', *British Educational Research Journal*, **26**(3), 375–91.

http://www.rtweb.info

Jackson, P. W. (1968) *Life in Classrooms*. New York: Holt, Rinehart and Winston.

James, A., Jenks, C. and Prout, A. (1998) *Theorising Childhood*. Cambridge: Polity Press.

Jamison, J., Johnson, F. and Dickson, P. (1998) *Every Pupil Counts: the Impact of Class Size at KS1*. Slough: NFER.

Jeffrey, B. and Woods, P. (1998) *Testing Teachers: the Effects of School Inspections on Primary Teachers*. London: Falmer.

Jenks, C. (1972) *A question of control: a case study of interaction in a junior school*. London: Institute of Education, University of London.

Johnson, D. (1990) *Parental Choice in Education*. London: Routledge.

Johnson, G., Hill, B. and Turnstall, P. (1992) *Primary Records of Achievement*. London: Hodder and Stoughton.

Jones, B. M. and Ghuman, P. A. S. (1995) *Bilingualism, Education and Identity*. Cardiff: University of Wales Press.

Jones, J. (1999) 'The implementation of the National Literacy Strategy: a response to Stainthorp', *The Psychology of Education Review*, **23**(1), 9–10.

Jones, K. and Charlton, T. (1992) *Learning Difficulties in the Primary Classroom*. London: Routledge.

Joseph Rowntree Foundation (JRF) (2000) *Poverty and Social Exclusion in Britain*. York: Joseph Rowntree Foundation.

Kagan, J. (1964) 'Information processing in the child: significance of analytic and reflective attitudes', *Psychological Monographs*, 78.

Karoly, L. A., Greenwood, P. W., Everingham, S. S. (eds) (1998) *Investing in Our Children: What We Know and Don't Know about the Costs and Benefits of Early Childhood Intervention*. New York: RAND.

Katz, L. (1995) *Talks With Teachers of Young Children*. Norwood, NJ: Ablex.

Katz, L. (1998) A development approach to the curriculum in the early years, in Smidt, S. *The Early Years: A Reader*. Routledge: London.

Kellmer-Pringle, M. (1974) *The Needs of Children*. London: Hutchinson.

Kerry, T. and Kerry, C. (1997) 'Differentiation: teachers' views of the usefulness of recommended strategies in helping the more able pupils in primary and secondary classrooms', *Educational Studies*, **23**(3), 439–57.

King, R. (1978) *All Things Bright and Beautiful? A Sociological Study of Infants' Classrooms*. Chichester: John Wiley and Sons Ltd.

Kingdom, J. (1991) *Government and Politics in Britain*. Oxford: Polity Press.

Kline, P. (1991) *Intelligence: the Psychometric View*. London: Routledge.

Kogan, M. (1978) *The Politics of Educational Change*. London: Fontana.

Kohl, H. (1986) *On Becoming a Teacher*. London: Methuen.

Kounin, J. S. (1970) *Discipline and Group Management in Classrooms*. New York: Holt Rhinehart and Winston.

Labour (1995) *Excellence for Everyone: Labour's Crusade to Raise Standards*. London: Labour Party.

Labov, W. (1973) The logic of non-standard English, in Keddie, N. (ed.) *Tinker, Tailor: the Myth of Cultural Deprivation*. Harmondsworth: Penguin.

Lacey, C. (1970) *Hightown Grammar: the School as a Social System*. Manchester: Manchester University Press.

Laevers, F. (1995) *An Exploration of the Concept of Involvement as an Indicator for Quality in Early Childhood Education.* Dundee: Scottish Consultative Council on the Curriculum.

Lareau, A. (1989) *Home Advantage: Social Class and Parental Intervention in Elementary Education.* London: Falmer.

Lareau, A., McNamara, D. and Horvat, E. (1999) 'Moments of social inclusion and exclusion: race, class and cultural capital in family–school relationships', *Sociology of Education*, 72(Jan.), 37–53.

Laslett, R. and Smith, C. (1992) *Effective Classroom Management: a Teacher's Guide.* London: Routledge.

Lauder, H. and Hughes, D. (1999) *Trading in Futures: Why Markets in Education Don't Work.* Buckingham: Open University Press.

Lave, J. and Wenger, E. (1991) *Situated Learning: Legitimate Peripheral Participation.* Cambridge: Cambridge University Press.

Lawlor, S. (1988) *Correct Core: Simple Curricula for English, Maths and Science.* London: Centre for Policy Studies.

Lawn, M. and Grace, G. (eds) (1987) *Teachers: the Culture and Politics of Work.* London: Falmer.

Lawn, M. and Ozga, J. (1981) The educational worker: a reassessment of teachers, in Ozga, J. (ed.) *Schoolwork: Approaches to the Labour Process of Teaching.* Buckingham: Open University Press.

Lawn, M. and Ozga, J. (1986) 'Unequal partners: teachers under indirect rule', *British Journal of Sociology of Education*, 7(2), 225–38.

Lawrence, D. (1987) *Enhancing Self-Esteem in the Classroom.* London: Paul Chapman.

Lawton, D. (1995) *The Tory Mind on Education: 1979–1994.* London: Falmer.

Lazarus, R. S. (1991) *Emotion and Adaption.* Oxford: Oxford University Press.

Lazarus, R. S. (1999) *Stress and Emotion: A New Synthesis.* London: Free Association Books.

Learmonth, J. (2000) *Inspection: What's in it For Schools?* London: Routledge Falmer.

Leithwood, K. and Aitken, R. (1995) *Making Schools Smarter.* Thousand Oak, CA: Corwin.

Leithwood, K. and Jantzi, D. (1990) Transformational leadership: how principals can help reform school culture. Paper presented to *AERA annual conference.* April.

Levine, D. and Eubanks, E. (1989) Site-based management: engine for reform or pipe dream? Unpublished MS cited by Fullan, M. and Hargreaves, A. (1992) *What's Worth Fighting For in your School?* Buckingham: Open University Press.

Lewin, K. (1946) 'Action research and minority problems,' *Journal of Social Issues*, 2, 34–6.

Light, P. and Littleton, K. (1999) *Social Processes in Children's Learning.* Cambridge: Cambridge University Press.

Lipman, M., Sharp, A. M. and Oscanyan, F. S. (1980) *Philosophy in the Classroom.* Philadelphia: Temple University Press.

Lonsdale, P. and Parsons, C. (1998) Inspection and the school improvement hoax, in Earley, P. (ed.) *School Improvement after Inspection.* London: Paul Chapman.

Louis, K. S. and Miles, M. B. (1992) *Improving the Urban High School: What Works and Why*. New York: Teachers' College Press.

Lucey, H. and Reay, D. (2000) 'Identities in transition: anxiety and excitement in the move to secondary school', *Oxford Review of Education*, **26**(2), pp. 191–205.

MacBeath, J. (ed.) (1998) *Effective School Leadership: Responding to Change*. London: Paul Chapman.

MacBeath, J. (1999) *Schools Must Speak For Themselves: the Case for School Self-Evaluation*. London: Routledge.

MacBeath, J. (2000) *Self-Evaluation in European Schools: a Story of Change*. London: Routledge.

MacBeath, J. and Mortimore, P. (eds) (2001) *Improving School Effectiveness*. Buckingham: Open University.

MacBeath, J. and Myers, K. (1998) *Effective School Leaders: How to Evaluate and Improve Your Leadership Potential*. London: Pearson.

MacGilchrist, B., Mortimore, P., Savage, J. and Beresford, C. (1995) *Planning Matters: the Impact of Development Planning in Primary Schools*. London: Paul Chapman.

MacGilchrist, B., Myers, K. and Reed, J. (1997) *The Intelligent School*. London: Paul Chapman.

MacGrath, M. (2000) *The Art of Peaceful Teaching in the Primary School: Improving Behaviour and Preserving Motivation*. London: David Fulton.

Maclure, M. (2000) 'Arguing for yourself: identity as an organising principle in teachers' jobs and lives', *British Educational Research Journal*, **19**(4), 311–22.

Maden, M. (1999) The challenge of children in the education system, in Tunstall, J. (ed.) *Children and the State: Whose Problem?* London: Cassell.

Maden, M. (ed.) (2001) *Success Against the Odds – Five Years On: Revisiting Effective Schools in Disadvantaged Areas*. London: RoutledgeFalmer.

Makins, V. (1969) Child's eye view of teacher. *Times Educational Supplement*.

Mangan, J. A. E. (1993) *The Imperial Curriculum: Racial Images and Education in the British Colonial Experience*. London: Routledge.

Manke, M. P. (1997) *Classroom Power Relation: Understanding Student–Teacher Interactions*. London: Lawrence Erlbaum Associates.

Marlowe, B. A. and Page, M. L. (1998) *Creating and Sustaining the Constructivist Classroom*. London: Sage.

Marsh, L. (1970) *Alongside the Child*. London: Black.

Marshall, B. (1994) *Engendering Modernity: Feminism, Social Theory and Social Change*. Cambridge: Polity.

Marshall, T. H. and Bottomor, T. (1992) *Citizenship and Social Class*. London: Pluto.

Maslow, A. H. (1954) *Motivation and Personality*. New York: Harper & Row.

Maude, P. (2001) *Physical Children, Active Teaching: Investigating Physical Literacy*. Buckingham: Open University Press.

Mayall, B. (1994) *Negotiating Health: Children at Home and Primary School*. London: Cassell.

Maylor, U. (1995) Identity, migration and education, in Blair, M. and Holland, J. (eds) *Identity and Diversity*. Clevedon: Multilingual Matters.

Maynard, T. (2001) 'The student teacher and the school community of practice: a consideration of learning as participation', *Cambridge Journal of Education*, **31**(1), 44–9.

Maynard, T. and Furlong, J. (1993) Learning to teach and models of mentoring, in McIntyre, D., Hagger, H. and Wilkin, M. (eds) *Mentoring: Perspectives on School-Based Teacher Education*. London: Kogan Page.

McFarlane, A. (ed.) (1997) *Information Technology and Authentic Learning: Realising the Potential of Computers in the Primary Classroom*. London: Routledge.

McGuinness, C. (1999) *From Thinking Skills to Thinking Classrooms*. Research Report 115. London: DfEE.

McIntyre, D. (1993) Theory, theorisation and reflection in initial teacher education, in Calderhead, J. and Gates, P. (eds) *Conceptualising Reflection in Teacher Education*. London: Falmer.

McIntyre, D. and Hagger, H. (eds) (1996) *Mentors in Schools: Developing the Profession of Teaching*. London: David Fulton.

McNamara, D. (1994) *Classroom Pedagogy and Primary Practice*. London: Routledge.

McNamara, D. (ed.) (2002) *Becoming an Evidence-Based Practitioner*. London: RoutledgeFalmer.

McNiff, J. (1988) *Action Research: Principles and Practice*. London: Routledge.

McPherson, A. and Raab, C. D. (1988) *Governing Education: a Sociology of Policy since 1945*. Edinburgh: Edinburgh University Press.

Mead, G. H. (1934) *Mind, Self, and Society*. Chicago: University of Chicago Press.

Meadows, S. (1992) *Children's Cognitive Development: the Development and Acquisition of Cognition in Childhood*. London: Routledge.

Measor, L. and Woods, P. (1984) *Changing Schools: Pupil Perspectives on Transfer to a Comprehensive*. Milton Keynes: Open University Press.

Mehler, J. and Dupoux, E. (1994) *What Infants Know*. Oxford: Blackwell.

Meighan, R. (1978) 'The learner's viewpoint', *Educational Review*, **30**(2).

Meighan, R. (1981) *A Sociology of Educating*. London: Holt, Rinehart and Winston.

Meighan, R. and Siraj-Blatchford, I. (1997) *A Sociology of Educating*. London: Cassell.

Menter, I., Muschamp, Y., Nicolls, P., Ozga, J. and Pollard, A. (1996) *Work and Identity in the Primary School: a Post-Fordist Analysis*. Buckingham: Open University Press.

Mercer, N. (1992) Culture, context and the appropriation of knowledge, in Light, P. and Butterworth, G. (eds) *Context and Cognition: Ways of Learning and Knowing*. Hemel Hempstead: Harvester Wheatsheaf.

Mercer, N. (1995) *The Guided Construction of Knowledge: Talk amongst Teachers and Learners*. Clevedon: Multilingual Matters.

Mercer, N. (2000) *Words and Minds: How We Use Language to Think Together*. London: Routledge.

Merrett, F. and Wheldall, K. (1990) *Identifying Troublesome Classroom Behaviour*. London: Paul Chapman.

Meyer, J. W. and Kamens, D. H. (1992) Conclusion: Accounting for a World Curriculum in Meyer, J. W., Kamens, D. H. and Benavot, A. with Cha, Y. K. and Wong S. Y. (eds) *School Knowledge for the Masses: World Models of*

National Primary Curricular Categories in the Twentieth Century. London: Falmer, pp. 165–75.

Meyer, J. W., Kamens, D. H. and Benavot, A. with Cha Y. K. and Wong S. Y. (eds) (1992) *School Knowledge for the Masses: World Models of National Primary Curricular Categories in the Twentieth Century*. London: Falmer.

Middleton, S. (2000) *Poverty and Social Exclusion in Britain*. York: Joseph Rowntree Foundation.

Miles, M. (1986) *Research findings on the stages of school improvement*. New York: Centre for Policy Research (mimeo).

Miller, J. (1997) *Never Too Young: How Young Children Can Take Responsibility and Make Decisions*. London: Save the Children.

Mills, C. W. (1959) *The Sociological Imagination*. New York: Oxford University Press.

Moll, L. C. and Greenberg, J. B. (1990) Creating zones of possibilities: combining social contexts for instruction, in Moll, L. C. (ed.) *Vygotsky and Education*. Cambridge: Cambridge University Press.

Moos, R. H. (1979) *Evaluating Educational Environments: Procedures, Measures, Findings and Policy Implications*. London: Jossey-Bass.

Morange, M. (2001) *The Misunderstood Gene*. Cambridge, MA: Harvard University Press.

Mortimore, P. (1991) The nature and findings of research on school effectiveness in the primary sector, in Riddell, S. and Brown, S. (eds) *School Effectiveness Research: Its Messages for School Improvement*. Edinburgh: HMSO.

Mortimore, P., Sammons, P., Stoll, L., Lewis, D. and Ecob, R. (1986) *Report of The Junior School Project*. London: Inner London Education Authority.

Mortimore, P., Sammons, P., Stoll, L., Lewis, D. and Ecob, R. (1988) *School Matters: the Junior Years*. Wells: Open Books.

Moyles, J. R. (1992) *Organising for Learning in the Primary Classroom: a Balanced Approach to Classroom Organisation*. Buckingham: Open University Press.

Moyles, J. R. (ed.) (1994) *The Excellence of Play*. Buckingham: Open University Press.

Moyles, J. R. (1995) A place for everything? The classroom as a teaching and learning context, in Moyles, J. (ed) *Beginning Teaching: Beginning Learning in Primary Education*. Buckingham: Open University Press.

Mosley, J. (1996) *Quality Circle Time in the Primary Classroom*. Wisbech: Learning Development Association.

Moyles, J., Suschitzky, W. and Chapman, L. (1998) *Teaching Fledgling to Fly? Mentoring and Support Systems in Primary Schools*. London: Association of Teachers and Lecturers.

Mroz, M., Smith, F. and Hardman, F. (2000) 'The discourse of the literacy hour', *Cambridge Journal of Education*, 30(3), 379–90.

Muijs, D. and Reynolds, D. (2001) *Effective Teaching: Evidence and Practice*. London: Paul Chapman.

Munn, P., Johnstone, M. and Chalmers, V. (1992) *Effective Discipline in Primary Schools and Classrooms*. London: Paul Chapman.

Murphy, P. (2001) Gendered learning and achievement, in Collins, J. and Cook, D. (eds) *Understanding Learning: Influences and Outcomes*. London: Paul Chapman.

Murphy, P., Davidson, M., Qualter, A., Simon, S. and Watt, D. (2001) *Effective Practice in Primary Science: a Report of an Exploratory Study funded by the Nuffield Curriculum Projects Centre.* Buckingham: Open University.

Muschamp, Y. (1994) Target setting with young children, in Pollard, A. and Bourne, J. (eds) *Teaching and Learning in Primary Schools.* London: Routledge.

Myers, K. (ed.) (1996) *School Improvement in Practice: Schools Make a Difference Project.* London: Falmer.

NAAIDT (1992) *Make It Safe.* London: National Association of Advisers and Inspectors of Design and Technology.

Nash, R. (1976) *Teacher Expectations and Pupil Learning.* London: Routledge.

National Commission on Education (1995) *Success Against the Odds.* London: Routledge.

National Assembly for Wales (2001) *Supporting New Teachers: Early Professional Development Including Induction.* Cardiff: The National Assembly for Wales.

National Research Council (1999) *Improving Learning: A Strategic Plan for Education Research and its Utilisation.* Washington, DC: National Academy Press.

Newell, P. (1991) *The UN Convention and Children's Rights in the UK.* London: National Children's Bureau.

Nias, J. (1989) *Primary Teachers Talking: A Study of Teaching as Work.* London: Routledge.

Nias, J., Southworth, G. and Campbell, P. (1992) *Whole-school Curriculum Development in the Primary School.* London: Falmer Press.

Nias, J., Southworth, G. and Yeomans, R. (1989) *Staff Relationships in the Primary School: A Study of Organisational Cultures.* London: Cassell.

Nichols, G. and Gardner, J. (1999) *Pupils in Transition.* London: RoutledgeFalmer.

Nieto, S. (1999) *The Light in their Eyes: Creating Multicultural Learning Communities.* London: Trentham Books.

Nisbet, J. and Schucksmith, J. (1986) *Learning Strategies.* London: Routledge and Kegan Paul.

Nixon, J. (1996) *Encouraging Learning: Towards a Theory of the Learning School.* Buckingham: Open University Press.

No Turning Back Group of MPs (1986) *Save Our Schools.* London: Conservative Party Centre.

Norman, K. (1990) *Teaching, Talking and Learning in Key Stage One.* York: National Curriculum Council.

Norman, K. (ed.) (1992) *Thinking Voices: The Work of the National Oracy Project.* London: Hodder and Stoughton.

Noss, R., Goldstein, H. and Hoyles, C. (1989) 'Graded assessment learning hierachies in mathematics', *British Educational Research Journal*, 15, 109–20.

NPC(SW) (1991) *Constructive Teacher Assessment: Progression in Children's Understanding*, PIPE No 6. Bristol: National Primary Centre (SW).

NPC(SW) (1991a) *Strategies for Classroom Assessment: INSET Pack.* Bristol: National Primary Centre (SW).

http://www.rtweb.info

Office for National Statistics (annually) *Britain: The Official Yearbook of the United Kingdom*. London: The Stationery Office.

Office for National Statistics (2000) *Britain 1999: the Official Yearbook of the United Kingdom*. London: The Stationery Office.

OFSTED (1995) *Guidance on the Inspection of Nursery and Primary Schools: the OFSTED Handbook*. London: OFSTED.

OFSTED (1999) *Handbook for Inspecting Primary and Nursery Schools*. London: HMSO.

OFSTED (1999a) *Primary Education 1994–1998: a Review of Primary Schools in England*. London: The Stationery Office.

OFSTED (2000a) *The National Literacy Strategy: The Second Year*. London: HMSO.

OFSTED (2000b) *The National Numeracy Strategy: The First Year*. London: HMSO.

O'Hear, A. (1991) *Education and Democracy: Against the Educational Establishment*. London: Claridge.

O'Keefe, D. (1988) A critical look at the national curriculum and testing. Annual Conference of the American Educational Research Association. New Orleans, April.

Opie, I. and Opie, P. (1959) *Children's Games in Street and Playground*. Oxford: Oxford University Press.

Osborn, A. F., Butler, N. R. and Morris, A. C. (1984) *The Social Life of Britian's Five-Year-Olds*. London: Routledge and Kegan Paul.

Osborn, M., McNess, E. and Broadfoot, P. with Pollard, A. and Triggs, P. (2000b) *What Teachers' Do. Changing Policy and Practice in Primary Education*. London: Continuum.

Osborne, J. and Simon, S. (1996) Teachers' subject knowledge: implications for teaching and policy. BERA annual conference. September.

Osler, A. and Starkey, H. (1996) *Teacher Education and Human Rights*. London: David Fulton.

Paley, G. V. (1981) *Wally's Stories*. Cambridge, MA: Harvard University Press.

Parker-Rees, R. (1999) Protecting playfulness, in Abbott, L. and Moylett, H. (eds) *Early Education Transformed*. London: Falmer.

Parkin, T. and Lewis, M. (1998) *Science and Literacy: A Guide for Primary Teachers*. London: Collins.

Parsons, T. (1959) 'The school class as a social system', *Harvard Educational Review*, 29, 297–318.

Pascal, C. and Bertram, T. (eds) (1997) *Effective Early Learning: Case-Studies in Improvement*. London: Hodder and Stoughton.

Pate-Bain, H., Achilles, C., Boyd-Zaharias, J. and McKenna, B. (1992) 'Class size does make a difference', *Phi Delta Kappa*, November, 253–5.

Paterson, L. (1998) 'The civic activism of Scottish teachers: explanations and consequences', *Oxford Review of Education*, 24(3), 279–302.

Pattanayak, D. P. (1991) Foreword, in Alladina, S. and Edwards, V. (eds) *Multilingualism in the British Isles*. London: Longman.

Perrot, E. (1982) *Effective Teaching*. London: Longman.

Peters, R. S. (1966) *Ethics and Education*. London: Allen and Unwin.

Phillips, T. (1985) Beyond lip-service: discourse development after the age of nine, in Wells, G. and Nicholls, J. (eds) *Language and Learning: an Interactional Perspective*. London: Falmer.

Piaget, J. (1926) *The Language and Thought of the Child*. New York: Basic Books.

Piaget, J. (1950) *The Psychology of Intelligence*. London: Routledge and Kegan Paul.

Piaget, J. (1951) *Play, Dreams and Imitation*. New York: Norton.

Piaget, J. (1961) 'A genetic approach to the psychology of thought', *Journal of Educational Psychology*, 52, 51–61.

Pinsent, P. (1992) *Language, Culture and Young Children*. London: David Fulton.

Plummer, G. (2000) *Failing Working Class Girls*. Stoke-on-Trent: Trentham Books.

Pointon, P. and Kershner, R. (2000) 'Children's views of the primary classroom as an environment for work and learning', *Research in Education*, **64**, 64–77.

Pollard, A. (1980) Teacher interests and changing situations of survival threat in primary school classrooms, in Woods, P. (ed.) *Teacher Strategies*. London: Croom Helm.

Pollard, A. (1982) 'A model of coping strategies', *British Journal of Sociology of Education*, **3**(1), 19–37.

Pollard, A. (1985) *The Social World of the Primary School*. London: Cassell.

Pollard, A. (ed.) (1987) *Children and their Primary Schools: A New Perspective*. London: Falmer.

Pollard, A. (1987a) 'Social differentiation in primary schools', *Cambridge Journal of Education*, **17**(3), 158–61.

Pollard, A. (1987b) Primary school teachers and their colleagues, in Delamont, S. (ed.) *The Primary School Teacher*. Lewes: Falmer.

Pollard, A. and Filer, A. (1996) *The Social World of Children's Learning: Case Studies of Pupils from Four to Seven*. London: Cassell.

Pollard, A. and Filer, A. (1999) *The Social World of Pupil Career: Strategic Biographies through Primary School*. London: Cassell.

Pollard, A. and Filer, A. (forthcoming, 2003) *Learning Differently: the Social World of Secondary Schooling*. London: Continuum.

Pollard, A., Broadfoot, P., Croll, P., Osborn, M. and Abbott, D. (1994) *Changing English Primary Schools? The Impact of the Education Reform Act at Key Stage One*. London: Cassell.

Pollard, A., Thiessen, D. and Filer, A. (eds) (1997) *Children and their Curriculum: the Perspectives of Primary and Elementary School Pupils*. London: Falmer.

Pollard, A. and Triggs, P. (1997) *Reflective Teaching in Secondary Education*. London: Cassell.

Pollard, A., Triggs, P., Broadfoot, P., McNess, E. and Osborn, M. (2000) *What Pupils Say: Changing Policy and Practice in Primary Education*. London: Continuum.

Popkewitz, T. (ed.) (1993) *Changing Patterns of Power: Social Regulation and Teacher Education Reform in Eight Countries*. New York: State University of New York Press.

Pring, R. A. (2000) *The Philosophy of Educational Research*. London: Continuum.

http://www.rtweb.info

Pringle, M. and Cobb, T. (1999) *Making Pupil Data Powerful: a Guide for Classroom Teachers*. Stafford: Network Educational Press.

Proctor, N. (ed.) (1990) *The Aims of Primary Education and the National Curriculum*. London: Falmer.

Prutzman, P., Burger, M. L., Bodenhamer, G. and Stern, L. (1978) *The Friendly Classroom for a Small Planet*. New Jersey: Avery Publishing.

Putnam, J. and Burke, J. B. (1992) *Organising and Managing Classroom Learning Communities*. New York: McGraw Hill.

QCA (1998) *Education for Citizenship and Teaching for Democracy*. Final report of the advisory group chaired by Bernard Crick. London: QCA.

QCA (1998a) *The National Curriculum: Handbook for Primary Teachers in England*. London: HMSO.

QCA (2000) *Assessment and Reporting Arrangements 2001 Key Stage 2*. London: QCA.

QCA (2001) *Respect for All*. London: QCA.

QCA/DfEE (2000) *Curriculum Guidance for the Foundation Stage*. London: HMSO.

Raffe, D., Brannen, K., Croxford, L. and Martin, C. (1999) 'Comparing England, Scotland, Wales and Northern Ireland: the case for "home internationals" in comparative research', *Comparative Education*, 35(1), 9–25.

Rampton, A. (1981) *West Indian Children in our Schools*. Report of the Committee of Enquiry. London: HMSO.

Reason, R. (1993) Primary special needs and National Curriculum assessment, in Wolfendale, S. (ed.) *Assessing Special Educational Needs*. London: Cassell.

Reay, D. (1998) *Class Work: Mothers' Involvement in Children's Schooling*. London: University College Press.

Reay, D. (2000) 'A useful extension of Bourdieu's conceptual framework? Emotional capital as a way of understanding mothers' involvement in their children's education?' *The Sociological Review*, 48(4), 568–85.

Reay, D. (2001) ' "Spice Girls", "Nice Girls", "Girlies" and "Tomboys": gender discourses, girls' cultures and feminities in the primary school classroom', *Gender and Education*, 13(2), 153–66.

Reay, D. and Wiliam, D. (1999) ' "I'll be a nothing": structure, agency and the construction of identity through assessment', *British Educational Research Journal*, 25(3), 343–54.

Reid, I. (1998) *Class in Britain*. Cambridge: Polity.

Resnick, L. and Resnick, D. (1991) Assessing the thinking curriculum: new tools for educational reform, in Gifford, B. and O'Connor, M. (eds) *Future Assessments: Changing Views of Apptitude, Achievement and Instruction*. New York: Kluwer Academic Publishers.

Reynolds, D. (1995) 'The effective school: an inaugural lecture', *Evaluation Research in Education*, 9(2), 55–73.

Reynolds, D. and Farrell, S. (1996) *Worlds Apart? A Review of International Surveys of Educational Achievement Involving England*. London: OFSTED.

Reynolds, E. (2001) 'Learning the "hard" way: boys, hegemonic masculinity and the negotiation of learner identities in the primary school', *British Journal of Sociology of Education*, 22(3), 369–86.

Richards, C. (1999) *Primary Education: at a Hinge of History?* London: Falmer.

Richards, C. (ed.) (2001) *Changing English Primary Education: Retrospect and Prospect*. Stoke-on-Trent: Trentham.

Richards, C. and Taylor, P. H. (eds) (1998) *How Shall We School Our Children? Primary Education and its Future*. London: Falmer.

Richards, M. and Light, P. (eds) (1986) *Children of Social Worlds*. Oxford: Blackwell.

Riding, R. J. and Rayner, S. (1998) *Cognitive Styles and Learning Strategies*. London: Fulton.

Rieser, R. and Mason, M. (1990) *Disability: Equality in the Classroom, A Human Rights Issue*. London: ILEA.

Rist, R. (1970) 'Student social class and teacher expectations', *Harvard Education Review*, 40, 411–51.

Roaf, C. and Bines, H. (1989) Needs, rights and opportunities in special education, in Roaf, C. and Bines, H. (eds) *Needs, Rights and Opportunities*. London: Falmer Press.

Robertson, J. (1996) *Effective Classroom Control: Understanding Teacher–Student Relationships*. London: Hodder and Stoughton.

Robinson, E. (1983) Meta-cognitive development, in Meadows, S. (ed.) *Developing Thinking*. London: Methuen.

Robinson, K. (1999) *All Our Futures: Creativity, Culture and Education*. London: DfEE.

Robson, C. (1993) *Real World Research*. Oxford: Blackwell.

Rogers, C. R. (1961) *On Becoming a Person*. London: Constable.

Rogers, C. R. (1969) *Freedom to Learn*. New York: Merrill.

Rogers, C. R. (1980) *A Way of Being*. Boston: Houghton Mifflin.

Rogers, C. R. and Kutnick, P. (1990) *The Social Psychology of the Primary School*. London: Routledge.

Rogoff, B. (1990) *Apprenticeship in Thinking: Cognitive Development in Social Context*. Oxford: Oxford University Press.

Rogoff, B. and Lave, J. (eds) (1984) *Everyday Cognition: Its Development in Social Context*. Cambridge, MA: Harvard University Press.

Rose, J. (1995) 'OFSTED inspection – who is it for?', *Educational Review*, 9(1), 63–6.

Rosenberg, M. (1989) *Society and the Adolescent Self-Image*. CT: Wesleyan University Press.

Rosenholz, S. (1989) *Teachers' Workplace: The Social Organisation of Schools*, New York: Longman.

Rosenthal, R. and Jacobson, L. (1968) *Pygmalion in the Classroom*. New York: Holt, Rinehart and Winston.

Ross, A. (1999) *Curriculum: Construction and Critique*. London: Routledge.

Ross, A. (2001) What is the Curriculum?, in Collins, J., Insley, K. and Soler, J. (eds) *Developing Pedagogy*. London: Paul Chapman.

Rottenberg, C. and Smith, M. L. (1990) Unintended effects of external testing in elementary schools. Conference of the American Educational Research Association. Boston, April.

Rowland, S. (1987) Child in control: towards an interpretive model of teaching and learning, in Pollard, A. (ed.) *Children and their Primary Schools*. London: Falmer.

Rubin, Z. (1980) *Children's Friendships*. London: Fontana.

Rudduck, J., Chaplain, R. and Wallace, G. (1996) *School Improvement: What Can Pupils Tell Us?* London: David Fulton.

Rudduck, J. and Hopkins, D. (eds) (1985) *Research as a Basis for Teaching: Readings from the Work of Lawrence Stenhouse*. London: Heinemann Educational Books.

Rutter, M. and Madge, N. (1976) *Cycles of Disadvantage*. London: Heinemann.

Rutter, M., Maughan, B., Mortimore, P. and Ouston, J. (1979) *Fifteen Thousand Hours: Secondary Schools and their Effects on Children*. London: Open Books.

Sainsbury (1998) *Literacy Hours: A Survey of the National Picture in Spring Term 1998*. Slough: NFER.

Sammons, P., Hillman, J. and Mortimore, P. (1995) *Key Characteristics of Effective Schools: A Review of School Effectiveness Research*. London: OFSTED.

Sammons, P. and Nuttall, D. (1992) Differential school effectiveness: results from a reanalysis of the ILEA's. Conference Paper for BERA. Stirling, September.

Sampson, J. and Yeomans, R. (1994) Analyzing the role of mentors, in Yeomans, R. and Sampson, J. (eds) *Mentorship in the Primary School*. London: Falmer.

Sarasin, L. C. (1999) *Learning Style Perspectives: Impact in the Classroom*. Madison, WI: Atwood Publishing.

SCAA (1995) *Planning the Curriculum at Key Stages 1 and 2*. London: School Curriculum and Assessment Authority.

Scardamalia, M. and Bereiter, C. (1983) Child as co-investigator: helping children gain insight into their own mental processes, in Paris, S. G., Olson, G. M. and Stevenson, H. (eds) *Learning and Motivation in the Classroom*. Hillsdale, NJ: Lawrence Erlbaum.

Schmuck, R. A. (1985) Groupwork, in Slavin, E. R. (ed.) *Learning to Cooperate, Cooperating to Learn*. New York: Plenum.

Schon, D. A. (1983) *The Reflective Practitioner: How Professionals Think in Action*. London: Temple Smith.

Schools Council (1983) *Primary Practice, Working Paper 75*. London: Methuen Educational.

Schultz, T. (1961) 'Investment in human capital', *American Economic Review*, 51, 1–17.

Scott, D. and Usher, R. (1996) *Understanding Educational Research*, London: Routledge.

Scott-Baumann, A., Bloomfield, A. and Roughton, L. (1997) *Becoming a Secondary School Teacher*. London: Hodder and Stoughton.

Scruton, R. (1988) The myth of cultural relativism, in Palmer, F. (ed.) *Anti-Racism: an Assault on Education and Values*. London: Sherwood.

Secord, P. and Backman, C. (1964) *Social Psychology*. New York: McGraw Hill.

Secretary of State for Health (1999) *Saving Lives: Our Healthier Nation*. London: Department of Health.

SED (1965) *Primary Education in Scotland*. Edinburgh: Scottish Education Department.

Sedgwick, F. (1988) *Here Comes the Assembly Man*. London: Falmer Press.

SEED (Scottish Executive) (2000) *The Structure and Balance of the Curriculum: 5 to 14 National Guidelines.* Edinburgh: Learning and Teaching Scotland.

SEED (2001) *Scottish Education.* www.scotland.gov.uk.

Selley, N. (1999) *The Art of Constructivist Teaching in the Primary School.* London: David Fulton.

Selwyn, N. and Bullon, K. (2000) 'Primary children's use of ICT', *British Journal of Educational Technology,* 31(4), 321–32.

Senge, P. (1992) *The Fifth Discipline: the Art and Practice of the Learning Organisation.* New York: Doubleday.

Sexton, S. (1987) *Our Schools: A Radical Policy.* Warlington: Institute of Economic Affairs.

Shallcross, T., Spink, E., Stephenson, P. and Warwick, P. (2001) 'How primary trainee teachers perceive the development of their own scientific knowledge; links between confidence, content and competence', *International Journal of Science Education.*

Sharp, R. and Green, A. (1975) *Education and Social Control.* London: Routledge and Kegan Paul.

Shepard, L. A. (1987) The harm of measurement driven instruction. Paper presented to the American Educational Research Association. Boston, April.

Shorrocks, D. (1991) *The Evaluation of National Curriculum Assessment at Key Stage One, Final Report.* Leeds: University of Leeds

Shulman, L. S. (1986) 'Those who understand: knowledge growth in teaching', *Educational Researcher,* 15, 1–14.

Siegler, R. S. (1997) *Emerging Minds: The Process of Change in Children's Thinking.* Oxford: Oxford University Press.

Sikes, P., Measor, L. and Woods, P. (1985) *Teacher Careers: Crises and Continuities.* London: Falmer.

Silver, H. (1980) *Education and the Social Condition.* London: Methuen.

Simco, N. (2000) 'Learning to comply: the impact of national curricula for primary pupils and primary trainee teacher on the ownership of learning', *Forum,* 42(1), 33–8.

Simco, N. (2000a) *Succeeding in the Induction Year.* Exeter, Learning Matters.

Simon, B. (1953) *Intelligence Testing and the Comprehensive School.* London: Lawrence and Wishart.

Simon, B. (1981) Why no pedagogy in England?, in Simon, B. and Taylor, W. (eds) *Education in the Eighties.* London: Batsford Educational.

Simon, B. (1985) *Does Education Matter?* London: Lawrence and Wishart.

Simon, B. (1992) *What Future for Education?* London: Lawrence and Wishart.

Simon, B. (1994) *The State and Educational Change: Essays in the History of Education and Pedagogy.* London: Lawrence and Wishart.

Simpson, M. (1997) 'Developing differentiation practices: meeting the needs of pupils and teachers', *The Curriculum Journal,* 8(1), 85–104.

Siraj-Blatchford, J. and Siraj-Blatchford, I. (1995) *Educating the Whole Child: Cross-curricular Skills, Themes and Dimensions.* Buckingham: Open University Press.

Sixsmith, S. C. and Simco, N. (1997) 'The role of formal and informal theory in the training of student teachers', *Mentoring and Tutoring,* 5(1), 5–13.

Skinner, B. F. (1953) *Science and Human Behaviour.* New York: Macmillan.

http://www.rtweb.info

Skinner, B. F. (1968) *The Technology of Teaching*. New York: Appleton.

Slee, R. and Weiner, G. with Tomlinson, S. (eds) (1998) *School Effectiveness for Whom? Challenges to the School Effectiveness and School Improvement Movements*. London: Falmer Press.

Slukin, A. (1981) *Growing Up in the Playground*. London: Routledge and Kegan Paul.

Smith, A. (1998) *Accelerated Learning in Practice: Brain-Based Methods for Accelerating Motivation and Achievement*. Stafford: Network Educational Press.

Smith, C. and Whitely, H. (2000) 'Developing literacy through the Literacy Hour: a survey of teachers' experiences', *Reading*, **34**(1), 34–8.

Smith, P. K., Cowie, H. and Blades, M. (1998) *Understanding Children's Development*. Oxford: Blackwell.

Smith, R. and Coldron, J. (1998) Thoughtful teaching, in Cashdan, A. and Overall, L. (eds) *Teaching in Primary Schools*, Cassell: London.

Smyth, J. (1991) *Teachers as Collaborative Learners*. Buckingham: Open University Press.

SooHoo, S. (1993) 'Students as partners in research and restructuring schools', *The Educational Forum*, **57**, 386–92.

Southworth, G. and Lincoln, P. (eds) (1999) *Supporting Improving Primary Schools: the Role of Heads and LEAs in Raising Standards*. London: Falmer.

Southworth, G., Nias, J. and Campbell, P. (1992) 'Rethinking Collegiality: Teachers' views'. Mimeo presented to the American Research Association, New Orleans.

Spender, D. and Sarah, E. (eds) (1980) *Learning to Lose: Sexism and Education*. London: Women's Press.

Squibb, P. (1973) 'The concept of intelligence: a sociological perspective', *Sociological Review*, **21**(1), 147–66.

Starkey, H. (1987) 'Human rights: the values for world studies and multi-cultural education', *Westminster Studies in Education*, **9**, 57–66.

Starkey, H. (1991) *The Challenge of Human Rights Education*. London: Cassell.

Statistics Office (1998) *Guidelines for Initial Teacher Education*. Edinburgh: Scottish Office.

Stenhouse, L. (1975) *An Introduction to Curriculum Research and Development*. London: Heinemann.

Stenhouse, L. (1983) *Authority, Education and Emancipation*. London: Heinemann.

Stephens, P. (1996) *Essential Mentoring Skills: a Practical Handbook for School-based Educators*. Cheltenham: Stanley Thomas.

Stoll, L. and Fink, D. (1996) *Changing Our Schools*. Buckingham: Open University Press.

Straughan, R. (1988) *Can We Teach Children to be Good? Basic Issues in Moral, Personal and Social Education*. Buckingham: Open University Press.

Stubbs, M. and Hillier, H. (eds) (1983) *Readings on Language and Classrooms*. London: Methuen.

Sukhnandan, L. and Lee, B. (1998) *Streaming, Setting and Grouping by Ability: a Review of the Literature*. Slough: NFER.

Sutton, R. (1995) *Assessment for Learning*. Salford: RS Publications.

Sutton, R. (2000) *Undoing the Muddle in the Middle*. Salford: RS Publications.

Sutton-Smith, B. (1998) *The Ambiguity of Play*. Cambridge, MA: Harvard University Press.

Swaffield, S. (2000) 'Record keeping', *Primary File*, 38, 61–4.

Swann, J. (1994) What do we do about gender, in Stierer, B. and Maybin, J. (eds) *Language, Literacy and Learning in Educational Practice*. Clevedon: Multilingual Matters.

Swann, J. and Graddol, D. (1994) Gender inequalities in classroom talk, in Graddol, D., Maybin, J. and Stierer, B. (eds) *Researching Language and Literacy in the Social Context*. Clevedon: Multilingual Matters.

Swann, M. (1985) *Committee of Inquiry into the Education of Children from Ethnic Minority Groups*.

Tabachnick, R. and Zeichner, K. (eds) (1991) *Issues and Practices in Inquiry-Oriented Teacher Education*. London: Falmer.

Tann, S. (1981) Grouping and group-work, in Simon, B. and Willcocks, J. (eds) *Research and Practice in the Primary School*. London: Routledge and Kegan Paul.

Tanner, J. M. (1978) *Education and Physical Growth*. London: University of London Press.

Tate, N. (1995) *National cultures*, mimeo. Speech to the Shropshire Secondary Headteachers' Annual Conference, July.

Tattum, D. P. and Lane, D. A. (1989) *Bullying in Schools*. Stoke-on-Trent: Trentham.

Taylor, P. (1990) The aims of primary education in world perspective, in Proctor, N. (ed.) *The Aims of Primary Education and the National Curriculum*. London: Falmer.

Tharp, R. and Gallimore, R. (1988) *Rousing Minds to Life: Teaching, Learning and Schooling in Social Context*. New York: Cambridge University Press.

Thomas, D. (ed.) (1995) *Teachers' Stories*. Buckingham: Open University Press.

Thomas, G. (1992) *Effective Classroom Teamwork: Support or Intrusion?* London: Routledge.

Thomas, N. (1989) The aim of primary education in the member states of the Council of Europe, in Galton, M. and Blyth, A. (eds) *Handbook of Primary Education in Europe*. London: David Fulton.

Thompson, M. (1997) *Professional Ethics and the Teacher*. Stoke-on-Trent: Trentham.

Thorndike, E. L. (1911) *Human Learning*. New York: Prentice Hall.

Thorne, B. (1993) *Gender Play: Girls and Boys in School*. Buckingham: Open University Press.

Tickle, L. (2000) *Teacher Induction: the Way Ahead*. London: Open University Press.

Tizard, B., Blatchford, P., Burke, J., Farquhar, C. and Plewis, I. (1988) *Young Children at School in the Inner City*. London: Lawrence Erlbaum.

Tizard, B. and Hughes, M. (1984) *Young Children Learning: Talking and Learning at Home and School*. London: Fontana.

Tomlinson, M. (2001) *The Fifth Medway Lecture*. Medway Local Education Authority, April.

Tomlinson, P. (1995) *Understanding Mentoring: Reflective Strategies for School-Based Teacher Preparation*. Buckingham: Open University Press.

http://www.rtweb.info

Tomlinson, P. (1999a) 'Conscious reflection and implicit learning in teacher preparation: implications for a balanced approach', *Oxford Review of Education*, 24(4), 533–44.

Tomlinson, P. (1999b) 'Conscious reflection and implicit learning in teacher preparation: recent light on old issues', *Oxford Review of Education*, 25(3), 405–25.

Torrance, H. (1991) 'Evaluating SATs: the 1991 pilot', *Cambridge Journal of Education*, 21(2), 129–40.

Torrance, H. and Pryor, J. (1998) *Investigating Formative Assessment: Teaching, Learning and Assessment in the Classroom*. Buckingham: Open University Press.

Tripp, D. (1993) *Critical Incidents in Teaching: Developing Professional Judgement*. London: Routledge.

Troman, G. and Woods, P. (2000) *Primary Teachers' Stress*. London: Routledge.

Troyna, B. and Hatcher, R. (1992) *Racism in Children's Lives: A Study of Mainly-White Primary Schools*. London: Routledge.

TTA (1999) *Supporting Induction of New Teachers*. London: TTA.

TTA (2000) *Improving Standards through Evidence-Based Teaching*. London: TTA.

TTA (2001) *Career Entry Profile: Notes of Guidance and Standards*. London: TTA.

TTA (2002) *Qualifying to Teach: Professional Standards for Qualified Teacher Status and Requirement for Initial Teacher Training*. London: TTA.

TTA/OFSTED (1996) *Review of Headteacher and Teacher Appraisal: Summary of Evidence*. London: TTA/OFSTED.

Turner-Bisset, R. (2001) *Expert Teaching: Knowledge and Pedagogy to Lead the Profession*. London: David Fulton.

United Nations (1989) *Convention on the Rights of the Child*. New York: United Nations.

Vincent, C. (1996) *Parents and Teachers: Power and Participation*. London: Falmer.

Vincent, C. (2000) *Including Parents? Education, Citzenship and Parental Agency*. Buckingham: Open University Press.

Vulliamy, G. (2000) New Labour and School Exclusions. *Inaugural Lecture*. University of York.

Vygotsky, L. S. (1962) *Thought and Language*. Cambridge, MA: Massachusetts Institute of Technology.

Vygotsky, L. S. (1978) *Mind in Society: the Development of Higher Psychological Processes*. Cambridge, MA: Harvard University Press.

Walberg, H. J. (ed.) (1979) *Educational Environments and Effect: Evaluation, Policy and Productivity*. Berkeley, CA: McCutchan.

Walkerdine, V. (1981) 'Sex power and pedagogy', *Screen Education*, 38, 1–24.

Walkerdine, V. (1983) It's only natural: rethinking child-centred pedagogy, in Wolpe, A. M. and Donald, J. (eds) *Is There Anybody There from Education?* London: Pluto Press.

Walkerdine, V. (1984) Cognitive development and the child-centred pedagogy, in Henriques, D. (ed.) *Changing the Subject: Psychology, Social Regulation and Subjectivity*. London: Methuen.

Walkerdine, V. (1988) *The Mastery of Reason: Cognitive Development and the Production of Rationality*. London: Routledge.

Wallace, M. (1994) Towards a contingency approach to development planning in schools, in Hargreaves, D. H. and Hopkins, D. (eds) *Development Planning for School Improvement*. London: Cassell.

Walton, J. (ed.) (1971) *The Integrated Day: Theory and Practice*. London: Ward Lock.

Watkins, C. (2000) *Managing Classroom Behaviour: from Research to Diagnosis*. London: Institute of Education.

Watkins, C. and Wanger, C. (2000) *Improving School Behaviour*. London: Paul Chapman.

Watt, D. (1996) 'An analysis of teacher questioning behaviour in constructivist primary science education', *International Journal of Science Education*, **18**(5), 601–13.

Webb, R. (ed.) (1991) *Practitioner Research in the Primary School*. London: Falmer.

Webb, R. (1996) *Cross-Curricular Primary Practice: Taking a Leadership Role*. London: Falmer.

Webster, A., Beveridge, M. and Reid, M. (1996) *Managing the Literacy Curriculum*. London: Routledge.

Weiner, G. (1990) Developing educational policy on gender in the primary school, in Weiner, G. (ed.) *The Primary School and Equal Opportunities: International Perspectives on Gender Issues*. London: Cassell.

Wells, G. (1986) *The Meaning Makers: Children Learning Language and Using Language to Learn*. London: Hodder and Stoughton.

Wells, G. and Nicholls, J. (eds) (1986) *Language and Learning: an Interactional Perspective*. London: Falmer.

Wertsch, J. V. (1985) *Vygotsky and the Social Formation of Mind*. Cambridge, MA: Harvard University Press.

Wertsch, J. V. (1991) *Voices of the Mind: a Socio-Cultural Approach to Mediated Action*. Cambridge, MA: Harvard University Press.

Wertsch, J. V. (1998) *Mind as Action*. Oxford: Oxford University Press.

Wexler, P., Crichlow, W., Kern, J. and Matusewicz, R. (1992) *Becoming Somebody: Toward a Social Psychology of School*. London: Falmer.

Wheldall, K. (1991) *Discipline in Schools: Psychological Perspectives on the Elton Report*. London: Routledge.

Whetton, C. E. A. (1991) *National Curriculum Assessment at Key Stage One: 1991 Evaluation, Report 4*. Slough: NFER.

White, J. (1978) 'The primary teacher as servant of the state', *Education 3–13*, 7(2), 18–23.

Whitebread, D. (ed.) (2000) *The Psychology of Teaching and Learning in the Primary School*. London: RoutledgeFalmer.

Whitty, G., Power, S. and Halpin, D. (1998) *Devolution and Choice in Education: the School, the State and the Market*. Buckingham: Open University Press.

Wilkinson, R. G. (ed.) (1986) *Class and Health: Research and Longitudinal Data*. London: Tavistock.

Willes, M. (1983) *Children into Pupils*. London: Routledge and Kegan Page.

Wiliam, D. (2001) *Level Best? Levels of Attainment in National Curriculum Assesment*. London: Association of Teachers and Lecturers.

http://www.rtweb.info

Wilson, E. O. and Lumsden, C. J. (1981) *Genes, Mind and Culture*. Cambridge MA, and London: Harvard University Press.

Withall, J. (1949) 'The development of a technique for the measurement of social–emotional climate in classrooms', *Journal of Experimental Education*. **17**, 347–61

Wolfendale, S. (1989) *Parental Involvement*. London: Cassell.

Wolfendale, S. (1992) *Involving Parents in Schools*. London: Cassell.

Wood, D. (1986) Aspects of teaching and learning, in Richards, M. and Light, P. (eds) *Children of Social Worlds*. Cambridge: Polity Press.

Wood, D. (1988) *How Children Think and Learn*. Oxford: Blackwell.

Woodhead, M. (1997) The social construction of children's needs, in James, A. and Prout, A. (eds) *Constructing and Reconstructing Childhood*. London: Falmer.

Woods, P. (1986) *Inside Schools*. London: Routledge and Kegan Paul.

Woods, P. (1988) Managing the primary teacher's role, in Delamont, S. (ed.) *The Primary School Teacher*. Lewes: Falmer.

Woods, P. (1990) *The Happiest Days? How Pupils Cope with School*. London: Falmer.

Woods, P. and Jeffrey, B. (1996) *Teachable Moments: the Art of Teaching in Primary Schools*. Buckingham: Open University Press.

Wragg, E. C. (ed.) (1984) *Classroom Teaching Skills*. London: Croom Helm.

Wragg, E. C. (1993) *Class Management*. London: Routledge.

Wragg, T. (1999) *An Introduction to Classroom Observation* (2nd edition). London: Routledge.

Wragg, T. (2000) *Class Management*. London: Routledge.

Wragg, T. and Brown, G. (1993) *Explaining*. London: Routledge.

Wright, C. (1992) *Race Relations in the Primary School*. London: David Fulton.

Wrigley, T. (2000) *The Power to Learn: Stories of Success in the Education of Asian and other Bilingual Pupils*. Stoke-on-Trent: Trentham.

Yeomans, R. and Sampson, J. (eds) (1994) *Mentorship in the Primary School*. London: Falmer.

Young, D. (1984) *Knowing How and Knowing That*. London: Birkbeck College.

Young, M. F. D. (ed.) (1971) *Knowledge and Control*. London: Collier-Macmillan.

Yussen, S. R. (ed.) (1985) *The Growth of Reflection in Children*. New York: Academic Press.

Zeichner, K. (1981/2) 'Reflective teaching and field-based experience in pre-service teacher education', *Interchange*, **12**, 1–22.

INDEX

The index covers the preface, introduction and chapters 1–18. It does not include the key readings at the end of each chapter, or author references.